D0161359

A HISTORY OF EUROPEAN MUSIC

THE ART MUSIC TRADITION OF WESTERN CULTURE

A HISTORY
OF
EUROPEAN MUSIC

THE ART MUSIC TRADITION
OF WESTERN CULTURE

David G. Hughes
Fanny P. Mason Professor of Music
Harvard University

Chapter Appendixes compiled by
Thomas F. Kelly
Wellesley College

Illustrations selected by
Mary R. Rasmussen
University of New Hampshire

McGRAW-HILL BOOK COMPANY

New York   St. Louis   San Francisco   Düsseldorf   Johannesburg   Kuala Lampur
London   Mexico   Montreal   New Delhi   Panama   Paris   São Paulo   Singapore
Sydney   Tokyo   Toronto

A History of European Music: The Art Music Tradition of Western Culture

234567890 VHVH 798765

This book was set in Melior by John T. Westlake Publishing Services. The editor was Robert P. Rainier; the designer was John T. Westlake Publishing Services; and the production supervisor was Judi Frey.
Von Hoffman Press, Inc., was printer and binder.

Library of Congress Cataloging in Publication Data

Hughes, David G
    A history of European music.

    1. Music—History and criticism. I. Title.
ML160.H87   780'.94   73-21597
ISBN 0-07-031105-6

CONTENTS

v

PREFACE

Recent years have produced a number of textbooks dealing with the history of Western music, each with its own methods and its own point of view. It is appropriate, therefore, that the reader be informed from the outset of what he may expect from this book, and how he or she may most efficiently make use of it.

In the first place, as is evident from the subtitle, this is a history of "art" or "serious" music, as contrasted with popular and folk musical traditions. Naturally this implies no judgement of value: the study of folk and popular music is both important and interesting, but it is not the subject of this book.

In the second place, the history of music is here presented almost exclusively as a history of musical styles. While there is occasional reference to general cultural trends, to events in the lives of composers, to the place of music in society, the primary emphasis is on the music itself. The numerous musical examples have been selected to demonstrate as representatively as possible the most important aspects of musical styles. Particularly in the earlier part of the book, the discussion is centered on specific works. In later chapters, the greater familiarity and availability of scores and recordings has suggested a slightly different treatment, and the works mentioned in the text may readily be replaced by other similar pieces.

In the third place, this text has been written in such a way as to be accessible to readers with little or no prior musical experience, while still preserving an undiminished value for musically trained users. Naturally, the reader wholly unversed in basic musical concepts will need to put in somewhat more effort than the musician if he is to profit fully from what he reads. It will be necessary for him to study carefully (and preferably with the aid of an instructor) the relevant sections of Appendix A as he proceeds. The material of this Appendix has been arranged so as to correspond with the chapters of the text. The reader should not attempt to swallow the Appendix whole, but rather to use only those parts of it that are needed for the full understanding of the chapter involved. The primary purpose of Appendix A is to make intelligible the musical examples contained in the text. The inexperienced user of this book may still need to decipher, rather than merely read, the music presented—but the process of deciphering will be quite adequate to make clear the essential points of the text. (A preliminary version of this book has been extensively tested in several colleges, with both trained and untrained students, and the results have clearly confirmed the claim just made.)

Finally, and perhaps most important, there remains the perennial problem of inclusiveness. There are far too many "facts" (dates, names, titles, etc.) in the history of music to be fitted into a single volume, whatever its purpose. The inclusion of large numbers of such facts makes for a complex narrative, difficult to read, and even more difficult to interpret as to the relative importance of the material included. Conversely, excessive omission of factual material greatly diminishes the reference value of a book, and may leave the reader with an oversimplified impression. Every text must represent an attempt to avoid these extremes. In the present case, the intent has been to keep the main text as clear and uncluttered as possible: names and dates there are, of course, as is necessary, but they are kept to a minimum. To compensate, most chapters are followed by a brief appendix, containing, often in schematic or tabular form, not only the "facts" already presented in the text, but a considerable amount of further material as well. These appendices may be useful both for purposes of review, and as a means of providing suggestions for further study. They were prepared, not by the author, but by Dr. Thomas F. Kelly of Wellesley College. In some cases, their point of view will be seen to differ from that of the main text. This is no disadvantage: at the least it may serve to illustrate the diverse interpretations that inevitably persist in the study of musical history.

Since most of the chapter appendices contain not only references to editions of music but also basic bibliographic references, there is no general bibliography for the volume as a whole. The serious student should have no difficulty in expanding his bibliographic background by making use of the references in the editions and books cited. For those contemplating the purchase of musical scores or recordings, the suggestions contained in Appendix B may be of some use.

There remains the conventional but always satisfying task of acknowledging the assistance of all those who have helped, in whatever way, to bring this book to its final form. First in order must come the members of my family, who have endured—the anxieties and the delays, and above all the often irritable ways of an author. Their contribution has also been more specific, especially in the case of my wife, who has read aloud seemingly endless pages of typescript during the correction of the galley proofs. Next must be recognized the help of present and former colleagues, whose advice has been of incalculable assistance. I mention first those whom I no longer see daily: Professor Nino Pirrotta, of the University of Rome; Professor Anthony Newcomb, of the University of California at Berkeley; Professor David Del Tredici, of Boston University. Those who remain have been no less helpful: Professor John Ward, Professor Elliot Forbes, and Professor Lowell Lindgren. Although A. Tillman Merritt, now Professor Emeritus at Harvard, has not been involved directly in the preparation of this book, his teaching, many years ago, lies at the very root of my musical thought. The graduate students (now mostly teachers themselves) who have helped me are unfortunately too numerous to list by name. Their contribution has ranged from mere casual but illuminating remarks to learned critiques of sections of the book. They will recognize themselves on reading these lines, and will know, I am sure, that my gratitude is no less because they remain nameless here. Thanks are also due to those under-graduates who have used the preliminary version of the book in courses at Harvard and elsewhere: many of them have offered comments of great value.

Counsel of a more general sort has come from many sources. I can, alas, no longer thank the late William Mitchell, formerly Professor of Music at Columbia University, for his help during the formative stages of this project. Professor Gordon Crain was the first to read the manuscript as a whole, and his provocative and informed comments were of great value. Mr. Gordon Gidley performed the final copy editing, and transformed many an obscure passage into what I must hope is its present intelligibil-ity. The staff of McGraw-Hill Book Company, including especially Mr. Robert P. Rainier, has contributed materially in giving the book its present shape. And finally I owe an especial debt to Professor Thomas Kelly, who not only provided the chapter appendices, but much sage advice as well, and Professor Mary Rasmussen, of the University of New Hampshire, whose unequalled knowledge of musical iconography produced the elegant and instructive illustrations that embellish and enrich this book. To all of these, and (with apologies) to those not mentioned here, my heartiest thanks: they have been friends in the time of my need, and they have been friends indeed.

David G. Hughes

INTRODUCTION

There are several ways of presenting an introductory course in Western music, all of them valid. Most familiar is the music appreciation method, which typically begins by offering music of a sort familiar to most students, and then gradually deriving from it the technical concepts necessary for understanding it properly. Less common is the theory course, in which the student is required to examine a composition very carefully, and then actually to compose a piece in similar style—beginning with simple models, and gradually progressing to works of greater difficulty. Even rarer is the purely analytic course, which concentrates on the detailed study of a relatively small number of works, but does not require the student to write any music himself.

This book however, is a history of music, and thus represents the commonest alternative to the appreciation method. Why history? There are certainly disadvantages: one must begin with music most students have never heard and are unlikely to feel immediate affection for. One must, in order to be reasonably inclusive, devote only a few pages to great composers about whom volumes could well be written. Yet the advantages seem even more important. First and most obvious, study of the history of music is a means of learning about Western culture that reinforces, refines, and in some cases reinterprets knowledge gained from political or literary history. Second, the student is exposed to the widest possible variety of styles, and frequently finds himself taking pleasure in music of whose very existence he had previously had no idea. Finally—and this is important from a practical point of view—it happens that the historical approach offers great pedagogical advantages. The earliest Western music, while by no means simple aesthetically, uses simple technical means. A knowledge of pitch notation and intervals is all that is needed for the first chapter; harmonic intervals and meter suffice for the next two or three; and the more difficult concepts of triads, non-harmonic tones, and tonality are not required until the reader has had a good chance to become thoroughly at home with simpler ideas.

The history of music, like that of literature or the fine arts, differs essentially from political, economic, or institutional history: its subject is a repertoire of works of art, each in its own way meant to give pleasure or create beauty. One may approve or disapprove of Napoleon's career, or of the development of the English Parliament; but few turn to such matters with love or affection—the response a work of art generally aspire to stimulate.

Thus, although the book is about history, it is even more about the works of art that, taken together, have created that history. Merely *reading* such a book is of relatively little use unless it is accompanied by the experience of hearing the music that is discussed (or similar works). Reading without listening is like learning tennis without ever picking up a racket and ball: the essential content is missing. Naturally not everyone will respond equally to all the music presented; but there is no *bad* music included, and ample rewards lie along every step of the way for anyone who is willing to receive them.

This book is, in fact, an invitation to enjoy such rewards; and it could perhaps be asked, "Why not simply give us the music to hear, and we shall have our aesthetic pleasures, and, by using our powers of inference, our history as well?" Ideally, this would be the best solution, but in practice, such a method almost invariably fails. It does so because music, over the years, has been written in widely different styles, and styles are like languages: they must be learned if one is to understand what is being said. For those with little or no previous musical experience, this means that some degree of explanation—of translation, if you will—is necessary throughout. To read German, one must be able to recognize a German verb: so also in a musical style, one must be able to recognize the critical elements of a thirteenth-century motet or a Mozart symphony. Those who have already had pleasure out of music will feel (quite correctly) that they already understand certain styles—that of Mozart, or Bach, or Stravinsky. But this sort of familiarity is almost always intuitive only, and an understanding of the grammar even of familiar styles will result in better comprehension and, above all, deeper enjoyment of music already well known. Further, the study of successive styles in their historical order is not only of interest in itself, but also serves further to illuminate the works treated. Thus it would be difficult to make sense of a late thirteenth-century motet without knowing the background of earlier motet history; and this in turn involves some knowledge of the liturgy and its chants. Or, to take a more familiar example: Mozart's later works are often deeply influenced by his encounter with the music of J.S. Bach. Knowing something about Bach therefore tells one something about Mozart.

Histories of music are, naturally, written by musical historians, or musicologists, to use the commoner term. But men become musicologists because they love music first, and learn history later. In almost all cases, their love for music was first awakened by the works one hears at concerts or on "classical" radio stations—music of Beethoven, Mozart, Bach, Schumann, and the other great composers of the eighteenth and nineteenth centuries. Thereafter came their acquaintance with other types of music —that of the Middle Ages or the Renaissance, or of non-Western cultures. This order of learning is almost inevitable, given the present-day practice of music. It leads, equally inevitably, to certain differences of attitude: if the reader detects, in the later chapters of this book, a warmth of enthusiasm less evident in the earlier ones, this is not to be taken as a judgement of value. One's first love creates a state of mind that can never be wholly duplicated.

Before beginning the study of musical history, we must first attempt to define music itself. "Organized sound" is the definition proposed by a twentieth-century composer, and it is not a bad one. Mere sound—squeaking brakes, falling rain, ordinary speech—is not music: it is the organization of sound that creates music. But what does "organization" mean in this context? Everyone would agree that a two-year old let loose on a piano does not ordinarily make music, although the piano is a musical instrument; but many would now contend that music can be made without the use of any conventional instrument at all out of "non-musical" sounds, properly organized. Yet mere mechanical or mathematical ordering cannot be meant here, for in that case almost everyone with a sense of order or a knowledge of mathematics could become a great composer; and this has not been the case.

We ordinarily speak, in English and in several other languages, of a "piece" of music, implying that each "piece" is in some sense complete. In the verbal arts, such completeness is usually fairly easy to identify: if we were to find a copy of a play by Shakespeare or a novel by Jane Austen from which the end was missing, we would at once be aware of the lack. But this is at least in part because words refer to objects and concepts of the "real" world—we know that the novel is incomplete because some event towards which the author has obviously been pointing does not occur. Musical tones, however, rarely convey any concrete meaning. Yet we can identify an incomplete piece of music as easily as an incomplete work of literature. This results from a peculiar property of sounds (considering only musical ones for the moment), which, when properly used, fuse together into an interacting system wherein certain pitches become important in varying degrees, while others remain clearly subordinate. Thus even the first four or five notes of a melody interact to create in the listener a pattern of expectations, and the remainder of the tune consists of the fulfillment of these expectations, usually interspersed with intentional deceptions that heighten the tension and make the ultimate fulfillment that much more satisfying. It is in this way that one may properly speak of the unity of a piece of music; and it thus becomes evident how an incomplete piece can be identified: the ear's expectations have not been fulfilled. (Once again, one must be familiar with the style to perceive these effects.)

A simple test will prove the point. Play or sing a familiar melody, such as "America," substituting some other note for the correct ending tone: the result is clearly impossible (although it could be made possible as part of a larger composition). The tones of the melody have arranged themselves into a hierarchy that demands certain continuations and a certain conclusion, and prohibits others.

Thus the organization we have been attempting to identify lies somewhere in the nature of sound itself, and the manner in which the ear reacts to sound. It is not clear why this should be so; but neither is it important for our purposes that we know why (musical theory makes some attempt to explain this matter). We may simply define a melody as a succession of tones so ordered that a pattern of tensions and relaxations arise—the release of all tensions marking, of course, the end of the melody. Music using more complex means than melody alone will normally employ numerous other ways of creating and relaxing tension, but these need not concern us for the moment. With the definition of melody, we are ready to turn to the essential matter of this book: the history of art-music in the Western world.

A HISTORY OF EUROPEAN MUSIC

THE ART MUSIC TRADITION OF WESTERN CULTURE

 I

GREGORIAN CHANT

The history of western Europe begins symbolically with the deposition of the last Roman emperor of the West in 476 A.D. From then on, even the pretence of a vast centralized empire governing the whole of the civilized world was lost. The West was split up into a number of tribal kingdoms—remote ancestors of the modern nations—each fiercely devoted to its own interests. What used to be called, with some justification, the Dark Ages had begun.

The Roman Empire had of course exerted enormous institutional and political influence on the huge territories it had come to control. It had also had a powerful cultural influence: while the arts of Rome were largely derivative, developed from those of Greece, the empire imposed its civilization along with its political control. Its "barbarian" subjects were apparently good learners: there still remain Roman theaters in many places in western Europe, and there is ample evidence that the arts in general flourished throughout most of the empire. But Rome's power as a civilizer was the result of its political power. Once the empire had fallen, its various peoples felt little or no need to emulate the artistic traditions of the former capital. Thus, with some exceptions—certain poets, for example, who remained faithful to the Roman ways regardless of the then current state of the arts—the cultures of the post-Roman world were essentially native ones, growing out of the gifts and inclinations of the peoples who had first invaded and then settled in imperial territory. From the Roman point of view, these arts were "barbaric;" but the peoples we are pleased to call "semi-civilized" had strong artistic styles of their own. Nothing comparable to the *Aeneid* or the Roman Forum was produced during the sixth or seventh century, but there remain splendid pieces of jewelry, a few important buildings, and probably the beginnings of a great tradition of epic verse.

The artistic styles of the various peoples—Franks, Burgundians, Lombards, Vandals, and so on—were by no means wholly diverse, but their separatist political ambitions certainly were. Warfare, both civil and external, was a normal condition: these

1

were bloody and changeful years, in which rulers and even states arose and disappeared with extraordinary rapidity. Only one institution stood above the perpetual turmoil: the Church. Under Constantine, Christianity had been established as the state religion of the empire in 313. Even before the empire's collapse, the authorities of the Church had acquired a moral (and legal) force superior to the power of the civil state. After the disappearance of central authority, the Church remained the sole international institution in the West, and its permanence and relatively high moral standards gained for it a respect that no temporal ruler could command. While a unified Christian empire like that of Byzantium was impossible for the deeply divided West tribes, it was the Church, increasingly dominated by papal authority, that served as their moral and intellectual center.

With the disappearance of the Roman ruling class, education was almost wholly restricted to the Church. Only priests and monks—and by no means all of these—had even a rudimentary education. Still, enough learning persisted to preserve much of the classical Roman literary inheritance, which remained an inspiration and a model to subsequent cultures. As a result, the history of Western literature from the beginning of the Middle Ages to the present is hardly comprehensible without some knowledge of the classical models on which this literature was—intermittently at least—based.

With music, however, the case is quite different. Nothing is known about the kinds of music practiced at Rome in antiquity, and not a note of written Roman music has come down. For here the Church played a different role. While it had cooperated, often with misgivings, in the preservation of literature, it refused to do the same for music. In the eyes of the Church, the musician, like the actor, was associated with the worst depravities of paganism. His craft was not encouraged, nor were its products worthy of preservation. Of the once flourishing tradition of musical antiquity, the West preserved only a few speculative theoretical treatises derived from Greek sources. These later came to have great influence on the development of medieval musical theory, but not one of them contains a note of music.

Thus while the history of literature exhibits a continuity that goes back as far as Homer, the history of music does not. The Church looked favorably only on its own music—the music for its ceremonies and rites. While this emergent Western music doubtless had some basis in earlier traditions (notably that of the synagogue), it was not "classical" at all, but a new art. The link with antiquity was broken.

THE EARLY MIDDLE AGES: THE ASCENDANCY OF THE ROMAN LITURGY

The early Middle Ages preserved its music orally, with the result that most of it is now lost, except for fragments that may be embedded in later documents. The earliest surviving notated manuscripts date from the ninth century and contain almost without exception music for the rites of the Church. There can be no doubt that the peoples of those times produced songs and dances—that there were songs for working, songs for weddings, songs of mourning, and the rest—but all of these have perished, and it is not possible even to speculate intelligently on what they may have been like. It is important to bear in mind that while only the Church succeeded in preserving its music, that repertoire was at the time only part of a musical culture much more varied.

In all cultures music and worship have been closely associated from the beginning. Christianity, despite its distrust of professional musicians, was no exception. From the time of Saint Paul, Christians expressed their piety in song. But the primary concern of the Church was the regulation of specifically liturgical music: the music officially appointed to be sung at its services.

In this respect, despite the international nature of the Church, considerable diversity was at first tolerated. Until Carolingian times, the several provinces of the Western Church practiced their own liturgies, under the nominal leadership of the pope. Northern Italy used the Ambrosian rite, named after the influential Saint Ambrose (d. 397); the Frankish lands used the Gallican liturgy; and the Iberian peninsula the Mozarabic (or Visigothic). These three usages had more in common with each other than with the Roman rite, and were followed by far more of the faithful than adhered to the relatively conservative liturgy of Rome.

Early Western liturgies

The ultimate predominance of the Roman liturgy was primarily the result of political, not ecclesiastical, circumstances. During the eighth century, the Frankish kings Pepin and Charlemagne needed the help of the papacy for the furtherance of their territorial ambitions. In order to gain it, they began introducing the Roman rite into their kingdom, at the expense of the native Gallican usage. The process was already well under way when Charlemagne was crowned Emperor of the West in 800, and the latter event gave added impetus to liturgical reform. If there were to be again, as in the days of the old empire, a single Western state, its political unity should be reflected in unity of forms of worship. As a result, the Gallican liturgy disappeared completely; the Mozarabic did not survive the reconquest of Spain from the Arabs; and the Ambrosian was reduced to a local usage employed only in the immediate vicinity of Milan. While the Roman liturgy did not escape unaltered from this expansion, its triumph was nearly total: it remained the sole important liturgy in Western Europe until the Protestant Reformation.

Whatever their differences, the liturgical practices of the Middle Ages can be traced back to two fundamental roots: the Last Supper and the Jewish synagogue service. The former gave rise to the Eucharist, or Mass, in which the Last Supper is in a way solemnly reenacted. The latter, too, left its mark on the Mass, but was also the ancestor of independent services of various kinds, which ultimately took their definitive shape as the Office, the daily round of services sung or said by monks and clergy. By the ninth century, when the earliest manuscripts containing music were written, both Mass and Office had achieved a fixed form in all essential matters. Full details concerning the structure of each are given in the appendix to this chapter. Here it need only be noted that in both Mass and Office, music could be employed in three different capacities: any reading or prayer might be delivered in a musical, rather than a spoken voice (this gives better audibility, and also modestly enhances the words thus sung); music might be used to accompany any kind of liturgical *action* (a procession, for example); or music might be employed for its own value, as a means of stimulating devotion.[1] It must also be observed that in any service there were some texts that were invariable, or "ordinary." Others were variable, or "proper," and their choice was determined by the day or season of the church year (again, see the appendix at the end of this chapter for details concerning the latter). Free choice played a very small role in the selection of liturgical texts, and practically none at all in the choice of melodies for

Liturgical music of the early Middle Ages

[1]Footnote appears on following page.

those parts of the service that were "proper." Moreover, the style of the music was, in almost all cases, determined by the particular liturgical function that the music was to fulfill.

Liturgical music was, in the early Middle Ages, exclusively vocal music. The Church still distrusted professional musicians and their instruments, and saw no need for instrumental accompaniment. It was also *monophonic* music—music, that is, in which two different pitches are never sounded simultaneously. Polyphonic or harmonic music, with its simultaneously sounded melodies and chords, was apparently little known until the ninth century. Such monophonic vocal liturgical music is known as "chant" (sometimes plainchant or plainsong). In the pre-Carolingian period, each liturgy developed its own repertoire: in those times, Gallican chant, Ambrosian chant, and Mozarabic chant flourished—as did the chant of the Roman liturgy, called Gregorian chant, in honor of the supposed role of Pope Gregory the Great (r. 590-604) in its composition or arrangement.

The origin of these chant repertoires is almost wholly obscure. It has been noted above that they are not direct descendants of the classical tradition, although they may well be offshoots of some common Mediterranean tradition. Almost as little is known of the date of their origin. There is evidence that certain categories of chant still sung today were known in the fourth, fifth, and sixth centuries, but since music was not written down at that time, the accuracy of the oral tradition can not be judged. Some scholars believe that many of the melodies that have survived reproduce accurately chants of the fifth or sixth century—that they are pre-medieval products of late Antique culture (perhaps of the "popular" rather than the learned sort). Others hold that the preserved melodies bear little or no relation to earlier prototypes, having been radically transformed by generations of oral transmission. In this view, the preserved melodies go back no further than the eighth century. It is, of course, awkward to be unable to date a substantial repertoire of music to within 400 years (as if we were not sure whether Beethoven was born in 1770 or 1370), but there is at present no way out of the difficulty.

Whatever their origins, the several chant repertoires suffered the fate of the liturgies for which they were created. Gallican chant largely disappeared. Mozarabic chant lasted longer, but very little survived long enough to be written down in a notation that can be accurately read. Ambrosian chant is still sung in Milan today, but its dissemination and influence were small. It was Gregorian chant that came to be sung throughout Western Christendom.

[1]The chapter appendix indicates the manner of performance of the various parts of the Mass and Office. For the purpose of the following discussion, the following summary may be found convenient:

Recitation or "musical speech"—readings from Scripture (lections), prayers, psalms and canticles of the Office

Accompaniments to liturgical actions—the introit, offertory, and communion of the Mass

Music used for its own sake—the gradual, alleluia, and tract of the Mass; the responsory of the Office (all these immediately follow a lection).

TYPES OF GREGORIAN CHANT

The simplest type of Gregorian chant[1] may be exemplified by the tone or recita- *Recitational chant*
tional formula in which the epistle of the Mass is sung (Ex. I-1). Most syllables of the text are sung to a single repeated tone—the reciting note—from which only occasional deviations are made. This constant repetition of the same pitch characterizes the recita-

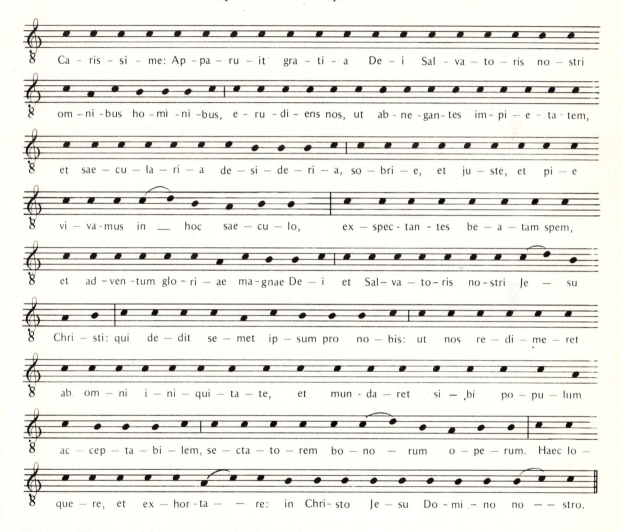

Ca - ris - si - me: Ap -pa - ru - it gra - ti - a De - i Sal - va - to - ris no - stri

om - ni -bus ho -mi -ni -bus, e - ru - di -ens nos, ut ab - ne -gan-tes im- pi - e - ta-tem,

et sae — cu — la — ri — a de — si — de — ri — a, so — bri — e, et ju — ste, et pi — e

vi — va-mus in __ hoc sae — cu — lo, ex — spec - tan - tes be — a — tam spem,

et ad —ven -tum glo-ri — ae ma-gnae De — i et Sal— va — to- ris no-stri Je — su

Chri — sti: qui de — dit se — met ip — sum pro no — bis: ut nos re — di — me — ret

ab om — ni i — ni — qui - ta — te, et mun - da — ret si — bi po — pu — lum

ac — cep — ta — bi — lem, se — cta — to — rem bo — no — rum o — pe — rum. Haec lo —

que — re, et ex — hor-ta — — re: in Chri- sto Je — su Do - mi — no no — — stro.

Brethren: The grace of God has appeared, of our Savior. . .   Ex. I-1

[1]For the sake of clarity, the various categories of chant are discussed in order of increasing musical complexity, without regard for their liturgical position. Nevertheless, the *aesthetic* effect of this music can be fully realized only by hearing (or singing) the chants in their proper liturgical context. Since liturgical celebrations using only chant have become rather rare, this objective cannot be fully achieved. The best substitute is the use of recordings that contain, not "selections" from the chant repertoire, but complete services.

tional style of chant. By this means, it is possible to chant a text of any length, merely by increasing or decreasing the number of repetitions.

But mere repetition of a tone does not make music: some means of articulation is required—some means of suggesting a beginning, a middle, and an end. This is provided by deviations from the repeated note. These always occur at some point of articulation in the sense of the text, and correspond almost exactly to the punctuation of ordinary speech. Each time a deviation from the reciting note occurs, the hearer is given the feeling that a certain unit of the recitation has been completed; thus the deviations give structure to what might otherwise be a shapeless and monotonous droning.

Cadence is the technical name for any musical device that gives the effect of closure, whether of a full stop, analogous to the period, or partial closure, like the comma. Two kinds of cadence are employed in the epistle tone, differing in function. One ends on the reciting note itself and is evidently the more final, since the entire chant ends with it. The other ends on b^1, and serves to mark a less important articulation. In addition to such cadences, there may also be deviations from the reciting note at the beginnings of phrases. These, called intonations, also have a form-producing effect: by creating a momentary feeling of instability, they give greater effect to the note repetition that is to follow. Thus the method of monotone recitation articulated by cadences can produce a satisfying musical whole, if a very simple one. It also has the advantage of being able to accommodate any text, of whatever length and structure: the singer need only deploy his cadences at the appropriate places, and chant the rest of the text on the reciting note.

Psalmody of the Office

In the psalm-chanting of the Office, the same principles are employed in a somewhat more complex and consciously artistic fashion, with correspondingly more richly musical results. The impetus for this more elaborate treatment lies in the nature of the psalms: they are poetry—not, to be sure, metrical poetry of the sort familiar from later ages, but poetry nonetheless. Each psalm is divided into a number of verses (from as few as three to more than twenty); and each verse is divided into two halves, not necessarily of equal length. The two halves of a psalm verse often express the same idea in two different ways ("Hear my cry O God/ attend unto my prayer" [Ps. 61:1]). Such a structure invites parallel musical treatment. Each verse is sung as a bipartite unit. While the reciting tone still predominates, the two different cadences are given more definite functions: one, called the mediation, always ends the first half of the verse; the other, the termination, ends the second half. Thus the cadences appear in strict alternation as one verse succeeds another (Ex. I-2). While the differing lengths of the verses and verse-halves preclude any feeling of metrical regularity, the symmetrical placement of cadences gives an effect of formality and balance that contrasts strongly with the free structure of the Mass recitation.

This balance is enhanced by the traditional mode of performance. The first verse of the psalm is sung by one half of the choir (and this verse only is begun with an intonation). The second verse is sung by the other half, the third by the first half, and so on in alternation. The two groups of singers normally face each other from opposite sides of the chancel. Thus another regularity, both audible and spatial, is added to the regularity within the psalm verse itself.

The antiphon

Nevertheless, a chanted psalm is never a musical entity in itself: it is always preceded and followed by a different sort of chant—the antiphon (in the earliest times, the

---

[1]In this and the following chapter, pitches are designated in the traditional manner. Capital letters represent the lower octave of the vocal range, lower case letters the higher octave.

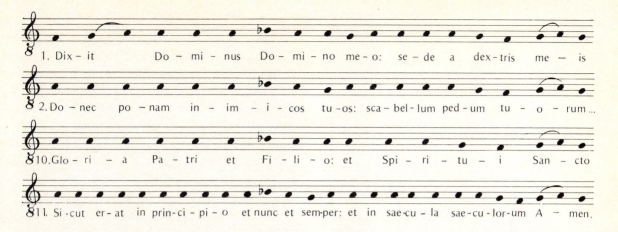

The Lord said to my lord, sit on my right hand, until I make your enemies a footstool for your feet. The Lord will send the scepter of your power out of Sion, to rule in the midst of your enemies. Glory be to the Father and to the Son, and to the Holy Spirit; as it was in the beginning, is now, and forever; and for ages of ages. Amen.

Ex. I-2

Function of the antiphon in psalmody

antiphon was also sung after each verse of the psalm). Thus the so-called termination never concludes anything, but rather leads on, either to the next psalm verse, or to the antiphon.

Example I-2 illustrates one psalm tone. The others employ exactly the same principles, but differ in the actual notes used. There are in all nine different tones: a standard set of eight, called first, second, third, and so on; and the *tonus peregrinus* (foreign, or wandering tone), used in certain special cases. Each tone has its own reciting tone and mediation, but may have several different terminations. Within any one psalm chant, only one termination is used. The choice of the termination to be used depends on the melody of the antiphon that frames the psalm, while the choice of the tone itself depends on the mode of the antiphon.

The liturgical climax of certain services of the Office is the chanting of a canticle (a scriptural poem not taken from the book of psalms). Since it is a general principle of the chant that the more solemn moments of the liturgy receive more ornate musical settings, the canticles are sung to tones related to the psalm tones, but using a few more notes: an intonation is used for every verse, and both mediation and termination may employ four or five notes each instead of two or three. For certain other liturgical occasions, even more ornate recitational formulas are used.

All the material thus far considered has been exceedingly modest in its use of musical resources. Often the number of different pitches used does not exceed three or four; and even within this restricted range, the melodic motion is almost wholly stepwise. Gregorian recitation stands at the borderline between speech and song, and any radical increase in its musical substance would defeat the very purpose for which it was designed—the intelligible delivery of text. These tones for recitations cannot be called "musical compositions" in the ordinary sense of the phrase, however profoundly musical their effect may be. They are instead formulas or directions for the correct and elegant rendering of musical speech.

The distinction becomes evident when we turn to the antiphons, chants that are still extremely simple, but are yet true and independent melodies, as defined in the Introduction to this book. Each is a complete musical entity, even though a very small one, with its own particular pattern of melodic tension and release. Consider the antiphon *Tecum principium* (Ex. I-3). Its vigorous opening motion creates a feeling of tension by giving special importance and different functions to the notes D and a. The second phrase ("in die . . .") partially resolves this in descending down to the D again, but this resolution seems incomplete, since the bold opening appears to imply a longer

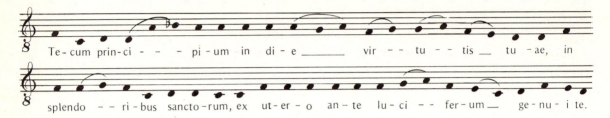

Te - cum prin - ci - - - pi - um in di - e _____ vir - - tu - - tis _ tu - ae, in

splendo - - ri - bus sancto - rum, ex ut - er - o an - te lu - ci - - fer - um _ ge - nu - i te.

The rule be with you in the day of your power; in the glory of the saints, before the morning star I have begotten you.

                                                                                    Ex. I-3

composition. The third and fourth phrases, accordingly, complete the process of achieving repose by echoing the pattern of the first two phrases, but in a less striking fashion. The ending of the antiphon is conclusive in a way that the psalm tones are not. The liturgical function of an antiphon is to serve as a frame for a psalm: in the complex antiphon-psalm-antiphon it is only the antiphon that needs to be conclusive, for it alone must serve as the ending of the entire complex.

The role of cadence in an independent melody such as *Tecum principium* is a most important one. The creation in the melody of a hierarchical pattern of pitches (in this case the notes D, a, and to some extent F are clearly more important than the others) causes the pitch on which a cadence is made to be of crucial importance. Only one tone can serve as a point of complete repose (in this case, D). Hence cadences made on that tone are almost certain to be more final than those made elsewhere. This is an important resource in all melody: cadences can not only articulate the music into phrases, but can also suggest distinctions in importance among such articulations.

Thus the role of the final tone of any melody—the only possible tone of complete repose—must be particularly significant. This was felt also by the singers and theorists concerned with Gregorian chant in the Middle Ages. They found that a chant ending on D was apt to create a pattern of important and unimportant pitches different from that produced by a chant ending on E or F. They therefore divided the entire repertoire of chant into four basic classes: one containing all chants ending on D, a second those on E, a third on F, and a fourth on G. (Chants ending on a were regarded as variants of the D or E class; those on c as variants of the F class.) Each such class was then further subdivided into two subclasses, one of which included melodies of relatively high range (called "authentic") and the other, those of low range ("plagal"). The resultant eight groups were called *modes*, numbered from "1" to "8," and every non-recitational chant was assigned to one of them. These modes (of which the theory will be discussed at the end of this chapter) had great practical importance.

Each mode has assigned to it a corresponding psalm tone, designed to fit as smoothly as possible with the melodies of the mode. (Or, since our knowledge of the early history of the chant is so limited, it may be that the nature of each psalm tone influenced the shape of the antiphons that were to be used with it.) Sometimes a psalm tone may bear a close relationship to one or more antiphons of the corresponding mode; in other cases, the relationship may be faint or imperceptible. In any event, however, knowledge of the modes was essential to the singer: he had to know the mode of any antiphon in order to sing the psalm according to the correct tone. He also needed to know which of the several terminations of the psalm tone to use. This choice, presumably dictated by a desire to secure a smooth transition between the end of the psalm and the beginning of the antiphon, had become traditional and obligatory at an early time. In the manuscripts, each antiphon is followed by the letters "euouae" (the vowels of "seculorum. Amen," the final words of the doxology, with which almost all psalms conclude). Above these letters the music for the proper termination was entered. This gave both pieces of information at one stroke, for every termination was used in one and only one mode.

While many chants of the same mode resemble each other quite closely, a given mode will also include a large number of pieces similar only in their general range and their final. The extent of this difference may be seen by comparing *Tecum principium* with the antiphon *Hodie Christus* (Ex. I-4). To some extent, this difference results from liturgical considerations, for *Hodie Christus* is an antiphon for the canticle *Magnificat*, the chanting of which is the liturgical climax of vespers. Since the tones used for the canticles are more elaborate than the psalm tones, it is natural that their antiphons will be more complex as well. Thus *Hodie Christus* is "neumatic" in style (uses two or three notes for many of its syllables), while *Tecum principium* is mostly "syllabic" (one note per syllable). But the two are also unlike in other respects.

Today Christ is born; today the savior appears; today the angels sing on earth, the archangels rejoice. Today the just exult, saying glory to God in the highest, alleluia.

Ex. I-4

Hodie Christus uses more complex compositional techniques than those we have so far seen: it is harder to hold together a long piece than a short one. The first half of the piece (through "archangeli") moves within the range of a fourth: the ear easily perceives the importance of a as a tone of suspense, but the role of the equally important F is not made clear. We are held in a purposeful state of uncertainty. Moreover, these first four phrases contain a good deal of repetition of melodic elements (e.g.,

"Christus natus est," "in terra canunt angeli," and "laetantur archangeli" all use the same melody). This sort of repetition, so common in later music, is by no means universal in Gregorian chant, but it may be used, as here, as a form-building element. It is only at the fourth "hodie" that the melody breaks out of its constricted range and achieves a climax. This at once clarifies the tonal functions of the piece and creates an expectation of the final D. By deliberately delaying the clarification, the unknown composer has created interest and intensity over a considerable span.

The medieval antiphon repertoire contains thousands of pieces. Since each occasion of the Church year requires from half a dozen to over twenty antiphons, the necessity for such a large number is evident. But by no means are all of the melodies different. Sometimes the same tune is used to set sixty or seventy different texts, with only minor deviations caused by differing numbers of syllables in the texts set. And even among melodies that are not the same, there are often strong family resemblances, as if, perhaps, all of them were descendants of some common and remote ancestor. This introduces an essential aspect of the Gregorian aesthetic: the chant composers, none of whom are known to us by name, did not feel that each piece had to have a sharply defined individuality of its own. They were, rather, entirely content to work with common, traditional materials, reshaping them to their needs.

The vast majority of the antiphons are similar in general style to the examples given and are, like them, intended for use with the psalms and canticles of the Office. A relatively small and separate class is formed by the antiphons used in liturgical processions. As a result of their special liturgical purpose, these antiphons generally are much longer and more ornate than even the canticle anthiphons. Apart from these, however, the stylistic homogeneity of the repertoire is remarkable—a clear instance of the force of liturgical propriety in the shaping of musical style.

Introit, offertory, and communion

The three "action-chants" of the Mass—the introit, offertory, and communion—are given more elaborate musical treatment than the antiphons. While the role of music remains subordinate to the action of the liturgy, the solemn character of the Mass calls for greater musical richness. Chants of these three types are basically in neumatic style (two to five notes for most syllables); and the offertories, which are the most elaborate, even contain occasional melismatic passages, that is, places in which a single syllable of text is given ten, fifteen, or even more notes. This increase in the number of notes is more important than it might seem, for it basically alters the hearer's perception of the text. As the number of notes grows, the aesthetic contribution of the text decreases, to the point that, in largely melismatic pieces (to be considered shortly), the words are reduced to little more than a subordinate understructure—a support for the flow of the music.

In the eighth and ninth centuries, the introit, offertory, and communion all had the same general form, consisting of the main part, a free melody, followed by a psalm verse, followed by the melody repeated, one or more psalm verses, each followed by the main melody, then the doxology, and the main melody again, which always formed the conclusion. These melodies thus functioned precisely like the Office antiphons, and are often so called: introit antiphon, offertory antiphon, communion antiphon. But while in the psalmody of the Office the entire psalm was sung, in the action chants only a part was used, the number of verses chanted being determined by the amount of time needed for the liturgical action. Thus on a high feast, with a lengthy and imposing introit procession, several verses might be required before the procession reached the sanctuary; while on a common weekday, a single verse would suffice. Later, from the tenth century on, most of the psalm verses disappeared: the shortening of the offertory ceremonial and the infrequency of lay communion reduced these chants to the antiphon alone. For some reason, the offertory reacquired verses—and very elaborate ones—for a while, but these too soon fell into disuse. The introit was reduced to a single verse and doxology, and ultimately lost the middle appearance of the antiphon.

Introit and communion verses share a set of eight standard tones, similar to, but more ornate than, those used in Office psalmody. Probably the offertory verses once used the same or similar formulas, but their replacement by the elaborate and non-formulaic melodies mentioned above has destroyed the evidence.

The action-antiphons are also somewhat similar to, but more ornate than, the Office antiphons. The introit *Dominus dixit* (Ex. I-5) is notable for its emphasis on a small number of pitches—primarily F and D. It is a peculiarity of Gregorian chant that the notes F and c are often singled out for a special emphasis, whatever the mode. The reason for this is entirely unknown. Its effect is to give each mode a particular flavor,

(Antiphon) The Lord said to me you are my son, today I have begotten you. (Verse) Why do the heathen rage, and the peoples imagine vain things? (Antiphon) The Lord said. . . . (Doxology) Glory be to the Father. . . . (Antiphon) The Lord said. . . .

Ex. I-5

depending on the relation of the tones F and c to the final and to other important tones. How strong—and how foreign to later styles—this flavor can be is especially apparent in the E modes, as in the opening of the fourth-mode introit *Resurrexi* (Ex. I-6). Here the conflict between the final E and the emphasized F is most striking.

Re-sur — — re - - xi   et _ ad - huc tecum sum,   al — le — lu — — ia.

I have arisen and am with you, alleluia.

Ex. I-6

In *Dominus dixit* (Ex. I-5), however, there is no such conflict, and the effect is much more tranquil. One may fairly compare the beginning of *Dominus dixit* with that of the communion *In splendoribus* (Ex. I-7). The openings are remarkably similar. But

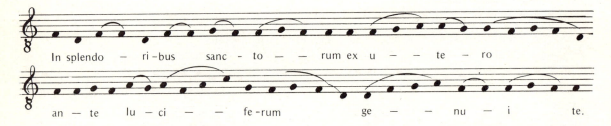

In splendo — ri–bus   sanc - to — — rum ex u — — te — ro

an — te   lu – ci — — fe -rum   ge — — nu — i   te.

In the glory of the saints, before the morning star I have begotten you from the womb.

Ex. I-7

whereas the introit continues to explore the initial D-F interval, *In splendoribus* exhibits the same intentional uncertainty of pitch functions found in the antiphon *Hodie Christus* (Ex. I-4). At first it would be nearly impossible to predict the final; it is only at the climax ("luciferum") that the tone functions are retrospectively clarified. At the same time, *In splendoribus* demonstrates another difference between Gregorian and later styles of melody: here the climactic phrase ranges from c down to D—the interval of a minor seventh. In later music, one would certainly expect the lowest note to be C, producing an octave range. But phrases outlining a seventh are entirely normal in Gregorian chant—more common, in fact, than those spanning an octave.

Offertories and their verses are rather more ornate than introits and communions. The verses, intended to be sung by soloists, are particularly bold in their melodic style, alternating widely leaping phrases with passages in which motion is kept to a minimum, with the melody revolving either around F or c.

Style of responsorial chant

The remaining classes of Gregorian chant to be considered also involve one or more soloists (often two to four singers acting as a small choir). These are the great responsories of matins, and the gradual, tract, and alleluia of the Mass, all called responsorial chants because the main chorus alternates with, or "responds to," the soloists. All the pieces in these categories are in part melismatic, having at least some syllables ornamented with melismas of over fifteen notes. All except the tracts contain a recurrent section for chorus (the respond) that alternates with a verse sung by the soloists. In the earliest times, the choral parts were probably simpler, but by the time of the first notated manuscripts, they had become almost as complex as the verses.

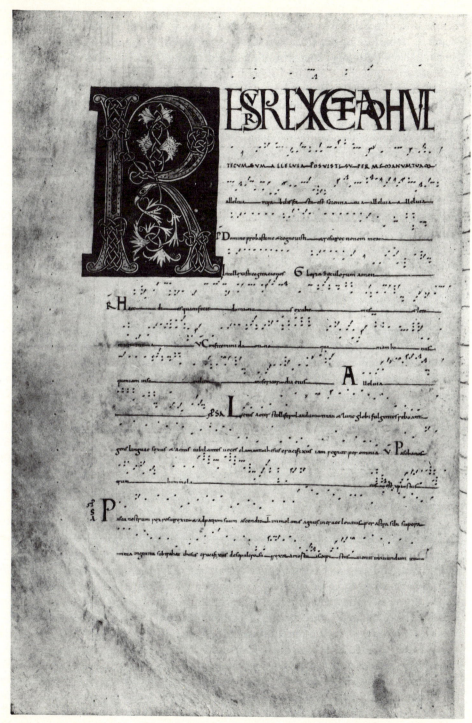

Fig. I-1: A page from an eleventh-century manuscript from southwestern France, showing the beginning of the Easter Mass (cf. Ex.I-6, which reproduces in modern notation the music of the beginning). (Paris, Bibliothèque nationale, MS Lat. 776.)

In addition, all these chants except the alleluias share a notable technique of composition: most of the melodies, instead of being individual and unique, are put together by stringing together certain standard melodic formulas.[1] Each category of chant had a repertoire of such formulas for each mode. Thus, for example, eighth-mode responsories have three or four different opening formulas, a number of different formulas for the immediate continuation, several for the first cadence, and so on. Most of the material of a normal eighth-mode responsory would be selected from this stock repertoire, with bits of free material to effect the connections. This technique is known as "centonization"—meaning patchwork, which is precisely what it is. Nothing could better illustrate the profound difference between our views about what music should be and those of the early Middle Ages than this unabashedly "plagiaristic" approach. Its origin is doubtless to be found in an early practice of solo improvisation, in which standard phrases would greatly simplify the improviser's task; and parallels to it can be found in literature (the standard epithets of epic poetry) and in painting (the copying of ikons in Byzantine art, or the duplication of pictorial motives in Western painting). It is a tribute to the earliest authors of the repertoire of melodic fragments that the results of this apparently unaesthetic way of "composing" are almost invariably of the highest quality.

Gradual

The graduals are perhaps the finest examples of the melismatic style. *Tecum principium* (Ex. I-8) is assigned to the second mode, but uses the final a instead of D, and shares a special repertoire of formulas with a group of melodically similar graduals. In this piece, the contrast between passages of vigorous melodic motion and stretches of almost static behavior—already mentioned in connection with offertory verses—is especially pronounced. In the respond, from "ex utero" on, the melody is almost entirely centered on c until "te," when it climbs laboriously to f before sinking to the final. In contrast, the beginning of the verse is recitational in style, almost like the intonation of an Office psalm chant (from which, perhaps, these ornate melodies may originally have derived). Such syllabic passages throw the melismas into stronger relief and show how variety in text-setting can be used to reinforce musical structure. Unfortunately the original ABA pattern of the gradual was destroyed before the thirteenth century: the custom grew up of omitting the repetition of the respond, and having the chorus join in at the end of the verse.

Tract

The tracts are similar in style to the graduals. They occur in only two modes, the second and eighth, and each mode has only a limited stock of formulas. As a result, the family resemblance between any two tracts of the same mode is very strong. The tracts differ from the graduals in manner of performance, for there is no recurrent respond: instead, the several verses are sung consecutively by soloists, without repetition.

Liturgically, the tracts function to replace the alleluia during seasons of penitence, most notably in Lent. Consequently, a number of them have texts of a rather dark and gloomy character. This is by no means, however, a universal characteristic: some texts are neutral or even rather joyous ("Praise the Lord, all ye heathen," for the second Sunday in Lent). Considering that all the tract melodies of each of the two modes used are closely similar, and that neither mode is regularly associated with any specific kind of text, another important aspect of Gregorian chant becomes evident: the music makes no attempt to reproduce the sentiments expressed in the words. It is hard to imagine a

---

[1]This bears an obvious relation to the "families" of melodies mentioned in connection with the antiphons.

Gradual
[Soloist]   [Choir]

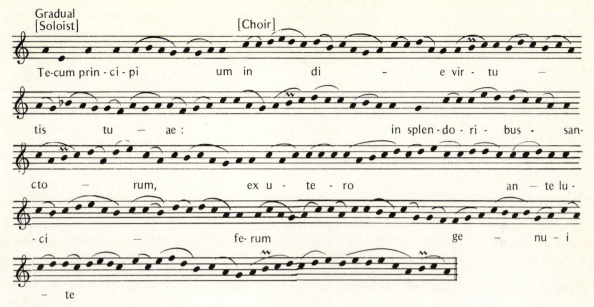

Te-cum prin - ci - pi   um in   di —   e vir - tu —
tis   tu — ae :   in splen-do-ri-bus · sancto —   rum,   ex u - te - ro   an - te lu-
-ci —   fe- rum   ge — nu - i
— te

The rule be with you in the day of your power; in the glory of the saints, before the
morning star I have begotten you.

Verse

Di-xit Do — mi-nus Do-mi-no me —   o: Se — — de a dex tris me —   is: do-
nec po - nam i-ni-mi — cos   tu - - os,   sca - bel —
— — — — — lum   pe — dum tu-o — —
rum.

The Lord said to my lord, sit on my right hand, until I make your enemies a footstool for
your feet.

Ex. I-8

composer of more recent times giving the same melody to "Lord, have mercy upon me" and "the truth of the Lord is everlasting," but precisely this happens in the tracts, and other examples may be found throughout the Gregorian repertoire.

This is not a defect, but rather a particular feature of the aesthetic of the chant. Music was expected to clothe and adorn the texts that it used, not to interpret them. Adornment in itself is emotionally neutral, and the formal clothes used for a funeral may be equally appropriate to a wedding or a diplomatic reception: the point is merely that a certain degree of solemnity is required. So also with the chant: the style of the "clothing" is always appropriate to the liturgical circumstances; the individual melodic garment was not, however, dependent upon the subjective emotions aroused by the text being set.

All categories of chant so far examined are remarkably homogeneous. There is evidence that all the proper chants of the Mass except the alleluia had been assigned to the appropriate liturgical occasions by the eighth century, probably with some form of the music that has survived. These may therefore be taken to represent "classical" Gregorian style, and their homogeneity to represent a constant tradition of composition. The case is otherwise with the alleluias of the Mass and the great responsories. The earliest manuscripts (unnotated sources of the eight and ninth centuries) do not contain identical alleluia repertoires, nor do they always agree as to the assignment of specific alleluias to specific Sundays and feasts. This suggests that the alleluias were at that time new compositions about whose disposition agreement had not yet been reached. Not surprisingly, therefore, they are different in style, both from each other and from the classical chants.

Alleluia

All alleluias have the same overall form: the word "alleluia" is sung by a soloist, then repeated to the same music by the choir. There follows a melisma, or jubilus, and then a verse (soloist), after which "alleluia" with its jubilus is repeated.

Within this general framework, considerable differences occur. Some alleluias closely resemble the classical style, and may have been composed at the same time as the other proper chants, or in close imitation of them. Others, however, such as the *Alleluia Surrexit Christus* (Ex. I-9), exhibit striking differences in style and details of form. There are numerous descending scale fragments, a feature for the most part absent from classical Gregorian melodies. Even more noticeable, however, is the extensive repetition of material. The end of the verse (melisma on "suo") is identical with the last two-thirds of the jubilus, and the beginning of the verse quotes from the beginning of the alleluia.

It is generally believed that alleluias resembling *Surrexit Christus* are a product of a period later than the one that produced the other proper chants. Confirmation of this supposition is provided by the general absence of centonization, so important for the graduals and tracts. While the same alleluia melody often serves for several different verse texts, it is the entire melody that is adapted, not a repertoire of standard phrases. Moreover, where adaptation is not in question, the melodies are generally entirely different—more diverse in style than the presumably earlier chants.

The alleluia repertoire is therefore a mixed one, containing some chants in the classical style and others in a different, more modern idiom. The mixture is even more pronounced in the case of the great responsories. The oldest responsories belong to the same period as the graduals. They are heavily dependent on centonization, almost certainly an early technique. Their verses are also regularly set to ornate standard tones,

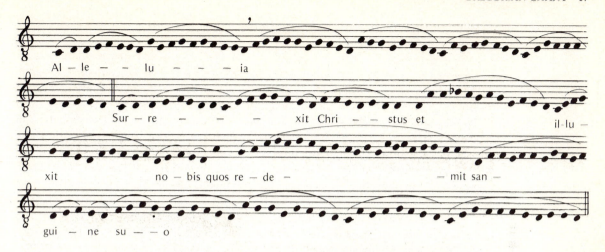

Al – le – – lu – – – ia

Sur – re – – – xit Chri – – stus et il-lu –

xit no – bis quos re – de – – mit san –

gui – ne su – – o

Alleluia: Christ has arisen and shone upon us, whom he redeemed with his blood.

Ex. I-9

a procedure not found in the other responsorial chants, but one suggesting an early date. Later responsories tend to ignore the repertoire of standard phrases in favor of free, newly created melodies, often showing some of the stylistic features of the later alleluias. In some cases, the verses abandon the standard tones and are given free melodies of their own. In these later responsories, as in the late alleluias, it is apparent that the old Gregorian aesthetic has been abandoned. In place of the older preference for the typical, which produced melodies centonized out of common material, the new view emphasized the individual.

The vast Gregorian repertoire, with its thousands of chants, is the oldest Western music that has come down to us, and has doubtless been in continuous use as long as any body of music whatever. Both in its influence and in its intrinsic value, it is one of the greatest of artistic achievements. It differs from later music in many particulars: in its manner of exploiting tonal relationships, its use of standard formulas, its avoidance of personal sentiment, and much else. These differences, taken together with the exceedingly modest means employed in the chant, may make it at first hearing rather inaccessible to the modern listener. But there is scarcely any music that more richly repays close study than the chant. The experienced hearer finds in it an inexhaustible treasure of melody. If it does not speak personally to the hearer, this is not because it is mute, but because it is directed to God rather than to man. Personality has no place in such a music.

THEORY AND NOTATION

Three matters connected with the chant remain to be mentioned. The first of these is the theory of the modes, developed in the tenth and eleventh centuries. Modal *practice* was understood much earlier: eightfold classifications of sacred chant may be found in Byzantine music, and even in pre-Christian rites of the near East. But even as late as the ninth century, the writer Aurelian of Réomé, while providing detailed

Classical modal theory

information on what tones and terminations to use, was unable to give a clear idea of what a mode actually is.

This lack of an adequate definition was bothersome, and the problem was increased by the medieval compulsion to find antique authority for contemporary practice. Among the few surviving classical treatises on music, the *De institutione musica* (roughly: principles of music) of Boethius (d. ca. 524) seemed to offer a theoretical justification for the medieval modal system. Boethius wrote of eight modes, most of them grouped into pairs similar to the authentic-plagal pairs of Gregorian modes. These modes had traditional Greek tribal names: Dorian, Phrygian, Lydian, and Mixolydian, with the prefix "hypo-" (e.g., Hypolydian) for the lower modes of a pair. In point of fact, they had no connection whatsoever with the modes of the chant, being derived from pre-Christian Greek speculative theory. Nevertheless, the outward similarity was tempting to medieval minds, and by the tenth century, serious attempts were made to reconcile Boethian teaching with medieval practice. These attempts, at first tentative and confused, finally succeeded, expecially in the work of Guido of Arezzo and Hermannus Contractus, both writing in the eleventh century.

The Church modes   As worked out by these and other theorists, the modal system was an elegant synthesis. Each pair of modes (first and second, third and fourth, etc.) shared a common final, and, in addition, certain "species" of fourth and fifth. Thus, for example, the fifth and sixth modes shared that species of fifth in which the semitone lies at the top. In the authentic modes, the fifth was reckoned up from the final, and the fourth up from the top note of the fifth. In the plagals, the fourth lay below the final instead. It can be seen from a diagram of the complete system (Ex. I-10) that each of the first seven modes has its own species of octave as well; that is, the sequence of tones and semitones is different for each of these modes. Since the diatonic octave can have only seven species, the eighth mode cannot have its own: it duplicates that of the first. But since it has a different final and a different species of fifth, its identity is adequately established.

This construction is highly ingenious and intellectually satisfying. It does not accurately represent what Boethius had in mind, but that is hardly surprising, since Boethius was describing something quite different from Gregorian chant. More important, however, it does not adequately represent the chant either. One may search the

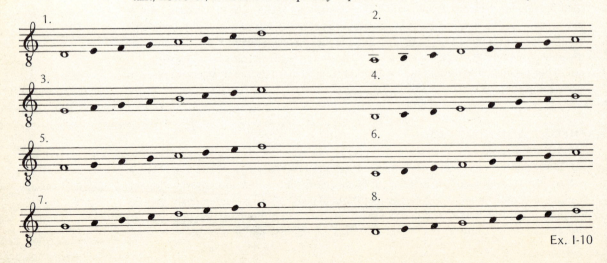

Ex. I-10

diagram in vain for traces of the common F-a-c pattern of the eighth mode, for the persistence of F and c in all modes, for the prevalence of patterns bounded by a seventh (not an octave), and the like. It is therefore undesirable to use terms such as "Dorian" for the chant, and it is rarely fruitful to use the concepts of modal theory in an attempt to "explain" Gregorian music.

Eleventh-century theory is, however, important in other respects. Its intellectualism, based on that of Boethius, set the tone for centuries of musical thought. For the Middle Ages and even after, the true "musician" was one who understood music as an intellectual discipline. The actual practice of music—composition and performance—was given a much lower status. Thus when theory and practice disgreed, the former had the advantage. Some Gregorian chants were revised in the eleventh century to make them at least somewhat more compatible with theory. Moreover, it is likely that the new music written in the tenth and eleventh centuries was influenced by the development of modal theory—or at least the product of a similar type of thinking.

The second matter to be considered is that of musical notation. While the chant *Notation* was initially transmitted orally, manuscripts with notation begin to appear from the ninth century on. Apparently the oral transmission had been extremely careful, for there is remarkable unanimity in the early notated sources.

It is generally believed that the first attempt at notation in the West was the addition of accent marks to the texts of lections. These served to mark the cadences of the lection tones. Since the grave accent (ˋ) was used to indicate a falling accent in speech, it was naturally employed in music to denote a lower pitch; the acute (ˊ), conversely, marked a higher pitch; and the circumflex (ˆ) a higher followed by a lower pitch. The exact notes to be sung could not be specified, but this was hardly important, as the singer would easily remember them.

By the ninth century, the accents were associated, at least in thought, with free melodies as well. Aurelian of Réomé speaks of a tune as being "acute" at one point, "circumflexed" at another. By the end of the century, fully notated manuscripts appeared. In these, the basic accents retain their original meaning, but, especially in ornate chant, they are less common than compound signs, made up of from two to five or more elements. These compound signs, or neumes, are written in a cursive fashion, *Neumes* and rarely look much like the accents from which they derive, but they show clearly enough the general contour of the melody, without, however, indicating exact pitches or intervals. The same ambiguity characterizes the rather obscure ornamental symbols which also appear in the music, indicating special vocal effects.

Thus the early manuscripts were and could be no more than mnemonic aids for singers who already knew the repertoire by heart. They could not communicate a new melody to a singer unfamiliar with it, nor could they preserve the old ones unaided by an accurate oral tradition. They must, however, have performed a great service in reducing the burden on the singers' memory: even now, a singer skilled in the chant can, with a glance at notation of this type, recognize a familiar melody and sing it.

The making of a singer in the tenth century was, then, still mostly a matter of memory. It was, in fact, a process that took several laborious years; indeed, without the presence in the chant of such devices as centonization and the use of the same melody for different texts, it would have taken a lifetime. The notation, which from the first was both calligraphically beautiful and extremely subtle in indicating elegant nuances of singing, helped, but not enough. Some means of conveying pitch more accurately was needed to shorten the period of a singer's training, and even more to help disseminate the mass of new music that was then being written.

The first attempts at a more precise notation are found in certain early manuscripts in which the neumes are written, not in a straight line above the text, but in an undulating fashion. This reproduces graphically the rise and fall of the melody: the height of a sign on the page has been taken as a metaphor for the "highness" or "lowness" of the music. Obvious and natural as this metaphor may seem, it was a novel and important achievement (neither the ancient Greeks or the Byzantines, for example, ever knew it). From there it was only a short step to drawing a straight line over the text, and arranging the neumes quite precisely with reference to that line. Once the pitch represented by the line was known, the pitch of any notational sign could then be easily determined. This transformation of the old neumes into an accurately "diastematic" (heighted) notation was accomplished independently in the southwest of France and in southern Italy in the late tenth and early eleventh centuries. Subsequently, other lines were added, parallel to the first, for even greater clarity. This produced what we know as the staff—basically no more than a refinement of the one-line system, but a very valuable one. Its invention is attributed to Guido of Arezzo.

Diastematic notation

Diastematic notation did not represent a pure gain for the chant. The necessity for accurate heighting required modification of the flowing shape of the early neumes, and many of the subtleties suggested by the earlier system simply could not be represented in the new. For example, it is certain that the chant once used tones in addition to those of the diatonic scale, and intervals smaller than a semitone for ornamental purposes. The former were not, and the latter could not be represented on a staff. Thus certain centers of chant continued to use staffless and unheighted neumes long after diastematic notation had become available. The famous monastery of St. Gall, in what is now Switzerland, which had produced some of the most important early manuscripts of chant, is a case in point: heighted neumes were not used there until late, when the monastery was in decline.

Staff notation

In France, during the twelfth and thirteenth centuries, staff notation acquired the form that it was to keep in liturgical books until the present. This form, known as "Roman chorale notation" or "square notation," served not only as a vehicle for accurate transmission of the chant, but also, from the late twelfth century, as the principal means of notating polyphonic music (see below, Chapter III).

The examples given in this book have been reproduced, not in traditional chant notation, but in modern notes without stems. This implies a manner of performance in which all notes are equal in duration. In fact, however, the rhythmic interpretation of the chant is one of its most controversial aspects. When in the nineteenth century the French monks of the Benedictine abbey of Solesmes began their great work of rescuing the chant from the neglect and corruption into which it had fallen, they became convinced that the chant had originally been sung with most notes rhythmically equal. This interpretation was therefore used in the numerous chant books published by them, and it eventually received the official approval of the authorities of the Roman Catholic Church.

Other scholars, however, were not convinced. There is evidence—obscure and difficult, to be sure—that in the tenth and eleventh centuries differing rhythmic values were in use, and that certain chants may have had some sort of metric regularity. The controversy has continued to the present time and shows no signs of resolution. On the whole, those favoring some sort of rhythmic differentiation seem to have the better case in theory, but they have never come to any agreement among themselves as to how the theory should be executed. As a result, anyone who actually wishes to sing the chant has very little choice: he may either attach himself to the opinions of one single scholar and use whatever method that scholar may advocate (and even then, he must make his own rhythmic versions of what he wants to sing), or he may use the "equalistic" method. The latter alternative is almost universally chosen; and the Solesmes interpretation is, in practice, victorious—not so much because of its scholarly merits, but because its adversaries cannot agree on any other.

The third and final matter concerning the chant is again theoretical, as was the first, but in a different way. Alongside the intellectual modal theory already discussed, there grew up a kind of practical theory aimed at helping the beginner to master the chant. This was based on yet another invention of Guido of Arezzo, amplified by later musicians. He observed that the six lines of a melody for the hymn *Ut queant laxis* (Ex. I-11) each began (1) with a different text syllable: ut, re, mi, fa, sol, and la; and (2) on

That your servants may sing with deeper notes of your wondrous deeds, St. John, cleanse the guilt of unclean lips.

Ex. I-11

successively higher notes: C, D, E, F, G, and a. The interval pattern formed by the six notes C to a was called a hexachord. Since the whole body of chant used only the range of notes beginning on low G and going up to the g two octaves higher, the hexachord, preserving its exact sequence of tones and semitones, could lie in only a few places: beginning on the low G, on C, on F (using a b flat), on the next G, and on the c above (in which case a high a must be added to the top of the range). The hexachords on C were called natural, those on G hard, and that on F soft (Ex. I-12). Within a hexachord, the notes were designated by the appropriate text syllable of the hymn. Thus in any hexachord, the first (lowest) note was ut, the second re, and so on. Most notes could belong to more than one hexachord, owing to overlapping. Thus the central G could be sol (C-hexachord), re (F-hexachord), and ut (G-hexachord). It was referred to in writing as G sol-re-ut.

Hexachords

Ex. I-12

Solmization   The singer learning a new piece would select a hexachord of appropriate range and sing, not the text, but the proper syllables to the pitches of the melody. If the melody exceeded the bounds of the first hexachord, he would "mutate" into a new one by using as a pivot a note common to both the old and the new hexachords, as shown in the solmization of the opening of the antiphon *Apertis thesauris* (Ex. I-13). This process of sight-singing was facilitated by the "Guidonian hand," a diagram in which each pitch was given a location on one of the joints of the fingers.

Ex. 1-13

Opening their treasures, they offered.

Obviously this is not "theory" in the same way as the modal system, but the system of "solmization" (so named after two of the designation syllables) had an immediate and lasting effect on musical pedagogy. With various modifications, it has remained in use from the eleventh century to the present day.

The Liturgical Year

The specific content of any service, whether Mass or Office, is in some part determined by the cycle of observances of the Christian Year. Each Sunday is a feast commemorating the resurrection, but specific events in the life of Christ are commemorated in a series of feast days and seasons, organized in two cycles of seasons, having similar organization and being grouped around one of the two central feasts of the year, Christmas and Easter. One of these seasons being fixed and the other moveable, the interlocking of the two cycles is assured by seasons of variable length to accommodate the beginning of the next cycle. The list below describes the two cycles.

I.   Feasts of Our Lord (The Proper of the Time)

Preparation	*Advent.* From the 4th Sunday before Christmas until Christmas. A season of penitence and preparation for the Nativity.
Central feast	*CHRISTMAS.* December 25. Commemorates the Nativity of Christ.
Period of rejoicing	Christmastide lasts 12 days.
Season variable in length	*Epiphany.* The 13th day after Christmas (Jan. 6). Commemorates the manifestation of Christ to the Gentiles, as symbolized by the visit of the Magi. The season lasts until the beginning of the Easter cycle.
Preparation	*Pre-Lent.* The three Sundays preceding Lent, with the intervening weekdays. *Lent.* The 40 weekdays (representing Christ's temptation in the wilderness) plus 6 Sundays preceding Easter. Begins on *Ash Wednesday.* The last three days of Lent are especially solemn, each having its own liturgical observances: *Maundy Thursday* commemorates the Last Supper and the institution of the Mass; *Good Friday* commemorates the crucifixion of Christ; *Holy Saturday,* the Easter Vigil, has since earliest times been the day for admission of new members by baptism.
Central feast	*EASTER.* The first Sunday after the full moon on or next after March 21. Commemorates the resurrection of Christ.
Period of rejoicing	A 40-day Eastertide of rejoicing, followed by *Ascension:* the 40th day after Easter. Ascensiontide continues for 10 days.
Season variable in length	*Pentecost.* Fifty days after Easter. Commemorates the coming of the Holy Spirit. Sundays after Pentecost continue until the first Sunday of Advent (generally five to six months).

II. **Feasts of the Saints**

    A.   The Proper of the Saints. Specific saints and events are commemorated on a fixed date, each year; each feast has its own proper chants, lessons, etc.

        1. Feasts of the Blessed Virgin Mary. Various feasts throughout the year commemorating events and qualities of the life of Mary, the mother of Jesus; for example, the Purification (Feb. 2), the Annunciation (March 25), the Visitation (July 2).

        2. Feasts of the saints. Certain saints, either because of their importance or because of the antiquity of their observances, have their own proper chants, prayers, and lessons. They are commemorated on fixed dates yearly. Some examples: St. Stephen (Dec. 26), St. Thomas, apostle (Dec. 21), the Conversion of St. Paul (Jan. 25).

    B.   The Common of the Saints. Because of the proliferation of the cult of the saints in the Middle Ages, and the impracticality of providing new propers for each feast, certain collections of proper chants, lessons, and prayers are used for several saints with common qualities. These groupings are as follows:

Apostles and evangelists
Popes
One martyr (bishop or non-bishop)
Two or more martyrs
Confessors (bishops or non-bishops)
Doctors
Virgins (martyrs or non-martyrs)
Holy women (martyrs or non-martyrs)

As an example, the Feast of St. Timothy, bishop and martyr, celebrated on January 24, uses the proper chants, lessons, and prayers for feasts of one martyr.

III. **Other observances.**

    A.   Ember weeks. The Ember weeks at the four seasons, being the Wednesday, Friday, and Saturday after (1) the First Sunday in Lent, (2) the Feast of Pentecost, (3) September 14, and (4) December 13, are set aside as special seasons of fasting and penitence.

    B.   Votive and occasional Masses. Propers are provided for special occasions or intentions that do not occur regularly; for example, weddings, burials (the Requiem Mass, named for the first word of its introit); Masses of the Holy Trinity, of the Angels, etc.

The Mass

The Mass, as the re-enactment of the Last Supper, has from earliest times been the principal act of worship of the Church. Its basic actions are the taking of bread and wine; the giving of thanks over both; the breaking of the bread; and the distribution to the faithful. These actions together form the basis of the Eucharist, or Holy Communion. From very early times the Eucharist was preceded by prayers and readings from scripture, so that the service as a whole might have an educational as well as a sacramental function. This fore-mass is concerned principally with what is said, while the Eucharist is concerned with what is done.

The following table lists the events of the Mass in order, and classifies them according to whether they are sung to a recitation formula or have a more purely musical construction. The musical pieces are further divided into *proper* (i.e., appropriate to the occasion by having a special text for each feast) and *ordinary* (i.e., having a fixed and unchanging text) chants. It will be noted that some chants are designed to accompany specific actions, while others have a purely musical function.

Certain later accretions (e.g., the blessing of Holy Water before Mass and the reading of a Last Gospel after the blessing) are omitted in the table.

Table 1. Structure of the Mass

Recitation	Proper (variable text)	Ordinary (fixed text)
	1. *Introit.* Action chant: during the ceremonial entrance of the celebrant	
		2. *Kyrie*
		3. *Gloria* (omitted in penitential seasons). These two chants are a standardized form of the litany sung at this point in earlier times
4. *Collect.* Prayer for the day		
5. *Epistle.* First reading		
	6. *Gradual* (replaced in Eastertide by an *Alleluia*)	
	7. *Alleluia* (replaced in Lent by a *Tract*) These two chants are the only purely musical events in the Mass	
8. *Gospel.* Second reading		
		9. *Credo.* A later addition; not used in Rome until the 11th century
	10. *Offertory.* Action chant: during the taking and preparing of bread and wine	
11. *Secret.* Prayer over offering		
12. *Preface.* Text partly fixed, partly variable with season; serves as introduction to *Sanctus*		
		13. *Sanctus*
14. *Canon.* Prayer of consecration; text invariable; spoken since the 8th century		
15. *Lord's Prayer*		

Table 1. Structure of the Mass (continued)

Recitation	Proper (variable text)	Ordinary (fixed text)
		16. *Agnus Dei.* During the breaking of bread
	17. *Communion.* Action chant: during the distribution of bread and wine	
18. *Postcommunion.* Final prayer		
		19. *Ite, missa est* (replaced by *Benedicamus Domino* in penitential seasons). Dismissal
20. *Benediction.* Spoken; a later (post-9th-century) addition		

The Office

The regular round of prayer and worship in monastic communities. The Rule of St. Benedict (6th cent.) first gave a fixed order to these services, which occur eight times daily:

1. Matins (during the night)
2. Lauds (before dawn)
3. Prime (*ad primam horam*, i.e., 6 a.m.)   ⎤
4. Terce (*ad tertiam horam*, i.e., 9 a.m.)   ⎟ The "little hours"
5. Sext (*ad sextam horam*, i.e., noon)   ⎟
6. None (*ad nonam horam*, i.e., 3 p.m.)   ⎦
7. Vespers (at sunset)
8. Compline (before retiring)

All offices contain the following elements:

1. Recitation of a portion of the psalter
2. Reading from the scripture, followed by a sung response. This can vary in elaborateness as follows:
   a. Prime, Terce, Sext, None, and Compline: a *capitulum* (as little as one sentence) followed by a simple versicle and response
   b. Lauds and Vespers: a *capitulum* followed by a *short responsory*
   c. Matins: nine lections, each of considerable length, and each followed by a *great responsory*
3. A hymn, which may come before (Matins, little hours), after (Lauds, Vespers) or between (Compline) the psalms and reading

In addition, some offices contain *canticles*, portions of scripture not from the Book of Psalms, but performed like psalms.

Table 2. Structure of the Roman[1] office

	The little hours	Compline	Lauds and Vespers	Matins
Introduction	Hymn			Invitatory psalm, with antiphon. Hymn
Psalms	Several psalms, the group preceded and followed by a single antiphon	3 psalms, the group preceded and followed by a single antiphon	5 psalms (at Lauds, one is a canticle), each with its own antiphon	Three nocturns. each containing: 5 psalms with 5 antiphons
Reading	Capitulum Versicle and response	Hymn Capitulum Short responsory	Capitulum Short responsory	3 lections with 3 Great responsories
Ending		Canticle, with antiphon	Hymn Canticle, with antiphon	(Originally the nocturns were separate offices, later united to form Matins)

[1]This arrangement is used by the church of Rome, by cathedral and other collegiate churches, and by certain religious communities, such as Dominicans and Franciscans. Another arrangement, called the Monastic office, is used by other groups, such as Benedictines, Cistercians, and Carthusians. The differences are minor, and concern mostly the numbers of things (psalms, antiphons, etc.) the offices contain.

Form and performance of musical pieces.

Chants may conveniently be divided into text-related (recitation formula) and musical forms.

I.   **Text-related forms.**

    A. Lections and prayers. Lections (capitulum, lection, epistle, and gospel) and prayers are chanted to recitation tones which accommodate themselves to the phrasing of the text to be chanted. Though there are several such tones, varying in elaborateness according to liturgical function, they all have a similar structure. Each tone usually recites on a single note, to which are added formulas for a full stop (period) and a pause (comma, semicolon), and a formula to signify the end of the lection.

    B. Psalmody. There are several different formulas for singing the psalms, but they all have a similar structure. Formulas consist of a single reciting pitch, to which are added melodic formulas for the beginning, the middle, and the end of the verse. For any psalm tone, the formula is repeated for each verse of the psalm.

II. **Musical forms.** These may be classified as *antiphonal* (alternating between two groups of singers) or *responsorial* (employing alternation between a soloist and the chorus.

    A. Antiphonal pieces.

        1. *Antiphon.* To be sung before and after the singing of a psalm or canticle (and originally sung between the verses as well). Antiphons are sung by the whole chorus, and the psalm is sung in alternate verses by the two groups.

        2. *Introit.* A rather elaborate antiphon used at the Mass for the entrance of the celebrant. Originally a whole psalm, the Introit now consists only of a single verse plus a doxology ("Glory be . . ."), preceded and followed by the antiphon.

        3. *Communion.* The antiphon sung at the distribution of communion at Mass. Originally a psalm was sung, but the antiphon is now used alone.

        4. *Offertory.* The antiphon sung during the preparation of the bread and wine at Mass. Originally consisting of an antiphon and several verses, the Offertory now consists of a single antiphon. The music (especially that of the now omitted verses) is so elaborate that the chant may never have been designed for choral singing.

        5. *Chants of the ordinary.* Settings of the unchanging sung portions of the Mass. These chants, of later medieval composition, employ no solo singers, but require the alternation of the halves of the choir. They are discussed in Chapter II.

        6. *Hymns.* Metrical, non-biblical poems. Alternate strophes are performed by alternate sides of the choir. See Chapter II.

B. Responsorial pieces. These are generally elaborate, as they involve the use of trained solo singers. The number of soloists employed (from one to four) increases with the importance of the feast.

1. *Responsory.* A refrain, sung by the chorus, precedes an elaborate verse (usually a fixed formula) sung by the soloists, which is then followed by a repetition of all or part of the refrain. Sometimes this is followed by a solo doxology and another repetition of the choral refrain. Short responsories and great responsories both have this structure, but the music of the short responsory is very simple, while that of the great responsory is elaborate.

2. *Gradual.* A great responsory sung at the Mass. The repetition of the refrain is now usually omitted, and the choir joins with the soloists for the conclusion of the verse.

3. *Tract.* A series of psalm verses sung to very elaborate musical formulas by soloists alternating with the full choir.

4. *Alleluia.* The soloists sing the word "alleluia," which is repeated by the choir, adding a long melisma or *jubilus*. The soloists then sing an elaborate verse, and the chorus repeats the original Alleluia with its *jubilus*.

Bibliography

A. Books containing chants.

The official editors of chant-books for the Roman Catholic Church are the monks of the Abbey of Solesmes, France. All of the books listed below (except the *Offertoriale*), in addition to a number of others, were produced by them.

The Liber Usualis with Introduction and Rubrics in English (Desclée no. 801), Tournai, 1963. A great compendium of music for both the Mass and the Office for the principal feasts of the year.

Graduale Sacrosanctae Romanae Ecclesiae (Desclée no. 696), Tournai, 1938, 1916. The complete music for the Mass for the entire liturgical year.

Antiphonale Sacrosanctae Romanae Ecclesiae (Desclée no. 820), Tournai, 1949. Music for the Office (except Matins) according to the Roman, or secular, rite.

Antiphonale monasticum pro diurnis horis (Desclée no. 818), Tournai, 1934. Music for the Office (except Matins) according to the monastic rite.

Liber responsorialis, Solesmes, 1895. Music for Matins of certain feasts, according to the monastic rite.

Processionale monasticum, Solesmes, 1893. Responsories, antiphons and other pieces for use in processions.

Carolus Ott, ed.: *Offertoriale sive versus offertorium*, Tournai, 1935. The offertories for the year, along with their verses, which latter are not preserved in the Solesmes books.

B. Books on chant.

Peter Wagner: *Einführung in die gregorianischen Melodien*, 3 vols., Leipzig, 1895–1921.

I. *Ursprung und Entwicklung der liturgischen Gesangsformen*, 1895; 2d ed., 1901;

　　　　3d ed., 1911. English translation of the 2d ed. as *Origin and Development of the Forms of the Liturgical Chant*, London, 1907.

　　II. *Neumenkunde*, 1905, 2d ed., 1912.

　　III. *Gregorianischen Formenlehre*, 1921.

　　　　Despite its age, the best general work on the chant, both historical and descriptive.

Willi Apel: *Gregorian Chant*, Bloomington, Indiana, 1958. A one-volume study in English, based largely on the study of the Solesmes books, and containing much valuable information of an analytical, descriptive, and statistical sort.

Paléographie musicale. The monumental series published by the monks of Solesmes, under the successive editorships of André Mocquereau, Joseph Gajard, and Jean Claire, 1889–　. The series presents facsimiles of important chant manuscripts, and the introductions present important studies on subjects of chant paleography and history.

POST-GREGORIAN CHANT

All the chant considered so far is termed "Gregorian," despite the stylistic innovations observed in some alleluias and great responsories. These innovations seem to have made their first appearance in the eighth or ninth century—precisely the period when the Gregorian repertoire was being disseminated through the Frankish kingdom. It is quite likely that the classical Gregorian style was essentially Mediterranean, while the newer elements were northern in origin.

For many years it was the custom to regard all the products of the post-Gregorian period as decadent and uncreative—to regard the music composed during the ninth, tenth, and eleventh centuries as pedestrian compared with the "inspired" Gregorian melodies. It would be at least remarkable if this judgment were correct—if three hundred years had produced no music of real value. But the evaluation is false. One may legitimately prefer Gregorian music to that which followed, but not because the former is "better." The output of the period in question was of enormous importance in its own right, both historically and aesthetically.

Characteristics of post-Gregorian music

The innovations mentioned may be found occasionally in the proper chants of the Mass, but truly new styles in the strict sense arose outside of those categories. By the ninth century, every liturgical occasion was already provided with its own music. The gradual *Viderunt omnes* was sung on Christmas throughout western Christendom, and a new composition for the same purpose was neither necessary nor indeed permitted. The traditional chants were regarded as divinely inspired, and their suppression would have been a kind of sacrilege. Only the occasional introduction of a new feast into the calendar might provide an opportunity for the writing of new music for the proper—and this was hardly an adequate outlet for generations of composers and poets.

It was inevitable, however, that the new styles should have been preserved solely in the area of sacred music. There was doubtless an abundance of secular music during this period, and it is quite possible that secular influences helped to determine new directions in sacred music. But for the educated—still for the most part the clergy—secular art was by nature "popular," and hence not worthy of serious study or (when notation was available) of preservation.

31

Fig. II-1: Choir of the cathedral of Autun, France, a superb example of Romanesque architecture dating from the early twelfth century. Other Romanesque buildings, especially those of southwestern France, are more heavily ornamented and less "classical" in style. (Photograph: Bildarchiv Foto Marburg.)

This left the composer with little apparent room for exploitation: chants for the ordinary of the Mass and melodies for the hymns of the Office would at first seem to be the only areas in which large-scale expansion could be undertaken. But this reckons without the medieval love of elaboration. Traditional literary or theological texts that have survived frequently bear extensive "glosses"—textual explanations and amplifications, far longer than the original text—carefully written in the margins of the page. In much the same way, the traditional chants of the liturgy, while they could not be replaced or altered, could be expanded and amplified by textual and musical additions. This process led to the creation of several new forms, and of a repertoire as large as the Gregorian and considerably more diverse.

It is this diversity that suggests the phrase "new styles" rather than "new style" for post-Gregorian music, called "medieval chant" by some scholars. Yet certain traits are common to most, if not all, of the repertoire. One, a fondness for repetition, has already been observed in the presumably late *Alleluia Surrexit Christus* given in the preceding chapter (Ex. I-9). Another is an increased reliance on the intervals of the perfect fifth and the octave above the final as fundamental organizing relationships within a melody. Yet another, less immediately tangible, is a preference for purposeful melodic motion towards a predictable goal. The static hovering characteristic of so many Gregorian chants (especially ornate ones), is almost never found in later music. Naturally some Gregorian traits persist in post-Gregorian music—which was, after all, composed by men who sang the traditional chants daily. The mixture of new and old varies from one piece to another, dependent, no doubt, on circumstances now wholly unknown.

THE ORDINARY OF THE MASS

The ordinary of the Mass was one obvious area in which new musical settings were welcome. The ordinary texts had been added to the liturgy at different times. Originally, it seems, they were sung to simple melodies by the whole congregation. Little or no true Gregorian music has survived for them. At a relatively early time, the choir took over the singing of the ordinary, and it was then possible to give the texts more elaborate musical settings. There was, of course, no reason to restrict each text to a single melody. Such a limitation was appropriate to the proper chants, many of which were sung only once a year; but texts sung daily could well afford to have multiple musical settings, both to avoid monotony, and to provide varying degrees of solemnity appropriate to different liturgical occasions.

Chants for the ordinary of the Mass

Composers took good advantage of this opportunity. Several hundred melodies survive for the Kyrie eleison alone, and while not all the texts of the ordinary were as popular, their settings, too, were numerous. The modern chant books give only a small selection from this repertoire, and present them in somewhat misleading fashion. They are arranged in cycles or "Masses," each Mass containing a setting of the Kyrie, Gloria, Sanctus, and Agnus Dei (the few settings of the Credo are given separately). The implication is that each Mass is in some way an organic whole. In fact, however, the melodies were written separately, without reference to each other. Their gathering together to form complete cycles was the work of the late Middle Ages.

The texts of the Kyrie, Sanctus, and Agnus Dei are all rather short, and were given largely melismatic settings. The Gloria and Credo, however, are relatively long, and could not be so treated without excessive length. Their melodies are therefore neumatic or syllabic.

The Kyrie given here (Ex. II-1) is clearly post-Gregorian in style. It is quite easy to predict from the opening notes what the final tone is to be. The melody is in constant, purposeful motion. This is particularly evident in the "Christe" section, where the first phrase ornamentally outlines the series c-b-a-G, then presents the same descent directly, and finally, by touching on F, attaches the loose E of the first "Kyrie" to the melodic web. Such directed melody appears in Gregorian chant, to be sure, but only intermittently, as a special device; here it is present constantly. The frequency of descending scale fragments, already noted in connection with the *Alleluia Surrexit Christus* (Ex. I-9), is another symptom of the new stylistic orientation. So also is the amount of repetition, but since this doubtless results at least in part from the repetitions within the text, it is perhaps of less significance in this case.

Lord have mercy; Christ have mercy; Lord have mercy.   Ex. II-1

Glory to God in the highest, and on earth peace to men of good will. We praise you, we bless you, we adore you, we glorify you, we give thanks to you.   Ex. II-2

It is evident also that this Kyrie conforms better to modal theory than does most classical chant. Indeed, if only it included the D below the low E, it would be a perfect theoretical specimen of the eighth mode. As it is, the proper species of fifth, G-d, is at least prominently displayed, whereas a Gregorian chant of the eighth mode would probably have emphasized the fifth F-c instead.

The Gloria (Ex. II-2; only the first part is given) is even more evidently late in style. Its mode is somewhat problematic, to be sure, as most of the chant appears to be on G, while the concluding "Amen" (not shown) ends on b. But again, the melody is constantly moving towards a specific goal, most often G, b, or d, but occasionally shifting suddenly to the A-e axis. There is a great deal of repetition, either nearly exact ("Laudamus te" and "Adoramus te") or somewhat varied. Gregorian elements are also present, as they are in much post-Gregorian music, but the overall impression is anything but Gregorian.

HYMNS

The composition of hymns for the Office afforded another outlet for poets and composers. Each Office service required a hymn, and there was no requirement that every church use the same text or tune on any given occasion. Consequently a large repertoire grew up, with complicated interrelations between poetry and music. The same text may have many different musical settings, and, conversely, the same tune may serve as a melody for many different texts.

Most numerous and most characteristic are the poems cast in the so-called Ambrosian meter (after St. Ambrose, the fourth-century Milanese bishop, who wrote several hymns using it). This meter may be illustrated by the lines

The Ambrosian hymn

> A sólis órtus cárdiné
> adúsque térrae límitém

where the marked accents show the pattern of iambic dimeter. (In iambic verse, each foot is traditionally reckoned as consisting of two iambs, not one. Hence this is dimeter, not tetrameter, despite the four accents.)

In the time of Ambrose, Latin verse may still have been quantitative, that is, based on the length of syllables rather than on their accentuation. But from the eleventh century or earlier, while quantitative verse was used for certain purposes, the newer style of poetry was preferred. In this, the placement of the verbal accent, especially at the end of the line, determined the meter. Most "Ambrosian" hymns are far later than Ambrose, and belong in this latter category. Their meter is based on accent, and they are written in a series of four-line stanzas, each having the rhythm shown above. Ambrosian hymns represent, therefore, the first poetic texts encountered here that are rhythmic in our sense of the word.

The melody writers supplied music for the first stanza of a hymn only. Succeeding stanzas were sung to the same music—a natural proceeding, since all stanzas had the same rhythm, and would fit the tune without difficulty. This method of setting a text is called strophic form, and once again emphasizes the characteristically post-Gregorian element of repetition.

Well over a thousand hymn melodies survive. Their style is generally syllabic or mildly neumatic, often with the usual post-Gregorian traits: purposeful direction of the melody; emphasis on the tone a fifth above the final; and, sometimes, internal repetition within the stanza. Some hymns exhibit another feature. When a text in Ambrosian meter is given a wholly syllabic setting, as is frequently the case, the resulting musical *rhythm* is a very familiar one:

$$\frac{4}{4}$$

A so-lis or-tus car-di-ne / ad-us-que ter-rae li-mi-tem

Although this rhythm is not notated as such in the manuscripts or in modern service books, it is certainly latent in the music. Thus, whatever the original rhythm of Gregorian chant may have been, and whatever rhythms may have been used in early polyphony (below, Chapter III), simple, regular metrical music was common in the liturgy of the Office as far back as the ninth century, and perhaps much earlier.

LITURGICAL ELABORATIONS

Musical elaborations

The post-Gregorian chant so far discussed was composed for use within the existing liturgy, and its use did not alter traditional liturgical practices. From the ninth century on, there also grew up a large body of sacred music that elaborated on or embellished the liturgy—a consequence of the medieval love of amplification mentioned at the beginning of this chapter. Poets and composers found that while the prescribed introit for a given feast could not be replaced by a new composition, it could be enlarged by the provision of an "introduction," and could even be subjected to interpolation—new phrases of text and music could be inserted between the phrases of the original. This and other types of liturgical amplification are often lumped together under the generic term "tropes," but, as will become apparent, there are sufficient differences of technique to discourage such a simplification. About the only term that comfortably accommodates all the types to be found is the awkward "para-liturgical compositions."

Perhaps the earliest embellishing technique was the addition of elaborate melismas to existing chants. It was a general rule that increased solemnity should be reflected by an increase in the number of notes assigned to the syllables of the text. For the medieval musician who wished to express the extraordinary solemnity of some special occasion (the patronal feast of his church, for example, or one of the great feasts of the Christmas season), the addition of an extra melisma to an already elaborate chant was a simple and logical means. The earliest and most famous of such added melismas was the triple "neume" ultimately assigned to the last responsory of Christmas matins, *Descendit de caelis.* The first section of this melisma (Ex. II-3), was sung at the end of the first singing of the respond, the second after the repetition of the respond after the verse, and the third and longest after the doxology. Such an addition gives extraordinary brilliance and majesty to the conclusion of the service.

Fa — brice　mun - di

Ex. II-3

Many other chants were similarly embellished, either occasionally or consistently, so that is is sometimes difficult to determine whether a given passage is an addition or part of the original chant. In some places there were standard melismas—one for each mode—that could be attached to any chant needing special emphasis. But this method of embellishment, for all its age and apparently widespread use, was of relatively minor significance compared with those techniques of elaboration that added new *text* to existing chants. Two principal methods were used: in one, new text was added to a melisma already present in (or already added to) an existing chant; in the other, the new text was supplied with its own new music, and both were added to the chant. The first produced the Kyrie "tropes," the *prosulae* of offertories, responsories, and other chants, and probably the "sequence" (or prosa). The second gave rise to the tropes to the proper of the Mass (introit, offertory, and communion), and to the other tropes of the ordinary, especially those of the Gloria in excelsis.

Textual elaborations

The shorter type of texted melisma was generally known as a "prosula" when applied to chants of the proper, but unfortunately usually called a "trope" when practiced on the Kyrie. Example II-4 is no more than the texted form of the Kyrie melody given in Example II-1. (Ex. II-4 shows only the first part of the texted version; the rest is similar in style.) Here the text is set in strictly syllabic fashion, and the length of the text lines is thus determined by the number of notes in the tune. This is not invariably the case, however: a few Kyrie melodies are texted in neumatic fashion. The words "Kyrie" and "Christe" may be omitted, as in the example, leaving only the "eleison" of the liturgical text. Performance practice seems to have varied. On some occasions, only the texted version was sung; at other times, each texted line was followed by the same music sung without text. In any event, the result is no more than a textual elaboration of the liturgical words: there is no musical addition.

Tropes and prosulae

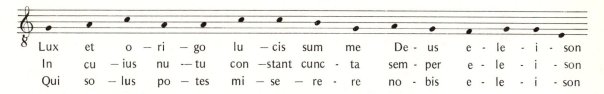

Lux	et	o – ri – go	lu – cis	sum	me	De - us	e - le - i - son
In	cu – ius	nu –– tu	con –stant cunc - ta	sem - per	e - le - i - son
Qui	so – lus	po – tes	mi – se – re - re	no - bis	e - le - i - son

Light and origin of light, highest God, have mercy. In whose will all things forever exist, have mercy. Who alone can take pity on us, have mercy.

Ex. II-4

The texting of Kyrie melodies has left one mark that has persisted to the present. Almost from the beginning, it became customary to refer to the tunes by citing the opening words of the associated text. Thus the melody of Example II-1 is regularly known as the "Kyrie Lux et origo" even in modern service books, although the "Lux et origo" text has not been used in the liturgy for centuries.

The assumption that syllabic versions like Example II-4 resulted from the texting of a preexistent melody long passed unchallenged. Often, however, the added texts are not in prose, but in strict quantitative verse, usually dactyllic hexameters. Thus, for example, the text

Cunctipotens genitor, Deus omnicreator eleison

is found set in strictly syllabic fashion to the tones of a well-known Kyrie melody. But, even given the flexibility of Latin hexameters (the number of syllables may vary somewhat), how did poets happen to find a preexistent melody that would happen to fit the metrical scheme of the poetry? It is more than possible that many—perhaps even most—of the new texts came into being at the same time as the melodies: in short, that the melismatic melody of *Lux et origo* is not the original form at all, but rather a "de-texting" of a syllabic original.

Other prosulae do not present this question: many are verifiably textings of preexistent melismas, most often from offertory verses or responsories. Most use strictly syllabic texting, without any change in the substance of the melisma. Thus the length of each "line" of text was predetermined by the length of the phrases of the melismas, and regular poetic forms were not possible. Nevertheless, poetic devices are not absent. One often finds that each text line ends with the same vowel that was originally sung throughout the melisma; as a result, there is assonance among the lines. In other cases, true rhyme is found at the end of some or even all of the lines. Latin poetry of the tenth and eleventh centuries often shows signs of a striving for clearer, more emphatic poetic articulation. The strength of this tendency is demonstrated by its (admittedly modest) appearance in the prosula—the most rigidly predetermined of musico-poetic types.

Introit and Gloria tropes

Even commoner than the prosula and its relatives—and of even greater importance historically—were what might be called the classical tropes: compositions in which new texts and new music were interwoven into the fabric of a preexisting chant. The introit and the Gloria in excelsis were the commonest recipients of such treatment (it is not rare to find a dozen different tropes for a single introit), but other parts of the ordinary and proper were also troped in this way. Example II-5 shows the introit *Puer natus,* of the third Mass of Christmas, with the trope *Quem nasci mundo.* The trope consists of a "prelude," leading up to the beginning of the introit, and of three interpolated phrases, each of which prepares the way for the liturgical phrase to follow: thus it is always the liturgical text that concludes. Here, as is often the case, the trope lines are in dactyllic hexameter, without rhyme or assonance. The musical setting seems to ignore the poetic rhythm (this too is normal). It is mostly neumatic, to match the text-setting of the introit, but does not sound especially Gregorian.

There is considerable technical variety in the trope repertoire. Some tropes make brief quotations from the chants, other achieve some degree of unification by varied repetition of their own material, while still others appear to be wholly free. In *Quem nasci,* both the opening G-d of the introit and the descent at "magni consilio" appear more than once in the trope (line 1, beginning, and "ordine;" line 3, "capitis," and "vertice"), thus providing connection both with the introit and between the trope lines.

It appears that in the earliest phase of troping, only introductory lines were used; nothing was interpolated into the body of a chant. Apart from this, it has so far been impossible to establish chronological or geographical patterns in the variety of procedures found in the tropes: their musical study has only begun.

One special technique of troping, rather later (eleventh and twelfth centuries) than the methods so far described, consisted in the interpolation, not of new words and music, but rather of quotations from other pieces, into a chant. A number of festal epistles were treated in this way (called "farsed" or "stuffed" epistles), and the same technique was occasionally used with other pieces. To the uninitiated, these might seem to be normal tropes, for the usual technique of line-by-line interpolation is always clear. But the sophisticated medieval singer would at once have recognized the interpolations as quotations from a wide variety of sources, both text and music being skillfully chosen to create a continuous and unified effect. This was clearly an art for the initiated, showing, perhaps, some of the subtlety and overrefinement of a late phase of the embellishing movement.

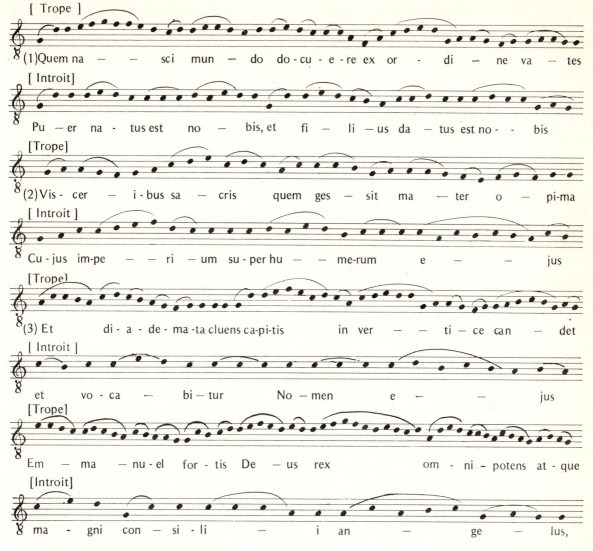

Whom the prophets taught would duly be born on earth,
A child has been born for us, a son has been given to us;
Whom the fruitful mother bore in her holy womb;
Whose authority will be on his shoulder,
And upon his head crowns will shine;
And his name will be called
Emmanuel, mighty God, almighty king and
Angel of mighty counsel.

Ex. II-5

Apparently most of the interpolative forms so far discussed were intended for so-loists; and since most of the troped chants were primarily choral, this created an audible alternation of musical textures corresponding to the alternation between chant and trope. This circumstance was influential in leading to the rebirth of Western drama. An early trope to the Easter introit *Resurrexi* begins with the words "Quem quaeritis"

(Whom do you seek?). In general technique and musical style, this resembles the trope discussed above (Ex. II-5), but for one thing: the text is cast in clear dialogue form.

> TROPE (Angel) *Whom do you seek in the sepulchre,*
> *O Christ-lovers?*
> (The three Marys) *Jesus of Nazareth, O*
> *Heaven-dweller.*
> (Angel) *He is not here. He has arisen as he had said before.*
> *Go and proclaim that he has arisen from the tomb.*
> INTROIT (chorus) I have arisen, and am with you. . . .

Liturgical drama

We do not know what sort of performance the author of this trope may have intended, but in the tenth century the trope was detached from the Mass and transferred to Easter matins. There it came to be set up as a miniature drama. Members of the clergy were assigned parts and given costumes; a section of the church was set aside as the scene and furnished with appropriate properties; and the singers made suitable motions and gestures while singing their parts. This was in fact the beginning of modern European drama, for the dramas of antiquity had long since passed out of practical stage use, and become merely literary texts to be studied by the learned.

The Easter play was soon expanded by the addition of further lines of dialogue, and, shortly thereafter, of whole scenes, involving new characters (e.g., Peter and John) and new incidents from the biblical narrative. The text for these additions could either be found in the liturgical repertoire (antiphons consisting of a single scriptural sentence that would serve as a dramatic "speech") or could be newly written. Dialogue tropes modeled on *Quem quaeritis* were also written for other feasts (Christmas, Ascension) and performed in a similar fashion. By the twelfth century, new themes and subjects, unrelated to any trope, were treated dramatically, and newly written material began to predominate over borrowings from the liturgy. At this point, the drama became primarily a lyric form, based on metrical poetry; its further history will be treated in Chapter III.

The last of the interpolative chant forms to be treated here, the sequence or *prosa*, was perhaps the most influential, and certainly the longest lived. Its origins are obscure. No later than the eighth or ninth century, it became customary to embellish the alleluia of the Mass with a lengthy melisma in addition to the melismas already contained in the Gregorian melody. (Here, too, there is some uncertainty, for it has already been pointed out that some Gregorian alleluias may well date from this period, and some added melismas quote from the alleluia to which they were added.) Such melismas had the usual purpose of enhancing the solemnity of the chant so treated. By the ninth century, texts were fitted syllabically to the melismas. Notker Balbulus, a ninth-century monk of St. Gall, says that he learned the technique from a monk of Jumièges who had fled southwards to escape the invading Normans. At Jumièges, the alleged purpose of adding text was to make the lengthy melodies easier to remember. In any event, the process soon generated an artistic form that far transcended any merely mnemonic purpose.

For over a century, manuscripts transmit both the melismas and their texted forms. This may reflect an early mode of performance, in which melismatic and texted versions alternated. Thereafter, the melismas disappear, and only the texted forms are found in the sources.

In the Middle Ages, the melisma was often referred to as a *sequentia* (presumably "something following the alleluia"), and the texted form as a *prosa* ("something with words"). This valuable distinction is often lost in modern studies, many of which use "sequence" for both. The conversion of a sequentia into a prosa may often have altered the original form of the melody, for the sequentia seems to have been rather free in structure, while the texts of most prosae were not. The typical early prosa consists of a series of paired lines, each member of a pair having the same or nearly the same number of syllables as its mate. Each line-pair may be of any length—some are more like paragraphs than lines—and the prosa as a whole may begin and end with a single unpaired line. This yields the textual form [X] AA BB CC . . . NN [Y]. Since textual pairing was regularly reflected by musical repetition, the sequentia, whatever its original shape, acquired the structure [X] AA BB CC . . . NN [Y] once it was texted.

Sequences and prosae

The principle of line-pairing is often reinforced by giving each member of a pair of lines the same or nearly the same phrase and accent pattern. But regular poetic meter, whether quantitative or accentual, and rhyme are entirely absent from the early prosa. The only poetical artifice commonly found is assonance: in most prosae of French origin, all of the lines, and many subdivisions of lines as well, end in -a, probably to assonate with the final -a of "alleluia;" but prosae from Germany often lack even this feature.

Example II-6 shows the first part and the ending of the prosa *Epiphaniam Domino*. The melody is one of the relatively few found in both French and German sources. The example gives the text found in French manuscripts, with the characteristic assonance in -a. The emphasis on repetition is especially evident. The opening line is not actually a member of a pair, yet its two halves are nearly identical. The paired lines proper begin at the number 2 ("Immensam . . .") and include five pairs of lines omitted from the example. The pairing in itself creates a great deal of repetition, and even more may arise from internal repetition within a line—as in the example, where in pair 3 the music for "assumeret" repeats that of "ita est"—or by borrowing fragments from one pair for use in another. Such intensified repetition, while by no means universal, is frequent in early prosae.

Another characteristic shared by many prosae is a wide melodic range, up to an octave and a fifth. Often the lower part of the range is used for the first sections of a prosa, and the climactic higher part appears only later on. This serves to enhance the vigor and energy of the melody.

The monasteries of St. Martial, in southwestern France, and St. Gall, in the German-speaking part of what is now Switzerland, were the earliest centers of prosa composition. The repertoires of these areas shared only a few tunes and hardly any texts: apparently the French and German schools developed independently. In both regions, the number of sequences (melodies) was at first rather limited, and expansion of the prosa repertoire was accomplished primarily by the writing of new texts to existing tunes. From the tenth century on, however, new melodies also became numerous. At the same time, other centers of prosa-writing became active, until almost all Europe was engaged in their production and dissemination. The total output has never been accurately counted, but many hundreds of pieces were made; and the more popular pieces survive in dozens of manuscripts, often of wide geographical and chronological distribution.

[1]

E - pi- phani - am Do-mi - no can-a--mus glor-i - o - sam   qua prolem De - i ve - re

[2]

ma-gi ad- o -rant (a) Im-mensam Chaldae - i   cu -ius Per -sae- que ve-ne- rant -ur po-ten-

(b) Quem cuncti pro-phe-tae prae-ci - ne - re ven-tu-rum gentes ad sal -

[3]

ti - am (a) Cu-jus ma - jes-tas i - ta est in -cli - na -ta ut assum - e-ret ser-vi formam

van-das (b) An- te   sae-cu--la qui De-us et   tempo- ra homo factus est in Ma - ri - a

[5 pairs of lines follow. Conclusion:]

Poscens ut per orbem regna om-ni - a   pro -te-gat in sae-cu - la sempi - ter -   na.

Let us sing to the Lord of the glorious Epiphany, when the magi truly adored the child of
God; whose great power is revered by Chaldeans and Persians; whom all prophets have
predicted would come to save the peoples; whose majesty was disposed as to take on the
form of a servant; he who was God before worlds and time was made man in Mary . . .
Asking that He protect all kingdoms of the world for ever.

Ex. II-6

From the eleventh century on, new tendencies began to appear in the prosa,
primarily in the area of versification. In the widely disseminated *Laetabundus*, for example, each of the longer lines of the text is clearly divided into two or three short
lines, and these short lines are given a marked rhythmic structure, often articulated by
rhyme. Thus, in the line-pair

Sicut sidus radium   Neque sidus radio
profert virgo filium   neque mater filio
pari forma   fit corrupta,

the first two of the three short lines are of identical accentuation, and this identity is
emphasized by the end-rhymes. The third short lines stand outside this scheme, but assonate with each other in -a. The melodic style of this and similar pieces is often somewhat softer and more lyrical than that of the vigorous early pieces.

In the twelfth century, the tendency towards full use of rhyme and regular meter
was fulfilled in the "Victorine" prosa, named after the poet Adam of St. Victor (a monastery in Paris), who made numerous and important contributions to the later prosa.

But this development, like the later history of the drama, is representative of a later sty-listic period, and will be treated in Chapter III.

With the consideration of the prosa and sequence, this survey of the medieval forms of chant is largely complete. A few isolated types have been omitted, and some practices, such as the re-use of authentic Gregorian chants with new texts for new feasts, have been ignored. But the essentials of a vast and important repertoire have been considered. That this music is on the whole still little known to the public should not be taken as a measure of its value: there is much of real worth here. What is more, two characteristics important for many centuries of later music became wide-spread. The first of these we have called "directed melody" a melodic style in which purposeful motion towards a foreseeable goal is the primary element. The second is the prominence acquired by the interval of the perfect fifth. Whereas in Gregorian chant various patterns of emphasized tones are used, medieval chant often eliminates all these in favor of emphasis on the final, its octave, and the fifth above the final. The fruitfulness of these principles was not exhausted until the end of the nineteenth century.

APPENDIX: Chapter II

1. HYMNS and their melodies may be found in Bruno Stäblein, *Hymnen*, Monumenta monodica medii aevi, vol. 1 (Kassel, 1956). They may also be seen at their places in the liturgy in the chant books for the Office listed in the appendix to Chapter I *(Antiphonale sacrosanctae Romanae ecclesiae; Antiphonale monasticum)*.

2. ORDINARY chants are readily found in any of the official chant books containing music for the Mass *(Liber usualis; Graduale Romanum)*; they are also published separately as *Kyriale*.

3. ADDED MELISMAS are not easy to find in modern edition. They are discussed and examples cited, in Jacques Handschin, "Trope, Sequence, and Conductus," in the *New Oxford History of Music*, vol. II (Oxford, 1954), pp. 130–46. Peter Wagner discusses them in his *Einführung*, vol. III, pp. 344–48 (see appendix to Chapter I).

4. TROPES are discussed in Paul Evans, *The Early Trope Repertory of St. Martial de Limoges* (Princeton, 1970), which includes transcriptions from a St. Martial troper. A large collection of introit tropes is found in Günther Weiss, *Introitus-tropen*, Monumenta monodica medii aevi, vol. 3 (Kassel, 1970).

5. LITURGICAL DRAMA is given full literary treatment in Karl Young, *The Drama of the Medieval Church* (2 vols., Oxford, 1933). An edition of some dramas, with music, is Edmond de Coussemaker, *Drames liturgiques du moyen âge* (Rennes, 1860; repr. New York, 1964). Performing editions of a number of liturgical dramas have been prepared for Oxford University Press by W. L. Smoldon; included are *Peregrinus*, *Planctus Mariae*, and *Visitatio sepulchri*.

6. PROSAE of the earlier period are included in *The Utrecht Prosarium*, ed. N. de Goede (Amsterdam, 1965). A few earlier prosae, along with many later metrical ones, are included in the facsimiles *Le prosaire de la Sainte-Chapelle*, ed. René-Jean Hesbert, Monumenta musicae sacrae, vol. I (Mâcon, 1952) and *Le prosaire d'Aix-la-Chapelle*, ed. R.-J. Hesbert, Monumenta musicae sacrae, vol. III (Rouen, 1961).

An important modern edition of the texts of medieval religious poetry is *Analecta hymnica medii aevi*, ed. Guido Maria Dreves, Clemens Blume, and Henry Marriott Bannister (55 vols., Leipzig, 1886–1922). There are thirteen volumes of prosa texts; vol. 47 contains tropes for the ordinary; vol. 49 contains proper tropes.

EARLY POLYPHONY
AND
THE MEDIEVAL LYRIC

All the music considered in the preceding chapters has been monophonic—music in which a single melody is the sole ingredient of the piece, whether performed by one voice or many, or indeed by one or more instruments. Many cultures have produced practically nothing but monophonic music, but it is one of the peculiarities of Western culture that from the early Middle Ages it has occupied itself extensively with polyphony, where either the sonorities produced by simultaneous sounding different pitches, or the simultaneous combination of two or more melodic lines—or both—are of importance equal to or greater than that of any one melodic line. Over the centuries, the West has produced a repertoire of polyphonic music unequaled by any other civilization.

The documented history of Western polyphony begins in the ninth century, at about the same time that the principal forms of post-Gregorian chant were being developed. This chapter will treat of polyphony from that time through the end of the thirteenth century, when polyphonic music had begun to outstrip monophony as the principal species of art music. Monophonic song, however—particularly that of metrical and lyrical character—enjoyed one of its most ample and gracious eras just before its virtual disappearance from the area of serious composition; and this development will be considered also, at the end of the present chapter.

THE DEVELOPMENT OF POLYPHONY THROUGH THE THIRTEENTH CENTURY

Polyphony in Western Music.　That the West has developed polyphony to a greater extent than other civilizations does not imply that elements of polyphony are found only in Western culture. Most non-European musics make use of at least simple polyphonic devices, and the techniques of early Western polyphony can be found in numerous other cultures. What is unique to the West is its continuing development of polyphonic techniques. Some loss necessarily accompanies this concentration: Western listeners are almost certainly less sensitive to subtle melodic nuances than are those whose musical experience has been primarily monophonic. But the loss is amply offset by the wealth of possibilities offered by polyphonic writing.

Consonance and dissonance

Polyphony inevitably introduces a new and fundamental element into the available musical resources: the relation between two or more simultaneously sounding pitches. For any given style, some intervals are consonant, or stable, requiring no motion to another interval; while others are dissonant or unstable, and must resolve sooner or later to a consonant interval. While in the last analysis it is style that distinguishes between consonance and dissonance, there is also a certain physical basis for the distinction. Since Greek antiquity it had been known that two strings of the same material and tension, of which one is twice the length of the other, would produce two tones an octave apart. Put in another way, this means that the octave may be represented by the ratio 2:1. Similarly, the fifth may be represented by 3:2, and the fourth by 4:3. These low ratios, as well as the strong affinities of the tones in these intervals, suggested to the Middle Ages that the octave, fifth, and fourth *ought* to be the chief consonances. The major third, perhaps more agreeable to modern ears, had the ratio 81:64 in the tuning then used, and seemed therefore to be less suitable for use as a consonance.

The consonance-dissonance dualism may clearly be used as a basic means of creating patterns of tension and release: dissonance will be confined to points at which tension is required, while consonance will, for example, enhance the effect of finality at the end of a phrase. Alternatively, consonance may be used throughout a piece of simple polyphony, its sonority being used for its own sake alone.

These options are evident in the primary techniques of simple polyphony. When the same melody is sung simultaneously at different pitch levels, the interval chosen will invariably be a consonance—in the Middle Ages, an octave, fifth, or fourth—and this interval will persist throughout, enhancing the sonority but not fundamentally altering the melody. In music employing a drone—an unchanging low note lying under a quickly moving melody—the intervals will change with each note of the melody; and while perception of these intervals will be weakened by the rapidity of their change, and by the very length of the drone, phrase endings will almost certainly be consonant, and dissonances will as certainly appear only in the interior of the phrase.

Relative motion of melodic lines

When, however, two different melodies are sounded at once, the intervals between them will of course change from moment to moment, and the effect of this continual change will be much stronger than in the case of the drone. Yet another important effect arises in the relative motion of the two melodies. Naturally this cannot always be parallel motion, for then the melodies could not be different. Instead, several types of motion are possible (Ex. III-1): parallel, similar (same direction but different distances),

parallel   similar   oblique   contrary   Ex. III-1

oblique (one melody repeats the same tone while the other moves), and contrary (the two move in opposite directions). The new dimensions of consonance versus dissonance and of relative motion of simultaneous melodic lines combined to provide an enormous area of exploration to medieval—and later—composers.

EARLY ORGANUM

Apparently, however, the duplication of a given melody at a different pitch, called organum, was the first standardized type of Western polyphony. The earliest surviving information comes from a ninth-century treatise, the *Musica enchiriadis* (musical handbook) and its accompanying *Scholia* (footnotes). The unknown author of this work gives rules for and examples of chant in parallel organum at the octave, the fifth, and, with important modifications, the fourth. A relatively simple example shows the chant (the *vox principalis*) invariably a fifth above the added or organal voice (*vox organalis*). In other examples, both the chant and the organal voice are duplicated in the octave above, partially obscuring the lower position of the organal voice. In either case, the parallelism is absolute: the added voice or voices exactly duplicates the melody of the chant at a different pitch.

Parallel organum:
Musica
enchiriadis

Such examples were not regarded as new compositions, but rather as a special and particularly solemn manner of performing the chant. The theorist merely gives the appropriate rules: once these are mastered, any chant whatsoever can be performed in the same way. Hence there are few notated specimens of polyphony from the ninth and tenth centuries. Polyphonic singing was still an art of improvisation on a given chant, and notation of the result was unnecessary.

In parallel organum at the fifth, it is of course necessary that all the fifths be perfect. The intrusion of a diminished fifth (B-F, for example) would spoil the effect. To ensure that all the fifths would in fact be perfect, the theorist constructed a curious scale (Ex. III-2) in which all fifths are perfect.

This scale guarantees perfect fifths, but at the same time causes problems with both octaves and fourths, since augmented—and hence undesirable—forms of these intervals occur at several places (e.g., the octave F-F♯, the fourths B♭-E, F-B). It is quite likely that this problem would never have bothered actual performers, who would merely have made instinctive modifications of the scale whenever they were necessary. But the author of the *Musica enchiriadis* was a theorist, not merely a performer, and was apparently attempting a system that was intellectually correct as well as musically satisfying. In trying to achieve this he hit on a device—or perhaps codified a practice —that had enormous influence on the history of polyphony.

Instead of constructing a different scale in which all the fourths are perfect, which would have been easy enough, he retains the scale given in Example III-2, and permits

Ex. III-2

the organal voice to depart from strict parallel motion in order to avoid augmented fourths. His rules are rather obscure, and his examples do not always follow the precepts given, but the result is clear enough. The organal voice, instead of duplicating the chant, often repeats a single pitch, as may be seen in the organum *Rex caeli* (Ex. III-3). Here the interval of the fourth is not reached until several notes after the beginning, and there are relatively few parallel fourths in the whole piece: the unison, on which the organum begins and ends, is actually the most important interval. As a result of the techniques used here, the distance between the two voices is by no means always the same, and, equally important, the melody of the organal voice is no longer a mere

Rex   cae — li   do — mi — ne   ma — ris   un — di — so — ni

Te   hu — mi — les   fa — mu — li   mo — du — lis   ve — ne — ran — do   pi — is

King of Heaven, Lord of the roaring seas, we your humble servants adore you in pious song.

Ex. III-3

duplication of the original chant. Two principles of the greatest importance are adumbrated in this example: the functional use of consonance and dissonance, and, less clearly, the combination of two different melodies in counterpoint.

Parallel organum in its strict form was doubtless extensively practiced in the ninth and tenth centuries, and probably long after. The partially parallel organum at the fourth proved, however, to be far more important. In the eleventh century, the influential chant theorist Guido of Arezzo devoted a small part of his most celebrated work, the *Micrologus*, to a treatment of polyphony. His method is clearly similar to that of the *Musica enchiriadis*, but there are certain differences. As in the earlier treatise, the organal voice nominally stands a perfect fourth below the chant; but Guido makes even greater use of repeated tones in the added voice and, in general, treats it more freely. Sometimes parallel motion disappears almost entirely, and in one example the organal voice consists entirely of repetitions of a single pitch.

Guido devotes several paragraphs to what he calls the *occursus*—the cadence. He prefers to end, not on the theoretically correct fourth, but on the unison—as was also the case in Example III-3—and he is obviously quite particular about the manner in which that unison is reached. In his text and in his examples, he explores the effects both of different intervals preceding the unison, and of different types of relative motion. He excludes parallel motion, to avoid preceding the final unison with another unison, and favors oblique or contrary motion.

In Guido's treatise, the organal voice has become even less a duplication of the original chant than it was in the *Musica enchiriadis* (although as yet it does not seem to have been considered a melody in its own right). Guido also shows a more refined sensitivity to the qualities of intervals and to the effects of the types of melodic motion. Although this makes the Guidonian organum a more flexible and truly polyphonic composition than the organum of the *Musica enchiriadis*, Guido still casts his discussion in the form of rules for improvisation, and still regards organum as merely a method of performance of the chant.

About the beginning of the eleventh century, the earliest surviving extensive collection of polyphony was made—the so-called Winchester Troper. This is not a theoretical work, but a manuscript intended for the use of singers at Winchester Cathedral.

Winchester Troper

Unfortunately, it is notated in staffless and unheighted neumes, so that unequivocal transcription is not possible. Still, the general style is clear enough, and the reason for notating a form that had traditionally been improvised is evident: the polyphonic techniques used are too complex to permit extempore performance. Probably something like Guidonian theory underlies the Winchester organa. The repeated tones and the unison cadences are still in evidence. In addition, however, there are clear instances of contrary motion at places other than the cadences. This permits more freedom for the organal melody, allowing it to develop more individuality. Nevertheless, a good deal of parallelism is still present.

The Winchester repertoire is a large one—it includes over a hundred organa, set to chants of a wide variety of liturgical functions—but it is unique for its time. Whether other such collections once existed cannot, of course, be known, but the existence of even one suggests that the cultivation of polyphonic singing had become an increasingly important area of musical endeavor. Other such suggestions may be found in the texts of many prosae, which seem to refer to polyphonic performance (the prosa *Caeleste organum* contains such a reference in its first words: "Today the celestial organum has sounded on earth"). Indeed, it is quite likely that by the eleventh century a great deal of the Gregorian and post-Gregorian chant of the greater feasts was sung polyphonically. Despite the various advances in technique, however, polyphony remained essentially a manner of performance of the chant: an organum was not so much a new composition as an embellishment of a given melody. Toward the end of the eleventh century, three developments took place that finally raised organum to the rank of original composition.

The first of these was more important than it might appear. The organal voice was removed from below the chant and placed above (some scholars believe that this had already happened in the organa of the Winchester Troper). By this simple stroke the chant ceased to be the focus of attention: the added voice acquired an equal or greater share of interest. The second development is witnessed by the theorist John of Afflighem in a treatise of about 1100. For John, contrary motion is *preferable* to parallel or oblique. Hence the organal voice ceases entirely to be a reflection or copy of the chant and becomes—must become—a melody in its own right, as is evident in the polyphonic *Kyrie Cunctipotens* (Ex. III-4). Such pieces are now generally called "free" organum, *Free organum* since the obligation to parallel motion no longer obtains. In Example III-4 it appears that the composer uses the new freedom less to obtain an effective melody in the organal voice than to explore the effects produced by constantly changing harmonic intervals.

Cun-cti - po - tens ge |- ni - tor   de - us   om - ni - cre — a — tor e - - - lei — son.

All-powerful father, all-creating God, have mercy.   Ex. III-4

The third development gave even greater freedom to the organal voice. Instead of being restricted to one note for each note of the chant, the organal voice was given the liberty of having two, three, or even more notes to a single one of the chant. With this further possibility available, the newly composed melody could develop almost at will. This introduces yet another element into the consonance-dissonance relation, for obviously those notes of the organal voice that coincide with a new note of the chant are more important harmonically than those that do not. Consonance will prevail when the chant moves, and almost any interval may safely be used elsewhere.

Cantus firmus

Multiplication of notes in the organal voice necessarily slows down the performance of the original chant and reduces the chant, at least in appearance, to the status of a structural support. The chant was now called "cantus firmus" (fixed song), a term that emphasizes its structural role. Yet its resultant diminished importance as melody should not be misconstrued. The "cantus firmus" remains the primary voice of a composition, and the voice added to it is related as a commentary or gloss is related to a passage of scripture—more voluminous and perhaps more immediately attractive, but still subordinate in principle.

These new techniques—the placement of the organal voice above the chant, the preference for contrary motion, and the increase in number of notes in the organal part—seem to have become established by the beginning of the twelfth century, although it is likely that different regions reacted at different times to the new stylistic developments. Polyphony prior to that time is known to us almost entirely from small and scattered sources: the Winchester Troper is the only large surviving collection. Doubtless local schools of polyphonic writing, each with its own style, existed; but almost nothing is known about them.

THE SCHOOL OF ST. MARTIAL

At the beginning of the twelfth century the musicians of the Abbey of St. Martial of Limoges, discussed above (Chapter II) in connection with their composition of tropes and prosae, began an extensive cultivation of polyphony. The school of St. Martial has left a considerable repertoire of organum, sharing evidently local characteristics. In addition, a twelfth-century manuscript preserves rather similar polyphony of a school connected with Santiago da Compostela, an important pilgrimage center in Spain. Taken together, the Santiago and St. Martial repertoires appear to represent the most progressive aspects of polyphony in the twelfth century (apart from the music of the slightly later school of Paris, which is discussed below).

Melismatic organum

The most striking innovation is an extension of a principle already discussed: in a few of the St. Martial pieces the organal voice occasionally has from five to more than a dozen notes to a single note of the cantus firmus. Organum using this procedure is called "melismatic" organum ("melismatic" refers in this case to the relation, not between music and text, but between the organal voice and the cantus firmus). Melismatic polyphony contributed further to the weakening of the cantus firmus as a melody, for the notes of the chant are often much protracted, and are irregularly spaced. It also makes available to the composer two clearly differentiated polyphonic textures: one, called "discant," in which the two voces move at approximately the same rate, having roughly the same number of notes; and another, called "organum" in the strict sense, in which the organal voice is melismatic.

Resonemus hoc natali, of which the beginning and end are given (Ex. III-5), is characteristic of St. Martial style. It is not strongly melismatic, but the smooth line of the organal voice consistently has more notes than the lower part and is the center of

Re — so — ne — mus   hoc   na — ta — li [per-] fi — — di — — — — — — e

Let us make music on this Christmas . . . treason

Ex. III-5

attention. The composer has apparently allowed himself considerable freedom in the choice of intervals between the two voices. (The qualification "apparently" is necessary since the sources do not show clearly how the two parts are to be fitted together, and a different transcription would yield somewhat different results.) Each new note of the cantus firmus may form one of the traditional consonances (octave, fifth, or fourth) with the organal voice; but thirds, sixths, and even dissonances such as the second also appear. The restrained use of ornamentation in *Resonemus* is typical: there are only a few St. Martial pieces in which the organal voice contains extended melismas, and quite a few organa are in note-against-note style throughout. The available styles seem not yet to have been consistently treated as form-producing elements, but rather as options to be employed at the composer's pleasure.

While earlier polyphony had been mostly liturgical, with some polyphonic tropes and prosae, the St. Martial school overwhelmingly preferred the setting of Latin lyric poems, still sacred in character, but with only loose liturgical ties. Such poems were, to be sure, used in the liturgy, often before lections at matins, and at the end of services of the Office, but they were rather arbitrary insertions, much less integral than the tropes or even the prosae. The melodies for these poems (the tunes that became the cantus firmi of the polyphonic settings) were presumably written first, simply as melodies. It is in some cases possible that the melodies were written directly for polyphonic setting, but since it had otherwise been the invariable habit of medieval polyphonists to use preexistent tunes for their cantus firmi, this is not probable.

Some words must be devoted to the question of the rhythm of these settings. While the notation used in the manuscripts is unequivocal with regard to pitch, it seems to give no indication of the duration of the tones. As a result, the rhythms actually employed are a matter of conjecture. In pieces largely in note-against-note style, there would seem to be no difficulty: the notes of the cantus firmus may be given equal values, and the upper voice fitted accordingly, using shorter notes where necessary. Where melismas occur, this leads to impossibly fast notes in the organal part. Since there is no evidence of systematic rhythm at this time and place—and since the very essence of southern French culture at this time seems to be an irregular, fantastic ornamentalism—the tones of the upper voice are usually transcribed as eighth notes, assuming a very free, rhapsodic style of performance. A more metrical transcription would also be possible.

THE SCHOOL OF PARIS

There have been occasions in history when favorable circumstances combined to produce an exceptional cultural flowering. One of those occasions was the "Gothic" period, from about the middle of the twelfth century to the end of the thirteenth. Centered in northern France, but radiating over much of western Europe, this "Renaissance of the twelfth century" produced the great cathedrals of Chartres, Reims, Bourges, Amiens, and many others, as well as comparable cathedrals in England and Germany, and many hundreds of smaller churches and public buildings. The art of the stained-glass window reached its apex in the later twelfth century. Sculpture, as an important element in church architecture, was extensively and impressively cultivated. The making of books, with elegant calligraphy and superb illustrations (miniatures), called forth the energies of painters. Literature, both in Latin and in the vernacular, also flourished; but the verbal arts were perhaps even more characteristically represented by the scholastic schools of philosophy and theology. The long-forgotten work of Aristotle again became known in the West, by means of Latin translations of Arabic versions (Arabs and Christians were in contact in Spain and in the Near East). The assimilation of rationalistic Aristotelianism into Christian thought posed a temendous challenge; and the vigorous response reached a climax in the work of St. Thomas Aquinas (1225-74), one of the greatest minds of all time.

If a single word can describe the spirit of this age, it is *system*. The spirit of systematization is evident in almost every product of the Gothic mind. Consider the facade of a cathedral, neatly compartmentalized into segments by horizontal and vertical dividers—which, moreover, clearly indicate the structure of the interior. Consider also that this is the age of the encyclopedic work—the systematic presentation of all that was known, whether of theology, as in the *Summa theologica* of Aquinas, or of some other subject. Even musical manuscripts give evidence of this preoccupation. Everything about them is neat and orderly. The notation, whether for monophony or polyphony, has become the regular "square" notation still used for the chant today. In most cases, the contents are carefully arranged according to some logical principle.

For this was one of the great ages of music as well, comparable in importance to the period that saw the creation of the Gregorian repertoire, or to that which saw the first flowering of tropes and prosae. For the first time, a huge repertoire of secular art music was brought into being (this will be considered below). Music for the church continued to be extensively cultivated, but, as might be expected, it was now polyphony that attracted most of the attention. Two periods may be distinguished: in the first, from the 1160s to about 1210, a huge new repertoire of organum was built up; in the second, from some time in the first quarter of the thirteenth century to about 1300, a new form, the motet, was created, and its possibilities exploited.

Notation of meter
It is not known whether the melismatic organum of the South, previously described, was familiar in the region of Paris. It probably was, as medieval communications were much better than is often supposed, and it may well have served as one of the stimuli to Parisian composers of the later twelfth century. But these latter were at work long before the school of St. Martial had finished its activity, and, from the beginning, their music is stamped with novel and different characteristics.

The epoch-making achievement of the early Parisian organum-writers was the notation of musical meter. Whether earlier monophonic or polyphonic compositions had been metrically performed (and that is not the issue here), musical notation had not previously had any means of helping the performers keep together. Hence composers attempted to develop, out of the notation already in use, a system by which the required durations could be indicated to the performer.

It appears that they started with the idea of a single fundamental rhythm, represented in modern notation thus: ♩♪♩ ♪♩♩♪♩ ♪ etc. Two rhythmic values are present, of which the greater (the "long") is twice the lesser (the "breve"). Now the polyphony in which these values were to be made manifest was largely melismatic, and written in the square note-group figures of the current plainsong notation. Such groups, called ligatures, could contain from two to as many as seven or more notes, the majority having from two to four. It became customary to regard a two-note ligature (ligatura binaria) as having a normal rhythmic value of breve-long (♪♩). Most of the fundamental rhythm given above could therefore be expressed by a succession of two-note ligatures. Only the beginning caused a difficulty, and this was solved by letting a three-note ligature (ternaria) having the value long-breve-long stand at that place. Thus the notation of the fundamental rhythm became: ternaria, binaria, binaria, and so on. The "opposite" rhythm, ♪♩ ♪♩|♪♩ ♪♩|♪, little used in the earliest period but important later, could then be notated binaria, binaria. . . ternaria. Here the two-note ligature keeps its breve-long value, but the three-note one now has the value breve-long-breve. This variability in meaning of certain ligatures is a normal feature of this type of notation. Other values could also be expressed, although not always without ambiguity. If notes shorter than the breve were desired, a ligature having more than three notes was written, and it was understood that this would have to be performed in the time allotted for a three-note group. A longer value could be indicated by interpolating a single note (simplex, which generally had the value of a dotted quarter in modern notation), or by certain special combinations of ligatures, notably two ternariae in succession.

The notational apparatus just described is apparently what was available to composers about 1160. Out of it grew the fully developed system of "rhythmic modes," of which the rhythmic patterns given above form a part. But the system in its entirety is not relevant to the earliest phase of Parisian polyphony, and consideration of it will be postponed until its appearance in the music.

An English theorist, now known only as "Anonymous IV," wrote (about 1260): *Master Leoninus, according to what used to be said, . . . made a great book of organum for the Gradual and Antiphonal, to increase [the solemnity of] the divine service. And [the book] was in use until the time of Perotinus the great, who shortened it and made many fine clausulae, for he was the best writer of discant, and better than Leoninus. . . . The books of Perotinus were in use . . . in the choir of the greater church of Notre Dame of Paris.*

Here we have the first reliable evidence about important individual composers, along with the place of their activity. Additional evidence indicates that Leoninus flourished about 1160-80, and Perotinus about a generation later. They represent the beginning of the school of Paris, or of Notre Dame, as it is sometimes called.

Of the "great book" (*Magnus liber*) of Leoninus, several copies survive, all much later than the time of Leoninus himself, in manuscripts that also include music of the period of Perotinus and even later. Nevertheless, it is possible to form a fairly clear idea of the nature of Leoninus's original work, which contrasts sharply with that of the St. Martial composers. In the first place, the repertoire of chants set to polyphony is entirely different: the *Magnus liber* restricts itself wholly to responsorial chants—the gradual and alleluia of the Mass, and the great responsory of the Office. For these it provides a fairly comprehensive cycle, giving organa for the chants of the greater feasts of the church year, carefully arranged in the calendar order of their celebration. The

Magnus liber organi: The style of Leoninus

collection is thus rigidly liturgical and is systematic in intent and arrangement—a sharp contrast to the St. Martial collections, which contain para-liturgical pieces, often in no discernible order.

The change in musical style is equally momentous, as may be seen in two excerpts from the organum *Exiit sermo* (Ex. III-6a, b). The chant on which this piece is based is the gradual for the feast of St. John the Evangelist (December 27). The sections set polyphonically are those that would normally be assigned to soloists—the intonation and the first part of the verse (by this time, the practice of bringing in the choir for the end of the verse already obtained). This same division of labor may be found in all the chants of the *Magnus liber:* polyphony is used for the solo sections, implying the use of plainsong for the choral parts. There may have been a practical reason for this, since elaborate polyphony was probably not within the competence of choirs at this time; but Leoninus has turned this to aesthetic advantage, by paralleling and reinforcing the solo-chorus alternation with a polyphony-monophony contrast.

Ex. III-6 (a)

Ex. III-6 (b)

Throughout most of the piece, the lower voice, which has the chant, is given exceedingly long notes—hence its name "tenor," from the Latin *tenere* (hold). The upper part, called "duplum," moves freely and rather rapidly over these dronelike tenor notes, using consonances at cadences and at points where the tenor note changes, but admitting any interval elsewhere. In the middle of the verse (Ex. III-6b) however, a quite different style appears: here the tenor moves more quickly, so that the two voices approach, at least, equality of motion. This latter style is, as has been said, called "discant," as opposed to the "organal" style of the sustained-tone sections; and a section in discant style is known as a "clausula."

The employment of these two contrasting styles within a composition is no arbitrary matter: the alternation is systematically determined by the nature of the chant being set. Whenever the chant is syllabic, or nearly so, organal style is used; whenever the chant is melismatic (as at the word "manere"), a clausula is written. By its very nature, a clausula could have only a few syllables of text—sometimes only a one-syllable fragment of a word.

The alternation of styles may also have had a practical origin, that of avoiding undue length. Certainly if every note of a gradual were set in richly melismatic polyphony, the resulting piece would be very long indeed. But more important is the exploitation of style contrast for structural purposes. Both styles gain in effect when used alternately, and the work as a whole is given a clear and logical shape.

The rhythm of the duplum reflects the contrast of styles as well. In the clausulae, the fundamental rhythm mentioned above ♩ ♪♪ ♪|♩) clearly predominates, despite numerous deviations from the strict pattern. In the organal sections, the rhythm is freer. Scholars are not agreed as to the details of transcription, but it is at least certain that the fundamental rhythm, if present at all, is much less insistently presented in the organal sections than in the clausulae. In view of succeeding developments, it is the discant style that represents the progressive element in the *Magnus liber*.

The treatment of consonance and dissonance in *Exiit sermo* is not different in essence from that found in earlier music, but appears more orderly. Most of the intervals formed on stressed long notes are perfect consonances. Occasionally, as at the very beginning of the piece, the consonance is preceding by a dissonance. The fourth is still treated as a consonance, but with decreasing frequency. Naturally enough, there is rather more dissonance in the melismatic or organal sections than in the discant, since the long-held tones of the tenor permit considerable dissonance without discomfort, while the moving tenor of the discant emphasizes whatever dissonance may occur. The imperfect consonances are still rather sparingly used, although a few major thirds occur in prominent places. Apart from the treatment of the fourth, this manner of handling intervals remained standard until about 1400.

The younger composer Perotinus was, according to Anonymous IV, the greatest writer of discant, while Leoninus had excelled at organum (i.e., melismatic style). Perotinus made various revisions in the *Magnus liber* and in addition composed many new clausulae in discant style. (It should not be assumed that all the surviving clausulae are by Perotinus himself, any more than that all the *Magnus liber* was by Leoninus. Doubtless many anonymous composers shared in the work.) This confirms the suggestion that discant was the progressive feature of the *Magnus liber*. As far as is known, no new melismatic sections of the Leoninian type were written after the period of Leoninus himself.

The style of Perotinus

Several hundred clausulae, meant either to replace the original clausulae of the *Magnus liber*, or in some cases perhaps to serve as independent compositions, survive in the same manuscripts that contain the work of Leoninus. From their style, it is evident that the system of rhythmic notation described above had undergone considerable further development, and this requires consideration before turning to the music itself.

The system of rhythmic modes, adumbrated in Leoninus and fully formed in the time of Perotinus, provided for six basic rhythmic patterns or modes, each with its own characteristic pattern of ligatures. The fundamental rhythm of Leoninus—long, breve,

Rhythmic modes

long, and so on—was the first mode, with the ligature pattern ternaria, binaria, binaria, . . . The second mode was the rhythm breve, long, breve, long, breve (with the accent on the breve): ♪♪ ♪♪ | ♪. Its ligature pattern was binaria, binaria, . . .ternaria. These correspond, at least superficially, to the trochaic and iambic feet of classical versification. The third and fourth modes correspond to the dactyl and anapest. They should therefore have the value long, breve, breve, and the reverse, musically ♩♪♪ ♪♪ and ♪♪♩ |♪♪♩. Such patterns, however, could not easily be combined with the ternary rhythms of the first two modes. To make such combinations possible, the third and fourth modes were so arranged that their long value was equal to the sum of the long plus breve of the first and second modes. This value (♩.) was called a perfect long, in contrast to the long of the first two modes (♩), which was called imperfect. The first breve of the third and fourth modes was equal to the breve of the first and second mode, but the second breve was twice as long (♩) and was called an altered breve. (The imperfect long and the altered breve are equal in length, but are used in different rhythmic contexts.) Thus the pattern of the third mode was ♩. ♪♩|♩.♪♩ , and that of the fourth (hardly ever used) ♪♩♩.|♪♩♩. . Their ligature patterns were simplex, ternaria, ternaria . . ., and ternaria, ternaria, . . . simplex.

The fifth mode consisted entirely of perfect longs, and was used mostly in the tenor. It was properly written in single notes, but when there was no danger of confusion, a series of ternariae could be used. The sixth mode was all breves and was regarded as a modification of the first or second mode. It was written quaternaria, ternaria, ternaria, ... The complete system was thus as follows:

Mode	Ligature pattern	Modern transcription
1	ternaria, binaria, binaria . . .	♩ ♪♩ ♪|♩ ♪♩ ♪|♩
2	binaria, binaria . . . ternaria	♪♩ ♪♩ |♪♩ ♪♩ |♪
3	simplex, ternaria, ternaria . . .	♩. ♪♩ |♩. ♪♩ |♩.
4	ternaria, ternaria . . . simplex	♪♩ ♩. |♪♩ ♩. |♪
5	simplex, simplex . . .	♩. ♩. |♩. ♩. |♩.
6	quaternaria, ternaria, ternaria . . .	♫♫ ♫♫ |♪

Rhythmic variety within a mode could be achieved by using a simplex or a ligature foreign to the standard modal pattern.

The composer of the Perotinian period had, then, a limited number of rhythmic formulas at his disposal. It is evident from the music that his chief interest was in the exploitation of their powerful motoric energy. It was just about this time—around 1200—that the patterns were most strictly kept. A given mode was maintained throughout a short piece, and for at least a considerable section of a long one: rapid change of mode does not occur. Simultaneous combination of two modes is, however, normal. The tenor is commonly in the fifth mode, while the duplum may be in the first, second, or third. Combination of second mode with third is also possible, but the first mode combines only with the fifth (or sixth). The effect is of tremendous, pulsating, almost dance-like energy.

The substitute clausula *Manere* (Ex. III-7) demonstrates this on a small scale. The cantus firmus is the melisma of *Exiit sermo* that was set as a clausula in the Leoninian organum (Ex. III-6b). In the Leoninian clausula, the tenor moves in perfect longs, irregularly grouped, while the new style gives the tenor a strict rhythmic organization, either (as here) in a regular pattern of perfect longs and rests, or in some other but

Manere

Ex. III-7

equally strict arrangement. The tenor pattern, once begun, persists throughout the piece, giving it a driving momentum, and also assuring its unity. In some clausulae, the entire tenor melody is repeated, sometimes so arranged that in the second appearance the pitches of the melody appear in a different part of the rhythmic pattern. Less often, the repeated melody is given a new rhythmic pattern. In any event, tenor repetition is obviously a means of increasing the size of the clausula.

The upper voices are more various in style, no doubt reflecting different composers and slightly different periods of composition. But the rhythm always adheres quite closely to the fundamental modal patterns. In the most elementary type of clausula the rhythms of the duplum serve to reinforce the pattern of the tenor, producing a powerful if simple effect. More subtle are those pieces in which the rhythms of the two parts overlap, at least at times: here there is no loss of strength, but a gain in delicacy and musical interest.

The clausulae were apparently intended to be performed in the appropriate organa in place of the Leoninian sections. This would have the effect of modernizing the older works, at least in part. In the manuscripts, groups of clausulae appear in the same liturgical order used for the *Magnus liber* itself. But it was also natural for composers to undertake the writing of wholly original works. This they did in the area of music for more than two voices. A number of three-voice organa (organa tripla) survive, some by Perotinus himself; and Perotinus was also the composer of two celebrated four-voice organa (quadrupla)—the only surviving long works for four voices from this period. All of these pieces, and especially the quadrupla, represent a kind of apex of the strictly modal style.

In principle, the tripla and quadrupla are organized on the Leoninian plan, with lengthy sustained tones in the tenor where the chant is syllabic, and with clausulae for the chant melismas. But the upper voices of the melismatic sections have become as strictly modal as the clausulae (only the tenor, of course, remaining stationary). The result is a pounding rhythmic energy almost unique in the history of music—an effect that must have been even more hypnotic when heard in the resonant interior of a stone church. The large dimensions of these pieces should not tempt one to imagine a corresponding *volume* of sound. Even this is soloists' music, and was probably performed with one singer to a part, with perhaps one or two extra (or an instrument) for the tenor.

Fig. III-1: *A page showing several short substitute clausulae. Because of their brevity, these were almost certainly designed to be used within the appropriate organum, and not for independent performance. Near the beginning and near the end of the page there are passages in organal style, perhaps reworkings of Leoninian originals. (Florence, Medici Library, Codex Laurentiana Pluteus 29.I.)*

There are relatively few works in this strictly modal style. A large number of clausulae (and parts of several three-voice organa) are considerably freer in rhythm. The prevailing modes remain clearly audible, but modifications of them are more frequently made. The tenor remains as rigidly patterned as ever, but the upper voice, while still remote from the flowing lyricism of Leoninus, has acquired more smoothness. From this time on, the general trend was to be in the direction of increasing freedom within the modal framework. While exact dates are not available, it would seem that the whole process, beginning with the pre-modalism of Leoninus, developing into the strict modalism of the quadrupla and related works, and continuing with the beginnings of modal dissolution, was contained in the years between 1160 and 1210.

The generation of Perotinus was also active in the production of a different type of composition, the conductus. In contrast to the strictly liturgical purpose of the Parisian organa and clausulae, the conductus (or conducti; both plurals were used) were settings of non-liturgical Latin lyrics, usually but not always of sacred character. In this respect, they were direct analogues of the polyphony of St. Martial. The conductus, however, did not employ preexisting cantus firmus, but was newly composed in all parts. To be sure, the tenor part was composed first. It was written, however, directly for polyphonic use. The other voice (or voices), added in the usual way, was given approximately the same rhythm as the tenor. Thus, while in organum and clausula the tenor differs in function and in sound from the other part(s), in conductus all the voices look about the same, even though the tenor is the primary melody. In the majority of conductus the text-setting is syllabic or nearly so, all voices declaiming the same syllables at the same time. The musical rhythm poses difficulties for the modern transcriber. The modal notation of the organa and clausulae was designed for melismatic music. When applied to syllabic pieces, it is reduced to an undifferentiated string of single notes, since a ligature cannot be used for more than one syllable. It is now generally agreed that these single notes are not to be read as equal values, but that the conductus are in modal rhythm, like other polyphony of the school of Paris. The choice of mode is based on a number of factors, including the rhythm of the text (most often trochaic), and the nature of the music and its relation to the text. In some cases, it is almost impossible to be certain what mode was intended by the composer.

In *Sol sub nube* (Ex. III-8), the choice of first mode leads to a close correspondence between musical and textual rhythms—something by no means always the case. The use of shorter values lends variety and interest to the rhythm. Later, at the penultimate syllable of the text, a fairly extensive melisma appears, contrasting sharply with what has preceded. Such melismas, often found in conductus, contrast with the prevailingly

Polyphonic conductus

Sol   sub nu — be   la - tu - it,   sed   e - clyp - sis   nes — ci - us,

The sun was hidden by a cloud, but unconscious of its eclipse.

From *Thirty-Five Conductus for Two and Three Voices*, ed. Janet Knapp, Department of Music, Yale University, 1965. Used by permission.

Ex. III-8

syllabic style. They appear most often at the beginning and just before the end, but occasionally in the body of the piece as well. Apparently in view of their frequently terminal function, they were known as *caudae* (tails). A few conductus, having numerous caudae and more melismatic text setting elsewhere, approach the melismatic style of the organum, but even in them, the characteristic sustained-note tenor, essential to the organum, is almost never present.

Organum, clausula, and conductus were the polyphonic forms of the later twelfth century in Paris. Apart from the melismatic sections of the two-voice organa, they shared many features of style. For the first time in musical history, a really large body of polyphony had been built up in which many basic compositional techniques were common. While each individual form had its own special requirements, and hence to some extent its own special techniques, what was common was far more important than what was different.

THE MOTET

Around the beginning of the thirteenth century a new form made its appearance. Just as the prosula had provided syllabic text for an extended chant melisma, the nearly textless substitute clausulae were now provided with syllabic or near-syllabic text. The result was called a "motet," from the French *mot* (word). In the earliest motets, the duplum of an existing clausula was provided with a Latin text related in meaning to the liturgical text from which the clausula syllables had been taken. This texted duplum was then called the "motetus." The original tenor was maintained intact, since it did not have enough notes to accommodate the new poetry. Motets such as these may have been performed within the organum for which the clausula was intended, as a kind of polyphonic trope, or separately, as a trope-like addition to the liturgy.

The motet of the thirteenth century

Since writing in three voices was extensively practiced by about 1200, it was not uncommon to enrich the texture of the early motet by adding a third part (triplum), rhythmically similar to the motetus, and sharing the same new text with it. The result is a hybrid-looking form, in which the top two voices have the look of a two-voice conductus, but the presence of a functionally different tenor unequivocally shows the piece to be a motet. The term "conductus motet" is sometimes used for this type, and a few such motets are given complete in one manuscript, and without tenor—that is, as true conductus—in another.

Shortly, however, the motet began to exhibit more radical tendencies. The chronology is not wholly clear. The conductus-like texture of the upper parts was soon abandoned, if indeed it had ever enjoyed general popularity. Two-voice motets remained popular. Then, a third voice was again added, this time, however, functioning as a new counter-melody, contrasting rhythmically with the other upper part. The three-voice motet thus produced became the standard texture for the remainder of the thirteenth century. The new style added part (triplum) had an important further peculiarity: in addition to providing rhythmic contrast, it was given an entirely different text from the motetus. "Polytextuality" was of course inherent in the earliest forms of the motet, since the tenor always retained its liturgical text fragment, and the motetus had new text. But the contrast thus produced was as nothing compared to the Babel-like complexity of two upper voices rapidly and simultaneously declaiming different words in different rhythms, over a functionally different tenor with its own (minimal) text. To compound the complexity, either or both of the upper-voice texts might be in French or in Latin. The motet could be polyglot as well as polytextual.

Some motets of this type were produced by the addition of a new and differently texted triplum to a two-voice piece that itself was merely a texted clausula. Others, however, were entirely new compositions. Although the tenors were generally selected from the traditional repertoire of melismas from responsorial chants, their rhythmic patterns were new, and both of the upper voices were freely composed.

Example III-9 shows the beginning of the motet *Lonc tans ai mise–Au commencement–Hec dies* (motets are named from the first words of their several texts, beginning with the top voice), illustrating the classical motet style of the thirteenth century (perhaps about 1250). The tenor is given a fixed rhythmic pattern, a trait inherited from the clausula, and generally maintained in the motet. In the complete motet, the tenor melody is sounded twice in the rhythm shown in the example, and then a third time in perfect longs. The two upper parts, each bearing a different French text, are added to the tenor according to the usual rules of consonance and dissonance. (The theorists assert that the motetus was first fitted to the tenor, and the triplum then superimposed onto the two-voice complex thus produced.) In Example III-9 fifths and octaves predominate, as is typical for the later motet repertoire. The fourth is rarely used as a consonance if its lower note is the lowest sounding pitch.

For a long time I have firmly decided to love her faithfully.

In the beginning of summer when the flowers grow in the green meadow

Ex. III-9

The upper voices are both in the first rhythmic mode, as is the tenor, but the composer has made every effort to give each of them a distinctive rhythmic profile. They begin together, but thereafter their phrases are of different lengths, and their cadences occur at different points. Moreover, both motetus and triplum are given as much individual melodic integrity as the technical difficulties of the form permit. Either one, sung by itself, is satisfying as melody. This independence is enhanced by the frequent textual and musical quotation in these parts of refrains from monophonic songs—quotations that the alert thirteenth-century listener would surely have recognized. Obviously much ingenuity was required of the composer to create independent, differently texted, and often partially preexistent upper parts that would fit properly with a wholly preexisting tenor. For the modern listener, the motet exhibits a texture of extraordinary complexity—the ear scarcely knows what to follow at first.

Motets of this type were regarded as music for the sophisticated: the theorist Johannes de Grocheo, writing about 1300, says

This song (the motet) ought not to be performed in the presence of common people, since they would not perceive its sublety, nor take pleasure in its sound; but rather in the presence of learned people and those who seek after subleties in art.

The classical motet is an ideal type of that sort of counterpoint that brings together in the unity of a single composition separate elements that are in themselves both disparate and complete, or nearly so: each of the upper voices, at least, is singable as a monophonic song. Such simultaneous ordering of distinct entities is as much a product of the temper of scholasticism as the harmonization of revelation with Aristotelianism found in the *Summa* of St. Thomas Aquinas.

Innovations in rhythmic notation: Franco of Cologne

In the second half of the thirteenth century the delicate balance of forces found in the classical motet began to be altered. The change was intimately related to innovations in rhythmic notation. We have seen that modal ligatures could not often be used in syllabic pieces. The undifferentiated single notes that replaced them caused enough difficulties in conductus and early motets. But as the motet grew in complexity, some means of notating rhythm in syllabic music became a necessity. This was found in a principle that has remained basic for rhythmic notation ever since: different note shapes were given specific rhythmic meanings. The long was represented by ⌐, the breve by ■, and shorter values (semibreves) by ◆. As was the case in modal notation, these were not absolutely fixed durations. The long could still be either perfect or imperfect (i.e., could have the value of three or two breves), and the breve could be doubled in length when altered, as in the rhythm ⌐■■⌐ ($\frac{3}{4}$♩♩♩|♩. ; later motets are usually transcribed in 3/4 rather than 6/8 meter, representing a tempo probably slower than that of the organa and clausulae). The semibreve was even more variable in length, as two, three, or four such notes could occupy the time of a normal breve.

The variability of the semibreve was the door through which new developments entered. Before about 1250, the semibreve had been used solely for ornamental flourishes (e.g., the sixteenth notes of Ex. III-9). A group of such notes, equal in length to a breve, might bear one syllable of text, but a syllable was never set to a single semibreve. The unit of textual declamation remained the breve and the long, arranged in the traditional modal patterns. Shortly after 1250, the celebrated theorist and composer Franco of Cologne introduced further novelties. He first gave definite values to the semibreve. If three semibreves took the place of one breve, each had the value of one third of a breve; if two semibreves replaced a breve, the first was worth one third, and the second, two thirds. A larger number of consecutive semibreves would have to replace two or more breves. Such groups were divided into subgroups of two, each having the value of a breve, with a final group of three if necessary. (Franco also treated of ligatures, still used extensively in the tenors, and often in the upper voices, giving each ligature form a specific rhythmic meaning.)

The theoretical stabilization of values of the semibreve was of course important, but even more important was Franco's willingness, in his compositions, to assign a syllable of text to each semibreve of a group of two or three, thus at times shifting the unit of declamation to the shorter value. This apparently minor innovation had profound effects, for it liberated textual declamation from the patterns of the rhythmic modes. Thus, in an example given by Franco himself

$$\frac{3}{4} \quad \textit{A- ve Ma-ri-a gra-ti-a   ple- na.}$$

modal rhythm has almost entirely vanished.

In practice, it was not generally found possible to attempt this more rapid declamation in both upper parts at once: the result would have been too nervous and too confusing. Instead, it was the triplum that became more animated rhythmically, while the motetus kept to the older motion in breves and longs. The result, of course, was to upset the equality of voices of the classical motet, and to focus the listener's attention on the triplum. The motet, only a few years earlier one of the most intensely contrapuntal of forms, was on the way to becoming an accompanied solo song.

After Franco, theorists began to assert that four or even more semibreves might take the place of a single breve—each semibreve capable of bearing a syllable of text. Franco's valuation of the semibreve had to be abandoned, and theorists disagreed as to the exact values to be assigned. For this discussion, it will be sufficient to regard larger groups of semibreves as effecting an aliquot division of the breve (e.g., if five semibreves stand in place of one breve, each equals one fifth of a breve).

This style, in which the triplum rapidly declaims its text in a subtle and flexible rhythm, while the two lower parts, moving much more slowly, serve as accompanists, is associated with the name of Petrus de Cruce, a composer active at the end of the century. Only a few motets of this type are preserved, and it is likely that not many were written. The beginning of *Aucun qui ne sevent–Iure tuis–Maria* is shown in Example III-10. Only the triplum shows the modern tendencies—the motetus and tenor could be

Petrus de Cruce

MARIA
No one who does not know how to serve love, or to carry on the sweet pursuit.

Ex. III-10

from a much earlier motet. The emphasis is on elegance and refinement, at the expense, perhaps, of much of the vigor of the earlier motet. There is a certain fin-de-siècle quality about such music, and in fact the early years of the fourteenth century brought about fundamental changes in the technical bases of polyphonic writing. The work of Petrus de Cruce stands as the terminus of the school of Paris, begun over a hundred years earlier by Leoninus. Both of these men had as their ideal a free, flowing melodic line, but there are profound differences in the means by which they achieved their goals. The graceful melodies of Leoninus, unfolding easily over a stationary tenor, are aesthetically and technically remote from the nervous elegance of Petrus. In the period between these two men, Parisian composers had exploited almost all of the possibilities of modal rhythm. The six rhythmic modes, apparently so limited in musical potential, had supplied the basic material of composition for over a century in one of music's most creative eras.

OTHER POLYPHONIC TECHNIQUES

Voice-interchange

The preceding pages have dealt with the main lines of polyphonic development. For the sake of completeness—and also to help suggest the richness and diversity of the thirteenth-century musical scene—certain less common techniques and devices need to be mentioned.

Beginning in the period of the three- and four-voice organa, passages may be found in which two upper voices share the same musical material in alternate phrases, producing a passage such as $\begin{smallmatrix} ab \\ ba \end{smallmatrix}$. This procedure, called voice-interchange (from the German *Stimmtausch*, which is often used even in English), was regarded as a kind of ornamental effect, to be used at the composer's pleasure, without special structural significance. Example III-11 shows a fragment from the four-voice *Viderunt omnes* of

Ex. III-11

Perotinus. Extended instances also occur, and there are entire motets in which voice-interchange is practically continuous. The resemblance of this to the later technique of imitation is obvious, but it must be noted that Parisian composers made no systematic attempt to exploit it. The essence of Parisian style lay in the manipulation of rhythm, and special melodic device rarely rose above the level of decoration.

Hocket

Another special technique, of apparently less importance, was in fact rather more intensely cultivated, precisely because it was basically rhythmic in nature. This was hocket, a procedure in which two or more voices alternate brief melodic fragments with short rests, combining to produce a single melody (Ex. III-12). This represents a kind of rhythmic virtuoso writing, and is not, in fact, at all easy to sing accurately. A few examples of hocket may be found before the beginning of the thirteenth century, but it was not easily notated in ligatures. It appears more frequently during the course of the

Ex. III-12

thirteenth century, and was one of the elements of the period that survived into the following century.

Tenor melodies

The tenors of most thirteenth-century motets were taken from the traditional reper- toire of clausula tenors—melismas from responsorial chants. Especially after 1250, exceptions to this general rule become numerous. As the motet lost its close connection with the clausula (and almost all connection with the liturgy), tenors from other parts of the liturgy were sometimes selected: a melody for the Kyrie, for example, or the *Alma redemptoris mater* (an elaborate antiphon in honor of the Virgin). This was natural, since the exigencies that had caused responsorial melismas to be treated in discant style had long since vanished, and there was no reason to adhere rigidly to a tradition whose basis had decayed. Some motets, however, went considerably further: there are motets with tenors identified as "Chose Tassin" or "Chose Loyset"—meaning "a melody of Tassin (or Loyset)". These tenors, originally independent instrumental tunes written for monophonic performance, were now serving as a support for conventional motet compositions. Other pieces have secular lyrics as their tenors, and one even uses a Parisian street cry ("Fresh strawberries"). Non-Gregorian tenors were not ordinarily subjected to the kind of rhythmic patterning found in the normal motet. They were, instead, usually left in their original rhythmic form. Since, however, regularity of rhythm was characteristic of almost all music of the period, the effect was not markedly different from that of the ordinary motet.

Motets with secular tenors were quite common in the second half of the century, and did not generally share the tendency of the "normal" motet to concentrate rhyth- mic interest in the triplum. A few even approach the texture of the old conductus, with all voices moving in roughly the same rhythms. The majority, however, resemble the classic motet style, with two active upper parts of approximately equal rhythmic in- terest, supported by a slower-moving tenor.

The musical primacy of Paris from the time of Leoninus on is indisputable. Al- though by no means all composers of the period were native Parisians, it is clear that Paris—the place where young men went to learn their art—was the center of their work and the market for the exchange of new musical ideas. It is likely that the practice of polyphony was centered in the University of Paris, and since this institution was a model for universities elsewhere, it is also likely that the radiation of Parisian musical influence to other places took place through academic channels. The force of this radiation must have been enormous. While it is certain that polyphony was extensively practiced in many places throughout Western Europe at this time, very little music survives that can definitely be attributed to composers indifferent to Parisian styles. In most places, the inherited, provincial techniques were abandoned in favor of methods imported from Paris.

Only in England is there clear evidence of the preservation of local peculiarities of style. English music of the thirteenth (and fourteenth) century is preserved in fragmentary fashion, but fortunately there are enough pieces to give at least an idea of the English schools. It is evident that the English gladly received the French influence—in fact, English musicians are known to have been active at Paris—and the familiar Continental forms, notably the motet, were cultivated in England. But local stylistic features persist, even when the overall technique is Continental. Perhaps the most striking of these local features is the British preference for large numbers of thirds and sixths. Because of this emphasis on the imperfect consonances, much English music of the period has a richer and fuller sound than contemporary French music.

Also noteworthy is the English preference for relatively simple rhythms among the upper parts of a motet. While some English pieces approach the rhythmic complexity of the French motet, others have upper voices that are rhythmically similar to one another, giving a more blocklike effect. Both these traits persisted in English music throughout the fourteenth century and into the fifteenth, when English style became an important ingredient of the new internationalism of the Renaissance.

It is ironic that the best-known piece of medieval music is an English one, and atypical even for English music: *Sumer is icumen in.* In this work, for six (!) voices, the upper four are in canon—that is, each has exactly the same melody as the others, but starts a little later. The lower two voices form a repeating accompaniment figure that persists throughout the entire piece. The combination of these two techniques is unique for this period, and unusual for any era, and the piece is clearly an exceptional one. Despite its deserved celebrity, it should not be taken as representative of thirteenth-century music. In England, as in France, it was the polytextual motet that occupied the central position in polyphonic music.

The Medieval Lyric.   It has already been observed in the discussion of the medieval drama and the prosa that, beginning in the eleventh century, new techniques of poetic versification began to be used. In place of the classical system of quantitative scansion (deriving poetic meter from the length of the syllables), and of the rather free technique of the early prosa, poetry began to depend more and more heavily on two devices familiar from more recent poetic works: scansion according to the natural accent of the words, and rhyme. The full and consistent deployment of these two devices—an achievement of the later eleventh and the twelfth centuries—produced a new flowering of poetry, of which the following stanza may serve as example:

Versification

> Éstuáns intrínsecús
> íra véheménti
> ín amáritúdine
> lóquar méae ménti
> fáctus dé matériá
> lévis éleménti
> símilís sum fólió
> dé quo lúdunt vénti

(Boiling inwardly with violent anger, I shall speak my mind in bitterness. Made of matter, light of substance, I am like a leaf with which the winds play.)

This stanza is followed by a number of others, all having the same pattern of stresses and the same rhyme scheme.

The importance of this new type of versification was enormous. It remained the basis of most European poetry until past the end of the nineteenth century. In music, it may well have been one of the sources of the rhythmic modes: in fact, if we assign long and short values to the stressed and unstressed syllables of the first two lines above, we arrive at the rhythm ♩ ♪♪ ♪|♩ ♪♪ ♪|♩ ♩ ♪♪ ♪|♩♩ ♩| —a pattern very characteristic of the Notre Dame clausula. The perfecting of new poetical techniques brought forth a flood of lyrical poetry, in Latin and in the vernacular tongues, and a great repertoire of monophonic melodies to which the new poems were sung.

THE LATIN LYRIC

A survey of this vast body of material may conveniently begin with the Latin lyric, since premonitions of the new style have already been mentioned in connection with the liturgical drama and the prosa. The type of prosa exemplified by *Laetabundus* (see above, Chapter II), often referred to as "transitional" in style, gave way to a fully metrical and rhymed type—the "Victorine" prosa, named after Adam of the monastery of St. Victor in Paris. Each line of the early prosa becomes a small stanza, and all the stanzas share the same regular rhythm. In fact, from the text alone, it would be difficult to distinguish a Victorine prosa from a hymn; but the melodies show the characteristic paired pattern AA BB CC . . . (without, however, unpaired lines at the beginning or end), instead of the strophic repetition of the same melody characteristic of the hymn. The late prosa often contains slight changes of metrical pattern from one stanza-pair to another, and this too is atypical for the hymn, in which all stanzas are metrically identical.

Adam of St. Victor, writing in the middle of the twelfth century, may be said to have brought the prosa to the terminal point of its development. While new works were written after his time, they are not of great importance, nor do they significantly expand the technical resources of the genre. But from about 1100 the prosa was joined by other sacred verse forms, and these, too, began to be extensively cultivated.

The "Victorine" prosa and the "versus" of St. Martial

In a miscellaneous manuscript of St. Martial dating from about 1100, there are a number of Latin poems entitled "versus." These are of two types, either wholly free sacred poems, often relating to one of the feasts of the Christmas season but lacking clear liturgical function; or poetic expansions of the "Benedicamus Domino—Deo gratias" ("Let us bless the Lord—thanks be to God") that occurs at the end of the Office services. Otherwise the two classes are quite similar: they employ the modern type of versification (not always, at this early date, consistently), usually in strophic form. Some are given simple, syllabic musical settings, while others receive quite ornate melodic dress. A few in this early manuscript, and rather more in later St. Martial sources, are polyphonic—in fact, the St. Martial polyphony discussed earlier in this chapter consists of polyphonic settings of *versus*.

In northern France, during the twelfth century, the term "conductus" was employed for the same type of poem. This, too, recalls the discussion of polyphony, for the polyphonic conductus was an important genre in the repertoire of the school of Notre

Dame. But the monophonic conductus also had an independent existence, being often used as an extra insertion in particularly splendid liturgical celebrations (the name conductus suggests that the form originally developed in connection with some sort of procession).

The notation of the sources gives no indication of rhythm. In monophonic music, ambiguity of rhythmic notation persisted longer than it did in polyphony. This may in part reflect the greater freedom of the single solo performer, who did not need to keep in time with another part or parts. It may also suggest that singers of monophony more often learned their songs from another singer than from a written source. The manuscripts would then function like the non-diastematic chant manuscripts: they could remind the singer of some, but not all, the elements of a melody (in the conductus manuscripts, of course, pitch is unequivocal, and only rhythm need be supplied by the performer).

Notation of rhythm

Despite the lack of indications in the manuscripts, such pieces seem to demand some sort of metrical rendition. Two possibilities are available. The first makes use of the rhythmic modes, assuming that the modal system was known to the singer, and that he could remember the proper mode to use, or choose the right one at sight. It is also possible that the syllables of a metrical poem were regarded as equal in length (with a few exceptions, such as the penultimate syllable of a line). Then the occurrence of several notes to a syllable would be a signal to the performer to sing these as fractions of the basic pulse, so that, taken together, they would be equal in time to one pulse-unit.

The liturgical drama

The new techniques of poetry were also applied to the liturgical drama, with results similar to those seen in the independent Latin lyric. The Beauvais *Play of Daniel* (late twelfth or early thirteenth century) is a highly sophisticated example of this type of drama. For the most part, the utterances of the characters are long enough to be cast into metrical, strophic poems, which are then given corresponding musical settings. In some cases, forms resembling the prosa are used. When short lines of dialogue cannot be grouped into stanzas, they are simply presented as isolated musical entities. In general, the music makes no attempt to mirror the emotions of the characters: except in Daniel's lament, it is an embellishment, not an interpretation of the text. (Performances and recordings of this and similar plays are generally cast in modal rhythm, although it is by no means certain that this was the original intention.)

After the thirteenth century, liturgical drama was apparently less actively cultivated. While there are many manuscripts that contain Latin plays, the writing of new liturgical drama of large dimensions seems to have practically ceased. One cause of this was the increased popularity of vernacular drama, which was not performed in the church, but rather in the square or market place. While the Latin drama had been sung throughout, vernacular plays were mostly spoken. They doubtless made considerable use of incidental music, but almost none has survived. It was not until the sixteenth century that music and drama were again as closely combined as they had been in the Middle Ages.

THE VERNACULAR LYRIC

Since Latin was the language of the clergy, it was natural that most Latin poetry should be sacred, or at least serious, in character. But Latin was also the language of the student; and students' minds were not always fixed on higher things. Some of these young men represented themselves as having no fixed residence, wandering from town to town and living as best they could. They referred to themselves as "Goliards," after their mythical patron saint, Golias. Whether their lives were as free as their poetry implies may be doubted. Their favorite poetical topics were the charms of women and wine, and their uninhibited verses are often extraordinarily fine.[1] Unfortunately, most of the poems have come down with music in undecipherable notation (or without any music at all), but the settings seem to have been in the same general style as the monophonic conductus.

The Goliards

Important as the Latin lyric was, it must take second place to the sudden efflorescence of vernacular secular poetry that began in the eleventh century. While sung vernacular poetry must always have existed, it had not earlier been thought worthy of preservation. In the eleventh century, however, it acquired a new dignity—the rank of secular art poetry and music—and from that time on, in the history of both literature and music, works in the common tongues began to be recorded and preserved with almost the same respect hitherto reserved for works destined for the Church.

The history of vernacular poetry begins in France, with the *Chanson de Roland* (second half of the eleventh century), the earliest and finest example of the *chanson de geste*, or heroic epic. This lengthy poem tells its story of warfare and chivalry—amply expanded from history by the unknown poet—in over 4,000 eleven-syllable lines. These are grouped into verse "paragraphs" of varying length, called *laisses*. In performance, the singer, usually a lower-class entertainer, needed to remember only two melodic phrases: one to be repeated for the words of every line of the *laisse* except the last, and the other for the concluding line. Since so little effort of memory was required, the music was not written down. Apparently the tunes were very simple and syllabic, although the performers may have embellished them, or perhaps accompanied themselves with an instrument. In any event, the music of the *chanson de geste* was a secondary matter: it was the story that counted.

The chanson de geste

The *chansons de geste* reflected a man's world—a hard world of battle and death, in which women were significant largely to the extent that they were able to influence affairs of state. This in turn reflected the realities of eleventh-century culture, mostly devoted to the difficult task of staying alive, and without much time or inclination for amenities. As the century drew to a close, however, and increasingly in the century following, there grew up more settled centers of civilization—petty courts where the nobility could live in safety and at ease. For such persons, the *chansons de geste* continued to exercise an appeal, as tales of heroism seem always to do; but the new manner of life was better mirrored in the lyric than the epic, and love became a matter of more immediate importance than war. There sprang up an extraordinary idealization of woman, and with this, the idea of *amor cortois* (courtly love)—an elaborate code of etiquette regulating the not always innocent love affairs of the upper classes. It would be difficult to imagine a more favorable soil for the cultivation of the secular lyric.

It was southern France that produced the first school of lyric poets—the troubadours. The origin of the name is uncertain; it may be connected with the Provençal *trobar* or French *trouver* (find, invent). The troubadours themselves wrote in Provençal, a language related to both French and Spanish. Their ideas were quickly taken

---

[1] The stanza from *Estuans intrinsecus* quoted above is an example. The rest of this poem, and a number of others, with excellent English translations, may be found in Helen Waddell's *Medieval Latin Lyrics*.

France: The troubadours and trouvères

up in northern France, where the poets—there called trouvères—wrote in an early form of French. These poet-musicians, almost all of them of the aristocracy, began the creation of a vast body of lyric poetry and music which, beginning about 1100 and continuing through the thirteenth century, eventually amounted to over 6,000 poems and 1,500 melodies. Eleanor of Aquitaine, wife first of Louis VII of France, then of Henry II of England, was an important figure, both in the elaboration of the etiquette of *amor cortois,* and in the interchange between southern and northern ideas. Her court at Poitiers (from 1170) was noted for its literary and musical brilliance.

Although the work of the trouvères differed from that of the troubadours in some particulars, both categories may here be considered together. Most of their poetry was concerned with themes connected with courtly love, ranging from simple love songs to dialogue debates on difficult points of etiquette. Many distinct poetic types were recognized, among which were the *alba* (or *aube*), an early morning song of lovers' parting; and the *pastourelle,* a tale of a knight attempting to gain the favors of a shepherdess. The poets showed great skill in versification, and their language is full of charm and elegance; but, on the whole, the poems are not marked by profundity of thought or feeling.

The great majority of the poems are strophic, the metrical arrangement and rhyme scheme of the first stanza being exactly repeated in subsequent ones. Both troubadours and trouvères were most ingenious in contriving new and different metrical patterns. (Indeed it was considered incorrect to imitate exactly a preexistent stanza form except when a poem was a direct answer to, or continuation of, an earlier one.) One general scheme appears in a large number of poems, especially of the trouvères; the first unit of two to four lines is answered immediately by the same number of lines having the same meter and rhymes, and is then followed by a free continuation. This yields patterns like: ababccddee, abc abc dedeff, and the like. The two opening sections are called *pedes* (sing. *pes*), and the concluding one *cauda.* In the terminology of the German Minnesänger, this is referred to as "Bar" form; there is no universally accepted equivalent term for the Romance languages, although the word "canzone" is frequently used.

Some poems have refrains—recurrent lines of text that appear in every stanza at the same place (most often the end). Others have what might be called pseudo-refrains, consisting of quotations from well-known songs—a different quotation for each stanza—appearing where one might expect the refrain to be. A few poems from this period are cast in what are called the "formes fixes" (fixed forms): the rondeau, virelai, and ballade; but the importance of these forms for the troubadour-trouvère period has been greatly exaggerated.

In the numerous large manuscripts containing the poetry of the troubadours and trouvères, music is given for some of the troubadour songs and for rather more of the trouvère songs. Many songs are attributed to known persons, usually members of the nobility. Ordinarily the first stanza of a strophic poem is written under the music, the remaining stanzas following without notation. Naturally the same music is used for these. The notation is wholly unambiguous with regard to pitch, but shows the same lack of rhythmic meaning already mentioned in connection with the Latin lyric. The rhythm must therefore be derived from the music itself, and from the rhythm of the poetry. This would have been easy enough for the medieval singer, even if he had not already learned the song from another singer (as was no doubt often the case), for he had in his head a living tradition of performance to guide him. For later scholars, the matter has not been so simple, and has given rise to considerable controversy.

The application of patterns derived from the rhythmic modes is the most commonly used solution, mainly because it is the easiest. There is no positive evidence that
this is what the composers intended. Moreover, in a number of cases this does not
produce good results (particularly for some of the earlier troubadour songs), and for
these, special methods have to be devised. The reader is warned that two transcriptions
of the same song may differ considerably from each other.

The music of the troubadour-trouvère poems, which was composed, or at least
caused to be composed, by the poets themselves, is distinguished first of all by its close
dependence on the structure (but not on the meaning) of the text. Its rhythmic dependence is accepted as an axiom in transcribing the melodies; its structural dependence is
evident by inspection. If, for example, in the "canzone" form mentioned above, the first
pair of lines is answered by a second pair having the same meter and rhyme scheme, the
music for the second pair will be a repetition (sometimes slightly varied) of that for the
first. In general, it may be said that the poetic structure of the stanza is clearly reflected
in the form of the music. Given the wide variety of poetic stanzas in use, this results in a
great richness of musical forms.

The song *Contre temps que voi frimer* (Ex. III-13) is cast in the common canzone
form. The first four lines consist of two pairs (*pedes*) with identical music. The remainder of the stanza (*cauda*) continues with new music, although there are subtle references to the earlier lines from time to time. The fifth relationship is especially important in this song and is used with great sophistication. The overall tonal center is
obviously D, and this is firmly established in the *pedes*. The first part of the *cauda*,
however, centers on a, providing both contrast and unity before the return to D in the
last three lines. This is an early instance of the deliberate change of tonal center within
a piece as a means of achieving tonal variety: many centuries later such a procedure
became known as modulation. (The transcription of the song given here is modal; other
rhythmic interpretations might be equally satisfactory.)

Example III-13 is typical of the major portion of the troubabour-trouvère repertoire.
There are, however, some songs that differ considerably in structure or style. A few, for
example, are provided with more ornate music. These are apt to cause considerable
difficulties in transcription, and hence are not often found in modern editions. The
musical effect of a melismatic song will differ markedly from that of one that is largely
syllabic, regardless of the method of transcription chosen. The rhythm of the text ceases
to act as a propulsive force governing the musical rhythm. In consequence, the symmetrical four-measure phrases so characteristic of the majority of the songs are much less
evident to the ear in the melismatic pieces.

A more numerous class comprises those songs that are not strophic. Chief among
these is the lai, a form having some resemblance to the prosa. In the lai, strophic
repetition is abandoned in favor of sectional construction. In some cases, the lai closely
follows the form of the prosa, having the pattern AABBCC . . ., in which A, B, and C are
not necessarily identical in versification. But a number of lais are freer in construction:
a section may be repeated several times, or may not be repeated at all; there may be
repetition of a section after the appearance of contrasting material, or there may be
internal relations among sections. About all that can be predicated of the lai in general
is its basically sectional character.

France was by no means the only country that produced lyric poetry in the twelfth
and thirteenth centuries: there are considerable repertoires in other languages, with
varying relations to the central Provençal-French school. Of these, the German reper-

About the time I saw the trees
freeze and whiten, I was
seized by the desire to sing . . .

Ex. III-13

Germany: The Minnesänger

toire, the work of the so-called Minnesänger (singers of courtly love), is perhaps the closest to the art of the troubadours and trouvères. While there had for long existed a tradition of German poetry, the marriage in 1156 of the Emperor Friedrich Barbarossa to Beatrice of Burgundy (herself the patroness of a French trouvère) provided a channel through which French influence could enter Germany. Thereafter, while the art of the Minnesänger never ceased to maintain its own individuality, French influence was increasingly accepted.

Like the troubadours, the Minnesänger were for the most part members of the petty nobility. They sang most often of love, although in a rather more abstract and idealized form than their French counterparts. For most of the poetic types current in France, German equivalents appeared: thus the Provencal *alba* became the German *Tagelied*, and the French *lai* the German *Leich*. The specifically German quality of the repertoire is clearly apparent in the versification. Romance poetry was based on the number of syllables in the line, while German poetry of this time counted the number of accents per line. As in later English poetry, the number of syllables between accents often varied. For this reason, purely modal interpretations of German songs are even more problematical than they are for the French repertoire.

Many Minnesänger are known to us by name. Both Tannhäuser and Wolfram von Eschenbach, who appear as characters in Wagner's *Tannhäuser*, were historical figures. Perhaps the most celebrated of them all was Walther von der Vogelweide, (ca. 1170-1230) who passed some time as a traveling entertainer despite his noble birth. The German songs, like those of France, are varied in form and style, although most scholars would agree that they share a specific if undefinable German quality. Differences in *rhythmic* style between the two repertoires should not be taken seriously, as the rhythms used in modern editions are necessarily conjectures of the transcriber.

Many German songs employ the canzone form, known in Germany as *Bar* form. The two pedes (Ger. *Stollen)* are normally identical, and the cauda (*Abgesang*) is different. Sometimes the *Abgesang* returns, after presenting contrasting material, to the music of the end of the *Stollen,* thus rounding off the form. In a few cases the entire melody of the *Stollen* is incorporated into the end of the *Abgesang*.

The other nations of Western Europe also made their contributions to the monophonic lyric. England appears to have produced relatively little, perhaps because the English nobility was still in part French-speaking and had little need for a native repertoire. Italy added more. The Provençal tradition was well known there and was still familiar in the time of Dante, in whose work several troubadours are mentioned by name. Nevertheless, there seem to be no surviving secular songs with music from the period. Instead, there remains a large number of Italian spiritual songs, the result of a widespread penitential movement that began in 1260. The wars and sufferings so universal in Italy had convinced many that God's wrath had to be propitiated, and companies of penitents traveled about the country, flagellating themselves, and singing songs called *laude* (singular: *lauda*). Naturally their textual content differed radically from that of the secular lyric, but the melodic style seems to be relatively similar to that of the other monophonic repertoires. Many *laude* had refrains, sung at the beginning and end, with contrasting verses between. (The refrain may also have been sung after each verse as well.) As in other monophonic types, the music of the verse might be wholly new, or might borrow material from the refrain.

The Italian penitents were not, for the most part, men of the nobility, although some of the *laude* make it evident that they included men of taste and education. In Spain, the aristocratic troubadour tradition was also known, but as in the case of Italy, few secular songs with music remain. Instead—again as in Italy—there has survived a large body of sacred monophony. This has been preserved in a collection made by Alfonso X, king of Castile and Leon from 1252 to 1284. These *cantigas,* as they are called, are for the most part in praise of the Virgin Mary, representing to some extent a translation of *amor cortois* into the Marian cult (something found, less often, in the French repertoire as well). The *cantigas,* like the *laude,* are usually songs with refrains; like them also, their style is to some extent individual, but not radically so. Indeed, one may say that the monophony of each of the nations treated here represents, not a musical language of its own, but rather a dialect of a single basic European style.

The extraordinary proliferation of monophonic song throughout Europe in the twelfth and thirteenth centuries is one more testimony to the artistic and intellectual vitality of the age. The builders of cathedrals, the scholastics, the miniaturists, the tellers of tales in verse and prose—all of these gave artistic shape to some aspect of the majesty or the delight of the world in which they lived. The musicians, whether learned polyphonists of Paris, elegant and noble troubadours, or perhaps even rather humble makers of songs, had the same aim and achieved the same success.

Other countries

EARLY POLYPHONY TO 1300.

I.   **Some stages in the rise of polyphony.**

    A.   *Musica enchiriadis.* Treatise, ca. 850, describes improvisation of parallel organum, and organum using oblique motion.

    B.   Guido of Arezzo, in his *Micrologus* (ca. 1040), describes and gives examples of basically parallel organum, but which begins and ends on the unison, hence implying some melodic independence in the added part.

    C.   Winchester Troper (Cambridge, Corpus Christi College Ms. 473); collection contains 164 two-voice organa. In note-against-note style, they employ much parallel motion.

    D.   John of Afflighem, in a treatise of ca. 1100, specifically advocates the use of contrary motion.

    E.   Chartres fragments. A few 11th-century pieces from Chartres show the added voice above the chant. The added part is melodically independent of the chant.

    F.   Codex Calixtinus. A 12th-century manuscript from Santiago de Compostela, including 21 two-voice pieces.

    G.   St. Martial polyphony. Four manuscripts (Paris, Bib. Nat. lat. 1139, 3719, 3549; Brit. Mus. Add. Ms. 36881), once owned by the Abbey of St. Martial at Limoges, contain 64 polyphonic pieces, some of which demonstrate "melismatic organum," the use of many notes in the organal voice against a single note in the principal voice.

II.   **Polyphony of the School of Paris**

    A.   Principal forms.

        1.   *Organum.* A polyphonic setting of a preexistent liturgical chant (usually a gradual, alleluia, or responsory). Solo sections set polyphonically, using chant as tenor; choral sections remain monophonic.

        2.   *Conductus.* A polyphonic piece *not* based on a preexistent chant (hence having no liturgical tenor); all voices move at approximately the same speed, have the same text.

        3.   *Substitute clausula.* A section in discant (see below) style originally designed to replace a similar section in an organum. Uses the same liturgical tenor as the clausula it replaces—usually the notes of a melisma.

    B.   Styles.

        1.   *Sustained-tone organum.* Tenor notes are enormously long, while upper voice or voices move at a faster rate. Used for syllabic and neumatic sections of original chant.

2. *Discant.* All voices (including tenor) move in regular rhythm, at nearly the same speed. Used for melismatic sections of original chant. This style is the basis for the motet.

C. Composers.

1. *Leoninus* (2d half of 12th cent.). Composer of *Magnus liber*, a collection of organa in two voices for major feast days. Sustained-tone sections are rhythmically free; discant sections are more rhythmically organized.

2. *Perotinus* (ca. 1160–ca. 1220). Composer of organa, many substitute clausulae for Leoninian organa, and conductus. Increased number of voices: most of his works are for three voices, some for four. Extreme regularity of rhythm and phrase.

D. Sources.

1. Wolfenbüttel, Ducal library Ms. 677. The oldest surviving source for the *Magnus liber.* A facsimile published by J. H. Baxter as *An Old St. Andrews Music Book*, London, 1931.

2. Florence, Bib. Laur. plut. 29.1. Another early source for the *Magnus liber*; also contains substitute clausulae, conductus, and early motets. A facsimile (2 vols.) published by Luther Dittmer, Brooklyn, New York, 1966.

3. Wolfenbüttel, Ducal library Ms. 1206. A slightly later source of organum. A facsimile published by Luther Dittmer, Brooklyn, New York (ca. 1960).

III. Thirteenth-century motet

A. Origins.

Developed from substitute clausula: text is added to upper voice (or voices) of clausula. If the same text is added in all parts, the result is called a "conductus-motet:" if different texts, simply a motet.

B. Characteristics of the "standard" mid-13th-century motet.

1. Voices, from first composed: tenor, motetus, triplum, quadruplum.

2. Each voice characteristically has its own text, Latin or French.

3. Tenor.

   a. Uses notes of an old discant clausula (i.e., a chant melisma).

   b. Frequently repeats the series of notes more than once.

   c. Generally organized in repeating rhythmic phrases.

   d. Generally has no text other than the syllable or two of the original chant.

4. Upper voices.

   a. Move at approximately the same speed.

   b. Have approximately the same range.

   c. Text is declaimed in modal rhythms.

   d. Phrase endings frequently do not coincide.

C. Composers.

1. Franco of Cologne (ca. 1260). His notational advances free voices from declamation in modal rhythms: the top voice (triplum) in particular uses

faster rhythm than duplum; the result is a three-speed motet—triplum is faster than duplum, which is faster than tenor.

    2. Petrus de Cruce (ca. 1280). The triplum declaims on very short note values. The result is an accompanied song effect: the triplum moves very fast, the duplum and tenor much more slowly.

D. Sources: motet collections.

    1. Montpellier, Bib. Universitaire Ms. H 196. A large and beautiful collection from the late 13th century. An exemplary edition was published by Yvonne Rokseth as *Polyphonies du XIIIe Siècle* (4 vols., Paris, 1935–39).

    2. Bamberg, Ms. Ed. IV 6. Facsimile and transcription by Pierre Aubry, *Cent Motets du XIIIe Siècle*, 3 vols., Paris, 1908.

    3. Burgos, Abbey of Las Huelgas. Facsimile and transcription by Higini Anglès, *El Còdex Musical de las Huelgas*, 3 vols., Barcelona, 1931.

E. Bibliography.

    1. Other modern editions.

        Husmann, Heinrich: *Die drei- und vierstimmige Notre-Dame-Organa.* Leipzig, 1940. Transcriptions of pieces in Perotinus style.

        Knapp, Janet: *Thirty-five Conductus for Two and Three Voices.* New Haven, 1965. Transcriptions from the Florence manuscript.

        Waite, William: *The Rhythm of Twelfth-Century Polyphony.* New Haven, 1954. A study of the Leoninus style, with transcriptions of many two-voice organa.

    2. Books

        Apel, Willi: *The Notation of Polyphonic Music.* Cambridge, Mass., 1953.

        Ludwig, Friedrich: *Repertorium organorum recentioris et motetorum vetustissimi stili.* Halle, 1910. An incomplete, but immensely useful, index to the organa and motets of this period.

        Reese, Gustave: *Music in the Middle Ages.* New York, 1940.

THE MEDIEVAL LYRIC.

I. **Important schools and areas of activity.**

A. Troubadours and trouvères (poet-musicians, often of high rank, in 12th- and 13th-century France).

    1. Troubadours. Their poems, of which ca. 2600 remain, are written in the *langue d'oc* (Provençal). About 260 melodies are preserved. Some composers:
Guillaume of Aquitaine, Count of Poitiers (1071–1127)
Marcabru of Gascony (d. ca. 1147)
Bernard de Ventadour (12th cent.)
Guiraut Riquier (d. ca. 1292)

    2. Trouvères. Active in northern France, where they wrote and spoke the

langue d'oil. About 4000 poems remain, and about 1400 melodies. Some composers:

Gace Brulé (d. ca. 1220)

Thibaut de Champagne, King of Navarre (d. 1253)

Conon de Béthune (ca. 1150–1224)

   3. Some standard types of subject matter for poetry.

      a. Love song *(canso):* knightly, chivalric love poetry.

      b. *Aube:* a morning song, sung by a friend to warn a pair of lovers of the approaching dawn.

      c. *Pastourelle:* a knight attempts to seduce a shepherdess, not always successfully.

      d. *Chanson de toile:* a lady at her needle work laments: her lost love, or her unhappy marriage, etc.

B. Minnesänger: contemporaries of the trouvères, they originated in Austria and Bavaria.

   1. Some composers:

Walter von der Vogelweide (ca. 1170–1230)

Neidhart von Reuenthal (ca. 1180–1250)

Heinrich von Meissen (called Frauenlob; d. 1318)

   2. Poetical forms and subjects. Similar to those of the trouvères. The basic musical form, the bar form, consists of two melodically identical *Stollen* followed by an *Abgesang.*

C. Spain. The Cantigas de Santa Maria, a collection of ca. 400 pieces collected by Alfonso X, King of Castile and León (d. 1284), consists of songs, mostly using refrain structures, recounting the miracles of the Virgin Mary.

D. Italy. *Laude spirituali,* vernacular religious songs, mostly employing refrain structures, date back as far as the late 13th century.

II. Modern and facsimile editions of secular monophonic music.

Aubry, Pierre: *Le chansonnier de l'Arsenal* (Arsenal Ms. 5198), facsimile ed., Paris, 1909.

Beck, Jean: *Le manuscrit du Roi* (Paris, Bib. Nat. Fr. 844), facsimile ed., 2 vols., London and Philadelphia, 1938.

————: *Le chansonnier Cangé* (Paris, Bib. Nat. Fr. 846), facsimile ed., 2 vols., Paris and Philadelphia, 1927.

Gennrich, Friedrich: *Rondeaux, Virelais und Balladen,* 2 vols., Dresden, 1921, Göttingen, 1927.

Denkmäler der Tonkunst in Oesterreich:

   Vol. XX.2. Songs of Frauenlob, Reinmar von Zweter, and Alexander. ed. Heinrich Rietsch.

   Vol. XXXVII.1. Songs of Niedhard von Reuenthal, ed. Wolfgang Schmieder and Edmund Wiessner.

Higini Anglès, ed.: *La Mùsica de las Cantigas de Santa Maria del Rey Alfonso el Sabio*, vol. 2 (transcriptions), Barcelona, 1932.

Fernando Liuzzi: *La Lauda e i primordi della melodia italiana*, 2 vols., Rome, 1935.

THE
FOURTEENTH
CENTURY

Until the end of the thirteenth century, monophonic music held its own as one of the primary types of art composition. Even in the late thirteenth century, however, the roles of polyphony and monophony began to diverge. Polyphony became the vehicle for the most challenging and progressive stylistic developments, while monophony was content with modest stylistic changes. After 1300, while monophonic music continued to be composed, the attention of serious musicians was devoted overwhelmingly to music for two or more voices. In Western culture—and Western culture alone—the history of art music became the history of polyphony.

POLYPHONIC MUSIC IN FRANCE AND ITALY IN THE FOURTEENTH CENTURY

France: The Ars nova.   By 1300, the motet was the principal polyphonic form, having undergone nearly a century of development. In the tripla, modal rhythm had been succeeded by a varied and often rapid textual declamation in semibreves. The semibreve remained the sole notational symbol available for short notes, and could vary in value from one-half of a breve to as little as one-ninth. Any further continuation in the direction of the style of Petrus de Cruce—any increase in the number of semibreves replacing a single breve—would merely have exacerbated a problem already much disputed by theorists: the proper value to be given a semibreve in a specific rhythmic context.

A new notational system was needed, one that would be flexible enough to permit further rhythmic experimentation, yet sufficiently logical to maintain an accurate relationship between the written symbol and its actual rhythmic value. This need attracted the attention of composers and theorists in the fourteenth century, and their solutions to the problem played a large role in determining important elements of musical style. Indeed throughout the fourteenth century musicians were deeply concerned with the notation of rhythm, and their music clearly reflects this preoccupation.

Notational reforms: Philippe de Vitry and the Ars nova

Instead of a fundamentally new system of notation, there appeared an expansion and rationalization of the old. The Frenchman Philippe de Vitry (1291-1361) is given the principal credit for this achievement, although he was not the only person involved. The authoritative formulation of fourteenth-century notational practice appeared in a treatise by de Vitry proudly entitled *Ars nova* (new art: primarily, but not exclusively, of notation). The emergence of a "new art" at this time may seem strange, for the fourteenth century in France is generally accounted a period of decline, during which architecture, philosophy, literature, and the fine arts added relatively little to the colossal achievements of the preceding century. It was also a period of unrest, marked by the long hostilities of the Hundred Years' War, and domestic tensions caused by the erosion of the previously stable feudal system. But the *Ars nova* may not have been quite as new as its practitioners believed, and there is in any case no reason to suppose that all the arts must show phases of energy and decline at exactly the same time.

The notational reform of the *Ars nova* appears more closely related to the theories of Franco of Cologne than to those of Petrus de Cruce. Its essential features were (1) the provision of new note forms to represent very short durations; (2) the extension of the Franconian rules governing the relation of the long and the breve to these shorter values; and (3) provisions whereby binary rhythms could be notated as easily as ternary ones.

During the thirteenth century, three basic rhythmic values had been in use: the long, the breve (short), and the semibreve (half or part of a breve). To these were now added the minim (♩; from Latin *minima*, least) and the semiminim (♪; half of a minim). This provided for a rational differentiation among short values, all of which had hitherto been represented by the semibreve. It also required rules concerning the relation of the new values to each other and to the old ones. These rules were as follows: a value might be ternary (equal to three of the next smaller value) or binary (equal to two of the next smaller value). In the former case, the Franconian rules applied, that is, the value might occur in either perfect (three-beat) or imperfect (two-beat) condition; but in the latter case, one of the next smaller value would be required to fill up the full three-beat space (e.g., ■■◆■ = $\frac{3}{4}$♩.| ♩ ♩|♩.|). If, however, the given value was basically binary, the inevitable triple meters produced by ternary division would be replaced by duple ones (e.g., ■■◆◆■ = $\frac{2}{4}$♩ |♩ |♩ ♩ |♩ |).

These principles governed the relation of the long to the breve (*modus*), the breve to the semibreve (*tempus*), and the semibreve to the minim (*prolatio*). Only the minim-semiminim relation was different, for the semiminim was always half a minim, never a third. The system was thus fertile in metrical possibilities, with a total of eight different combinations, ranging from ternary division at all levels to wholly binary division. Example IV-1 shows the possible meters (not the rhythms which, as will be seen, were quite complex).

The contrast between this flexibility and the relative rigidity of the thirteenth-century rhythmic modes is obvious. So, too, is the greater reliance on shorter note values. Music was not actually becoming faster, but the longer values were now reserved for special purposes, and the semibreve and minim were the "normal" notes of the fourteenth century.

The formulation of the new system appears to have occupied the first two decades of the century. There is, fortunately, one source in which old and new notations—and hence old and new styles—appear side by side. This is the *Roman de Fauvel*, a long

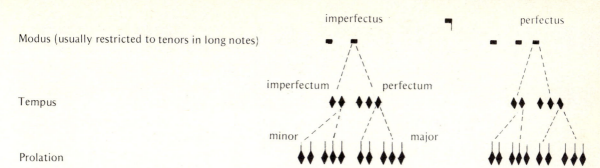

For each modus, the following combinations were possible:

> tempus perfectum, prolatio major (9/8 meter)
> tempus perfectum, prolatio minor (3/4 meter)
> tempus imperfectum, prolatio major (6/8 meter)
> tempus imperfectum, prolatio minor (2/4 meter)

Ex. IV-1

poem castigating the vices of contemporary society, which appears in one manuscript (1316) with a large number of musical interpolations, both monophonic and polyphonic. The interpolations are related to the main text by their subject matter: they too deal with the wrongdoings of noblemen and prelates. Indeed the motet at this time appears to have been a primary vehicle for social commentary.

Roman de Fauvel

   Most of the pieces in the *Roman de Fauvel* are in the style of the thirteenth century, but several are works in the newer manner, some perhaps by Philippe de Vitry himself. An anonymous example is the motet *Super cathedram–Presidentes–Ruina* (Ex. IV-2). This was originally written, not in *Ars nova* notation, but in a transitional fashion, with all the smaller values still written as semibreves, as in the works of Petrus de Cruce. At some later time, someone revised the notation, adding stems to some of the semibreves and making them minims. There is no way of knowing whether this corresponded with the composer's original intention, but the reviser doubtless knew more about the matter than is known today.

   The piece is more than twice as long as the average motet of the thirteenth century. The cause of this expansion may readily be found in the structure of the tenor. This voice doubtless takes its melodic substance from some preexistent chant, although no source has yet been found: what is new is its rhythm. The entire tenor is built up of repetitions of the pattern: ¾ ♩|♩♩♩|♩.|♩.|♩♩♩|♩.|▬| . These repetitions, while they may not be immediately audible, guarantee the coherence of the entire work; and, since the pattern itself is lengthy, the motet is long also, reaching a size hitherto achieved only by the great four-voice organa of the twelfth century.

   Repetition of tenor rhythms was not new. Repeated rhythmic patterns are found in the tenors of most clausulae and motets of the thirteenth century. But such patterns were short and invariably modal: their function was to supply a clearly audible rhythmic drive against which the freer upper voices could be contrasted. The present example shows a more subtle and intellectual use of the device. Here the pattern is too slow to

Ex. IV-2

On the throne of Moses there hides beneath hypocrisy the modern shepherd of prelates.
What truer witness than the external king of paradise?
Those who today sit upon thrones.

sound strongly modal, nor is it prominently heard. It is, rather, an organizing device, a method by which the composer can ensure the unity of his composition. In *Super cathedram*, the pattern is still simple enough to be audible to an attentive listener. The longer, slower, and more complex patterns of later motets suggest that composers came to use this constructive principle for its own sake, without expecting it to be heard. While such a procedure is certainly intellectualistic, it is by no means without parallel: there are several periods in the history of music when composers employed complex devices inaudible to most hearers.

Isorhythm   However composers may have thought of it, this method of treating the tenor was basic to the French motet of the fourteenth century, and is known as isorhythm. The example is therefore an "isorhythmic motet." The rhythmic pattern is known as the *talea* ("cutting"), and the cantus firmus melody is called the *color*. In an isorhythmic motet, the *talea* is invariably repeated, and the *color* may be also. Special complexities may arise from the combined repetitions of both.

Isorhythm is in part new, in part old, being in fact an up-to-date treatment of a technique originating in the twelfth century. The upper voices of *Super cathedram* show the same sort of mixture. In one sense, they are traditional. Each voice has its own text, as in the thirteenth century, and each is given a thoroughly independent melodic setting. In the treatment of consonance and dissonance, also, the upper voices use the same intervals in much the same way that the thirteenth century did. Even in rhythm, the motetus, at least, is traditional, being largely in the second and third rhythmic modes. The triplum, however, is clearly in a new style. Almost entirely free from modal rhythm, and yet (in this version) more clearly ordered than the tripla of Petrus, it reflects almost as clearly as the tenor the aesthetic of the "new art."

Rather more is known about the leading composers of the fourteenth century than of preceding ones. Of Perotinus and Leoninus only the names survive: their lives are wholly obscure. Of de Vitry much more is known. He was a poet, diplomat, churchman, a friend of the poet Petrarch. His work as a musical theorist has already been discussed. He was equally famous as a composer. His settings of secular songs were much admired in his time, but none of them has survived. His motets were also well known, and a few of these, at least, are extant. They are isorhythmic and show a profound feeling for structure, as well as an even greater independence from thirteenth-century methods (especially in rhythm) than *Super cathedram.*

Even more is known of Guillaume de Machaut (1300-77), the most famous French musician of the century. He, too, was famous both as a poet and a composer. Although he was a cleric, he spent most of his life in the service of princely patrons; nor did his clerical orders prevent him from devoting at least his poetic attention to the faded but still enticing attractions of *amor cortois.* It is also symptomatic of the times that Machaut supervised the production of accurate manuscript editions of his works, both literary and musical. Although by no means unknown earlier, the personality of the artist was an increasingly important factor.

Guillaume de Machaut

Machaut wrote over twenty motets, most of them isorhythmic. In some tenors, the *talea* and *color* are of different lengths, so that repetition of both brings the notes of the *color* into new rhythmic positions (Ex. IV-3). Often the last two or three *taleae* are given in diminution, that is, with their note values systematically reduced. Owing to the nature of *Ars nova* notation, this does not always produce a mathematically uniform reduction by a factor of one-half or one-third; the principle is, rather, that each long of the original becomes a breve in the diminution, each breve a semibreve, and so on. Since the *modus, tempus,* and *prolatio* may change at the same time, the result in modern notation may be a seemingly irregular shortening of the notes. The purpose of such diminution is of course audibly structural: the tenor increases in speed towards the end of a piece, creating an effect of climax.

Machaut's motets

Ex. IV-3

Another such audible structural device may be often found in the upper voices towards the end of a *talea,* where they frequently abandon their free melodic motion for passages in hocket. This again is an old technique, familiar from the end of the twelfth century on, but its use here—to increase the melodic animation at the end of the *talea,* thus signaling an important structural moment to the listener—is new. Since the rhythmic possibilities of hocket are rather limited, it was quite natural that such passages be rhythmically (not melodically) identical in succeeding *taleae.* Thus the principle of isorhythm, conceived for the tenor, begins to make its appearance in the upper voices as well.

In a number of Machaut's motets, as in some of de Vitry's, a fourth voice is added to the three traditional parts. This fourth voice is called the contratenor. As its name implies, it is more closely related to the tenor than to the upper voices, although it is not always isorhythmic. The addition of the contratenor is noteworthy for several reasons: it increases the sonority of the work, giving it added harmonic richness; it can also serve as a support to the upper voices during the frequent rests in the tenor *talea*; finally, and most important, it can, by moving freely above or below the tenor, permit the use of different notes in the upper voice than would be possible with the tenor alone. The last point, which is of great significance for the future, deserves fuller explanation.

Contratenor

Fig. IV-1: *An illustration from one of the Machaut manuscripts, showing singers reading from a "rotulus" or scroll (very few manuscripts of this format survive). The picture is entitled "Rondiau," but it does not appear that the artist attempted to depict any real music on the scroll. (Paris, Bibliothèque nationale, MS frç. 9221.)*

Suppose that at a given moment the tenor note is A (since the tenor is a preexistent chant, the composer has no choice about this). The usual notes for the upper voices are then

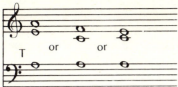

No other notes are available, since those given exhaust the available consonances (third, fifth, sixth, octave). The fourth was by now considered a dissonance when it occurred between the lowest sounding part and any higher voice, so that a D could not be used in this instance as a consonance. Now if the contratenor takes either the F or the D below the tenor, the situation is changed. The available notes become

This means that the tenor need no longer govern entirely the choice of notes for the upper parts: the presence of the contratenor permits more flexibility.

Such flexibility was the more important at the time, since certain interval succes- *Cadential patterns* sions were becoming standardized, particularly at cadences. Most important of these was the progression

or its analogue on other pitches. This cadential succession is particularly urgent in sound when both upper voices rise by a semitone, as in the second form given. To ensure this at any pitch level, fourteenth-century composers frequently added sharps before the penultimate notes of the upper voices (unless their motion would naturally be by a semitone, as E-F). There is reason to suppose that such sharping of penultimate notes may have been practiced in the thirteenth century as well, though it was seldom notated then. The manuscripts of the fourteenth century mark the beginning of a trend towards more explicit notation in this respect: not only at cadences, but throughout pieces, sharps and flats are to be found. Their use is, however, by no means consistent, even in different sources for the same piece. Meanwhile, theorists from the thirteenth through sixteenth centuries refer frequently to "musica ficta" ("imaginary notes," be- *Musica ficta* cause they were not part of any normal hexachord), assuming that performers would quite normally have to add sharps and flats beyond those given in the notation. Unfortunately their rules for the use of musica ficta are not clear enough to permit unequivocal decisions by modern scholars, whose transcriptions may legitimately vary considerably; there is little likelihood that any single "correct" solution will ever be found.

The problems of musica ficta are especially critical at cadences, precisely because cadential progressions were becoming increasingly standardized, and the exact form, particularly of the penultimate chord, strongly influences the total effect. The doubly sharped version is called a double leading-tone cadence, so named because each of the two upper voices *leads* by a semitone to the note of resolution.

While this cadence undoubtedly came into being as a consequence of the motion of the individual voices, the two sonorities involved acquired functions in their own right. The second sonority, consisting of a fifth and an octave, is fully and perfectly consonant, and was the natural choice for the ends and beginnings of phrases, although it could occur in mid-phrase as well. The preceding sonority consisting of a third and a sixth, became identified as a "chord of suspense," leading up to the second. It was used as the penultimate sound in the phrase, and elsewhere when an effect of tension was required. If a phrase were, by exception, to *end* on such a sound, a strong feeling of tension would result—a powerful propulsion toward the beginning of the next phrase.

Note that this is not merely a matter of consonance and dissonance, for all the intervals concerned are consonant. It is, rather, the selection of certain sonorities as being conclusive or inconclusive, and using this property as a means of shaping the phrase. This type of musical thinking may be termed "harmonic," as opposed to contrapuntal or polyphonic. While it had to some extent appeared before the fourteenth century, the *Ars nova* gave new emphasis to it. It was to continue, with increasing importance, until the end of the nineteenth century and even beyond.

Machaut's *Tu qui gregem—Plange regni—Apprehende* (Ex. IV-4) is an isorhythmic motet with a free introduction for the upper voices alone. The example shows the measures immediately following the introduction. The upper voices are frequently ornamental, settling on a consonance with the tenor and contratenor, then weaving around that note, thereby providing melodic and rhythmic variety. The contratenor begins above the tenor, then drops below it (although Machaut does not take advantage of its low D, which could have supported a D in the motetus, instead of the dissonant E).

Ex. IV-4

The end of the example shows an enriched and ornamented form of the double leading-tone cadence: the triplum inserts a D between the fundamental E and F, while the contratenor duplicates the E-F motion an octave below.

The free use of dissonance is characteristic of Machaut's style. The underlying interval structure remains clear, however, since the ear automatically follows the interval functions and accepts the ornamental tones as subordinate.

Machaut's motets are important, but they seem on the whole to represent a fairly conservative aspect of his style. His personality as a composer can be more immediately seized from his secular works to French texts. For these, Machaut wrote both the music and the poetry, in the tradition of the earlier trouvères. But by now, the real trouvère tradition was dead or dying. The comparatively fresh and spontaneous lyrics of the preceding century gave way to a more consciously literary art. The content of the poetry remained restricted largely to courtly love, but the language and versification became more complex. Originality in versification was an important aim, but most of Machaut's poetry operates within the stanza-structures known as the *formes fixes* (compare the formal freedom of the trouvères and the troubadours).

Machaut's secular works to French texts: rondeaus, virelais, ballades

The *formes fixes* remained important in the history of music for well over a hundred years. There were three basic forms, all strophic, and each with a fixed scheme of rhyme, refrain, and music. The rondeau has a two-unit refrain, the music for which also served for the remaining lines of the stanza, after the pattern ABaAabAB (capital letters designate the refrain; small letters, lines with the same rhyme and music). The virelai has the pattern ABccabAB. The ballade, descended from the trouvère canzone, has a repeated opening section and a refrain at the end: aabC.

Machaut wrote in all these forms, composing both monophonic and polyphonic virelais, and polyphonic rondeaus and ballades. In these works, no cantus firmus is used, nor is there ordinarily any use of isorhythm. Thus Machaut is free from the restrictive compositional requirements of the motet, and his music here has a melancholy emotional quality absent from the more austere motets.

In the excerpt from the virelai *Plus dure que un dyamant* (Ex. IV-5), the tenor, normally the fundamental voice in medieval polyphony, is reduced to a mere accompan-

Da — me vo pu — — re biau — té qui tou — tes pas-se
simple et plein d'u - mi — — li - té de dou — ceur fi —

a mon gré et vo sam – blant
ne pa – ré en sou - ri — — ant

Lady, your pure beauty, which to my taste exceeds all others, and your appearance— simple and full of the humility of sweetness, well adorned with smiles.

Ex. IV-5

imental function. The text-bearing voice, with its elaborate melody and subtly various rhythms, is clearly the center of attention. Just as certainly, the tenor exists merely as a support, supplying important consonances, providing rhythmic contrasts, and the like. This is the first style in which the tenor is both newly composed and subordinate: the tenor of the conductus is newly composed, but it is the principal melody; the tenor of the late thirteenth-century motet is in a way subservient, but it is preexistent.

In both the ballades and the virelais, Machaut supplies two different endings for those sections whose music is directly repeated, since the first singing of such sections leads back to a repetition of the same music, while the second leads on to the next part of the form. The first or *ouvert* (open) ending is made less conclusive, either by ending on a note other than the ultimate final, or by ending on an imperfect consonance, or both. The second or *clos* (closed) is more final. Thus in the ABccabAB form of the virelai, the use of the *ouvert* at the end of the first "c" and the *clos* at the end of the second helps to weld the two lines into a solid block of music, and to indicate to the listener that the second "c" concludes a major section of the form.

The provision of alternative cadences, though not new to the fourteenth century, first became a regular feature at that time. The use of pitch differences and different types of sonorities to distinguish the two cadential types again illustrates the tendency of the fourteenth century to functionalize such elements—or, to re-use the term, to think harmonically as well as contrapuntally.

Dame vo pure biauté is a relatively simple example of Machaut's secular style. Works for three and four voices are naturally more complex. The combination of three or four independent and fairly active voices leads to a complex contrapuntal texture in which the vocal part is less overwhelmingly dominant. The beginning of the ballade *Se quanque amours* (Ex. IV-6) illustrates this more elaborate style. Note the leap of a major seventh in the tenor—clear proof that this is a subservient voice, not a principal one. The top voice is here called by the traditional name of triplum, but it is textless and, with the contratenor, provides a rich counterpoint to the vocal line. The four-note motive that appears in the contratenor and triplum in measure 2 and in the contratenor in measure 4 recurs sporadically throughout the piece, providing an overall stylistic unity.

Ex. IV-6

In a few of the secular pieces, the intellectualism of the motets is evident. The rondeau *Ma fin est mon commencement* (my end is my beginning) displays the rarely used and difficult technique of cancrizans, or "crab," writing: the second half of the piece is the first half read backwards. But by and large, the secular music of Machaut is intuitive and expressive, rather than intellectual.

One other work of Machaut must be mentioned: a four-voice setting of the ordinary of the Mass. This is apparently the first complete polyphonic setting of the Mass ordinary by a single composer, and thus stands at the head of an immense list of polyphonic Masses by many composers up to the present day. The *proper* of the Mass, so important for Parisian polyphony of the late twelfth century, was no longer set in polyphony, with very few exceptions. Perhaps the application of complex polyphonic techniques to a chant and text that would be performed only once a year seemed wasteful. And perhaps the ordering of monophonic chants of the ordinary into cycles, typical of the later Middle Ages, drew the attention of composers to the use of such chants. In any event, from this time on, the word "Mass" applied to a polyphonic composition means a setting of the ordinary.

Machaut seems to have conceived of his Mass as a cycle—a unified piece. Nevertheless, a wide variety of techniques may be found: cantus firmus, with or without isorhythm; free declamatory passages for the long texts of the Gloria and Credo; and, perhaps most interesting, the persistent appearance in several movements of short motives like ♩♩♩ and ♩♩♩ . The second of these is the same as the pervading motive of *Se quanque amours*, suggesting that one should not think of these as "themes" in the modern sense—strongly individualized tunes conceived for a particular work—but rather as common elements of Machaut's style. Yet their use does apparently stem from Machaut's wish to make cohesive a long and complex score.

Imposing as it is, Machaut's Mass seems to have had little immediate influence. It remains alone in its time, isolated but prophetic.

Italy: Music of the trecento.   Up to this point, the history of polyphony as presented here has been primarily a history of French polyphony. While other centers—notably in England—were also active, it was Paris that took the leadership and kept it. Indeed the fame of Paris and its university had made it an exporter not only of music, but of architecture, philosophy, and literature.

In the fourteenth century, however, a polyphonic repertoire came into being which, in aesthetic and technical importance, could offer a serious challenge to the primacy of Paris. Italy developed its own *Ars nova*, often called "trecento" music (from the Italian for three hundred, the last three figures of 1300). It is well known that polyphony was extensively practiced in Italy before 1300, but little music survives. What there is shows a wide variety of styles, ranging from rather primitive organum to adapted copies of Parisian works. But in the fourteenth century there occurred in Italy one of those prodigious outbursts that lead to a new art—an outburst almost comparable to the rise of Parisian polyphony in the twelfth century.

Already, at the end of the preceding century, there had been a similar flowering in Italian poetry, leading to the "dolce stil novo" (sweet new style) and culminating in the work of Dante. But while the lyric poetry of the new school was doubtless sung (little music has survived), it was sung monophonically. Italian polyphony was the product of a different circle—perhaps a predominantly clerical one.

Italian rhythmic notation: Marchettus of Padua

At about the same time that Philippe de Vitry was systematizing the notational methods of the French *Ars nova*, the Italian theorist Marchettus of Padua was devising for Italian polyphony its first viable rhythmic notation. Marchettus, like de Vitry, based his system on thirteenth-century French notation; but he took the work of Petrus de Cruce, not Franco of Cologne, as his point of departure. For Marchettus, as for Petrus, the basic unit of time was the breve, divisible into almost any reasonable number of semibreves. But Marchettus devised new rules and notational characters that fixed the exact values of the shorter notes, thus eliminating the ambiguity inherent in the Petronian system. While Italian notation often closely resembles the French in practice and even in appearance, the two are quite different in theory. Instead of the hierarchy of *modus, tempus,* and *prolation,* the central factor in Italian notation is the division *(divisio)* of the breve, into four, six (both 2 x 3 and 3 x 2), eight, nine, and twelve semibreves. When fewer than the prescribed number of semibreves (or their equivalent) take the place of the breve, those occurring at the end of the group are lengthened. If lengthening is wanted elsewhere, special characters are used.

Italian composers generally preferred more open and natural rhythms than their French contemporaries. In consequence, the type of syncopation that consists in tying a note over a bar line, which was common in French music, was not needed. Italian notation, therefore, provides no convenient method of notating this device: each breve (measure) is marked off from its neighbors by a dot (the *punctus divisionis*), and a new measure must begin with a new note except when a long occupies two or more measures.

Jacopo da Bologna; Francesco Landini

The Italian school produced a considerable number of composers, in contrast to the French, where de Vitry and Machaut were unchallenged leaders. The earlier phase of Italian polyphony seems to have been centered in north-central Italy. Jacopo da Bologna (ca. 1300-ca. 1360) may be taken as representative of this stage. (Note that the addition of a place-name to the given name implies, in both French and Italian, that the composer worked, or was at least known, in cities other than his birthplace.) Later, Florence took over the leadership: Francesco Landini (1325-97), the blind organist who is considered the greatest Italian composer of the century, lived and worked there. While these two men—and also the numerous other known composers—had recognizable personal styles, the Italian repertoire shows considerable cohesiveness. Intensely personal characteristics are rarely found.

Forms and stylistic traits of trecento music

Italian composers had little use for artifice, and as a result, neither cantus firmus nor isorhythm is often found. Instead, the repertoire consists almost entirely of settings of secular poetry, thus emphasizing the "free" element of composition considerably more than in the "intellectual" North. There are three principal Italian forms. The first, and most peculiarly Italian, was the madrigal, a poem consisting of two or three tercets followed by a distich. The second was the ballata, in structure identical with the French virelai. The third was the caccia, or hunting poem, which had its own special musical technique. It also had a French analogue, the chace.

The essence of Italian style may be seen most clearly in the madrigal. *Fenice fu',* by Jacopo da Bologna (Ex. IV-7), is set for two voices, both texted. In French music, a two-voice piece is normally a vocal solo with instrumental accompaniment. Here both voices are sung (although instruments may well have joined in the performance), and are hence more nearly equal in importance than is customary in French music. While the tenor moves more slowly and less ornamentally than the top part, and while its

Ex. IV-7

function is still that of a supporting part, it is still a melody in its own right. In this sense, Italian music is more truly contrapuntal than French: its ideal is the cooperation of two more or less equal voices, rather than the primacy of a single one. While such cooperation may be found in French motets, it is there supported by a cantus-firmus tenor. Italian style is close to that of the conductus. It has even been suggested that ultimately the conductus is the root of trecento music, but the evidence for this is not convincing.

Both the preference for all-vocal texture and the relative equality of the parts can be traced back into the fragmentary remains of pre-*Ars nova* Italian music, and can thus be regarded as authentically Italian predilections. To these is related a third and newer characteristic: at certain points a phrase is begun, not by the two voices together, but by one alone at first, joined after a moment by the second. In addition to emphasizing the equality of the two voices, this serves as a strong articulating device: the immediately audible reduction of the texture to a single voice calls attention to the beginning of the new phrase. While this technique is by no means universal in Italian music, it is frequent and is symptomatic of Italian musical thought.

These three devices, together with the difference in rhythmic style, are perhaps the most important native Italian techniques. But the Italian school, vital and vigorous as it was, did not long escape French influence, especially toward the end of the century. This influence was doubtless stimulated by Franco-Italian contacts both during the papal residence at Avignon (1305-78) and, more especially, by the return of the papacy to Rome in 1378.

Clear evidence of French influence may be found in rhythm and notation. French practices began to appear in Italian notation, in order to express French rhythms. It is in the ballata that the newer tendencies are particularly clear. While monophonic ballate were known in the thirteenth century, the vogue for polyphonic setting of these lyrical poems occurred in the latter part of the fourteenth. While there is nothing French about the ballata in itself (the formal identity with the French virelai is probably no more than the result of descent from a common dance ancestor), it served as a suitable vehicle for the incorporation of typically French stylistic elements. Ballate for three voices were set

French influence

for two vocal parts and an instrumental contratenor—the latter being a clearly subordinate voice. When only two voices were used, the tenor was often instrumental. Both types differ from the all-vocal madrigal, which was by this time less actively cultivated, and the difference suggests acquaintance with French practice.

The difference in *style* may be observed in Landini's *Nella mia vita* (Ex. IV-8). The rhythms here are more complex than in *Fenice fu'*, obviously owing something to French style, although still preserving some of the relaxed and vocal quality characteristic of earlier Italian music. In some works, Landini goes considerably further and writes music of intense rhythmic complexity, but this is part of a more general tendency towards virtuoso rhythmic writing by both French and Italian composers late in the century, to be considered below.

In my life I feel [my heart] leave me.

Ex. IV-8

The treatment of the text is approximately the same in both the Italian examples and not very different from the text treatment in French music. There appears to be no attempt whatever to mirror the sense of the words in the music. Instead, the text lines are treated as structural units, generally articulated by means of melismas at the ends (and sometimes the beginnings), with more syllabic treatment in between.

Caccia and canonic technique   In the caccia, the case is rather different. The poems are lively, realistic descriptions of the hunt or of other outdoor scenes. There appears to be some connection between the prevalence of hunting poems and the basic musical technique of the caccia: just as in a hunt the hunters pursue their quarry, following on the same path, so in the caccia does one vocal part follow the other in canon, using exactly the same melody. The two canonic parts, separated by a time interval of two or more measures, are usually supported by an instrumental tenor. The overall form is like that of the madrigal (of which the caccia may be regarded as a subspecies): there are two sections, of which the second is generally the shorter. The second section often begins a new canon at a different time-interval.

The use of canonic technique may have been suggested by the subject matter, but most composers of cacce go further in integrating text and music. The shouts of the hunters are realistically set, often in hocket. When the canon causes such passages to overlap, the effect is boldly naturalistic, as well as vivacious and compelling.

Such passages, which occur in most cacce, are important as an early—if isolated —attempt to let the meaning of the text, not merely its structure and rhyme scheme, function as a determining factor in a composition. In later periods, this was often a primary consideration in text setting. Here it is clearly exceptional, since it occurs only in certain parts of a specific type of composition.

One writer has characterized the difference between the French and Italian styles in the fourteenth century as southern "sweetness" versus northern "subtlety," but the difference between the two styles should not be allowed to obscure fundamental technical similarities. Both French and Italian composers regarded music as consisting of a basic two-voice skeleton—the progression of consonant intervals between the top voice and the tenor. To give flesh to this skeleton, the upper voice (and, in secular pieces, the tenor also) was decorated with elaborate melodic embellishments, and a third and even a fourth voice might be added to give further richness. Example IV-9 shows the process applied to the last part of Machaut's *Se quanque amours* (compare Ex. IV-6). This is not to say that composers actually worked in this fashion: they probably did not. Yet their musical thinking was clearly conditioned by this approach, and especially by the idea of the fundamental two-voice framework as generator of the entire composition. Such a theory leads naturally to inequality of function among the voices of a piece. The top voice carries the principal melody; the tenor supports this; the contratenor and any other added parts "fill in" with less essential material. Certain forms, notably the motet and the caccia, require modifications of these functions but do not alter the principle of inequality; even the Italian near-equality of melodic activity preserves a disparity of function.

Comparison of French and Italian styles

Two-voice skeleton

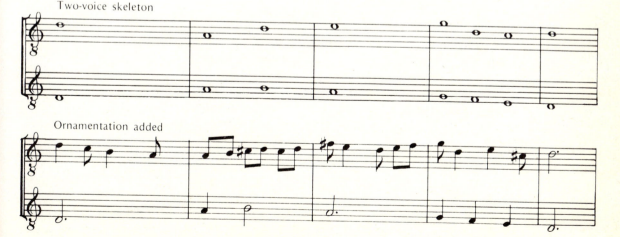

Ornamentation added

Ex. IV-9 (continued on following page)

Skeletal third and fourth voices added

Final form

The concept of the two-voice framework also permits a high degree of complexity, which can be achieved merely by making the overlay of embellishment more elaborate. The ear will still perceive the underlying framework under the apparent confusion, because that framework is simple and orderly.

The late fourteenth century.   Most of the fourteenth-century music so far considered has been fairly complex; but towards the end of the century intricacy became an end in itself, and composers went to extraordinary lengths to write music that was both difficult to perform and difficult to understand.

Part of the reason for this was technical: the prevalent system of composition permitted it. But part was social. The end of the fourteenth century marked the end of the medieval world in many respects. The first stirrings of the Renaissance were being felt in Italy, and the feudal society of the North was crumbling. Even the Church, for so long the core of medieval civilization, seemed to collapse. While the transfer of the papacy to Avignon had perhaps been no more than a scandal, its return to Rome was marred by the Great Schism, in which rival popes, elected by cardinals of their own creation, excommunicated each other and all who dared to doubt their claim. Secular society, beset by wars and economic troubles, was in no better condition. Extreme refinement in the arts was, for some at least, a way of escape from an unattractive world.

What ordinary people—even those of some education—sang in those days is not known. Most of the music that remains is of such intricacy that it could have served only for the delectation of sophisticated courts. Some pieces were written for the papal court at Avignon; others for lesser, secular courts. A few works seem to have been academic showpieces, written to exhibit the triumph of the composer's technique over compositional difficulties.

Most of the pieces are settings of French secular texts, although several of the known composers were Italian. The favored form was the ballade. Complexity developed chiefly in the area of notation and rhythm. The French notational system of the *Ars nova* remained the basis, but onto it were grafted new elements, some of them doubtless suggested by Italian notation. Special note forms, with special rhythmic meanings, were introduced: one form might have the value of one and one-half eighth notes in 6/8 meter, another the value of one-third of an eighth. Liberal use of such notes was combined with extensive use of syncopation. And syncopation itself was given an expanded meaning. In its simple form, it may be regarded as the placing of a longer value at a point where the meter requires a short one. Thus a fourteenth-century musician would read ♪♪♪ as ♪♪♪ ,the brackets showing the interpolated or syncopated note. Entire groups of notes, sometimes measures in length, were inserted in this way, the inserted passage thus being out of position metrically by a beat or two. In ♪♪♪ (in our notation ♪♪♪), ordinary rhythms are merely shifted over by one beat. But composers of this time also employed far more complex syncopations, for which modern notation is awkward and unsatisfactory.

When complex rhythms in different voices are combined, a texture of extraordinary complexity is produced, creating perhaps the most difficult music ever composed before the twentieth century, at least from the point of view of rhythm. Example IV-10 gives an idea of the style, including an especially clear instance of interpolation. The underlying two-voice structure is still solid and logical, once the rhythmic displacements have been ironed out.

It is also possible to see (and hear) behind the formidable technical artifice of this music a striving for expression. In performance, the rhythmic complexities take on the sound of an intensely expressive, almost mannered rendition of a basically simple line. And many pieces of the period make extensive use of prominent dissonance as well, almost certainly with the aim of achieving intense pathos.

Thus while works such as these must have had a limited appeal—they require highly skilled performers and sophisticated listeners—they form a fitting conclusion to the study of medieval polyphony. From the time of Leoninus, rhythm, above all the other elements of music, most attracted the attention of composers. Indeed, the history of polyphony from 1150 to 1400 can be regarded as chiefly a history of rhythm. By the end of the fourteenth century, the exploitation of rhythmic effect had reached a peak, and perhaps also a limit. The further development of musical style was to proceed along different lines.

En   at —   ten —   dant

es — pe — ran — ce con — for —   te   L'om —   me qui   vult

Ex. IV-10

THE PERFORMANCE OF MUSIC IN THE MIDDLE AGES

That little has been said concerning the actual performance of music in the Middle Ages reflects the unfortunate lack of knowledge about the matter. Not a single musical score of the period provides all the information needed to reproduce the music accurately in sound. The earliest manuscripts do not even make clear what pitches are to be used. After pitch was accurately notated, the rhythms remained unclear. And even when, during the thirteenth and fourteenth centuries, rhythmic notation was developed, many essentials continued to be omitted from scores: the performing medium, the tempo, the degrees of loudness and softness, and a host of other details that go into the production of real music. This was not the result of carelessness: the living tradition of performance was known to every musician, and there was no need to write down what was common knowledge.

In consequence, scholars are forced to depend on various kinds of indirect evidence in any attempt to reconstruct the actual sound of medieval music. Some literary sources describe musical performances; some works of painting and statuary depict it. But even these cannot be fully trusted, as the writer or painter may have misrepresented his subject for any one of a number of reasons: symbolism, rhetorical exaggeration, or even musical ignorance.

For Gregorian chant, the medium at least is certain: chant was sung, not played, and the roles of soloists and chorus are known. Instruments may have been used on occasion, but about this next to nothing is known. Post-Gregorian monophony was largely intended for soloists. Tropes, for example, were performed by one or two singers alternating with a chorus singing the Gregorian chant to which the trope had been added. Prosae may have been another matter. Their texts abound in references to instruments, and these references, while they may have been merely symbolic, may perhaps reflect actual performance practice. In the latter case, one or more instruments may have played along with the singers, either at the same pitch, or an octave higher or lower. The liturgical dramas seem to invite instrumental participation also, and modern performances of them generally employ many instruments. But the sources say nothing of them, and there is no way of knowing how—or even if—they were used.

Early polyphony seems to have been intended for vocal soloists, although it is at least curious that the word "organum" should mean "instrument." In the organa of the school of Paris, an instrument might well have helped out with the long-sustained notes of the tenor part, although a purely vocal performance is by no means impossible. By the time of the early motet, the tenors were very likely assigned to instruments; and even one or both of the upper parts could also be played, at the pleasure of the performers.

Instruments were quite possibly used in the performance of secular songs. The singer of the monophonic troubadour and trouvère songs may have accompanied himself on an instrument, or may have had accompanists. Thus the melody would have been played (perhaps with slight variation) as well as sung, and it is possible that free interludes were improvised between the stanzas. In polyphonic songs of the fourteenth century, the lower parts were intended either solely for instruments (as in French music) or for a combination of voice and instrument (as in some Italian music).

Instruments

But all this is still rather unsatisfactory. What instruments were used? And what did they sound like? Literary evidence makes clear that medieval practice was both colorful and variable. The same piece could be performed in different ways on different occasions, depending on the forces available and the taste of the audience. The music itself offers no clues, for composers almost never tried to write music especially suitable or idiomatic for a certain instrument. Therefore the question of what instruments were used must be answered by a list of instruments available, with the remark that any of them might be employed where appropriate.

In the fourteenth century, and for some time thereafter, instruments were grouped into two classes: *haut* (literally "high," but here meaning loud), and *bas* ("low," i.e., soft). Those of the first class included military and hunting instruments—horns and trumpets—and were largely used outdoors. It is likely that polyphonic music was more often entrusted to the "soft" instruments, of which there was a considerably variety. Bowed stringed instruments were represented by the vielles, ancestors of the modern violin family, but with a thinner and more nasal tone. They were made in various sizes so that they could play music of differing ranges. Plucked stringed instruments, such as the lute and psaltery, were popular. Among the woodwind instruments the flutes (really recorders) and the shawms (related to the oboe) were perhaps the most important. They also were made in different sizes.

The organ has been known since the early Middle Ages, but it did not much resemble the present-day instrument. It had only one keyboard, and no pedals. There was apparently no way of achieving tonal variety by means of drawing different stops: instead, when a key was depressed, all the pipes tuned to that note sounded. The small organ known as the portative was much used, both as a solo instrument and as an

Fig. IV-2: Giotto (ca. 1266–ca. 1337), The Banquet of Herod (detail), showing a fiddler entertaining during the feast. Note that there is no written music. (Florence, Santa Croce; photograph Alinari.)

accompanying force in polyphony. During the fourteenth century, a stringed keyboard instrument called the *echiquier* (chessboard) came into existence. It was the ancestor of the harpsichord and clavichord. In addition to these instruments of fixed pitch, a number of percussion instruments seem to have been in regular use.

In general, medieval musicians seem to have preferred mixing sharply contrasting sounds. Thus a three-voice song by Machaut might have been executed by a high male voice (singing in a thinner, more nasal manner than is now the custom), with a shawm playing the tenor and a vielle the contratenor. Such a setting, properly balanced in volume, would accentuate the difference in function among the parts and provide a total sound rich in color.

Color—bright and contrasting—was the main goal. There are not a few passages in medieval polyphony that look very ordinary on paper, but take on surprising life when given sufficiently colorful settings. It seems reasonable to suppose that this is the way they were played in their own day.

On great occasions, large numbers of players were sometimes brought together in a kind of large-scale "orchestra," but, unfortunately, how such forces were used is unknown. Did all the instruments play together, creating a great volume of sound? Did each type of instrument take one part of a polyphonic piece, maintaining the purity of that group's tone color? Or were different instruments only used successively, to provide variety among different pieces? It seems unlikely that these questions will ever be answered.

In addition to music in which both voices and instruments participated, the Middle Ages also knew purely instrumental pieces. It is likely that any piece originally conceived for voices, or for voices and instruments, could on occasion be played by instruments alone. The clausulae of the period of Perotinus, for example, sound very well when executed instrumentally. But there was also music specifically conceived for instrumental performance—music that was never intended for voices.

In this category falls most dance music (although some dances were sung as well as played). Unfortunately relatively little of this has survived. The dance tunes were mostly monophonic, and the players merely kept them in their memory. A few such pieces from the thirteenth and early fourteenth centuries have been preserved. Most are cast in the form of the estampie, and consist of a number of repeated sections called *puncta*, sometimes with a recurrent cadence. Even less common are polyphonic dances. Their style is not markedly different from that of many clausulae. *Dances*

Not all instrumental music was intended for dancing, however. Certain manuscripts in which thirteenth-century motets are preserved contain instrumental works of a different character. These are few in number, compared to the vocal pieces—three or four instrumental pieces to over a hundred motets would be a typical proportion. Their appearance is that of textless three-voice motets, and indeed that is what they are. In style, they do not differ much from ordinary motets, although they do show a fondness for hocket. This technique of rapidly alternating voices is easier to execute with instruments than with voices, and its use is natural enough. Only in this respect, however, does the nature of the medium seem to have caused a difference in the musical style of the instrumental pieces; although of course performers may have demonstrated their skill by improvising typically instrumental ornaments on the written music.

In the fourteenth century, the beginnings of an independent art of instrumental composition make their appearance. The Robertsbridge Codex, a fragmentary manu- *Independent instrumental compositions* script of about 1325, preserves polyphonic estampies for keyboard, in which a clear attempt is made to take advantage of the instrument's ability to make rapid skips easily. It also contains keyboard arrangements of three motets, two of them from the *Roman de Fauvel*. These are the first known examples of a genre that was to acquire enormous importance in succeeding centuries: the arrangement for solo instrument of a vocal original. Here too, the unknown arranger has capitalized on the ability of his instrument to execute rapid ornamental passages, as a comparison with the original motet shows (Ex. IV-11).

Ex. IV-11

Almost a hundred years later, another and much larger manuscript, the Faenza Codex, provides a large repertoire of such keyboard settings, many of them based on works by composers like Machaut, Jacopo da Bologna, and Francesco Landini. Their style is a good deal more complicated than that of the Robertsbridge pieces, but the basic principles remain the same: the melody of the original is overlaid with a rich coat of ornamentation, while the tenor is left more or less as is. Extra notes are sometimes added for a fuller sound, but contratenors of three-voice originals are not included in the keyboard versions.

Even by the end of the fourteenth century, instrumental music still occupied a distinctly subordinate place, but its importance was gaining and was to continue to grow until, by the sixteenth century, the two branches of composition stood on an almost equal footing.

I.   Vocal music.

A.   France.

1. The *Roman de Fauvel*. A satirical poem by Gervais du Bus, finished in 1316. One copy of a version expanded by Chaillou de Pessetain (Paris, Bib. Nat. Ms. f. fr. 146) has a large number of musical interpolations with Latin and French texts.

    Many are much older pieces: liturgical items, monophonic versus, 13th-century motets.

    There are 34 polyphonic pieces, most for 3 voices, all called motets. Perhaps as many as 10 are by Philippe de Vitry.

2. Philippe de Vitry (1291–1361), Bishop of Meaux, friend of Petrarch, one of the best-known statesmen and musicians of his day.

    Most of his works do not survive. Pieces must be attributed indirectly. Perhaps 17 surviving motets can be attributed to him, some 10 from the *Roman de Fauvel*.

3. Guillaume de Machaut (ca. 1300–ca. 1377). Contemporary of Chaucer (who quoted him) and Petrarch, he was secretary to John, King of Bohemia, and other high personages. Became a canon of Reims cathedral. In his later years, an amorous correspondence with Péronne d'Armentières gives insight into his compositional process.

    Machaut was his own editor, arranging his complete poetical and musical works in large manuscript collections. He grouped his compositions by genres, according to the following plan:

    Lais: There are 19, of which 2 are 3-part canons, one is for 2 voices, the rest monophonic. They typically have 12 long strophes, each divided into 2 sections sung to the same music. In 13 cases, the last strophe is the transposition to the upper fifth of the music of the first strophe.

    Motets: There are 23, 4 for 4-part voices and 19 for 3. Only 3 have no isorhythm, their tenors being secular songs. French texts predominate: only 6 motets are all Latin, 2 are mixed, and 16 are all French.

    Mass: "La messe de nostre dame" consists of settings of Kyrie, Gloria, Credo, Sanctus, Agnus Dei, and Ite missa est. All but the Gloria and Credo employ isorhythm.

    Hoquetus David: A unique instrumental piece employing hocket.

    Ballades: There are 42, of which one is monophonic, 15 for 2 voices, 18 for 3, 8 for 4. Form is aabC, where C is a textual refrain in each strophe. In each piece only one voice has text (the others being performed on instruments?), except for the three *compound ballades*, which provide two or more separate texts simultaneously.

    Rondeaux: There are 21, all polyphonic: 7 for 2 voices, 11 for 3, 3 for 4. Form is ABaAabAB (except one, which lacks the opening AB). More florid than the ballades, these pieces also have only one texted voice.

Chansons balladées (Machaut's name for the virelai): There are 33, of which 5 are for 2 voices, 2 for 3, and the rest are monophonic. Form is ABccabAB. Usually 3 strophes, with AB refrain sung once, not twice, between. Relatively simple, singable melodies.

In addition to these pieces, his didactic *Le Remède de Fortune* contains one composition in each genre (except Mass and Hoquetus), plus a *chanson royale* and a *complainte*.

4. Other sources.

   a. *The Mass.* Several settings of the ordinary of the Mass, known from their sources as the masses of Tournai, Toulouse (lacks Gloria and Credo), Barcelona, and Besançon, are extant. All are evidently put together from pieces not apparently composed together. These are difficult to date, as are the numerous individual Mass movements, because their style may be a slightly archaic one.

   b. *Motets.* The manuscripts of Ivrea and Chantilly, in addition to a few other sources, complete the small repertory of French music not composed by Machaut or Vitry. Similar in style and in subject matter, they contain some 35 motets from this period that do not appear elsewhere.

B. Italy.

   1. Sources. Little is known about the history or chronology of Italian *Ars nova* music. The extant manuscripts may give a distorted picture since, most of them being Florentine, they give the impression that Florentine polyphony was most important. Actually it would appear that Northern music was better known: Northern pieces appear elsewhere; Florentine pieces seldom do. Some important sources:

      Vatican Ms. Rossi 215: The earliest Ms.; fragmentary, but a good source of Northern Italian music. Florence, Bib.Naz. Panciatici 25: A large (151 pieces) source of earlier music.

      Florence, Bib. Medicea-Laurenziana Ms. Pal. 87: Called the Squarcialupi Codex after its 15th-century owner, this beautiful volume is the single most important source of trecento music, containing 358 exclusively Italian pieces, including the largest single collection (145 pieces) of Landini's works.

   2. Some composers (dating is difficult owing to a lack of biographical information and to stylistic uniformity.) Two main groups may be distinguished, earlier and later.

      a. Earlier composers:
      Maestro Piero
      Giovanni da Cascia (= Johannes de Florentia)
      Jacopo da Bologna
      Gherardellus de Florentia (d. ca. 1362)

      b. Later composers:
      Niccolò da Perugia
      Donatus de Florentia
      Francesco Landini (1323–1397); blind Florentine organist, the greatest

trecento composer; more than one-third of all remaining 14th-century Italian music is his.

Andrea da Firenze (d. 1415)

Bartolino da Padua

3. Principal forms of trecento music.

   a. *Madrigale* (madrigal). Form is aab (cf. French ballade). The favorite form of the earlier composers. Generally in two voices; usually quite florid.

   b. *Ballata*. Form is AbbaA (cf. French virelai). Became increasingly popular later in the century. Sometimes monophonic; generally less florid than the *madrigale*.

   c. *Caccia*. Usually a three-part piece, in which the upper two parts are in canon above a supporting tenor. Usually in two sections, each beginning a new canon. Texts characteristically are descriptive, narrative, and excited.

II. Music of the late 14th century.

A. Geography and composers.

   1. The papal court of Avignon was the scene of artistic activity including the works of such composers as Tapissier, Chipre, Perrinet.

   2. Interpenetration of French and Italian influences.

      a. Frenchmen in Italy: Baude Cordier, a composer in the Machaut style, is thought to have traveled in Italy; Johannes Ciconia, the leading composer in early 15th-century Italy, was a Northerner.

      b. Italians in the North: Many of the composers most typical of Northern activities were Italians: e.g., Anthonellus da Caserta, a leading Mannerist; Mateus da Perugia, one of the most forward-looking of composers in the North.

B. Styles.

   1. Mannerism.

      The manuscripts Modena, Biblioteca Estense L.568, and Chantilly, Musée Condé 1047, contain a small repertory of pieces in which the intricacies of notation and rhythm are exploited as stylistic elements. Probably no more than a short-lived and localized phenomenon, the "mannerist" style, represented by composers including Jacopin de Selesse, Anthonellus da Caserta, and Trebor, employed extravagant syncopation and elaborate rhythmic complications.

   2. Modern style.

      Most other composers, including the Avignon group, employed a style more clearly derived from 14th-century practice. Characteristically modern were an increased gracefulness and regularity in melody, and the use of a subordinate, harmonically-oriented contratenor voice. Clear examples of this style are to be found in the music of Mateus da Perugia.

III. **The principal remains of medieval instrumental music.**

A. "Kalenda maia," a texted estampie by the troubadour Raimbault de Vaqueiras.

B. Many 13th-century motets presumed to imply instrumental performances; among them, 8 untexted pieces, 5 of them with the same tenor, from the end of the Bamberg motet codex, ca. 1260.

C. The St. Victor Ms. (Paris lat. 15139): 40 textless clausulae.

D. London, British Museum Ms. Harley 978: 3 two-voice textless pieces.

E. The "Manuscrit du Roi" (Paris, f. fr. 844): 10 monophonic dances, entitled *danse* (2) or *estampie royal* (8).

F. The Robertsbridge Codex (British Museum Add. Ms. 28550): 6 pieces, 2 fragmentary, for keyboard. They include arrangements of pieces from the *Roman de Fauvel*.

G. British Museum, Add. Ms. 29987: 17 monophonic dances, including "istampite," "saltarelli," and two pairs of dances with individual titles.

H. Faenza, Biblioteca municipale Ms. 117. An important source of organ music from the early 15th century, this manuscript contains arrangements for organ of trecento vocal pieces, including pieces by Landini.

THE
FIFTEENTH
CENTURY

The word Renaissance (rebirth) was coined to describe the complex of new ideas and attitudes developed in the fifteenth century. It suggests that culture was truly reborn at this time through a unique rediscovery and reinterpretation of the arts of antiquity. Most modern scholars would prefer to regard this rediscovery as one among several—including "renaissances" in the ninth, twelfth, and eighteenth centuries. Nonetheless, the fifteenth century, while not unique in its preoccupation with antiquity, was a decisive era in cultural history, marking the end of medieval civilization and the beginnings of the modern world.

Italy, and Florence in particular, led the way. Painters and sculptors, poets and playwrights developed new styles based on the abundant physical and literary remains of ancient culture. Some lesser men were content to produce mere slavish imitations of their models, but the majority used antiquity as an inspiration for an artistic interpretation of their own world. A striking characteristic of the new spirit was its concentration on man and the finite, as opposed to the medieval preoccupation with God and the infinite. The Renaissance was a humanistic age, not necessarily irreligious, but convinced of the dignity and value of man. One may compare, for example, a thirteenth-century Italian crucifix with a Renaissance painting of the same subject. In the former, the figure of Christ is remote and hieratic: the signs of suffering—the wounds and the nails—are there, but He does not suffer as we do. In the Renaissance painting, it is a *man* who is nailed to the cross. While the divinity of Christ is not denied, it is his humanity that is stressed.

The Renaissance also saw the beginnings of historical inquiry. The Middle Ages had produced not history but chronicles—the bare record of events that had happened. While true historiography did not fully appear until the nineteenth century, Renaissance scholars began to adopt a new and more genuinely historical view of the past. Along with the exaltation of ancient glories, there went necessarily a condemnation of the "barbarism" of the Middle Ages: history was not the mere continuation of a single state of affairs, but a process that could produce results of varying quality. And while the Renaissance inevitably continued the medieval tradition of seeking "authority" in classical precedents, it did so in a different way. The ability to read Greek became, if not universal even among the learned, at least fairly common, and the number of available authoritative works was greatly enlarged by the inclusion of many Greek classics not hitherto translated.

Naturally this new profusion invited at least elementary historical investigation: older authors had to be distinguished from later, derivative ones. It also provoked a new attitude towards the received texts. While a few earlier scholars (notably Petrarch) had compared different manuscripts of the same work in an attempt to discover the purest version, this method came into extensive use in the Renaissance. A flood of critical editions of classical authors began to appear, made accessible to a large public by the relatively low cost and wide diffusion of printed rather than handwritten books.

The spread of learning from books was partially paralled by an increase in knowledge of nature. The real revolution in scientific thought was still well in the future, but the careers of both Columbus and Copernicus fall in the Renaissance, illustrating the desire to extend the boundaries of the known, whether by physical or purely intellectual means. The visual arts also give evidence of a different approach to nature. The use of perspective gives a painting the illusion of depth, permitting objects to be shown as they appear to the eye—not, as in much medieval painting, according to a fixed and predetermined scheme. And the increasing importance of landscape as an ingredient in painting demonstrates an enjoyment of the natural world for its own sake.

From antiquity the Renaissance derived its watchwords: clarity, balance, moderation—the golden mean. The old delight in symbolism, in mathematical approaches to the arts, did not disappear, for the Renaissance was more dependent on its antecedents than was then imagined. But artifice was subordinated to suavity and naturalness of content. A work had first of all to be pleasing, whatever hidden meanings it might be intended to convey.

Music had its share in the new attitudes and tendencies of the fifteenth century, but with some important differences. The notorious difficulty of verbally describing musical qualities left the connection between Renaissance ideals and musical practice rather loose. And music gained nothing from the rediscovery of the monuments of antiquity, at least until near the end of the sixteenth century. The music of classical times remained undiscovered. What little survived did so in a notation that could not then be read, so that one of the central factors in Renaissance thinking had very little influence on music. Nonetheless, the fifteenth century saw the creation of a new musical style, which, if it remained unaffected by antiquity, still faithfully reflected the attitudes of the times.

English music. A principal source of this style was English music, which has not yet figured prominently in these pages. From the twelfth century on, England was, musically speaking, a dependent of France, although a very active and creative one. English composers generally wrote in French forms, notably the motet, but their work was strikingly individual. Two recurrent characteristics are important for present purposes: a preference for having all the voices of a polyphonic piece move in the same rhythm; and a marked emphasis on the imperfect consonances (thirds and sixths), producing a simple but sonorous effect.

At some time, perhaps during the fourteenth century, English musicians began to introduce into the traditional improvisation on a cantus firmus a consistent use of imperfect consonances. There is some dispute as to the exact method used, but the result was apparently a chain of full sonorities—called "sixth-chords" in later theory—preceded and followed by the conventional octave and fifth (Ex. V-1).

Ex. V-1

There are numerous sources of thirteenth- and fourteenth-century English music, but almost all are fragmentary. From near the beginning of the fifteenth century, however, there survives a large collection of English compositions, the so-called Old Hall Manuscript, that contains motets, hymns, and, more significantly, polyphonic settings of various parts of the ordinary of the Mass. Numerous styles and techniques —isorhythm, canon, rhythmic and notational intricacy—may be found, showing that the composers were in touch with contemporary developments in France and Italy. But the peculiarly English traits mentioned are also present, as are others, such as the use of a cantus firmus that "migrates" from one voice to another within a single piece.

Old Hall Manuscript

The Old Hall Manuscript is convincing evidence of the vitality of English music in the early fifteenth century, but few of its composers are of great historical importance (even King Henry V, who contributed music to the collection, is important for nonmusical reasons). The principal English composer of the period, John Dunstable (d. 1453), who was primarily responsible for making English style known all over western Europe, is represented by only one piece in Old Hall. Most of his work is known from Continental sources, and indeed he may have done much of his composing abroad.

Dunstable's output, almost wholly sacred, includes both motets and settings of parts of the Mass ordinary. In some respects his music is conservative. He makes considerable use of isorhythm, of polytextuality, and of the fourteenth-century type of contratenor that weaves disjunctly above and below the tenor. But other features of his style, clearly English and clearly personal, are advanced beyond anything known on the Continent at the time.

The music of John Dunstable

Dunstable's *Regina caeli* (Ex. V-2) is what is now termed a motet, although it does not resemble any motet so far examined. Its texture resembles that of a fourteenth-

Regina coe-li   Lae- ta –   (-re

Rejoice, queen of Heaven.

Ex. V-2

century secular song, but its text is Latin and sacred. Moreover, while there is no isorhythm, there is a cantus firmus—not in the tenor, but in the vocal part. Dunstable does not merely assign the notes of the plainsong antiphon to this voice, but intersperses them with decorative notes of his own invention, thus producing a "paraphrase" of the original—a melody that is new, yet firmly and audibly based on a pre-existing chant. Paraphrase technique is not original with Dunstable, but it assumes great importance in his work and thereafter.

The presence of a cantus firmus, however decorated, justifies the designation "motet" for this piece. From this time on, the motet again becomes a sacred composition, ordinarily to a single Latin text, as it had been in the early thirteenth century when the term was first used. Motets of this type were, of course, perfectly suitable for use in church and found extensive liturgical employment in the fifteenth century and thereafter.

Dunstable's elegant melodic style is evident in the upper voice. The angular contours of fourteenth-century melody are here softened in favor of a flowing, vocal effect. The lower parts are subordinate and instrumental, as in the song-texture from which this type of piece ultimately derives.

Perhaps more important even than the melodic style is that of the counterpoint. Momentary dissonant clashes between parts, a regular feature in music of the fourteenth century, are here entirely absent. What dissonance there is is carefully controlled. It is either restricted to the weak part of the beat, or given the form of the suspension—a device that permits dissonance, but minimizes its harshness. A suspension (Ex. V-3) is made by introducing a note as a consonance on a weak beat, then

Ex. V-3

sustaining that note while the other voices move to notes dissonant with it on a strong beat, and finally moving it stepwise to the nearest consonance. This may be done with or without ornamentation.

There is good reason for this more restrictive treatment of dissonance. Dunstable's music, like English music in general, uses thirds and sixths a great deal. As long as the basic intervals are octaves, fifths, and fourths, as in earlier music, casual dissonances may be freely used: the perfect consonances are so strong that the ear clearly perceives what is fundamental and what is ornamental. When, however, thirds and sixths predominate, the addition of unregulated dissonance produces confusion: the ear loses track of the basic intervals in a harsh and bewildering cluster of sounds. Thus control of dissonance, an important aspect of Dunstable's style, is a necessary consequence of his fondness for the imperfect consonances.

Dunstable wrote a number of motets in the general style of *Regina caeli*. He also continued, however, in the more conservative tradition of the isorhythmic motet. His works in this form are traditional in technique—sometimes extending the isorhythmic principle so that all voices are isorhythmic throughout—but show his characteristic smoothness of melody and counterpoint.

Like other English composers, Dunstable made no complete settings of the Mass ordinary, for English composers did not set the Kyrie. His Mass music consists of isolated settings of single movements of the ordinary, paired pieces in which the Gloria and Credo or the Sanctus and Agnus Dei form a bipartite musical unit, and one cycle including all the ordinary except the Kyrie. The paired pieces and the cycle are of particular interest, since they frequently show attempts at musical unification of the movements, ranging from mere similarity of meter and identity of final tone, to the recurrence of musical material from one movement to another. In some pairs the unifying principle is isorhythm: the tenor of the Gloria is repeated, like a very long *talea*, for the Credo, and new upper voices are added. In the four-movement cycle, the melody of the Gloria is retained for the other movements, but its rhythm is not. Like many Mass pieces of the period, some of Dunstable's treat the longer texts in curiously telescoped fashion: phrases of the text that should properly occur successively are sung simultaneously by different voices.

Dunstable's style as revealed in the whole corpus of his works is remarkably self-consistent. Despite differing forms and techniques, the essential sound of the music remains much the same. Perhaps this stylistic solidity, together with Dunstable's great artistic achievement, helped earn for him the leadership in the English musical influence on the Continent.

The early northerners: Dufay and his contemporaries.   Little is known of the Continental composers of Dunstable's time. The complex and intricate music of the late fourteenth century was a transient style, although one that exercised considerable influence (e.g., the notational intricacies of the Old Hall Manuscript). One important trend appears to have begun early in the fifteenth century. The region comprising what is now northeastern France, Belgium, and the Netherlands started to become an exporter of musicians. For several generations, this area was the leading producer of singers and composers, until almost all of the important musical posts, and many of the lesser ones as well, from the English channel south to Naples, were filled by men born in this region—men who will be referred to here as "northerners."

The rise of the northerners

One of the earlier ones about whom at least something is known, Johannes Ciconia (ca. 1335-1411), was active mostly in Italy. He has left one work—perhaps an early composition—in the complex style of the late fourteenth century, but the rest of his music is simpler. Without departing radically from traditional methods, Ciconia managed to achieve a clarity and freshness of style in which both French and Italian elements can be detected. Like Dunstable, he wrote interrelated movements for the Mass ordinary. On occasion, he marks the connection between movements by the use of a "head motive"—a salient opening melodic idea (Ex. V-4a, b). It is prophetic of later developments that here Ciconia has borrowed the head motive for these movements from one of his own motets.

A far more important figure, whose significance exceeds even that of Dunstable, was Guillaume Dufay (1400-77), a northerner in whose work all the stylistic currents of the age are reflected. The reflection is that much clearer because, for almost the first time, it is possible by combining stylistic and external evidence to arrive at a reasonably accurate chronology of the composer's works. His beginnings in conventional Continental style his absorption of English influence, and his own mature contributions can be examined in their proper order.

Guillaume Dufay

Dufay wrote both sacred and secular music. Since the secular song remained more closely attached to traditional styles than did sacred forms (especially the Mass), it is

Ex. V-4

Stylistic elements of Dufay's secular music

logical to consider his secular music first. Dufay's early manner is evident in an excerpt from his ballade *Resvellies vous* (Ex. V-5). The rather angular melismas and restless rhythms in 6/8 meter are a direct inheritance from the French *Ars nova*. Even here, however, the voices are more homogeneous than in earlier French music, and there are more thirds and sixths.

A fifteenth-century poem by Martin le Franc tells us that Dufay and several others "followed Dunstable, and put on the English manner," thus achieving great merit. Dufay did not do so in *Resvellies vous* (Ex. V-5), and it is likely that there was never any instantaneous conversion, but rather a gradual adaptation of stylistic elements found in Dunstable (and elsewhere). The extent to which this adaptation altered and enriched Dufay's style may be seen by comparing the measures from *Resvellies vous* with two excerpts from the celebrated rondeau *Adieu m'amours* (Ex. V-6a, b). Almost all vestiges of *Ars nova* technique have been banished from this later work, leaving a style that was to be the root of Renaissance music.

Ex. V-5

Farewell, my love, farewell my joy
To say farewell wounds me so

Ex. V-6

To take the "English manner" first, it can be seen that in *Adieu m'amours* the number of thirds and sixths has increased, to the point where the open sound of the fifth is rarely heard except at cadences. In addition, dissonances have been almost totally eliminated, except for those achieved by suspension and those on unaccented parts of the measure. Both of these traits doubtless derive from Dunstable, and the smooth, flowing, and vocal style of the text-bearing parts may also. The replacement of the nervous rhythms in 6/8 by more relaxed patterns in 4/4 is less specifically English: it was a general tendency in the period after about 1420.

There is more to *Adieu m'amours* than the French *Ars nova* enriched with English elements. The texture—two vocal parts and an instrumental voice—recalls that of the Italian ballata. Since Dufay, like many other northern composers, lived and worked for part of his life in Italy, the derivation is likely enough. Even more important for the future is the way in which the voices are interrelated. They begin together in the traditional way, but on several occasions thereafter they enter successively, as in many Italian works. Here, however, each entering voice begins by imitating the first few notes of the first voice (Ex. V-6b), a procedure not usual in Italian music. This process of imitation has obvious structural values. As in the Italian prototypes, the momentary reduction of the texture to a single voice provides clear articulation of the sections—it serves as a kind of punctuation. Adding the element of melodic imitation also enhances unity; and as it does so, it strikes a telling blow against the *Ars nova* concept of separate functions for separate voices. Imitation promotes *equality* among the voice parts of a composition.

Imitative writing

The symmetrical balancing of the phrases found in *Adieu m'amours* will not be found in Dunstable—or often in Dufay's early works. To some extent it is the result of setting a metrical text: it is natural to set each line as a single phrase of music. But Dufay liked the effect for its own sake, as it can be found in works with prose texts also (e.g., settings of the Mass ordinary). The presence of clear and frequent cadences, often at four-measure intervals, gives clarity and balance to the music.

In *Adieu m'amours* Dufay incorporates into his personal style elements from the three principal national traditions of the fourteenth century: form and basic concept from the French *Ars nova*; texture and voice-interrelationship from the Italian trecento; and controlled dissonance, operating in music dominated by the imperfect consonances, from Dunstable and the English tradition.

Gilles Binchois

Dufay's contemporary Gilles Binchois (ca. 1400-60) was almost a specialist in the composition of secular songs. He too was held in high esteem by the musicians of his time. A typical song of Binchois sets a text in rondeau form for one vocal part and two instruments. The melodic interest is concentrated in the vocal part, which moves in short phrases, usually of four measures. The other essential part is the tenor, slower moving and not especially melodious, which supplies the essential intervallic support. The contratenor fills in where required, as was customary, enriching the sonority and providing rhythmic variety. Although Binchois sometimes uses imitation, he obviously did not regard it as an essential device: in some pieces it is absent altogether.

Such a description could be applied without significant change to many French secular works of a hundred years before. Despite the changes in musical language, and the freshness and vitality achieved by masters like Dufay and Binchois, the secular song remained a traditional form, looking almost as much to the past as it did to the future. Progressive devices such as imitation could be used in it, and often were; but the song accepted them as extra enrichments, not fundamental alterations of its nature.

The important innovations of the fifteenth century were largely concentrated in works for the Church—in the motet and, particularly, the Mass. In these areas, as in the secular song, it was Dufay who led the way. At the beginning of his career, two basic forms of sacred composition were available to him: the large-scale motet with a cantus-firmus tenor in long notes, generally isorhythmic, and two upper parts, with different texts; and a smaller motet type, in which the texture and style of the secular ballade were applied to a Latin sacred composition. The latter might be altogether without cantus firmus, or might have a Gregorian melody (perhaps paraphrased) in the upper voice, or even elsewhere. Both of these forms could be adapted to serve as vehicles for setting the ordinary of the Mass. Dufay could also observe around him the new interest in setting the Mass and, especially, in unifying the separate sections of the ordinary into a cyclical whole of some sort. To these circumstances, he applied his own inventiveness.

Dufay's Masses: stylistic innovations

Dufay wrote at least eight settings of the Mass ordinary, spanning almost the entire length of his creative career. He began in a style similar to that of the secular song, without cantus fimus and without much effort to unify the movements. He then experimented with the use of cantus firmus, both in long notes in the tenor, and in paraphrase in the upper part. In order to give shape to the longer movements, he introduced alternations in texture: passages for two voices alternate with passages for four; and specific directions in some manuscripts suggest that choral polyphony sometimes alternated with polyphony sung by soloists. (Sections in two voices occur in much English music, and Dufay may have adopted the practice from England; choral polyphony appears to have been Italian in origin.)

These devices did not, however, produce the kind of overall unity Dufay desired, and in his later Masses he turned to another procedure: the use of a single cantus firmus underlying all movements of a Mass. The recurrence of the same melody, stated in long notes in the tenor, in every movement of the Mass of course creates a clear and audible unity of effect—which Dufay could, when he wished, increase still further by beginning each section with a recurrent head motive, as in the Ciconia example above (Ex. V-4).

Cantus-firmus technique

The natural choice for such cantus firmi was plainsong; but since the same chant was to be used in each movement, a melody from the ordinary would not be suitable: it would be incongruous, for example, to sing the words of the Gloria or Credo while a Kyrie chant was sounding. A chant from the proper would not create this problem, although it would strongly relate the entire Mass to the feast from which the proper chant was chosen (e.g., a Mass based on a Marian antiphon would hardly be suitable for performance on any but a Marian feast). While Dufay did in fact make use of proper chants, he more often took a secular tune as cantus firmus. Thus the *Missa L'Homme armé* (Masses are named for their tenor melodies) is based on what seems to have been a popular song, and the *Missa Se la face ay pale* uses the tenor of one of Dufay's own polyphonic songs. Although the use of secular material as cantus firmus was not new, it was primarily Dufay's example that established the practice as a normal one. For a hundred years thereafter, secular songs, with all their worldly associations, were regularly woven into the web of liturgical polyphony, until finally the Council of Trent (1545-63) ordered the practice stopped.

Whether sacred or secular, the cantus firmus was made audible in the traditional way. It appeared in the tenor, in notes generally longer than those used in the other parts. In the longer movements of the Mass, the Gloria and Credo, the melody often appears two or three times, sometimes so arranged that each appearance is in progressively shorter note values—no doubt an inheritance of the diminution technique of the isorhythmic motet. In other movements one statement of the melody may be sufficient—that statement usually being divided into two or more parts by sections during which the tenor is silent. Occasionally, less straightforward techniques are used: in one case, Dufay has the melody sung backwards (cancrizans, or retrograde) in one of its appearances.

Dufay's adoption of cantus-firmus technique transformed the polyphonic Mass from a loosely organized succession of unrelated movements into a grandiose multi-movement cycle, unified both by recurrent cantus firmus and by recurrent head motives. At the same time, important textural changes appeared in his style. The number of voices was increased to four: the old disjunct contratenor was, as it were, split into two separate voices—the contratenor altus (whence our "alto"), which was a texted part similar to the top voice; and the contratenor bassus (bass), which lay *below* the tenor.

While such a scheme may also be found in the fourteenth century, Dufay's use of it was new. He took intense interest in certain successions of sonorities, especially at the ends of phrases. These were possible only when the lowest sounding part had a specific, rather disjunct shape. Since a preexistent melody, whether sacred or secular, would be unlikely to have such a shape, the placement of the contratenor bassus below the tenor permitted Dufay to employ both the cantus-firmus principle and his preferred successions of sonorities.

In the first Agnus Dei from the *Missa L'homme armé* (Ex. V-7), Dufay's treatment of the voice parts shows vestiges of both new and old techniques. The top voice has most of the melodic interest. The contratenor altus lies consistently above the tenor. It does not pretend to independence, like the motetus of an isorhythmic motet, but is given a melodious, if modest, part. The tenor carries the secular song, in notes only slightly longer than those of the two contratenor parts. The contratenor bassus is disjunct and angular, betraying a special function. It is not always below the tenor, but is mostly so. Its wide skips at the end of the excerpt are the direct result of its harmonic role at the cadence (this point will be discussed more fully below).

This passage resembles the texture of the secular song, but with the primacy of the top voice somewhat reduced. It also resembles the traditional motet, but with a new, still partly nascent role assigned to the motetus (here = contratenor altus). From these models, however, Dufay has fashioned the beginnings of something quite new. It is merely a step from Example V-7 to a polyphony in which three active and approximately equal parts are set against a slower moving tenor. Dufay took this step in some of his works, and sometimes even the tenor, having finished its statement of the cantus

Ex. V-7

firmus, continues freely in the style of the other voices. But here his ideal is still at least partly traditional—in his ears, the sounds of the old forms still ring—and the ancient concept of voices with particular functions is not abandoned.

This may be shown by Dufay's attitude towards imitation. It is hardly present in the Agnus Dei (Ex. V-7)—not nearly so much as in *Adieu m'amours*. A really consistent use of imitation implies the abolition of separate voice-functions. Dufay does not make that consistent use. He is content to add imitation as a kind of decoration when he feels it appropriate; but his style does not require it, and it is often absent.

Dufay's interest in functional sonorities has been mentioned. He made two important advances in this area, one transient (although at the time, very important), the other so important that its implications had not been exhausted until about 1900. The first was concerned with the handling of the imperfect consonances—the thirds and sixths. English improvisation based on these intervals has already been illustrated (Ex. V-1): each phrase begins and ends on a fifth and an octave above the lowest part; all the other sonorities consist of a third and a sixth above the lowest voice. Apparently about 1426, Dufay systematized this into a method known as fauxbourdon. In this, the top voice and the tenor (here the lowest part) were written down. The third voice was improvised merely by singing a perfect fourth below the top part. In the excerpt from Dufay's *Ad coenam agni* (Ex. V-8), fauxbourdon is combined, as was customary, with paraphrase technique. The top voice incorporates a hymn melody, slightly decorated. Writing in this manner was relatively easy, and yet produced a rich and agreeable sound. Dufay wrote many smaller works in fauxbourdon and incorporated its basic sound—the chain of thirds and sixths—into other pieces. The idea was quickly taken up by other composers and proved extremely popular for several decades.

Functional sonorities

Fauxbourdon

Ex. V-8

Fauxbourdon was enormously influential, but Dufay's other discovery, while it attracted less attention, was more important. The principal cadential progression of the fourteenth century had been the expansion of a sixth above the lowest tone to an octave (Ex. V-9). Part a of the example shows the fundamental form, part b the addition of a

Cadential progressions

Ex. V-9

third voice and the sharping of both upper parts (double leading-tone cadence). This cadence apparently survived unchanged into the fifteenth century, although it is possible that the inner voice was less often sharped after about 1420. Fifteenth-century composers, and especially Dufay, found that a more satisfying cadence could be made from the succession of sounds shown in Example V-9c. The difficulty with this was that a cantus firmus would almost never end with a descending fifth, and it was traditional for the tenor to be the lowest note in the last sonority. Even in pieces without cantus firmus, it was customary to end by moving the tenor stepwise down to the last note. This problem was at first solved by putting the contratenor, regularly a very disjunct voice, to work (Ex. V-9d). Here the desired succession of sounds is preserved, along with the traditional treatment of the tenor. Still later, when four-voice writing became customary, and when it became desirable for each voice to have a reasonably vocal style, the octave leap in the contratenor was eliminated (Ex. V-9e). All the cadences given in the example may be found in Dufay, but he clearly came to feel that the last one was the most satisfactory: he uses it at the ends of most movements and major subsections in his mature works. The importance of this cadence is twofold. In the first place, it represents a radical extension of the primacy of the fifth-relationship. The importance of the relation of the fifth in melody has already been noted; here it appears in what may now properly be called harmony as well. The penultimate chord of the cadence is (in the example) built on the tone D; the last one on G—a fifth down (or a fourth up). To use later terminology, the two chords are related as dominant to tonic, a progression later known as an authentic cadence. Naturally, the same relationship can be established on other degrees of the scale: the cadence could be set up to end on A, in which case the preceding chord would be built on E, and so on. This relationship of dominant to tonic is so rich in possibilities and implications that its manipulation remained at or near the center of every composer's attention for several hundred years: starting at the cadence, the relationship gradually spread to other parts of the musical phrase, until it permeated every part of a composition.

The same cadential formula also began to undermine a principle of polyphonic writing that had been fundamental since the twelfth century: the idea that the basis of polyphonic writing lay in the essential intervals between two principal voices (top voice and tenor). To be sure, the underlying sixth-to-octave progression inherited from the fourteenth century is contained in the new cadence, but it is obscured by the presence of the contratenor below the tenor. It is now the lowest part—the bass—that is fundamental, not the tenor. But there is still more: chord formations like the penultimate one, D-F♯-A, began to be heard as entities in themselves, three-note sonorities that had independent existences, quite apart from the interval-relation of the top voice and tenor. Theoretical recognition of these "triads," as they were later called, had not yet come, nor is it likely that composers like Dufay thought in such terms. But the beginnings of new ways of thinking about music were already present, waiting to be developed by later generations.

Dufay's motets and hymns

If, during the early fifteenth century, the secular song was on the whole a rather conservative medium, and the Mass a relatively advanced one, the motet stood somewhere between. Isorhythmic motets of the traditional type were still written, almost invariably as occasional pieces to celebrate some important event. Dufay provided motets of this type for the signing of a peace treaty between the Pope and the future Holy Roman Emperor (*Supremum est mortalibus*, 1433), another for the consecration of the Cathedral of Florence (*Nuper rosarum flores*, 1436), and others as well. While strongly infused with fifteenth-century stylistic elements, their structure remains similar to the old design cultivated by de Vitry and Machaut. The isorhythmic motet was a dying genre, and its restriction to extremely formal occasions merely confirms its obsolescence.

Dufay also wrote motets that do not employ isorhythm. A few of these resemble his later Masses in texture, having a tenor in longer notes with more active upper voices. More numerous, however, are the pieces in which the principal melody is in the upper part, normally a paraphrase of a plainsong melody. These are similar in technique to Dunstable's *Regina caeli* and, like the latter, derive ultimately from secular models. Dufay's celebrated *Alma redemptoris mater* is a particularly fine example of paraphrase. The plainsong antiphon, itself extremely attractive, is reworked into a fully characteristic and much longer line. The motet ends with a succession of sustained chords—another indication that vertical sonorities were becoming an object of special interest.

Dufay's hymns also use paraphrase technique, as was evident in *Ad coenam agni* (Ex. V-8). Some are entirely in fauxbourdon, while others have freely composed lower voices. The hymns differ from the paraphrase motets in being shorter and, of course, in using the same music for different strophes of the hymn text. Usually, polyphonic stanzas alternate with monophonic ones.

Without disrespect to his contemporaries, it may be said that Dufay stands as the central figure of his era. He contributed to all categories of musical composition, leaving works of the highest value in each. His mature style contains almost all the elements that were to form the bases of music until the end of the sixteenth century; and, while his use of them was to a degree conservative, his innovations opened all of the principal paths for those who came after him.

The later fifteenth century.   Among the composers of the generation following Dufay, the most eminent was Johannes Ockeghem (ca. 1425-ca. 1495). Like Dufay, he was both a northerner and a man highly esteemed by his contemporaries and successors. (It is even possible that some of Dufay's later works were affected by Ockeghem's influence.) While Ockeghem wrote a few secular pieces and about ten motets, most of his work was concentrated in setting the ordinary of the Mass. Almost a dozen complete Masses by him survive, as well as a number of fragmentary settings.

Ockeghem in general continued along the lines drawn by the Masses of Dufay, but with strongly developed personal idiosyncrasies. The structural procedures used in his Masses are various. There are some tenor Masses using cantus firmi more or less in Dufay's manner. In one of these, based on the song *Fors seulement*, composed by Ockeghem himself, not one but two voices of the original song are drawn upon, the material being mostly presented in succession, not simultaneously. In this work, for four voices, the tenor is nearly as active as the other voices. The cantus-firmus material is also rather freely treated: in the Gloria, Ockeghem first gives the opening measures of the chanson tenor, along with a few measures of its top part (not, however, the first measures); then the first notes of the top part appear, followed by the beginning of the tenor again; and so on, in a rather irregular pattern. In consequence, the modern ear, at least, does not easily distinguish the preexistent materials from the rest of the texture.

There are also Masses that are unified, not by recurrent musical material, but by a consistent technical device. The best known of these is the *Missa prolationum*

Ockeghem's style

(Prolation Mass), in which Ockeghem, with enormous ingenuity, combines two two-voice canons simultaneously. Since the notation used was essentially the same as that of de Vitry, with its perfect and imperfect, normal and altered values, the application of the different prolations (meters) yields slightly different rhythmic results in canons that are exact as to pitch. The ability to write aesthetically satisfying music while conforming to such stringent technical conditions confirms Ockeghem's status as a major master.

Surprisingly, there are also Masses with no consistent unifying devices at all. Among these is the *Missa Mi-mi*. This has a brief head motive consisting of the notes E and A (both "mi"—the first in the natural hexachord, the second in the soft), but the rest appears to be freely composed. The coherent effect it makes on the listener is the result of internal consistency of style and expression.

Almost all of Ockeghem's stylistic traits so far mentioned are rather personal ones, shared by few other composers. Yet he was greatly revered in his own time and enjoyed a highly successful career. It is possible that his reputation rested less on the idiosyncratic features so far described than on his innovations in the area of musical texture. It was Ockeghem who finally took the step to a completely vocal texture, in which all parts (except a long-note tenor, if one was present) were of roughly equal melodic activity. The old concept of separate roles for each voice had now very nearly disappeared—again, except for the tenor. (The "vocalization" of all the parts does not necessarily mean, however, that all parts were in practice sung. It is fairly certain that instruments continued to participate, either reinforcing or even replacing one or more of the voices.)

Moreover, there was an almost insoluble obstacle to creating a complete equality among the parts. While Ockeghem seems to have been less interested than Dufay in harmonic functions, he still made extensive use of the authentic cadence. This, of course, requires a disjunct bass line, ending with an upward fourth or downward fifth, while the upper parts move by steps. In the interior of a piece, such skips could be and often were eliminated by artful manipulation of voice entrances. But at the ends of movements and major sections, all voices were normally present, and the bass could not evade its harmonic responsibilities. While composers made every effort to integrate the bass into the style of the other voices, it was impossible for them to succeed entirely, and the bass continued to have a character slightly different from that of its fellows.

Ockeghem came as close as any composer to reducing that difference to a minimum. His preference is for an intensely contrapuntal texture, in which each voice is given a long and complex arching melody. While in Dufay, balanced and symmetrical phrases are normal, they are largely absent in Ockeghem. His phrases are long and asymmetrical, with few and relatively weak cadences. The rarity of cadences naturally reduces the harmonic obligations of the bass line and allows it greater melodic freedom.

This is evident in the Agnus Dei from the *Missa Mi-mi* (Ex. V-10). In this period, pieces ending on E have a special character of their own, in part because they do *not* end with the now-familiar authentic cadence. The authentic cadence is of course possible on any pitch, but the fifteenth century, unlike the fourteenth, was conservative in its use of (notated) sharps and flats. The D♯ required for an authentic cadence on E was generally avoided. Instead, either or both of two different cadential formations was used: the Phrygian and the plagal (Ex. V-11a, b; the relation between the names of cadences and modal terminology is the result of theoretical speculation and may safely

no —

mi — — — se — re — — re

re — — — — — re no —

— — — — — — — — re no —

— bis.

no — — — — — — — — — bis.

— — — — — — — — bis.

— — — — — bis.

Have mercy on us.

Ex. V-10

a) Phrygian   b) Plagal

Ex. V-11

be ignored). The Phrygian cadence was designed for and largely limited to cadences on E (or A, if B♭ was used). It avoids the need for disjunct motion in the bass, but is less conclusive than the authentic. The plagal cadence was often added after the Phrygian for greater finality, and could be added to the authentic as well, since it was available at any pitch. In Example V-11, two forms of each are shown, the first ending on a complete triad, the second on an open fifth. Whatever the type of cadence, composers of the fifteenth and early sixteenth centuries preferred to end a movement or an entire piece on an open fifth. Hence the first forms are for internal cadences, the second for final ones.

Ockeghem's fondness for special—most often dark—colors is evident in his choice of E endings in the *Missa Mi-mi* (Ex. V-10) and, in other pieces, by his frequent use of unusually low vocal ranges. An equally striking effect is produced by the relentless intensity of the counterpoint, especially in the long complex melismas preceding the cadence. Such complex counterpoint needs occasional relief, and Ockeghem regularly provides it by thinning out the texture to three or even two voices between fuller passages like those in the example.

Imitation in Ockeghem is generally quite inconspicuous. Even when it does occur, it seems to be more decorative than structural in function. In the *Missa Mi-mi*, devoid (as far as is known) of preexistent material, the result is a polyphony that is entirely free-composed. Ockeghem appears to be fascinated with music-making in its purest form, independent of all technical considerations except the musical intuition of the composer.

While the Agnus Dei cited is typical of much of Ockeghem's music, it does not exhaust his resources. In some places, as a relief from the complexity of his usual manner, he turns briefly to a style in which the voices momentarily give up their rhythmic independence and move together rather slowly in block chords. While Dufay also uses chords in this way, Ockeghem does so more frequently. The emphasis in such passages is not on the separate contrapuntal lines, but on the sonority of the chords themselves—all triads—and on the nature of the chord-succession. For some time to come triads,whether occurring in "block-chord" passages of several measures or as "accidents" in contrapuntal passages, were generally so disposed that the *root* was in the bass; that is, if one imagines the three different tones of the triad as two superimposed thirds—for example, C-E-G—the lowest tone of this imaginary disposition will regularly be the lowest sounding tone in the actual music. The third and fifth above the root might be (and were) disposed in any desired position, and either tone might be omitted or sounded by more than one voice.

It is unlikely that even fifteenth-century ears would have heard purely triadic passages as reinforced series of intervals between tenor and top voice. The richness of triad progressions was as great as that of fauxbourdon, and the almost infinite variety of possibilities inherent in the successions of triads on different roots far surpassed fauxbourdon in potential. While musicians may not yet have come to think in terms of triads, their music was increasingly dominated by triadic successions.

Ockeghem was by no means the only important composer working in the second half of the fifteenth century. He was without doubt the greatest, but he was also something of an isolated figure, for all his fame. His contemporaries did not share his nearly exclusive interest in sacred music, for in the later part of the century, it was once again the secular song that was most intensively cultivated. A large number of composers was involved, many of them connected with the brilliant Burgundian court; and many manuscript collections of songs (called *chansonniers*) have been preserved.

Secular forms in the later fifteenth century

In the second half of the fifteenth century, the *formes fixes* began to lose their popularity as determinants of musical structure. Many rondeaus and virelais (the latter usually reduced to a single stanza and called *bergerettes*) were still written, but there was an increasing preference for settings in free musical forms. The traditional texture—one vocal part with two accompanying instruments—was retained, but the increasing equalization of the parts already observed in sacred music was felt in the song as well. The accompanying parts came to approach the main melody in style, so that they could well be sung, and doubtless on occasion were. Imitation, too, became frequent but was still by no means obligatory.

In *Joie me fuit*, by Antoine Busnois (d. 1492), perhaps the most celebrated contemporary of Ockeghem, the beginning is in imitation in all three voices (Ex. V-12). At the entry of the second line of text, however, the contratenor does not share in the imitation, and in the third line there is no imitation at all.

Antoine Busnois

Joi-e me fuit et dou-leur me queurt

Joy flees me and sadness seeks me.

Ex. V-12

In technique, this song hardly differs from Dufay's *Adieu m'amours*. It shows, however, a number of progressive features. The new harmonic functions are very much in evidence: the contratenor is often almost entirely a chord-supporting voice. The use of duple meter is also a reflection of later date. While many songs continued to use the familiar triple rhythms, their dominance was on the decline. Also new is the low register of the three voices, especially the contratenor. The fondness of Ockeghem for the dark colors of low voices has been mentioned; here is another instance showing the interest his generation took in exploring sounds hitherto unused. While songs like this are not typical—most are set considerably higher—the territory thus explored was retained and made common property, so that the sixteenth century inherited a much wider tonal space than did the fifteenth.

In the last decades of the fifteenth century, composers began to write with increasing frequency for four voices, rather than the traditional three. This change had already taken place in the Mass and the motet, and doubtless reached secular music from them. Old songs were provided with an additional voice, to modernize them, and more and more new ones had four parts to begin with. At the same time—and also apparently from the same source—secular music began to make more frequent use of preexistent material. A composer might, for example, take over the tenor of a previously composed song and write fresh parts around it. Or he might choose a popular tune for this purpose. The given material might appear either in the tenor or in the top voice, or even in two voices, by treating the material in canon.

Four-voice texture

Both tendencies—writing in four rather than three voices, and employing preexistent material—indicate a greater interest in artifice towards the end of the century. The simpler possibilities had been fully explored, and composers turned toward more intricate settings. Nevertheless, the songs apparently held the interest of a considerable audience, not only in French-speaking areas, but elsewhere as well. This strikingly emphasizes the international diffusion of northern music during the fifteenth century. As in the thirteenth, a single, internationally appreciated style had achieved a position of dominance—one which was to continue through most of the sixteenth century.

Confirmation of this dominance may be seen in the earliest printed music. In 1501, Ottaviano Petrucci published the first book of music printed from movable type, the *Odhecaton* (hundred songs). Although it appeared in Italy, it contained almost exclusively songs to French texts by northern composers, and the same is true of two similar volumes that followed in the next few years. Petrucci knew his public well, and apparently knew that Italians would rather buy French music than the product of native composers.

Naturally, the invention of music printing was important for other reasons. Printing houses soon became established in the major cities of Europe, and their products were widely circulated. The audience for music was certainly enlarged by the convenience and economy of printed music, and composers also benefited in becoming more easily acquainted with the work of others—even those working at a great distance. Finally, the modern student of music derived his own advantage: a work printed in several hundred copies was more likely to survive than one copied in only a few manuscripts. While handwritten music continued to be widely used through the eighteenth century and even beyond, the invention of music printing was an indispensable ingredient in the development and diffusion of musical ideas from 1500 on.

Instrumental music in the fifteenth century. Instrumental music, which had been groping towards the status of an independent art in the fourteenth century, moved closer to that goal in the fifteenth, although knowledge of it is still far from exact. Pictorial evidence shows that instruments continued to be widely used for the dance, but much dance music must have been monophonic and played from memory, or perhaps improvised; almost nothing survives in writing.

An important exception must be made for the *basse dance* (low dance—perhaps because it was performed with gliding, rather than leaping, steps). This was a slow and stately dance, often followed in performance by a quicker dance. It was popular in both France and Italy towards the end of the fifteenth century. A considerable repertoire of tunes for the *basse dance* has been preserved. The manuscript sources give the melodies in the form of a long series of notes without any differences of rhythmic value—paradoxically enough when one considers the importance of rhythm for the dance. The explanation is simple: these tunes were used as cantus firmi in long notes, and what a modern listener might call the "real music" was improvised above them.

If the *basse dance* proper and the quicker dance following used the same melody, as was often the case, the musical result was what might be called a dance-pair—two musically related dances of different rhythmic character. In various ways, this was to become an important feature of dance music of the centuries following.

The *basse dance* emphasizes the importance of improvisation for instrumental music of the time. Indeed, the surviving music probably represents only a minute fraction of what was actually played. But there was, of course, composed music for instruments also. It seems clear that chansons and even music for the church might on occasion be played by instruments alone, without alterations except for embellishments that the players could introduce. Some songs from the end of the century seem, indeed, to be more suitable for instruments than for voices.

Moreover, the tradition of arranging vocal works for keyboard performance (often called "intabulating," after "tablature," a form of keyboard and lute notation) remained alive. The surviving documents are German, and their music is intended for the organ,

Fig. V-1: Israel van Meckenem (d. 1503), "Household music," showing a small organ suitable for domestic use. (Kunstsammlung, Veste Coburg.)

which at this time was beginning to acquire those special characteristics—two or more manual keyboards, a pedal keyboard, and stops to permit variety of tone color—that set it apart from other keyboard instruments.

Keyboard music:
Buxheimer
Organ-Book

The principal source is the Buxheimer Organ-Book (ca. 1470). The vocal works intabulated are of considerably earlier origin, belonging to the Dufay generation rather than to that of Ockeghem. The technique of arrangement is rather complex. The settings are mostly in three voices, not two. The top voice is a freely decorated version of the song tune. The other voices are slow-moving and are either freely invented or related in one way or another to the lower voices of the song. Passages idiomatic to the keyboard—rapid scales and trills, repeated notes, and the like—are freely used in the decorated voice, but are largely absent from the others.

The same source also includes a number of settings of liturgical cantus firmi, doubtless written down because they were considered more complex and sophisticated than what would normally have been improvised. They do not, on the whole, look much different from the song settings, although here the upper part is freely composed and the tenor has a given melody. Of particular interest for the future are some of the settings of chants for the ordinary of the Mass in which music is provided for some, but not all, of the cantus firmus. This is evidence of a practice that was to have considerable importance in the next century: the performance of the ordinary by choir and organ in alternation. This meant that half of, say, the Gloria text was never sung, its chant being merely elaborated polyphonically at the organ. Despite what may seem serious liturgical disadvantages, the "organ Mass" was already popular in the fifteenth century and became more so later.

Perhaps most important of all are those pieces that employ no preexistent material: these are among the first wholly free and purely instrumental compositions. Example V-13, *Praeambulum super fa* (prelude [piece before the service] on F), gives an idea of

Ex. V-13

this style. The ingredients are simple: rapid figural passages, occasionally relieved by solemn chords. The musical content may seem slight compared to contemporary vocal works, but the powerful sounds of the organ help to compensate. The piece is a study in sonority, not composition. And, in any event, the importance of such works lies less in their musical value than in their example: they show the emergence of instrumental music as a separate branch of composition, with its own resources and its own forms.

APPENDIX: Chapter V

Bibliography

Basic to the study of this period is Gustave Reese, *Music in the Renaissance,* revised edition (New York, 1959). The very full bibliography found there will refer the reader to the many specialized studies of the music of this era. Listed below are some modern editions of fifteenth-century music.

Droz, E., Yvonne Rokseth and Geneviève Thibaut, eds. *Trois chansonniers français du XVe siècle.* Paris, 1927. A good collection of fifteenth-century chansons.

Dufay, Guillaume. *Opera omnia,* ed. Heinrich Besseler. Rome, 1961-1966.

Dunstable, John. *Complete Works,* ed. Manfred Bukofzer. London, 1970 (Musica Britannica 8).

Hewitt, Helen. *Harmonice Musices Odhecaton A.* Cambridge, Mass., 1942. An edition of an important collection of secular pieces published 1501.

Obrecht, Jacob, *Opera omnia,* ed. A. Smijers and M. Van Crevel, Amsterdam, 1953-   .

Ockeghem, Johannes. *Collected Works,* ed. D. Plamenac. Second ed. New York, 1950-   .

Rehm, W., ed. *Musikalischer Denkmäler II: die Chansons von Gilles Binchois.* 1957.

Smijers, A., ed. *Van Ockeghem tot Sweelinck.* Amsterdam. 1939-   . A collection of music from the later fifteenth and early sixteenth centuries.

A Comparison of the Works of Some Fifteenth-Century Composers

COMPOSER	John Dunstable (ca. 1383-1453). Elder contemporary of Dufay, his style exerted much influence on later 15th-century music.	Guillaume Dufay (ca. 1400-1474). Long associated with cathedral of Cambrai, he was several times in Italy, serving the Malatesta family (ca. 1420) and the Papal choir (ca. 1430).	Binchois (Gilles de Binche, ca. 1400-1460). Served ca. 30 years at Burgundian court.
MASSES	An important prelude to cyclic mass settings is Dunstable's grouping of pairs of movements (Gloria-Credo; Sanctus-Agnus) on a common cantus firmus.	Three early masses à 3: Sine nomine; Sancti Antonii; Sancti Jacobi (includes some Ordinary sections; Communion is earliest known written example of fauxbourdon). Three middle masses (La Mort de Saint Gothard; Caput; Se la face ay pale) all à 4; all feature a cantus firmus and a head motive which recur for each movement, and have two slow-moving untexted lower voices. Three late masses (L'Homme armé; Ecce ancilla domini; Ave regina caelorum), each with cantus firmus and head motive, have nearly equal activity in all voices. Several (mostly early) individual and pairs of mass movements, most à 3.	No complete mass settings are known. A few isolated movements.
MOTETS AND CHURCH MUSIC	A number of isorhythmic motets, including the impressive Veni sancte spiritus; several songlike sacred pieces, often employing melodic paraphrase.	A number of ceremonial isorhythmic motets, including Nuper rosarum flores, for dedication of Florence cathedral, 1436; settings à 3, many employing fauxbourdon, of alternate strophes of hymns. Song-like motets, many of them settings of votive Marian antiphons.	Motets, hymns, magnificats, mostly in treble-dominated song style. Melodic paraphrase, fauxbourdon sometimes employed.
CHANSONS	A song style featuring supple melodic syncopation with accompanying voices in thirds and sixths produces a treble-dominated song style which set the pace for the century.	Except for a few Italian and Latin songs, almost all are in French. Typically à 3, they are cast in the formes fixes: ballades, virelais, and (most often) rondeaux. Sometimes only treble has words; often two parts are texted, accompanied by a textless contratenor. Many chansons include textless (instrumental?) interludes. Occasional use of imitation.	Widely admired for his chansons. Generally they are in formes fixes, mostly rondeaux. Usually only upper voice is texted. His best songs have a remarkably rich lyricism.

Johannes Ockeghem (ca. 1420-1495). Chaplain and composer to the kings of France.	**Antoine Busnois** (d. 1492). Priest, poet and musician. Worked at Burgundian court and in Flemish churches.	**Jacob Obrecht** (ca. 1450-1505). Dutch composer, a conservative contemporary of Josquin.
Eleven complete mass cycles; a Requiem; several incomplete cycles and individual settings. A close texture with few cadences made of long, sinuous melodies, often includes a tenor cantus firmus paraphrased to approximate the other voices (masses *Ecce ancilla domini; De plus en plus; Au travail suis*); cantus firmus melody sometimes permeates to other voices. Mass *Fors seulement* has a Gloria which borrows from several voices of the chanson model. Some masses do not use cantus firmus: Masses *Mi-Mi, Cujusvis toni* (which can be sung in several modes), and *Prolationum* (employing double mensuration canons).	One mass, *L'Homme armé*, à 4, known to be his. Uses cantus firmus in tenor and head motive.	Twenty-five masses, generally à 4. Cantus firmus treatment often divides melody into melodic cells which are freely combined (e. g. mass *Maria zart*; some use of parody technique (e.g. mass *Fortuna desperata*).
Ca. 10 motets, some à 5 and à 6. Several votive Marian antiphons. Ockeghem's typical dense, non-imitative texture occasionally disguises a paraphrased chant melody (e. g. *Alma redemptoris mater*).	A few motets, some employing ostinato tenors (one, *Anthoni usque*, has a single bell-note tenor).	Ca. 25 motets. Imitation rather rare, which is unusual at this period. Some pieces have long-note cantus firmus.
Ca. 20 chansons, most à 3. Little imitation (an exception is *Prennez sur moi*, a famous three-part canon that can be sung in several modes), duple rhythm predominant.	Ca. 70 chansons, many in *formes fixes* (mostly rondeaux). Much use of imitation; frequent parallel thirds and tenths. Metrical contrasts between sections of some songs.	Ca. 30 pieces, about half with Dutch titles. *Formes fixes* lose their fixity, songs begin to have individual formal structures. Texture becomes motet-like. Much use of sequence, and of parallel tenths and thirds.

VI

VOCAL POLYPHONY
OF
THE SIXTEENTH CENTURY

While the earlier sixteenth century still clearly belongs to the Renaissance period, continuing and elaborating upon the tendencies noted at the beginning of the preceding chapter, the 1500s as a whole were more agitated and turbulent. Again, as in the fourteenth century, serious stresses appeared in many aspects of the social order. The most significant of these was the Reformation: in Germany and elsewhere, religious reformers challenged the authority of the Roman church. For the first time, this resulted in permanent divisions within Western Christianity. Earlier reformers had been either absorbed into the Church, or destroyed; but Luther, Calvin, and others founded churches independent of—and in deadly rivalry with—the Church of Rome. Much of Germany (especially the northern regions) became solidly Lutheran; Calvin established churches in Switzerland; and Protestantism in one form or another gained footholds in France, the Low Countries, and the British Isles.

Rome was forced to take the Reformation seriously. Its answer was a "Counter Reformation" of its own, intended to neutralize the gains of the reformers by somewhat modernizing its still medieval attitudes and correcting some of its more flagrant abuses. The Counter Reformation also encouraged fervent individual piety, to match that of the Protestants.

The Reformation demonstrated that spiritual matters need not center about the pope. The "revolution" of Copernicus showed that in the physical heavens, the earth could no longer be regarded as the center of the universe. While Copernican theory was accepted only gradually, the mere existence of such thinking was unsettling. Magellan's voyage (circumnavigation completed in 1522) had proved that the earth was not flat; Copernicus now claimed it was not even stationary.

Intellectual shocks such as these were especially disturbing to a society that itself was changing. The middle classes were continuing their increase in power. Many a prince or duke maintained his court only by the assistance of the bourgeois banker who lent him the necessary money. The largely agrarian economy was giving way to one in which trade and manufacturing were increasingly cultivated. This of course furthered the interest of the middle classes, while often adding to the misery of the poor.

In the arts, there is a clear progression from the Renaissance classicism of about 1500 to something quite different fifty to seventy-five years later. Raphael is still purely a Renaissance painter, but in Michelangelo, who lived until 1564, there are obvious elements that transgress the Renaissance ideals of clarity and harmony. Intense personal expression, particularly in Michelangelo's later works, overpowers classical restraint. The painters of the late sixteenth century are known as mannerists: their work, less intense than that of Michelangelo, is characterized by willful distortions. Figures are exaggeratedly elongated, or seen in unnatural postures, or from peculiar perspectives.

Much the same may be said of literature. In Italy, the early sixteenth century rediscovered and imitated Petrarch. The same period produced the great poet Lodovico Ariosto (1474-1533), whose *Orlando furioso* treats the medieval theme of the Crusades, much romanticized by tradition, with Renaissance elegance. Later in the century Torquato Tasso (1544-95), in his *Gerusalemme liberata,* wrote on the same general theme but in more passionate vein. He also wrote the *Aminta,* an example of idealized pastoral life that was much admired and much imitated. The pastoral genre, while based on classical precedents, became a stylized escape literature; and poetry in general turned either to the pastoral or to intense rhetorical passion. In either case, the diction tended to be complex and artificial, heavily spiced with metaphor and sudden antitheses.

SACRED MUSIC

The formulation of sixteenth-century style: Josquin and his contemporaries.   While much of the best music was written for and in Italy during the sixteenth century, the principal composers continued to come from northern France and the Low Countries. The "Netherlandish Schools" would have achieved lasting celebrity merely because of the extraordinary number of first-class musicians produced by this area in the fifteenth and sixteenth centuries. But the North was also the birthplace of one of the greatest composers in the history of music: Josquin des Prez.

Josquin's career

Josquin was born about 1440 somewhere in northern France. Little is known of his early life, although he is said to have been a pupil of Ockeghem. Like many other northerners, Josquin spent much of his life in Italy, and apparently did not return to the North for long until about 1500. He died in 1521.

Josquin achieved a celebrity that few composers have equaled. Writers on music throughout the sixteenth century agree in calling him the prince of musicians, his work the standard against which all other music had to be measured. The first volume of printed music limited to works by a single composer was a collection of Josquin's Masses (1502); and the printer Petrucci later published two more volumes of his Masses (1505 and 1514). Modern critics universally share this high estimate of Josquin's ability: his name would certainly appear on any list of the greatest composers of all time. But it was the contemporary recognition of his importance that naturally made him a critical historical figure as well. His style and his techniques became the chief legacy inherited by the sixteenth century.

Josquin's style

Josquin was by no means the creator of a revolutionary new style, although he did make important innovations. His work is better regarded as a synthesis of fifteenth-century developments, in which all the procedures then known were given their fittest formulation. In Josquin's music, the equality or near-equality of parts emphasized by Ockeghem was confirmed and strengthened, as was the essentially vocal quality of all the parts. From Josquin's time on, differing functions for different voices were eliminated in contrapuntal vocal music, with exceptions for voices carrying a cantus firmus and for the bass, which of course had its harmonic function to fulfill. Along with this there naturally went a more systematic use of imitation—since imitation is an ideal expression of the equality of the voices.

Many pieces by Josquin (although by no means all) are cast in a shape that was to become normal for the sixteenth century. The text was divided up into a suitable number of phrases; a characteristic musical motive was assigned to each phrase; and for each motive an imitative section, called a "point of imitation," was built up, terminating in a cadence, but generally overlapping in such a way that the new imitation had begun by the time the cadence was finished. In pieces of this type, imitation is for the first time raised to the level of a fundamental structural principle, rather than used as a decorative device. Its structural function is two-fold: on one hand, it unifies the individual section, since the section is based on a single piece of musical material; on the other, it contributes towards the unity of the whole by providing consistency of technique.

In the numerous pieces in which imitation is not used in such consistent fashion, the overall unity, while apparent to the ear, is not always as easy to explain. In many cases, modal unity is observed, for sixteenth-century composers still thought of their music as being in one or another of the modes of Gregorian chant (above, Chapter I), usually regarding the mode of the tenor as determining that of a polyphonic piece. Thus a work beginning on D would also end on D, and make extensive use of triads related to D by fifths and fourths (A, G). Probably more important was the unity provided by the continuous sense of the text, which supplies both a principle of cohesion and a kind of justification for the sectional structure: each member or phrase of the text generates a corresponding section of music. And behind all of these points there lies an intuitive unity, apparently inaccessible to analysis—a continuing fitness or congruence of parts evident when, for example, a vocal piece of Josquin is played by instruments alone: the text is not present, but the music still makes sense.

Josquin was also fond of employing canon in his works. Canon is, of course, no more than a special case of imitation—one where the imitation continues exactly and at length. In its effect, however, canon differs somewhat from other imitative counterpoint precisely because it does continue throughout. The canonic voices, usually two out of the total of four or five, function as unifying elements merely by their adherence to the canon. Josquin applied canonic technique both to freely invented material and to preexistent melodies (the latter requires considerable ingenuity, as indeed does all canonic writing). His liking for this device is a reflection of the delight in artifice that was a continuing characteristic of northern music of the fifteenth and sixteenth centuries.

Use of canon

The word canon itself conceals symptoms of this attitude. It means, literally, a rule or law. From the early fifteenth century and even before, composers had commonly written out only the first of the canonic parts, adding a verbal instruction (canon) specifying the information necessary to derive the second voice. Often this was done merely to save time and space, but in many cases the instruction is deliberately enigmatic, amounting to a puzzle—sometimes a very difficult one—that the performer must solve. Needless to say, the best canons, such as those of Josquin, are more than mere puzzles: they have full artistic validity as well. But the element of artifice is prominent all the same.

In one important respect, Josquin departed from Ockeghem's practice: he avoided the extremely long phrases and weak cadences of the older master in favor of a much more clearly articulated style. Josquin's cadences are stronger and more frequent, and his designs thus clearer and more open.

Texture and textural change

This clarity is further reinforced by Josquin's frequent textural changes, which serve the double purpose of providing variety of sound and underlining the structure of a composition. A favorite device is the temporary reduction of the texture to two voices, often answered by the same or similar material in two other voices, called duetting. Even when imitation is used in such duets, their thinner sound provides relief from the more complex sonorities of the full ensemble.

Alternatively, Josquin often abandons contrapuntal writing in favor of successions of triads, with all voices having the same rhythm. While there is ample precedent for this type of writing in Ockeghem, Josquin expands its use, sometimes allowing it to dominate an entire composition. More often, however, he exploits the contrast between contrapuntal style and chordal, or "familiar," style as another means of emphasizing structure.

The force of these textural contrasts is enhanced by Josquin's preference for larger ensembles. Few of his works are for three voices—by now an old-fashioned texture. Many are for four, and a large number for five or six. (This does not, however, imply performance by a large chorus. Fifteen to twenty-five singers would have been fully adequate for a five- or six-voice sacred piece, and one singer to a part for a secular song.)

Text and music

Nowhere is Josquin's genius more evident than in his invention of musical motives designed to fit specific words or phrases of text. The music is so conceived as to fit not only the natural accentuation of the words, but also their sense. At times, this is no more than simple pictorialization: a word meaning "to rise" is set to an ascending motive. In other cases, the connection is a psychological one. The appropriateness of the music is evident, but the reasons for its suitability are not. This closer relation between words and music results in an increased individualization of each work. Josquin's music shows a greater range of expressivity than that of his predecessors.

This point is eloquently illustrated by the beginnings of two secular songs (Ex. VI-1a,b). For the first, Josquin has written somber music of great power, transcending by far the rather trivial text. For the second, he has given an equally trivial but lighthearted poem a gay and delicate setting.

In spite of their sharply different character, both *Faulte d'argent* and *Douleur me bat* are based on the same fundamental techniques. In each, two voices engage in a canon at the fifth throughout the piece (the canon begins just after the excerpts quoted), while the other voices surround this with a web of frequently imitative counterpoint. The specific quality of each piece is determined not by form or technique, but by the nature of the musical materials employed.

Cadential patterns

In these pieces, and throughout the work of Josquin, the authentic cadence, normally ornamented by a suspension, is nearly universal at major articulations, and common at less important ones. The standardization of cadential types, already well advanced in the fifteenth century, is confirmed in Josquin's work. Apart from the authentic cadence, one finds the Phrygian (as before, limited to pieces or sections on E) and plagal cadences, as well as the traditional sixth-to-octave cadence, in use for cen-

Grief strikes me.   Ex. VI-1(a)

Lack of money is a sorrow without equal   Ex. VI-1(b)

turies, but now—consistently employing a sharped sixth and an unsharped inner voice—used and heard as a weaker variant of the authentic. The infiltration of cadential progressions into the interior of the phrase is also more common than in earlier music; but Josquin, like other composers of the period, still employs a wide variety of internal chord progressions: sixteenth-century music is by no means "tonal" in the later sense of the word. A few of Josquin's pieces end not with the traditional open fifth, but with a complete major triad—another indication of increasing recognition of the triad as the basic sonority, replacing the two-voice framework of the fourteenth century.

Josquin's Masses

Josquin composed about twenty settings of the Mass, transmitting in them the principal Mass-types of the fifteenth century, and adding new techniques of his own. Of the three basic types cultivated by Josquin, the cantus-firmus Mass, in which each movement is built around one or more statements of a single preexisting sacred or secular melody, is perhaps the most conservative, although Josquin is not always conservative in his treatment. Of greater importance for the future is the so-called parody

Parody Mass

Mass. (The term has here a purely technical meaning and does not suggest any kind of irreverence.) In a Mass of this type, not merely a single tune, but the entire polyphonic complex of a preexisting work serves as a model for the composer, who takes the material and reworks it to suit his fancy—altering the relationships between the parts, adding extra voices, splicing in new material, and so on. Although Josquin wrote no Masses that use parody technique consistently, as did later sixteenth-century composers, he went further in this direction than any of his predecessors. The *Missa Mater patris* (based on a motet by Antoine Brumel, a younger contemporary) set an example that was to be widely followed. A comparison of the beginning of Brumel's motet with that of the Agnus Dei of the Mass (Ex.VI-2a,b) shows Josquin's procedure to be quite simple: he quotes the motet literally at first, then continues freely, adding a fourth voice. Later examples of parody are often more complex.

Ex. VI-2

Paraphrase Mass:
Missa Pange
lingua

Josquin's third type, the "paraphrase Mass," is also forward-looking. Here preexistent melody is used, but not as a cantus firmus. No voice presents the melody in its entirety, but all voices use it as a source of musical materials. The motives used for imitation are derived from the chosen tune, often with free embellishments. This again emphasizes the equality of voices: in Dufay, a paraphrased tune was confined to a single voice that dominated the texture; in Josquin, the tune permeates the entire musical substance. This permeation by elements of a given melody is also characteristic of some of Josquin's cantus-firmus Masses: the tenor presents the cantus firmus complete, while the other voices derive much of their material from it.

In fact, Josquin appears to have written only one true paraphrase Mass, the *Missa Pange lingua*, one of his latest and finest works. Josquin's treatment of paraphrase may be seen by comparing the hymn melody on which the Mass is based (Ex. VI-3a) with the beginning of the Kyrie (Ex. VI-3b). Since the melody may be regarded as tripartite in

Speak, tongue, of the mystery of the glorious Body, and of the precious Blood, which, fruit of a noble womb, the King of the nations poured out as ransom of the world.

Ex. VI-3(a)

Ex. VI-3(b)

structure, Josquin assigns part one to the first Kyrie, part two to the Christe, and part three to the second Kyrie. (The tripartite structure of the Kyrie text is universally recognized in polyphonic settings, which consist of three sections, called Kyrie I, Christe, and Kyrie II.) The opening of Kyrie I is obviously based on the beginning of the hymn, but in measure 9 the bass introduces a motive derived from the music for "corporis" in the hymn. In order to preserve unity, Josquin casts this new motive in a shape closely related to that of the opening one, even though the two are based on different chant materials. Similarly sophisticated techniques are used throughout the Mass, which is closely unified—despite much difference in the details of paraphrase use—by the consistent recurrence of chant-derived material.

In addition to the elegant use of paraphrase, Example VI-3b demonstrates other important elements of Josquin's style. The opening provides an example of overlapped duetting: measures 5-9 repeat in the upper voices the material of measures 1-4 in the lower. The latter, however, is extended so that in measures 5-6 three, then four voices sound together. The duets open in imitation, but in each of these it is the higher of the two parts that makes full use of the hymn tune; the lower merely quotes its opening notes.

Another type of repetition may be found in Kyrie II of this Mass and in other works of Josquin. This consists in reiterating a small amount of musical material at successively different pitches—often a second lower each time—and is called sequence (Ex. VI-4). Sequence is an excellent way of achieving cohesion on a small scale, and Josquin makes much use of it. It is less often found in vocal music of the later sixteenth century, but becomes a fundamental technique in the late 1600s and thereafter.

Ex. VI-4

Josquin's treatment of cadence is especially characteristic. The end of a movement or major section is generally prepared by vigorous intensification of the rhythmic movement in all the voice parts, a device already common in Ockeghem. Despite the limited stock of cadential formulas, the cadences themselves are varied and often complex. In the *Missa Pange lingua* the first Kyrie ends with an authentic cadence on G, the concluding tone of the first section of the chant. The Christe ends on D, which could also be easily reached by an authentic cadence. But Josquin prefers a "deceptive" one: the expected triad on D is momentarily replaced by one on Bb, and arrives a measure late. Even then, the tenor continues to move about for two measures—a favorite Josquin habit. The second Kyrie must end on E, the final of the chant, and must therefore, as has been seen, employ a Phrygian cadence. This duly appears, but Josquin's fondness for post-cadential motion keeps both alto and bass in action for two more measures, to produce a plagal cadence in the last measures. The variety of cadence types in a single Mass movement is a small-scale reflection of Josquin's mastery of a wide range of musical techniques of all sorts.

Several of Josquin's Masses are based on musical motives that are not preexistent, but rather specially invented for the purpose. The *Missa La Sol Fa Re Mi* uses the note series E-D-C-A-B—the pitches having the names given in the title when the "hard" hexachord (on G) is used. The series appears as a long-note cantus firmus, and also serves as a source of motives for imitation. The *Missa Hercules dux Ferrariae* derives its basic material in an ingenious way: the vowels of "Hercules dux Ferrariae" (Hercules [I], duke of Ferrara, to whom the Mass is dedicated) are equated with the solmization syllables having the same vowels, so that "e" becomes re, "u" ut, and so on. The series of notes thus produced, called a *soggetto cavato,* is then used as a cantus firmus. Also indicative of Josquin's interest in abstract technical procedures is the *Missa L'Homme armé super voces musicales,* in which the famous tune appears a tone higher in each movement of the Mass. In some of these works (most of them apparently early), one senses that Josquin's primary interest is in technique; but this is by no means true of all of them, and as he grew older, his technical command was so great that no artifice could interfere with his style.

Great as Josquin's Masses are, his motets are, on the whole, even finer. Perhaps stimulated by the diversity of texts he set, Josquin here exhibits a diversity of technique and of expression surpassing even that of the secular songs and the Masses. At one end of the spectrum are small pieces set entirely in chordal, or familiar, style, in which continuity is maintained only by Josquin's keen feeling for meaningful chord-successions, and by the sense of the text. At the other stand imposing works for six or even more voices, employing cantus firmus, imitation, and canon, and textures of great complexity.

Josquin's motets

A representative motet, one of two Josquin settings of the psalm *De profundis,* is given in part in Example VI-5. The use of a psalm text, rather than a strictly liturgical one, or one written for a particular occasion, is indicative of a new trend. Although relatively little is known concerning the actual use of motets in services of the Church at this time, it is evident that they were seldom liturgical in the strict sense of the word. The texts of the Mass proper, for example, were rarely set polyphonically. But Josquin was only one of many composers who began to turn increasingly to the Bible, and especially to the psalms, for motet texts. Perhaps the use of polyphony at vespers may account at least for the psalmodic motets, for vespers consists largely of psalms. But until more information becomes available, reasons for the change of emphasis must remain speculative.

De profundis contains no preexistent material. It is basically sectional in character: each phrase of the text is given an individual musical setting, ending with some sort of cadence, during or after which new material is introduced for the next phrase. The first section is imitative, although influenced by Josquin's preference for paired voices (Ex. VI-5a; there is a considerable pause between the entries of the first two voices and those of the others). The second section consists of a duet for the lower voices, repeated in the upper ones. There follows an imitative duet. Duets, imitative sections, and passages in familiar style (Ex. VI-5b) are then used in artful alternation for the remainder of the piece.

Works of this sort, despite their variety of techniques and their sectional construction, are heard as fully unified, yet it is not at all easy to explain how the impression of unity is created. Musical structures that do not significantly depend on repetition of sections are sometimes called progressive forms, as opposed to "closed" forms such as the *formes fixes.* In progressive forms, the unity must be supplied by the composer's

From the depths I have called to thee, Lord.   Ex. VI-5(a)

And because of thy law.   Ex. VI-5(b)

intuition: one section succeeds another because the composer knows intuitively that it
should. In monophony and in melody-dominated polyphony this may be a relatively
simple matter. But in complex polyphony of the type cultivated by Josquin, where the
musical interest lies in the combination of simultaneous lines in large-scale musical

paragraphs, unity is a more complex matter. Perhaps this is why such polyphony depended for so long on cantus firmus—and continued at times to do so throughout the sixteenth century. Yet with Ockeghem, and even more with Josquin, the possibility of freely composed polyphony, without obvious external unifying devices, was realized.

All the Josquin examples cited here, as well as those of Ockeghem in the preceding chapter, represent what is essentially very complex music. This complexity is manifested not only in techniques such as canon and imitation, but also in the very basis of the style—equal-voiced polyphony. The ear does not hear simultaneous melodies as easily as it does simple chords or a melody with subordinate accompaniment. Moreover, the melodies themselves, rather than being simple, symmetrical tunes, are subtly balanced constructions, with fluid, asymmetrical rhythms. They are combined in such a way that their rhythmic disparity is accentuated. The overall rhythmic pulse is simple enough, but the rhythmic detail is not. In addition, the successive entries of different voices regularly cause the text to appear in different voices at different times (for example, at one point in De profundis, each of the four voices is singing a different syllable).

This is not said in disparagement: great music is apt to be complex on some levels. But the intricacy of musical style at the beginning of the sixteenth century had two important historical consequences. For one thing, it almost guaranteed the subsequent emergence of simpler, more popular styles as an alternative to the learned richness of the northern art. For another, it assured its own longevity. For, unlike the mannered complexities of the late fourteenth century, which could mean little to anyone except the connoisseur, this was an art that could be experienced on various levels: even the musically ignorant could delight in the splendor of its sounds. But for the sophisticated—and above all for the composer—its very complexity afforded an almost infinite richness of possibilities. The sixteenth-century theorist Glareanus (1488-1563) referred to the work of Josquin as an *ars perfecta*—a perfect art. It was in any case a perfect stylistic basis, and for this reason stylistic change proceeded slowly in the sixteenth century, at least in traditional categories such as the Mass and motet.

Influence of Josquin's techniques

For this reason also, there arose a great number of composers. The techniques of Josquin's style were not difficult to learn, and were of vast potential for individual development. There was, moreover, an enormous market for new music: every court, every major church was expected to have a substantial musical establishment. Among the singers and players, at least one or two would be composers, capable of supplying the music needed for ceremonies and services. Thus, much of the music performed at any locality was produced on the spot—although, of course, the diffusion of printed music made it possible to use works of other, perhaps more famous composers also, when this was desired.

Within a limited space, it would be neither possible nor desirable to attempt to enumerate all or even many of the competent composers of the period. This discussion treats instead a few figures who represent significant trends of the times.

Certain men of the period of Josquin must be mentioned. One of the most celebrated was Jacob Obrecht (ca. 1450-1505). Although younger than Josquin, he did not live as long, so that many of the more progressive features of early sixteenth-century style are not to be found in his work. He was, in any case, of a somewhat conservative disposition. His Masses constitute the largest part of his output. Most of them are of the cantus-firmus type, often using extremely ingenious methods of treating the chosen

Jacob Obrecht's style

melody. Like Josquin, Obrecht took a keen interest in technique for its own sake. Other Masses are based on polyphonic compositions, and frequently draw upon more than one voice of their originals, thus anticipating parody technique, as Josquin also did. Neither canon nor imitation in general seems to have held much interest for Obrecht, although occasional examples may be found. His delight in euphony finds expression in the frequent employment of pairs of voices moving in parallel tenths—a continuing characteristic of his style.

Heinrich Isaac: Choralis Constantinus

Contemporary with Obrecht was Heinrich Isaac (ca. 1450-1517). Important as a composer of secular pieces to French, Italian, and German texts, and also of Masses and motets, Isaac is best known for a unique collection of sacred polyphony, the *Choralis Constantinus,* on which he worked from 1508 until his death. This is music for the Mass, but for the proper, not the ordinary. It consists of polyphonic settings of the complete propers for Sundays and greater feasts, using the appropriate plainsong melodies as cantus firmi. Part of the work was the result of a commission from the Cathedral of Constance; the remainder appears to have been intended for the Imperial Chapel at Vienna. It was not printed until the 1550s, long after Isaac's death. It is the first complete set of polyphonic propers—even the twelfth-century *Magnus liber* contained only graduals and Alleluias for the Mass—and is particularly remarkable for an age that in general neglected the proper in favor of settings of the ordinary and motets.

From the point of view of musical style, the *Choralis Constantinus* is a kind of compendium of northern techniques of the time. Isaac's music is here complex and intellectual, but not to the point where musical values are threatened by technique. Like the best of his contemporaries, Isaac well knew just how far he could go in indulging his fondness for technical games.

Post-Josquin northerners to 1550.   During the remainder of the sixteenth century, both motet and Mass continued to be central preoccupations of most composers of vocal music. Indeed, the century was one of the great ages of sacred music, ranking with the latter part of the twelfth century and the earlier part of the eighteenth in this respect. Of the literally hundreds of competent composers, and dozens of outstanding ones, many were northerners; but increasingly the other nations began to produce their own musicians, ultimately including some of the greatest of all. Musical style, however, remained predominantly northern, and the northern composer living and working in Italy—as so many from Dufay on had done—remained typical until after the middle of the century.

The technical foundations of sixteenth-century sacred music had been laid by Josquin, so thoroughly that there is little in the repertoire that cannot be traced to him. Yet Josquin's style was extremely rich and various, with possibilities far too numerous to be fully realized by any one man. Thus, later composers were able to create personal styles, often by concentrating on a single feature of the basic style and developing this intensively.

Nicholas Gombert's style

This can clearly be seen in the work of Nicolas Gombert (before 1500-1556), known primarily for his motets. Gombert's chief interest was in the creation of a dense and continuous contrapuntal texture. Such a texture may, of course, be found in Josquin, but it is usually relieved by duets, familiar style, or some other simplification. In Gombert, such alternatives are almost entirely absent. Imitation begins in the opening measures, and contrapuntal writing prevails uninterrupted until the end. As in Josquin, a new motive is introduced for each new phrase of text, so that the basic construction is sectional; but Gombert minimizes the sectional feeling. The internal cadences are unemphatic, and are so arranged that the new imitation has already begun before the cadence is completed. While one voice or another may occasionally drop out for a few measures, it is more typical for the parts to continue with relatively infrequent pauses.

For Gombert, the succession of points of imitation was sufficient as a form-producing dvice. Hence neither cantus firmus nor strict canon, nor any of Josquin's more abstruse technical devices, had any appeal for him.

Gombert's motet *Quae est ista* is actually the second part, or movement, of the two-part motet beginning *O gloriosa Dei genitrix*. (It was quite common at the time to divide a longer text into two or even more parts and compose each part as an independent piece. Such movements do not differ from ordinary motets.) It begins with a point of imitation, with alternating entries on D and A, so that the motive will lie comfortably for different voice ranges. But where Josquin would probably have come to a cadence shortly after the fourth entry, Gombert extends the section further by adding new entries of the motive. A new motive, to the next phrase of text, enters inconspicuously, without benefit of a cadence to mark the separation of sections (Ex. VI-6, "sicut au-

Who is she who arises like the rising dawn?

Ex. VI-6

rora"). Gombert makes frequent use of various forms of deceptive cadence, a device that naturally emphasizes continuity and minimizes articulation. The authentic cadence, with its implication of finality, appears less often than in Josquin (except, of course, at the ends of entire pieces).

Gombert's approach to his text continues and strengthens tendencies found in Josquin. The first motive, on the words "quae est ista quae ascendit" ("who is she that ascends"), is quite naturally set to a strongly rising line spanning just over an octave. The impression of "ascending" is strengthened by rising melismas in the inner parts. This type of text treatment, in which the music illustrates not the sentiment but the action specified in the text, was to become a prime preoccupation in the later sixteenth century, especially in secular music. In Gombert's time, it was hardly more than on occasional diversion.

The treatment of the phrase "electa ut sol" ("chosen, like the sun"), which occurs later in the text, is a kind of musical pun. Both *ut* and *sol* are solmization syllables as well as Latin words, and Gombert has given them their appropriate pitches. The attraction that such technique-oriented diversions continued to hold for composers testifies to the enduring intellectuality of sixteenth-century style.

Adrian Willaert

With his single-minded pursuit of contrapuntal continuity, Gombert represents one phase of post-Josquin sacred music. Adrian Willaert (ca. 1490-1562) represents another—one that is not so easily defined. Willaert settled definitively in Italy, spending the last thirty-five years of his life as director of music at St. Mark's in Venice. During this time, he trained a large number of young composers, mostly Italians, and is perhaps the most important figure in the transmission of northern style to Italian musicians.

Willaert's mature style, clearly descended from that of Josquin and best revealed in his motets, is very different from Gombert's. Willaert often builds his music on cantus-firmus canons, as does Josquin; but he is relatively indifferent to the consistent use of imitation as a structural principle. While his voices generally enter successively, they do not consistently present the same material. On the other hand, Willaert rarely employs the strictly chordal style. Since, like Gombert, he avoids frequent cadences, his music, too, unfolds in a uniform texture, but one in which imitation is only an occasional feature.

In his later works especially, Willaert seems to be working toward a greater conciseness of style. Melismas are few in number and small in size. The text is carefully declaimed, often to melodies containing numerous repeated notes. In each voice part, therefore, the words come out clearly and intelligibly, but since the voices are put together in the usual northern way, rarely singing the same syllables at the same time, the increase in clarity means more to the singer than to the listener.

Willaert also contributed to the expansion of available musical resources, as Josquin had before him. He made occasional ventures into tonal areas seldom used before, using tones remote from the normal scale, like A♭. When such excursions are combined with the dark colors of the lower voices, the result is an expressive intensity hardly matched up to his time.

Much more celebrated is Willaert's occasional use of a technique that was to acquire great importance in the work of his successors: the employment of two complete choruses, situated in different parts of the church. By writing so that the two choruses alternate, only occasionally singing together, a new spatial dimension can be added to music. The idea was by no means an invention of Willaert, but he—perhaps stimulated by the two facing choir lofts of St. Mark's—appears to have been the man who made of it a Venetian specialty. Later composers, mostly Venetian, were to expand the possibilities of the new medium to a spectacular degree.

Double-chorus writing

With Willaert, however, double-chorus writing remained fairly simple. He invariably chose a psalm for his text, doubtless because even in chant a psalm was performed by alternating choruses. The first chorus was given the first verse of the psalm, the second chorus the second, and so on. Often the two choirs (generally of four voices each) joined together for the final doxology, producing a climax of eight-part writing. But Willaert's style in his double-chorus writing is quite different from his usual manner. Here the music is in chordal style, with few melismas and little contrapuntal interest. Obviously, Willaert felt that the physical effect of the double-chorus medium was so important that complex contrapuntal music was unnecessary or even out of place. The effect in sound must be heard in an appropriate setting to be fully experienced.

As a third representative of sacred style around the middle of the century, Jacob Clement, known as Clemens non Papa, may be considered. Another northerner, he was born around 1510 and died not long after 1550. Like his contemporaries, he achieved a clearly personal style, based ultimately on that of Josquin, but with special characteristics of its own. Like Gombert, Clemens favored imitation, but unlike him, he permits himself fairly frequent internal cadences. As a result, Gombert's contrapuntal intensity is replaced by a clearer and more open character.

Clemens non Papa's style

Clemens wrote both motets and Masses in considerable numbers. The Kyrie from the Mass *Jay veu le cerf* not only gives an idea of his style, but also provides an example of the technique that by this time dominated Mass composition: parody.

As has been seen, composers as early as Ockeghem had approached the parody-Mass type by employing, in addition to a cantus firmus, sporadic quotations from other voices of a polyphonic setting of the cantus firmus tune. Nevertheless, the extensive cultivation of this type of cyclic Mass began with the generations after Josquin. By the middle of the century, most Masses were written in this way. The reasons for the rapid rise in popularity of the parody Mass are not clear. Apparently the cantus-firmus Mass had lost its appeal, but the idea of using preexistent material had not. Parody seemed the only solution.

Parody technique

The technical possibilities were endless. The only "rule" of parody technique was that a preexisting motet or polyphonic song be chosen as the basis of the Mass. Thus, the composer could quote literally from his model and expand the quotations by means of new material. Or he could, as it were, dissect the model, extracting its salient motives, and recombine these in new ways. Or he could retain the important chordal progressions of the original and elaborate these in a new way. All these methods were frequently used.

The procedure used in Clemens's Kyrie is in part dictated by the nature of the model—a setting by Pierre de Manchicourt (a composer born about 1510) of what may have been a traditional French drinking song. The tune itself is based on repetitions of two main motives, the first occurring at the beginning, and the second, a scalewise descent from C to F, first appearing slightly later. Manchicourt has skillfully created a four-voice imitative texture based almost entirely on these motives. The result is a tightly unified composition.

In taking over such a piece as a model, Clemens was almost compelled to use the "dissection" method. Thus the beginning of his Kyrie (Ex. VI-7b) quotes the chanson beginning (Ex. VI-7a) closely for three measures, then adds a third entry of the motive (the Kyrie is for five voices, rather than the four of the model). The entries of the two lower voices are like those of the model, but they come a little later; and instead of resting, the upper voices continue with new material. More important, Clemens does not introduce the second motive anywhere here, preferring to replace it with further entries of the first motive. Only later does the second motive, somewhat disguised, make its appearance.

Conversely, the Christe uses the second motive and avoids the first; and the final Kyrie the first and not the second. In this way Clemens achieves variety with very restricted materials.

This is a relatively free example of parody technique, fairly typical of Clemens's usual method. Other composers frequently adhered much more closely to their models, often incorporating large portions of them into their Masses without substantial alteration.

The Clemens Kyrie also contains two other techniques, very different from each other, with important subsequent histories. At the beginning of the first Kyrie and of its model, the imitation is not exact: the first note of the alto should properly be B♭, not C, to preserve the exact shape of the motive. As it stands, the initial perfect fifth is imitated by a fourth instead. This is not the result of indifference or incompetence: Clemens doubtless could have contrived a continuation for the upper voice that would have permitted the B♭ in the alto. It results rather from an interest in tonal cohesion. The interval F-C answered by C-F produces a more unified tonal impression than would be given by strict imitation: the former restricts the opening pitches to members of the triad on F, while the latter yields the non-triadic set of notes F-B♭-C. An imitation altered for this purpose is known as a tonal answer, and the increasing use of such answers by many composers at this time testifies to the growing importance of the dominant-tonic relationship in all parts of the musical texture.

Tonal answer

I have seen the stag bound forth from the forest and drink at the fountain.

Ex. VI-7(a)

Lord have mercy

Ex. VI-7(b)

The second Kyrie of the same Mass is an example of a special type of musical structure, called basso ostinato, in which a continuously unfolding piece is built on a constantly repeated figure in the bass. In this piece, the tenor and bass share the task of presenting the bass figure. The tenor has it first, but not in its definitive form: on first appearance it seems merely to be a suitable harmonic bass for the main motive in the first soprano. The bass then presents it in its final form, and it is repeated six more times, beginning either on C or on F, before the end of the piece. Ostinato clearly is a convenient way to give unity to a work, and is also an excellent test of a composer's ingenuity in finding constantly new material for the upper parts. Josquin was especially fond of the technique and used it frequently. It appears occasionally in sixteenth-century vocal music by other composers, but found its most congenial home in instrumental music, discussed in Chapter VII.

Basso ostinato

The Later Sixteenth Century.   In the latter half of the sixteenth century, sacred music in general tended toward conservatism, and stylistic advances were concentrated in the secular field. This may in part result from a natural traditionalism often ascribed to music for the Church; but even more important was the role of the Counter-Reformation, and, specifically, of the Council of Trent (1545-63). This great gathering of Roman prelates was summoned (rather reluctantly) by Pope Paul III with the object of coming to a settlement of the Protestant problem, of reformulating certain doctrines disputed by the reformers, and of curtailing abuses within the Roman Church. Church music was subjected to scrutiny under the last of these headings. The Council (and a slightly later commission that met at Rome) approved the use of polyphonic music in church, but directed that it be free from all worldly associations, that it be so ordered that the sacred words could clearly be understood, and that it avoid distracting extremes.

Council of Trent

The first of these recommendations, if followed strictly, would have precluded the use of parody Masses based on secular models. The second would have discouraged imitation in favor of chordal writing. The third, while somewhat vague, would certainly have tended to prohibit novel or experimental techniques. In practice, the action of the Council had relatively little effect. Parody Masses on secular songs continued to be written, but were often published with the designation "Missa sine nomine" (Mass without a name) to disguise their secular connection. Imitation continued in general use: here composers seem to have paid little attention to the opinion of the Council. Distracting novelties are, to be sure, rather rare in sacred music, but whether this is a result of the Council or of a generally conservative attitude toward music for the church cannot be easily determined.

Conservative or not, the period from 1550 to 1600 produced some of the greatest music ever written for the church—it has often been called the Golden Age of sacred polyphony. This suggests that originality is not the sole criterion of musical value, and it confirms the extraordinary vitality of the stylistic legacy bequeathed by Josquin and his contemporaries.

During this time, composition became a truly international art. While the northerners continued to predominate, they lost their exclusive position. National schools, already well begun by 1550, flowered in the decades following. For the most part, such men will be considered in the next section of this chapter, but one of them, Giovanni Pierluigi da Palestrina (1524-94) must be mentioned here; for although an Italian, his style was supranational.

Born near Rome, Palestrina lived and worked in that city for most of his life. Virtually all his attention was devoted to sacred music. He produced over a hundred Masses and several hundred motets, but only a few secular pieces. His reputation, great in his own day, became even greater after his death, when he was, as it were, canonized as the perfect master of his time. His works were held up as models of perfection, and have formed the basis of instruction in vocal counterpoint up to the present. His exaltation to such a quasi-unique position was in part mere historical accident: he was not that much better than the best of his contemporaries. Still, there can be no doubt that his music admirably fulfills the requirements of music for the divine service, and conforms to the spirit, if not always to the letter, of the ideals of the Council of Trent.

Palestrina

Palestrina, working with the same materials Josquin and his successors had used, achieved his own musical character by means of an extraordinary purity of style. He combines extreme smoothness of melodic line, ideally suitable for the voice, with

Fig. VI-1: The Sistine Chapel in the Vatican, with frescos by Michelangelo (1475-1564).
Many celebrated singers and composers, including Palestrina, served here. (Photograph Alinari.)

Palestrina's style

counterpoint so designed as to eliminate all possibility of dissonant collisions between the parts. His treatment of dissonance is so restrained and so systematic that it was natural for his style to have been selected for purposes of instruction. Compared with that of Josquin, Palestrina's style is rather more harmonic. The need for a persistent presence of triads throughout a composition, and for certain triad successions at specific points in the phrase, has become for Palestrina so important that even the conduct of the individual parts must yield precedence. It is the genius of Palestrina that he was able to reconcile the harmonic and the linear elements of music so perfectly.

In the realm of expression, Palestrina's music seems rather more reserved, less wide-ranging, than that of many other composers. There is much less difference between a sombre piece and a gay one by Palestrina than there is in Josquin. For Palestrina, purity of sound and style was more important than any direct musical interpretation of the text. And, precisely because of his reserve, Palestrina gains an expressive advantage: a special turn of phrase that might pass unnoticed in another composer has in his music the effect of a major musical event.

The Agnus Dei of the *Missa O admirabile commercium* provides both an illustration of Palestrina's style and a further example of parody technique. The Mass, first printed in 1599, is based on one of Palestrina's motets, published thirty years earlier. The use of a motet rather than a chanson as model is characteristic of Palestrina: only a few of his pieces are on secular songs. (It should not be inferred from this that Palestrina was typical of his period, for the secular parody was still very much alive, despite the Council of Trent.)

The motet *O admirabile commercium* is largely in an ornamented chordal style (Ex. VI-8a), with very little imitation. This texture was, for Palestrina as for Josquin, used mainly for contrast within a piece, rather than as an end in itself. The average motet is more apt to be imitative. The Agnus Dei demonstrates Palestrina's consummate skill at preserving a recognizable relation to his model, while at the same time producing music that is completely fresh.

O splendid exchange.   Ex. VI-8(a)

The opening of Agnus Dei I (Ex. VI-8b; like the Kyrie, the polyphonic Agnus Dei is regularly composed as a tripartite movement) is based on free imitation of the suspension idea found in the quintus part of the motet. At the same time, the cantus of the motet is retained, but with its time values doubled (augmented) to allow time for the imitation. The cantus later joins in the imitation, so that the whole first section is very

Lamb of God.

Ex. VI-8(b)

like a normal motet beginning. The rest of the Agnus Dei is based in varying ways on motives and textures drawn from later sections of the motet, displaying an ingenious mixture of free and borrowed material.

Palestrina represents an apex of Renaissance music, as Josquin had before him. But while Josquin stood alone, in that no other composer of his time could equal him, Palestrina must share his honor with some of his contemporaries. Chief among these was the northerner Orlando di Lasso (1532-94; also known as Roland de Lassus). Lasso spent much of his life in Germany, passing nearly forty years at Munich; but he was a true international, who wrote music to French, Italian, and German secular texts with equal ease. As a composer of sacred music, his reputation rests chiefly on his several hundred motets, his Masses being on the whole less important.

Orlando di Lasso

Less conservative than Palestrina, Lasso speaks a more vigorous musical language, while still employing the standard materials of sixteenth-century technique. The motet *Taedet animam meam* opens with an elaborate point of imitation (Ex. VI-9a),

[Two lower voices enter later]

My soul is disgusted with my life.

Ex. VI-9(a)

but the motive, with its skip of a minor sixth, reaches a degree of dramatic expression that Palestrina does not seek. Also to be noted is the harmonic nature of the motive: its first three tones are the notes of the minor triad on C—another indication of the increase in triadic thinking to be found in most music of the late sixteenth century.

The section on "loquar in amaratudine" ("I shall speak in bitterness") begins with a sudden slowing down of the rhythm, for expressive reasons. The curious fauxbourdon-like passage (Ex. VI-9b) following is also textually motivated. Fauxbourdon itself was long since out of fashion, and by the time of Lasso the triad in "sixth-chord" position (with the third, rather than the root, as the lowest note) was felt to be harsh-sounding: its insistent use here suggests the bitterness of the speaker. Lasso's declamation is also crisp, as may be seen in the repeated notes of the opening motive.

In bitterness.   Ex. VI-9(b)

Lasso is more interested than Palestrina in the vigorous depiction of his texts, even if his style is necessarily a little less "pure" on that account. As might be expected, he often chose for his motets texts that offered good opportunities for illustration, especially those expressing penitence and sorrow, for which he finds dark musical colors that are admirably appropriate.

General tendencies of late sixteenth-century sacred music

The general tendencies of sacred music of the late sixteenth century may be regarded as intensifications of procedures found earlier. Imitation may be more complex; the harmony richer; the text may exert a greater influence over the nature of the music; the number of voices may increase (in works for more than six voices, most composers made some use of the double-chorus technique discussed above in connection with Willaert; this will be discussed in Chapter VII). For perhaps the first time in the history of western music, a polyphonic style had been evolved that permitted the composition of a vast number of pieces, each different enough from all the others to be in some sense original, yet remaining within fairly narrow stylistic limits. The mere volume of well-constructed music composed during the period is staggering: thousands of Masses, and many more motets. While much of this music represents no more than expert craftsmanship, the best stands on a level with the best music of any period. That so much could be achieved with so little fundamental stylistic change testifies to the vitality of the basic principles employed: imitation, the triad as basic sonority, the typical cadential progressions. Moreover, by the end of the sixteenth century, not one of these principles had yet been exhausted. Used in different ways and given new meanings, they were to remain vital for several hundred years.

SECULAR VOCAL MUSIC

France: The Chanson.   The history of sacred music during the sixteenth century is, on the whole, simpler than that of secular music. Although local and individual styles are clearly recognizable, the motet and the Mass form an international repertoire based on northern techniques. Secular music presents a radically different picture. For one

Fig. VI-2: *Three women making music, by the so-called Master of the Female Half Figures (fl. ca. 1530). The music, identifiable from the open part-books, is that of Claudin's chanson Jouyssance vous donneray. The lutenist has either memorized or is improvising an accompaniment, presumably based·on the music of the two closed part-books at front. (Photo Meyer K. G., Vienna.)*

thing, it developed along national lines, so that each major musical nation brought forth secular forms and styles of its own, written to poetry in the vernacular. For another, secular music came to be the principal vehicle for innovative tendencies during the sixteenth century—tendencies that were largely prevented by conservatism from entering the motet and the Mass. In consequence, secular music presents a rich and almost bewildering variety of types, varying from nation to nation, from composer to composer, and even from work to work within the production of a single musician.

This contrasts somewhat with the period immediately preceding. Despite the existence in the fifteenth century of native German and Italian styles (which will be discussed below), the chanson—a secular song to a French text, composed in contrapuntal style by a northern musician—was considered throughout Europe to be the most sophisticated expression of secular art music. Two characteristics are often found in late fifteenth-century songs: the delight in technical artifices such as canon; and the use of preexistent musical material, chiefly songs of a popular nature. Both canon and popular songs are found in the secular works of Josquin, and the setting of popular tunes in either three- or four-voice versions was especially common in the first two decades of the sixteenth century.

Thereafter, freely composed chansons of a contrapuntal type, usually without underlying canons but employing free imitation, continued to be written: most of the northern composers whose sacred music was discussed in the first part of this chapter produced such works. These pieces were naturally affected by the general stylistic currents of the times: they tended towards a larger number of voices, a richer harmonic effect; and they were influenced by other trends to be considered shortly. Nevertheless, the artful, imitative chanson had a fairly continuous history during most of the sixteenth century.

The Parisian chanson

There was, however, a brief but important interruption in this history. This is best symbolized by the lack of any publication containing chansons by Josquin between the early years of the sixteenth century and 1540. During this period the contrapuntal chanson suffered at least a partial eclipse, and a much simpler type of piece came into vogue. Since most of the composers who worked in this new style were connected with the French court at Paris, the new genre is generally referred to as the Parisian chanson.

The origins of the Parisian chanson are not wholly clear. It was, in part, a reaction against the complexity of the art song of northerners such as Ockeghem and Busnois. Also influential was the poet Clément Marot (1496-1544), who rejected the complex, rhetorical style of his predecessors for a simple, unaffected diction quite close to popular speech. Such poetry naturally suggested a musical setting free from artifice. Then, too, influences from Italy may well have been at work, for the Italians had (as will be seen) been practicing for some decades a secular art song quite different from the art songs of northern composers. In any event, the new Parisian style proved immensely popular. During little more than a decade beginning in 1528, the Parisian printer Pierre Attaingnant published nearly two thousand pieces of this sort.

Claudin de Sermisy

Claudin de Sermisy (ca. 1490-1562) was perhaps the most representative composer of the Parisian chanson. While his numerous works are by no means monotonously similar to one another, they are remarkably consistent in style. Almost all are four-voice settings of poems of the Marot type—simple in diction; sentimental, suggestive, or even obscene in content. The music is predominantly chordal, although melismatic flourishes and brief imitative passages are frequent. The structure of the music is clearly and audibly based on that of the text. Each line of text receives a phrase of

scanned according to the ancient meters). He arbitrarily assigned long and short values to the syllables of French words, and then applied the principles of classical versification. His poetry was of little artistic importance, but Baïf was fortunate in obtaining the interest of major composers in setting his verse to music. Chief among these was Claude le Jeune (ca. 1530-1600), who, with other musicians, set Baïf's poetry to what they called *musique mesurée à l'antique,* which reflected exactly in musical rhythm the long and short syllables of Baïf's versification. Since classical poetic meters are by no means restricted to regular successions of two-, three-, or four-unit groupings, the result, exemplified by the beginning of Le Jeune's *La bel' aronde* (Ex.VI-13), is a mixture of rapidly changing meters unique for its time.[1] In order to bring out the novel rhythmic effect as clearly as possible, the chordal texture of the air is used (indeed many of Le Jeune's pieces are entitled "air"). Since many of the poems have refrains, a setting in *musique mesurée* frequently consists of a musical refrain alternating with contrasting sections, in a pattern like AbAcAdA.

Musique mesurée: Claude le Jeune

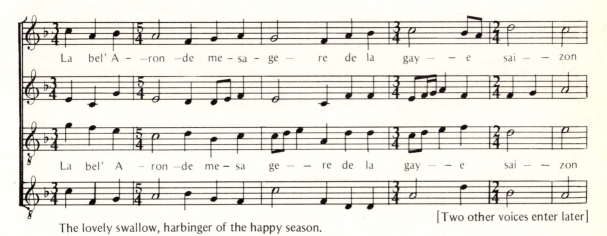

The lovely swallow, harbinger of the happy season.

[Two other voices enter later]

Ex. VI-13

Thanks chiefly to the talent of Le Jeune, *musique mesurée* was able to transcend the rather limiting academicism of its theory and to achieve real freshness and originality. Yet this manner of composition remained the preoccupation of a minority. Its chief significance, apart from the value of the best works written in the style, is in showing the strength of the tie between musician and poet in the later sixteenth century — something demonstrated in a different way by the secular music of Italy.

Italy: The madrigal and other secular forms.   In Italy, the reaction against the learned art of the North began half a century before it did in France. As has been said, northern composers were living and working in Italy throughout the fifteenth century, and during that time there were few native Italian composers of any consquence. While northerners occasionally contributed to indigenous forms (Isaac, for example, made settings of Florentine carnival songs), for the most part they cultivated the contrapuntal chanson to French text.

The late fifteenth century

[1] Medieval and Renaissance music usually contains some indication of meter, but does not make use of bar lines. The latter have been regularly added in the examples given in this book, for greater ease of reading. In Example VI-13, both bar lines and meter are editorial, but are fully justified by the intent and effect of the music.

Much as these works were admired, the complexity of their style encouraged the development of a simpler native secular art. This arose in the last quarter of the century and had its chief center at the brilliant court of Mantua, presided over by the highly cultivated Isabella d'Este. The development of the new style in Italy required, as in France, the cooperation of poets and musicians. The former produced vast quantities of verse, mostly of very mediocre quality. The subject is usually love, the tone alternately literary and popular (although this is the "popular" tone of the aristocrat aping the manner of his inferiors). While the poems had a number of generic names, depending on their structure, the most characteristic was *frottola*, and this title is often, if rather loosely, applied to the entire repertoire.

Frottola

All of this was poetry to be sung, not merely read or recited. Chief among the composers of music for the frottola were Bartolomeo Tromboncino (d. ca. 1535) and Marchetto Cara (d. ca.1530), although many other musicians worked in this genre; there are, as well, numerous anonymous compositions. As a musical form, the frottola stands in sharp contrast to the chanson, for which all-vocal performance was at least possible. The frottola is intended to be performed by a single singer (sometimes two) accompanied by instruments. In consequence, it consists of a simple melody, usually cast in symmetrical phrases of two or four measures; a bass part whose function is almost entirely harmonic; and two subordinate nonvocal inner voices, sharing the same range and contributing both harmonic richness and a certain amount of rhythmic animation. Imitation is absent, and there is no attempt at giving the voices equal importance. The poems are generally strophic, so that in performance a piece of some length results from the repetition of a short section of music for each strophe of the text.

In the excerpt from the anonymous *L'amor donna ch'io* (ExVI-14), the primacy of the top voice is evident, as are the differing functions of the other parts. The rhythmic lilt of the melody, with its alternation of 6/8 and 3/4, is also characteristic. As in the example of *musique mesurée* above, the meters are not indicated in the original (indeed a musican of the time would not have thought in such terms), but the actual rhythmical effect is accurately given by the transcription.

Lady, the love I bear you I would willingly disclose.   Ex. VI-14

While pieces such as this are far removed from the high art of the northerners—it is doubtful if the frottola composers could have coped with the technical problems of the learned chanson—they have a charm of their own. And in their strongly harmonic style, with clear-cut cadences, they are in a sense progressive.

The vogue of the frottola lasted through the first two decades of the sixteenth century. The printer Ottaviano de' Petrucci produced eleven books of such compositions, and there are many manuscript sources as well. After 1510, a change in literary taste began to be reflected in the frottola: the poetry selected for musical settings was increasingly serious in content and literary in style. But the musical style remained essentially unchanged. Thus Tromboncino, for example, set serious poetry of Petrarch in much the same manner as he set the trivial verses of his fellow courtiers. In fact, the music of a frottola never pretended to be a musical interpretation of a poem, but merely a manner of performing it. Some frottole are indeed frankly described as "a manner of singing a sonnet"—meaning that any sonnet, not just the text given with the music, might be sung to that tune.

The change in literary taste ultimately drove the frottola out of existence. Higher literary standards were set: Petrarch was held up as a model of excellence, and the frivolous versification of the frottola poets was disdained and forgotten. But the new poetry needed a musical vehicle more imposing than that provided by the frottola: music was now to be not merely a vehicle for poetic declamation, but also a kind of image of the poem—its equivalent in tones.

For this, the musical technique of the frottola offered inadequate resources. It was therefore natural for Italy to turn to the North and to northern musicians as it labored to create a new style. Elements of the frottola were retained and combined with features of the French chanson and the motet, the result being the sixteenth-century madrigal, the most important secular form of the period.

The new madrigal shares only its name with the madrigal of the fourteenth century (above, Chapter IV). Strictly speaking, the term is a literary one, denoting a short, epigrammatic poem, usually with some special twist in its last two lines. Like "frottola," however, "madrigal" came to be applied to a certain kind of musical setting, regardless of the form of the text, and it is in this sense that the word will be used here.

Madrigal: Origins and characteristics

The madrigal, although partly the descendant of the frottola, differed profoundly from its parent, precisely because of its northern, contrapuntal elements. While actual performances often made use of instruments, the madrigal was written in a manner that at least admitted of all-vocal performance. It was, like the chanson, a kind of vocal chamber music, designed more for active participation than for mere listening. Typical pictorial representations depict five or six singers (no more) sitting about a table, singing from their music.

Thus in the madrigal, each voice was given text, and each had a meaningful melodic line. While the early madrigal was often as chordal as the frottola, the careful declamation and the flowing melody in each voice show a new attitude on the part of the composer. The madrigal also abandons the strophic setting characteristic of the frottola and, in an effort to achieve an ideal harmony between music and text, provides fresh music for each new line of text. The overall form is therefore like that of the motet—a succession of short sections, each using new musical material invented specifically to accommodate the line of text being treated.

In its early stages, the madrigal was cultivated mostly by northern musicians. One of the earliest was Philippe Verdelot (d. ca. 1540), apparently a Frenchman. His *Ogn'hor per voi sospiro* (Ex. VI-15) first appeared in print in 1537, only seven years after the term "madrigal" had begun to be used. Although the piece employs a good deal of chordal writing, the smooth melodic lines of the inner parts clearly differentiate

Early madrigal composers

Every hour I sigh for you, Lady, since I do not dare to reveal my faith.   Ex. VI-15

it from the frottola. The typical symmetrical phrasing and tuneful melody of the frottola
are also absent. Yet it is by no means merely a northern motet with an Italian secular
text. It is shorter and more concise than a motet. Though contrapuntal, it is far less
obviously so than most sacred music. And there is a special, almost affectionate relation
between text and music. The madrigal has already acquired a stylistic identity of its
own.

   Along with Verdelot, Jacques Arcadelt (ca. 1504-after 1567) was another important
northern composer of Italian madrigals. Indeed the only important Italian of the early
period was Costanzo Festa (d. 1545). This state of affairs was not, however, to endure.
The madrigal quickly acquired enormous popularity. The singing of madrigals became
a favorite pastime of the educated, creating a constant demand for new music. It was
inevitable that native composers should eventually arise to challenge the northern
domination, particularly in a genre making use of the vernacular.

   This was the more to be expected as a result of composers' increasing preoccupation with the treatment of their texts. While early madrigals (up to about 1550) differ
from each other mainly in the amount of imitation used, ranging from almost wholly
chordal settings to motet-like pieces, in the second half of the century composers

Fig. VI-3: "Four singers," attributed to Adam de Coster, active in Antwerp in the early seventeenth century. Despite the late date, one may imagine that a madrigal or chanson is being performed with voices alone — compare the mixed medium shown in the preceding illustration. (Hampton Court Palace.)

sought to reflect the meaning of the text with more and more precision and force, daring almost any technical innovation to do so.

Nonetheless, the first and most important composer of this sort was also a northerner: Cipriano da Rore (1516-65). Rore's attitude toward his texts was serious: he set only dignified and literary poetry, and endeavored in his settings to delineate as dramatically as possible the changing moods portrayed in the texts. This naturally led to stylistic innovations. Tones remote from the diatonic scale appear more frequently; unusual melodic intervals (such as the major sixth) are found; slow passages are immediately juxtaposed with rapid ones; unusual spacing of the voices may be found—the bass very low, for example, while all the other voices are high. These and other stylistic elements have since become so common that it is difficult for the modern ear to recapture the sense of shock they must have caused sixteenth-century singers; but there is no difficulty in grasping Rore's basic principle that interpreting the text was more important than following the normal rules of musical grammar.

Innovations in the madrigal: Cipriano da Rore

The broadened stylistic vocabulary made available the means for increased contrast, and in fact there is generally strong contrast among the sections of a single Rore madrigal. This may be seen in an excerpt from his *Ov' è'l silentio* (Ex. VI-16), the second part, or movement, of a sonnet-setting. The wide tonal range is immediately evident: triads on B are practically unknown in sacred music. Their use here testifies to Rore's desire to increase tonal space in the interest of expressivity.

Which habitually follow you with uncertain footsteps, weary . . .   Ex. VI-16

Music and text

In fact, everything in this setting depends on expressivity. The text is, as it were, dissected into its expressive components, and each of these is given music of the highest appropriateness. There is at one point a startling change from a triad on C to one on B, emphasizing the word "lume" (light); and, later, impassioned declamation gives way to a long sigh at "lasso" (weary). This is a world far removed from that of Verdelot. Here the music depends entirely on its text for continuity: without the words the frequently violent musical changes would be meaningless. Yet purely musical values are not neglected, however great the importance of the text. Abstract devices such as imitation are regularly present, as is also the "staggered" declamation resulting from independent melodic lines. Music, though already the dependent of the text, is not yet the absolute servant she was to become at the end of the century.

Rore's intensely personal mirroring of the emotional meaning of the poetry he set was not the only possible reaction to a text at this time. Many composers were attracted less by this serious approach than by a half-playful, pictorializing reaction to individual words, in which music was made to suggest not only the emotions, but also the objects and actions of the external world. Even Rore was not untouched by this, despite his basic seriousness. But what was for him an occasional indulgence became for others a major preoccupation. Any word suggesting ascent or height was set to a rising line or an upward skip; and words like "inferno," "fall," and the like were given opposite treatment. Mention of grief or pain called forth dissonant suspensions. Happiness and singing were rendered by quick little melismas. Should the poem mention waves, an undulating figure would appear in the music.

Madrigalisms

Some of these "madrigalisms,"as they have come to be called, were not even audible: they were apparent only to the eye of the performer. Thus "night" and "darkness" were often set to "black" notes—notes with filled-in heads, like present-day quarter notes, but not necessarily quick. That such "eye-music" was extensively cultivated demonstrates not only the profoundly pictorial nature of the later madrigal, but also its intent as music addressed not as much to listeners as to performers, who enjoyed the wit of the composer, as well as his musical skill.

The best of the later madrigalists integrated the madrigalistic clichés into convincing and expressive works of art. For them, pictorialism was an agreeable ornament. The Venetian composer Andrea Gabrieli (ca. 1520-86) begins the madrigal *Due rose fresche* *Andrea Gabrieli* (Ex. VI-17) with the voices entering in pairs, illustrating the "two fresh roses," and soon

Two fresh roses, plucked in paradise.

Ex. VI-17

rising to achieve a brillant high sonority at "paradiso." The music remains convincing, however, despite two pictorialisms in less than ten measures. The madrigals of lesser men are often no more than strings of such clichés—elegant and fashionable, but without much meaning.

Probably the greatest of the later madrigalists whose work remains within the limits of Renaissance style was Luca Marenzio (1553-99). Like Gabrieli, he was an *Luca Marenzio* Italian, and his fame was a symbol of the passing of musical leadership from northerners to native Italian musicians. While northerners like Lasso, Philippe de Monte, and Giaches Wert were important madrigal composers, the tide by now had turned: Italy was now the central musical nation, and two centuries of northern hegemony had ended.

Marenzio's choice of texts is typical for his time. Petrarch is still represented, but less often than Giovanni Battista Guarini and other poets who wrote in the fashionable rich and mannered style, full of complex metaphors and sudden antitheses. The poems are frequently pastoral, peopled with amorous nymphs and lovesick shepherds. Indeed, one of the favorite sources for madrigal texts of the later period was Guarini's play *Il pastor fido* (the faithful shepherd), a more mannered intensification of Tasso's *Aminta*.

For this elegantly artificial verse, Marenzio contrived a style of the utmost refinement and delicacy. While he never failed to take advantage of any pictorial opportunity presented to him by the text, he kept his madrigalisms subordinate to an expressive rendering of the substance of the poetry. His madrigals may be divided into two large classes: the pastoral proper, light and graceful in tone; and the serious type, in which deep emotions predominate.

The first class is represented by his setting of *Due rose*, which Marenzio begins by quoting the opening of Andrea Gabrieli's setting of the same text—a gracious gesture of deference to the older composer—and then continues freely. The texture is freely contrapuntal, with occasional imitation and two or three brief chordal passages. The music flows with an effortless grace that only a great master can achieve.

Marenzio's style

Naturally, madrigalisms abound: the word "duo" (two) provokes three little duets; immediately thereafter "egualmente" (equally) is symbolized by the use of chordal style; and "diviso" (divided) is divided from the preceding words by rests in all voices. All of this is routine procedure for composers of the time, although Marenzio rises far above routine in his execution. What follows is also pictorial, but illustrates an important new stylistic resource. The word "dolce" (sweet) was generally illustrated by some special harmonic effect. That is what Marenzio chooses to do here (although he animates the harmony by staggering the declamation slightly): the lowest sounding voice is given the tones C-B-C-C♯-D-E♭, in which all the intervals are semitones, with an altered form of a tone following immediately on the unaltered (C-C♯). This use of altered scale degrees in direct conjunction with unaltered ones is known as chromaticism. An important expressive device in the hands of later madrigalists, it came to be used regularly to depict extremes of emotion, especially (but not always) painful ones.

Marenzio's serious style may be seen in his *Dolorosi martir*. Its text dwells exclusively on pain and suffering, and Marenzio's music rises to equal intensity. The first dozen measures are a long chain of dissonant suspensions, depicting the torments described in the text. On several occasions Marenzio uses triads with the third in the bass, which, as has been noted, were felt to convey an idea of harshness. Chromaticism is sparingly but effectively employed. Marenzio does not hesitate to take any liberty that will help him illustrate his text. Thus (Ex. VI-18) for "triste voci" (sad voices), he uses a motive based on the normally unvocal skip of a seventh; and the melismas on "urlie" (shrieks) are intentionally awkward. The word "amara" (bitter) evokes another favorite device, the use of the augmented triad (composed of two major thirds, and hence dissonant) in a prominent place. The mention of "vita" (life) in the line immediately following calls forth a little sparkle of quick melismas. Only a superb technician could give unity to such a diversity of devices, and Marenzio was certainly that.

Yet a piece like *Dolorosi martir* shows clear signs of the imminent end of an era, although it is one of Marenzio's earlier works. The principle of vigorous and dramatic text-illustration, first systematically followed by Cipriano da Rore, has by now stretched the musical fabric nearly to the breaking point. Goaded on by the mannered

Sad voices, complaints, howls.

Ex. VI-18

antitheses of the poets, composers reached for ever more extreme musical means, combining these in a single piece so that the contrast among them would enhance their shock value. This sort of extremism—this pushing-to-the-limits of a style—is symptomatic of an approaching change: the reader will remember that the rhythmic intricacies both of Petrus de Cruce around 1300 and of the Avignon composers nearly a century later were followed by a radical stylistic reorientation.

Thus despite the superb musical quality of Marenzio's work, he must be regarded as a twilight figure—a practitioner in a style with much past, but relatively little future. Not, to be sure, that this was the end of the madrigal's path. Marenzio himself went further, and so also did other composers. But with works such as those we enter the musically turbulent years of the very end of the century, in which Renaissance style finally collapsed, to be replaced by something quite different.

Although the madrigal was by far the most important Italian secular form of the sixteenth century, it was by no means the only one. The need for light, easily comprehensible music that produced the Italian frottola towards the end of the fifteenth century and the Parisian chanson in the second quarter of the sixteenth was not satisfied by the madrigal, which, even in its lighter moods, was too sophisticated and complex. After the passing of the frottola, many of its characteristics survived in the villanesca (first known appearance in 1541; later called "villanella"). In the second half of the century, other types appeared also, called "balletto," "canzonetta," or by names derived from cities (veneziana, etc.). While these differed somewhat from each other, they shared certain basic qualities. Their texts were non-literary poems, often humorous or obscene, and often in a local dialect (hence the types named after cities). The poems were strophic, usually with refrains, and their forms were clearly reflected in the music, which was simple, predominantly chordal in style, and vigorously rhythmic in

Other Italian secular forms

a dancelike fashion, with many repeated notes. The basic texture was similar to that of the frottola: a melody with a harmonic bass and one or more harmonic inner parts. As if to emphasize the light, "artless" character of such pieces, composers often utilized deliberately incorrect part-writing, especially parallel fifths. Pieces of this kind generally have a musical refrain, which alternates with one or more contrasting sections. The emphasis on repetition of sections also underlines the light and popular nature of this genre.

In one sense, however, such trifles were more progressive than the serious madrigal. The homophonic rhythm directs attention to the triad progressions, and the incisive rhythms to short melodic motives rather than long lines. Both of these elements were important ingredients in the new style of the seventeenth century.

MUSIC IN OTHER COUNTRIES

As has been seen, Italy became the leading musical nation in the second half of the sixteenth century. Its leadership continued for two centuries, but was not absolute, like the primacy of Paris in the thirteenth century and that of the northerners in the fifteenth. England, Germany, France, and Spain all developed musical cultures in the sixteenth century and continued them in the years following. While these regional styles were often modeled on Italian ones, and often employed imported Italian musicians, native composers were also plentiful: Italy was in fact a *leader,* not a sole source of supply.

Sacred music: Morales and Victoria

Spain. In Spain, an important school of sacred polyphony flourished, producing a number of distinguished composers, including two of international fame: Cristóbal de Morales (ca. 1500-1553) and Tomás Luis de Victoria (1548-1611). Both were primarily composers of sacred music, and both received training in Rome. Like the lesser Spanish masters of the period, they based their styles on the fundamental northern techniques of the time. Morales seems to stand closer to Josquin, Victoria to Palestrina, as is natural enough given their dates. Yet each achieved individuality and, besides, seemed to impart a particular Spanish flavor to the northern idiom. This often, but by no means always, was expressed in a style of mystical, somber intensity.

Secular music: Juan del Encina

Secular music was also actively cultivated in Spain. Throughout the fifteenth century and into the sixteenth, the leading secular form was the villancico, a fixed poetic structure resembling the French virelai. In the earlier period, music for the villancico was rather simple in style. The main melody was in the top voice, with two or three subordinate accompanying parts below, a texture similar to that of the Italian frottola. In *Ya na quiero* (Ex. VI-19), by Juan del Encina (1468-1529), the text is a vernacular devotional poem addressed to the Virgin Mary, rather than a strictly secular one; but this is not uncommon. Only the top voice is given text, the lower two presumably being intended for instrumental performance.

During the sixteenth century, Spanish secular music was much affected by influences from abroad—first by the ubiquitous pressure of northern techniques, then by the novelties of the Italian secular style. Some composers wrote madrigals in the Italian manner, and even the villancico was converted to a style similar to that of the madrigal or motet, with voices of equal melodic importance and often with extensive use of

Ya no quie-ro te — — ner fe, Se – ño – ra sino cun vos

I seek to keep faith only with you, lady.

Ex. VI-19

imitation. Although such pieces retain detectable local flavor, and are not mere imitations of foreign style, their technique has become international.

Music in German-speaking regions; music of the Protestant churches.   In Germany the musical situation was more complex. This was owing both to the Reformation, which created a need for sacred polyphony for the Lutheran north as well as for the Roman Catholic south, and to the persistence of native traditions dating back to the Middle Ages.

The most striking of the latter was the continued cultivation of monophonic song by the Meistersinger (master-singers). These men in a sense continued the tradition of the Minnesänger (above, Chapter III), but unlike their aristocratic predecessors, the Meistersinger were tradesmen and artisans—townspeople of the middle class. Their art reflected the somewhat limiting conservatism that characterized their society, and their melodies seem rather stiff in comparison with those of the Minnesänger.

Secular music:
The Meistersinger

The Meistersinger preserved a number of traditional melodies *(Weisen)*, often later versions of Minnesänger tunes. A Meistersinger might write a new text to an existing melody, or invent an entirely new melody with new words. The latter was of course regarded as the higher artistic achievement.

The texts were often paraphrased from the Bible, and proper versification and rhyme were considered to be of the greatest importance. The melodies, whether new or old, are mostly in Bar form (AAB). They are generally simple in style, but occasionally break out into little melismas (*Blumen*, flowers).

The Meistersinger were organized in guilds, and any town of importance had at least one such society. Each guild developed an elaborate system of regulations aimed at defining "correctness" in both poetry and music. The pedantry of these rules was hardly conducive to the production of original or important music. Even the famous Hans Sachs (1494-1576; central character in Wagner's historically accurate opera *Die Meistersinger von Nürnberg* of 1867) remains a relatively minor figure in the history of German music. Perhaps the greatest importance of the Meistersinger guilds was their fostering of music among people of the middle class, thereby helping to lay a foundation for the German musical pre-eminence that came about in the second half of the eighteenth century.

More representative of the best of German music was the Lied—the polyphonic secular song to German text. In the fifteenth century, such pieces occur in manuscripts

Lied

that also contain works by Franco-Flemish composers.[1] These earlier Lieder differ from the latter in their conservatism, and sometimes also in less skillful compositional technique. By the end of the century, however, the Lied had become a highly important secular form, with a well-developed technique of its own. Among the many composers of Lieder were Heinrich Isaac, whose sacred music has already been discussed earlier in this chapter, and Paul Hofhaimer (1459-1537). Hofhaimer's *Nach willen dein* (Ex. VI-20) is also in bar form. The main melody, probably preexistent, is in the tenor. The

According to your wish, to prove myself in all truth to you alone, [since] you are worth all the world to me, I give myself to you for your own.

Ex. VI-20

---

[1]The term "northerners" hitherto used for composers from northern France and the Low Countries is ambiguous in a discussion of German music. It is therefore replaced here by "Franco-Flemish:" no change in meaning is intended.

other voices surround it with active non-imitative polyphony somewhat in the manner of the contemporary French-language chanson. The form is clearly articulated by cadences. Apart from the tenor, the voices are nearly equal in importance and activity—an indication of relatively advanced style, as earlier pieces are often for only three voices, or have an alto part that is clearly subordinate.

Lieder continued to be written throughout the sixteenth century. In those of Ludwig Senfl (ca. 1490-?1556), a pupil of Isaac, the influence of the northern motet is evident. The main melody is still in the tenor, but all voices are more nearly equal in importance, and imitation is often used extensively. A number of Senfl's Lieder are for five and even more voices.

During the latter half of the century, the Lied was even more strongly affected by foreign influence—now mostly from Italy. Both the Italian madrigal and the lighter forms such as the villanella were known and enjoyed in German-speaking nations, and the Lied gradually lost its own character to take on that of the foreign importations. This is already visible in the Lieder of Lasso, and is even more marked in those of Hans Leo Hassler (1564-1612), the most prominent composer of Lieder at the end of the century. Hassler actually entitled his volume of Lieder printed in 1596 "German Songs after the Manner of Italian Madrigals and Canzonets;" and, as he had studied in Venice, he knew the "manner" well enough to copy it with fidelity and charm. Thus the Lied, beginning as an indigenous form with its own techniques, ended by becoming a Germanized version of an Italian style; but while the later pieces may lack the sober strength of Hofhaimer or Isaac, their quality is such as to raise them far above the level of mere imitations.

The known history of German sacred polyphony begins rather late, and shows clearly that Germany stood at some distance from progressive musical currents until the sixteenth century. There is evidence that in some places two-part organum similar to that used in the eleventh century was sung as late as 1500. This was naturally not a universal practice, and there exists music by fifteenth-century German composers that is modeled on more nearly contemporary styles—for example, Masses from the end of the century that resemble works of Dufay. But on the whole the fifteenth century produced little sacred music of historical or artistic importance.

With the sixteenth century, this situation changed radically. Musical establishments comparable to those of Italy sprang up, and important composers of Franco-Flemish origin came to direct or to take part in them—the best known being Isaac in the first half of the century and Lasso in the second. Native composers also appeared in great numbers, and with fully adequate technical equipment. In consequence, German sacred music for the Roman Catholic church reflected promptly and accurately the styles cultivated by composers elsewhere. This is particularly evident in the work of Lasso, who was a master of every form known to his time. In writing madrigals, chansons, or Lieder, he puts on the stylistic dress appropriate to the genre. In his sacred music, however, he remains faithful to the international Franco-Flemish style, whether he is writing for the court at Munich or for some other place.

Sacred music for the Roman Catholic church

Although there were significant native composers, much of the best music for the Roman Church was written by men from the Franco-Flemish area. Chief among them, after Lasso, was Philippe de Monte (1521-1603), a gifted and prolific musician who worked for some time at the Imperial Court at Vienna. Jacobus Kerle (1531-91) may also be mentioned. He had composed music for the *preces speciales* (special prayers) at the

Council of Trent, thereby helping, it is said, to overcome the prelates' antipathy to polyphonic church music. Thereafter he passed much of his carer in Germany.

Music in the Protestant churches

In addition to works actually produced in Germany, the Roman Catholic churches there could and did make use of compositions written elsewhere, since the liturgical requirements and the liturgical language were universal. The same is not true—or at least not wholly true—for the Protestant churches. The reform movement, from its official beginning in 1517 (the date of Luther's ninety-five theses), showed varying attitudes to liturgy and music at different times and places. Luther himself was an admirer of music—particularly the music of Josquin—and felt that art polyphony performed a valuable function in divine service. Since his attitude towards the liturgy was liberal, permitting retention of most of the Latin Mass under certain circumstances, some Lutheran churches were able to make considerable use of music written for the Roman Catholic service. But Luther also encouraged the use of German in church, and favored congregational participation in the singing. For both of these purposes, new music had to be written, or at least adapted.

Other reformers took more extreme views. Zwingli and Calvin, two leaders in Swiss Protestantism, banned polyphony from their churches, requiring instead tunes to which the congregation could sing (in unison) the psalms in the vernacular. Between Luther's position and that of Calvin and Zwingli, almost every intermediate attitude found proponents. Such positions had this much in common: to a considerable extent, at least, the new churches would have to create their own music.

Lutheran music

The first Lutheran music to appear consists of monophonic tunes set to Protestant devotional poems. The poems, many by Luther himself, are in some case wholly original; others are translated and adapted from Latin hymns. Of the melodies, some were newly written (a few perhaps by Luther himself) while others were adaptations of plainsong melodies or even secular Lieder. The latter, when associated with their new texts, are contrafacta—a generic term for the retexting of an earlier composition, whether monophonic or polyphonic. While the use of contrafacta goes back to the twelfth century and beyond, it was particularly important in the sixteenth: by this means, secular madrigals could be made into motets, or Catholic motets into vernacular German pieces.

Chorale

Ultimately a great number of Lutheran melodies accumulated. They came to be called "chorales," because at that time the word "choraliter" denoted unison singing by congregation and choir, the use for which these tunes were intended.

In view of Luther's tolerance for art polyphony, it was natural that the chorale melodies should be used as bases for polyphonic compositions. The first collection of such pieces, by Johann Walther (1496-1570), appeared in 1524. The technique is that of the secular Lied: the chorale melody is given to the tenor voice of a four-part setting. The other three voices either may have more active figuration, or may move chordally with the chorale. The latter type (Ex. VI-21) is the direct ancestor of the characteristic chorale settings of the seventeenth and eighteenth centuries. It differs from its descendant, however, in its freer treatment of harmony and rhythm, as well as in its placement of the melody in the traditional tenor position, rather than on top, as later became the custom.

The chorale setting was the Lutheran counterpart of the secular Lied. While the simple chordal type continued to be composed, more elaborate settings also appeared, paralleling the increasing influence of Franco-Flemish style on the Lied during the sixteenth century. Pieces of this more complex type were in fact motets with German texts. Lutheran composers also produced motets not based on chorale tunes. While both these and the more elaborate chorale settings are in the general motet-tradition of the sixteenth century, Lutheran music rarely approaches the complexity achieved by some of the music for the Roman church.

Ex. VI-21

Lutheran musicians also made extensive use of music written for the Roman Catholic liturgy, and composers often set Latin texts as well as German ones. In consequence, the total repertoire available was rich and various.

Other denominations

The same can hardly be said for some of the more severe Protestant denominations, notably those of Switzerland, Holland, and France. Here the determining factor was the opposition of religious leaders to art polyphony. Both French Switzerland and Holland produced music to accommodate these severer views. Clemens non Papa, whose Catholic music is discussed in the first part of this chapter, wrote a collection of *Souterliedekens* (little psalm ongs). The texts are metrical Dutch translations of the psalms, intended for devotional use. The translations had been carefully designed to be sung to preexistent monophonic tunes of a popular nature. Clemens provided these melodies with very simple three-voice settings, the given tune appearing in either the top or middle voice. The music, well within the reach of amateur singers, was designed to be used in the home, not in church.

The Calvinists, centered in Geneva, had the psalms translated into French verse. The poems were then fitted to meodies—mostly adaptations of existing tunes from a wide variety of sources—by the musician Louis Bourgeois (ca. 1510-1561). Despite Calvin's disapproval, simple polyphonic settings of these melodies were often made, both by Bourgeois himself, and later by the important composer Claude Goudimel (killed in the massacre of the Huguenots at Lyons in 1572). The melodies used for the Genevan Psalter, as it is called, became permanently attached to the translations and gained a wide diffusion among Protestants: Bourgeois's tune known to England and America as "Old Hundredth" is still sung in thousands of churches. It was, in fact, in the area of monophonic melody that sixteenth-century Continental Protestantism most enriched music: the psalm-tunes and especially the chorales were to be of great importance in the future: they were to become, in simply harmonized form, the primary substance of Protestant hymnbooks; and the chorales were to serve as cantus firmi for a great repertoire of later Lutheran polyphony.

England.   The history of English music is a curious one, showing, between times of great activity, more periods of stagnation than is the case in most other countries. The work of Dufay, his contemporaries, and his immediate successors is hardly thinkable without Dunstable. But after achieving so much in the early fifteenth century, English music seems to have gone into decline for several decades (a fact remarked on by at least one Continental writer).

From the fifteenth century there survive a number of polyphonic "carols" (sacred songs with refrains; the term was not then restricted to Christmas music). These, however, are modest and conservative little pieces, in a style not too far from that of Dunstable. At the end of the century, the situation began to change. From around 1500, *Eton Choirbook* there survives a manuscript—the Eton Choirbook—containing a large repertoire of motets and Magnificat settings by English composers. While quite conservative compared with Continental music, this is music that shows a high level of technical competence and a distinct individuality. Characteristic traits are: an infrequent use of imitation; a predilection for large numbers of voices (many pieces are in six, eight, or even more voices); and well-defined sectional construction, the different sections often scored for different combinations of voices. Many of the Eton pieces contain large and complex passages set to a single word or syllable of text, producing a rich and imposing effect.

The music of the Eton Choirbook demonstrates that the period of English stagnation was over, and during the rest of the sixteenth century, the music of English composers nearly equals that of Continental musicians in both quality and variety.

Sacred music   English sacred music was at first little affected by the separation of the Anglican church from Rome (1534). Henry VIII, who initiated the break with the papacy, was, unlike Luther and Calvin, no reformer. At first the Anglican liturgy retained most of the features of the Latin Mass. Gradually, however, Protestant ideas began to take root in England, as many Continental reformers took refuge there from persecution. By the time of the brief and futile return to Roman Catholicism, under Mary (r. 1553-58), the first two versions of the *Book of Common Prayer* had already been issued, and all services were expected to be held in English. With the accession of Elizabeth I (r. 1558-1603), the independent Anglican church was restored, now largely Protestant in belief, but still to some extent Catholic in practice.

As a result, sixteenth-century English composers produced sacred music both with English text and with Latin—the latter often for the Roman rite, but sometimes for the *Anthem* Anglican. The chief English-language form, the anthem, was in most cases simply a motet with English words. The services, settings of the canticles for morning and evening prayer, often approximate in their treatment of text the style of the Gloria and Credo of the Latin Mass. Anglicanism retained (in translation) most of the Latin ordinary, and this, too, was frequently set to music. In addition, various settings, both monophonic and polyphonic, were made of the various items of the Anglican liturgy for which Latin equivalents were missing (the most famous set of these being John Merbecke's *Booke of Common Praier Noted* of 1550); and adaptations were made of the Continental metrical psalms.

The chief glories of English sacred music of the time, however, are to be found in the traditional categories of Latin Mass and motet and, to a lesser extent, in the anthem. The greatest composer of the earlier part of the century was Thomas Tallis (ca. 1505-85), most of whose surviving music is to Latin texts. Tallis was a master of all the techniques of his time, and used them to produce music of great expressivity. In his *In jejunio et fletu*, a somber motet on a somber text, Tallis makes sparing use of imitation, doubtless for expressive reasons. One characteristic mannerism of English polyphony is very prominent—the use of cross-relation, in which two forms of the same note (e.g., G and G♯, or B♭ and B♮) appear in different voices either simultaneously or in direct succession (Ex. VI-22). While cross-relation may be found occasionally in Continental music, it is much commoner among the English, who apparently relished the sharply dissonant effect produced. Even English composers do not use it gratuitously, however: it is always the product of logical melodic motion in the two voices concerned.

Cross-relation

par - ce po - pu- lo tu - o

par - ce po - - pu-lo   tu - - o { par - ce   po - pu-lo   tu - o

Do — mi — ne

par - ce po - pu-lo tu - - o   par - ce po - pu-lo

par — ce   po - pu- lo tu - - o   par — ce po - pu-lo

Spare thy people, Lord.

Ex. VI-22

William Byrd (1543-1623) is the equal of such men as Lasso and Palestrina. Although he remained faithful to the church of Rome all his life, he suffered none of the persecutions that were common in Elizabethan England. He held high positions in Anglican churches and produced fine music for the national church, although his works for the Roman rite are even better.

William Byrd

His style, like that of his predecessors and contemporaries in England, is a somewhat conservative version of the international style current all over Europe. Certain

English preferences may be discerned: fondness for cross-relation, and for scoring successive sections of a large piece for different combinations of voices; but the overall technique is similar to that of Continental music.

Byrd appears, however, to have been the first to write "verse anthems"—pieces in which passages for full chorus alternate with others for one, two, or several solo voices accompanied by organ (or other instruments). Verse anthems and verse services became a common and important genre in English church music.

For the Roman church, Byrd wrote three Masses, all employing the head-motive technique, and thus suggesting a certain conservatism. Much of his best music may be found in his motets, of which he published several collections between 1575 and 1607. *Tollite portas* appeared in the first part (1605) of Byrd's *Gradualia*, a collection of settings of texts of the Mass proper (Byrd, like Isaac, was one of the few composers of the time to give serious attention to the proper). The late date of the publication should be noted. While new stylistic trends were well on the way to displacing Renaissance style in Italy by 1605, the musical Renaissance in England had not yet run its course. *Tollite portas* could, at least as far as overall style and technique are concerned, have appeared in a Continental publication of the 1560s.

The piece sets the text of a gradual for Advent, but the associated plainsong melody is not employed. The basic technique is imitation, rather freely handled. In setting the text of the gradual verse, Byrd uses only three voices (Ex. VI-23), reintroducing the other two only at the final Alleluia, thus articulating the form by means of the typically English device of contrasted scoring. That Byrd was fully aware of Continental practices is shown by the motive he uses for "quis ascendit" (who will ascend)—an emphatically rising line that shows the influence of the madrigalists.

Who shall ascend the mountain of the Lord, and who shall stand in His holy place?　Ex. VI-23

There is good reason for the appearance of madrigalisms in English music of this time, for toward the end of the sixteenth century the Italian madrigal was imported into England and there domesticated. There had always been a continuing tradition of polyphonic secular song in England, but relatively little such music survives, and what there is is of secondary artistic importance. In 1588, two publications of the greatest moment appeared: William Byrd's *Psalmes, Sonets and Songs...,* and the *Musica transalpina,* edited by Nicholas Yonge. In the first, Byrd offered both sacred and secular pieces to English text, set for five voices; these are mostly reworkings of songs originally conceived for a single voice with instrumental accompaniment. In the second, the editor presented to the English public a considerable anthology of Italian madrigals, with texts translated into English. Although Byrd's pieces are by no means Italianate, they are often not too far from the madrigal in structure; and the appearance in print of such works by the most distinguished English composer doubtless gave impetus to the composition of secular music. The *Musica transalpina,* moreover, found a ready market (so much so that several other anthologies were published in the years immediately following), and the immediate reaction of English composers was to challenge the Italian imports with madrigals of their own.

Secular music: The English madrigal

Musica transalpina

In 1593, Thomas Morley (1557-1602?) published the first English madrigal collection, misleadingly entitled *Canzonets, or Little Short Songs to Three Voyces,* in which Italian style and technique were blended with native English qualities. This was the beginning of a flood of English madrigal publications by a considerable number of composers—a flood most concentrated in the years just after 1593, but continuing until 1627. Again, there is something of an anachronism here, for the English began to

English madrigalists

Ex. VI-24(a)

Ex. VI-24(b)

cultivate the madrigal just as it was entering its last phase in Italy, and they continued doing so long after it had been abandoned there in its traditional style.

The English madrigal was based entirely on Italian techniques: Marenzio was perhaps the "transalpine" master most admired. In general the English preferred the lighter, pastoral vein to the passionate style, although there are some notable exceptions in individual pieces. Many madrigals incorporate features that belong properly to the lighter genres of Italian secular music—the villanella and the balletto. Thus we find sections using the syllables "fa la la" (from the balletto), as well as unaltered repetitions of whole sections of music (from most of the lighter forms). Nevertheless, all of these Italian devices were thoroughly assimilated by native composers; the English madrigal has a style of its own.

Two of the leading composers were Thomas Weelkes (ca. 1575-1623) and John Wilbye (1574-1628). The latter left relatively little, but that little is of high quality. His *Stay Corydon*, first printed in 1609, shows the English madrigal at its finest. The pastoral text is handled with exquisite delicacy, and the abundant madrigalisms are always musically as well as textually appropriate. Particularly inventive is the repeated final section, where the text presents "follow" and "fly" in two successive lines. Wilbye twice uses the conventional close imitation, but in two refreshingly different ways (Ex. VI-24a, b).

The sudden flowering of the English madrigal is one of the chief jewels in the crown of Elizabethan culture. The abundance of its achievement is all the more astonishing when one considers that at the same time two other such creative outbursts were going on in English music—in the lute song and in music for keyboard (below, Chapter VII)—and that music was by no means the only art to be so productive.

SIXTEENTH-CENTURY VOCAL MUSIC.

I. **Principal forms.**

A. Mass. The cyclical Mass remained a principal form for composers throughout the century. Almost all the composers listed below wrote numerous
Masses. A typical unifying technique is the use of the same borrowed material in each movement; such material may be treated in the following ways:

Cantus firmus. By now an old-fashioned technique. Presentation of the borrowed melody in long notes in a single voice (or, occasionally, moving
from voice to voice).

Paraphrase. The preexistent melody serves as a source of melodic material
for all the voices; from it they derive motives for imitation, counterpoints,
etc. (Note how this differs from the single-voice elaboration paraphrase of
Dunstable, Dufay, etc.)

Parody. The use of a preexistent polyphonic composition as borrowed material, drawing on several or all voices at once as a source of musical
material.

B. Motet. Polyphonic compositions on liturgical, biblical or other sacred texts
were a principal type of 16th-century sacred music. They have no set form or
procedure: most of the prevailing techniques of the day are used for motets.
A chant melody may be used for paraphrase or cantus firmus (parody is not
generally used). Of particular importance, in motets and elsewhere, is the
use of persistent imitation, in which each phrase of text has its own melodic
motive imitated in all voices. Almost all the composers listed below wrote
many motets.

C. Chanson. The term applied to any secular piece with French text; the *formes
fixes* had lost their fixity by the end of the 15th century. Some chansons (by
Josquin, Clemens, Gombert, etc.) are polyphonic and motet-like. Another
sort, called "Parisian chanson," was begun in the 1520s by Claudin de Sermisy and Clément Janequin; this type, predominantly chordal, syllabic, and
involving repetition of sections, was cultivated throughout the century.

D. Madrigal. The vogue in Italy for the frottola (simple, harmonic settings for
performing—but not expressing—poetic texts) gave way ca. 1520 to the
madrigal, characterized by superior poetry. The madrigal remained the
principal form of Italian secular vocal music throughout the century. In its
early period (before 1550) it is characterized by a uniform mood throughout
a composition: principal composers of this type of madrigal are Costanza
Festa, Jacques Arcadelt, Philippe Verdelot, and Adrian Willaert. The later
madrigal is increasingly concerned with precise expression of the changing
meaning of the text. Not only is general mood conveyed, but individual details are depicted by various technical devices. Composers in this style in-

clude Cipriano de Rore, Giaches Wert, Luca Marenzio, and Claudio Monteverdi. The English importation of the Italian madrigal led to a late 16th-century English school of madrigal writing, including Thomas Morley, William Byrd, Thomas Weelkes, and John Wilbye.

II.   Composers.

Agricola, Alexander (ca. 1446–1506). Composer in the Netherlandish style who worked in Italy, Burgundy, and Spain; Masses, motets, and chansons.

Arcadelt, Jacques (ca. 1505–ca. 1560). Northerner who worked in Rome; Masses, motets, chansons, madrigals.

Byrd, William (1543–1623). English Roman Catholic, who wrote both Anglican and Catholic Church music, in addition to secular and instrumental pieces; pupil of Tallis, and co-holder with him of music-printing monopoly for England. See section III for a comparative view of his output.

Cara, Marco (d. ca. 1530). A frottola composer of the court of Isabella d'Este; simple, chordal pieces with repetitions designed as vehicles for poetic texts.

Clemens, Jacobus (Clemens non Papa; ca. 1510–ca. 1550). Netherlandish composer of Masses, motets, chansons, madrigals; many psalm settings; much imitation, but more cadences, clearer than Gombert.

Des Prez, Josquin (ca. 1450–1521). Best and most famous composer of his age; among his numerous Masses, the *Missa Mater Patris* may be the first complete parody Mass; motets of exceptional beauty and variety.

Dowland, John (1562–1626). English lutenist and composer, also widely known on the Continent; especially known for his lute music and his solo songs with lute accompaniment (see Chapter VII).

Festa, Costanzo (ca. 1490–1545). Roman composer; Masses, motets, hymns, madrigals.

Gabrieli, Andrea (ca. 1520–86). Possibly a pupil of Willaert; organist of St. Mark's in Venice; composer of madrigals, Masses, psalms, and motets (many in the polychoral style for which St. Mark's was renowned).

Gabrieli, Giovanni (ca. 1555–1612). Pupil of his uncle Andrea Gabrieli; second organist of St. Mark's; Venetian polychoral motets, and pieces which combine vocal and instrumental groups.

Gesualdo, Carlo (ca. 1560–1613). Italian composer, primarily of madrigals. His passionately expressive style employs extremes of chromaticism.

Gibbons, Orlando (1583–1625). English organist and composer; much Anglican Church music, including "verse" anthems (pieces containing accompanied solo sections); also secular vocal and instrumental music.

Gombert, Nicolas (ca. 1500–56). Northerner who served the Imperial Chapel; composed mostly motets; dense, continuous texture, imitative and contrapuntal.

Hassler, Hans Leo (1564–1612). Pupil of Andrea Gabrieli; chief musician of Nuremberg, later serving the Elector of Saxony; Masses, motets, Lieder and madrigals, in a graceful style emphasizing light melodies.

Isaac, Heinrich (ca. 1450–1517). International master of all current styles; Masses, motets, and secular pieces; composer of *Choralis Constantinus*, a complete setting of Mass propers for Sundays and feasts of the year, using chant as cantus firmus or paraphrase.

Janequin, Clément (ca. 1485–ca. 1560). French composer; Masses, motets, Parisian chansons, including long descriptive ones.

La Rue, Pierre de (d. 1518). Born in Picardy, served in the Spanish Netherlands; composer of Masses, motets, chansons, an outstanding Requiem.

Lasso, Orlando di (1532–94). Very prolific composer, widely traveled and celebrated; worked in Italy and in Antwerp and Munich. For a comparative view of his works, see section III.

Le Jeune, Claude (ca. 1530–1600). French composer; a member of Baïf's Académie, he wrote musical settings reflecting the quantitative meters of "vers mesurés à l'antique."

Luzzaschi, Luzzascho (1545–1607). Ferrarese madrigalist, pupil of Rore; five books of madrigals; also some famous madrigals for one, two, or three sopranos with keyboard accompaniment.

Marenzio, Luca (1553–99). Italian madrigalist; worked mainly in Rome; 16 books of madrigals, 5 of *villanelle*; motets.

Monte, Philippe de (1521–1603). Belgian composer; worked in Italy, England, Germany; madrigals, motets, Masses.

Monteverdi, Claudio. See appendix to Chapter VII.

Morales, Cristóbal de (ca. 1500–53). A Spaniard who also worked in Rome; Masses, motets, Magnificats, lamentations.

Morley, Thomas (1557–1602). Pupil of William Byrd, edited English versions of Italian madrigals and *balletti*, author of *A Plaine and Easie Introduction to Practicall Musicke* (1597); wrote many madrigals and ballets of his own.

Mouton, Jean (ca. 1470–1522). French composer, teacher of Willaert; Masses, motets, a little secular music; smooth melodic contours.

Palestrina, Giovanni Pierluigi da (1524–94). Worked in Rome; principally a composer of sacred music. His style is thought to be the epitome of Renaissance vocal polyphony. For a comparative view of his works, see section III.

Rore, Cipriano da (1516–65). Flemish composer; worked in Italy, mainly in Ferrara. His madrigals have a particular expressive quality which set the style for later madrigalists.

Senfl, Ludwig (ca. 1490–ca. 1556). A composer who served the Bavarian court; pupil of Isaac, he completed the *Choralis Constantinus*. Masses, motets, Lieder.

Sermisy, Claudin de (ca. 1490–1562). French composer; Masses, motets, Parisian chansons.

Tallis, Thomas (ca. 1505–85). English composer, co-holder with William Byrd of music-printing monopoly from 1575; much Latin church music, including a famous 40-voice motet.

Tomkins, Thomas (ca. 1571–1656). English composer, organist at Worcester Cathedral; Anglican Church music, almost all contained in *Musica Deo Sacra*, printed 1668; also secular vocal and instrumental music.

Tromboncino, Bartolomeo (d. ca. 1535). Composer at Mantuan court of Isabella d'Este; the principal composer (with Marco Cara) of the poetry settings known as frottola, strambotto, sonetto, etc.

Verdelot, Philippe (d. ca. 1550). Northern composer who worked in Venice; about 100 madrigals, one Mass.

Victoria, Tomás Luis da (1548–1611). Spanish composer who spent much of his life in Rome; principally sacred music. For a view of his output, see section III.

Weelkes, Thomas (ca. 1575–1623). English composer of madrigals. Also some church music.

Wert, Giaches de (1535–96). Northerner who worked in Italy, principally in Mantua and Ferrara; his principal output is his 12 books of madrigals.

Wilbye, John (1574–1628). English composer, especially noted for madrigals of a serious, expressive character.

Willaert, Adrian (ca. 1490–1562). Northerner who composed in Venice; Masses, motels, chansons, madrigals; not consistently imitative; smooth melodic lines. An influential teacher.

III.   Comparative output of four late-16th century composers.

A. Giovanni Pierluigi da Palestrina (1524–94).

105 Masses: about half parody, the others mainly paraphrase
265 Motets
 68 Offertories in motet style
 45 Hymns
     Liturgical music: 8 Magnificats, 11 Litanies; Lamentations; etc.
 60 Spiritual madrigals
163 Madrigals

B. Orlando di Lasso (1532–94).

 54 Masses survive: mostly parody
516 Motets
123 Magnificats
     Miscellaneous liturgical music
148 French chansons
176 Italian madrigals, villanellas, etc.
 93 German Lieder

C. Tomás Luis da Victoria (1548–1611).

 21 Masses
 61 Motets
 35 Hymns
     Liturgical music for Holy Week (incl. Lamentations)
  7 Psalms
 18 Magnificats

D. William Byrd (1543–1623).

  3 Masses: all freely composed

240 Motets (incl. 2 books of *Gradualia*, settings of Catholic Mass propers)
84 Anthems (English-language motets), incl. several "verse" anthems—
    pieces which include sections of accompanied solos
   Miscellaneous English liturgical music
91 Madrigals
45 Pieces of instrumental chamber music
   Many pieces of virginal (solo keyboard) music

IV. Bibliography

Reese, Gustave: *Music in the Renaissance*, rev. ed., New York, 1959. The basic
book for this period; it provides exhaustive bibliographical references.

V. Editions of Music.

Modern editions of much music of this period are available only in large, multi-
volume works or in monumental series. In the list below, a number of these publications have been cited in abbreviated form, as follows:

CMM   *Corpus mensurabilis musicae*, ed. A. Carapetyan. Mostly collected editions of the music of 15th- and 16th-century composers.

DdT   *Denkmäler deutscher Tonkunst*, ser. 1, 65 vols, 1892–1931.

DTO   *Denkmäler der Tonkunst in Oesterreich*, 115 vols. to date, 1894–   .
Publications in this series are numbered both by volume and, up to volume 83, by year (Jahrgang, abbrev. Jg.). Many year designations are
subdivided, eg., V:1.

EDM   *Das Erbe deutscher Musik*, ser. 1

EMS   *The English Madrigal School*, ed. E. H. Fellowes, 36 vols, 1913–24; rev.
ed., *The English Madrigalists*, ed. Thurston Dart, 1958–   .

ESL   *The English School of Lutenist Song Writers*, ed. E. H. Fellowes, 1920–
32; rev. ed., *The English Lute-Songs*, ed. Thurston Dart, 1951–   .

MMRF *Les maîtres musiciens de la Renaissance française*, ed. Henry Expert.

Agricola
   Opera omnia, ed. E. R. Lerner, CMM 22 (1961–   ).

Arcadelt
   Opera omnia, ed. Albert Seay, CMM 31 (1965–   ).
   The Chansons of Jacques Arcadelt, ed. E. B. Helm, *Smith College Music Ar-
chives* vol. 5, 1942.

Byrd
   The Collected Works of William Byrd, ed. E. H. Fellowes, 20 vols., 1927–50.
   Psalms, Sonnets, and Songs of Sadness and Piety, EMS vol. 14.
   Songs of Sundry Natures, EMS vol. 15.
   Psalms, Songs and Sonnets, EMS vol. 16.

Cara
   Le frottole nell' edizione principe di Ottaviano Petrucci, libri I, II, e III, ed.
      G. Cesari et al., *Instituta et Monumenta* ser. I, vol. I, 1954.

Des Prez
   Werken, ed. A. Smijers, 49 vols., Leipzig, Amsterdam, 1921–62.

Dowland

>The English School of Lutenist Song Writers, ed. E. H. Fellowes, 1920–32; rev. ed., The English Lute-Songs, ed. Thurston Dart, 1951–
>
>First Book of Airs, 1597, ESL vols. 1–2.
>
>Second Book of Airs, 1600, ESL vols. 5–6.
>
>Third Book of Airs, 1603, ESL vols. 10–11.
>
>A Pilgrim's Solace, ESL vols. 12, 14.
>
>Ayres for Four Voices, transcribed by E. H. Fellowes, ed. Thurston Dart and Nigel Fortune, Musica Britannica vol. 6, 1953.

Festa

>Opera omnia, ed. A. Main, CMM 25, 1962.
>
>Hymni per totum annum, ed. Glen Haydon, Monumenta polyphonica italica, vol. 3, 1958.

Gabrieli, Giovanni

>Opera omnia, ed. Denis Arnold, CMM 12, (1956–   ).

Gibbons

>Orlando Gibbons, Tudor Church Music, vol. 4, London, 1925.
>
>Verse Anthems, ed. D. Wulstan, Early English Church Music, vol. 3, London (ca. 1964).

Gesualdo

>Sämtliche Werke, ed. Wilhelm Weismann and Glenn E. Watkins 1958–

Gombert

>Opera omnia, ed. J. Schmidt-Görg, CMM 6 (1951–   ).

Hassler

>Werke I: Cantiones sacrae, ed. H. Gehrmann, DdT vol. 2, 1894.
>
>Werke II: Messen, ed. J. Auer, DdT vol. 7, 1902.
>
>Werke III: Sacri concentus, ed. J. Auer, DdT vols. 23–24, 1906.

Isaac

>Choralis Constantinus liber I, 1550, ed. E. Bezecny and W. Rabl. DTO Jg 5: 1 (vol. 10), 1898.
>
>Choralis Constantinus liber II, ed. Anton von Webern, DTO Jg. 16: 1 (vol. 32).
>
>Choralis Constantinus Book III, ed. L. Cuyler, Ann Arbor, Mich., 1950.
>
>Weltliche Werke, ed. Johannes Wolf, DTO Jg. 14: 1 (vol. 28), 1907.

Janequin

>Chansons polyphoniques, ed. A. Tillman Merritt and François Lesure.
>
>Chansons (Attaingnant, 1529?), ed. Henry Expert, MMRF vol. VII, 1898.

Lasso

>Sämtliche Werke (incomplete). ed. F.X. Haberl and A. Sandberger, 21 vols., Leipzig. 1894–1926; new ser., Kassel, 1956–

Le Jeune

>Octonaires de la vanité du Monde (IX–XII); Pseaumes des Meslanges de 1612; Dialogue à sept parties, ed. H. Expert, Les Monuments de la musique française au temps de la Renaissance, vol. 8, 1928.
>
>Dodecacorde (1598), pt. I, MMRF vol. XI, 1900.
>
>Le Printemps, pts. I–III, MMRF XII–XIV, 1900–01.

Marenzio

>Sämtliche Werke, ed. A. Einstein, 2 vols., publ. in Publikationen älterer Musik . . . der deutschen Musikgesellschaft, Jg. V:1 (1920) and VI (1931).

Monte

 Opera, ed. C. van den Borren and J. van Nuffel, 26 vols., (Düsseldorf, 1927–35).

Morley

 The First Book of Canzonets to Two Voices; Canzonets or Little Short Songs to Three Voices, EMS vol. 1.

 First Book of Madrigals to Four Voices; Two Canzonets to Four Voices, EMS vol. 2.

 Canzonets or Little Short Airs to Five and Six Voices; Two Madrigals, EMS vol. 3.

 First Book of Ballets to Five Voices, EMS vol. 4.

Palestrina

 Le opere complete, ed. R. Casimiri, 30 vols., Rome, 1939–62; an older ed. by T. de Witt, F. X. Haberl, et al., 33 vols., Leipzig, 1862–1907, repr. 1968.

Rore

 Opera omnia, ed. B. Meier, CMM 14, 3 vols., 1959–63.

 The Madrigals of Cipriano de Rore for Three and Four Voices, ed. G. P. Smith, Smith College Music Archives vol. 6, 1943.

Senfl

 Sieben Messen, ed. E. Löhrer and O. Ursprung, EDM vol. 5, 1936.

 Deutsche Lieder, ed. A. Geering, EDM vol. 6, 1938.

 Motetten, ed. W. Gerstenberg, EDM vol. 13, 1938.

 Deutsche Lieder, zweiter Teil, ed. A. Geering and W. Altwigg, EDM vol. 15, 1939.

Tallis

 Thomas Tallis, Tudor Church Music vol. 6, 1928.

Tomkins

 Thomas Tomkins, Part I: Services, ed. A. Ramsbotham, Tudor Church Music vol. 8, 1928.

 Songs of Three, Four, Five and Six Parts, EMS vol. 18, 1922.

 Musica Deo Sacra, pts. I and II, ed. Bernard Rose, Early English Church Music vols. 5 and 9, London (ca. 1959).

Tromboncino

 See Cara.

Verdelot

 Opera omnia, ed. A.-M. Bragard, CMM 28 (1966–   ).

Victoria

 Opera omnia, ed. F. Pedrell, 8 vols., 1902–13.

Weelkes

 Madrigals, EMS vols. 9–12.

Wert

 Collected Works, ed. C. MacClintock, CMM 24 (1961–   ).

Wilbye

 Madrigals, EMS vols. 6–7.

Willaert

 Opera omnia, ed. H. Zenck, CMM 3 (1950–   ).

VII

SIXTEENTH CENTURY INSTRUMENTAL MUSIC
AND PROGRESSIVE TENDENCIES IN THE LATE 1500s

In the sixteenth century, instrumental music achieved a position as a separate and independent art, capable of producing works that, at their best, could rival the best vocal works of the period. An instrumental repertoire of enormous size and great diversity began to accumulate, slowly at first, but with increasing rapidity as the years passed. This apparently radical change from the modest nature of preserved fifteenth-century instrumental music can be traced to several causes.

The increased importance of cities assured the rise of the middle class, and prosperous merchants quite naturally attempted to imitate the social patterns of the aristocracy. The use of music had long been a prominent feature of aristocratic life, and thus passed by way of emulation into the life of the bourgeoisie. While this favored vocal as well as instrumental performance, it was perhaps more influential in the case of the latter. The presence of hired players at a middle-class banquet was an almost automatic guarantee of exalted social standing for the host.

The invention of music printing in the first years of the century permitted the wide diffusion of music at relatively small cost. This at least permitted, and quite probably encouraged, amateurs to learn to play instruments. In any event, there arose a demand for instrumental music suited for amateur performance (a demand that has continued virtually to the present day).

Finally, and perhaps most important, the virtuoso performer achieved greater importance than ever before. Many virtuosi became true celebrities, who could command large fees from wealthy lovers of music. While at the same time the tradition of instrumental improvisation continued, it no longer seemed suitable to allow such improvisations to perish without leaving any record. Thus means of notation were improved in order to record instrumental music of great complexity, and, in turn, performers often became serious composers, who relied only in part upon improvisation. (The compositions of a virtuoso performer were generally issued in print only upon the retirement or death of the composer: no virtuoso was inclined to supply competitors with his own music.)

These factors help to explain the phenomenal rise of sixteenth-century instrumental music; and they help account as well for the increased interest in such music on the part of the churches, the courts, and the houses of the wealthy — the first requiring liturgical polyphony, the others dance music and entertainment music.

Types of sixteenth-century instrumental music.   Considering the various factors that contributed to the growth of instrumental music in the sixteenth century, it is not surprising that the repertoire is large and complex, with wide divergences of style, function, and medium. At one pole stands dance music, functional in origin, and structurally conditioned by its function. At the opposite extreme stands music conditioned by nothing other than the composer's fancy. Between these extremes lies a considerable range of instrumental types, most of which are related in one way or another to vocal music. While styles varied considerably from place to place and from time to time during the century, certain basic categories may be distinguished in the instrumental repertoire.

Music based on vocal models

One common practice was the instrumental performance of a piece originally composed for voices. Performances of this sort may on occasion have been absolutely identical with the vocal originals. A motet for five voices, for example, might simply be played by five instruments having the appropriate ranges. Since the players would merely use the music printed (or written) for singers, the details of such performances — how often vocal music was so rendered, and with what instruments — cannot be known with certainty. Indeed many publications of the sixteenth century carry subtitles indicating that their content was suitable both for singing and for playing; and a few contain wholly textless music, with directions suggesting that the pieces could be sung, using solmization syllables instead of words, as well as played. Vocal and instrumental music still were not always mutually exclusive categories.

Instrumental performance of vocal works had, however, two limitations. In the first place, it was in practice limited to use by instrumental ensembles, since vocal music appeared in separate partbooks, one for each voice, and it is exceedingly difficult for a soloist to read out of several books at once. Secondly, it takes no account of the peculiar qualities and abilities of instruments, most of which can easily produce rapid ornamental figures different from the kinds of ornaments congenial to the voice (this despite claims that the music was "apt for voices or instruments").

For these reasons, specifically instrumental revisions of vocal pieces were often made, either for ensemble or for solo instrument. In some cases, the change was to a mixed medium, rather than a wholly instrumental one: typical are the many arrangements for solo voice and lute of secular pieces originally intended for vocal ensemble. In the transcription of Tromboncino's four-voice *Poi che'l ciel* (Ex. VII-1), the transcriber followed the original faithfully, merely omitting one inner voice to make the lute accompaniment less difficult.

Even commoner, however — and more significant — are vocal pieces revised for wholly instrumental performance. In these, the substance of the original is maintained, but it is usually overlaid by rich and specifically instrumental ornamentation.

Diminution

Naturally the type of ornamentation — or diminution, as it is often called — is determined by the type of instrument involved: one does not write for lute as one does for organ. But certain basic devices — scales and rapid trill-like passages — are common to all types of diminution.

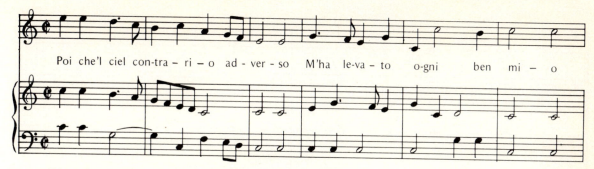

Poi che'l ciel con-tra – ri – o ad – ver-so M'ha le-va – to o-gni ben mi – o

Since the adverse heavens have taken from all my good.

Ex. VII-1

Dance music

The sixteenth century produced vast quantities of dance music — pieces that could actually be used to accompany dances, but that could also be played and enjoyed simply as music. (In fact, music for actual dancing was probably more often improvised than composed.) Dance music was composed both for instrumental ensemble, and for solo instruments such as the lute or harpsichord. Whatever the medium, such music is necessarily conditioned by the nature of the steps to be danced: the number of phrases and their lengths are determined by the dance pattern. In practice, this almost invariably results in music of regular rhythm and fairly short phrases. Thus dance pieces are usually built out of relatively short sections; but it is common to find two or more different dances linked together in a loose sequence to form a larger piece — the most common arrangement being a sedate dance in duple meter followed by a quicker one in triple meter. In many cases, the dances in such a group share nothing but the same final tone and a general similarity of style. Often, however, they are more closely interrelated. In Example VII-2, showing the first section or "strain" of each of two dances forming a set, the music of the second dance is merely an altered form, or variation, of the first.

Variation types

The technique of variation acquired great importance in sixteenth-century instrumental music, often, but by no means always, in connection with the dance. Several types of variation may be distinguished. In one, the variation shares with its original (called the "theme" when variation is the essential technique of the piece) the same phrase structure and, in addition, the same basic harmonies at the same points in the

Pavan

Ex. VII-2(a)

Galliard

Ex. VII-2(b)

phrase. The melody of the variation(s), however, is different from that of the original. In another type the variation maintains some form of the original melody as well as the harmonies and phrase structure. Example VII-2b belongs to this class: it achieves variety by casting the melody in a new rhythm and meter. But it is equally possible to keep the original meter and achieve variety by applying diminution (Ex. VII-3).

Ex. VII-3

Somewhat apart from these two variation types stands another variety that is rarely found in dance music, but more often in instrumental music intended for sacred use. In this type, a melody is maintained intact in every variation, in the manner of a cantus firmus — which it very often is. The materials used by the other voices are not necessarily related from one variation to another (although they may be). In the cantus-firmus type variation, the phrase structure of the variations is not necessarily constant.

In the sixteenth century, an especially important type of variation was that based on certain well-known, standard harmonic progressions. These are often considered to be "ostinato" compositions — that is, variations on a given bass line. In fact, however, the bass parts of such variations are generally quite free in appearance, although they do touch upon certain obligatory notes (one at the beginning of each measure, for example) in a predetermined order.

Each of these standard harmonic progressions had a latent upper voice as well as a bass, but the actual melodies make such ingenious use of ornamentation that the underlying line is — to modern ears, at least — scarcely apparent. Three of the most popular of these standard progressions were the *passamezzo antico*, the *passamezzo moderno*, and the *romanesca*. Example VII-4a shows the abstract two-voice structure of the *romanesca* (still familiar as the basis of the popular tune "Greensleeves"), and Example VII-4b the first of a set of variations on the *romanesca* pattern. Here the bass of the pattern is entirely clear, and the upper voice hardly less so. Later variations in the same set treat the traditional material more freely.

Variations on standard harmonic patterns

Ex. VII-4(a)

Ex. VII-4(b)

In the case of these standard progressions, the usual criterion of variation form — the presence of two or more sections sharing certain common features — may disappear: a single variation may be written on the *passamezzo antico*, for example. Any sixteenth-century musician would recognize this as a variation on a familiar theme, although a modern hearer might discern no connection with the idea of variation.

While sacred cantus firmi were sometimes used as the basis for variations, they were also set — most often for organ but also for other instruments — in non-variational fashion for actual liturgical use. The fifteenth-century tradition of the organ Mass (above, Chapter V) was continued and strengthened in the sixteenth, the basic principle — alternation of choral plainsong with composed polyphony for the organ — remaining the same. Instrumental cantus-firmus settings do not generally resemble vocal treatments: they are freer and less tightly organized, and the cantus firmus itself is often treated with considerable liberty.

Treatment of sacred cantus firmi

There remains a large and various body of pieces which are free both in form and (frequently, at least) in function. In many cases, no consistent formal principle whatever is apparent, save for the desire to show the instrument(s) off to best advantage. Most pieces of this sort are solo works for lute or keyboard. Like their fifteenth-century

Free pieces: fantasia, toccata, ricercare, canzona

ancestors, they are apt to rely heavily on scales and ornamental figuration. Example VII-5, from an early composition for lute, shows this quasi-improvisatory style at its freest.

Ex. VII-5

Another free type of instrumental piece borrows from the motet its basic structural method of successive points of imitation, even though the actual materials are freely invented, and often idiomatically instrumental. Later in the sixteenth century, the improvisatory and imitative styles were combined to produce works in which free ornamental sections alternated with slower passages in imitation.

The nomenclature employed for these types is confusing and inconsistent. Since the essential characteristic of all such pieces was their freedom from any preexistent materials or conditions, the most appropriate term was "fantasia" (i.e., depending solely on the composer's fancy). This term was, in fact, often used, for both improvisatory and imitative pieces. So also were the titles ricercare and (later) canzona. Both of these ultimately came to be associated with imitative pieces, as did "fantasia" as well. "Toccata" was generally restricted to pieces with prominent improvisatory or virtuoso elements. "Intonation" and "prelude" both refer to function (usually the setting of the pitch for a subsequent vocal piece), but such pieces were also generally "free" in style, although smaller than the toccata.

The sixteenth-century instrumental repertoire.   The principal forms used by composers of sixteenth-century instrumental music have been examined. It remains to survey some of the vast extant literature in a historical rather than typological fashion. This survey will concentrate primarily on music for solo instruments: the reader may assume the flourishing of an ensemble tradition (especially for dance music) throughout the century.

Italy took and kept a position of leadership in instrumental music long before she did in vocal music. At a time when the modest frottola was Italy's only contribution to the vocal repertoire, Italian players were already in demand both at home and abroad, and a school of Italian instrumental composers was flourishing. The first printed instrumental music appeared in 1507, and the remainder of the century saw the appearance of an enormous number of publications for various media. Lute music stood first in popularity, but music for keyboard instruments and for ensemble was also actively cultivated.

Many early compositions for lute (apart from dance music) are called fantasia or ricercare. The earliest surviving specimens of this type are short improvisatory pieces of rather modest interest (see Ex. VII-5). Development was extremely rapid, however, and by the time of Francesco da Milano (1497-1543), the fantasia had become a serious and important art work. Francesco, called "the divine" by his contemporaries, was a celebrated lutenist and the first great Italian composer of the Renaissance. Of his considerable output, most consists of pieces entitled fantasia or ricercare, the rest being lute versions of vocal works. (Such versions are called "intabulations," after "tablature," the type of notation employed for lute music.)

A few of Francesco's fantasias are reminiscent of the early, simple type, but the majority are both complex and impressive. The excerpt given in Example VII-6 is

Italian lute music

From *The Lute Music of Francesco Canova da Milano*, ed. Arthur Ness, Harvard University Press, 1970. Used by permission.

Ex. VII-6

stylistically typical. The piece from which it is taken is sectional, in the manner of the vocal motet; but the absence of text — and hence of any reason to introduce distinctively new material for each section — permits a tighter continuity. Over half of the fantasia is devoted to the elaboration of the initial melodic idea. Imitation is prominent, but often informal, dissolving frequently into virtuoso passages.

The rest of the century saw a rich continuation of Italian lute music, but hardly any composer whose work surpassed that of Francesco. The repertoire includes fantasias, dance pieces, and variations, but much of the music remains unpublished, and its detailed history remains to be written.

Italian keyboard music, especially that for organ, is better known, if only because the repertoire is much smaller. The organ at this time was not exclusively a church-related instrument, and chamber organs were often used for dance and other secular music. There is also a considerable amount of music that may have been played on either the organ or the harpsichord: the sources give no information. Still, it is as a church instrument that the organ called forth the most important music. In addition to the organ Mass, there also arose organ pieces less strictly functional in nature, among others the ricercare, which developed along much the same lines as the lute fantasia, with the difference that the organ's ability to sustain tones made possible a more complex and explicit polyphony than was possible on the lute. Related to the ricercare was the canzona, which, as its name suggests, derived ultimately from the French chanson. Thus it was lighter in character than the ricercare and often incorporated repetition schemes, as did its vocal model. Pieces like these had no formal place in the liturgy, but could be played at any time during a service when music was felt to be

Italian keyboard music

Fig. VII-1: *Annibale Caracci (1560-1609), Lute Player. The instrument, the positions of the hands, and even the notation are all realistically depicted. (Photograph Alinari.)*

appropriate. (Ricercari and canzone were also written for instrumental ensemble — indeed the same piece may appear in rather simple style for ensemble, and in a more ornamented version for keyboard.)

Of especial interest is the toccata, for in pieces of this type the sonorous capacities of the organ can be exploited in an especially effective way. While the toccata was bound by no formal scheme, composers of the second half of the century generally favored a form in which passages in rapid and elaborate figuration alternated with chordal or imitative sections — thus taking advantage of the organ's agility, as well as its power to sustain tones indefinitely. The latter quality lends particular force to dissonant suspensions, with the result that a few toccatas are built almost entirely of chains of suspensions, with no rapid passages at all. One characteristic of later organ music was generally absent from Italian works of the period: the regular use of the pedal keyboard. Since many Italian organs were not equipped with pedals, their employment had to be at most optional.

One of the best-known Italian organ composers was Claudio Merulo (1533-1604): the beginning of one of his toccatas is shown in Example VII-7. Merulo passed much of career at Venice, where organ and other instrumental music was especially actively

Ex. VII-7

cultivated. As has been noted (above, Chapter VI), Venetian composers had often written for two or more vocal choirs, taking advantage of the spatial effects possible in the great church of St. Mark's. It was natural to translate this type of effect to instrumental music, and there were, significantly, always two official organists at St. Mark's. The most characteristic Venetian specialty was music for two or more instrumental ensembles. Thus, near the end of the century, canzone for eight, twelve, or even more instruments, grouped into antiphonal choirs, were composed. Such works, are, however, intimately linked to similar compositions employing both voices and instruments, and showing signs of a new stylistic orientation, to be treated later.

Spain

Spain also produced an important body of instrumental music during the sixteenth century. The most favored instruments were the organ and the vihuela, the latter a relative of the guitar (Spain stood alone in its lack of interest in the lute). The first publication for vihuela dates from 1536, but the sophistication of the music suggests considerable development earlier. The principal forms are the free improvisatory piece (commonest in the earlier publications, and similar to the earliest Italian lute fantasias), the imitative fantasia, intabulated vocal music, and a number of remarkable sets of variations ("diferencias") on traditional tunes or harmonic progressions (Ex. VII-4b is an instance). In addition to these purely instrumental genres, settings for solo voice and vihuela were made of works originally written for vocal ensemble, and original songs for voice and vihuela were composed.

Antonio de Cabezón

Although the harpsichord is known to have been used in Spain, the surviving keyboard music is intended for the organ. Spanish organ music is dominated by another major Renaissance composer, Antonio de Cabezón (ca. 1500-66). Cabezón's style, though rather restrained and severe, nonetheless takes good advantage of the technical possibilities of the organ. His works include compositions in the forms employed by the vihuelists (keyboard fantasias are called tientos), as well as cantus-firmus settings intended for church performance.

France

From France and the Low Countries, on the other hand, there survives an abundance of lute music, but it is mostly of a rather modest sort — dances and simple intabulations. Although native virtuosi are known, the most famous lutenists in France were foreigners such as Albert de Ripe, an Italian whose works were posthumously published in France. In addition to music for solo lute, the *air de cour*, or song with lute accompaniment, was extensively cultivated.

French keyboard prints began in 1531, and contain for the most part transcriptions of motets and chansons, with some dances, and a few liturgical pieces. For some time thereafter, little keyboard music survives. While it is known that some Frenchmen were active as builders of organs and harpsichords, and some as performers — and thus almost certainly as composers — their music is lost. Only Jean Titelouze (1563-1633) is known as a composer for organ — a late and isolated figure who produced cantus-firmus settings in a severe, contrapuntal, and (for their date) conservative style.

Germany

While Germany produced a good deal of lute music (mostly dance music and arrangements of songs), German organ music is on the whole more important, if only in prefiguring the enormous output of music for organ produced during the following century and a half. An organ publication by Arnolt Schlick appeared as early as 1512, containing for the most part cantus-firmus settings in thoroughly idiomatic organ style. Several important composers of vocal music also wrote for organ, but little of this repertoire is now extant. In the later sixteenth century, the process of diminution or "coloration" — the addition of more or less stereotyped ornamental figures to a given melody — became the central concern of most organ composers, and there are many pieces that are little more than series of scales and trills, without much musical imagination. The reaction to the relative sterility of the "colorists" was not to come fully until the seventeenth century.

Naturally the Roman-Lutheran division in Germany led to a certain separation of repertoires: Lutheran composers set chorales, while Catholics remained faithful to the Gregorian repertoire. But there was no radical difference in technique, and the instrumental music of both confessions is approximately the same in style.

The Netherlands: Jan Pieterszoon Sweelinck

The Netherlands produced an extremely important composer of keyboard music: Jan Pieterszoon Sweelinck (1562-1621). An organist by profession, Sweelinck wrote fantasias, variations, and other works for organ, as well as a considerable quantity of distinguished vocal music. An important feature of Sweelinck's style is his frequent employment of consistent melodic-rhythmic figuration throughout several consecutive measures. This abstract "pattern music," as it has been called, was to serve as an important ingredient in the seventeenth century, both in instrumental and in vocal music.

Sweelinck was also important as a teacher, and many German organists of the next generation had their training with him. But his connection with England was equally important. His music was widely known there, and appears in British manuscripts along with music by English composers.

Indeed Sweelinck was clearly influenced by English composers of instrumental music, who produced a distinguished repertoire that parallels, both in its quality and its relatively late date, English vocal music of the late sixteenth and early seventeenth centuries. Many English sources are devoted to the lute song, a genre intended for solo voice with lute accompaniment, but often published in an alternative version for vocal ensemble as well. In the latter form, the lute song bears a superficial resemblance to the contemporary English madrigal, but there is no real relationship. The versions for lute and voice are clearly the original ones; the songs are strophic, often with internal repetitions; the melodies are simple and symmetrical, and the music seldom attempts to illustrate the text in madrigalian fashion.

The finest composer of songs of this type was the lutenist John Dowland (1563-1626). His work is distinguished by exceptional harmonic and contrapuntal richness in the accompaniment, and by a frequently melancholy melodic charm. *I saw my lady weep* (Ex. VII-8) is also notable for its chromaticism.

The English lute school: John Dowland

Dowland was also an important composer for solo lute. His works for the instrument include many dance pieces, as well as a number of long and serious fantasias of the imitative sort. The latter represent some of the finest lute music ever written.

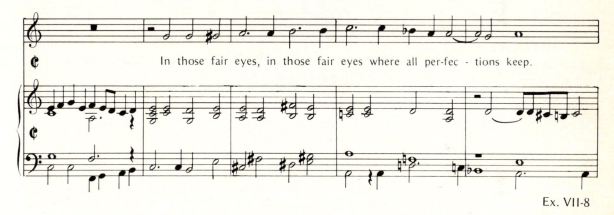

In those fair eyes, in those fair eyes where all per-fec - tions keep.

Ex. VII-8

Nevertheless, English lute music is less widely known than the much smaller keyboard repertoire — perhaps because the latter is more easily accessible in modern editions. The keyboard tradition was already well established in England by the middle of the sixteenth century, but the full flourishing of the English school coincides with the rise of the madrigal — the end of the sixteenth century and the beginning of the seventeenth. While much of the music of that time was playable on (and some intended for) the organ, the chief instrument was the virginal, a type of harpsichord.

English keyboard music

The contents of the virginal manuscripts (the first printed source did not appear until 1611) show a familiar range of types, with certain English peculiarities. There are relatively few intabulations of vocal pieces. Most of the repertoire consists of dances, sets of variations, and free pieces of both the imitative and the virtuoso types. There are also cantus-firmus settings, but the cantus firmi chosen are often melodies used only by English composers. One finds, for example, dozens of settings of an "In nomine," from a Mass by the Englishman John Taverner (and even more such settings for instrumental ensemble). Also notable is the English treatment of dance forms. While some English dances may have been intended for actual dancing (as were some Continental pieces), most are highly stylized music, meant to be heard only. They use the familiar rhythmic patterns and phrase structures, but their textures are too complex for practical dance use. Most common is the pavan-galliard pair, a slow dance in duple meter followed by a quicker one in triple. Each member of such a pair is made up of several short strains, and each may be immediately followed by its varied and ornamented repetition: AA' BB', and so on. In some cases, the galliard uses materials from the pavan preceding, at least to the extent of quoting the beginning of the pavan, altered to suit the new meter. In the celebrated "Lord of Salisbury" pavan and galliard by Orlando Gibbons (Ex. VII-9), only the galliard has repeated strains, and its quotation of the pavan's beginning is partly concealed in the inner voices. The work is a fine specimen of English virginal music, rich in texture and harmony, and brilliantly suited to the instrument.

Ex. VII-9

Variation principle in English keyboard music

Although the variation principle is not uncommon in Continental dance music, it is especially prominent in English dances. It is thus not surprising that formal sets of variations, most of them unconnected with the dance, form an important part of the virginal repertoire. Composers were especially fond of taking a simple popular tune and then subjecting it to a highly sophisticated process of variation. William Byrd, who was as important for his instrumental works as he was for his vocal music, produced such a set in *Jhon come kisse me now*. The simple presentation of the tune at the beginning (Ex. VII-10a), with a bass closely related to one of the standard Renaissance harmonic patterns (the *passamezzo moderno*), is followed by fifteen different settings, in almost all of which the original melody is discernible, however diverse the figuration. In some variations, Byrd takes advantage of the AA' structure of the tune to employ one kind of figuration in the first half and another in the second. Thus the first phrase of variation 5 is really answered only by the second phrase of variation 6, the two intervening phrases being more animated and linked to each other (Ex. VII-11b,c). As in the Gibbons work, the writing is highly idiomatic for the virginal, and demands considerable technique. Even when methods primarily associated with vocal music — notably imitation — are employed, the style remains clearly instrumental.

Ex. VII-10(a)

Ex. VII-10(b)

Ex. VII-10(c)

Summary. The importance of sixteenth-century instrumental music is generally underrated, perhaps because it is not played as often as motets and madrigals are sung. Yet it is a repertoire of great aesthetic value — one that definitively established instrumental composition as equal in importance to vocal writing. Moreover, it made a significant contribution to the formation of Baroque style. The abstract rhythmic-melodic patterns of instrumental music, stylistically transformed, became an essential ingredient in the musical thought of the seventeenth and eighteenth centuries.

PROGRESSIVE TENDENCIES

The second half of the sixteenth century, and more especially its last two decades, saw the rapid development of ideas and methods that were to varying degrees radical in nature. In the area of musical theory, there was a new interest in Greek music. In practice, one finds an increased use of chromaticism; a strengthening of musical contrast by the simultaneous presentation of different motives; an intensified interest in virtuoso singing, whether notated or improvised; and an intentional (as opposed to optional) combination of voices and instruments in a single work, often involving polychoral effects as well. While all these originated and for a time remained within the conventions of sixteenth-century style, they were in the end hostile to the balanced and moderate ideals of the Renaissance; and it is owing largely to them that the beginning of the seventeenth century brought forth profound changes in basic techniques of composition.

The renewed interest in Greek music was radical primarily in its consequences. In its formation, Renaissance musical style owed almost nothing to the revival of interest in antiquity, being in this unlike the visual and verbal arts. The total ignorance of the sound of ancient (Greek) music continued throughout the sixteenth century; but musicians became increasingly fascinated with the idea, at least, of ancient music.

Sixteenth-century composers and theorists could read, in Plato and elsewhere, of the phenomenal power that Greek music apparently had — power to move the hearer to

Influence of Greek musical theory

laughter or to tears, and even power to cure drunkenness and insanity. The music of their own time, on the contrary, had no such power. It could cause interest, delight, even emotion; but it lacked the elemental force that Greek music seemed to have had. It was natural enough to ask why this was so. Various answers, often conflicting, were proposed. One was offered by Vincenzo Galilei (1533-91; father of the scientist). Galilei's position, apparently derived largely from the ideas of the classicist Girolamo Mei (1519-94), was essentially this: music of the present time was ineffective compared to that of the Greeks because "singing several airs together" — that is, using an imitative, contrapuntal texture — left the ear distracted and perplexed. Galilei uses a curious metaphor to express the inadequacy of counterpoint. If a column is pulled at from several directions with equal force, it will not move; if it is pulled with the same force, but from one direction only, it will fall. Thus if a verbal text is associated with a single, forceful melodic line that clearly projects its meaning, the hearer will be moved; if it is set in counterpoint, the situation is that of the column being pulled in several directions: the effect of one melody will neutralize that of the others.

Thus Galilei, a Florentine writing in 1581, advocates an end to contrapuntal writings and urges the concentration of expressive force in a single melody with a distinctly subordinate accompaniment. Galilei himself was an excellent musician, and he and other Florentines experimented actively in an attempt to forge a viable musical style out of this precept. These efforts ultimately succeeded, but during the sixteenth century proper, they were not very influential.

Other musicians, sharing the enthusiasm for Greek antiquity, took a different tack. They learned from the surviving Greek and Latin books on musical theory that the Greek tonal system was based on the interval of the fourth, the tetrachord, which might be filled in in three different ways, called genera (sing. genus). The first or diatonic genus (Ex. VII-11a) might be a fragment of an ordinary Western scale; but the second and third genera (Ex. VII-11b and c) called chromatic and enharmonic, correspond poorly with Western music of the period. (In the enharmonic genus, the second F stands for a pitch midway between F and E.) Both the latter genera use intervals larger than the major second as scale steps; and the enharmonic also uses an interval smaller than a minor second.

Ex. VII-11

Knowledge of the ancient Greek genera has been common among well-educated musicians since the Middle Ages, but no one had seriously attempted to reintroduce them into musical practice until the sixteenth century, when Nicolò Vicentino (1511-72) devoted much of his life to advocating their employment. To facilitate the understanding of the quarter-tone intervals inherent in the enharmonic genus, he had special keyboard instruments constructed that were capable of performing them. He published an important theoretical treatise, *L'antica musica ridotta alla moderna prattica* (ancient music revised for modern practice; 1555), and a number of compositions. The latter show that his primary concern was for effective rendering of the text. Unlike Galilei, however, Vicentino continued to employ the conventional contrapuntal style as a basis.

Vicentino's theories were not widely accepted, nor were his compositions especially influential. His importance is largely symbolic: his career was dedicated to the late sixteenth-century ideals of recovering the lost art of antiquity and of creating a musical style that would best serve to express the emotions suggested by a literary text.

Chromaticism of the Greek sort never achieved practical importance in sixteenth-century music, but the use of altered tones in general became a fundamental tool of Italian madrigalists from the time of Cipriano da Rore. While there is mild chromaticism in the Marenzio madrigals discussed earlier, Marenzio and other composers of the time often went much further. An unexpected altered chord might appear in an otherwise predominantly diatonic context to create a special effect, or a whole passage might be built on a chromatic basis. The latter usage is illustrated in the beginning of Marenzio's celebrated *Solo e pensoso* (Ex. VII-12). The top voice proceeds in a steady

Use of chromaticism in madrigals

Ex. VII-12

ascending chromatic scale (extending well beyond the passage quoted). All such passages are, of course, textually motivated: chromaticism is associated with painful or amorous emotions, or with the astonishing and the mysterious.

Carlo Gesualdo

The most extreme practitioner of the chromatic style was Carlo Gesualdo (ca. 1560-1613), who in his madrigals sacrificed almost every rule of counterpoint and euphony to an intensely personal portrayal of the text. In *Moro, lasso*, the first few measures (Ex. VII-13) show a characteristic alternation between slow, violently chroma-

I die weary of my grief, and she who can give me life.   Ex. VII-13

tic passages and rapid diatonic ones — an alternation called forth by the abrupt and typical antitheses of the text ("moro," die — "vita," life). The chromaticism, hardly surpassed until the nineteenth century, is not at all speculative or theoretical, but results from Gesualdo's passionate desire to extract every possible drop of emotional content from his text. The same desire produces a number of dissonances not normally found in sixteenth-century vocal music.

Clearly the extensive use of chromaticism tends to destroy the bases on which sixteenth-century style is built, if only because these bases are normally diatonic. "Consistent use of the abnormal" is a contradiction in terms, and yet it represents more or less what Gesualdo was doing.

Other disintegrative forces were also at work. In the beginning of Marenzio's *Solo e pensoso*, the top voice — the one bearing the chromatic line — is wholly set apart from the other four, so that in effect two different kinds of music are being combined simultaneously. This introduces a new element into the characteristic texture of equally important voices: a tension caused by the presence of disparate materials that seem almost to compete with each other. The Marenzio work is an example (perhaps extreme) of a practice increasingly common in the late madrigal: in a single section, two or even more contrasting motives, often set to successive phrases of text, are presented and manipulated at once. This adds to the contrast between sections — a feature of almost all madrigals from Cipriano's time — an internal contrast within a section. Preoccupation with forceful expression of the text has become so great that the musical continuity is on the point of disintegrating.

Inner tension is particularly marked in the madrigals of Claudio Monteverdi (1567-1643), and it is significant that he went on, beyond the polyphonic madrigal, to become the greatest composer in the new style of the seventeenth century. Monteverdi makes use of all the new techniques — chromaticism, free dissonance, contrasting motives — but for a different purpose. For Monteverdi, the madrigal becomes a species of dramatic recitation: the lyrical element is frequently suppressed in favor of declamation, only to reappear with additional power because of the contrast.

Si ch'io vorrei morire (published in 1603) begins with a purely declamatory passage (Ex. VII-14a): the five voices appear for the moment to be a single singer, rhetorically displaying his passion. And while musical devices of the earlier madrigal, notably imitation, appear from time to time in the course of the piece, they are wholly subordinate to the urgency of dramatic expression. Even more than Gesualdo, Monteverdi ignores rules when it pleases him: the clustered dissonances (Ex. VII-14b) are indefensible in theory, but essential to the proper expression of the text.

Madrigals of Claudio Monteverdi

So that I wish to die.

Ex. VII-14(a)

Ah dear sweet tongue.

Ex. VII-14(b)

Indeed it would seem that Monteverdi is also trying to recapture the power of antique music, although still within the context of the polyphonic madrigal. His works in this medium are the finest of the period, in part because he was not a technical specialist (as, for example, Gesualdo was a specialist in chromaticism), but used every tool available that would further his purposes.

Monteverdi was perfectly conscious that he was breaking new ground. When the reactionary critic G. M. Artusi published in 1600 an attack on the "defects" of the new music, Monteverdi wrote a defiant letter in reply, which he published in 1605 as preface to his fifth book of madrigals, and again two years later with copious, and certainly authorized, annotations by his brother. He claims that the rules he has broken are indeed valid for what he calls the *prima pratica* (first practice or style), exemplified by the music of Ockeghem, Josquin, and others up to Willaert: in that style, music is mistress of the word. But, Monteverdi asserts, there exists also a *seconda pratica* (second practice), in which the words are mistress of the music; in this, the old rules can be freely treated when the text justifies such a license. With acute historical sense, he traces the beginning of the *seconda pratica* to Cipriano, and mentions, among others, Gesualdo and the Florentine group as followers of it. He makes no attempt to deprecate the older music; he merely insists that his own is something different, to be differently judged.

Prima pratica and seconda pratica

The virtuoso performer

The cult of the virtuoso also had profound effects on sixteenth-century style. Virtuoso performance, whether vocal or instrumental, had by this time a long history. Josquin is said to have complained of singers who added improvised embellishments to his music, and no doubt many sixteenth-century pieces were performed with abundant, if not always tasteful, additions. In self-defence, some composers began to write appropriate ornaments directly into their music, both to prevent irrelevant embellishment by tasteless performers, and to use ornamentation as still another means of achieving more intense expression of the text. Three women at the court of Ferrara became known all over Italy for the matchless beauty — and agility — of their singing. Many composers, Monteverdi included, wrote madrigals for three soprano parts and two lower voices, certainly inspired by the Ferrarese singers or by one of the numerous similar groups that were formed to emulate them.

Luzzasco Luzzaschi's use of ornamentation

While the three-soprano madrigals of Monteverdi do not appear to differ greatly from his other madrigals, those of Luzzasco Luzzaschi (1545-1607), who worked at the court of Ferrara itself, hardly look like madrigals at all. Luzzaschi has adopted the simple solution of eliminating the subordinate lower vocal parts in favor of a keyboard accompaniment, so that the skill of the virtuose will shine forth the more clearly. The vocal lines are clearly designed to exhibit that skill, but they are expressive as well (Ex. VII-15). No doubt many actual performances of madrigals printed in unembellished versions may have superficially resembled the Luzzaschi example. It is not the ornamentation that is new, but rather its deliberate incorporation into the music by the composer himself, as an expressive as well as a decorative device.

The madrigal was the chief vehicle for advanced tendencies in the late sixteenth century. It was not, however, the only one. Many composers wrote motets and even Masses in a style only a little more conservative than that of their madrigals. Moreover, some important areas of experimentation found a more congenial home in sacred rather than secular music.

Sacred music

One of these arose from practical problems of performance. It had long been the custom, when circumstances required, to use instruments to reinforce or replace one or more voices in polyphonic vocal music. The organ, in particular, could effectively support a small group of singers, since the organist could, at need, play all the voices — provided that he first copied them out of the separate partbooks in which they were printed, and wrote out for himself a score or intabulation. This was not usually neces-

on — de sempr'ar — ' — — — — — do

cre-sce la fiam — ma

e cre - sce la fiam — — — ma

And the flame with which I always burn increases.

Ex. VII-15

sary, but partial support often was. Instead, therefore, of going to the considerable trouble of copying out all the parts, the organist might extract from the parts a "basso seguente" (following bass) that would duplicate the vocal bass part, and, when that was silent, whatever was the lowest sounding voice. The result was a composite and continuous part consisting of the lowest sounding notes throughout the piece. Using this, the organist could easily imagine and play the appropriate chords sounded by the other parts. Thus a passable performance of a four- or five-voice motet could be managed by one or two singers and the organist with his basso seguente — and doubtless such performances often took place. But as in the case of improvised ornamentation, the result was unpredictable: it became evident that music written directly for the specific performing forces at hand would be desirable.

Basso seguente

The composer Lodovico Grossi da Viadana (1564-1645) undertook to supply such a repertoire. In 1602, he published *Cento concerti ecclesiastici* — a volume of 100 sacred pieces for from one to four singers, plus a bass part for the organ, to which the organist was expected to form a complete accompaniment by adding the appropriate chords. In general style, Viadana's work is relatively conservative — far more so than that of Monteverdi or Gesualdo. But the medium of small vocal ensemble with partially improvised keyboard accompaniment was to be one of the most progressive features of early seventeenth-century style.

At the opposite end of the spectrum lies the repertoire of music for two or more choirs. Polychoral writing, to which reference has already been made in connection with Willaert, was not in itself necessarily advanced or radical. Conservative composers such as Palestrina wrote extensively for two or three choirs, usually adopting for this purpose a simplified chordal style, and skillfully exploiting the spatial effects available from alternating and combining the performing forces. At Venice, however, polychoral writing took on special characteristics. This was in part owing to the special place held by St. Mark's in Venetian life. It was not only a church, but also a kind of civic showplace, in which the glory of the Venetian republic could be displayed to the greatest possible effect. The processions held in the Square of St. Mark's on major feasts of the church year and on civic occasions were as magnificent as money and talent could make them, and the festal services inside the church were not less so.

For the Venetian composer, therefore, there was every motive to exploit brilliance and richness of sonority as much as possible; and he was given ample means to do this. It appears that, at St. Mark's at least, a number of instrumentalists participated in the performance of motets along with the singers — frequently an orchestra of sixteen or twenty was available. The Venetian school, therefore, went much farther in the exploration of sonorous possibilities than did composers elsewhere.

This is not always immediately evident from the scores. In the vocal works of Andrea Gabrieli (ca. 1515-86), the leading Venetian of the generation after Willaert, there are many pieces for two and three choirs, but the writing does not appear to differ from that in other polychoral music. While it is quite certain that instruments were used in the performance of such pieces, the printed music itself does not mention instruments, nor can one tell from the notes whether a given part was intended for vocal or instrumental performance. Doubtless such matters were settled at rehearsals, and it is quite likely that several different modes of performing a single work would have been acceptable to the composer.

Giovanni Gabrieli

Andrea's nephew, Giovanni Gabrieli (ca. 1555-1612), was a composer of even greater importance. In his early works, he continued in the tradition of his uncle, but increasing preoccupation with special sound effects and with forceful musical rendering of his texts ultimately led him to a style in which Renaissance limits are left far behind.

The ingredients leading to this post-Renaissance style are several, most of them not striking in themselves. For example, while earlier composers generally wrote for two choirs of similar range, Giovanni Gabrieli often prefers contrasting choirs — one of higher voices and one of lower, for example. Doubtless this contrast was reinforced by choosing instruments of contrasting timbres to play along with the singers. The alternation of such choirs is often almost dazzlingly rapid, creating a chiaroscuro of tone colors foreign to the older style.

For these alternations, Gabrieli uses, of necessity, a basically chordal style; and he generally chooses to emphasize a few chords of particular harmonic importance — the triad on which the piece is to end, and the triads whose roots lie on a fifth above and a fifth below that of the final triad. In such passages, Gabrieli renounces the rich variety of chord successions typical of most Renaissance music, but the resultant tonal focus and stability provide full compensation.

Gabrieli is also fully aware of the modern resources of chromaticism, contrasting motives, and the whole gamut of extreme procedures designed for textual expression. To these he adds his own contribution: a type of melodic line, often sequential, made up of short, rapid figures. This doubtless derives from contemporary instrumental practice, but Gabrieli does not hesitate to assign such music to the voice as well. The beginning of his eight-voice *Hodie completi sunt* (Ex. VII-16) may serve to illustrate Gabrieli's mature style. Here the two choirs are similar, not contrasting. Their alternation begins before the first group has finished its first note, and continues in short phrases until a great pseudo-imitative buildup of sound, based on motives that seem

Ex. VII-16

Ex. VII-16

instrumentally conceived, takes place. Later passages are even more instrumental in style, often making use of sequence.

In some late works, Gabrieli makes the contrasts even more explicit. Certain parts are designated as instrumental, others as vocal: the choice is no longer left to the performer. Instrumental style is contrasted with vocal; and in vocal passages, a simple manner of writing may be contrasted with an ornate one fit only for trained soloists.

Concertato style

The term used then for works that explicitly mixed instrumental and vocal parts was "concertato." Thus the pieces of Viadana mentioned above, despite their conservatism, are concertato works, and their title "Concerti" suggests this. But concertato generally suggests also the use of up-to-date style, as well as the modern mixed medium. Thus the later works of Gabrieli ideally represent the concertato style, both in the opulence of their sound, and also in the musical tension resulting from their affective treatment of the texts.

Italian influence in Germany

The progressive tendencies just described originated in Italian music, but quite naturally had influence abroad as well. German musicians, especially, studied Italian developments carefully, and assimilated them into their own works. Most progressive German composers, however, were Lutherans, and were therefore committed to the use of chorale melodies; the chorale having acquired the same kind of authority in the Lutheran liturgy the chant had once had in the Roman church.

Fig. VII-2: Canaletto (1697-1768), view of St. Mark's, Venice, showing musicians in the gallery at right, with a similar gallery visible further back. (Photograph Ralph Kleinhempel, Hemburg.)

Simple chorale settings suitable for congregational singing continued to be made, with the significant difference that the melody was now usually placed in the top voice, not in the tenor. But such settings scarcely allowed for the employment of modern stylistic devices. It was in freer pieces, which used the chorale primarily as a source of musical material (occasionally as a cantus firmus), that German composers could best find room for the new Italian trends.

Michael Praetorius

Michael Praetorius (1571-1621) is most noted for his polychoral works. His *Polyhymnia caduceatrix* (1619) contains pieces modeled on those of Giovanni Gabrieli, although rather less venturesome. Praetorius draws his texts and much of his musical substance from chorales, carving characteristic motives out of the beginnings of chorale phrases. His music is not, however, as tense or dramatic as that of Gabrieli. As in some earlier Venetian polychoral works, the richness of the medium may have been sufficient novelty. Other composers, working with more limited resources, often produced more genuinely modern work. One of the most important was Johann Hermann Schein (1586-1630). A distinguished composer of both vocal and instrumental works, Schein regularly employed chorale melodies in his sacred music. But his *Opella nova* (1618, 1626), for few voices and instrumental bass, treats the traditional tunes freely, with loose imitation, sequence, and careful attention to textual expression. The sacred vocal music of his contemporary Samuel Scheidt (1587-1654) shows a clear progression from the traditional polyphonic motet texture to a medium in which a small vocal ensemble is supported by an instrumental bass. It is evident from the work of such men that modern Italian procedures found ready acceptance in Germany, where they flourished primarily in the area of Lutheran sacred music. The new German style was, however, no mere slavish copy of Italian music: the chorale left its own special imprint, as did the individual characters of German composers, few of whom embraced the extremes of Italian radicalism.

Johann Hermann Schein and Samuel Scheidt

In other countries Italian practices were not so readily accepted. England, still in the midst of its belated Renaissance flowering, remained largely unresponsive to radical ideas. Later, when innovations might have been favorably received, the country was suffering from the internal dissensions that resulted in the establishment of the Commonwealth — a government largely hostile to the arts. France never looked favorably on Italian extremism, for French taste generally favored restraint and moderation.

The end of the sixteenth century found Italy in the position of musical leader: to the extent that other countries failed to observe Italian developments, such countries remained to some extent provincial, perhaps even backward. This situation persisted for more than a century: it was only after about 1750 that Italy ceased being the chief exporter of new musical ideas. The age of the northerners had come to a close.

Such a change in primacy cannot, perhaps, be fully understood, but the preceding pages contain at least some clues. The essence of the northern art had been the contrapuntal combination of long, asymmetrical melodic lines, and every progressive tendency described above was in some sense foreign to that essence: strong chromaticism, violent dissonance, extreme opulence of sound, or, conversely, restriction to one or two voices with subordinate accompaniment. The *prima pratica*, though it flourished all over Europe, was a creation of Franco-Flemish composers. The *seconda pratica* was Italian by birth.

SIXTEENTH-CENTURY INSTRUMENTAL MUSIC. (For vocal music of the late 16th century, see appendix to Chapter VI.)

I.   **An overview by countries.**

   A. Italy.

      1. The publisher Petrucci produced six volumes of lute music 1507-11: two books of vocal transcriptions and ricercari, a book of dance music, and two books of frottola accompaniments and ricercari.

      2. Early keyboard sources are a 1517 book of frottola intabulations published by Andrea Antico, and a 1543 book of liturgical organ music by Girolamo Cavazzoni.

      3. The later part of the century produced the lute music of Francesco da Milano and many others, the keyboard music of Claudio Merulo and Andrea Gabrieli, and the ensemble pieces of Giovanni Gabrieli.

   B. France.

      1. The numerous collections published by Pierre Attaingnant beginning in 1529 provide music for lute, keyboard, organ, and ensemble.
         a. Many chanson and motet intabulations.
         b. Many ensemble dance pieces.
         c. Few abstract forms (prelude, fantasia, etc.)

      2. In the 1550s, the publications of Le Roy and Ballard provided much music for lute, cittern, ensemble.

      3. No keyboard music was printed in France after the publications of Attaingnant until the 17th century.

   C. Germany. Many tablatures for lute (Judenkünig, ca. 1510, 1523; Gerle 1532, etc.) and keyboard (Schlick, 1512; manuscript organ tablatures of Hans Kotter, Fridolin Sicher, Leonhard Kleber, etc.) were produced throughout the century. Many are instructional books, designed for the dilettante, and they typically contain many highly ornamented transcriptions of vocal pieces. The music is largely derivative: not the most distinguished 16th-century repertoire.

   D. Spain.

      1. First printed instrumental source is *El Maestro* of Luis Milán, a book of music for *vihuela* (a double-strung guitar).

      2. Seven or eight other vihuela tablatures appear in the 16th century, including those of Narváez, Mudarra, Pisador.

      3. Two large organ tablatures, those of Cabezón (1578) and Henestrosa (1557).

      4. Very little ensemble music, and practically no dances.

   5. At least half of repertoire is vocal arrangements; variations are a favorite technique; a wealth of accompanied song—all the vihuela tablatures contain some.

E. England.

   1. Almost all 16th-century English instrumental music is preserved in manuscripts, of which, however, a large number exist. There are many lute manuscripts, including a collection in the Cambridge University Library. Keyboard music is preserved in such collections as the *Mulliner Book* (ca. 1540), the *Fitzwilliam Virginal Book* (ca. 1615), and *My Lady Nevell's Book* (by William Byrd). In addition, a significant amount of "consort" (i.e., ensemble) music is preserved.

   2. There are few arrangements of polyphonic vocal pieces to be found in English sources, and few abstract pieces such as fantasias and ricercari.

   3. Favorite forms seem to be dances (mostly pavanes and galliards) and variations.

II. **Forms of 16th-century instrumental music.**

A. Intabulations. A large part of the repertory consists of arrangements of vocal pieces, often with a great deal of added figuration.

B. Free forms. Independent of vocal pieces, improvisatory forms—called "ricercare," "prelude," "fantasia," "toccata," "tiento," etc.—began to be written in the 16th century. By the latter part of the century some of these names had taken on more specific meaning:

   Ricercare ultimately became a monothematic imitative piece, the ancestor of the fugue.

   Toccata came to mean a keyboard piece with fiery, rhapsodic sections, but often including imitative sections, as in the toccatas of Merulo.

   Canzona, for most of the century the name for an intabulated vocal chanson, came ultimately to be a separate instrumental piece, with several sections, modeled on the vocal chanson, and livelier than the ricercare.

C. Variation forms.

   1. Dances. These were often presented in pairs (e.g., pavane-galliard), of which the second was often a metrical variation of the first. In addition, the individual dance movement was generally constructed as a series of strains, with each strain being repeated in varied form immediately after its presentation.

   2. Variations on tunes. Popular tunes, hymn tunes, and other melodies frequently served as the basis for sets of variations, especially for lute and keyboard music.

   3. A number of standard repeating harmonic patterns, many of which had names, such as the *Passamezzo antico*, served as the basis for instrumental pieces. In addition, original ostinato basses were sometimes used.

III. **Bibliography:** some modern editions of 16th-century instrumental music.

Cabezón, Antonio de: *Obras de musica,* Ed. Felipe Pedrell; rev. ed. Higinio An-glès, *Monumentos de la Música Española* 27-29, Barcelona, 1966.

Expert, Henri, ed.: *Les maîtres musiciens de la Renaissance française,* vol. XXIII: *Claude Gervaise, Estienne du Tertre, et Anonymes: Danceries,* Paris, 1908.

Fuller-Maitland, J. A., and W. Barclay Squire, eds.: *The Fitzwilliam Virginal Book,* Leipzig 1899; repr. New York, 1963.

Gabrieli, Andrea: *Orgel- und Klavierwerke,* ed. Pierre Pidoux, 5 vols., Kassel, n.d.

Heartz, Daniel, ed.: *Preludes, Chansons and Dances for Lute,* Paris, 1964. In-cludes transcriptions of Attaingnant lute music.

Jeppesen, Knud, ed.: *Die Italienische Orgelmusik am Anfang des Cinquecento,* Copenhagen, 1943; 2d ed. 1960. Music from two early 16th-century Italian or-gan publications.

Kanazawa, Masakata, ed.: *The Complete Works for Lute of Anthony Holborne,* Cambridge, Mass., 1967-

Narváez, Luis de: *Los Seys Libros del Delphin,* ed. E. Pujol, *Monumentos de la Música Española,* vol. 3, Barcelona, 1945.

Ness, Arthur, ed.: *The Lute Music of Francesco Canova da Milano (1497-1543),* Cambridge, Mass., 1970.

Rokseth, Yvonne. *Deux livres d'orgue.* Paris, 1925. Transcriptions of Attaingnant organ music.

VIII

THE EARLY BAROQUE
YEARS OF EXPERIMENTATION

Like "Gothic," the word "Baroque" originated as a term of disparagement, coined by eighteenth-century rationalists to condemn what they regarded as the disordered products of the preceding age. Although the term has lost its pejorative connotations, it remains true that the seventeenth century was a period of considerable disorder and violence. The religious revival that had produced the Reformation and the Counter Reformation produced religious wars as well, and some of the bitterest of these—the Thirty Years' War in Germany and the Civil War in England, for example—were fought in the seventeenth century. Indeed, as our own time amply demonstrates, intensely held emotional convictions are very likely to lead to strife.

The seventeenth century was also an age of political absolutism, aptly symbolized by the reign of Louis XIV, a monarch whose power and ostentation were envied—and, when possible, imitated—by princes everywhere. Under such circumstances, it is perhaps surprising that this was also one of the great ages of philosophy and natural science: Descartes and Newton may stand for a large number of important minds active in these areas.

Intense convictions may also produce their own reaction in the form of hedonism and cynicism, and they did so during the seventeenth century. Not everyone can be a saint, and even among saints there may be an occasional need for diversion. Thus while some men fought for their beliefs and their lives, others passed their time in indolence, catering only to their own pleasures.

This duality is clearly expressed in the arts. Some artists strive for intense expressivity, and aim by one means or another to overwhelm; but there is also much art that is intended only to amuse. Still other works attempt to achieve both goals, if not simultaneously, at least in different sections.

Naturally this does not apply closely to architecture, which rarely has amusement for its goal. Baroque architecture is usually complex and often overwhelming. Bernini's colonnade for St. Peter's in Rome is a good example of the "colossal Baroque." Even those Baroque churches not conceived on a grandiose scale were designed so as to produce complex interactions of space and light, combined with rich and often fantastic decoration. Typically Baroque is the illusionistically painted ceiling vault, contrived so that the eye is carried far beyond the physical limit of the building and on into the painted "space" beyond.

Baroque painting also exhibits the rhetorical character of the age. The voluptuous figures of Rubens seem to be at the point of moving. In the works of Caravaggio, mysterious effects are produced by a single strong light, casting deep shadows (a technique also exploited by Georges de la Tour). Even in Jan Vermeer, whose works do not otherwise seem Baroque at all, it is the mysterious character of the light that contributes most to the exquisite overall effect.

In literature, while one thinks first of the complexity and power of Donne and the best of the metaphysical poets, and of the majesty of Milton's vision in *Paradise Lost,* there are many lesser metaphysical poems that are mere entertainment—complicated indeed, but light and frivolous in content. Moreover, especially in France, a continued interest in antiquity tempered Baroque rhetoric with classical restraint. The supreme examples of this blending may be found in the plays of Racine, which the French call "classical," not Baroque.

The Baroque does not lend itself to generalization, therefore, as easily as the Renaissance; and this raises in a particularly acute form a question that has been so far deliberately left unasked: what in fact constitutes a "period" of artistic style? The answer is generally formulated somewhat as follows: a span of time is regarded as a "period" if the works produced within it are related to each other by some common fundamental technique, in such a way that their similarities are more important than their differences. Thus, for example, the period of Parisian polyphony may be thought of as unified by a continuing interest in rhythmic effects based in some way on the rhythmic modes.

Yet the matter is not always so simple. An isorhythmic motet by Dufay, although it prominently displays a fourteenth-century technique, is not for that reason fourteenth-century music, nor even music that stands somehow outside its proper period. Technique is not the sole criterion: all factors that go to make up style, whether or not they are amenable to exact definition, are involved. Dufay's isorhythmic motets belong, with his other works, to the early Renaissance. Despite their use of an archaic technique, their overall sound is that of early Renaissance music.

Still, it may be argued that while Josquin sounds a good deal like Palestrina or even Marenzio, Dufay does not sound much like any of them, although all are considered Renaissance composers. Such difficulties are frequently avoided by dividing each period into three sub-periods: an early period of experimentation (exemplified by Leoninus in the late twelfth century and by Dufay in the fifteenth); a middle or classical period (Perotinus and Josquin); and a late or mannered period (Petrus de Cruce and Gesualdo). This approach can be useful in clarifying the historical position of composers and their works, but only if two precautions are taken. First, words like "early," "experimental," "classical," and "mannered" must be divested of all connotations of value. It is the quality of a work, not its position in a historical scheme, that determines its aesthetic value. Second, no preconceived details may be imposed on such a pattern. Thus the classical phase of the Renaissance was a long one, owing to the fruitfulness of the techniques perfected by Josquin. But if Perotinus is taken as representing the classical phase of Parisian polyphony, that phase was quite short. And the French *Ars nova* seems to have had no early period at all. Some scholars have attempted to fit the history of music into a scheme of regular and orderly cycles, but such attempts appear arbitrary and false to the facts, and have not been generally accepted.

Nevertheless, the division of a large period into sub-periods helps to explain why Dufay does not sound like Palestrina. The early phase of a style is likely to be formative: basic techniques that will later dominate the period are not yet fully formulated. Its music will therefore sound rather different from that composed during later phases of the same period. Leoninus does not sound much like Franco of Cologne; nor Dufay like Palestrina; nor, as will become apparent, Monteverdi like Bach.

The early seventeenth century provides a particularly apt instance of an early, experimental phase. The tendencies described at the end of Chapter VII arose within the context of Renaissance style, even though they were all in some measure inimical to it. In the first three decades of the seventeenth century, most composers found that the observation of traditional norms of composition was no longer desirable: the ideal of equal-voiced polyphony, controlled dissonance, and sectional construction based on short phrases of text came to appear inadequate in some or even all respects. As a result, musicians, while for the most part continuing to use the modern devices of the late sixteenth century, more and more frequently discarded the bases on which music had previously been built. This naturally led to a search—sometimes almost frantic—for new but comparable bases. The period was thus one of discovery, in which stylistic differences between composers—even between different works of the same composer—were abnormally great. There is scarcely anything else in the history of music that gives so vividly the impression of a style—or better, a variety of styles—in the exuberance of youth.

At the same time, a new and curious phenomenon makes its appearance: the old style, and particularly the conservative style of Palestrina, continued to be cultivated, regularly by a few conservative composers, for particular purposes and occasions by others, and by almost all as a means of educating young musicians into the technique of their art. There were good reasons for this: the extremes of the new style were not always appropriate, especially for sacred music; and the absence of a generally accepted body of new techniques made the retention of the old almost necessary as a teaching device. Nevertheless, this persistence of Renaissance technique introduced for the first time a significant new element into the history of music. It made musicians conscious of style *as* style. From this time on, almost all composers were able to write in two different styles—the one current in their own time, and the "petrified" style of Palestrina. In a sense, they could speak two different musical languages, whereas their predecessors had supposed that only one existed. In consequence, they became style-conscious in a way their predecessors were not. Renaissance composers naturally varied their style to suit the genre or the occasion, but this variation took place within relatively narrow limits. Baroque composers, with two entirely different styles at their command, could and occasionally did undertake changes of style on a fundamental level.

Nonetheless, this represents only an exceptional element in Baroque musical practice. Palestrina and a few others were revered, preserved, occasionally performed, and sometimes imitated (although the imitations were generally more modern than their authors supposed). There was, however, no widespread revival of interest in "old music." For the most part, as in earlier periods, new music was written whenever music was needed, and was forgotten or even discarded shortly after it had fulfilled its function. Systematic musical antiquarianism did not begin until well into the nineteenth century.

The development of a dramatic style and the beginnings of opera. By 1600, the year usually given as marking the beginning of the Baroque period, Monteverdi had gone a long way in the process of reshaping the madrigal into a dramatic, rather than a lyrical, composition; and Gabrieli was at work on those mixtures of sonorities and textures that were to transform the polychoral motet just as radically. But 1600 is chosen as a beginning for a quite different reason: it is the date of the first preserved musical drama.

The use of music in connection with dramatic presentation was not by any means new. The liturgical drama of the Middle Ages was sung throughout, and most Renaissance dramas were performed with generous musical embellishment. But no attempt had been made to integrate music into the fabric of the drama—to use music as an aid in the transmission of specifically dramatic emotion. A sixteenth-century dramatic performance might use dance music and perhaps include choruses commenting on the action, but the principal business of the play was carried on in speech.

Madrigal comedy

An apparent exception to this rule was the madrigal comedy, a genre cultivated around the turn of the century and chiefly associated with the composers Orazio Vecchi (1550-1605) and Adriano Banchieri (1567-1634). The madrigal comedy used a succession of polyphonic pieces, mostly of the lighter sort like the villanella, to set a dramatic text of the commedia dell' arte type. But the music itself is hardly dramatic: it is mostly light and witty, and individual characters are musically represented by several singers at once. Thus the madrigal comedy may properly be said to be a dramatic application of music, and perhaps a musical reflection of spoken comedy, but it is not true musical drama.

The Florentine camerata

The latter resulted from the line of thought pursued by Vincenzo Galilei (above, Chapter VII) and by a number of other Florentines, both musicians and amateurs, during the last decades of the sixteenth century. These men are often referred to collectively as the "Florentine camerata," but they were by no means a unified group. They were, rather, rivals, each anxious to claim the maximum credit for reviving the legendary effectiveness of Greek music.

Since Greek drama was one of the chief proofs of the power of ancient music, it was natural for the Florentines to turn to dramatic composition as one of their aims. The central problem was, of course, to find a musical style suitable for the delivery of dramatic dialogue. There was ample precedent for solo singing, but no solo style current at the time was capable of conveying the changing emotional content of dramatic speech in a realistic manner.

Monody: Characteristics of the stile recitativo

The solution was simple but radical. The solo voice was given a melodic line less songlike than ordinary melody, and yet more melodic than even rhetorical speech. This was accompanied only by chords played by a lute or other suitable instrument. The melody was made absolutely subservient to the natural declamation of the text; and, while it was expected to convey the state of mind of the character singing, there were no distracting madrigalisms. Ideally, the music was to imitate as closely as possible the delivery—impassioned as the occasion might require—of a fine actor.

Various names were given to this new style of singing. The one that ultimately prevailed—*stile recitativo* or recitative—is not wholly satisfactory, as it suggests to the modern reader characteristics typical of much later music. The term "monody," though not used by the Florentines, might be more useful, except that it is also applicable to quite different and non-dramatic styles of the period. The Florentines themselves often used "stile rappresentativo" (i.e., theatrical style), but this, too, came to be applied to non-dramatic works as well.

Whatever its name, the new Florentine style was a fundamental departure. Its novelty lay not in the medium, as accompanied solo singing was common enough; nor even in its basically declamatory character, for declamatory madrigals go back at least as far as Cipriano da Rore; but rather in the almost total submission of the music to the demands of the text. Even in the most extreme declamatory madrigal, purely musical processes appear: words are repeated, for example, to make possible the repetition of musical motives. In the new style, word-repetition is allowed only for an exceptional dramatic effect; and the melodic line carefully avoids characteristic motives, for these would arouse musical expectations that could not be fulfilled.

With the new style of singing as a tool, it became possible to set wholly to music almost any drama, and to perform the result—the *dramma in musica*—in the normal theatrical way, with costumes, scenery, and singing actors. But it is to be noted that the Florentine poets and composers made no attempt to revive the high style of Greek tragedy. Instead, they chose subjects for which the still fashionable pastoral treatment was suitable: the earliest musical dramas, or operas, to use the later name, were based on the stories of Apollo and Daphne, and Orpheus and Euridice. Such choices in part reflect current poetic trends, and perhaps also a certain hesitation at attempting to cope with grandiose figures such as Oedipus or Orestes. At the beginning, the Florentines wisely chose plots involving characters who were also *singers*.

Euridice, the earliest opera that has survived complete, was commissioned for performance in Florence to celebrate the wedding of Henry IV of France and Maria de' Medici (1600). The text of this *Euridice* was by Ottavio Rinuccini, the music by Jacopo Peri (1561-1633). At the first performance, some of Peri's music was replaced by that of a Florentine rival, Giulio Caccini (ca. 1546-1618). Both composers quickly brought out complete versions of their scores.

The first opera: Jacopo Peri and Giulio Caccini

Two brief excerpts (Ex. VIII-1) give an idea of the new "recitative" style as practiced by Peri. In the first, from the very beginning of *Euridice*, Tragedy introduces the action. The second is from one of the most intense moments in the work, when Dafne enters to break the news of the death of Euridice. In some respects the two passages are very similar. The voice is given a declamatory line that carefully avoids any suggestion of normal melody. The accompaniment consists of only a few chords, changing rarely. There is nothing to distract the attention from the sung declamation of the poetry, nothing to impede complete understanding of the text.

Yet there are considerable differences between the two excerpts. The first, emotionally relatively neutral, is given a correspondingly cool setting. But the second, representing Dafne in anguish, must convey something of her despair. Peri portrays this in the by then traditional manner, introducing chromaticism and dissonance, as well as a more varied, agitated rhythmic declamation (the line beginning "Miserabil beltate" is an especially good example).

In addition to the realistic speech-rhythms of the vocal part, the chief means of conveying intense emotion is the harmony—the chords used in the accompaniment, and their relation to each other and to the voice. Only the basic identity of a chord, not its precise form, was important. If a triad on G was needed, it made no difference whether it was played with G in the top voice, or B, or D. There was thus nothing to be gained by writing the accompaniment out in full. It was enough to write the bass:

Accompaniment: The basso continuo

Io che d'al – ti sos – pir va – ga e di pian – – ti

I, fond of deep sighs and tears.

Ex. VIII-1(a)

Las – sa che di spa – ven – to e di pie – ta – – te ge-la-mi il cor nel se – no

Mi – se – ra – bil bel -ta – te com' in un pun – to ohi – – me

Sad, for fear and pity froze my heart in my breast. Unfortunate beauty, how in an
instant, alas. . .

Ex. VIII-1(b)

the accompanying players would understand that each bass note represented a complete triad with that note as root. In the few cases where this was not so—when a note
other than the root was used in the bass, or when a momentary dissonance in the accompaniment was required—numbers could be placed above or below the bass note,
specifying the intervals to be played above the bass.

The accompanist (or accompanists, since more than one might be used) had before him only a bass part, like the basso seguente described in the preceding chapter,
sprinkled here and there with figures, from which he was to improvise or "realize" a
chordal accompaniment. Example VIII-2 shows a fragment of such a bass part with
two different realizations, one very simple, the other embellished. The type used depended on the circumstances. This method of performance is called figured bass, thor-
ough bass, or basso continuo. It quickly became standard procedure in all kinds of music, and remained in universal use throughout the Baroque period. Its employment in
the earliest surviving operas vividly symbolizes the rejection of counterpoint on
which much early Baroque music was largely based.

While declamatory passages such as those quoted above were the most radical
novelty of the musical drama, they were by no means its sole ingredient. The dramatic

Ex. VIII-2

style found room for choruses in a simplified madrigal style, and solo songs, some-times quite lengthy, in which simple, symmetrical melody replaces declamation. The inclusion of these more conventional sections is carefully justified dramatically: it is only natural that Orpheus, the greatest of singers, should sing a real song of joy when he successfully rescues Euridice from the dead. But they were necessary in any case. The novelty of the recitative could be far better appreciated when heard in contrast with music of a different kind.

Drama was the most spectacular product of the Florentine musicians, but it was not the only one. In 1601, Caccini published a collection entitled *Le nuove musiche* (new music), containing pieces some of which may date from before 1600. The me-dium—solo voice plus figured bass—is the same as that used in the drama, but the texts are lyrical, not dramatic. There are two groups of pieces, one called madrigals, the other arias. The madrigals look very like dramatic declamation, but in fact they have much stronger musical continuity: the chords change more rapidly, and the phrases of the vocal part are more nearly symmetrical and tuneful. The arias, even more strongly musical, are mostly simple, tuneful, and invariably strophic songs that resemble, not the dialogue, but the songs in the dramas.

Caccini's Le nuove musiche

Both Caccini and Peri were singers as well as composers, and Caccini, especially, often wrote elaborate ornamentation into his vocal parts. This is in no way a violation of the otherwise austere Florentine aesthetic, but rather another case of a composer making use of ornament for expressive purposes, rather than allowing the performer to invent his own, possibly irrelevant, embellishments.

The new dramatic style was enthusiastically received, and attracted a great deal of attention. A sacred work, *Rappresentazione di anima e di corpo* (Representation of soul and body) was given in Rome in 1600. The composer, Emilio de' Cavalieri (ca. 1550-1602) had also been active in Florentine circles, and hurried his work into print —for he also claimed credit for the invention of the new style. In fact, however, the mu-sic of the *Rappresentazione* is less novel than that of Peri and Caccini. Cavalieri makes less use of musical declamation, and more of formal songs and choruses.

Emilio de' Cavalieri

After 1600—the year of Cavalieri's work and the two settings of Rinuccini's *Euridice*—relatively few musical dramas were written. Practical considerations may have had some share in this: operas were associated with brilliant entertainments of the aristocracy, organized to celebrate ducal weddings, accessions, and the like. They required much rehearsal and were extremely expensive to produce. It is also possible, however, that the new dramatic style was still felt to be somewhat problematic—a vehicle whose potentialities had not yet been fully realized.

*Monteverdi's
Orfeo*

This realization took place in 1607, when Monteverdi wrote his *Orfeo*, one of the greatest works of musical drama, for the ducal court at Mantua. Monteverdi was entirely in accord with the Florentine principle that music should be the servant of the words, not their mistress. Outwardly, *Orfeo* resembles the Florentine operas: it is a pastoral version of the Orpheus myth, with sung declamation intermixed with songs and choruses. But Monteverdi was a far better composer than either Peri or Caccini, and his work both transcended and transformed that of the Florentines.

Orfeo differs from its predecessors not only in quality, but also in the use made of the various components of dramatic style. While the dramatic action is still entrusted to declamatory recitative, there are more songs and choral pieces, longer and more complex than those of *Euridice*. They are again carefully woven into the dramatic fabric, and are not mere decorations. In addition, there is a large amount of purely instrumental music. (The Florentines left relatively little independent instrumental music for their dramas, although more may have been used in actual performance.) Some of the instrumental pieces, called ritornelli, are recurrent, and help both to articulate the shape of the drama and to set an appropriate tone for the action. They may also have served the practical function of allowing time for the changes of scenery between acts.

Fortunately, details of the exact instrumentation used in the performance have survived—generally in a form such as "this ritornello was played by viols," indirectly suggesting that other choices might also have been possible. Monteverdi calls for organs, lutes, harpsichords, and bowed strings to perform the basso continuo, and employs almost all the instruments then in use for the songs, choruses, and ritornelli. The effect must have been extraordinarily rich and colorful, but it was not necessarily novel, for large orchestras had often been used in court entertainments during the sixteenth century.

Monteverdi's talents are amply demonstrated in his treatment of dramatic dialogue. He made no theoretical innovations in this work, but he faced and solved ideally the central problem of recitative, finding a style that is neither too dry and unmusical, nor so musical that it threatens to dominate the text.

Although the second act of *Orfeo* is not formally divided into scenes, three sections may be distinguished. In the first, Orfeo and the shepherds are rejoicing; in the second, a messenger enters and recounts the death of Euridice, after which Orfeo sings and leaves to seek her in the world below; and in the third, those left on stage comment on the action. Thus only the middle scene contains any real action; the other two are dramatically static, and function as a frame for the central crisis. While there are several prominent unifying devices in the act, and in *Orfeo* as a whole (the phrase "Ahi, caso acerbo" recurs almost as a refrain; and the ritornelli create obvious linkages), there is even greater emphasis on musical and dramatic continuity.

The climax of the act naturally comes with the tale of Euridice's death and Orfeo's reaction to it. Here Monteverdi's dramatic sense, active for years in his madrigals, is

ployed in some arias, producing an effect more complex than that of a simple strophic song. When the repeated bass line is short enough and has sufficiently striking musical character to be readily perceived, it is a basso ostinato: in such a piece a largely continuous melody unfolds over a frequently repeated bass. Ostinato technique was common in sixteenth-century instrumental music, but first became popular in vocal music in the early seventeenth century.

Arias of large size came to be called "cantatas" (sung pieces). They were sometimes further enlarged by the insertion of an instrumental ritornello after each strophe of the poem. Thus, with rather modest means, a fairly ample structure could be achieved.

Occasionally a single poem was divided into two parts, the first being set in recitative, the second in aria style. In such cases, the light tone of the aria was frequently replaced by a more serious type of melody, often in triple meter with broad, flowing lines and graceful melismas. This style was increasingly used in arias (whether with or without recitative) from 1620 on.

In opera, Florence did not maintain her position of leadership for long. While occasional new operas appeared there during the second and third decades of the century, it was Rome that came to predominate from about 1620 until the late 1630s, largely owing to the patronage of the powerful Barberini family, in whose palace a 3,000-seat opera theater was opened in 1632. Owing no doubt to ecclesiastical influence, Roman composers produced sacred as well as secular dramatic works, the most important being Stefano Landi's *Il Sant' Alessio* (1632). Secular works included pastoral operas similar to those of the Florentines, and comic operas as well. The comic type was in part the work of the poet Giulio Rospigliosi, whose service in Spain led him to follow to some extent the example of the Spanish playwright Calderón.

Roman opera

The chief characteristic of the Roman style, however, was the serio-comic plot. Often both complex and fantastic, this consisted of a basically serious story interspersed with more or less relevant comic scenes, the whole calling for extensive and impressive scenic effects. (In 1644, the Barberini were temporarily driven from Rome. They took their artistic entourage with them to France, where they implanted an ineradicable love of spectacular scenery in French audiences.)

Musically, the Roman operas are also less rigorous than the Florentine works. While the recitative style is still extensively used, it is often less expressive than the Florentine type, being in some cases no more than a declamatory vehicle by which the words may clearly be heard. The Roman composers preferred to concentrate their efforts on the solo songs—which may now properly be called arias, since they share the style of the monodic arias—and on choral pieces. The resulting alternation between declamatory recitative and self-sufficient songs was to crystallize as the basic structure of Baroque opera.

Perhaps the finest product of the Roman school was yet another *Orfeo*, this one by Luigi Rossi (1598-1653). The text is a typically Roman mixture of serious and comic scenes, of little dramatic value, but Rossi's music is elegant and varied: the composer has all but ignored the drama, using it merely as a frame for attractive (and, to be sure, appropriate) music.

Luigi Rossi

The Roman school did not long survive the expulsion of the Barberini, and even their return in 1653 failed to renew it. Operatic leadership passed to Venice, where, in 1637, the first *public* opera house was opened. From that time on, Venice was never without several active opera houses, supported, not by the patronage of a wealthy court, but by the income received from the sale of tickets and subscriptions. The implications of this change of audience—from an invited gathering of (presumably) connoisseurs to a paying crowd drawn from various levels of society—are obvious, and the consequences will be apparent in Chapter IX, in which the bulk of Venetian opera will be discussed.

At this time, however, Monteverdi's later contributions to opera should be considered, if only to keep the works of this critical figure as close together as their diversity permits. After *Arianna,* Monteverdi wrote no more operas until 1617, but thereafter he composed the music (now lost) for a number of stage works for Venice and other northern Italian cities. In his old age, he wrote two major works for the Venetian theaters, *Il ritorno d'Ulisse in patria* (The Return of Ulysses to his Homeland; 1641), and *L'Incoronazione di Poppea* (The Crowning of Poppea; 1643), both fortunately still extant. Of these, the second is a masterpiece equal to *Orfeo,* but entirely different from it in style and technique.

Monteverdi's Venetian operas: L'Incoronazione di Poppea

The differences begin with the subject matter, which in *Poppea* is taken from ancient history, not mythology, although mythological characters still appear. The tale of the lustful emperor Nero and his ambitious mistress Poppea is told in an almost realistic fashion. There are many characters, including some comic ones, whose interrelationships are unfolded in a rapid succession of short scenes, very much in the manner of Shakespeare. The result is an excellent libretto that gives ample opportunity for the display of a wide range of passionate emotions.

Monteverdi's score clearly demonstrates the stylistic changes that had taken place since his *Orfeo.* There are several arias of the newer type, with flowing ornamental lines, usually in quick triple meter. Some are built on ostinato basses: the concluding ostinato duet sung by the triumphant lovers is a superb example of an extensive aria justified by dramatic circumstances. Having achieved their aim, the two characters lyrically expand their emotions into a piece of some length—as in the great soliloquies or love "duets" in Shakespeare or Racine, which also are dramatically static, but illuminate inner feelings.

Poppea is not, however, a simple alternation of declamatory recitative and reflective arias. Monteverdi still uses recitative for some of the most intense moments of the drama, and his recitative still has the emotional power it had in 1607. In many scenes, recitative and fragments in aria style are mixed in rapid succession, richly painting the sudden flickerings of contrasting passions aroused by the rapid flow of incidents in the plot.

In one such scene (I, 9), Poppea asks Nero three coy questions. The first of these is in recitative, as are all of Nero's answers; but the second and third questions are in aria style, although much too short to be real arias. The power of the recitative is vividly demonstrated in Nero's passage beginning "Poppea, respiro appena" ("Poppea, I hardly breathe;" Ex. VIII-5): the impassioned declamation and chromatic harmonies ideally portray Nero's passion. Later in the same passage, the recitative is enriched by musical devices—repetition and sequence—and becomes a type later known as arioso. There follows a true aria for Poppea: the action pauses, and her state of mind can be depicted at length. The remainder of the scene maintains the same flexibility of dramatic technique. For Monteverdi, the text remains mistress of the music, despite the changes in musical style and in subject matter.

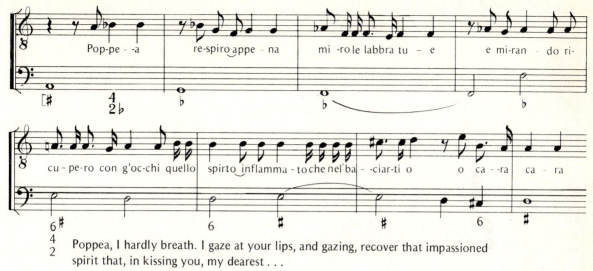

Poppea, I hardly breath. I gaze at your lips, and gazing, recover that impassioned
spirit that, in kissing you, my dearest . . .

Ex. VIII-5

In one respect *Poppea* appears less opulent than *Orfeo*: there are far fewer instrumental pieces, and those that there are seem less imposing than the ritornelli of *Orfeo*. In part, this doubtless results from practical considerations. The court operas could have whatever the patron was willing to pay for; and since they were generally meant to be extremely impressive, no expense was spared to make them so. But the commercial opera houses could not afford such extravagance if they were to make a profit, and Monteverdi, like other Venetian composers, had to write for the forces available. The spectator, however, is not likely to feel any impoverishment. The relatively slow dramatic motion of *Orfeo* invites—indeed demands—both musical and visual pageantry. In *Poppea*, such display would merely impede the rapid flow of incident and emotion.

The new counterpoint.   Opera and monody were the most obviously modern genres of the early seventeenth century, but music of several other types flourished as well. Even the monody publications usually include a few pieces for two or even more voices (plus the inevitable basso continuo), and many operas contain duets, as well as choruses. In such pieces, some sort of polyphonic treatment is necessary, as the musical interest must be divided among two or more vocal parts. Hence the rejection of counterpoint, characteristic of monody, cannot be regarded as absolute. In music for several voices, counterpoint is not rejected, but transformed.

Monteverdi was a leader in this area also. In the two excerpts shown in Example VIII-6, both for the common medium of two vocal parts and basso continuo, two aspects of the transformed contrapuntal style can be seen. The first bears some resemblance to the style of recitative (notice particularly the static bass part), but here characteristic motives appear that can then be treated in loose imitation. In the second, (Ex. VIII-6b), the rapid sequential figures clearly show influences from instrumental music, as in the concertato works of Giovanni Gabrieli. Indeed Monteverdi, who lived and worked in Venice from 1613 until his death in 1643, was the true heir of Gabrieli's legacy, just as he had been the true heir of the Florentines.

And I do not dare, alas, disclose.   Ex. VIII-6(a)

Ex. VIII-6(b)

The most profound of the many differences between the new and old contrapuntal styles lies in the treatment of rhythm. The use of a wide variety of rhythmic values, frequent clusters of very short notes (often in sequence), and metrical patterns emphasizing regularity of pulse (so that from now on the bar line does in fact mark a truly strong beat) created a counterpoint wholly remote from the long, flowing lines of the sixteenth century.

The new rhythmic freedom is in part possible because the underlying chordal structure is made so clear by the basso continuo. This harmonic clarity also permits a freedom of dissonance that Renaissance style could not tolerate. Emphasis on the triad as an entity in itself allows the ear to hear sharply dissonant clashes without becoming confused as to the identity of the chord against which they occur.

While the new style of counterpoint was most at home in music for two to four voices, the many works of Monteverdi's Venetian period include a number for much larger forces. The medium varies considerably: as many as eight vocal parts may be used, often with independent instrumental parts as well (two violins are often specified), and of course the basso continuo. Significantly, these pieces often contain passages for smaller ensembles, in which ornamental or semi-dramatic counterpoint can be used. Many of the secular works are called madrigals, and some of the sacred ones motets, although their connection with the sixteenth-century prototypes is rather slight.

A special effect invented by Monteverdi must also be briefly described. He himself says that he found music lacking the power to depict warlike or wrathful passions. For this purpose he devised a special kind of music, involving rapid reiteration of a single note and retention of the same chord (or of two alternating chords) over a long period. This he termed *stile concitato* (excited style; not to be confused with the unrelated term "concertato"). The most famous monument of the *stile concitato* is the *Combattimento di Tancredi e Clorinda* (1624), a semi-dramatic setting of an episode from Tasso's *Gerusalemme liberata;* but *concitato* elements appear in other works also, when called for by the text.

Stile concitato

The madrigal *Hor ch' el ciel e la terra* illustrates various aspects of Monteverdi's handling of the many-voiced medium, including the *stile concitato.* The opening, a superb portrayal of the stillness of night, is stylistically modern only in the addition of violin parts and basso continuo to the vocal ensemble. Thereafter, however, the style is enriched by elements from the drama and from the concertato. There is a passage in quasi-recitative style for two tenors (Ex. VIII-7a), interrupted by exclamations from the other voices. Modern affective harmonies are used in a slightly later passage. *Stile concitato* appears twice, prompted by the word "guerra" (war; Ex. VIII-7b). The repeated notes and sustained harmonies are clearly in evidence, especially in the string parts. The two *concitato* sections alternate with two exquisite chordal sections depicting inner peace. As in the drama, the text is mistress of the music, but in a much different way. For all the up-to-date technical equipment, a piece such as this remains attached to the tradition of the sixteenth-century madrigal: both types are based on sectional structure and lyrical expansion of words or phrases of the text. And in fact, despite the numerous distinguished works Monteverdi wrote for this type of medium, the concertato madrigal for many voices was a dying genre. The richest possibilities lay in works for smaller forces.

I wake, I think, I burn, I weep. And she who undoes me.

Ex. VIII-7(a)

War is my state.

Ex. VIII-7(b)

Sacred music.   Except for a brief mention of Roman sacred opera, only secular music has so far been considered in this chapter. This is justifiable, in that most of the progressive tendencies of the period made their first appearance in secular music; but it should not be taken to suggest that sacred music had no share in innovation. While some composers maintained a conservative style in their sacred works, others did not hesitate to use the most modern techniques.

Venice was the chief center of modern sacred music. Monteverdi produced a large quantity, mostly using the same techniques employed in his secular works. His so-called *Vespers* of 1610 is a kind of compendium of concertato church music; but even that celebrated work seems almost slight beside his two great collections of sacred music printed in 1640 and 1651. The Mass ordinary, psalms, the Magnificat, and other sacred texts are here set with all the resources that the modern style could offer. In Venice, at least, conservatism laid no constraint on music for the church.

Monteverdi's sacred music

As has been seen in the preceding chapter, Italian developments were carefully studied by German composers, many of whom went to Italy to study the new styles at first hand. The greatest of these was Heinrich Schütz, after Monteverdi the finest composer of his time. Schütz went to Venice in 1609 to study with Giovanni Gabrieli. There he published a book of superb five-voice madrigals (1611), the last of the great madrigal collections in the old style. He returned to Germany in 1613, and there introduced into sacred music the polychoral concertato style (*Psalmen Davids*, 1619) and the passionate vocabulary of the late madrigal (*Cantiones sacrae*, 1625). In 1628 he went again to Venice, this time to observe the work of Monteverdi. During this second visit, he mastered the techniques of monody and of the new style of counterpoint, neither of which had been extensively used in his earlier publications. In 1627, he

Heinrich Schütz (1585-1672)

had composed music for a German translation of Rinuccini's *Dafne* (the text previously set by Peri and Caccini), thus producing the first German opera. Unfortunately the music has not survived.

The music of Schütz

He adapted monody to German needs in his *Kleine geistliche Konzerten* (small sacred concertos; 1636, 1639), two collections of works for one to five solo voices plus basso continuo. The modest resources called for reflect the impoverishment of Germany during and after the Thirty Years' War: for some time, large musical forces simply could not be thought of.

In the rather few one-voice pieces in these collections, Schütz makes only occasional use of purely declamatory style, preferring in general a more melodic idiom in which the bass part has some share of the musical interest (as in the Gagliano excerpt given earlier). In works for two or more voices, the new style of counterpoint is used, often in combination with the expressive chromaticism Schütz had employed in his madrigals.

In the three books of *Symphoniae sacrae* (sacred "symphonies" or concertos; 1629, 1646, 1650), the medium is enlarged to include independent instrumental parts as well as solo voices. (The third set also has reinforcing parts for chorus and instruments.) In consequence, the style is also to some extent modified, in order to take advantage of the varied capabilities of the performing forces.

Veni de Libano, from the first book, is set for two violins, two solo voices, and basso continuo. This flexible medium permits either voices or instruments to form a trio texture with the bass, a device Schütz uses constantly, reserving the full forces for climaxes. Apart from the purely instrumental sections, the form of the piece is that of the traditional motet: each phrase of text is given suitable musical material, which is worked out at length; then a new text phrase is introduced with new music; and so on. But if the form is traditional, the style is thoroughly modern. The adroit handling of the performing forces, the idiomatic instrumental writing, the short phrases built up out of little rhythmic motives, the constant sequences—all of these show Schütz's mastery of contemporary techniques (Ex. VIII-8).

Schütz's use of dramatic techniques

Schütz's output includes a considerable body of sacred vocal music in addition to the collections already mentioned. Of particular importance are those works in which Schütz applies dramatic techniques to sacred subjects. The *Historia von der Geburt Jesu Christi* (Story of the birth of Jesus Christ; 1664) is the most "operatic" of these. The recitative, with its many short repeated notes, is strongly declamatory, although by no means lacking in expression. When the nature of the text requires, the declamation is changed to the flowing and melodious arioso style, midway between recitative and song.

Recitative is used to set the narrative parts of the Biblical story. The words of actual characters (Herod, the Wise Men, the choir of angels, etc.) are set as self-contained musical pieces. Schütz calls these *intermedia,* but they are in fact arias (or duets, trios, choruses—according to the number of persons speaking). Each of these has a well-defined character, owing not only to the nature of the musical material, but also to the instrumentation: the shepherds are given flutes, Herod a trumpet, the high priests trombones, and so on. Despite the late date of the *Historia,* the newer Italian melodic style in flowing triple meter is not much in evidence: most of the music is closer to Schütz's own earlier works than to contemporary Italian models. There is also a freshness and vitality in the music that is remarkable for a composer of Schütz's age.

Ex. VIII-8

Come, come, you will be crowned.   Ex. VIII-8 (cont.)

His other late works are of a different sort. He composed, late in life, three settings of the Passion story. In these, he deliberately renounced the modern techniques that had served him so well, and wrote in an austere, controlled style superficially resembling that of the sixteenth century. The solo parts are not in recitative, but in an unaccompanied monody not unlike a plainsong psalm tone. The choral sections are also unaccompanied, although they have in them a kind of urgency that sets them clearly apart from sixteenth-century music. From the evidence of these and other works, and from direct statements by the composer himself, it is clear that the aging Schütz almost regretted having been one of the leaders in bringing the new Italian style to Germany. It appeared to him that young composers were beginning to write in the modern style before they had mastered their craft (i.e., learned the *prima practica*): in these late works, Schütz demonstrated how much could be achieved even then by a master who willingly submitted to the old rules.

Schütz's late works

Instrumental music. In instrumental music, the difference between sixteenth- and seventeenth-century styles is far less striking than it is in vocal music, in part precisely because many of the new vocal resources were borrowed or developed from instrumental practice. There were, to be sure, changes in instrumental style at this time, but there was nothing comparable to the invention of monody or the transformation of vocal counterpoint.

In fact, music in traditional forms accounts for a large part of the output of the early 1600s. In dance music, there are few fundamental differences between pieces published in the early seventeenth century and works thirty years older. In other areas, tra-

ditional forms were retained, but invested with new content. Nowhere is this more evident than in the music of Girolamo Frescobaldi (1583-1643), organist of St. Peter's in
Rome, and the greatest keyboard composer of his time. Almost all of Frescobaldi's
works bear titles or employ methods inherited from the sixteenth century: there are
toccatas, ricercari, and canzone, as well as cantus-firmus settings and variations.

A toccata by Frescobaldi is, like one by a sixteenth-century composer, a freely sectional work in which passages of ornamental figuration alternate with passages in contrasting styles, usually but not always involving imitative counterpoint. Into this traditional mold Frescobaldi pours an intense rhetorical expressivity wholly characteristic
of his time. The combination of chromaticism, sharp dissonance, and an irregular, unpredictable texture produces a high degree of tension (Ex. VIII-9). The overall effect is

Ex. VIII-9

improvisatory (such pieces were sometimes used as organ "meditations" during the
Mass), but the music is in reality carefully calculated. It is evident from the abundance
of written-out ornamental passages that Frescobaldi, like other composers of the time,
wished to press melodic embellishment into service as an expressive, not merely a
decorative, device; hence he leaves no room for improvised ornamentation.

The figural style of the toccata represents one extreme of Frescobaldi's style. The
other is represented by his imitative ricercari. These too are traditional in general technique, being strongly contrapuntal, usually monothematic pieces. But the chromatic
harmonies and dissonances, and often the use of intrinsically chromatic themes, result in a style that is wholly modern. Between the two extremes stands the canzona,
which combines the sectional construction of the toccata with the imitative texture of
the ricercare. Frescobaldi's canzone are lighter in style than his ricercari. They are divided into three or more clearly demarcated sections, the first and last ordinarily imitative, but in a lively and figural style. Occasionally snatches of the ornamental style of
the toccatas appear at the end of a section. Since each section is based on musical motives normally unrelated to the materials of other sections, and since the sections
generally differ sharply from each other in texture and in meter, the overall effect is
one of discontinuity.

Keyboard music represents almost the only important repertoire for solo instrument in Italy in the early seventeenth century. The immense popularity of the lute apparently declined, and while the easier and more convenient Spanish guitar was much played, little serious music was written for it. Music for instrumental ensemble, however, was actively cultivated. Two basic types may be distinguished: one for large ensemble (generally used polychorally), and a second for smaller groups. The instrumental works of Giovanni Gabrieli are the climax of the first type. These are monumental pieces scored for from eight to over twenty parts. Most are entitled "canzona," but a few are called "sonata" (a term that will be discussed shortly). All are sectional pieces like the keyboard canzone, differing mainly in that they employ rather less imitation—a natural consequence of the extremely rich medium.

Gabrieli's instrumental music

Such pieces are instrumental counterparts of contemporary polychoral vocal pieces. As in vocal music, however, the richest possibilities lay in music for smaller ensembles. This was the more true in instrumental music because the new harmonic freedom caused serious problems of tuning and pitch for almost all except stringed instruments: the rich and varied sonorities of Gabrieli (or of Monteverdi's *Orfeo*) became difficult to achieve unless the harmony was kept extremely simple.

The increasing cultivation of the small instrumental ensemble coincided with a gradual and inconsistent change in terminology. During the early seventeenth century, the term "canzona" was applied to a wide variety of pieces having in common only relatively superficial characteristics: they were sectional, purely instrumental, and had at least some faint resemblance to the French chanson (from which the term derived). Since the newer pieces for small ensemble rarely bore any resemblance at all to the chanson, the word "sonata," meaning simply "something played," came to be used more frequently. An early seventeenth-century sonata is a sectional instrumental piece, for one to four melody instruments plus basso continuo, having no functional purpose but the delectation of the hearers.

The style of the early sonata was extremely various: experimentation and novelty were not confined to vocal music. The violin sonatas of Biagio Marini (1597-1665), for example, are relatively modest pieces, both in size and in the technical ability required of the players. They are generally cast in several sections, each of which employs free imitation and sequence in a manner characteristic of the new style of counterpoint. The bass part, while subordinate, often has a fairly active role, and the chords prescribed by the basso continuo are an essential part of the total sound (unlike the situation in works for many voices). Such pieces clearly illustrate the Baroque polarity between top voice and bass—a polarity that found its first expression in vocal monody.

The early sonata: Biagio Marini

Out of the variety of styles in the first decades of the century, the beginnings of a standard pattern ultimately appeared. The sonata came to consist of alternate lively and slower sections, the quicker ones generally being imitative, the slower ones shorter and often chordal. During the first half of the century, the sections remained rather short, and were apt to exhibit the same kind of discontinuity found in vocal music of the period. The expansion of these sections into larger structures based on a single piece of musical material was an achievement of the middle years of the seventeenth century.

German composers were also active in instrumental music. While dance music was extensively cultivated, Germany's greatest contribution lay in organ music, and

German organ music: Samuel Scheidt

specifically in music connected with the chorale. The central figure was Samuel Scheidt, whose *Tabulatura nova* (1624; the title "new tablature" refers to Scheidt's adoption of the modern Italian manner of keyboard notation) was the most important organ publication of the time. A pupil of Sweelinck, Scheidt took as his primary aim the reform of the German "colorists"—those for whom organ composition was merely a matter of loading virtuoso embellishments on a preexistent melody. In consequence, some of his works suppress ornament almost altogether, and use a contrapuntal style in which only the persistence of small, rhythmic motives and the occasionally intense harmonic language suggest modernity. Others are ornamental and figural, but their ornament is treated as an essential element of the music, rather than as a decorative overlay.

The two excerpts in Example VIII-10 illustrate these methods. The first shows a characteristic insistence on the rhythm ♫ ♩. Page after page of the *Tabulatura nova* is filled with "pattern music" of this kind. The second was labeled by Scheidt himself "imitatio violistica" (imitation of stringed instruments). It is an early instance of the transfer of the idiom of one instrument to the technique of another, a principle that was to be extraordinarily fruitful for the Baroque.

Ex. VIII-10(a)

Ex. VIII-10(b)

Scheidt's use of the choral variation

Most of Scheidt's instrumental work is in some way based on preexistent material. For the most part, chorales or plainsong melodies are used as traditional, long-note cantus firmi. Several settings of the same melody may then be grouped together to form a set of chorale variations. Thus, for example, his *Vater unser* has nine variations, differing in the number of voices used, in the placement of the chorale tune (soprano, tenor, bass), and in the type of treatment (i.e., contrapuntal or figural accompaniment to a long-note chorale, or figuration applied to the given melody itself). In works like these, Scheidt laid the foundations for over a century of German organ technique.

Summary. As the preceding pages have shown, the early seventeenth century was an age of intensive experiment and rapid stylistic change. Each composer formed his own idea of what was valid among the new ideas, and what older techniques were still fruitful. The resulting variety of styles was naturally very great, but one feature remains constant in almost all music of the time: the explicit dependence on the triad as the fundamental building block of musical composition. The emergence and rapid spread of the basso continuo is both a symbol and a consequence of this. In many pieces, or sections of pieces, the triads are so ordered as to produce the effect known as tonality: one triad, the "tonic," acts as a central sonority, and all the others are related to it in specific and well-defined ways. Nevertheless, while all good music of the time has some sort of tonal cohesion, tonality in this sense is not a necessary or consistent attribute of early seventeenth-century music. Most composers still enjoyed and made use of the rich variety of chord-relationships inherited from the late sixteenth century, and expanded by the early seventeenth. Such richness was at the time incompatible with tonality as it developed later in the century. One of the central accomplishments of the next generation of composers was the selection from the harmonic vocabulary of those triad successions that could most strongly convey an unequivocal tonal feeling.

APPENDIX: Chapter VIII

EARLY BAROQUE

I. **Styles.** The late 16th-century tendency toward polarization of upper voices and supporting bass led to the creation of two basic elements of Baroque style: basso continuo and recitative style.

A. Basso continuo. A bass line that is the harmonic foundation of the music. The harmonies implied by the bass line, or specifically required by the use of figures, are realized by a chord-playing instrument. Thus a composition for solo voice and basso continuo would require at least three (not two) performers: a singer, one instrumentalist to play the bass line ('cello, bassoon, viola da gamba, etc.), and one or more to play the harmonies (lute, harpsichord, organ, etc.).

B. Recitative style. Invented in Florence in the years preceding 1600. An attempt to revive classical Greek musical declamation, designed to make music subservient to words. Stylistic features:

1. A single solo voice declaiming in a relatively free rhythm based largely on the prosody and the sense of the text.
2. Expressive devices: unusual rhythms; dissonances between voice part and bass; unusual skips in the voice part.
3. Accompaniment limited to a frequently rather static basso continuo line.

II. **Forms.** Formal categories were not always well defined in early Baroque music: definitions must be somewhat tentative.

A. Monodies. Pieces in recitative style. Many collections were published in the early 17th century. Individual pieces were usually called "aria" (strophic) or "madrigale" (through-composed). Some composers: Giulio Caccini, Sigismondo d'India, Claudio Saracini, Alessandro Grandi.

B. Cantatas. Longer (and slightly later) pieces of solo vocal music with basso continuo, occasionally also with melody instruments. Text is usually secular. Frequently made up of smaller sections, some of which are more musically interesting than others; the latter are nearer the pure recitative style, while the former are the precursors of the later *aria* (not in the sense of strophic monody, as above, but in the sense used by Bach and Handel: a big, musically interesting song, as distinguished from a recitative). Composers include Salomone Rossi and Giacomo Carissimi.

C. Oratorios. Large dramatic (but not staged) pieces, usually on religious subjects. They often include chorus, instruments, several solo singers, one of whom may be a *testo*, or narrator. Composers include Carissimi, Heinrich Schütz, and, later, Marc-Antoine Charpentier and Alessandro Stradella.

234

D. "Concertato" pieces. The term is applied to most pieces that involve several singers, or singers plus instruments, or (sometimes) several instruments. Such pieces characteristically have several short sections involving solo singing, instrumental refrains, ensemble sections, etc. Some composers: Claudio Monteverdi, Giovanni Gabrieli, Lodovico da Viadana, Schütz, Johann Hermann Schein.

E. Opera. The invention of the Florentine monodists. The earliest operas, by Caccini and Peri, had long stretches of music in recitative style. Later opera often added more elements of purely musical interest. The growing separation of dramatic and musical elements (the later Baroque distinction between recitative and aria) is felt first in opera. Some composers: Caccini; Giacomo Peri; Claudio Monteverdi; Steffano Landi; Luigi Rossi.

F. Instrumental music.

1. Ensemble. Early pieces are not clearly defined: pieces named "sinfonia," "sonata," "canzona" were designed for instruments and might consist of several short sections. The favored Baroque texture of two equal upper parts plus bass is sometimes used. Composers include Biagio Marini and Francesco Turini.

2. Solo keyboard. Rhapsodic pieces (toccata, *intonazione*, prelude) and more contrapuntal ones (canzona, ricercare) continue in favor; they are sometimes quite long, with contrasting improvisatory and imitative sections. Composers include Trabaci, Girolamo Frescobaldi, Schein.

III. Composers.

Caccini, Giulio (ca. 1546–1618). Italian singer and composer. His *Le nuove musiche*, a collection of monodies, set the pattern for many other such collections; the expression of the text, particularly by means of affective vocal ornaments, is discussed in the important preface to this publication.

Cavalieri, Emilio de' (ca. 1550–1602). Roman aristocrat, associated with the Florentine theorists and composers ca. 1600. Used elements of the recitative style mixed with more traditional materials in the "sacred opera" *La rappresentazione di anima e di corpo* (Representation of the soul and the body; 1600).

Frescobaldi, Girolamo (1583–1643). Organist of St. Peter's, Rome. Composer of much imaginative instrumental music for organ, harpsichord, and instrumental ensemble.

Landi, Steffano (ca. 1590–ca. 1655). Italian composer, active at Rome. His opera *Sant' Alessio* (1632) shows the beginning of the Baroque division of text into neutral recitative and musically interesting song (aria).

Marini, Biagio (1597–1665). Italian violinist and composer. One of the earliest composers of Baroque violin music and concerted instrumental pieces.

Monteverdi, Claudio (1567–1643). Prolific and innovative, he bridges, in his music, the gap between Renaissance and Baroque. He produced imaginative masterpieces in all genres except instrumental music: madrigal, opera, concertato vocal music, monody, and sacred music.

Peri, Jacopo (1561–1633). Italian singer and composer. His setting of *Euridice* (1600) is more dramatic, less inclined to vocal display, than that of Caccini.

Praetorius, Michael (1571–1621). German composer, noted for his concertato vocal music. Author of an important treatise, *Syntagma musicum* (1618), dealing, among other things, with musical instruments and their use.

Scheidt, Samuel (1587–1654). German composer, active at Halle. Composer of much liturgical organ music, and of concertato music.

Schein, Johann Hermann (1586–1630). German composer, cantor at Leipzig. Like Schütz, he was a pioneer in the new concertato style of vocal music in Germany.

Schütz, Heinrich (1585–1672). German composer, court musician at Dresden. The pupil of Giovanni Gabrieli and of Monteverdi, he imported Italian innovations into Germany, and wrote vocal music (almost exclusively sacred) of great charm.

Viadana, Lodovico da (1564–1645). Italian composer. One of the earliest to employ a (somewhat conservative) type of monody in sacred music.

IV. **Bibliography.**

A. Books.

Blume, Friedrich: *Renaissance and Baroque Music*, New York, 1967.

Bukofzer, Manfred: *Music in the Baroque Era*, New York, 1947.

Palisca, Claude: *Baroque Music*, Englewood Cliffs, N. J., 1968.

B. Music: A selected list of publications containing early Baroque music.

Benevenuti, Giacomo, ed.: *I classici musicali italiani*, vol. 1, Milan, 1941. Early 17th-century organ music.

Caccini, Giulio: *Le nuove musiche*, 2 facs. eds., Rome, 1930, 1934. Modern ed. by H. Wiley Hitchcock, Madison, Wisc., 1970.

Jeppeson, Kurt., ed.: *La Flora*, 3 vols., Copenhagen, 1949. An anthology of monodies.

Peri, Jacopo: *Euridice*, facs. ed., Rome, 1934.

Monteverdi, Claudio: Complete works, ed. Francesco Malipiero, 16 vols., Asolo, 1926–66.

Schütz, Heinrich: *Neue Ausgabe sämtlicher Werke* (in progress), Kassel, 1955–   ; an older edition, ed. P. Spitta et. al., 18 vols., Leipzig, 1885–1927.

IX

THE LATER
SEVENTEENTH CENTURY
DEVELOPMENT OF A COMMON
PRACTICE

In the years from 1640 to about 1690, Italy kept the musical leadership it had recently acquired. Germany developed an increasingly important musical culture, based primarily on Italian models, but with strong native elements as well. France, having rejected the Italian innovations of the early 1600s, stood in musical isolation; and England also remained, though in a different way, outside the central development of style. This divergence of national styles, despite certain common elements, is a striking feature of seventeenth-century music, especially when contrasted with the international quality of much Renaissance music, and the gradually increasing internationalism of the eighteenth century. This chapter therefore will consider first the development of tonality and the music of Italy, then French and English music to about 1700, and finally German music of the later seventeenth century.

The years after 1640 were a time of selection and clarification, as might be expected after decades of experimentation and novelty. For the best composers of the early 1600s, every work was an individual problem, requiring its own particular solution. What was now needed was the integration of selected new techniques into a new common practice, comparable in stability to the common practice of the sixteenth century, so that the same procedures could be used and re-used in different works, each time with fresh content.

PRINCIPLES OF TONALITY

The basis of an emergent common practice was the gradual elaboration of the principles of tonality—principles adumbrated but by no means fully established in many works of the early seventeenth century. As early as the fifteenth century, certain chord progressions had become standardized as cadential forms, the authentic cadence being the most important of these. During the sixteenth century, music came to be based almost as much upon successions of triads as upon the combination of lines. In a Palestrina Mass or motet, for example, the contrapuntal texture may be and often is extremely complex, but it also invariably produces a series of triads. The basso seguente was a tacit admission of this underlying triadic structure, and the basso continuo an explicit one.

Tonality, however, does not automatically result from the use of triads: it requires the use of triads in specific ways, which derive ultimately from the fifth-progression inherent in the authentic cadence. The theory of tonality begins with the assumption that a single tone may be made in some way central in the structure of a piece of music. This, of course, is nothing new: such an assumption may be found in much Western music of all periods. But in the seventeenth century, the primacy of a certain tone automatically assured the primacy of the triad built on that tone—the tonic triad. Normally, the progression found in the authentic cadence was used to establish the identity of a given triad as tonic: the desired tonic triad was preceded by a triad built on a tone a perfect fifth higher—the so-called dominant triad. The chords in the progression dominant-tonic (or V-I, to use the later shorthand designation) are not, however, wholly unambiguous. If the two triads are played in the reverse order, for example, it is not at all clear that the first chord is the tonic. What is required is still a third chord, the subdominant (IV), lying a fifth below the tonic, as the dominant lies a fifth above. Arranged in the order IV-V-I, these triads unequivocally specify the tonal center, and since the tonic usually begins as well as ends a tonal phrase, such a phrase will generally have the structure shown in Example IX-1.

Establishing a tonal center (margin note)

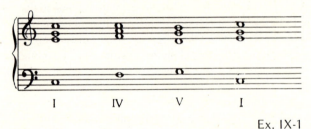

Ex. IX-1

Now this basic progression can be established on any tone whatsoever as tonic. When the tonic is C, the progression is in the key of C; when it is A, it is in the key of A. Moreover, any tonic triad can have one or two different forms: it may have a major third above the tonic note (as in C-E-G), or a minor third (as in A-C-E, or C-E♭-G). This comes about because two basic scales are available for each tonic. Those keys having the tonic triad with major third are called major keys; and those having the minor third, minor. Example IX-2 shows the basic progression in a number of different keys, together with the scales implied by those progressions and the normal key signature—the sharps or flats that occur regularly in music of that key, and hence are written at the beginnings of the staves, instead of each time they occur. (Note that in minor keys, the raised seventh degree of the scale is not included in the signature.)

Major and minor (margin note)

The basic progression [I . . .] IV-V-I may define a tonic, but it does not automatically produce music. To supplement the unifying effect of the central tonal harmonies, there must also be provision for harmonic variety. Such variety may be achieved in several ways.

Harmonic variety (margin note)

First, the root of the triad need not always be in the lowest voice. Any triad may under appropriate circumstances be presented with its third or (more rarely) with its fifth in the bass. These two forms of a triad are called its first and second inver-

Ex. IX-2

sions, and while they lack the solidity of the root position form, they provide not only variety, but also opportunity for writing smooth and melodious bass parts.

Second, even the chords of the basic progression may to some extent be replaced by related sonorities. This is especially fruitful in the case of the subdominant, for which several substitutes are available, but even the dominant may occasionally be replaced by a related chord. Such replacements are often not triads, but seventh chords: triads to which a further third has been added on top. Seventh chords are necessarily dissonant, and hence useful in heightening harmonic tension.

Third, all the various possible chords of a given key (i.e., the triads and seventh chords built on each of the seven scale degrees) may be used in the interior of a phrase without reference to the basic progression, in successions that have their own harmonic logic. Such successions are most often sequential, since sequence is the easiest way of achieving the necessary coherence.

Fourth, any major or minor triad of a key may be preceded by its own dominant, called a secondary dominant, in contrast with the true dominant of the key. This usage generally involves the momentary introduction of tones foreign to the basic scale of the key, and can produce much harmonic richness without weakening the centrality of the tonic.

The use of a secondary dominant implies that a non-tonic triad is for an instant treated as a tonic. When a chord is so treated for an extended period of time—when,

Modulation

that is, the original tonic is temporarily suppressed in favor of another tonic—the resulting change of key is called modulation. Modulation is of enormous utility, for it permits a kind of harmonic traveling—a journey from the tonic to one or more related keys, culminating in a return to the starting point. Such a scheme combines unity with variety in ideal fashion, and makes possible the maintenance of tension (caused by the absence of the original tonic) over large stretches of time.

In seventeenth-century music, modulation is generally restricted to keys closely related to the original tonic (i.e., those that share several triads with the original). The change of tonal center is achieved by the use of a chord common to both keys, which is aproached as if it were in the old key, but left as if it were in the new one. This gives a smooth and gradual effect. Occasionally, for special purposes, two remotely related chords may be directly juxtaposed, producing a much more sudden and striking modulation.

While the principles of tonality are founded on triads and seventh chords, tonal music freely admits the regular presence of *nonharmonic* tones—tones foreign to the triad or seventh chord sounding at any given moment. These, which the ear easily distinguishes from the chordal background, can serve to animate the rhythmic texture, provide dissonance, and, in general, add still further variety without compromising the basic tonal unity.

Needless to say, a technique of such potential complexity—only the simpler aspects of tonality have been summarized here—was not formulated instantly. It came into being by slow and sometimes uncertain steps. The proof of its increasing strength is shown by a basic trend in the music of the seventeenth century. While music of the early decades is generally made up of relatively short units, so that even a lengthy piece turns out, on examination, to consist of many short sections, the later 1600s expand these sections, separating them into independent movements, often of considerable length. It was above all the organizing power of tonality that permitted this.

MUSIC IN ITALY

Venetian opera

The public opera houses of Venice proved to be an enormous success, and opera quickly became one of the principal types of public entertainment in Italy. Opera singers, in particular, acquired great fame, often far more than that achieved by either librettists or composers. Especially in demand were the castrati, male singers who were emasculated before their voices changed at puberty. However questionable such a procedure may seem on moral grounds, the aesthetic results were apparently spectacular. The castrati retained the soprano voices of boys, but developed a power unattainable by either boys or women; and their long and rigorous training (shared by all singers of the time) made them capable of vocal virtuosity unmatched before or since.

Given the popularity of opera and the adulation of singers, it is hardly surprising that composers and librettists were interested primarily in pleasing the public. The librettists, for their part, aimed consciously at entertainment, not edification. Their libretti are similar in form to that of Monteverdi's *Incoronazione di Poppea*: there is a prologue, followed by three or more acts, each consisting of up to a dozen or more short scenes. The plots are freely based on ancient history or, less often, mythology, so adapted as to permit special emphasis on disguise in general and transvestism in

Fig. IX-1: A stage-setting, designed by Giacomo Torelli, for a seventeenth-century opera. The scene represents the palace of Apollo. (Harvard Theatre Collection.)

particular. Comic characters and scenes are freely mingled with the serious action. While the bizarre and preposterous results are not distinguished literature, the libretti are carefully contrived to make the basic passions of the chief characters stand out with great force and clarity.

The music also continued in the tradition of *Poppea*, but with clear signs of a new direction. At first, Monteverdi's flexible dramatic method was retained: any scene might be a mixture, determined by the dramatic situation, of recitative, short aria sections, and music too lyrical for recitative but too fragmentary for aria. Gradually, however, composers came to cast most scenes in a regular pattern of alternation between recitative and aria, and to concentrate most of the musical interest in the aria, which served not only the dramatic function of conveying emotion, but also the less exalted one of displaying the singer's ability. Opera, which had come into existence in order that music should be the servant of the drama, was moving towards a new balance, in which musical values came first to equal, and then to exceed in importance the dramatic substance.

The chief Venetian opera composer after Monteverdi was one of his pupils, Francesco Cavalli (1602-76), many of whose forty-odd operas were so successful in Venice that they were subsequently produced in other Italian cities. In Cavalli's work,

Operas of Francesco Cavalli

the recitative often retains the affective force it had had in earlier opera, although there are also many pages of rather neutral declamatory writing. In some scenes, the flexible scene structure just mentioned is maintained; in others, recitative and aria are clearly separated, both in style and in function. Although some arias are fairly long, their length is generally achieved by the repetition or alternation of rather short musical units. There are strophic arias, often with an instrumental ritornello after each strophe; arias on an ostinato bass (a form especially favored for laments); and arias in several sections, freely fashioned according to the demands of the text.

Instruments in addition to those executing the basso continuo are also significantly employed in Cavalli's operas. The instrumental *sinfonia,* or overture, with which every opera began, was by this time a piece in several sections contrasting in tempo; those of Cavalli are scored for a five-part orchestra, presumably of strings. Instruments *Cavalli's arias* are also used, of course, for the ritornelli of arias. In a few arias, instrumental accompaniment is called for within the aria itself. Such arias "with instruments," as they are called in the scores, are still relatively rare: in most arias, only the basso continuo accompanies the singer. But the technique is a progressive one, and in later operas, the number of such pieces is larger.

In Example IX-3, the beginning of an aria "with instruments" from Cavalli's *Erismena* (1655), the ritornello is a musically complete unit, as was customary. But here a new unity is achieved, for Cavalli has made the opening of the ritornello identical to the beginning of the vocal section. Later in the aria, the voice and the instruments are heard together. Thus integration of texture is achieved by instrumental participation in vocal sections, and integration of musical material by relating the ritornello thematically to the vocal part. This is the first step in a development that was ultimately to make the voice and orchestra nearly equal participants.

Cavalli's treatment of harmony here shows what had been achieved in the realm of tonality, and, by implication, the lines along which further development would take place. The emphasis on the chords of the basic progression (I . . . IV-V-I) is striking: the first three measures consist of that progression only, and the three following repeat the same progression a fifth higher.

The tonal clarity of the ritornello prevails throughout the aria as a whole. The first section is solidly in G; the middle section makes modulations to various related keys; and the last section is merely a restatement of the first, also in G. Although this is for its time a rather long aria, Cavalli achieves length by the still traditional means of juxtaposing small-scale elements (the ritornello is 12 measures long, the first vocal section 20). Only the middle section is at all extended (45 measures). This is natural: the numerous modulations not only provide harmonic variety, but also a means of extending the musical material. It had become easy enough to establish a key, and easy enough to modulate; but it was not yet easy to write extensive passages within a single key. Hence tonal structures remained relatively small until means were discovered by which to expand from within—to write phrases not of three or four measures, as here, but of eight or sixteen.

The overall form of this aria is ABA', in both text and music. Although ABA form was to become the normal aria structure two generations later, it was by no means a regular choice with Cavalli, who employed it as only one among many possible forms.

Cavalli's recitative may be studied in an excerpt from the same scene (Ex. IX-4). It is still carefully written and forceful, if not as passionate as that of Monteverdi. Emo-

Aldimira

Va — — ghe stel — le — lu — — — ci bel — le —

Ex. IX-3

Aldimira   Erismena

So- gna il mio bene   co-sì co-sì la tua Er-is-me-na fiero I-dra-spe tra-di-sti?

co- sì co-sì fel-lon scher — ni-sti chi l'hon-or tua ti die — de?

Aldimira: My beloved is dreaming. *Erismena*: Thus, proud Idraspe, you have betrayed
your Erismena. Thus, villain, you have scorned her, who gave you your honor.

Ex. IX-4

Cavalli's recitative
tional intensity is produced, as in earlier recitative, by harmonic means, notably by the introduction of remote and unexpected chords. Thus, in the example, Aldimira has a few words, ending on an E major triad. (The actual triads do not, of course, appear in the score: they were supplied from the bass line by the accompanist.) Erismena breaks in with her first question on the remotely related triad on C. Her second question ("Così, così fellon") returns as abruptly to E major. These sudden shifts are unpredictable to the ear, and create strong tension. Thus while recitative may contain a large number of normal tonal progressions, unexpected harmonic shocks such as these tend to neutralize any overall tonal unity: the changes of key are here based on textual, not musical, considerations. While some recitatives, particularly those of the soliloquy type, are tonally unified, most are not; it was sufficient that a recitative end in a key closely related to that of the aria that was to follow.

Accompanied recitative
In a very few cases, the recitative was accompanied, not merely by the basso continuo, but by stringed instruments as well, Use of this effect was reserved for one or two climactic scenes of an opera. The enriched accompaniment naturally enhances the musical—and hence the affective—force of the declamation, and "accompanied recitative," as it is called, with ample musical means to portray quickly changing emotions, was a tool of great dramatic potential. It was, however, seldom employed, as the overall trend was in favor of musical, rather than dramatic, values.

This trend is evident in the work of Antonio Cesti (1623-69), an enormously popular composer who set the style for musicians all over Italy. In his operas the recitative has lost still more of its once focal position, as still more of the musical interest has been transferred to the arias. This tendency may have been connected with the increasing popularity of the cantata, a genre extensively cultivated by Cesti. The cantata, a direct descendant of early seventeenth-century monody, was a setting for relatively small forces, of a lyrical or dramatic poem, and was intended for non-stage performance before a small and presumably cultivated audience. Although the cantata, like the opera, employed both recitative and aria, it was naturally less dramatic in purpose.

Look at me, drunk with endearments, rich with oaths, loaded with promises, swollen with hopes, and then left alone in despair.

From *Antonio Cesti, Four Chamber Duets*, ed. David L. Burrows, A-R editions, 1969. Used by permission.

Ex. IX-5(a)

Otherwise, the two remained closely related, both in style and in forms: a cantata from the middle or late seventeenth century looks very much like a fragment of an opera.

In the case of Cesti, the smaller form could well have influenced the larger. Such an influence could have operated in only one direction. The opera, generally a large-scale work with a complex plot and lavish scenery, could still afford to use music in a subordinate role if the composer so chose. But the cantata was an almost purely musical type, and needed all the resources that elegant singing and rich harmony could provide. In Cesti's cantata *Pria ch' adori*, excerpts from which are given in Example IX-5, while the recitative is impressively affective, it leads up to the following duet as to a

The cantata: Antonio Cesti

Sad crowds who weep, fix in your thoughts the bitter way of my misfortunes.

From *Antonio Cesti, Four Chamber Duets*, ed. David L. Burrows, A-R editions, 1969. Used by permission.

Ex. IX-5(b)

climax. It is the duet, with its flowing triple-meter lines, that is the primary focus of interest. The elegant lyricism of such pieces has earned the name "bel canto" (beautiful song) for the style of the period. Repetition of words for purely musical reasons is a clear and common sign of the predominance of musical over textual values. In the complete cantata, the proportion of aria to recitative is even greater than indicated by the example, and some cantatas lack recitative almost entirely.

Cesti's operas

Transferred to the operatic stage, such a style inevitably increases emphasis on the aria there also. While Cesti's operas contain much recitative, some of it as intense as that of *Pria ch' adori*, in drama there is necessarily a great deal of text that is not affective in nature. For this, Cesti uses a neutral and declamatory recitative, against which the melodious arias and duets stand out the more strongly. While Cesti remains faithful to the concept of opera as musical drama, in that his arias are dramatically justified as lyrical expansions of dramatic emotion, his operas point to a style in which music—especially singing—predominates. It is only a step from Cesti to the "singer's opera," in which the drama is merely an excuse for the display of the composer's melodic gift, and, even more, for that of the singer's virtuosity.

Cesti's most famous work,*Il pomo d'oro* (The Golden Apple; 1668) is not entirely typical. Since it was written for an imperial wedding at the Viennese court, it was, like the earliest operas, largely freed from practical constraints. *Il pomo d'oro* contains all the normal ingredients of opera, but is much longer and more lavish. More characteristic of Cesti are *Orontea* (1649) and *La Dori* (1661), the first written for Venice, the second for Florence. That the three operas cited were composed for three different cities, one outside Italy, is an indication of the wide diffusion both of Cesti's work and of Italian opera in general. By mid-century, an operatic common practice had in fact been achieved, and its products were in demand not only throughout Italy, but in much of Austria and southern Germany as well.

Among Cesti's numerous successors, Giovanni Legrenzi (1626-90) and Alessandro Stradella (1644-82) may be mentioned. In their works, and in those of their contemporaries, the tendency towards primacy of music over drama continued, with the aria assuming more and more importance. As it increased in importance, the aria also grew in diversity. From about 1670 on, the characteristic triple-meter bel canto style began to give way to a greater variety of aria types. Different types of aria texts began to receive more sharply contrasting musical settings, each representing a particular emotion. Thus, to join the lament, which had been a recognized aria type since the beginning, there arose many more classes, expressing a range of emotions from despair to exuberant joy.

Agostino Steffani

This and other aspects of Italian opera near the end of the century may be illustrated by the work of two composers who worked in quite different circumstances: Agostino Steffani (1654-1728), who passed most of his career writing Italian opera for German courts; and Alessandro Scarlatti (1660-1725), who began his work in Rome but later spent much time in Naples and in other Italian cities (Scarlatti's later works will be considered below). Steffani was little known in Italy. His ability to achieve success abroad testifies to the popularity of Italian opera in Germany, but it also hints at the primacy of musical values over dramatic ones. While German court audiences may well have been educated, compared to many who frequented public opera houses in Italy, it may be doubted that all of them understood sung Italian well enough to follow the intricacies of a libretto: the continuing German interest in Italian opera thus suggests that the music was the principal attraction.

Steffani's operas are generally serious and carefully wrought, with considerable contrapuntal as well as melodic interest. Three aria beginnings (Ex. IX-6) from his *Alarico* (1687) show clear differentiation among aria types. The first is a solemn prayer; the second a lyrical piece; and the third, accompanied by trumpets, a typically martial one. Each continues by developing, through use of sequence, modulation, and varied repetition, the materials of the beginning. In this way, each maintains a consistent mood, and projects a single emotion.

Nume_a-la-to   Nume_a-lato dammi pace

Se non   vo-glio_in a- - mo- rar-mi

Schie –   re in -vit-te non tar - da- te

Winged god, give me peace   Ex. IX-6
If I don't wish to fall in love
Unconquered hosts, do not delay

By this time, the pattern ABA, with slightly contrasting material for the middle (B) section, had become the most common form for the aria. At the same time, the internal expansion of the aria had also begun; and while many of Steffani's arias are still quite short, some are of a size that would have been unlikely in 1650. The combination of increased length with the necessarily static ABA pattern emphasizes the essential nature of middle and late Baroque dramaturgy. Action can take place only in recitative: the arias, which by now take up most of the score, serve only to express emotional states. The vitality of Baroque opera depended on their effectiveness in doing this both faithfully and appealingly.

Steffani represents the aristocratic type of late seventeenth-century Italian opera, which found its most congenial home in the courts of Austria and southern Germany. Italy itself preferred a slightly different type, in which comic scenes more often continued to be inserted into predominantly serious plots, and in which vocal melody and vocal virtuosity were even more strongly emphasized than in the court opera. The early work of Alessandro Scarlatti may be taken as representative of the native Italian opera, not because he is the most typical composer, but because he is the one best known now, and because he was probably the most talented. Others, whose music is simpler

Alessandro Scarlatti's early operas

and less demanding, were more successful in their own day; but their work is now almost wholly inaccessible, while Scarlatti's is at least in small part available.

At first glance, a Scarlatti score looks much like one of Steffani. There is the same regular alternation between recitative and aria, with the former carrying primarily the narrative, the latter the affective portion of the text. Only in a few climactic scenes is a more flexible construction used. There is also the same increased individuality of aria types, characteristic of the late 1600s. But in Scarlatti's operas (and others intended for Italian audiences) there are also comic scenes, with special aria types of their own. Moreover, the music has a certain sensuous quality, not absent from the court opera, but more pervasive here. This quality, not easily definable, is most apparent in the graceful and charming vocal melody, and in the relative lack of emphasis on counterpoint.

In the aria "Ah crudel," from Scarlatti's *La Rosaura* (1690), the voice is accompanied by a four-part string ensemble. The instruments, while fully integrated into the texture, are given for the most part brief interjections, not continuous contrapuntal lines. The singer is the center of attention, and the instruments support, but do not compete with the voice.

This aria also is in ABA form, as are most in the operas of the period. As is regularly the case, the B section is based on material similar or identical to that of A, but treated in different keys—another instance of the role of tonality in articulating form. Occasionally, for textual reasons, the B section may contrast more sharply with A, but the inevitable return of the A section still prevents any true dramatic progression during the aria: the music and text of the end will be those of the beginning, at least on the printed page. In actual performance, it was customary for the singer to improvise (or to have prepared) embellishments for the second occurrence of the A section, which would thus become at least a musical climax for the aria as a whole.

Scarlatti begins "Ah crudel" with an effect that came into common use in his time. The first utterance of the voice, here at the very beginning of the piece (Ex. IX-7), is a brief and preliminary statement of the main melodic idea, which is then repeated and continued. An aria beginning thus is often called a "motto aria," the preliminary statement being the motto or epitome of what is to follow. Here both the initial statement and its repetition are immediate; in other arias, a brief instrumental section may precede and follow the first statement.

Motto aria

The motto aria is a particularly striking illustration of the composer's desire to focus his music precisely on a single emotion: the motto sums up in a few notes the whole meaning of the aria, of which the remainder is a musically necessary and agreeable expansion. It should be noted that while musical materials—whether used as a motto or not—were expected to express as exactly as possible a specific emotion, they were not intended to be "original" in the modern sense of the word. A triumphant aria by Scarlatti may sound very like an aria to a similar text by some other composer. As long as both conveyed the intended sentiment, their similarity was not regarded as a defect.

In short, music was to present a gallery of emotional types. Ultimately, under the influence of the seventeenth-century belief that music could produce specific emotional reactions in the hearer by the use of specific musical means, a belief prominent in the mechanistic psychology of René Descartes (1596-1650), a whole theory of such types—the "Doctrine of the Affections"—grew up. In the theoretical formulations of this "doctrine," most of which date from the eighteenth century, attempts were made

Doctrine of the Affections

Ah, crudel, Ah, cru-del di che bel van--to te sarebbe la pie-tà

Ex. IX-7

to derive general rules by which music might be made to express certain emotions: small intervals, for example, were found appropriate for grief; large ones for joy. But as early as the 1690s, composers were devising appropriate musical figures intuitively, without reference to abstract theory.

Both opera and cantata were, in the vast majority of cases, secular in subject matter. Indeed, opera was most at home in the festive carnival season immediately preceding Lent. In penitential seasons, opera was not performed, but the popularity of musical drama encouraged the development of an analogous sacred form, the oratorio, in which contemporary musical styles could be used in the unstaged presentation of a sacred story. Two types of oratorio were cultivated, the *oratorio volgare* (oratorio in the vernacular), and the Latin oratorio. Both had obvious resemblances to the opera, and even more to the cantata: in all these genres, an action was represented musically; and in the cantata and oratorio the action was imagined, not seen by the listener. The oratorio, however, differed from the secular forms in its use of a *testo* (narrator), a soloist who sang the non-dialogue portions of the text, and in its emphasis on the chorus, which, especially in the Latin oratorio, continued to be of primary importance even after it had largely disappeared from opera.

Oratorio

The *oratorio volgare* developed from sacred dialogues that followed the sermon in religious services of a popular nature. In the late sixteenth century, such dialogues (between God and the soul, for example) were sung polyphonically. In the early seventeenth century, monody was used where appropriate—for single characters and for the narrator—and choral polyphony for groups of characters and for devotional texts.

The Latin oratorio was closely connected with the Brotherhood of the Santissimo Crocifisso in Rome, a largely aristocratic religious fraternity. It was the custom of this group to have Latin motets performed at its meetings—motets that, by the early seventeenth century, were in concertato style. When the Scriptural motet texts contained dialogue (as often happened), their latent dramatic possibilities were exploited by assigning different singers to the several characters of the text, and composing the parts in the new monodic style. The motet was too small a framework, however, for the presentation of a complete Scriptural story in a single continuous composition. The large Latin oratorio, consisting of a number of "scenes," provided a convenient solution to this problem.

Giacomo Carissimi

Domenico Mazzocchi (1592-1665) was an important composer of vernacular oratorios, but the most celebrated oratorio writer of the century was Giacomo Carissimi (1605-74), whose Latin oratorios—based on Old Testament stories—are settings of Biblical texts expanded by newly written material. The added text is most often of a lyrical cast, since the Bible usually gives only the bare narrative. Carissimi's recitative is, at climactic moments, as impassioned as that of the earliest operas; and even in the arias and duets, his music provides a carefully wrought realistic depiction of the story. In one duet from his *Abram et Isaac,* the two characters are so overcome by emotion that their words come out in little clusters of notes separated by rests—a graphic portrayal of emotional incoherence. In other, less intense situations, Carissimi employs the flowing triple-meter lines characteristic of the mid-century.

Carissimi's choral writing generally avoids complex polyphony in favor of simple texture, animated by forceful rhythms based on the textual stresses. The result is brilliant and sonorous: the choral conclusions of the oratorios are among his finest efforts.

After Carissimi, oratorio was cultivated mostly by opera composers, who at first maintained a specific oratorio style for their sacred pieces. By the end of the century, however, the oratorio was no longer composed as part of a religious service, but had become an independent sacred opera in concert form, for use during Lent. Even the narrator and the chorus—the two primary features that had distinguished oratorio from opera—disappeared in the course of time, leaving only the sacred subject matter and the absence of staging as real oratorio characteristics.

Other Italian sacred music

Apart from the oratorio, Italian sacred music of the seventeenth century is little known. Many settings of the Mass, of vesper psalms, and the like were written—often by composers whose operatic or instrumental music is more familiar. These works ranged from modest "motets" for solo voice with basso continuo, through more elaborate pieces with instrumental ritornelli, up to huge polychoral works in the concertato tradition, with soloists, one or more choruses, and instruments. On the basis of the scanty information available, it would appear that sacred music, while naturally influenced by contemporary developments in opera, was primarily descended from the concertato style of the earlier part of the century. Long texts, like the Gloria of the Mass, were naturally set in sections; and, in later works, the sections were longer and more clearly characterized. Neither recitative nor aria was of much importance in liturgical music. Aria-like sections occur, but only as subordinate parts of a larger design.

Instrumental Music. The seventeenth century was as important for instrumental music as it was for vocal music; and, in general, the same stylistic features appear in both repertoires. This is not surprising, since, for almost the first time, there were important composers who were equally active in both fields. The rise of instrumental music to a position of equality was accomplished in the seventeenth century. In another hundred years, it was to surpass vocal music in importance.

The chief instrumental vehicle during the later seventeenth century was the sonata, a term by this time applied to two different kinds of pieces, each of which might be written for varius media. The *sonata da camera* (chamber sonata) was a succession of dance pieces. The *sonata da chiesa* (church sonata) was the successor of the abstract type of sonata described earlier. Either might be scored for one or more melody instruments plus basso continuo. The terminology is thoroughly confusing. A sonata for one melody instrument and basso continuo is called a solo sonata (but may require three performers—one for the bass line, another for the realization of the figured bass, and a third for the melody part). A sonata for two instruments plus basso continuo is, however, called a trio sonata, the nomenclature being based here on the number of contrapuntal parts (the trio sonata generally requires four performers). Sonatas for larger ensembles are designated *à* 4 (three melody instruments and continuo), *à* 5 (four instruments and continuo), and so on.

The Baroque sonata: terminology

The chief centers of instrumental composition were in northern Italy: Venice, Modena, and especially Bologna. The founder of the Bolognese school was Maurizio Cazzati (ca. 1620-77), also a prolific composer of sacred music. In his instrumental works, Cazzati most often chooses the trio sonata medium. This preference is symptomatic. A contrapuntal common practice was needed as much as a harmonic one, and it could be achieved neither in the solo sonata, always prone to virtuoso display, nor in the many-voiced medium, which was too thick in texture. The open texture formed by two high melodies sounding over a distant bass—already exploited by Monteverdi—was ideal for contrapuntal development.

Cazzati's sonatas stand between the canzona and the experimental sonatas of the early 1600s on the one hand, and the fully developed trio sonata of his successors on the other. The dimensions are still very small, but each section is large enough to be considered an independent movement. In many movements, the two violins engage in imitation (not shared by the basso continuo) as is almost demanded by this kind of medium (Ex. IX-8). Indeed, imitation became a fundamental device of Baroque music, although its function was fundamentally different from that of Renaissance imitation. Baroque imitation is based on what has here been called the new counterpoint—lines built out of short rhythmic motives, often sequential. These motives arise from and contribute to the underlying tonal harmony, and their employment is conditioned by

Trio sonatas of Maurizio Cazzati

Imitation in Baroque music

(continued on following page)

Ex. IX-8

Ex. IX-8

the harmonic plan. In Renaissance music, counterpoint is the essential element, producing a harmonic succession that is of lesser importance. These positions are reversed in Baroque style: it is the succession of triads that is fundamental, and to this succession contrapuntal devices, conditioned by the harmony, may be added as desired.

The mature trio sonata: Giovanni Maria Bononcini and Giovanni Battista Vitali

Still nascent with Cazzati, the interest in imitative counterpoint heightened in the works of his two principal successors, Giovanni Maria Bononcini (1642-78) and Giovanni Battista Vitali (ca. 1644-92). Bononcini wrote a number of sonatas in canon, and Vitali's *Artifici musicali* is a kind of textbook of elaborate contrapuntal devices.

Such works were, however, extremes. The trio sonata entered with Vitali and Bononcini a classical phase, in which imitation played an important but not overwhelming part. Out of the rich variety of canzona sections, three types of movement crystallized: the quick imitative type, usually in duple meter; a slow type, generally featuring striking harmonies and dissonant suspensions; and a quick type in triple meter, loosely imitative, with dance-like rhythms. These types may also be seen in Cazzati, but without the individuality and homogeneity found in Vitali and Bononcini.

The opening measures of a Vitali sonata are shown in Example IX-9. The lengthy theme (or "subject") in the first violin part begins by clearly defining the key of A minor, then exploits the variety inherent in all the chords of that key before returning to an A minor cadence. Overlapping this cadence, the theme is then presented in the second violin. Thereafter, the movement alternates between modulating sequences and presentations of the theme in related keys (ending, of course, in the original tonic, A minor). Since the material of the sequences is drawn from fragments of the theme, the result is tightly unified.

Ex. IX-9

Most of the sequences are of a type that became a fundamental staple of Baroque harmonic practice—that in which the roots of successive chords descend by a fifth. (This may be seen in the bass of the theme itself, in the last two beats of the second measure, and the first two of the third.) Sequences based on this progression of roots *Use of sequence* are effective with both triads and seventh chords and all their inversions. They can be animated by all sorts of motivic decorations to assume a multitude of melodic shapes. Even more important, they are extraordinarily useful in modulation (Ex. IX-10). They occur in thousands of pieces of the later Baroque.

Ex. IX-10

Instrumental music also flourished at Venice, where Giovanni Legrenzi, already mentioned as an opera composer, printed important collections of sonatas. While the majority of his works are for two violins and basso continuo, some are scored for larger ensemble, including a few that continue the polychoral tradition of the early part of the century. Legrenzi's sonatas are particularly noteworthy for their crisp and concise themes (Ex. IX-11), clearly instrumental in character and sharply individual. In his manner of shaping movements, Legrenzi is more traditional than the younger Vitali. The opening subject is frequently not the sole source of material for a movement, and Vitali's alternating subject-sequence construction is often absent.

Ex. IX-11

Characteristics of the sonata da camera

The *sonata da camera* was cultivated by the same composers who wrote church sonatas. The sequence of dances in these "suites" was not yet standardized, although there are frequent occurrences of certain series. The chief dances were the allemande (moderate speed, duple meter), the corrente (quick triple meter), the sarabande (slower triple meter), and the gigue (quick triple or compound meter). Each had characteristic rhythmic figures as well as a normal tempo and meter.

Some of the dances written at this time were apparently used to accompany actual dancing, while others were stylized, and intended as chamber music for listening only. In either case, most are cast in binary form, in which the first section achieves a modulation away from the home key, and the second a return to the tonic (often by way of other keys). The texture is usually lighter and less contrapuntal than that of the *sonata chiesa*.

Keyboard music

After Frescobaldi, Italy was on the whole less productive of keyboard music than of vocal or instrumental ensemble music. There was, nevertheless, a continuing tradition of composition for both organ and harpsichord. The best-known composer of the second half of the century was Bernardo Pasquini (1637-1710), a pupil of Cesti, who spent his life as an organist in Rome. Although the sources of Pasquini's keyboard music date from the beginning of the eighteenth century, many of the pieces are doubtless considerably earlier. The traditional categories of toccata, canzona, and variation are still represented, as are also the dance suite and sonata. A number of the sonatas are given as figured basses only, either for one harpsichord or in some cases two. The performer(s) had to improvise the upper voices on the basis of the figures.

The style of Pasquini's music varies somewhat according to the category. The toccatas are conservative, even retrospective, containing passages based more on the free chord progressions of the sixteenth and early seventeenth centuries than on tonality. In the sonatas and dance pieces, the style is more modern. Indeed, the dance suites seem to have been modeled on the ensemble dances just discussed. Pasquini was also a well-known composer of operas, although it is largely through his keyboard music that he is known today. Conversely, Alessandro Scarlatti made extensive contributions to the keyboard literature, which are now largely ignored in favor of his operas.

Summary. In general, the separate genres treated in the preceding pages show parallel developments. The gradual exploitation of the potential of tonality made possible not only the progressive enlargement of individual movements, but also the reintroduction of contrapuntal devices into the texture whenever these were appropriate. It was also tonality that permitted the increased individualization of thematic material, and hence of entire movements: almost all late seventeenth-century melodic motives are in some sense derived from, and expressive of, the chords of the basic tonal progression, I...IV-V-I. The common practice required after the experimentalism of the early seventeenth century had thus been achieved, but the potentials of this practice were as yet far from being fully realized. A composer reaching maturity about 1600 or 1700 was in a position similar to that of an immediate successor of Josquin. He had before him a settled technique, rich with as yet unexplored possibilities. It is not surprising that the late Baroque was another of the greater ages of music.

MUSIC IN OTHER COUNTRIES

France. French culture was in general hostile to the extremes of Baroque ideals; or, when it did accept Baroque methods, it did so in transforming and "classicizing" them. Thus the work of the painter Nicolas Poussin (1594-1665) is dominated by classical tendencies; and the plays of Corneille, Racine, and Molière are, as mentioned earlier, considered "classical," not Baroque.

Hence, the great musical revolution that swept over Italy and, later, Germany was little felt in France. The passionate intensity of the new monodic style introduced by Peri and Caccini in 1600 provoked no more interest among the French than had the affective pictorialism of the late sixteenth-century Italian madrigal. That the cultivation of such traditional categories as dance music and the *air de cour* continued uninterrupted reflects the French notion that the role of music was to give pleasure, rather than to excite profound emotion. An index of French conservatism is provided by the organ works of Jean Titelouze mentioned above (Chapter VII): their style is extremely reserved for music produced in the 1620s.

Opera, the most characteristic Italian product of the time, had at first no success in France. Caccini himself visited Paris; the exiled Barberini brought their troupe to France in 1644; Rossi's *Orfeo* and several works of Cavalli were performed in Paris. But the French remained satisfied with their own entertainments: the spoken drama and the ballet. The ballet, with a tradition going back well into the sixteenth century, was a presentation that combined elaborate dancing, music, and costumes with recitation, the latter spoken at first, but later often sung. A celebrated early ballet was the *Balet comique de la royne* (1581; the title means "comic ballet of the queen," but "comic" here merely means that there is a plot). Many others followed, usually written for some event at the royal court, whence they became known as *ballets de cour*. While ballets often had plots of a sort, and hence could almost be regarded as operas, no attempt was made to use music for dramatically expressive purposes: it remained a decorative element, like the scenery and costumes. The musical interest of the ballets was

Ballet de cour

in fact rather modest, since music was only one—and not the most important—of the factors contributing to the total effect.

An important new French style appeared first in music for the lute and for the *clavecin* (harpsichord). The lute, for which little solo music was written in Italy after 1600, acquired new popularity in seventeenth-century France, where it became a favorite instrument of the aristocratic salons. The most important lute composer was Denis Gaultier (ca. 1600-72), whose treatment of lute-writing, known as *style brisé* (broken style), was an innovation of enormous consequence. In *style brisé*, the notes of a chord, instead of being sounded together, are broken up and distributed throughout the measure. This serves both to keep alive the quickly fading tone of the lute, and to suggest the presence of inner contrapuntal voices below the melody. (The original notation merely gives the notes as they occur, but modern polyphonic transcriptions represent fairly what is actually heard.)

The lute music of Denis Gaultier

Another striking feature of Gaultier's texture is the presence of numerous *agreménts* (ornaments), indicated by stenographic signs or by small notes. By breaking up a long note into a number of shorter ones, *agréments* also help to counteract the rapid fading of the tone, but their aesthetic effect—the elegance they lend to the melodic line—is more important than their practical function. Example IX-12 shows a few of the *agréments* and the symbols that later became more or less standard for them.

Ex. IX-12

Gaultier's *La rhétorique des dieux* (the rhetoric of the gods) was compiled about 1655, although many of the pieces in it may be considerably earlier. It is made up primarily of dance pieces arranged in groups or "suites" (Gaultier does not use the latter term) sharing the same key. Many of the dances are given picturesque titles, such as "La belle ténébreuse" (the beautiful shadowy girl), or even descriptive "programs:" "Diana. The chaste goddess, in this energetic speech, urges all lovely ladies to acquire virtues, and particularly to preserve their virginity intact." These designations, however, appear to be merely whimsical additions: the music makes no real attempt to portray the subject given in the title.

There is no set order of dances within a group. Most groups contain one or more allemandes, courantes, and sarabandes; and other dances are also frequently found. Almost all of the dance pieces are in two-part form, except for occasional tripartite pavanes, and a few pieces "en rondeau," in which a recurrent section (R) alternates with contrasting material (RaRbRc . . . R). There are a few "preludes"—improvisatory opening movements notated almost entirely in whole notes, to which the performer is to give appropriate rhythms. The several "tombeaux," or laments, honoring a deceased friend or patron, are generally slow dance pieces.

The *Allemande grave* whose beginning is given in Example IX-13 is a "tombeau" dedicated to Gaultier's late wife. The grave and somber tone is thus particularly appropriate, although it is common in Gaultier's work generally. It is evident from the delicacy of this music—its refusal to be interested in the physical act of dancing—that this is chamber music based on stylized dance rhythms rather than music for the ballroom. The different dances have already become genres, preserving only rhythmic reminiscences of their origins.

Ex. IX-13

Jacques Champion de Chambonnières (ca. 1601-167-) transferred both the *style brisé* and the *agréments* to the *clavecin* (harpsichord), an instrument he seems to have regarded as a kind of lute played by remote control (striking the key taking the place both of stopping the string and of plucking it). Since the harpsichord also has a short-lived tone that benefits from ornamentation, it has been alleged that Chambonnières had primarily practical motives in transferring lute techniques to the keyboard, but this may be doubted. Ornamentation is peculiarly congenial to the harpsichord, even when it is not practically necessary: a richly embellished line is a pleasure to both the hand and the ear.

The clavecinistes: Jacques Champion de Chambonnieres

Since the harpsichord has a greater range than the lute, and since it handles large chords more easily, the music of Chambonnières has a richer and fuller sound than that of Gaultier; otherwise the work of the two men is quite similar. There is the same concentration on dance pieces arranged into suites, there are the same forms, the same use of descriptive titles.

The beginning of a courante and of its "double" are given in Example IX-14. A double is merely an ornamental variation of a dance (cf. the varied strains of

Ex. IX-14(a)

Ex. IX-14(b)

Elizabethan virginal music, Chapter VII) occurring either as a separate piece (as is the case here), or with the varied sections following directly on the unvaried ones (AA'BB'). The rather complex rhythm of the courante, with its fluctuation between 3/2 and 6/4 meter, was to remain typical of the French courante for the next hundred years. Chambonnières exploits not only the ornamental, but also the contrapuntal possibilities of his instrument: despite the "broken style," there is a good deal of genuine polyphony.

While Gaultier had no important successors, Chambonnières established a long dynasty of French harpsichord composers, or *clavecinistes*. The second generation is well represented by two of his pupils: Louis Couperin (1626-61), a member of an important musical family; and Jean-Henry d'Anglebert (1628-91). Both men, as well as a large number of lesser figures, carried on the style of their teacher. Their treatment of tonality is more advanced than that of Chambonnières, and their music often more clear cut. In recompense, they do not often achieve the freedom and fantasy of their teacher.

Like Gaultier, both Couperin and d'Anglebert wrote preludes. The appearance of these on the printed page is startling: the notation consists largely (in Couperin's case entirely) of whole notes, separated into groups by curved lines. It was for the performer to impose on this skeleton a rhythm of his own choosing, presumably at sight. Example IX-15 shows the beginning of a Couperin prelude, and one of the innumerable ways in which it might have been played. The existence of such unmeasured preludes suggests that earlier performers had preceded their suites by an entirely free improvisation.

The art of the *agréments* continued to flourish: the preface of d'Anglebert's one printed collection (1689) lists twenty-nine different signs for ornamentation. For all its decoration, however, the music of this generation is still solid and serious; under its delicate surface, there is considerable polyphony. With the beginning of the eighteenth century, a simpler style became popular, in which the chief emphasis was on a gracious and elegant melody.

The *clavecinistes* based their art solidly on the capacities of the instrument they wrote for. This is another instance of a general Baroque trend towards idiomatic instrumental writing. But the style of the *clavecinistes* originated in Gaultier's lute music; and their *agréments* passed on into the work of French composers for the organ. Thus the transference of idiom from one instrument to another was as typical for the Baroque as the development of the idioms themselves.

Other clavecinistes

Ex. IX-15

French organ music of the seventeenth century shows a remarkably homogeneous repertoire, of a rather cheerful and unproblematic character, with well-differentiated types of pieces based on different ways of using the instrument. Thus there is the *récit*, in which a solo register (stop) is given a melody, supported by a softer accompaniment; the *dialogue*, in which contrasting registrations alternate; the *plein jeu*, for full organ, with great chords and suspensions; and so on. From the end of the seventeenth century, variations on Noëls (popular Christmas songs) were also composed—one of the few types that did not arise from a particular organ registration.

French organ music

Much of the repertoire is distinguished more by charm than profundity: indeed, some modern ears might find the music rather light for church use. The beginning of a *récit* by Nicolas Lebègue (1631-1702; Ex. IX-16) gives an idea of the style, but it should be noted that there are also many obviously "serious" pieces as well.

Ex. IX-16

Although Italian opera was a failure in France, the few performances that did take place seem to have stimulated French musicians to create a native operatic style, free from Italian eccentricities; and in 1671-72 the first French operas appeared, with music by Robert Cambert (ca. 1628-77). While these were successful, Cambert was at once forced by political machinations to give place to Jean Baptiste Lully (1632-87), an Italian who was brought to France at the age of fourteen. An adroit courtier and a man

French opera

Jean Baptiste Lully

Fig. IX-2: *A performance of Lully's* Alceste *at Versailles. Note the large orchestra, divided into two groups at either side of the front of the stage. (Harvard Theatre Collection.)*

of great ambition, he had been the principal composer of *ballets de cour* until the success of Cambert tempted him into the field of opera. Lully managed to obtain from Louis XIV a monopoly over operatic performances, and having thus driven Cambert out of competition, he dominated the operatic stage from 1672 until his death, producing some twenty operas, or *tragédies lyriques,* as they were called.

Lully, a fine artist as well as a courtier, forged his French style out of elements he knew to be agreeable to Louis XIV and his favorites. Spectacular stage effects and dances—both much liked by the French court—were always provided in abundance. Despite his Italian origin, Lully kept within the bounds of French taste, never attempting to emulate the intense expressivity or the vocal display of Italian opera.

In the age of Racine, the French demanded that even an opera should have a respectable literary text: dramatic values were, if anything, more important than musical ones, provided that adequate allowance was made for dancing and for scenic effects. Most of Lully's libretti were written by Philippe Quinault, a competent minor poet, who treated his classical subjects seriously and logically, while at the same time ingeniously providing reasonable pretexts for the obligatory machines and ballets.

The importance attached to the literary aspect of opera inevitably meant that recitative was given a good deal of prominence, since it is in recitative that literary values can most easily be discerned. Lully carefully based his recitative on the natural declamation of the text, even alternating duple and triple meter when this seemed desirable (Ex. IX-17). While he rarely attempted to give it strong expressivity, it is generally a little more melodious—and more carefully written—than Italian recitative of the same period: Lully succeeded in creating a new French style of dramatic declamation. *Lully's recitative*

Je vais par-tir bel-le Her-mi-o-ne Je vais ex-é-cu-ter Ce que l'a-mour or-don-ne malgré le pé-ril qui m'at-tend Je veux vous dé-li-vrer ou me per-dre moi même

I shall depart, lovely Hermione. I am going to do what love commands despite the danger that awaits me. I wish to save you or to be lost myself.

Ex. IX-17

The importance Lully attached to his recitative is demonstrated by the occasional passages (chiefly in his later works) in accompanied recitative. The solemn and splendid effect produced by the string accompaniment is striking, and Lully makes, on the whole, more use of the device than most Italian composers.

If Lully's recitative is slightly more melodious than that of the Italians, his arias ("airs" in French) are rather less so. Some are light pieces in dance-like rhythms, descendants of a long tradition of French song. Others are dignified and solemn. Most are quite short and are accompanied only by the basso continuo. (As in Italian music, arias for bass voice generally give the same music to the singer and to the continuo.) The more solemn arias, however, are often given orchestral accompaniment, as may be seen in an excerpt (Ex. IX-18) from *Amadis* (1684): this aria is one of Lully's grander conceptions. *Lully's arias*

Whatever the type, the Lullian aria contains neither the exuberant flowing melody of the Italian style, nor the elaborate coloratura passages. There are small scale *agréments*, to be sure, and the singers may well have added more in performance. But Lully's style is restrained and severe, his expressive range limited. The contrast between recitative and aria is considerably less marked than in Italian opera—to the point that one Italian visitor to Paris claimed that he had sat through an entire evening of Lully waiting for the first aria to begin.

Neither recitative nor air would have sufficed to ensure Lully's success had his operas not contained much of the spectacular as well. This took both visual and musical form, and included elaborate scenic effects and costumes, numerous dances, and monumental choral scenes. With these means, Lully was able to transform what might otherwise have been a thin and bloodless entertainment into an imposing spectacle worthy of the Sun-king's court.

Close forever, my eyes, my sad eyes. I lose what I love best: The light is to be taken from me.

Ex. IX-18

Lully's use of the orchestra

Instrumental music naturally played an important part in all this, if only to accompany the dances. The basis of Lully's orchestra was a string section divided into five parts, to which other instruments could be added when appropriate (e.g., flutes for pastoral scenes, trumpets for battles). The five-part string writing produces a rich, thick texture, tending, like so much else, to emphasize splendor and majesty. The dance pieces are in the same forms and styles as those of the *clavecinistes*, although of course the ensemble medium precludes the use of *style brisé* and of elaborate ornamentation.

Lully's most important contribution to instrumental literature was a new type of operatic overture. This, the "French overture," was one of the few manifestations of French musical style that became widely popular outside France. The French overture consists of two sections, a slow and solemn opening, making much use of dotted notes, followed by a quick section employing at least some imitation. In some overtures, part or all of the opening section recurs at the end. While this form was devised to introduce a musical drama, pieces in French overture style and form came to be used for other purposes as well.

French overture

Lully's success was so great that his operas continued to be performed for nearly a hundred years after his death, although later generations often altered his scores to accommodate changes in taste. The permanence of the Lullian repertoire had a kind of petrifying effect on French opera: each new production was compared to Lully, and, where it differed, was found defective. The most interesting—and successful—later works for the French musical stage were not true operas at all, but rather "opéra-ballets," in which dramatic content was all but eliminated in favor of dancing and spectacle. The music for the opéra-ballets was rather lighter than that of Lully—whose exalted, Baroque manner was more revered than closely imitated—and admitted at least a modest element of Italian influence. André Campra (1660-1744) introduced the new manner in the opéra-ballet *Europe galante* (1697), and France produced no new serious dramatic opera until nearly forty years later.

Lully's influence

The special characteristics of French style are most clearly evident in opera and in keyboard music. In sacred music, French composers were active enough, but the music is less specifically French in sound. Lully himself wrote a number of *grands motets*, usually for two choirs, soloists, and string orchestra. Some are imposing works, but they lack the individuality of his stage music.

French sacred music: Marc Antoine Charpentier

I shall strike the shepherd, and [the flocks] will be dispersed.

Ex. IX-19

Perhaps the best composer of sacred music at the time was Marc-Antoine Charpentier (1634-1704), a pupil of Carissimi. He composed Masses, motets, and oratorios, as well as works for the secular stage. In all of these, both his French nationality and his Italian training are evident. His oratorios are clearly modeled on those of his teacher, although they tend towards larger dimensions and clearer tonality, as is natural for works of the time. In Example IX-19, from an oratorio on the denial of St. Peter, the pictorial melisma on "dispergentur" (will be scattered) is wholly Italian in appearance. But Charpentier's works, many of them very fine ones, seem not to have been influential—perhaps because they were too Italian. He remains an isolated figure.

England.   While France enjoyed prestige and domestic calm during the second half of the seventeenth century, England had to wait until near its end before emerging from civil and religious disorders. In 1649, Charles I was beheaded, and the brief and not over-popular Commonwealth was established. After Cromwell's death, Charles II was invited to return (1660), but he and his successor James II so alienated their people that James was driven from the country. The throne then passed (1688) to the Dutchman William of Orange, whose English wife was next in line after James. Despite these difficult times, English musicians produced a great deal, much of it fully worthy of comparison with Continental music.

In the first two decades of the century, England was still in the midst of its late Renaissance flowering, and while the new Italian styles may have been known, they were not immediately imitated. With the accession of Charles I (1625), English music began to enter the Baroque age. Walter Porter (ca. 1595-1659) studied in Italy, perhaps with Monteverdi himself, and brought back with him the florid ornamental vocal style.

The music of William and Henry Lawes

More important, however, were the brothers Henry (1595-1662) and William (1602-45) Lawes. Henry concentrated on vocal music, producing songs and duets with basso continuo, which stand between recitative and song: the accurate declamation in his vocal writing derives from the recitative, but there is a constant tendency for real, if fragmentary, tunes to insinuate themselves into the melodic line.

William wrote mostly instrumental music—dance pieces and fantasias directly descended from Elizabethan prototypes, but now filled with Baroque contrasts and personal eccentricities. Some of William's pieces are set for the traditional consort of viols; others are for one or two violins, bass viol, and organ. The organ parts are fully written out—a practice common in English instrumental music at the time. While Henry's music is clearly an English version of Italian recitative style, William's is part of a native instrumental tradition, and seems untouched by any influence from Italy.

Another important composer of instrumental music was John Jenkins (1592-1678). Many of his pieces are "fancies" (fantasias) for viols—serious, imitative works more conservative than those of William Lawes. Others, scored for two melody instruments (perhaps violins rather than viols) plus basso continuo, show Italian influence in the choice of medium. In musical substance, however, even these remain within the English tradition.

The first half of the century produced no attempt at an English opera. As in France, both spoken drama and dancing were in considerable favor, and musical drama did not appear to be an urgent necessity. Corresponding to the French *ballet de cour*, the

Masque

English had the masque, an entertainment that included dancing, singing, spoken recitation, and elaborate scenery. Although recitative was used in masques from 1617 on, it was not the only vocal style: both solo songs and choruses were also employed. Many composers, including the Lawes brothers, contributed music to the masques.

The Commonwealth put an end to the court masque, although less ostentatious masques continued to be produced in private houses. Puritan influence had forced the closing of public theaters as early as 1642, and the resultant unavailability of spoken drama, very popular in England, finally aroused interest in the creation of English opera—which, oddly, the Puritans were willing to tolerate. In 1656, Sir William Davenant produced his *Siege of Rhodes*, a "representation . . . of declamation, after the manner of the ancients"—a description reminiscent of the language of the early Florentines. The music, written by Matthew Locke (ca. 1630-77) and others, is unfortunately lost, but it apparently contained recitative of a dramatic type. Some idea of the style may be derived from the opera-like masque *Cupid and Death* (1653), to which Locke contributed much of the music. The recitative is especially interesting, for it resembles the powerful affective style of the early 1600s. Chromaticism is the chief means employed to create intensity: in one instance a sudden change from E major to G minor duplicates exactly an impressive stroke by Monteverdi in his *Orfeo*.

English opera: Matthew Locke

Although *The Siege of Rhodes* was successful, the years following brought few operas of importance. Instead, the theaters, which reopened with the Restoration, were the focus of attention. Nevertheless, music had a considerable role in the spoken drama. New plays were designed, and old ones altered, to incorporate large amounts of music, in the form of songs, dances, choruses, purely instrumental pieces, and often entire masques. At the time, some of these plays were actually advertised as operas; they have since been described as "semi-operas" or "dramatic operas." They differ from the true opera in that the main action of the plot is generally carried on in speech, the musical sections being embellishments of varying degrees of relevance.

The next significant true opera did not appear in England until about 1682 (the exact date is not known), with the *Venus and Adonis* of John Blow (1649-1708), and even this impressive work is subtitled "a masque for the entertainment of the king." It is, nevertheless, a real opera, though it is one of small dimensions. In it, Blow combines a number of stylistic traditions. It begins with a French overture, but the songs and dances that follow are purely English in sound, and partly Italian in technique. The most distinguished feature is the recitative, which continues and even intensifies the highly affective type found in Locke's *Cupid and Death*. The third and last act, a long dialogue between Venus and the dying Adonis, is composed wholly in this style, in which violence of expression takes precedence over all other musical values. Blow convincingly portrays the grief of the heart-broken Venus through use of irregular phrases, jagged melodic leaps, and chromaticism (Ex. IX-20).

John Blow

Apart from this one work, Blow wrote little for the theater, preferring to devote his energy to ceremonial and sacred music—areas that were of considerable importance in England after the Restoration.

The types of Anglican church music had been established early in the seventeenth century. The most important were the service—a setting of the invariable parts of morning and evening prayer—and the anthem, which corresponded to the Roman Catholic motet. Orlando Gibbons had popularized the verse anthem, in which solos and instrumental accompaniment were used as well as choral sections, and it was this type that was principally cultivated by later composers. Full anthems (those for full chorus throughout) continued to be written, often as display pieces, intended to show the contrapuntal skill of the composer—a function that underlines their archaic quality.

Anglican church music

A - - las Death's sleep thou art too young to take. My groans ___ shall reach the heav'ns; oh ___ pow'rs above Take pi-ty on the wretch - ed Queen of love!

Ex. IX-20

The Commonwealth frowned on any kind of elaborate church music: choirs were disbanded, and many English organs were destroyed on order of the authorities. Naturally this attitude created a kind of gap in the production of music for the church; and the gap was accentuated at the Restoration, for Charles II insisted that the music of the Chapel Royal be thoroughly modern in style. Composers reacted by grafting elements of the new secular dramatic style onto the traditional forms of the verse anthem, even introducing independent instrumental "symphonies" when the king's presence was expected. But outside the royal presence, more traditional attitudes prevailed. Many composers, including most of those already mentioned, contributed works in a wide variety of styles to the repertoire of sacred music. Among the progressive techniques employed were the accompaniment of solo sections in verse anthems by the basso continuo instead of viols, and the occasional use of affective chromaticism in the Italian tradition. For the most festive occasions, there are great anthems for orchestra and one or more choruses, with or without soloists. These may have been suggested by the king, or by the example of Lully's *grands motets*. Among the best of these are Blow's brilliant and festive coronation anthems, in which French and Italian techniques are subordinated to English expression.

Despite the troubles of the times, seventeenth-century England produced a body of music well able to bear comparison with Continental works. But England had the still better fortune of producing Henry Purcell (1659-95), a composer who stands far above not only his English contemporaries, but also above almost all other musicians of his time. This great man, in his pitifully short career, became at once the culmination of the English tradition and its last well-known representative.

Henry Purcell

All the currently cultivated English genres are represented in Purcell's works: music for strings, anthems, odes for various state occasions, one opera, and much music for plays. In his music, the native English style is felicitously combined with techniques borrowed from France and Italy. This synthesis was a conscious one: Purcell was well aware of the virtues of all major styles then being cultivated, and set about quite deliberately to combine their best features.

Among Purcell's earliest works are a group of fantasias for viols—a retrospective, not to say archaic choice of medium and form (they are the last known to have been written). They follow the old tradition in their structure and in their severely polyphonic writing, although their harmonic language is tense and modern, with much use of chromaticism and sharp dissonance. Only shortly afterwards, he published a collection of trio sonatas for violins (1683; a second set appeared posthumously). In the preface to this publication, Purcell says that he has tried to imitate the most famous Italian composers; and these sonatas, although strongly personal, are, in fact, wholly Italian in texture and form. Purcell obviously had studied the works of men like Vitali and Bononcini, and had quickly mastered their methods. His own musical personality and the force of the English tradition are manifest in the generally tighter construction of the sonatas. There is much less reliance on sequence, and more intensely contrapuntal writing. English also are the occasionally audacious harmonies, and the frequent modulations to relatively remote keys. The slow movements are often notable for sharp and irregularly treated dissonance. The quick ones employ Italianate themes, but these permeate the movement more than is usual in Italian sonatas: the basso continuo participates in the imitation as well as the two upper voices, and the sequential episodes are smaller.

Purcell's instrumental music

Although Purcell was a superior composer of instrumental music and a distinguished contributor to the then current genres of English church music, it is in his music for the theater that his best work is found. His one true opera, *Dido and Aeneas* (1689), written for performance by the girls at a boarding school, is a chamber opera similar to Blow's *Venus and Adonis*. Like its predecessor, it is short, and employs only modest resources. But it far surpasses Blow's work and, despite some weak scenes, stands as one of the permanent masterpieces of the musical stage. Purcell's internationalism is evident. From France comes the form of the overture, and a passage of recitative accompanied by strings that was doubtless suggested by similar passages in Lully. But much of the style is Italianate, as is the approach to ABA form in some of the arias. The frequent use of basso ostinato is ultimately of Italian origin, but Purcell had long since made this one of his favorite (and most effective) devices. Wholly English are the styles of the many dances, the characteristic speech rhythms of the vocal declamation, and the extensive use of the chorus, as well as many of the tunes, which have a direct simplicity that instantly betrays their origin. Dido's celebrated lament, "When I am laid in earth," written on a chromatic descending ostinato, is a masterpiece of Baroque pathos, too easily accessible to require quotation here.

Dido and Aeneas

The fame of *Dido and Aeneas* has tended to eclipse the rest of Purcell's dramatic music, but much of his finest work may be found in his incidental music to plays. Especially in the dramatic music of his last years, the various national elements, formerly harnessed together, are fused into a completely individual style.

Purcell's incidental music

In Purcell's music (probably composed in 1695) for John Dryden's *The Indian Queen*, almost every aspect of the composer's mature style may be found. There is recitative, often highly expressive or pictorial—or both (Ex. IX-21a; note the melisma on "discord," and the melodically, not textually motivated B-B♭ conflict on "arise"). There are arias, Italian in basic technique, but freer than most Italian pieces in their juxtapositions of unrelated sections to create a single large form (Ex. IX-21 b and c show the openings of two of the three sections of such an aria). Indeed Purcell uses standard formal patterns in his vocal music only when they suit his purpose. While there are a large number of ostinato pieces, many of the arias, duets, and choruses are freely constructed.

Purcell's idiomatic declamation of English has often been remarked on, and is evident in the examples just cited. It is regrettable that a composer with such superb

... and see what men are doom'd to do where el-e-ments in dis — — —

(a) — cord dwell Thou God of sleep a — rise and tell

(b) violins By the croaking of the toads in their caves that make a-bode

(c) From thy sleep — ing man — sion rise

Ex. IX-21

gifts for writing vocal, and specifically dramatic, music worked at a time when the demand for true English opera was minimal. The end of the century did indeed see a demand for opera in England, but it was Italian opera that was wanted. After the death of Purcell, English music was temporarily submerged in a flood of Italian importations.

Germany. Although German music of the later seventeenth century was dependent primarily on Italian models, the degree of that dependence varied. In Austria and southern Germany, both largely Roman Catholic, Italian musicians were imported to fill major court and church positions, and their music, both sacred and secular, differed little from that produced on Italian soil. Needless to say, German taste was not the same as Italian, and a Mass or opera written for the Imperial Court at Vienna was not identical in style to one written for Venice or Rome. But from the historical point of view, such differences as did exist are of relatively small importance.

The situation was quite different in the Protestant north, where neither Roman Catholic service music nor Italian opera was in great demand. North German composers concentrated their attention on music for the Lutheran church, following in the footsteps of Schütz, Scheidt, and others—but always with an eye open for new developments in Italy.

Franz Tunder

Among the Lutheran composers was Franz Tunder (1614-67), a pupil of Frescobaldi who spent most of his life in the North German city of Lübeck. Tunder's music includes organ compositions, as well as "sacred concertos," which continue the tradition of the *Symphoniae sacrae* of Schütz. (Such pieces are now often called "cantatas," but the term was not used by the composers themselves, and is better reserved for a different type of church composition, to be considered below.) These works, for from one to five vocal parts, with instrumental accompaniment as well as basso continuo, are constructed in sections based on the phrases of the text. Compared to Schütz's own works, Tunder's are characterized by denser textures (the instrumental sections are often scored for five or six parts), and generally longer sections. Tunder often uses a chorale, either as a cantus firmus, or as a source of musical motives that are then used in imitation.

*Dietrich
Buxtehude*

Tunder's successor at Lübeck was the more important Dietrich Buxtehude (1637-1707), another composer who devoted most of his effort to providing music for the Lutheran church. By Buxtehude's time, Lutheranism was severely troubled by internal dissension: traditional or orthodox Lutheranism had become in many places dogmatic and formalistic, rather like the Roman Catholicism it had replaced. The Pietists, advocates of a more personal, subjective, and emotional approach, attacked the orthodox establishment with the crusading vigor of reformers, winning many converts, and often influencing those who remained within the orthodox camp. Like the English Puritans, whom they somewhat resembled, the extreme Pietists denounced elaborate church music in favor of simple unison singing by the congregation. Hence, most important Lutheran music continued to be written for orthodox churches; but Pietistic influence may often be seen either in the choice of mystical and devotional texts, or in the intimate fervor of the music—both of which traits may be found in Buxtehude.

*Buxtehude's
sacred concertos*

Otherwise, Buxtehude's sacred concertos continue along the lines established by Tunder: the sections are longer and more sharply individuated, and the style is clearer and more strongly tonal. Italian influences are evident in the bel canto style of many of the vocal melodies and in the trio-sonata texture often used for instrumental ritornelli. The overall forms are so diverse as to defy generalization. Some chorale settings are no more than simple harmonizations with instrumental interludes after each line. Others are more complex, and use the chorale as a basis for ornamentation and elaboration. The pieces not based on a chorale (and these are in the majority) show even more diversity; but, except for those built on ostinatos, all exhibit the traditional sectional structure. Typical ingredients are instrumental sections (called sinfonia or ritornello) often for two violins and continuo, and sometimes for larger ensembles; bel canto type solos, with or without independent instrumental parts; homophonic, declamatory choral sections; and freely constructed larger sections in which the voices and instruments alternate and combine. Such larger sections are often divided into several subsections, each based on a different text phrase and different musical material. Buxtehude frequently uses thematic relationships to unify long compositions: the last section may, for example, be a varied repetition of the first, or may use the same material in different treatment. It is above all, however, the regulating power of tonality that permits Buxtehude to achieve large dimensions without loss of clarity.

Some idea of Buxtehude's vocal style may be derived from two excerpts taken from the large-scale sacred concerto *Das neugeborne Kindelein* (the newborn child). The first (Ex. IX-22a) displays his effective chordal writing for chorus (the melody in the soprano is derived from a chorale). In the second (Ex. IX-22b), after a majestic cadence for voices

Ex. IX-22(a)

Ex. IX-22(b)

and instruments, the word "singen" (sing) calls forth a melismatic figure treated in imitation—almost as a kind of madrigalism. Later, following the words "Ist Gott versöhnt und unser Freund," the opening ritornello appears for the first time in a major key; the line "Es bringt das rechte Jubeljahr" (it brings the true year of rejoicing) calls forth trumpet-like figures in the vocal bass and the strings, suggesting a triumphant celebration. The preoccupation with musical symbolism was a continuing one for German composers, who liked to reinforce the general affection of a passage with more specific textual interpretation.

Buxtehude's style as exemplified in this piece is clearly influenced by Italian practice. An Italian contemporary would doubtless have thought such music old-fashioned, for it lacks the concise clarity cultivated by Italian composers after 1680. Such a judgment would, however, miss the point. German composers were interested in Italian music for its technical devices, which they employed to achieve goals of their own. The warmth and mysticism of German music were quite foreign to the Italian ideal.

The sacred concerto is the most important form of German vocal music in the seventeenth century, but not the only one. Several German composers cultivated the aria, a strophic secular song accompanied by the inevitable basso continuo. Perhaps the best known of the aria composers was Adam Krieger (1634-66), a poet as well as a composer. His arias, mostly for one or two voices, are provided with instrumental ritornellos to be played between the strophes. The vocal lines are simple, but warmly expressive.

Despite its name, the aria had nothing to do with opera, and indeed truly German opera was slow to develop. After the lost *Dafne* of Schütz (1627), few German operas, and none of real importance, were written until the end of the seventeenth century. In part this resulted from the calamitous Thirty Years' War (1618-48), which left the German states impoverished, embittered, and (oddly) more interested in foreign than native culture. After the war, when some recovery had been achieved, the Southern German courts imported Italian opera (as has been seen) rather than encouraging native products.

Opera in Germany

Finally in 1678 a public opera house was opened at Hamburg, intended specifically for the production of German operas. At first a number of sacred operas were performed, doubtless to convince the Lutheran authorities that opera was not as immoral as it was said to be. Thereafter, most of the works produced there were secular, with libretti modeled on or actually translated from Italian ones. The music was also largely based on Italian models, although some signs of French influence and some purely native traits may be seen in it. The inability or unwillingness of imported Italian singers to sing in German occasionally caused these German operas to be sung either wholly or partly in Italian, but most performances were in German.

The lack of opera composers of the first class prevented German opera from acquiring the degree of stylistic individuality achieved by its Italian and French analogues. For the same reason, it failed to produce any enduring masterpieces. But the opera house at Hamburg founded an important tradition, which was to reach its full fruition in the eighteenth century.

German instrumental music of this period may be divided into two principal branches: chamber music and keyboard music, the latter subdivided into music for

*German
instrumental
music*

harpsichord (or clavichord) and music for organ. The chamber music is strongly influenced by Italian models. Although several distinguished composers contributed trio sonatas and dance suites for various combinations of instruments to the chamber repertoire, Germany's best and most original instrumental music was written for keyboard.

*Johann Jakob
Froberger's
keyboard works*

Here the extent of Italian influence, while not negligible, is somewhat less, as keyboard music was not a central preoccupation of most important Italian composers after Frescobaldi. The outstanding keyboard master of the early period, a pupil of Frescobaldi himself, was Johann Jakob Froberger (1616-67). In his toccatas Froberger continues the brilliant improvisatory style of his teacher, but with a difference. The violent contrasts are still present, but the wildness of the early Baroque has given way to a more thoughtful, rational style. The same applies to the canzone: they are still sectional, imitative pieces, as are those of Frescobaldi; but the sections are now regularly linked by the use of variations of the theme of the first section in succeeding parts, and the themes themselves are more clearly tonal in their implications. A comparison of a chromatic theme by Frescobaldi with one by Froberger (Ex. IX-23) shows the former deliberately seeking to mystify, and the latter rationalizing his chromaticism into a tonal framework.

Frescobaldi

Froberger

Ex. IX-23

Froberger's fantasias and ricercari, on the other hand, are strictly imitative and almost archaic in style. Notable is the strongly characteristic, and strongly tonal, nature of their themes. These pieces, like the capriccios, use transformations of the opening subject as material for later sections. In these works Froberger approaches the monothematic and non-sectional fugue, which was to be a major category of German music of the late Baroque.

This much of Froberger's work can be seen as a continuation of his teacher's tradition, but the same cannot be said of his dance suites for harpsichord. In these, Froberger employs the forms and the *style brisé* of his older French contemporaries Gaultier and Chambonnières. The suites contain allemandes, courantes, and sarabandes, often with an interspersed gigue (later seventeenth-century editions placed the gigues at the end, the place it finally came to occupy in the suite). The dances are in the usual two-part form. The *style brisé* is prominent, but the details of the harmony are on the whole more Italian than French.

*Other keyboard
composers*

Froberger, in fusing the French and Italian styles, created an amalgam that served as model to many later German composers; but another important stylistic current was also operative in German keyboard music. This was the abstract "pattern music" first developed by the Elizabethan virginalists and transmitted to the Continent by Sweelinck. Use of repeated rhythmic patterns is not wholly foreign to the style of Froberger himself, but the abstract style is more characteristic of northern German musicians. Example IX-24 shows the beginnings of two variations on the then popular

Ex. IX-24

song "Die Meyerin," the first by Froberger, the second by the North German Johann Adam Reinken (1623-1722). The two are similar in meter and texture, but Froberger treats his material rather freely, while Reinken, having chosen a pattern, sticks relentlessly to it.

Keyboard suites continued to be written throughout the seventeenth century, all based to some extent on Froberger's model, and most influenced by contemporary French pieces as well. The sequence allemande—courante—sarabande—gigue emerged as standard, with any additional dances placed after the sarabande. Later suites show the trend towards greater length, greater regularity, and stronger tonality that is characteristic of later seventeenth-century music in general.

Even more important than this repertoire is the vast German production of organ music, mostly intended for use in Lutheran churches. The several different genres of organ composition were descended more or less directly from late sixteenth- and early seventeenth-century prototypes, with varying degrees of change. Among the free pieces (i.e., pieces not based on a chorale) were the prelude, generally improvisatory in style, serving either to give the pitch for a vocal piece following, or in general, to introduce something else; the fantasia, now again a free piece, similar to the prelude; and the toccata, a virtuoso display piece marked by brilliant figuration. (These names were not always used in consistent fashion.) Quite different was the fugue, an imitative piece descended from the canzona, but more and more in a single section and on a single subject. A fugue was often added to or combined with a prelude, fantasia, or toccata, to form a larger complex. Especially congenial to organ technique were pieces on ostinato basses (usually called chaconne or passacaglia) as the recurrent bass could be played on the pedals with a special tone color.

Equally important was organ music based on chorale tunes. It was always the congregation's prerogative to sing the chorale, but the organist could and did precede the singing by an organ setting of the same melody, both to give the pitch, and to remind the people of the tune. Hence the term chorale prelude came to be applied to a large and diverse repertoire of chorale settings intended for this purpose. The various possible chorale treatments had almost all been established by Scheidt earlier in the

German organ music

Fugue

Chorale prelude and other works using chorale tunes

century, and included the motet-like setting, built of successive points of imitation based on motives derived from successive lines of the chorale; the chorale fugue, based on a subject derived from the beginning of the chorale and including a long-note presentation of the entire tune; the figural setting, in which the melody sounds against an independent accompaniment based on a characteristic motive *not* derived from the chorale; and the melody type, in which an ornamented version of the tune is heard over a subordinate accompaniment. Somewhat different was the chorale partita or variation set, in which the tune was presented in several different types of settings, each being a separate movement or variation. (A single variation from a chorale partita is often indistinguishable from an independent chorale prelude.) Finally there was also the chorale fantasy, which, as the name implies, treats the chorale in free, unpredictable fashion.

Buxtehude's organ works

One of the most important of the organ composers was Buxtehude, and his organ works reveal a new side of his musical character: they seem bolder and freer than his vocal works. This Baroque side of his temperament is evident in his chorale fantasias —lengthy pieces showing a rich variety of styles and textures within a single movement; the chorale melody appears and disappears in one voice after another, now in long notes, now overlaid with elaborate ornamentation. There are also a number of shorter chorale preludes, in which the melody, modestly embellished, is given to the top voice, while the lower parts support it with figural counterpoint, generally based on motives derived from the chorale; and there are sets of chorale variations, in which each variation maintains a fairly consistent texture and technical procedure.

The best of Buxtehude's organ music, however, is to be found in his free works. There are three superb ostinato pieces; a number of canzonas, closely related to those of Froberger; and almost thirty pieces generally known as preludes and fugues (or toccatas and fugues: there is little significant difference between the two types in Buxtehude). In one prelude and fugue in A minor, for example, there are four sections. The outer two are free and rhapsodic, and the inner two imitative. The second of the imitative sections uses a theme derived from that of the section preceding. Thus the "prelude" and the "fugue" are not separate movements, but merely ingredients of a continuous piece.

The preludial sections are characterized by figures idiomatic to the organ, such as the alternation of thick and thin textures, sustained pedal tones, and wide leaps for the pedal, as well as less obvious traits that derive from pedal technique. The result is an impressive, flickering stream of sound, shaped by the composer into a grand, rhetorical design.

The two fugal sections are more closely knit and less discontinuous. In the first of them, the subject is almost always present, but variety is achieved by presenting it in melodic inversion as well as in its original form, and by varying the counterpoints and the tonality. The second fugal section is much the same, but includes a short sequential section near the end, and the start of an overlapped entry of the subject. This latter device, known as stretto, can be important in creating intensity in fugal writing. Compared with the Italian method of alternating imitative entries with sequences, Buxtehude's technique is conservative, comparable, perhaps, to Purcell's adaptation of Italian techniques in his early trio sonatas.

Johann Pachelbel

Buxtehude is the most prominent representative of the North German organ school. Central Germany (the south, being largely Roman Catholic, is not important in this connection) produced a leading organ composer in Johann Pachelbel (1653-1706), whose music is marked by clarity and smoothness that contrast sharply with the rhapsodic mysticism of the north. Although he also wrote toccatas, preludes, and the like, Pachelbel's best work is found in his chorale settings, and in his nearly one hundred fugues "on the Magnificat" (pieces intended to serve as intonations for the Magnificat at Lutheran vespers). He was a master of smooth and melodious counterpoint that, while idomatic to the keyboard, has a certain vocal quality. Most of his chorale settings employ imitation in some fashion. The opening of the chorale tune may be formed into the subject of a fugue; the accompanying voices may imitate a freely invented subject; or the chorale-derived fugue may be combined with a long-note presentation of the melody. In the last instance, the fugue usually subsides into free contrapuntal accompaniment once the chorale has entered.

Especially when not constrained by a chorale melody, Pachelbel is able to invent subjects of concise tonal forcefulness (Ex. IX-25). In order to preserve tonal unity, the second entrance of the subject (the "answer") is often slightly different from the subject itself (Ex. IX-25a,b). Such a modified or "tonal" answer had by this time become a regular choice in fugues whose subjects touched on the fifth degree of the scale at or near the beginning. The modification helps smooth the transition from the tonic (key of the subject) and the dominant (key of the answer). Subjects not using the fifth degree near the beginning do not need modification, and are given exact ("real") answers.

Ex. IX-25

In his fugues, Pachelbel does not insist quite so much on the subject as does Buxtehude. There are often brief sections, called "episodes," during which the subject is not heard. This is a progressive feature, and episodes become larger and more important in later fugues. In another respect, Pachelbel is conservative: his subjects appear almost exclusively in the tonic and dominant keys. (Buxtehude, in contrast, often introduces entries in other related keys.) This, combined with the shortness of the episodes, restricts the range of modulation and keeps the non-chorale fugues quite short, as is normal for the seventeenth century.

Pachelbel almost never subjects chorale melodies to ornamentation, nor does one find in his music the French *agrément* signs. Both these traits are more characteristic of

North Germany, where French influence radiated out from French-imitating petty courts. The extent of this influence may be seen in the music of Georg Böhm (1661-1733), who composed harpsichord suites almost wholly French in style, and organ works (including several sets of chorale variations) in which French ornamentation is applied to the chorale.

While German composers made worthy contributions in other genres, notably instrumental chamber music, the most important German music of the seventeenth century falls into the categories here discussed—the sacred concerto and the various forms of keyboard music. In contrast to the predominantly secular orientation of the known Italian repertoire, in which only the trio sonata could rival (at a distance) the opera, German music was turned more to the church, and many of the best composers devoted most of their effort toward providing music, both vocal and instrumental, for Lutheran services. This automatically involved them with the chorale and with the organ. The chorale, was, of course, wholly foreign to the Italian tradition, and organ music was by no means a leading genre of composition in Italy. As a result, German music, while basically founded on Italian techniques, had no difficulty in achieving an individual character of its own.

MIDDLE BAROQUE

I. **Overview.** The middle Baroque was in many respects an era of consolidation. The experimentalism of the early Baroque gradually disappeared, as forms, styles, and techniques of composition became standardized. Italy remained the most progressive musical nation, and Italian influence was felt everywhere except in France, where an indigenous French style developed.

   The most important technical advance was the development of tonality—the means by which a single triad could be made the tonal center of an (eventually quite extended) composition.

II. **Forms.** In general, most of the forms current in the early Baroque continued, acquiring more specific characteristics.

   A. Opera. By the 1640s, the distinction between declamatory recitative and melodious aria had become fully clear. Musical interest centered increasingly in the arias. Plots were complex and bizarre. Italian opera was popular not only in Italy, but also elsewhere (especially in German-speaking countries). French opera developed only late in the 17th century, with a rather severe style of its own.

   B. Oratorio. Both Latin and vernacular oratorio were cultivated. The latter, particularly, came to reflect current operatic practice.

   C. Cantata. Relatively short, lyrical, or semi-dramatic poetry set as a succession of recitatives and arias for one or more singers plus accompaniment. Most cantatas were composed by opera composers, and reflect operatic trends, but in a more sophisticated and refined fashion.

   D. Instrumental music.
       1. Ensemble music. The sonata: a piece in several movements for one (solo sonata), two (trio sonata), or more melody instruments plus basso continuo. The *sonata da chiesa* (church sonata) was an abstract piece, sometimes employing complex imitation; the *sonata da camera* (chamber sonata) was a succession (suite) of stylized dance movements.
       2. Solo music. The suite: a series of stylized dance movements, for lute, harpsichord, or clavichord. The fugue: an imitative movement on (usually) a single theme (subject), for keyboard. The prelude (toccata, fantasia, etc.): a free composition for stringed keyboard instrument or organ; often used to precede a fugue. The chorale prelude: an organ setting of a Lutheran chorale melody for organ.

III. **Composers.**

   D'Anglebert, Jean Henry (1628–91). French composer of music for clavecin (harpsichord).

Biber, Heinrich (1644–1704). Bohemian violinist and composer. Court musician to the Archbishop of Salzburg. Composed violin sonatas of considerable difficulty, often using double-stops and scordatura (unusual tuning).

Blow, John (1649–1708). English composer. His *Venus and Adonis* is an important early English opera. Also composed songs, church music.

Buxtehude, Dietrich (1637–1707). Danish organist and composer. He was organist at the Marienkirche, Lübeck, where his concerts were widely admired. Composed virtuosic, improvisatory organ music; imaginative and idiomatic instrumental music; and sacred vocal music.

Carissimi, Giacomo (1605–74). Roman composer of chamber cantatas and of oratorios. His style of dramatic oratorio writing served as the model for many later composers.

Cavalli, Francesco (1602–76). Venetian opera composer; pupil of Monteverdi. A solid, direct style, less musically and psychologically adroit than that of his master, is typical of his 41 operas.

Cesti, Pietro (often Antonio or Marcantonio; 1629–69). Italian composer of many operas and cantatas. Melodic gracefulness and rhythmic and harmonic regularity combine with increasing emphasis on the lyrical portions of the vocal line at the expense of the recitative element.

Chambonnières, Jacques Champion de (1602–ca. 1672). French court harpsichordist and composer. The founder of the French tradition of harpsichord composition, he composed suites of dance pieces in a refined style derived from courtly lute music.

Charpentier, Marc-Antoine (1634–1704). French composer, pupil of Carissimi. Overshadowed in his lifetime, his numerous operas, oratorios, and sacred compositions are now beginning to emerge from undeserved neglect.

Couperin, Louis (ca. 1626–61). French organist, violinist, and composer, uncle of François Couperin. Composer of harpsichord pieces on a grander, more dramatic scale than those of his master Chambonnières; also organ music.

Froberger, Johann Jakob (1616–67). German organist and composer, pupil of Frescobaldi. Composer of organ and harpsichord music, in which both Italian and French elements may be seen. Especially notable are his suites of stylized dance pieces.

Gaultier, Denis (ca. 1600–1672). The greatest of the French court lutenists of the 17th century, his pieces for lute, including the large collection *La rhétorique des dieux*, consist for the most part of suites of stylized dance pieces with fanciful titles.

Jenkins, John (1592–1678). English composer, noted for his "fancies" for viols.

Legrenzi, Giovanni (1626–90). Italian composer of operas, cantatas, and instrumental music.

Lully, Jean Baptiste (1632–87). Italian-born French composer. A favorite of Louis XIV, he exercised a tyrannical authority over French musical activity and taste during his lifetime, and established an operatic style in his lyric tragedies and comedy-ballets that set French standards for a century.

Pachelbel, Johann (1653–1706). German composer, noted especially for his fugues and chorale preludes for organ.

Purcell, Henry (1659–95). English composer, active in the theater, the court, and the Chapel Royal. His music combines Lully's forms with Italian melody and ornament in a particularly English and personal style. Theater music, songs, anthems, and occasional pieces.

Reinken, Johann Adam (1623–1722). North German organist and composer. Organ and chamber music.

Steffani, Agostino (1654–1728). Italian composer, active in Germany. His works, with their clear tonality and sharp individuality, represent a stage intermediate between middle and late Baroque.

Stradella, Alessandro (1642–82). Italian composer. His four operas and his many cantatas and oratorios show a melodic gracefulness unusual among his contemporaries.

Tunder, Franz (1614–67). German composer, predecessor of Buxtehude at Lübeck. His "sacred concertos," many of which employ chorale melodies, represent a link in the chain running from Schütz through Buxtehude to J. S. Bach.

IV. Bibliography.

A. Books.

Bukofzer, Manfred: *Music in the Baroque Era*, New York, 1947.

Palisca, Claude: *Baroque Music*, Englewood Cliffs, N. J., 1968.

B. Editions of music. In the following list of modern editions, some publications are cited in abbreviated form:

DdT *Denkmäler deutscher Tonkunst* ser. 1, 65 vols., 1892–1931.

DTB *Denkmäler deutscher Tonkunst* ser. 2: *Denkmäler der Tonkunst in Bayern*, 38 vols., 1900–38. Publications numbered by year (*Jahrgang*, abbrev. Jg.); many numbers are subdivided, e.g., Jg. 2:1.

DTO *Denkmäler der Tonkunst in Oesterreich*, 115 vols. to date, 1894– Publications in this series are numbered both by volume and, up to volume 83, by year (*Jahrgang*, abbrev. Jg.). Many year designations are subdivided, e.g., Jg. 12:2.

D'Anglebert. *Pièces de clavecin*, ed. M. Roesgen-Champion, Paris, 1934.

Biber. *Sechzehn Violinsonaten*, ed. E. Luntz, DTO Jg. 12:2 (1905).

Buxtehude. *Werke*, ed. W. Gurlitt, G. Harms, and H. Trede, 7 vols., (Hamburg, 1927–37). *Sämtliche Orgelwerke*, ed. J. Hedar, 4 vols., Copenhagen, 1952.

Carissimi. *Opere complete* (incomplete), ed. L. Bianchi, vols. 1–8 in *Istituto italiano per la storia della musica, Monumenti* 3, Rome, 1951–   . *Six Solo Cantatas*, ed. G. Rose, London, 1969.

Cavalli. *Giasone:* Prologue and Act I, *Publikationen älterer praktischer und theoretiker Musikwerke*, ed. R. Eitner, vol. 12 (Berlin, 1883).

Cesti. *Il pomo d'oro*, DTO, vols. 3:2 and 4:2, ed. Guido Adler, (1896). Several cantatas printed in *The Italian Cantata 1: Antonio Cesti, The Wellesley Edition* no. 5, ed. David Burrows, Wellesley, Mass., 1963.

Chambonnières. *Oeuvres complètes*, ed. Paul Brunold and André Tessier (Paris, 1925).

Couperin, Louis. *Oeuvres complètes*, ed. Paul Brunold, Paris, 1963. *Pièces de clavecin*, ed. Alan Curtis, Paris, 1970.

Froberger. *Keyboard works*, ed. Guido Adler, DTO Jg. 4:1 (vol. 8), Jg. 6:2 (vol. 13), Jg. 10:2 (vol. 21).

Gaultier. *La rhétorique des dieux et autres pièces de luth*, Publications de la Société française de musicologie ser. 1, vols. 6–7 (Paris, 1932).

Jenkins. *Fancies and Ayres*, ed. Helen Joy Sleeper, Wellesley, Mass., 1950.

Lully. *Oeuvres complètes* (incomplete), ed. H. Prunières, 10 vols., Paris, 1930–39.

Pachelbel. *Klavierwerke*, ed. M. Seiffert, DTB Jg. 2:1, Leipzig, 1901.

Purcell. *Works*, London, 1898–1965.

Steffani. Opera *Alarico*, duets, cantatas, ed. A. Einstein and H. Riemann, DTB Jg. 11:2, Jg. 12:2, Leipzig, 1905, 1912. Opera *Tassilone*, ed. G. Croll, *Denkmäler rheinischer Musik* vol. 8, Düsseldorf, 1958.

Tunder. *Vocal works*, ed. M. Seiffert, DdT, vol. 3, Leipzig, 1900; rev. ed., Wiesbaden, 1957.

THE
LATE
BAROQUE

Italian Instrumental Music: The Concerto.   The third and final phase of Baroque music began in Italy during the 1680s, and somewhat later in other countries. It lasted through the first decades of the eighteenth century, only to be gradually eroded away by a new stylistic and aesthetic orientation, as the heroic-pathetic rhetoric of the Baroque was abandoned in favor of refinement and elegance. For if the seventeenth century was the age of emotion, the eighteenth was the "age of reason," and reason is no friend of the grand gesture.

Nevertheless, in the few decades of its ripeness, the late Baroque produced some of the greatest music ever written, and vast quantities of lesser work that can still be heard with much pleasure. It was, like the sixteenth century, a time when basic techniques had developed to the point where lesser composers could turn out acceptable music without great difficulty, and where great ones consistently produced masterpieces. Indeed, among music-lovers, the word "Baroque" often means specifically "late Baroque," but this is an unfortunate usage: the admirable technical assurance of late Baroque music should not be allowed to obscure the virtues of the preceding styles.

During this time, Italy maintained her position of musical leadership, and Italian styles were exported all over Europe—even to France, which had resisted Italianization for so long. But although no one could have foreseen it at the time, the days of Italian supremacy were numbered. The two greatest composers of the age, Johann Sebastian Bach and George Frideric Handel, were not Italian, but German; and two others of the first rank, François Couperin and Jean-Philippe Rameau, were French. Italy continued as teacher, but her pupils surpassed their mistress.

It was, however, an Italian, Arcangelo Corelli (1653-1713), whose work established the chief style and the principal forms of late Baroque instrumental music. In Corelli's hands, the trio sonata and solo sonata developed along the lines laid down by Vitali and Bononcini, gaining, however, in richness and in size. Corelli was one of the first composers in whose works tonality is consistently used as the basic organizing principle. Compared to his predecessors, he commanded a larger repertoire of sequences and a sharper sense of overall tonal structure. With these as a basis, he was able either to

Arcangelo Corelli: The concerto grosso

281

achieve a polyphony that was at once complex and clear, or, when he preferred, to abandon counterpoint entirely in favor of brilliant figural writing (the latter especially in the solo sonatas). At the same time, the solidity of the tonal basis permitted movements to be longer than they had generally been earlier. Corelli often uses no more than four movements (slow—fast—slow—fast), each one of considerable length.

Trio and solo sonatas—both church and chamber type—make up the bulk of Corelli's rather small output, and they alone would have sufficed to establish him as a master of the first rank. But late in life (the exact year is not known), he published a volume of works he called "concerti grossi." From the evidence of the German musician Georg Muffat, it appears that at least some of these pieces had been written by the early 1680s. Corelli was therefore one of the earliest practitioners of a substantially new and immensely important Baroque form: the concerto.

The concerto is orchestral music—music, that is, in which each written part is normally played by more than one performer, and one of its central principles is the exploitation of the contrast in sound between the full orchestra and a smaller body of solo players. This was by no means new. Trio sonatas were doubtless often performed with several players to a part; and a number of seventeenth-century composers had experimented with contrasts in medium. But in Corelli's concertos, the solo-versus-orchestra contrast acquires new importance.

For Corelli, a concerto is an orchestral sonata, of either the church or chamber type. The main body of strings, the ripieno, or tutti, consists of two sections of violins, one of violas, and one of 'cellos, basses, and keyboard continuo. Against this four-voice orchestra is set the concertino, consisting of two solo violins and a solo 'cello, in obvious imitation of the trio sonata. For this mixed medium, Corelli writes movements that closely resemble those of his sonatas, except that a movement of any type may be enriched by the contrast between ripieno and concertino.

Corelli's concertos

The first of his concertos is in seven movements, alternately slow and fast, with an extra fast one at the end. In the first and fourth of these, the concertino invariably plays along with the ripieno: there is thus no contrast of medium. Except for the viola part, they might be movements from a trio sonata. The other movements contain passages in which the concertino alone is sounding, and the special effect produced thereby is employed in a surprising variety of ways. While later composers often adopted standard solutions—for example, soft or figural passages for the concertino, loud and cadential areas for the ripieno—Corelli appears to have taken a free and experimental approach. Thus the rapid figuration of the fourth movement might seem appropriate to a soloist, but it is given to the ripieno; conversely, the severe contrapuntal style of the sixth would hardly suggest contrast in medium, but it appears all the same. And the first movement, with its written-in dynamic contrasts, seems almost to cry out for alternation between ripieno and concertino, but all of it is given to the full orchestra. In choosing less obvious and perhaps more subtle scorings, Corelli reveals himself as an innovator, writing before the conventions of the form had hardened.

This concerto may also serve to demonstrate some other aspects of Corelli's style. The first movement virtually summarizes the late Baroque method of handling tonality. The first two measures present key-defining harmony (Ex. X-1). The dominant chord is here reached by way of its own dominant. There follows a rising sequence, which also makes use of secondary dominants; another cadence; then (not shown) another sequence, and the final cadence (here the last chord is the dominant, not the tonic, in order to

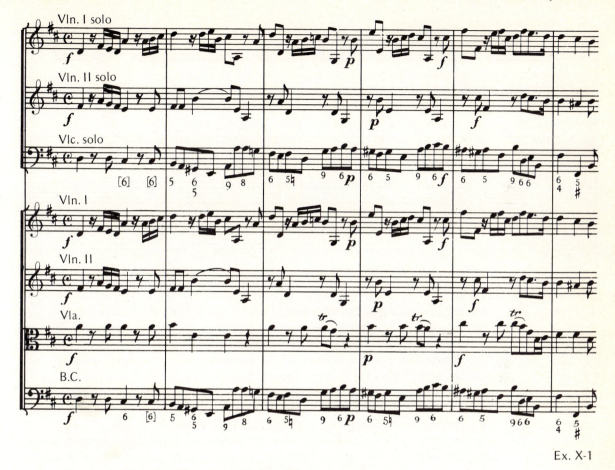

Ex. X-1

increase the tension). The same plan of alternating sequences and cadences appears in the second movement, where it is reinforced by contrast of medium: the sequences are given to the concertino, the ripieno joining in at the ends and at the cadences. In this plan lies the essence of late Baroque tonal writing: every cadence is immediately followed by material that threatens to leave the key just established. Thus, once the first modulation has been made, there follows an almost continual tonal instability, relieved only occasionally by cadences in keys other than the tonic. The tension built up in this way is sufficient to support works of considerable length.

Vivid proof of the vitality of tonal principles may be derived from the fourth movement of the same concerto. Here both melody and counterpoint seem to be entirely absent: there is nothing but the constant figuration of the first violin part, which is nothing more than a series of broken chords (Ex. X-2). Although the brilliant sound created by the figuration is an important part of the effect, the principal structural resource of a piece like this is the solidity and logic of the harmonic process.

In sharp contrast to this stands the sixth movement, which is imitative throughout. It differs from the German fugues examined in Chapter IX by the presence of substantial episodes in which the subject is not present. These two movements, the fourth and the sixth, represent the two poles of late Baroque texture: non-contrapuntal figuration, and

Ex. X-2

rich imitative counterpoint. They should not be regarded as mutually contradictory, for they merely represent two different ways to give animation and interest to a succession of chords arranged in a satisfactory tonal order.

Nevertheless, it was in the concerto that non-contrapuntal writing found a particularly congenial home. The concerto came to be related to the sonata much as the opera was to the concerto: both concerto and opera preferred bold and vigorous gestures to the refinements of chamber music. Concerto themes, with their powerful rhythms and harmonically derived melodies, typically give important material only to the top and bottom voices; and even these are related not so much contrapuntally as harmonically (i.e., as melody and harmonic support). Simplified textures of this sort became a hallmark of the concerto, although imitative movements did not entirely disappear.

The mature concerto grosso

The forms of the concerto movements, still experimental in Corelli's work, gradually became more regular. The typical concerto is in three movements: the outer two quick; the middle one slow. While the slow movement may be of almost any shape, the quick ones are generally in some variant of the form R a R b R c . . . R (in which R denotes the recurrent tutti section, or ritornello, and the lower case letters the sections given to the concertino). The tutti entrances are thus further emphasized by the use of approximately the same material each time. The complete ritornello usually appears only twice, at the beginning and at the end. The internal tutti sections are usually abridged, in order to avoid prolixity, and appear in keys other than the tonic.

The contrast of medium is brilliantly made to serve structural ends: the tutti utterances are similar enough to be recognized as pillars of the structure, while the concertino sections combine the function of providing sonorous contrast with that of effecting modulation from the key of one ritornello to that of the next—purposes to which their content, largely figural sequences, is ideally suited.

Solo concerto

It is evident that the concerto grosso proper, with its sonata-derived concertino of two violins and 'cello, is by no means the only medium in which the concerto can be realized. Almost from the beginning, other possibilities were explored. Most popular was the solo concerto, which employed a single instrument in place of the concertino.

The violin was the preferred instrument for the solo concerto, but other instruments were also used: the flute, the oboe, the trumpet—or indeed almost any instrument except the harpsichord or organ, for which concertos were written only later. Solo concertos are generally similar in style to concerti grossi, except that the thinner texture of the solo sections, and doubtless an interest in virtuosity, gave rise to especially complex figuration for the solo instrument. Particularly noteworthy is the frequent use of a single line to suggest a complete chord or even a contrapuntal combination of several lines (Ex. X-3).

Ex. X-3

Concertos were also written for groups of from two to four similar or diverse instruments. Like the solo concertos, these are similar to the concerto grosso in form and style. Somewhat different is the "concerto for orchestra," from which the apparently basic principle of contrasting media is absent. In some concertos of this type, the forms of the concerto grosso are retained, and the role of concertino is played by the full orchestra: concertino and tutti sections are recognizable by their style, not their instrumentation. In others, even the style contrast is reduced, and each movement is a relatively homogeneous continuum, marked principally by the recurrence of the opening idea, and by the functional difference between cadential harmony at such points and sequences in between. When the opening idea is imitative in nature, such movements take on the aspect of an orchestral fugue.

Italy produced an enormous repertoire of sonatas and concertos in the years from 1690 to 1730. An important early writer of concertos was Giuseppe Torelli (1658-1709), apparently the inventor of the solo concerto. Torelli's concertos, although progressive in their treatment of the medium, still maintain a connection with the sonata: movements often begin with an imitative due over a harmonic bass. Such contrapuntal treatment occurs less frequently in the works of later composers.

The greatest master of the concerto in its mature form was Antonio Vivaldi (ca. 1675-1741), author of nearly five hundred concertos, as well as operas and oratorios. About half of his concertos are for violin, but the remainder employ a wide variety of instruments, including unexpected ones such as the mandoline. Some concertos are grouped into cycles, with implications that the music is to depict extra-musical ideas: one such set provides a concerto for each of the four seasons. The majority, however, are abstract instrumental works, and even the programmatic pieces rarely depart radically from Vivaldi's normal style.

The last movement of Vivaldi's celebrated concerto for four violins is cast in an overall form that is clearly a variant of the normal ritornello structure described above. The first motive of the ritornello is vigorously characteristic and strongly tonal. It is also wholly non-contrapuntal. There follows a sequence on a related motive, and then

Antonio Vivaldi

Ex. X-4

several more related motives (Ex. X-4). The wealth of motivic material, which is typical of Vivaldi, permits a large number of options in constructing the rest of the movement—fragmentary recurrences of the ritornello are easy to manage, and the concertino sections may borrow motives from the ritornello without danger of redundancy. In this case, the concertino sections are figural, brilliantly exploiting the possibilities of the medium.

Perhaps the most significant aspect of a work like this is its lack of sustained contrapuntal writing. The late Baroque concerto is simultaneously the culmination of what had preceded it and a sign of change to come. The vigorous revival of counterpoint in the seventeenth-century Italian sonata is already a thing of the past, and the signs begin to point ahead to a time when accompanied melody will be the dominant style. As yet, however, the signs are no more than signs; in everything but its disinterest in polyphony, the concerto is thoroughly Baroque—in its driving, motoric rhythms, its motivically constructed melodies, its handling of tonality, and, especially, its noble and rhetorical aesthetic.

Opera in Italy.   In opera, the Italian late Baroque inclined toward a melodious but still partly contrapuntal style. The best-known composer—and one of the finest Baroque opera composers—was Alessandro Scarlatti, whose early work was discussed in the preceding chapter. Since many of Scarlatti's operas were written for Naples, early eighteenth-century Italian opera is often called "Neapolitan opera," a misleading designation that is better avoided.

Scarlatti is said to have written more than a hundred operas; he was also the author of about six hundred cantatas, a considerable amount of church music, and some instrumental works. Very little of this vast production is available in modern editions, and it is not easy to trace the development of his style from the early works—similar in style to those of Stradella and Legrenzi—to the operas of his maturity. Whatever the process, his operas after about 1690 exhibit a fairly constant pattern—one also found in the equally little-known works of his contemporaries and successors. The pattern is of course inherent in the libretti of the time; and while it may be said that Scarlatti and others merely reflected in their music a literary phenomenon, it remains true that composers apparently complied readily enough with the conventions of the libretti, and hence consented at least implicitly in their rather formalized structure. The principal elements in the late Baroque operatic pattern include the almost exclusive use of da capo (ABA) form for the aria; the consistent alternation of recitative and aria, with little use of chorus, ensemble, or independent instrumental music; the frequent use of strings (and in later works especially) other instruments to accompany the voice in the arias. These elements were not new, but the consistent way in which Scarlatti and others combined them was. In addition, Scarlatti, while employing "secco" recitative (recitative accompanied only by the continuo) for by far the greatest part of the dialogue, was able to make especially effective use of recitative accompanied by the orchestra for moments of extreme dramatic tension.

In Scarlatti's operas the aria is often expanded to imposing dimensions, in keeping with the general late Baroque tendency toward enlargement of forms. The aria normally opens with a ritornello for orchestra, establishing the basic affection and setting up a repertoire of rhythmic and melodic motives upon which the rest of the piece will be based. The ritornello cadences in the tonic, after which the voice enters to sing the first stanza of the text. This section is often quite lengthy, with frequent melismas and

*Later operas of
Alessandro
Scarlatti*

*Characteristics of
the Scarlatti aria*

Fig. X-1: George Friedrich Schmidt (1712-75), "Executio anima compositiones," perhaps representing the performance of a secular cantata, or of an aria taken from an opera. (Kunstsammlung Veste Coburg.)

repetitions of words or phrases. The voice is given full prominence, and is supported either by the basso continuo alone, or by brief and fragmentary interjections from the orchestra. There follows another ritornello, either a repetition or a modification of the initial one. If the aria is in da capo form—as are the majority of Scarlatti's—the B section then follows, after which the A section is repeated in its entirety. In most cases the singer was expected to add improvised embellishments to this repetition.

This scheme, with its ritornellos and its emphasis on the contrast between vocal and orchestral sections, is closely related to the concerto. In fact, the aria may be thought of as a miniature concerto for voice—an analogy strongly fortified by the vocal virtuosity that Scarlatti often demands of his singers.

The aria "Se Il trono", from *Mitridate Eupatore* (1707), begins with an opening ritornello ten measures long. The principal vocal section, though built primarily out of alternation between areas of cadential harmony and sequences (Ex. X-5a), also includes expansions within cadential areas—another device that permits enlargement of the form with no sacrifice of tension. The A section ends with a shortened version of the ritornello; the B part, using almost exactly the same kind of material, achieves contrast by purely tonal means, passing through the darker key of B minor (Ex. X-5b). Although this aria is much longer than the average aria of Scarlatti's predecessors, the effect is still compact and concise.

If I demand the throne, from heaven or by my sword, I want to reign only with her whom I adore.

Ex. X-5(a)

Ex. X-5(b)

For much of his career, Scarlatti was extremely popular, and this popularity was certainly well deserved: the best of his work represents late Baroque Italian opera at its highest level. Although his operas are scarcely ever staged today, this should not be taken as a measure of their value.

Toward the end of his life, Scarlatti appears to have declined in public favor. Although he made some attempt to adjust to changing public taste, his music came to be found less interesting, perhaps because it was too complex (compared to newer styles) to be enjoyable. Thus, although Scarlatti is often regarded as the founder of a new school of opera, a school committed to rigid recitative-aria alternation and to vocal virtuosity, it is more reasonable to consider him as representing the end of an era—as one of the last Italian opera composers whose work still manifests the heroic grandeur of the Baroque. For Scarlatti, despite the charm of his melodies and the brilliance of his vocal writing, has by no means turned away from polyphonic writing (as can be seen even more clearly in his cantatas); nor has he forsaken the exalted ideals of the Baroque. His successors, on the other hand, were more concerned with elegance than with grandeur. Their work is not Baroque in any real sense.

George Frideric Handel.   Scarlatti did, however, have one successor, at least in spirit: George Fridiric Handel (1685-1759), one of the greatest of composers. Handel was born in Germany, had his musical education there, and in 1703 was employed by the German opera at Hamburg, then under the leadership of Reinhard Keiser (1674-1739), its finest composer. At Hamburg, both Italian and French styles were known and practiced. Handel was successful in Hamburg, but left in 1707 for Italy, where he spent three years assimilating the newest developments of Italian style. His Italian visit produced a number of Italian cantatas. After a brief return to Germany, Handel first visited (1711) and then settled (1712) in England, where he spent the rest of his life—a naturalized German, the foremost representative of Italian music in England.

Handel's life

This much biographical information is essential to an understanding of Handel's music. His style is the product of a diversity of antecedents: the German formation, rich in learned counterpoint; the Hamburg opera, sophisticated and up to date; the brilliance of Italian style; and, not least, the lifelong practice of music in England, a country whose musical energies were at their weakest, but where the musical past, exemplified by Purcell and even by the Elizabethans, was held in sincere respect.

Handel's Italian operas

Handel began his English career primarily as a composer of Italian opera, then very fashionable in London. From 1705 (even before he settled in England) until 1741, he devoted most of his efforts to this genre, even when disappointing financial results suggested that English taste was taking a different direction.

Handel's operas owe much to those of Alessandro Scarlatti, and follow the dramaturgical conventions established at the end of the seventeenth century. The libretti are serious in tone and complex in incident, deriving either from ancient history or from legend. But Handel, working with conventional forms, was able by his genius to transcend them. In his arias, the commonplace rhetoric of the verse is swallowed up in the intensity of the musical expression.

For Handel, the aria was both an abstract musical scheme and a vehicle in which the emotion of the character was transmitted to the audience. His arias are large and vigorously individual, in the Baroque sense of sharply realizing a given affection, rather than in the modern one of conveying a unique personal experience. Handel effortlessly combines German contrapuntal facility with the sensual warmth of Italian melody, with the result that his textures are in general more complex than those of his

Italian contemporaries. The forms are large: the first section of a da capo aria is often a bipartite structure, in which the initial ritornello is followed by a vocal section modulating to a related key, then by a transposed and shortened ritornello, a second vocal section returning to the tonic, and finally a repetition of the initial ritornello. As is normal in this period, the middle (B) section of an aria is generally much smaller, and may omit the orchestra in favor of accompaniment by the continuo alone.

As in Scarlatti, the concerto-like aspect of the arias is often enhanced by brilliant vocal writing, posing extremely difficult problems for modern performers: only recently have acceptable performances of Handel's operas been presented and recorded, and such performances are still rare. An extreme example of vocal virtuosity may be seen in the Italianate aria "No, no I'll take no less," from Handel's *Semele* (1744), a pseudo-opera with English text. Example X-6 reproduces the first vocal section of the aria, toward the end of which the violin seems actually to compete with the voice in the

Ex. X-6

execution of brilliant figuration. The virtuosity here may result in part from the words "in full excess" of the text, and in part from Handel's desire to portray Semele as a vain character.

While essentially conservative in his dramatic use of music, Handel occasionally takes liberties with accepted forms in order to make a particular dramatic point (as indeed do other composers of the time). There are da capo arias in which the B section is, for dramatic reasons, wholly unrelated to the material of A; as well as arias in which da capo form is renounced in favor of some other scheme. Also important are the arioso, an abridged aria in which an intense affection is concisely presented without extensive ritornellos or large scale repetition; and the accompanied recitative, which permits the forceful portrayal of rapidly changing emotions. Although it is clear that Handel took his dramas seriously, and did not regard them as mere pretexts for agreeable concerts, the value of his operas lies primarily in the greatness of their music, not in any dramatic innovations. It requires a certain conscious adjustment on the part of the modern listener to accept Handelian dramaturgy.

It is therefore fortunate that Handel's operatic career did not in the end yield the success promised by its beginning. At first there were troubles with rival opera companies, but soon Handel had to contend with a decline of English interest in Italian opera of any sort—a decline probably hastened by the success of Pepusch and Gay's *The Beggar's Opera* (1728). This was a satiric piece—in English—with simple, unpretentious music; and its impact may have made it more difficult for audiences to respond to the grandiose rhetoric of Handel's operas. Still, it was not until 1741 that Handel definitively gave up opera in favor of English oratorio, a genre that turned out to be perfectly suited both to Handel and to his public.

Handel's oratorios

The basic form of the oratorio as cultivated by Handel is similar to that of the opera: most oratorios have a plot, often from Biblical history, and clearly defined characters. Narrative is given in recitative, and reflective text is set as an aria. But many of Handel's oratorios give considerable prominence to the chorus, something almost unknown to Italian opera, in which the few vocal ensembles were generally sung by the soloists. In consequence, Handel is able to enrich his style further with elements of the strong English choral tradition from Byrd to Purcell. Moreover, the chorus, by providing a different medium, gives new variety to the oratorio, not only in sonority, but also in form, since there were no stereotyped forms—either textual or musical—for choruses as there were for arias.

While even in the arias Handel uses a considerable number of freely invented forms, and relies less on the standard da capo pattern, it is in the choral movements that formal variety is greatest. These range from through-composed pieces of the anthem type, in which successive sections are based on different material, to severe choral fugues employing a single subject. In addition to these types (and others intermediate between them), one finds also what may be called choral arias, in which the chorus fulfills the function of the soloist in a solo aria. Whatever the form, Handel's superb instinct for effective choral writing is always evident, and the mere sound of his choral music is marvelously rich and effective.

Handel's choral inventiveness is ubiquitous in the oratorios. The double chorus "I will sing unto the Lord" from *Israel in Egypt* (1739) begins with a solemn theme that suggests contrapuntal treatment, but what follows is neither especially solemn nor particularly contrapuntal. Graceful melismas and declamatory writing are used more than the original idea, but all three reappear throughout the movement (i.e., it is not divided into successive sections based on different materials). Near the end, there are brilliant homophonic passages for the full double chorus, splendidly demonstrating Handel's command of sonority.

Handel's contribution to instrumental music is on the whole less important than his work in opera and oratorio. Although he was a celebrated virtuoso at the harpsichord and the organ, he must have relied heavily on improvisation, for his surviving keyboard works—probably teaching pieces—do not require the formidable technique he must certainly have possessed. More characteristic are his trio and solo sonatas and, especially, his concertos, which contain some of his finest music. His organ concertos, among the earliest concertos for a keyboard instrument, were intended for performance as interludes between sections of his oratorios. More conventional are the concertos for wind instruments and the concerti grossi, although in the latter Handel deviates from the typical Vivaldi scheme by restoring the initial opening slow movement, and by often including a dance movement near the end. Both the characteristic concerto style and a more severe contrapuntal manner may be found in the concerti grossi, which are among the best contributions to this genre.

*Handel's
instrumental
music*

Handel stands in majestic isolation, far above almost all of his contemporaries. But in time he also stands behind them, for he took almost no interest in the new stylistic tendencies that began to appear in Italy after 1725. Only in a musically conservative city like London could a composer have fallen so far behind the times and still remained so successful. Handel's residence in England may be regarded as providential. It allowed him to refine his command of late Baroque techniques in the great Italian operas of the 1720s and 1730s, and then to transfer these techniques, further enriched by elements of the English choral tradition, to the even greater English dramatic works of his later years.

Music in France. Handel's successful cultivation of an Italo-German style in England is one vivid example of the musical internationalization that reached a peak in the eighteenth century. The musical situation in France provides another. Throughout the seventeenth century, the French had jealously preserved their own national styles, and had for the most part resisted the powerful forces emanating from Italy. But about 1700, France opened her doors, and Italian influence entered in force. French composers began writing sonatas and concertos in addition to—or even instead of—the traditional categories of opera and keyboard music. At almost the same time, French taste began to incline to the elegant and decorative, rather than the heroic. The change in taste was not, however, absolute, and one may often find Baroque grandeur and the new "rococo" daintiness side by side in the works of a single composer.

The greatest French musician of this period was François Couperin (1668-1733), called "le grand" to distinguish him from other members of his large and musically illustrious family. Couperin was active in most of the principal musical genres except opera, and has left chamber music, sacred works, and above all, pieces for the *clavecin*, on which his fame chiefly (if not quite fairly), rests. Like the earlier *clavecinistes*, he grouped his pieces into suites, or *ordres*, in a single key. Many of the movements are still clearly in the rhythmic style of the traditional suite dances—allemande, courante, and so on. But Couperin usually avoids noncommittal designations like "allemande" in favor of fanciful titles—"The Knitting Women," "The Mysterious Barricades," "The

François Couperin

Victorious Muse"—or proper-name titles intended as compliments to aristocratic pat-rons. Such titles had long been used by the *clavecinistes*, although few of the earlier ones were as imaginative as those of Couperin.

Couperin's forms are those of his predecessors: the binary form is most frequent, al-though the rondeau is also used. The unmeasured prelude, however, does not appear. The style is clearly marked by the growing French taste for elegance as opposed to grandeur: Couperin's textures are much less dense than those of D'Anglebert. But this is still in essence Baroque music, and rests firmly on contrapuntal and harmonic princi-ples not very different from those of Corelli. "La convalescente," from Couperin's last suite, is one of his nobler and more serious works. The texture is simple: a melody over a bass, with occasional free inner voices, the whole decorated by numerous *agréments* (Ex. X-7). But the bass is characteristically Baroque in style, and the melody is also, in its spinning out of basic rhythmic motives (unlike the simple non-motivic tunes that were soon to come into favor).

Ex. X-7

Couperin's debt to Italy can be seen more clearly in his chamber music than in his keyboard works. The chamber music medium was itself foreign to French style, which had preferred the large-scale drama or the keyboard miniature. Some of Couperin's chamber pieces are given explicitly Italian titles, or utilize well-assimilated Italian techniques. Alongside an "Apotheosis of Lully" is an "Apotheosis of Corelli," in which Corelli's manner can clearly be recognized, in a sophisticated French translation.

Operas of Jean-Philippe Rameau

It has been mentioned that French opera fell into a period of relative decline after the death of Lully. This ended in 1733, when the 50-year-old composer and theorist Jean-Philippe Rameau (1683-1764) began a long and distinguished operatic career with his *Hippolyte et Aricie*. Rameau was profoundly committed to French operatic ideals as exemplified in the works of Lully, but his style, enriched by Italian influences and his own theoretical researches, has far more substance and variety than that of his predeces-sor. Indeed, only the generally poor libretti of these works, coupled with the great difficulty of performing them, prevents their being staged more frequently.

Like all French operas of the time, Rameau's contain a large amount of "divertissement"—dancing and spectacle nearly or wholly irrelevant to the action.

Although these sections contain much fine music, they are of less importance than the dramatic parts, in which Rameau shows himself capable of responding magnificently to dramatic values. His recitative—directly descended from that of Lully, but fortified by a generous admixture of Italian passion—is capable of great emotional flexibility, and his serious arias have an amplitude and a richness lacking in earlier French music. But more important, Rameau is bound to no rigid dramaturgical scheme: he freely mixes recitative, aria, and chorus whenever the dramatic situation requires.

At the end of Act IV of *Hippolyte et Aricie*, a monster appears out of the sea (spectacular stage effects were still much loved) and apparently devours Hippolyte. Then Phèdre appears and bitterly reproaches herself for having been the true cause of his "death." Rameau's music closely follows every nuance of the action, making no use of set forms. While one's first impression might suggest that the brilliant treatment of the orchestra is the most noteworthy feature of this excerpt, it is in the end Rameau's attentive treatment of the drama that is more important. In Phèdre's monologue, especially, vocal declamation and orchestral accompaniment combine to convey faithfully every aspect of her changing emotional states (Ex. X-8). Opera—and Italian opera especially—was shortly to be made the object of a "reform," and Rameau's musical dramas were to be an important source of reform ideas.

What frightful thunder! Let us flee! Where can I hide? I feel the earth shake.
Hell [opens below me].

Ex. X-8

Johann Sebastian Bach. The history of German music during the first half of the eighteenth century is dominated by an extraordinary paradox: Germany produced, in the person of Johann Sebastian Bach (1685-1750), one of the supreme musical geniuses of all time, surpassed by no one and equaled by only a very few. Yet it is doubtful whether a German musician in 1725 would have included Bach's name in a list of the five best composers of the time. Bach was not unknown in his own age: he had a great reputation as an organist, and his compositions were admired by a number of serious musicians and amateurs. Many others, however, found his music too complex and intellectual, and his reputation never reached that of lesser composers such as Georg Philipp Telemann (1681-1767).

This is the first time—but not the last—that a composer's contemporaries made such a serious error in judgment. In earlier times, masters of the first rank—men like Perotinus, Dufay, Josquin, Palestrina, Monteverdi—were acclaimed as such by their colleagues, and had no need to wait for posthumous fame. With Bach the case is different: he was recognized, but only as a good musician, not as the transcendent master he was. This raises a problem for the historian. If he presents the period as those living at the time understood it, he will necessarily forfeit the insights later generations have contributed, and will be forced to concentrate his attention largely on music of very modest aesthetic value. Yet if he merely selects for presentation the works posterity has canonized, he runs the risk of falsifying the nature of the times.

Every serious scholar is aware of this difficulty. The advanced student of Elizabethan literature cannot simply read Shakespeare and stop there. He must know the lesser men as well, thereby learning not only what literature meant to a cultivated Elizabethan, but also how far Shakespeare transcended his times. On a more elementary level, such comprehensiveness is not possible: if only one Elizabethan author can be considered, then that one must be Shakespeare: "important," in the long run, means important aesthetically, whatever contemporaries may have thought. Thus, for the purposes of this book, music in Germany in the first half of the eighteenth century is the music of J. S. Bach. If this distorts the musical experience of Bach's contemporaries, it does so in the sense of replacing what actually was by what might have been—in the best of possible worlds. And the reader interested in the lesser men will come to no harm: anyone with a good knowledge of Bach can turn easily to the work of Bach's contemporaries. He will have in hand more than enough to understand them.

Bach's life   Bach came from a family that produced a large number of musicians—being in this like Couperin. The Bach family was deeply rooted in Lutheran Germany, and Johann Sebastian's early formation was dominated by the North German Lutheran tradition. His life was not outwardly eventful. After holding a number of positions, most as church organist, but two as court musician (at Weimar and at Cöthen), he became director of music at St. Thomas Church in Leipzig (1723), where he remained until his death. The principal event of his musical biography was his discovery, fairly early in life, of the modern Italian instrumental style. This enabled him to fashion crisp and concise themes that contrast with the often rambling ones of his North German predecessors.

Since Bach spent much of his life in the service of the church, it is not surprising that sacred music forms a large part of his output. Yet there were also important stimuli for the production of secular and instrumental music: his years as a court musician; his membership, late in life, in the Leipzig Collegium Musicum (an association of musicians); and his continuous preoccupation with teaching both the members of his numerous family (several of his sons were composers, two of them very important ones) and other pupils. Thus, while Bach's piety and his devotion to the church are beyond question, it is a mistake to regard him as a "church composer." He was a musician, and wrote in all the forms and media of his time except opera.

Like many late Baroque composers, Bach was prolific. His works are, as it were, a musical continent—in which it is all too easy to become permanently (if delightfully) lost. In attempting to survey this great mass of material, it will be well to start by following some of the steps Bach himself used in introducing his pupils to the art of music. He began by giving them very simple bipartite pieces—either dances or "preludes"—for clavier (harpsichord or clavichord). He wrote some such pieces himself, but often used works of other composers, since at such a modest level the work of any competent musician would serve.

The next step, however, was peculiarly Bach's own. He wrote a set each of two-voice "inventions" and three-voice "sinfonias" (often called three-part inventions). Each set contains fifteen pieces, arranged in ascending order of major and minor keys, only the commoner keys being used. Bach himself preceded them with this introduction: "A correct introduction, whereby amateurs of the clavier . . . are shown a clear fashion not only (1) of learning to play cleanly in two voices, but also after further progress (2) of proceeding in three voices rightly and well; and at the same time not only to get good *inventiones* (ideas) but also to develop the same well, and above all to achieve a *cantabile* (singing) style in playing, and to receive a strong foretaste of composition." The pedagogical intent is obvious, but there is nothing academic about these pieces: in them, the whole art of Bach is expressed in miniature. The Sinfonia in F major (Ex. X-9) is a perfect blending of solid tonal harmony with complex but lucid counterpoint. The structure is characteristic: the first three measures contain three statements of the theme, one in each voice. Then a sequence based on elements from the theme modulates to the dominant and cadences there (the theme itself appears in the

Bach's didactic works: Inventions and Sinfonias

Ex. X-9

middle voice just at the cadence). A new sequence now begins, and the remainder of the piece alternates sequences, presentations of the theme, and cadences. The demands of unity and variety are wholly filled. This piece, with its alternation of modulatory sequences and entrances of the subject, could be called a fugue, but Bach did not choose to give it that title. For him, a fugue, though a piece of precisely this sort, was generally a work on a somewhat larger scale.

Well-Tempered Clavier

After the student had mastered the inventions and the sinfonias (no easy task), he might next set to work on Bach's most famous keyboard work, the *Well-Tempered Clavier*[1] a collection of twenty-four preludes and fugues, one in each major and each minor key. (Late in life Bach made up a second collection of the same sort, now generally known as the second part of the *Well-Tempered Clavier.*)

Nowhere is the diversity of Bach's genius more evident. The preludes range from wholly figural pieces depending entirely on harmonic progression for their coherence (such as the first one), to pieces as contrapuntal as the fugues themselves. The fugues are very nearly as diverse—so much so that they were the despair of later pedants who, trying to codify the "rules" of the fugue, could do so only by regarding many of Bach's as incorrect. Nevertheless, all of Bach's fugues share one common trait: their subjects are all perfectly individual (in the Baroque sense), each one introducing the hearer into the unique world of that single composition (Ex. X-10).

Ex. X-10

Bach's fugues

In all this diversity, however, certain basic categories may be distinguished. First there is the simple fugue, whose subject is of such musical interest that its periodic reappearance after an episode is—when combined with the unity and variety afforded by the tonal architecture—sufficient to give the work momentum. Such fugues often have a countersubject as well as a subject, the countersubject being the material that appears in the first voice when the second voice presents the answer, and that subsequently recurs whenever the subject or answer does. The countersubject must always combine with the subject and the answer in "invertible counterpoint at the octave."

---

[1]"Well-tempered" here merely means tuned in roughly equal semitones. The older tunings of Bach's time did not permit playing in keys such as F♯ major and E♭ minor.

That is, either must be capable of being moved one or more octaves up or down, so as to sound either above or below the other. Thus, if the fugue begins

subject	countersubject	free material	
	answer	countersubject	*Invertible*
		subject	*counterpoint*

it must be possible in later entries to lower the countersubject or raise the subject (or answer) to produce the position

subject
countersubject

sounding equally well.

Invertible counterpoint can be extended to three voices ("triple counterpoint") to produce another type of fugue, always in three voices. In this type, the nucleus of the fugue—not stated at the outset—is a three-voice complex consisting of the subject in one voice, a countersubject in another, and a second countersubject in the third. Each of these three elements must have a recognizable melodic identity of its own, so that the complex will sound not only well but different in any of its six possible positions:

S	S	CS_1	CS_1	CS_2	CS_2
CS_1	CS_2	S	CS_2	S	CS_1
CS_2	CS_1	CS_2	S	CS_1	S

Such a fugue will invariably begin in what appears to be a normal fashion:

S	CS_1	CS_2
	A	CS_1
		S

Only later will it become apparent that the three-voice counterpoint is in fact fully invertible, and the remainder of the fugue will present some or all of the possible inversions in various keys, with modulating episodes between. (Quadruple counterpoint and invertible counterpoint at invervals other than the octave are both possible, but even Bach uses them only occasionally.)

A third type of fugue is that based on stretto, or overlapped entries of the subject. *Stretto fugue* Such overlapping, in which one or more entries are begun before a preceding entry is finished, has a powerful climactic effect, especially when the overlapping can be tightened by gradually decreasing the time interval between entries as the fugue progresses. Any subject's possibilities for stretto can be increased by using the devices of augmentation (doubling or otherwise increasing the time values of the subject); diminution (halving or otherwise decreasing the time values); and inversion, in which ascending invervals of the subject are replaced by corresponding descending ones, and vice versa. This must not be confused with the contrapuntal inversion just discussed.

In stretto fugues, especially when many different overlappings are possible, the episodes are apt to be much diminished in size, and may sometimes disappear altogether.

Finally, the double fugue and triple fugue should be mentioned. In a double fugue, *Double and triple* an apparently normal fugue is begun, only to be interrupted after a while by the *fugue* exposition of a new subject (or, in the case of the triple fugue, by successive expositions of two new subjects). The subjects are then combined. Like the stretto fugue, this can be made into a highly dramatic form.

*Bach's keyboard
suites*

In each of the collections considered so far, Bach's intent is clearly didactic and systematic. In his suites for keyboard, however, specifically didactic purposes seem to recede in favor of the pure pleasure of music-making. Apart from a few separate suites, there are three principal sets of six each: the "French" suites, the "English" suites (these rather meaningless titles were added after Bach's time), and the partitas—so named by the composer himself. Bach generally keeps to the standard late Baroque suite pattern: allemande, courante, sarabande (extra dances, if any), gigue. The English suites and partitas begin with splendid introductory movements, some in the form of the French overture, some concerto-like movements for keyboard, and others of still different types. The dances themselves are regularly in the normal binary form, often "rounded," in that the end of the B section repeats in the tonic what had appeared at the end of the A section in the dominant or relative major. In style, the suites are richer and more complex than most works of the time: Bach's contrapuntal facility and his virtuoso keyboard technique combined to produce a density that many musicians of his time found excessive. There is, however, evidence that Bach wrote down his music much as he wanted it played, while other composers expected the performer to embellish their scores, not only by adding little ornaments in the French manner, but also by elaborating more seriously on the written text. Thus Bach's contemporaries may not have sounded as simple as their written scores suggest. Bach's suite movements are in any event far too complex for actual dancing. They are dances only in the by now familiar sense: while they preserve the characteristic rhythms of the dance types that give them their names, their music is abstract and stylized.

In addition to his solo clavier music, Bach also wrote pieces for unaccompanied violin and unaccompanied violoncello. In these works, virtuoso technique is not an optional luxury, but a real necessity, for the player must create the illusion of a rich musical texture on an instrument whose basic language is monophonic. Bach accomplishes this in two ways. In the first place, he makes extremely extensive use of double, triple, and quadruple stops, carefully placing his music so that these resources may be frequently and effectively used. Secondly, he is especially ingenious in achieving the effect of polyphony even within a single melodic line by writing compound lines suggesting complete chords or two or more contrapuntal lines. The technique is that of Example X-3 (above), but Bach's use of it is generally denser and more complex. (Indeed the rich texture of all of Bach's music often owes much to the use of compound lines.) With these means, Bach is able to write for solo stringed instrument music that is hardly less rich than his works for keyboard or orchestra.

Chamber music

Such pieces, although they have antecedents, are somewhat unusual. And Bach's chamber music, although it maintains many traditional features, is also in part surprising. Most noteworthy is Bach's almost complete neglect of the trio-sonata medium. Instead, Bach either wrote solo sonatas for violin, flute, or viola da gamba, with basso continuo, which was conventional enough; or solo sonatas with written-out harpsichord parts, which was not conventional at all. In some movements of these latter sonatas, the harpsichord is chiefly an accompanimental instrument, and its part may well represent the kind of continuo playing Bach employed when improvising from a figured bass. But in other movements (more often the quick ones), the harpsichord is given two contrapuntal parts while the melody instrument supplies the third. Thus the trio-sonata texture is in fact preserved, but for two players rather than the traditional four. The reduction in the number of players is significant: the contrapuntal and harmonic richness of the music make it possible to dispense with the harmonic filling of the conventional basso continuo. Excerpts from the first two movements of a violin sonata illustrate both uses of the keyboard, and provide examples of both the noble and the lyrical side of Bach's style (Ex. X-11).

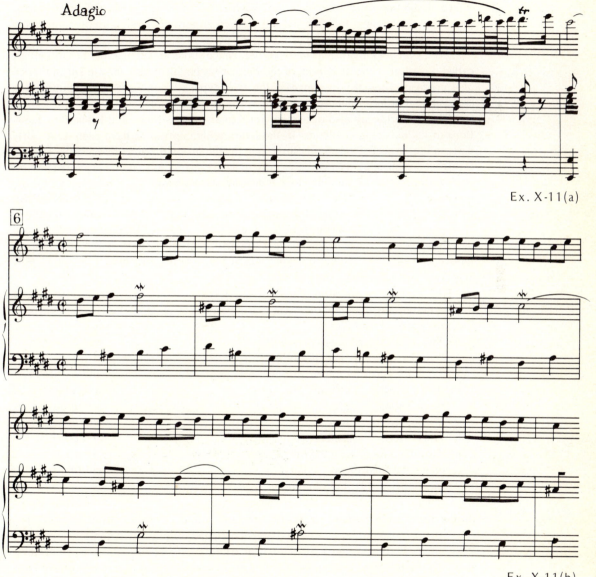

Ex. X-11(a)

Ex. X-11(b)

In writing for orchestra, Bach follows Italian models, but in a German fashion that is also influenced by French practice. His basic orchestra consists of the usual four string parts (two violins, violas, 'cellos and basses) plus the basso continuo. But German orchestral usage had long accorded wind instruments a greater role than they

Bach's orchestral works

normally played in Italy, and Bach often adds flutes or oboes (or both), horns, and, for festive effects, trumpets and timpani. Occasionally the winds merely double the string parts, but more often they have independent parts of their own. The trumpet and horn parts are of especial interest. The instruments then in use depended solely on the player's lip for changes of pitch, and hence could be used melodically only in their highest register, where the available notes are close enough together to make reasonable melodic lines possible. Players of Bach's time had developed the technique of playing in this register to a fine art; and modern performers, even with the much more flexible valve instruments, often find Bach's parts no easy problem.

Bach's orchestral music is of two types: dance suites and concertos. The former are called "overtures," because each of the four suites begins with a movement in French overture form. There follow dances of the usual type, althogh Bach is less bound to the conventional order of dances here than in the keyboard suites.

The concertos are also of two sorts: original compositions, and keyboard adaptations of Italian string concertos. In the latter, which appear to have been done fairly early in life, as part of his apprenticeship to the Italian style, Bach preserves the original form, but enriches the solo string writing so as to create a polyphonic keyboard part for each violin part of his model. These concertos, for from one to four harpsichords, are certainly the first important harpsichord concertos, and may be the first altogether. Later, Bach, perhaps stimulated by his adaptations, wrote original harpsichord concertos as well. Several of his concertos survive in two forms: in a striking exemplification of late Baroque idiom transfer, Bach rearranged for keyboard original pieces first intended for violin solo, and also made concertos for solo melody instrument out of what were originally keyboard concertos.

His most famous concertos, however, are the set of six dedicated to the Margrave of Brandenburg, and invariably known as the Brandenburg concertos. Each of these is differently scored, as follows:

Brandenburg concertos

1. Two horns, three oboes, bassoon, "violino piccolo" (small violin)	and orchestra
2. Trumpet, recorder, oboe, violin	and orchestra
3. Three violins, three violas, three 'cellos	and basso continuo
4. Violin, two recorders	and orchestra
5. Flute, violin, harpsichord	and orchestra
6. Two viole da braccio, two viole da gamba (instruments related to the violin family, but of an older type)	and basso continuo

(In the above table, "orchestra" means the conventional four-part string ensemble.)

These differ from the normal Italian concerto not only in instrumentation, but also in structure. In numbers 3 and 6, there is no true ripieno: the tutti effect is achieved by using all the instruments at once, and that of the concertino by using only one or two. The others employ the normal concertino-ripieno contrast, but in complex ways. Solo sections often have a certain amount of orchestral accompaniment, and in general the alternation of medium is less regular than it usually is in Vivaldi. The first movement of the second concerto, for example, has a clear enough ritornello, but this is followed, not by an extended solo passage, but by several brief solos interspersed with orchestral fragments of the ritornello. Thereafter, solo sections often have orchestral accompaniment (the longest orchestral silence is only eight measures long), although the functional distinction between solo and tutti remains clear. In the second movement of the same concerto, the orchestra is omitted altogether; and in the last, a kind of informal fugue, it functions as a kind of expanded continuo section, supplying harmony, but rarely taking part in the melodic material enounced by the solo instruments. In short, the Brandenburg concertos are very free adaptations of the Italian concerto principle: Bach gives to each movement an individual form, without troubling with precedent.

The preceding paragraphs have surveyed the chief areas of Bach's activity as an instrumental composer, with one major exception: music for organ. Since the organ was the Lutheran church instrument par excellence, it forms a natural bridge from the secular to the sacred, and thereby also from the instrumental to the vocal.

Bach's organ music: Preludes and fugues

There are two principal categories of organ music: the free works, and those based on chorale melodies. Most unusual among the free pieces is a set of six trio sonatas for organ solo (these may possibly have been written for a harpsichord provided with a pedalboard like that of an organ). Here Bach's economy is again evident: the traditional four performers of the trio sonata have been reduced to a single (if very busy) executant. Most of the other free pieces derive from the North German organ tradition of Buxtehude, although there are important stylistic differences, stemming from Bach's acquaintance with the new Italian style. The chief form is the prelude (or toccata or fantasia) and fugue. For Bach, these are two-movement works whose parts no longer interpenetrate as they did in Buxtehude. Their plan is similar to the preludes and fugues of the *Well-Tempered Clavier*, although the organ pieces are generally larger and weightier. Bach was himself a celebrated organist, and his writing for the instrument is wholly idiomatic; of all his music, this is perhaps the most congenial for the performer (although it is by no means easy). The subject of the great fugue in G minor, for example, is playable on all sorts of instruments, but a careful look will show that it is peculiarly adapted to the organ's pedal keyboard: most of it can be played easily by alternate feet (Ex. X-12; "L" and "R" indicate "left foot" and "right foot").

If the free organ pieces represent the fusion of the North German tradition with the modern Italian style, the chorale-based organ works are a coordination of almost all the known traditions of chorale treatment. One may find the old motet-like chorale, consisting of a series of little fugues on successive lines of the tune; the more unified monothematic fugue with superimposed chorale cantus firmus: the ornamented cantus-firmus type; a concerto-like type in which a ritornello appears between the lines of the chorale; chorale fantasias, in which the melody is subjected to free and often fragmentary treatment; and other types as well (including, significantly, movements in trio-sonata texture incorporating chorale phrases). Perhaps the most characteristic form is one associated with Bach's *Orgelbüchlein* (Little Organ Book), an unfinished collection of chorale preludes dating from the years up to 1723. Many of the pieces in this collection look like single variations from chorale variation sets. (Bach did not much

Bach's chorale-based organ works

cultivate the writing of complete sets.) The melody appears without interludes, usually in the top voice, sometimes in two voices in canon, accompanied by consistent figuration in the other parts. In some cases, the figuration is hardly more than motivically animated harmony. In others there is more contrapuntal complexity. Thus, in *Durch Adams Fall* (By Adam's Fall), the inner parts have one type of figuration, while the bass (pedal) part has a different motive of its own.

For Bach, such motives are not derived from purely abstract musical processes. Here, as in almost all his chorale works (and, as will be seen, in his vocal works also), the motives delineate musically the chief ideas or affections of the text, whether the latter is only implicit, as in this case, or actually sung. In *Durch Adams Fall,* the pedal motive symbolizes the Fall of Man: most of its intervals are diminished, or otherwise dissonant—the theological implication is obvious. The sinuous and partly chromatic lines of the inner voices suggest both the serpent and the misery caused by the Fall. The piece is thus a musico-theological portrait of extraordinary compactness and intensity.

Naturally, not every text invites such specific treatment, and many of Bach's chorale preludes attempt nothing more than a general delineation of mood. But it is characteristic of Bach to seize wherever he can on concrete rather than abstract imagery.

This principle of Bach's style, clear enough in the chorale preludes, is even more striking in his vocal church music. His output in this area is enormous: over 200 cantatas (the term is discussed below), mostly for the church, are preserved, and many more are known to have been written. There are two settings of the Passion, a great Mass, several smaller ones, a Magnificat, several motets, and other lesser works.

Bach's sacred vocal works

Bach wrote sacred vocal music from his early years on. At first, his works continue the tradition of Buxtehude and others. The texts, usually from the Bible or from a chorale, are set multisectionally, with solos, duets, choruses, and so on, as the text and the musical occasion require. These are, in fact, "sacred concertos," whose ultimate ancestry may be found in the works of Heinrich Schütz; but in Bach's case, they are invariably, if wrongly, called cantatas.

The true Lutheran cantata originated with pastor Erdmann Neumeister (1671-1756), who in 1700 published a collection of texts, in German and on sacred subjects, but built on the lines of Italian secular cantata texts or opera libretti. Neumeister's poetry was for the most part newly invented, and was so arranged as to call for recitatives, arias, and choruses as clearly separate units. When set to music, the new-style cantata differed from the old sacred concerto both textually (since little of the poetry was Biblical or from a chorale) and structurally (since its parts were separate movements, not sections of a single movement). What is more, the new texts permitted the importation into Lutheran music of the newest elements of the Italian operatic style.

Characteristics of Bach's cantatas

Most of Bach's sacred cantatas are of the new type. The majority date from his first years at Leipzig (1723ff.). For several years he produced a complete annual cycle of about sixty such works every year—an almost incredible feat. The principal types may be distinguished thus:

I. Solo cantatas (i.e., those without concerted choral movements)
II. Cantatas with chorus
    A. "Free" cantatas
    B. Cantatas employing a chorale cantus firmus

Certain elements are common to all of these categories (if not necessarily to every cantata within them). One is the operatic alternation between recitative and aria. Another is the use of a simply harmonized chorale to conclude the cantata, which suggests that even for the solo cantata a chorus of some sort was also available. Still another is the treatment of instrumental forces. The full orchestra is that of the purely orchestral music: strings (usually in four parts) and basso continuo, with other instruments added for expressive or symbolic purposes. (Thus triumphant texts call for trumpets and tympani; pastoral ones for flutes or oboes; and so on.) The full orchestra is regularly used to accompany choral movements, and sometimes for arias as well. But the majority of the arias are scored for chamber ensemble: two oboes and continuo, solo violin and continuo, or any of a large number of such combinations. Here again, the choice of instruments is often determined by symbolic considerations.

The arias (the term here includes duets and trios as well) are generally of considerable length. Many are in traditional da capo form, some in modifications of da capo form, and others in free forms of Bach's own devising. Especially in the arias scored for voice and chamber ensemble, Bach delights in treating the vocal part and the upper instrumental part(s) as equals, weaving their lines together in complex but transparent polyphony. Late Baroque transfer of instrumental idioms reaches another peak here, as the soloist is expected to execute figuration derived now from the technique of the violin, now from that of the flute. It has been objected that Bach's music was abstractly conceived— that it does not sound as well as it looks on paper. This is simply not true in the vast majority of cases. The music sounds ideally—but it is very difficult to sing.

If Bach's arias are an intensification and translation to the sacred domain of the ordinary Italian opera aria, much the same can be said of his recitative. It is more expressive—more jagged and less euphonious—than its Italian counterpart, but its basic means are the same. One of Bach's supreme abilities is his treatment of arioso, that hybrid style standing between recitative and aria. Here, unhampered by the normal needs of musical continuity, Bach can give full expression to every word of the text while at the same time making use of the full range of music's expressive powers.

The solo cantatas alone—and they are a minority—would constitute a priceless treasure of sacred music, but Bach's cantatas with chorus must be assigned an even higher rank. In structure, they resemble the solo cantatas. There are generally from six to ten movements, mostly recitatives and arias, with a concluding chorale. The opening aria, however, is regularly replaced by a monumental concerted movement for chorus and orchestra, and another such movement may occur later on.

In the so-called chorale cantatas, the opening choral movement employs a chorale melody as cantus firmus, and is in effect a large chorale prelude scored for chorus and orchestra. Many of the forms found in the chorale preludes may be found in these choruses as well. In the first movement of *Wachet auf* (Cantata 140), the orchestra begins with a free ritornello, which reappears in various modifications after each line of the chorale. The chorale melody is given to the soprano section of the chorus, while the lower voices have contrapuntal, but not imitative material. The last line, however, is preceded by a fugal exposition on a free subject. In this movement the chorale melody appears only as a cantus firmus, and does not affect the other musical materials used. A later movement of the same cantata (which survives also in a version for organ solo) also uses a free ritornello to separate the phrases of the cantus firmus.

*Bach's chorale
cantatas*

At an opposite extreme stands *Ein Feste Burg* (Cantata 80), which is saturated throughout by the chorale melody. In the first movement, the tune is played in canon by oboes and continuo, and each of its lines is preceded by a fugal section for chorus, the subject for which is derived from the chorale line that is about to be heard. Other chorale movements stand between these two extremes, insofar as the penetration of the chorale melody into the general texture is concerned, and also vary greatly in their level of contrapuntal complexity. There are a few special solutions as well, such as the magnificent *Jesu der du meine Seele* (Cantata 78), in which ritornello, ostinato, cantus firmus, and imitative writing are all combined. The result testifies to Bach's ability to solve the most formidable contrapuntal problems while at the same time maintaining the most intense expressivity.

The choral movements that do not utilize chorale melodies at all are even more various. There are huge da capo choruses, wholly in the form of the da capo aria, but enriched by the choral sound and the intricate polyphony of the choral and orchestral writing. There are austere choral fugues. There are movements in which an aria-type chorus develops into a central fugal passage before returning to a less imitative style at the end. And there are various types of two-part choral movements, often resembling a prelude and fugue.

Herr, gehe nicht ins Gericht (Cantata 105) is of the latter type. The chromatic anguish of the slow opening section precedes a vigorous but despairing choral fugue. The soprano aria shows how far Bach was willing to go in portraying his texts musically: the text speaks of "tottering," and Bach responds by omitting the basso continuo—the foundation upon which music should be based. The concluding chorale sums up the spiritual progress—from despair to confidence—that has been the theme of the entire text. Bach achieves this musically by gradually slowing down the initially agitated accompaniment until, in the final measures, it seems to reach a state of rest.

In this and in many other cantatas, Bach, who never wrote an opera, projects real dramatic values with great power. For even more dramatic compositions, one must *Bach's Passion* look, not to the so-called Easter and Christmas oratorios (which are really a cantata and *settings* a cantata cycle), but to the two extant settings of the Passion, one "according to St. John" (before 1724), the other "according to St. Matthew" (1729). In these great works the familiar story is projected forcefully (St. John) or poignantly (St. Matthew) with a technique that would certainly have made Bach the greatest—if not the most popular—opera composer of his day.

Bach's Passion texts are related to older ones much as the new-style cantata is related to the sacred concerto. The narrative of events is given in the words of the Gospel, but numerous chorales and free poems are interspersed. The poems are emotional and contemplative, with the result that the characteristically operatic alternation of action (recitative) and reflection (aria) prevails. In the St. Matthew Passion, Bach's setting systematically defines the roles of the participants. The Gospel narrative is set for the "Evangelist," often very powerfully, in secco recitative, as are the words of individual characters (Peter, Pilate, etc.). Groups (the high priests, the crowd) are represented by the chorus. The words of Christ, however, are set in recitative accompanied by a "halo" of sustained notes in the strings, which fails only at the words "My God, why hast thou forsaken me?" Apart from the opening and concluding devotional choruses, the free poems are set as accompanied recitative verging on arioso, or as arias. The chorus is also used for the chorales, but the simple chorale harmonizations are easily distinguishable from the complex choruses of the crowds.

It is in these latter that Bach's dramatic mastery is most evident. Many of them are quite short—down to a mere two beats in the paralyzing shout "Barrabas"—and make no pretense at being complete pieces of music. They give the listener only a fleeting glimpse of turbulent men and women shouting. It is, however, remarkable that Bach, whose musical structures are usually lengthy and perfectly developed, was willing to sacrifice musical values to dramatic ones in a way almost never found in contemporary opera. When to this dramatic power is added the poignant, lyrical beauty of the arias and the noble simplicity of the chorale settings, it is small wonder that the St. Matthew Passion is regarded as one of Bach's supreme masterworks.

Bach also contributed to three other types of vocal music: the motet, the secular cantata, and sacred music to Latin texts. The motets, most of which were written for funerals, are on German, not Latin, texts. They are notated as for unaccompanied chorus, but it is likely that in performance instruments were also used. The secular works are humorous works or tributes to patrons. They are full of charm, and reveal a lighter side of Bach's style.

The Latin church music calls for more extended comment. Although there is not a great deal of it, the category includes two works that occupy exalted places in the Bach canon. One is the Magnificat, a brief and enchanting setting for soloists, chorus, and orchestra of the traditional text. Structurally, this is like a cantata without recitatives. Bach takes each verse of the text and sets it as an aria, duet, or chorus.

Bach's Latin church music: Magnificat

The other great Latin work is the Mass in B minor, a complete setting of the Latin ordinary put together, in 1733, partly out of new material and partly out of adapted and revised versions of cantata movements. The work is immense—far too vast for inclusion in any actual church service—but its grandeur is such as to put to flight any questions regarding practical purposes. Here again the form is that of a cantata without recitatives. The texts are broken up into units of convenient length (the Kyrie, for example, has three sections, the Gloria eight), and each unit is set as a chorus, aria, or duet. It is easy to speak of the supreme technique demonstrated in this work—the effortless five- and six-voice choral polyphony, the masterly fugues, the retrospective use of Gregorian cantus firmi in two movements of the Credo—or to point to the numerous pictorial and symbolic devices it contains. More important is the profundity of the music. Hardly anywhere else, even in Bach, can one find movement after movement maintaining the same depth of expression.

Mass in B minor

In his later years Bach's interest in system and artifice became even more pronounced. In 1742, in addition to compiling the second part of the *Well-Tempered Clavier*, Bach wrote a set of thirty variations for harpsichord—the so-called Goldberg Variations. The theme is a bipartite sarabande, and Bach's technique of variation consists in retaining the principal harmonies and the phrase structure of the theme, not its melody. There are ten groups of three variations each. In each group, the first variation is free as to style, the second a brilliant display piece (except in the first group) and the third is a canon—the first canon being at the unison, the next at the second, the next at the third, and so on until variation 30, in which the expected canon is replaced by a variation in which two folksong melodies are combined. Then the theme is repeated, for a final touch of symmetry. It should be noted that each variation makes perfect sense as an independent piece: Bach is here the architect, fitting finished blocks into an exquisite design.

Bach's late works

Five years later there appeared two works in which canon and variation are both prominent. The first is a set of chorale variations for organ on the melody *Vom Himmel*

Musical Offering

hoch. Each of the variations illustrates a different type of canon against the melody as cantus firmus—an extremely difficult technical problem, solved, of course, without the least appearance of effort. The second, the *Musical Offering,* resulted from Bach's visit to Frederick the Great of Prussia. The king, a performer and composer himself, gave Bach a subject on which to improvise a fugue. Bach immediately played a three-voice fugue but, when asked for one in six voices, preferred to use a subject of his own rather than Frederick's. After returning to Leipzig, Bach wrote out his improvised three-voice fugue, added a six-voice one, a trio sonata, and two sets of canons, all of which employ Frederick's theme in some way. Bach's architectural thinking is obvious in the plan of the work:

fugue à 3	5 canons (theme as c.f.)	trio sonata	5 canons (made out of theme)	fugue à 6

Bach called the fugues "ricercare," a retrospective touch; but it is interesting that although most of the *Musical Offering* is in a severely Baroque contrapuntal style, there are places in the first fugue and in the trio sonata that show a more open and relaxed manner. Perhaps Bach was here deferring to Frederick's preference for modern simplicity.

Art of the Fugue

If so, it was no more than a momentary gesture. Bach's last major work, the *Art of the Fugue,* is once again systematic, didactic, and profoundly contrapuntal. It was Bach's plan to demonstrate in this work the various possibilities of fugal and canonic writing in a series of pieces all based on the same subject. He did not live to complete it, although only one entire fugue and part of another are lacking. What is extant is unequaled testimony to the combination of incredible contrapuntal skill with profound expressivity. These fugues, while they no longer exhibit the dramatic fire of Bach's earlier works, are no less beautiful, despite the severest technical problems. Every conceivable contrapuntal device is used: stretto, inversion, augmentation and diminution, invertible counterpoint at the tenth and twelfth, and even mirror writing (in which an entire fugue is turned upside down, note for note, to make a new fugue)—but the result, while often severe, is always poetic.

When Bach died in 1750, he had already outlived his time. A new style had become popular (he knew it perfectly well, and mocked it in one of his secular cantatas), and learned counterpoint was out of fashion. Bach was quickly forgotten by all but a few, and his works remained in oblivion until the nineteenth-century Bach revival—by which time much had been irretrievably lost. His music had little influence on his contemporaries and still less on his successors. It happens that the major composers of the next period, Haydn, Mozart, and Beethoven, came to know something of "the old Bach" (as he was called to distinguish him from his more famous sons), but they acquired their knowledge almost by accident, and the general musical public had by then forgotten him entirely. Nevertheless, seen from a distance of two hundred years, he stands high above all those around him, at an altitude very few have ever reached.

LATE BAROQUE.

I.   **Composers.**

Bach, Johann Sebastian (1685–1750). German composer, cantor at Leipzig, now acknowledged as the greatest composer of his age; see the list of his works elsewhere in this appendix.

Corelli, Arcangelo (1653–1713). Italian violinist and composer; worked in Rome. His clear, regular, idiomatically written solo and trio sonatas and concerti grossi set standards and established models of form and style for his successors.

Couperin, François (1668–1733). Nephew of Louis; organist of St. Gervais, Paris; court musician; harpsichordist and teacher. Composer of sacred music, including two organ Masses, trio sonatas, and much harpsichord music, arranged in "ordres" (suites). His style is characterized by a graceful elegance and supple ornament.

Graupner, Christoph (1683–1760). Court conductor and composer at Darmstadt. Composed operas for Hamburg; church music; much orchestral and chamber music.

Handel, George Frideric (1685–1759). Raised in Germany, trained in Italy, lived and worked in England; he is the best example of a universal high Baroque style that has never lost its appeal. See the list of his works elsewhere in this appendix.

Hasse, Johann Adolf (1699–1783). Kapellmeister and opera director at Dresden. Enormously successful composer of opera whose works were performed everywhere; not an innovator, his works follow all the operatic conventions of his time.

Keiser, Reinhard (1674–1739). An influential figure in German operatic history as director of the Hamburg opera and composer of ca. 100 operas, many produced there.

Kuhnau, Johann (1660–1722). German organist, theorist, and composer; cantor of Thomaskirche, Leipzig. Particularly known for his keyboard compositions, which include many multi-movement sonatas.

Leclair, Jean Marie (1697–1764). The greatest French master of Baroque violin music. Five books of virtuoso solo sonatas.

Rameau, Jean-Philippe (1683–1764). French theorist and composer, chiefly of opera. His operas have a rich and imaginative orchestration and use much instrumental music.

Scarlatti, Alessandro (1660–1725). Italian composer, father of Domenico Scarlatti. His many operas and cantatas established a style widely emulated by other opera composers.

Telemann, Georg Philipp (1681–1767). German composer; worked at Leipzig, Frankfurt, Hamburg. Enormously prolific, he composed ca. 40 operas, 12 annual cycles of cantatas and motets, hundreds of pieces of chamber music.

Torelli, Giuseppe (1658–1709). Bolognese violinist and composer. His instrumental music includes concertos for one and two violins, which make innovative use of ritornellos in the construction of movements.

Veracini, Francesco Maria (1690–1750). An international violin virtuoso; composer of difficult violin sonatas.

Vivaldi, Antonio (ca. 1675–1741). Priest and composer; worked at the Pietà Conservatory in Venice. He composed much sacred vocal music and many operas, most of which are now unknown. His more than 400 concertos, with their rhythmic drive, their imaginative orchestration, and their melodic freshness, assure him a permanent place among the foremost Baroque composers.

Zachow, Friedrich Wilhelm (1663–1712). German composer known primarily for his sacred vocal music, which shows certain resemblances to that of J. S. Bach.

II.   **The works of Bach and Handel.**

    A.   Principal works of J. S. Bach.

       1. Vocal.
        Many cantatas, mostly sacred
        Mass in B minor.
        4 Lutheran masses (Kyrie and Gloria only)
        Magnificat in D
        6 motets
        St. Matthew Passion; St. John Passion

       2. Instrumental (except solo keyboard)
        Orchestral:
        6 Brandenburg concertos
        4 orchestral suites
        2 concertos for violin
        Concerto for two violins
        7 harpsichord concertos (3 are transcriptions)
        3 concertos for two harpsichords
        2 concertos for three harpsichords
        Concerto for four harpsichords (transcription of a Vivaldi concerto for four violins)
        Concerto for flute, violin, and harpsichord
        Solo and chamber works:
        6 unaccompanied violin sonatas
        6 accompanied violin sonatas

6 suites for unaccompanied viola da gamba

3 sonatas for viola da gamba

6 sonatas for flute

4 trio sonatas

3. Solo keyboard

Organ:

Many preludes and fugues, toccatas and fugues, fantasias and fugues; Passacaglia and fugue; Pastorale; Canzona.

Chorale preludes

18 Leipzig chorales

17 "Catechism" chorales (*Clavierübung*, part III)

46 Orgelbüchlein chorales

6 "Schübler" chorales (all are transcriptions of cantata movements)

Other miscellaneous chorales

6 trio sonatas for organ

4 chorale partitas (sets of variations)

Harpsichord:

The Well-Tempered Clavier: two sets of 24 preludes and fugues, in all the major and minor keys

Air and thirty variations (The "Goldberg" variations; *Clavierübung*, part IV)

6 English suites

6 French suites

15 two-part Inventions

15 three-part Sinfonias

6 partitas (dance suites; *Clavierübung*, part I)

Italian concerto (*Clavierübung*, part II)

Various individual toccatas, preludes, fugues, suites

4. Miscellaneous.

Musical offering: a series of pieces for various media on a theme of Frederick the Great.

The Art of Fugue: fugues and canons treating a single theme.

B. Principal works of George Frideric Handel.

1. Vocal

Operas:

3 early works for Hamburg, including *Almira*, 1705

2 works in Italy, including *Agrippina*, 1709

37 operas in London, most for the King's Theatre, 1711–1741, including:

Giulio Cesare, 1724

Rodelinda, 1725

Sosarme, 1732

Alcina, 1735

Serse, 1738

Oratorios: 19 in all; all are in English except for 2 early Italian works.
They include:

La Resurrezione, 1708
Saul, 1739
Israel in Egypt, 1739
Messiah, 1742
Samson, 1743
Belshazzar, 1745
Judas Maccabaeus, 1747
Solomon, 1749
Theodora, 1750
Jephtha, 1752

Passions (in German)

St. John Passion, 1704
Brockes Passion, ca. 1716

Other secular vocal works:

Acis and Galatea, ca. 1720
Alexander's Feast, 1736
Ode for St. Cecilia's Day, 1739

Church music:

6 "Chandos" anthems
4 coronation anthems for George II
Other anthems, canticles, etc.

Miscellaneous:

22 Italian duets
ca. 100 Italian cantatas

2. Instrumental

Orchestral:

Water music, ca. 1717
Fireworks Music, 1749
6 concerti grossi, Op. 3
12 concerti grossi, Op. 6
18 organ concertos
Miscellaneous other concertos

Solo and chamber:

18 solo sonatas
26 trio sonatas

Much harpsichord music, including many suites.

III. **Editions of music.** In this list of modern editions, the following publication is cited in abbreviated form, as follows:

DdT *Denkmäler deutscher Tonkunst*, ser. 1, 65 vols., 1892–1931

Bach, Johann Sebastian. *Werke*, 47 vols., Leipzig, 1851–1899; *Neue Ausgabe sämtlicher Werke* (in progress), Leipzig, 1954–

Corelli. *Les oeuvres de Arcangelo Corelli*, ed. J. Joachim and F. Chrysander, 5 vols., London, 1888–1891.

Couperin, François. *Oeuvres complètes*, ed. M. Cauchie, 12 vols., Paris, 1932–33.

Graupner. *Ausgewählte Kantaten*, ed. F. Noack, DdT vols. 51–52 (1926); rev. ed., 1960

Handel. *The Works of George Frederic Handel*, ed. F. Chrysander, Leipzig, 1858–1902; new ed., *Hallische Händel-Ausgabe* (in progress), Kassel, 1955–

Keiser. *Croesus*, ed. M. Schneider, DdT vols. 37–38 (1912); rev. ed., 1958.

Kuhnau. Keyboard works, ed. K. Päsler, DdT vol. 4 (1901).

Rameau. *Oeuvres complètes* (incomplete), ed. C. Saint-Saëns, Paris, 1895–1924.

Scarlatti, Alessandro. *La Griselda*, ed. O. Drechsher, Kassel, 1960; *Eraclea*, ed. D. J. Grout, *The Operas of Alessandro Scarlatti*, vol. 1, Cambridge, Mass., 1974.

Vivaldi. *Opere*, Milan, 1947–[1950].

Zachow. *Gesammelte Werke*, ed. M. Seiffert, DdT vols. 21–22 (1905).

XI

THE
CLASSICAL
PERIOD

Opera seria and opera buffa.   By about 1730 in Italy, and somewhat later elsewhere, Baroque style had lost its vitality. The "Age of Reason" had arrived, and its goals were not the lofty, rhetorical ones of the seventeenth century, but rather the rationalistic aims of clarity, order, naturalness, elegance. Baroque intensity came to be regarded as a sin against good taste; and Baroque complexity (especially in counterpoint) as artificial and contrary to "nature."

The inevitable change in musical style that such a change in disposition must produce was anticipated by a literary reform that had important consequences for the history of opera. Many seventeenth-century Italian men of letters had deplored the poor literary quality of the opera libretto, and by about 1690 their criticisms had become strong enough to produce changes. Comic scenes and characters were eliminated from serious actions; the number of arias was decreased; and the placement of the aria at the end of a scene, to be sung by a character just about to leave the stage, was regularized. Fewer characters were used, and the incidents were made more plausible. There was also a change in favor of more elegant and less fantastic language. The new type of libretto was brought to perfection in the works of Pietro Metastasio (1698-1782), an immensely influential writer who was regarded by his contemporaries as the equal of Petrarch and Dante.

Pietro Metastasio

In Metastasio's libretti all is order, moderation, and elegance. The structure is always clear, the alternation of recitative and aria being carefully built into the poetry itself. Although the stories still deal with the exploits and trials of the ancient great, the characters always express themselves with refinement and good taste: emotions they have, but not so strongly that decorum is forgotten.

This type of opera is known as "opera seria" (in contrast to comic opera, which will be treated later). Opera seria became firmly established by about 1730, and continued in vogue (although eventually with declining popular success) until the turn of the century and even beyond. Although it is possible to consider Alessandro Scarlatti as the first important composer of opera seria, his musical style was still too saturated in Baroque elements to express fully the new ideals. It was the next generation—men born

Opera seria

Fig. XI-1: The Teatro Regio, Turin, probably during a performance of Leo's opera Arsace in 1740. (Archivio fotografico, Museo Civico, Turin.)

in the 1690s and after—that produced music in a style which perfectly matched that of the Metastasian libretto. The work of these men is even less known than the music of Scarlatti. There were, of course, many composers of the day who enjoyed great popularity: Leonardo Vinci (1690-1730), Francesco Conti (1682-1732), and especially the Italianized German Johann Adolph Hasse (1699-1783). But their music is not well known now. The only opera composer of the time whose name has remained celebrated is Giovanni Battista Pergolesi (1710-36), and there is no reason to suppose that he was the most important of his time. Still, despite the scarcity of information, some generalizations may be risked. In the first place, the structure of the opera seria remained that used by Scarlatti: regular alternation of recitative (mostly secco) and aria; prevalence of da capo form for arias, often of large dimensions and with virtuoso writing for the voice; few ensembles; little or no independent instrumental music; emphasis on musical values at the expense of the drama. What was new, at least in part, was the musical language, which differed in three important respects from that of Scarlatti: it almost entirely lacked contrapuntal qualities, interest being focused on the melody alone; the melody itself was apt to be a symmetrical "tune," arranged in pairs of two- or four-measure phrases, rather than a long line spun out of small rhythmic motives; and the changes of harmony—fairly regular and rapid in Baroque style—were slowed down, as if each single chord were to be savored at length. These qualities are all apparent in Example XI-1, an excerpt from an aria in Pergolesi's *Il prigionero superbo* (1733). Baroque dynamism has yielded to a sweet and elegant tunefulness.

Ex. XI-1

Italian opera of this sort was enormously popular all over Europe. We have seen that Handel wrote Italian opera for London, although his works are still firmly Baroque in style. Other Italian composers, some of them writing in a post-Baroque idiom, were also active there. Vienna was a particularly important Italian stronghold: it was there that Metastasio spent much of his life. Opera seria penetrated as far west as Spain, and as far as Russia to the north and east. In its popularity, it was liable to abuse. The Metastasian libretto, despite its formal elegance and acceptable if not intense dramatic content, was incapable of withstanding powerful pressures from audiences, and more especially from singers. The best opera singer, many of them castrati, acquired enormous fame and wealth; and their influence, far greater than that of either librettist or composer, often led to abuses of dramatic propriety in a structure already weak enough in that respect. A superfluous aria might be inserted into a scene merely because a famous singer wanted something to sing at that point; or a simple and serious piece might be stifled by a singer's virtuoso ornamentation. These and other abuses of opera seria are amusingly satirized in Benedetto Marcello's *Il teatro alla moda* (1720), but little was done about the problems until after mid-century, when yet another operatic "reform" was undertaken.

Yet Italy was already producing a different type of opera—one more concerned with dramatic values. This, the "opera buffa" (comic opera), was ultimately to supplant the opera seria. Two traditions of Italian comic opera may be distinguished. The first, opera buffa proper, reaches back almost to the beginnings of opera. It was merely a variant of the serious opera, differing in that its libretto was primarily rather than incidentally comic. Such operas are not especially numerous, but they may be found scattered throughout the repertoire of the seventeenth century and into that of the eighteenth. (One of the few Scarlatti operas available in a modern edition, *Il trionfo dell' onore*, is of this type.) They use essentially the same forms and procedures as contemporary serious opera, and often include parodies of serious style.

The second comic tradition is that of the "intermezzo." It stems from the seventeenth-century custom of including comic scenes in serious operas. Some of these scenes were entirely irrelevant to the main plot, and often involved stock characters such as the stutterer, the amorous serving woman, the coward, and so on, as opposed to the emperors and princesses of the serious scenes. Such irrelevant comic scenes came to be placed at the end of each act except the last and, precisely because of their irrelevance, could easily migrate from one opera to another. Thus it was not unusual to find an opera by one composer provided with comic scenes (or intermezzi) by another.

Since serious operas had three acts, there were normally two intermezzi—one after the first act, the other after the second. While the earlier intermezzi merely presented stock characters and situations, later ones integrated these into a more or less coherent plot—one that continued from the first scene through the second. Thus the intermezzo had in effect become an independent opera, and by the 1730s could be performed separately. The tendency towards independence was strengthened by the success of

Pergolesi's *La serva padrona*. This intermezzo was written to be performed between the acts of the composer's *Il prigionero superbo*; but while the serious opera was a failure, *La serva padrona* was soon performed all over Italy. At about mid-century the intermezzo, for reasons not wholly clear, ceased to be performed. Thereafter Italian comic opera was represented by the opera buffa, although some traits of the intermezzo persisted.

La serva padrona is typical of the intermezzo type of comic opera. The musical forces are modest: a small orchestra and only two singing parts. The characters are from the middle or lower classes; the setting is contemporary Italy. The plot is simple enough, but demands real acting from the singers: mere posturing, often sufficient in the opera seria, is not enough. The dialogue is set in recitative of a rapid and declamatory kind. The arias are mostly short and quick. Their principal motives are derived from the natural speech-rhythms of the words employed. While da capo form appears, it is not used to produce lengthy arias like those of serious opera. In the rapid movement of the comic style, long ritornellos and coloratura passages would be out of place. The end of the first aria of *La serva padrona* (Ex. XI-2) is characteristic—in its use of the bass voice (rare in serious opera); in its homophonic, often unison accompaniment; and in

To wait and have no one come, to lie in bed and not sleep, to serve well and not give pleasure, these are three awful things.

Ex. XI-2

its patter-like word repetition, which here has real comic purpose, in contrast to the merely artificial repetitions in opera seria.

La serva Padrona ends with a formal duet: the action is concluded, and the use of a set piece in which the two characters express their satisfaction is perfectly natural. More often, however, a comic plot multiplies dramatic complications just before its end (or just before the end of an act). Neither recitative nor a formal aria, duet, or trio would serve ideally in such scenes: the former because it would be musically anticlimactic; the latter because any of them would necessarily be static. Shortly after Pergolesi's time a new solution was found for this difficulty—the finale. This was an informal musico-dramatic construction in which short, unrelated sections of music, each appropriate to a given moment in the drama, follow each other in a succession determined solely by the needs of the libretto. There is no attempt at real musical unity (although the finale often conforms to a unified tonal plan); instead, coherence is guaranteed by the progress of the drama, aided by the tendency of the finale to increase in number of characters involved, speed, and volume of sound. While the early finales contained little music of great value, the principle involved was an important one, as it provided a new and flexible tool by which dramatic action could realistically be set to effective music.

The buffo finale

At about the same time—around mid-century—the opera buffa began to attract the interest of literary figures, especially the important Italian dramatist Carlo Goldoni (1707-93). In his libretti, what had been mostly sub-literary farce was often elevated to the level of true comedy. While the prevailing tone remained light, sentimental and serious characters became important elements of comic opera, and the scope of its subject matter was extended to include almost anything in contemporary life that the librettist wished to treat. Although it was not apparent at the time, this change sealed the ultimate doom of the opera seria. The Metastasian libretto now differed from a serious "comic" libretto only in its structural rigidity and in its preference for semi-legendary heroes of antiquity over characters of (approximately) the present day. Neither characteristic proved, in the end, to be an advantage.

Instrumental music: The early symphony. By mid-century the operatic scene was complex. Not only were there two species of Italian opera, the seria and the buffa, but other countries had also evolved (or were beginning to evolve) comic opera styles of their own. In addition, the signs of impending reform of Italian serious opera were becoming clearer. These developments will, however, be better understood if the state of instrumental music in the 1730s and the decades following is examined first.

Domenico Scarlatti

In doing so, a momentary digression is necessary to consider a unique figure—an exact contemporary of J. S. Bach, and like him, a composer of little immediate influence but great artistic importance—Domenico Scarlatti (1685-1757). This Scarlatti, the son of Alessandro, was a harpsichord virtuoso, who spent much of his life in the service of the courts of Portugal and Spain. His fame rests almost entirely on his 550 "sonatas" (or "exercises," as he called them in his one published collection) for harpsichord. For Scarlatti, the sonata was a single movement in binary form—often in the "rounded" binary, in which the latter part of the A section (in the dominant or the relative major) recurs in the tonic at the end of the B section. Thus a Scarlatti sonata is often formally identical to a Bach suite movement, with the difference that the sonatas rarely depend on conventional dance rhythms. Each sonata is musically complete in itself, but Scarlatti often pairs two sonatas in the same key to create a two-movement piece.

Scarlatti's genius lies less in formal innovation than in his idiomatic writing for the harpsichord, and in the rich, even eccentric, variety of the musical content of his work. Few composers have ever written as imaginatively for the harpsichord as Scarlatti. His music exploits all the possibilities of the instrument, extracting from it every imaginable color of sound. Many passages that seem relatively undistinguished when seen on paper, or even when heard in performance on the piano, are wholly transformed when the harpsichord is used: rarely in earlier music has the effect been so dependent on the medium. Naturally, such music is often difficult to play, but the resulting brilliance of sound is ample reward for the performer. (One may compare some of J. S. Bach's fugues, in which contrapuntal considerations often create vicious problems for the player—which are, however, mostly imperceptible to the audience.)

Scarlatti's musical style is so diverse as to defy definition. It is clearly post-Baroque in essence, for it makes little use either of the grand Baroque gesture or of the resources of contrapuntal writing. Also anti-Baroque and innovative is the frequent presence of strongly contrasting themes within a single movement: it would be difficult to take any of Scarlatti's mature sonatas as the expression of a single affection. The Sonata in G (K. 260, to use the identifying number in Ralph Kirkpatrick's recent catalogue of the sonatas), while more radical harmonically than most, is otherwise typical (Ex. XI-3). The opening measures are on the whole unremarkable (although the wide leaps in the left-hand part are typical of Scarlatti's harpsichord style). But in measure 20 there begins a passage of wildly eccentric harmony, tenuously held together by the stepwise bass. This leads to the orthodox dominant, not without causing some astonishment at the chosen manner of arriving there. Scarlatti marks the arrival in the new key by new thematic material, as is his frequent custom. But the relative calm is broken by another harmonic explosion before the end of the first section, and by two more in the second. The violent contrast between the cheerful diatonicism of the tonally stable parts and the eccentric chromaticism and dissonance of the modulations is the essence of the piece.

The superficial similarity between pieces such as this and sonata movements written half a century later has misled some writers into supposing a causal connection. Scarlatti's mature work, however, was almost unknown outside the Spanish court. His music was in some senses prophetic, but the prophecies were not heard until long after the events foretold had occurred.

The principal developments in the mainstream of instrumental music were taking place in Italy, France, and Germany. Perhaps the most important of these was the creation of an immensely significant new musical genre—one whose name has served almost as a synonym for serious music in the past two centuries: the symphony.

Origins of the symphony

Around 1730, the dominant form of public instrumental music was the concerto, which by then had a history of nearly half a century behind it. No one knows why composers at this time turned their attention from the concerto (at least to some extent) to a new form: perhaps the concerto seemed too closely bound to the old Baroque style to function effectively as a vehicle for the new manner. In any event, the earliest independent symphonies date from about this time. The qualification "independent" is necessary here, for at this time the overtures to Italian operas were also called "symphonies." By the time of Alessandro Scarlatti, such overtures had settled into a three-movement form in the pattern fast-slow-fast. Since an overture had no musical connection with the opera it preceded, such a symphony could be separated from one opera and used with others, or, if desired, played separately.

Ex. XI-3

The earliest independent symphonies also had three movements in the pattern fast-slow-fast, and shared other characteristics with the overture-symphonies. While it would seem reasonable to suppose that there was some connection between the two, the present evidence is to a certain extent contradictory. Even the earliest symphonies are not much like overtures in style, suggesting that influences from other genres—the orchestral suite, the sonata, or the concerto, perhaps—may also have played a part in the formation of the symphonic idiom. At present, the early repertoire is too little known to permit definite conclusions.

Symphonies of Giovanni Battista Sammartini

The first well-known composer of independent or concert symphonies was Giovanni Battista Sammartini (1700-75), whose early works date from the 1730s or perhaps even earlier. Despite the date, these symphonies are remarkably secure in their mastery of form and style. They are set for either three- or four-part string orchestra with basso continuo (although they could have been played by string trio or quartet: the distinction between chamber music and orchestral music was by no means absolute at this time). Each is in three movements, fast-slow-fast. The basic musical material generally consists of themes—often real tunes—rather than long asymmetrical lines spun out of small rhythmic motives. The texture is largely homophonic, with many unison passages, although some contrapuntal writing appears, especially in sequences.

While the form of the slow movement varies from one symphony to another, the outer movements are regularly in rounded binary form, with a "rounding" often more extensive than that found in earlier works:

Rounded binary form

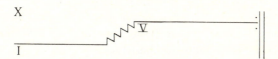

Thus the first section, with its two tonal levels, tonic and dominant, recurs more or less complete at the end, but changed so that it stays in one key, the tonic. In the above diagram, the dots preceding this return represent a modulatory area normally based on the materials of the first section.

The treatment of tonality is characteristic of the new style. Instead of the more or less constant tonal flux found in Baroque music, Sammartini prefers to set up tonal plateaus—substantial areas solidly rooted in a single key. Thus the first section of such a work might be represented as:

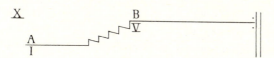

that is, a tonally stable area in the tonic, followed by a modulatory passage leading to the dominant, and then another tonally stable area in the latter key. If in addition the arrival in the new key is signaled by the use of new thematic material, the result is:

This, when it recurs at the end of the second section, becomes:

Here the change of theme calls attention not to a change of key, but to the absence of such a change—to the solidity and persistence of the tonic.

This form is clearly an adaptation of the Baroque binary that accommodates the new approach to harmony—an approach based on less frequent chord changes and a relatively restricted repertoire of chords. The tonally stable areas often contain nothing but the three basic chords of the key—tonic, dominant, and subdominant. These areas often mix major and minor tonics and subdominants on the same roots, a device that achieves harmonic variety without leaving the key.

Sonata form

Considerably later, this structure acquired the name "sonata form," and its parts acquired names as well. The first section, with its two tonal levels, was the exposition, as it exposed the basic thematic material; the modulatory area after the double bar was the development, as it normally utilized further—or "developed"—the themes of the exposition; and the remainder, the recapitulation, since it restated the material of the exposition. Although late in origin, these are useful terms, and they will be used here. It should be emphasized, however, that the presence of three definable elements in sonata form—exposition, development, and recapitulation—must not suggest that this is a three-part form, like the ABA of the da capo aria. The repetition scheme, invariable in most symphonies until about 1800, proves that there are really only two sections:

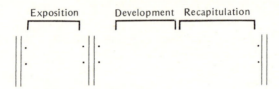

—of which the second is further subdivided into two functionally different subsections.

In the first movement of Sammartini's early Symphony in D, the overall structure conforms to the pattern just described, except that the opening material does not appear in the recapitulation—an omission not infrequent at the time, and probably dictated by the extensive use of this material in the development.

Style galant

The style is as important as the form. Like the Pergolesi aria, this symphony embodies the predilections of the post-Baroque generation. The first eight measures (Ex. XI-4) in particular are like a paradigm of the new approach: there are two symmetrical phrases of four measures each, almost entirely in unison, with the implied harmonies tonic (first four measures) and dominant (second four). While there are snatches of imitation later, these are purely decorative, and do not alter the fundamentally non-contrapuntal nature of the music. This new manner of writing is known as the *style galant*. It is the eighteenth-century realization of the ideals of clarity, simplicity, and elegance. The contrast between this music and that of Corelli or Vivaldi (who was still composing)—to say nothing of J. S. Bach—shows how wide the stylistic gap had become, even at this early date.

From *The Symphonies of G. B. Sammartini*, ed. Bathia Churgin, Harvard
University Press, 1968. Used by permission.

Ex. XI-4

Sammartini was highly regarded by his contemporaries, for his works were widely disseminated. Whether he was in fact the founder of the symphonic tradition, or merely one of its earliest practitioners, is still uncertain: too little is known of the other composers of his time. In any event, he remains an isolated figure, since—although his own work developed considerably during his long career—it was in Germany and France that the symphony was most actively cultivated during the remainder of the century. Again, only a few of the many composers have been studied, and any account must be a tentative one.

The best-known symphonic center in Germany was at Mannheim. Here Johann Stamitz (1717-57) had trained an orchestra internationally known for the accuracy and fire of its execution. For this virtuoso instrument Stamitz and a number of other composers wrote a large and important repertoire of symphonies. As might be expected, exploitation of orchestral effects was characteristic of the Mannheim style. One finds sudden juxtapositions of loud and soft passages, wide-ranging lines for the strings (Ex. XI-5), and, most famous of all, the crescendo, or gradual building up of sound from soft to loud. This latter device was largely foreign to Baroque style, in which a movement either maintained approximately the same dynamic level throughout, or contrasted loud and soft areas as a means of defining structure. The Mannheim crescendo not only testifies to an interest in exploiting a physically exciting property of music, but also shows a new approach to dynamic contrast—and implicitly, to contrast in general: mere juxtaposition, which was fundamental to the middle and late Baroque, has begun to give way to gradual transition.

The Mannheim school: symphonies of Johann Stamitz

Ex. XI-5

Stamitz's treatment of form is rather different from that of Sammartini. Stamitz's symphonies are often in four movements rather than three: the original fast-slow-fast has a minuet inserted after (sometimes before) the slow movement. The minuet was the only overt dance movement that ever found a place in the symphony, although there are fast movements that resemble gigues; and it is not clear why this should have been the case. No doubt it hints at a connection with the earlier orchestral suite, since in both suite and symphony the minuet is regularly followed by a second minuet, and then by a repetition of the first minuet, to make a larger ABA movement. The second minuet is called "trio" because at one time it was written in three- rather than four-part harmony, but the symphonic trio was never restricted to any number of parts or instruments.

Stamitz's fast movements do not appear to be derived directly from rounded binary form, as they lack the characteristic repeat signs that almost all other composers used. It may be that there is some connection with the ritornello structure of the concerto here: the development regularly begins with the opening theme(s) in the dominant, so that the opening material occurs three times in all, like a ritornello; and the B theme(s) often feature solo writing for woodwinds or horns. Whatever its origin, Stamitz's symphonic form is still not essentially different from that of Sammartini. Stamitz also writes expositions presenting two contrasting tonal areas, developments that employ the material of the exposition in new keys and new ways, and recapitulations that restate all or most of the exposition with whatever modifications are necessary to keep everything in the tonic. There are also new features: compared with early Sammartini, Stamitz's orchestra is larger, and his movements longer. Both of these characteristics are typical of a slightly later date: by the 1740s, the symphony had already begun to expand.

Expansion of the orchestra

The enlargement of the orchestra was accomplished by adding woodwind and brass instruments to the basic four-part string texture. The added instruments might be employed in three different ways. They could sustain harmonically important tones while the strings had more active material (this was often the only possibility for the brass, which were technically limited to a small number of notes, since the Baroque art of playing melodies in the highest register appears to have been lost). They could play along with, or "double," a melody of the strings, thus providing both reinforcement and a change of orchestral color. Or they could be given essential melodic material while the strings accompanied or were silent. Stamitz uses all three methods, and thereby achieves a rich and varied orchestral color.

The use of woodwinds and brass to sustain harmony tones had an important side effect, for this kind of textural filling-in greatly diminished the need for the basso continuo. While keyboard instruments continued to be employed in symphonic performances until late in the century, their raison d'être gradually disappeared. In consequence, the leadership of the orchestra passed from the continuo player to the leader of the first violins.

Other symphonic centers

Mannheim was by no means the only important symphonic center. A major school of composers practiced at Vienna, where the strength of Italian influence favored a style more melodious and elegant than that of Mannheim. Paris was another principal center, where works by native composers competed with importations from abroad. In the latter half of the century, Parisian composers often specialized in the *symphonie concertante*—a symphony containing important display passages for solo instruments, and hence a hybrid descended from both symphony and concerto.

In London, Johann Christian Bach (1735-82), a son of Johann Sebastian, wrote symphonies and concertos, as well as Italian operas. He had studied in Italy, and his style is marked by smoothly flowing melodies of a singing type—melodies that held a great attraction for the young Mozart.

North Germany produced a most important composer in Carl Philip Emmanuel Bach (1714-88), Johann Sebastian's greatest son. While this Bach was active in most forms of instrumental (and indeed also vocal) music, his most characteristic medium was the keyboard, and it is as a keyboard composer that he will be considered here. His name is inseparably linked to the *empfindsamer Stil* (sensitive style)—a North German stylistic trend of which he was the leader. This had as its aim neither the charm and elegance of the French and Italian styles, nor the brilliance of the Mannheimers, but rather a flickering, intimate expressivity—a delicate musical portrayal of the composer's inmost sentiments.

Empfindsamer Stil: C. P. E. Bach

For this reason, Bach's preferred instrument was not the brilliant harpsichord, but rather the clavichord, which, although very small in tone, was capable of dynamic variation. Also suitable was the still-new pianoforte (literally, soft-loud), which had the same ability, and had also sound enough to be used in concerts as well as in the drawing room.

C. P. E. Bach's keyboard music consists of sonatas, rondos, and fantasies. The sonatas, to which we shall return, are in a sense symphonies for keyboard instrument. The other terms require explanation. The rondo is a single-movement work deriving from the rondeau of the French *clavecinistes*: in it a recurring section alternates with contrasting episodes in different keys, as, for example, ABACADA. Bach's rondos are more complex than their French prototypes, and their use of developmental material (i.e., new treatments of ideas from the recurrent section) in the episodes relates the form to that of the sonata. The fantasy is what its name implies: a free improvisatory piece bound by no fixed rules, in which the sequence of events is determined only by the whim of the composer. It is possible that some of these fantasies are written out records of actual improvisations.

The sonatas represent all phases of C. P. E. Bach's lengthy career. Among the most influential were those of the first set (1742), called the Prussian sonatas after their dedication to the king of Prussia. These are vigorous pieces in three movements, to be performed, according to the title page, on the harpsichord. (Later collections are labeled "for clavier"—a neutral designation; still later ones specify the pianoforte.) The treatment of sonata form is still conservative: Bach shows little interest in exploiting the striking contrasts employed by many of his contemporaries. His contribution lies, rather, in the nature of his style. His striving for expressivity is manifest in a slow movement in which an already highly pathetic phrase is interrupted by a passage in instrumental recitative: the instrument is required to imitate the inflections of passionate speech. In a much later sonata, the expressivity is less urgent, but the juxtaposition of three different elements in the space of a few measures gives the music a serious, almost problematic tone (Ex. XI-6). Very striking here is the treatment of tonality: a movement in F major begins on a chord of C minor. Even in the key of F minor, this would more often than not be a major triad, since true dominants are major triads in tonal music. In using the minor form here, Bach further extends the free interchange between chords of major and minor keys on the same tonic, first mentioned above in connection with Sammartini. Without departing from the key of F major, Bach creates a striking effect of harmonic color by "borrowing" a chord from F minor. (The reverse process—borrowing chords from the major when the basic key is minor—was not at the time as fruitful.)

C. P. E. Bach's keyboard sonatas

Ex. XI-6

The importance of C. P. E. Bach's work lies above all in its pervading seriousness. The stock tools of many *galant* composers—the pretty tunes, the brilliant but empty passage work, the conventional accompaniment figures—are largely absent. One finds, rather, a musical substance in which every note contributes to the expressiveness of the whole. Bach demonstrates that the new formal and stylistic means can transcend mere entertainment: that they are capable of bearing a profound message.

Operatic Reforms.   Bach was not, however, entirely alone in this attitude. By mid-century the first, largely negative reaction to the Baroque was at least partly spent. Simplicity and elegance, though engaging, could not by themselves be enough. The inclusion of serious scenes in the Italian opera buffa by about 1750 has already been mentioned: it is symptomatic of a new direction, not only in music, but in the other arts as well. In literature, for example, Voltaire (1694-1788), the often humorous skeptic, is typical of the earlier reaction against Baroque grandeur and intensity. Characteristic of the late eighteenth century is the work of Goethe (1749-1832), from which the skeptical air is largely absent: serious method is joined with serious—and indeed profound—content.

It may seem slightly incongruous that some of the clearest manifestations of this tendency towards greater depth are evident in the genres of comic opera. The French opéra comique is a case in point. Early in the eighteenth century it consisted of non-literary farce in which spoken dialogue was interspersed with simple preexistent songs, to which appropriate new texts had been added. Gradually, the literary quality was improved, and new music, especially composed for the purpose, was more often used. Then, in 1752, several Italian comic operas (including Pergolesi's *La serva padrona*) were performed in Paris, setting off a noisy literary quarrel over the relative merits of French and Italian styles. In the same year, Jean-Jacques Rousseau (1712-78), an ardent Italophile, produced his *Devin du Village*, a comic opera using not spoken dialogues, but sung recitative as in Italian comic opera. The songs, however, are in

National schools of comic opera: opéra comique, ballad opera, singspiel

typically French taste. While this work—for which Rousseau provided both text and music—was successful, opéra comique of the later eighteenth century reverted to the earlier spoken-dialogue type, enriched, however, with more elaborate music, for the most part newly composed. Many comic operas of this later period exhibited traits that were to become important in the future: exoticism (use of a setting remote in time or place); an idealized peasantry as collective hero; and more or less veiled social criticism.

The English counterpart of opéra comique was the ballad opera, the most successful of which was *The Beggar's Opera* (see above, Chapter X). The ballad opera underwent a development from farce to sentimental comedy not unlike the French and Italian forms. But important composers were lacking, and a strong tradition of English opera was not established.

In 1743, a ballad opera entitled *The Devil to Pay* was performed in Berlin in German translation. Its success led to numerous imitations, encouraged by the current popularity of simple strophic secular songs (*Lieder*; sing. *Lied*). The resultant musical plays are known as singspiels. Like the French and English types, the singspiel began simply, as a spoken play with occasional songs, the latter in a folk-like idiom, suitable for performance by actors who were not primarily musicians. In time, two types developed: a sentimental type, using lyrical music similar to folksong; and a more lively, sophisticated type, with music strongly influenced by the style of the Italian opera buffa. The first prevailed in northern Germany; the second in the south and in Austria, where Italian music was widely admired.

The great vitality of national comic opera after 1750 or thereabouts posed a serious threat to the international opera seria. Audiences who had experienced the dramatic effectiveness of comic opera at its best tended to become dissatisfied with conventional Metastasian opera. The principal objects of discontent were the excessive dominance by virtuoso singers, the overabundant and often tasteless ornamentation in the vocal parts, the dramatically static da capo aria form, dull recitative, and, in general, lack of real dramatic force.

Several composers attempted improvements within the general framework of opera seria, particularly Italian composers working under foreign influence. Niccolò Jommelli (1714-74), for example, spent a number of years at the court in Stuttgart, and in the operas he wrote there music is given a more clearly dramatic role than in the average opera seria. This is evident in his extensive use of orchestrally accompanied recitative, dramatically meaningful duets and choruses, imaginative orchestral effects, and, above all, in his willingness to sacrifice musical structure to dramatic effect. Thus, in the thirty-odd pages of score that make up the latter part of Act II of his *Fetonte* (1768), orchestral music, recitative, and more formal vocal sections are freely intermingled. The technique is reminiscent of the dramaturgy of Rameau, and in fact there was considerable French influence at Stuttgart. It may also owe something to the opera buffa finale.

Opera seria: the beginnings of reform

Another progressive composer was Tommaso Traëtta (1727-79), who worked at the court of Parma, which was also strongly receptive to French ideals. Traëtta even set Italian adaptations of French libretti used by Rameau, and, like Jommelli, he made every effort to enhance the specifically dramatic contribution of his music.

Yet neither of these men attempted radical reforms. Their works remain in the tradition of opera seria; and, while they succeeded to some extent in restoring the drama to a larger share of its rightful place, the underlying conventions remained unchanged. Their operas are still singers' music, with much virtuoso ornamentation; and the prevailing tone is still one of Metastasian elegance, through which genuine emotions penetrate only with difficulty.

Christoph Willibald Gluck

A more basic operatic reform was achieved by Christoph Willibald Gluck (1714-87). Gluck was born in Bohemia, studied in Italy with Sammartini, and made a considerable reputation as a composer of conventional Italian opera. From 1755, he made arrangements of French comic operas for performance at Vienna, often contributing to them some new music of his own. There was as yet nothing to suggest that he was more than an unusually versatile opera composer.

But new ideas were in the air. There was a new feeling for nature and the natural, most clearly in the work of Jean-Jacques Rousseau. There was the revival of the serious approach to the arts, already mentioned. And, especially relevant to the case of Gluck, there was yet another burst of interest in classical—and especially Greek—antiquity, leading ultimately to Winckelmann's important treatise, the *Geschichte der Kunst des Alterthums* (History of the Art of Antiquity; 1764). Taken together, these three trends of thought laid the foundation for an aesthetic far different from that of the opera seria.

Reforms of Gluck and Calzabigi: Orfeo ed Euridice

In 1761 there arrived in Vienna the poet Raniero Calzabigi (1714-95), a man with strong ideas concerning musical dramas—ideas of enormous importance to Gluck, who later gave Calzabigi much of the credit for his operatic reform. The two collaborated, and their first work, *Orfeo ed Euridice*, appeared in Vienna in 1762. In this, and even more in their *Alceste* of 1767, there is evident a radical break, both in form and in style, with the opera seria.

The external signs of the reform are by no means wholly new. They include use of the overture to prefigure the coming action; exclusive use of recitative accompanied by the orchestra; drastic shortening of most of the arias, few of which are in the da capo form; suppression of vocal ornamentation, whether written out or improvised; extensive use of ensembles and choruses; and, most important, flexibility of musical forms, so that recitative, aria, chorus, and instrumental sections might be freely intermingled whenever the dramatic situation required. All of this, however, is only a little more than what Jommelli and others were doing. The true achievement of Gluck and Calzabigi lay quite as much in the area of style, both literary and musical.

Alceste

For *Alceste*, to take a particularly obvious example, Calzabigi derived his story from the play of Euripides. But the latter—Greek though it may be—was not classical enough for his taste. The drunken Hercules and the rather disgusting Pheres are neither attractive nor "natural." Therefore Calzabigi omitted them entirely in his version, which is noble and statuesque throughout. This classical repose is musically rendered by a style of severe simplicity coupled with lyrical sweetness. The music is vigorous, graceful, or solemn, as the occasion requires, and gives the impression of profound sincerity. It is evident that Gluck was by no means the most imaginative musician of his time: his genius lay rather in his ability to create music perfectly adapted to the dramatic situation—music that was, once again, the servant of the drama. Thus, many scenes that seem uninteresting on a reading of the score, or even in recorded performance, spring vividly to life on the stage.

The aria "Chiamo il mio ben così" from *Orfeo* is strophic: three stanzas of text are set to the same music. But Gluck inserts a passionate recitative after each stanza, thus building a scene of considerable size without resorting to the large aria forms of opera seria. The style is also characteristic (Ex. XI-7). There are no lengthy instrumental ritornellos, only brief and poignant echos; the melody is simple and natural: one feels in fact that one is listening to Orpheus, and not merely to to a singer.

After *Alceste*, Gluck wrote several works for Paris, and made French versions of both *Orfeo* and *Alceste*—adaptations that could be made without much difficulty or

Thus I call my love when the day appears; when it vanishes. . .

Ex. XI-7

distortion, since most of Gluck's reform procedures either derived from or had counter-parts in French operatic practice. In the later works, music is allowed a somewhat greater share of attention: they are musically richer and more interesting, while still adhering faithfully to the basic ideals of *Orfeo*. Although with his reform works, Gluck became a celebrated and successful composer, he had no real followers, nor did his work have much immediate influence. The imprint of his ideals, if not his style, may be seen in Mozart's *Idomeneo* and, much later, in the thought of Berlioz and even Wagner. The effectiveness of his music, however, is so much a function of his personal manner, impregnated as it seems to be with a kind of moral elevation, that he could be imitated only superficially. Furthermore, despite Gluck's achievement, the old serious opera was in irreversible decline. His contribution, however noble, could not alter this. Yet Gluck remains a figure of major importance, not only for the intrinsic value of his works, but also as the first composer whose music is fully representative of the classic style of the late eighteenth century.

HAYDN AND MOZART: THE MATURE CLASSICAL STYLE

Classicism.   The last decades of the eighteenth century were for the most part domi-nated by classical ideals. The ornamental elegance of the mid-century fell into disfavor, to be replaced by styles emphasizing simplicity and dignity. In the visual and literary arts, direct influences from Greek antiquity are common. This classicism, however, flourished only briefly, and was always on the verge of a more frankly emotional approach. Thus Goethe, the greatest of the literary classicists, began his career with works like the novel *The Sorrows of Werther* (1774), in which the dominant aesthetic is that of the *Sturm und Drang* (storm and stress) movement—a brief irruption of passion-ate artistic intensity that flourished in the 1770s. Only later did he turn to a more disciplined, truly "classical" style. Moreover, by 1798, the romantic movement had begun in German literature, and the arts began to turn to explicit subjectivism. The classical decades were a brief period during which the claims of reason and emotion, of form and content, were in perfect equilibrium.

This equilibrium, encouraging both clarity of form and intensity of expression, proved to be ideally suited to music; and the historical situation was equally favorable. New forms and styles had been brought to a point of reasonable stability, so that a young composer could build his own personal style on the basis of a well-defined common practice. Thus it is not entirely surprising that this period includes the activity of three of the greatest of composers: Joseph Haydn (1732-1809), Wolfgang Amadeus Mozart (1756-91), and Ludwig van Beethoven (1770-1827). The work of these three men constitutes one of the supreme achievements of Western music. There is some reason for referring to this achievement in the singular. While, as will be seen, each of these composers was deeply original, all of them had careers based primarily in Vienna, and their styles are interconnected by important influences. Haydn and Mozart learned much from each other, and Beethoven was both a student of Haydn's and an admirer of Mozart. Many other worthy composers were also active during these years, not only at Vienna, but also in other musical centers all over Europe. The classical style was, like that of the late Baroque, an international one, and its practitioners included Czechs and Spaniards as well as Germans and Italians. Following the precedent set in Chapter X, however, discussion will here be confined to music of the highest aesthetic importance. This section will consider the work of Haydn and Mozart, and Beethoven will be treated in the following chapter.

Joseph Haydn.   Haydn, the oldest of the three, received some musical education during his years as a choirboy in Vienna, but had no systematic instruction in composition. Upon leaving the choir at the age of seventeen, he supported himself by giving lessons and accepting what employment he could find. Gradually his name came to be known among music-loving Viennese. He served briefly in two noble households, and in 1761 was appointed assistant conductor of the orchestra of Prince Esterházy, later becoming director of the prince's musical establishment. Since the prince was immensely wealthy this establishment was a very large one, capable of producing any sort of music that might be desired, and Haydn remained contentedly in this post until the musicians were disbanded in 1790. The prince spent much of his time at his remote palace of Esterház, and Haydn was "cut off from the world . . . and forced to become original," to use his own words. While there is no doubt as to his originality, Haydn was also receptive to influences from the styles of other composers, notably C. P. E. Bach and, later in life, Mozart. By 1790, Haydn's reputation was international. Except for two highly successful visits to England (1791 and 1794), he passed the remainder of his life, honored, well-to-do, and independent, in Vienna.

Haydn's life

Although Haydn worked in almost all the genres then current, including opera, his chief accomplishment was in instrumental music, especially in the symphony and the string quartet. The latter term requires explanation. In the earliest years of the symphony (up to ca. 1750), there was no clear distinction between orchestral and chamber music. Regardless of its title, a piece for four string parts might be played either by an orchestra or by four string soloists. Modern scholars generally regard brilliant, homophonic pieces as conceived essentially for orchestra—they are, then, symphonies—and more intricate and detailed works as basically intended for chamber performance. The latter, then, are "quartets for strings," or string quartets.[1] The differentiation between the two styles grew stronger as the years passed, but even in Haydn's own Opus 1, composed in the late 1750s, and supposedly a set of string quartets, the fifth work is in fact an arrangement of a symphony.

Haydn's quartets

Although the string quartet ultimately came to share the same four-movement structure of the symphony—fast, slow, minuet, fast—in Haydn's case it arrived there by a different route. Haydn's early quartets are more closely attached to a flourishing tradition of entertainment music—light pieces usually scored for small groups of strings and/or winds, and written to order for performance at private parties. Music of this sort was known by a wide variety of names, of which divertimento and serenade were perhaps the commonest. Such pieces contained some movements in symphonic

---

[1]The somewhat confusing terminology employed for serious classical compositions depends primarily on the medium, since forms and styles are largely the same in all the media. Works for orchestra are symphonies; those for two to eight instruments are duos, trios, quartets, etc. If instruments other than strings are used, the title generally makes this clear: a "quartet" means a string quartet; an "oboe quartet" means a quartet for oboe plus three strings; a "woodwind quartet" is one for four woodwinds; and a "piano quartet" is one for piano with three strings. Works for piano solo or piano and one instrument (most often violin) are called sonatas: piano sonata and violin sonata in the cases cited. Many sonatas are in three movements, omitting the minuet.

style and form, but usually included two or more minuet-trio movements, and often one or two marches. Thus there were generally more than four movements—and might be as many as ten.

Haydn's first quartets are related to the divertimento in that most of them have the order: fast, minuet, slow, minuet, fast. Thereafter he dropped one of the two minuets, and the quartet took on the aspect of a chamber symphony for four instruments. It continued to differ from the true symphony in style, however; as in the pairs cantata-opera and sonata-concerto, the chamber style is more delicate and finely wrought, and often more contrapuntal.

The last point is particularly relevant in Haydn's case, for in many of his works he shows an affinity to certain Baroque procedures, notably the spinning-out of long melodic lines from rhythmic motives, and the use of imitative counterpoint. Several of the quartets end with a formal fugue rather than the customary light-hearted finale, and many other movements have strong contrapuntal elements as well.

The six quartets of Opus 20 (1771) are Haydn's first masterpieces in this genre. The fifth of these, a dark and foreboding work, may help dispel the common impression that Haydn excelled only in cheerful and unproblematic music; it is, however, characteristic of his treatment of form, medium, and style. Example XI-8 shows the beginning of the first movement, through the establishment of the new key and into the second part of the exposition. After presenting a first theme in the key of F minor (mm. 1-4) and an expanded variant of it (mm. 5-10), Haydn moves almost at once to the contrasting key of A♭. The intervening measures, which include a partial and therefore deceptive presentation of the opening theme in A♭, are designed as it were to obliterate the initial tonality in favor of the new one. The new tonal plateau must be so solidly prepared that the listener will accept it as an area of considerable repose. The final establishment of the new key is signaled by a new group of themes (mm. 28ff), although Haydn often uses his first theme again for this purpose. The development, of considerable length, is no longer merely a means of return to the tonic: it is a primary focus of dramatic tension. This is shown clearly by the way in which Haydn chooses to introduce the recapitulation. While earlier composers had often ended their developments with a formal cadence in a related key, and begun afresh in the tonic with the recapitulation, Haydn moves to the dominant of the home tonic and prolongs that chord for four full measures; its final resolution, as the recapitulation begins, comes as a real fulfillment. This movement ends with a coda, a final section often added at the end of the recapitulation, primarily to stabilize the tonic still further, but also to permit further development of thematic material.

The remainder of the quartet presents a minuet, a profound slow movement in binary form, and a grim and learned fugue, in the course of which Haydn utilizes a countersubject, melodic inversion, and stretto—all carefully identified as such in the score.

The date of this work is in part a clue to its deeply emotional character: the 1770s were the years of the *Sturm und Drang*, and much of Haydn's music of this time was influenced by it. This is demonstrated not only by the passionate style of the music itself, but also by Haydn's frequent choice of extremely unusual keys (e.g., a symphony in F♯ minor, a piano sonata in C♯ minor). After 1780, the wave of emotionalism receded, leaving in Haydn's music, however, an enlarged expressive breadth, now more tightly disciplined. From 1780, in full possession of his technical mastery, and

Ex. XI-8

Ex. XI-8 (cont.)

both stimulated and influenced by the music of his friend Mozart, Haydn composed an astonishing succession of masterworks in all genres: symphonies, operas, quartets and other chamber music, piano sonatas, oratorios, and Masses—which met with enthusiastic approval from audiences all over Europe.

Haydn's symphonies

Haydn began rather modestly as a composer of symphonies, and the gradual deepening of his concept of the form is reflected not only in the intangible area of profundity of musical language, but also in more specific ways, of which two are considered here: orchestration, and the nature of the final movement.

Haydn's use of the orchestra

From the beginning, Haydn employed a standard orchestra of four string parts (two groups of violins, one of violas, and a fourth of 'cellos and basses; the latter two instruments playing the same part and usually also doubled by a bassoon), two oboes, two horns, and often a flute. To these, trumpets and timpani were sometimes added for especially festive pieces. In the early symphonies, the basso continuo was always needed as well. At first, Haydn concentrated all the musical interest in the string parts—especially the first violins—and used the other instruments either to double or to add weight by sustaining the harmony tones. On those occasions when the wind or brass instruments were used alone, they received virtuoso parts more appropriate to a concerto than a symphony.

Gradually, Haydn began using the winds more independently, without, however, introducing concerto-like elements. An important melody might be assigned to the flute or oboe, with the strings providing accompaniment; or the parts assigned to the winds, while still fundamentally harmonic in purpose, might be given some melodic interest as well—thus adding contrapuntal as well as sonorous values. As has been said, one effect of this more sophisticated orchestration was the gradual elimination of the need for the basso continuo. The written-out parts for strings, winds, and brass supplied all the notes needed for unequivocal definition of the harmony. During his visits to London Haydn did, indeed, himself direct his latest symphonies from his seat at the keyboard; but this was merely a courtesy, in giving a prominent and visible place of honor to the by then renowned composer.

Fig. XI-2: A performance of chamber music, ca. 1750. (Photohaus Hirsch, Nördlingen.)

Haydn's treatment of the orchestra in his later works, with its enormous enrichment of sonorous possibilities, is one kind of evidence of his preoccupation with broadening the scope of the symphony. His treatment of the last movement (finale) is a matter of a quite different sort, but testifies to the same preoccupation. The natural places for expressive weight in the symphony were the first and slow movements. The minuet had its own character, and was almost invariably lighter in tone. The last movement should be light (or at least not problematic) but rousing, and it should also balance the first movement. Lightness was not difficult to achieve: a lively tempo and tuneful themes cast in symmetrical phrases will almost automatically produce it. But the question of form remained. Two options were available: sonata form and rondo form. The former would of course balance the first movement, but would result in three or even four movements in binary form. The rondo avoided that problem, but left no room for development, a process increasingly important in Haydn's music.

Haydn's finales: the sonata-rondo

Fig. XI-3: *A concert in Amsterdam in 1792. Since not only the audience, but also most members of the orchestra (in the rear) are conversing, this is presumably an intermission. (Harvard Theatre collection.)*

Neither of these objections was overwhelming, and Haydn wrote many successful finales both in sonata form and in rondo form. His most characteristic finale-type, however, is one in which sonata and rondo elements are blended into a rondo-sonata or sonata-rondo. Consider the symmetrical rondo: ABACABA. The key of the first B section will naturally be related to the key of the first A, probably the dominant, so that A and B together resemble an exposition. When AB recurs near the end, the linkage between the two sections can be rewritten so that B will now lie in the tonic, and AB will function as a recapitulation. If, then, C is made developmental in character, using themes from A and B, the hybrid form is fully achieved. It differs from sonata form fundamentally, in that A recurs, in the tonic, just before the development. This recurrence, by dissipating the tonal tension normally felt at this point, also lightens the form and makes it more sectional.

Haydn's mature symphonic style is particularly evident in the "Paris" and the "London" symphonies—the former commissioned for Paris, the latter written for the two London visits. Symphony No. 85 (1785 or 1786), called *La reine* (the Queen), because it was said to be a favorite of Marie Antoinette's, begins with a slow introduction. Such introductions had become common in the late eighteenth century, serving as solemn or mysterious preludes to the quick movements that followed. In this case, Haydn chooses to display clear thematic connections between the introduction and the sonata form following, but this was by no means a regular feature.

The "Paris" and "London" symphonies

The treatment of the second key area is characteristic of Haydn's mature style. After a brief outburst in minor, Haydn presents, not a new theme, but a new version of the first theme. As he grew older, Haydn increasingly preferred to emphasize the unity of his sonata-form movements by means of this sort of thematic economy. Movements of this type are a particularly clear proof that the essence of the sonata-form exposition lies in its tonal contrasts, rather than its thematic ones.

Extremely important is the length and the "weight" of the development section: it is nearly as long as the exposition, and actually longer than the recapitulation. In addition, it has become, not merely a means of achieving harmonic variety leading ultimately to the original tonic, but the psychological climax of the entire movement. Haydn's developmental procedures are too numerous to be catalogued in full. They include: restatement of themes from the exposition, in different keys and the opposite mode, often with different orchestration; fragmentation of themes into short Baroque-type motives treated contrapuntally or sequentially (or both); enrichment of previously heard themes by new contrapuntal materials; and even the introduction of entirely new thematic material (this last being relatively infrequent).

In the symphony under consideration, a particularly fine example of contrapuntal enrichment occurs in the development (Ex. XI-9b), where the violas and 'cellos in unison play an echo-like accompaniment to the first theme (note also that here the string basses are given an independent part). The ultimate return to the tonic is achieved in a manner quite different from that used in the quartet Opus 20, no. 5. There the dominant of the home key was reached and strongly emphasized; here it is the dominant of G minor that is the apparent goal. Only twenty measures later does Haydn, by means of a simple chromatic descent, reach the key of B♭. Surprises of this sort are common: the listener may be fooled into believing that the recapitulation has already begun, when further events show that it has not; or an obviously impossible key (here G minor) may be extensively prepared, which a brief bit of sleight of hand converts into the true tonic. Either device may be used humorously or dramatically.

Ex. XI-9(a)

Ex. XI-9(b)

The development section of this movement is quite long, and it may at first seem surprising that the recapitulation is considerably shorter than the exposition. This sort of condensation is not, however, unusual, especially when materials from the exposition have been extensively developed, as is the case here. It is also noteworthy that the contrapuntally amplified form of the first theme, introduced in the development, is used again in the recapitulation, making another link between the parts of the movement.

In the finale (to pass over for the moment the two middle movements), there is evident the characteristic fusion of sonata and rondo elements, as well as considerable thematic economy: much of the material in the so-called contrasting episodes is clearly connected with the opening theme. The movement's relation to the sonata principle is centered mainly in the strongly developmental character of the middle section, while its lightness and gaiety is assured by the nature of the material and by the character of the phrasing. Thus at the very beginning, an 8-bar phrase is directly repeated, followed by a 16 (8+8)-bar phrase also repeated exactly. Comparison of such structures with the more complex and asymmetrical beginning of most first movements will make clear the relation between tuneful symmetry and lightness on the one hand, and irregular phrasing and seriousness on the other.

The slow movement, which comes second in Symphony No. 85, is cast in the form of variations on what was apparently a French folk-tune ("La gentille et jeune Lisette").

While the variation principle is of considerable antiquity, having been extensively cultivated from the sixteenth century on, its classical manifestation has special characteristics. The theme is generally a simple symmetrical tune in binary form (not a bass pattern, as was so common in the Baroque). In general, the process of variation leaves the phrasing and harmonic structure of the theme intact, varying the degree of melodic ornamentation, the texture, and (in at least one variation) the mode. The total number of variations in a single set is normally small—between four and six being about average. In the present example, Haydn remains unusually faithful to the substance of the original melody: there is hardly any rapid ornamental figuration, and variety is achieved mainly by the use of contrasting tone colors. Two short sections stand outside the general variation scheme: a transition from the minor variation back to the major; and the closing measures, which are in effect a coda.

Slow movements in general constitute the only exception to the overall tonal unity of a multi-movement complex like the symphony or string quartet. The first and last movements must of course be in the principal key of the work, and the minuet is almost invariably in the tonic also. In a Baroque suite, all movements are normally in the tonic; the classical preference for using a related key, rather than the tonic, for the slow movement—and sometimes for the trio of the minuet—is another example of the large-scale tonal thinking characteristic of the period as a whole.

The minuet and trio movement invites special comment. Haydn himself once wistfully remarked that someone should write a really new minuet, not realizing, perhaps, that it was he who continued to pour into this modest form an extraordinary variety of style and content. The persistence of a dance movement in the otherwise abstract scheme of the symphony is curious. In general, the minuet functions as a kind of relief between the larger forms of the movements on either side of the movements on either side of it: its sections are short and clearly articulated, its phrases often symmetrical, and its content usually unproblematic. Nevertheless, the refinement of detail —especially rhythmic detail—raises the minuet above the level of a "mere" dance, and gives it a rightful place in the symphonic plan.

Symphonies such as Haydn's established the genre as the chief vehicle for serious musical expression in public concerts (the string quartet occupying the same position for smaller gatherings). Haydn himself went on to write nearly twenty more symphonies, masterworks of the first order, and it is a pity that many of them are hardly ever performed today. Although credit must be given to many lesser composers for their contributions to the symphony, it was Haydn who did most to raise the form from a galant trifle to a musical utterance of often profound significance.

Strangely enough, after Haydn's second visit to London, he abandoned the symphony entirely. Although he continued to compose some instrumental music—a few string quartets and piano sonatas—his principal concern became vocal music, the most notable works of his late years being six great Masses and two large oratorios, The Creation (1798) and The Seasons (1801).

Haydn's late vocal works

The second half of the eighteenth century was not one of the great ages of sacred music: neither the rationalistic spirit of the times nor the lightness of the style galant was propitious. Most composers wrote their Masses and motets in a more or less operatic style, including, as a gesture to the past and to the solemnity of the occasion, a few sections in strict counterpoint. These fugal passages were by virtue of their archaic musical language felt to be peculiarly appropriate to the church.

The mature
Masses

    Somewhat the same thing can be said of Haydn's mature Masses, although their basic style must be described as symphonic, rather than operatic. It is as if Haydn merely transferred his symphonic energies, with the appropriate changes necessitated by the vocal medium, to the Mass. This is not to say that overtly symphonic forms appear in the Masses, but rather that the entire musical substance is pervaded by the symphonic spirit and continuity. The chorus and soloists take their place as additional "instruments" in an again expanded orchestra.

    The Gloria of the *Missa in Angustiis* (also called the Lord Nelson Mass; 1798) demonstrates this symphonic approach to the Mass. It is cast in three large sections, of which the first and third make use of the same principal themes. Thus this is not, like the B minor Mass of J. S. Bach, a "cantata Mass" made up of successive unrelated movements. Within each section, the music is continuous: choral, solo, and orchestral passages are freely intermingled. (An especially effective series of juxtapositions occurs in the choral responses throughout the slow section.) While the entire fabric is strongly contrapuntal, Haydn includes only one formal fugal section, at the words "In gloria Dei patris," a traditional place for a fugal passage. The concluding, "Amen," however, is not part of the fugue, but is set to the second principal theme of the opening section, thereby providing a typically Haydnesque unifying feature.

Fig. XI-4: A performance of Haydn's opera L'incontro improvviso *at the theater at Esterház. (Courtesy of the Theater-Museum, Munich.)*

While in London, Haydn had the opportunity of hearing some of Handel's choral music, and was apparently deeply impressed that such works had so long outlived their composer. He resolved to write an oratorio by which future generations would remember him. For his text, he had the help of Baron van Swieten, a wealthy Viennese musical antiquarian, who adapted and translated an English poem based on Milton's *Paradise Lost*. Van Swieten was an ardent champion of J. S. Bach and Handel, at a time when the former was almost wholly forgotten and the latter known only in England. But Haydn did not allow Van Swieten's enthusiasms to exercise serious influence on his own musical style. While *The Creation* contains a few Handelian touches, it remains triumphantly Haydnesque.

The oratorio is cast in a basically operatic form, with recitatives, arias, and choruses—including several "arias with chorus" that recall the formal flexibility of Haydn's late Masses. The large orchestra is throughout treated symphonically, serving as a companion to the vocal part, not a mere accompaniment. *The Creation* is one of Haydn's finest works and, along with the equally fine *Seasons*, would indeed have served to immortalize its composer's name, had not that purpose long since been achieved by his symphonies and quartets.

The Creation and The Seasons

Haydn brought to his oratorios the experience gained in writing a considerable number of operas, hardly ever heard today. Although these works contain much music of the first order, it was not Haydn's lot to be the supreme representative of late eighteenth-century opera: this was a place reserved for Mozart, his younger contemporary and friend.

Wolfgang Amadeus Mozart.   Mozart's career was almost the opposite of Haydn's. The son of a sound provincial musician, Mozart was a child prodigy—a traveling pianoforte virtuoso by the age of six, and a competent composer soon after. Although Mozart's father, Leopold, in his intensive training of the boy, doubtless had mercenary motives at least in part, the result was in the end fortunate. The young Mozart's gifts ripened at the earliest possible moment, thus enabling him to make the most of the pitiably few years of his life.

Mozart's tours as a child and adolescent took him throughout Germany and Austria and to France, England, and Italy, thus exposing his uniquely receptive musical mind to the widest possible variety of stimuli. Ultimately he settled down—to a degree—as an employee of Archbishop Colloredo of Salzburg, for whom his father also worked. But Mozart found he could tolerate neither the provincial atmosphere of Salzburg nor the despotic character of the archbishop. Finally he broke loose and settled in Vienna (1781) as a free-lance musician, intending to earn his living by giving concerts and lessons, and through receiving commissions and publishers' fees. At first he was successful, but the fickle Viennese public did not long continue their support, and by the time of his death he was poor, exhausted, and almost forgotten.

Mozart's life

It would be impossible to catalogue all the ingredients Mozart assimilated into his style: he had heard too much, and remembered it too well. Certain influences, however, were especially important. In his early years, the principal one was Johann Christian Bach, a son of Johann Sebastian who, as has been seen, had studied in Italy and fully mastered the Italian style before settling in London, where he wrote operas as well as instrumental music. From this Bach, Mozart learned the art of suave and graceful melody. Later in life, Haydn also exercised a major influence on Mozart—as Mozart's

Influences on Mozart

mature works did on Haydn. Then Mozart also met van Swieten, and learned from him of the riches contained in the work of the "old Bach." On the whole, however, while Haydn gives the impression of having forged for himself a personal style out of years of experience and thought, Mozart appears to have been born with a style of his own—but one that he was constantly expanding and enriching by his knowledge of the music of others. No other composer in the history of music had greater skill in hearing music, nor more perfect technique in accomplishing his own musical purposes.

Mozart's works

In his short life Mozart composed over 600 works, ranging in size from little ballroom dances to lengthy operas. By no means all of them are masterpieces, although hardly any are less than perfect technically. His greatest works are chiefly in the categories of the opera, the symphony (especially the later ones), the string quartet and quintet, the piano concerto, and music for piano solo; but towards the end of his life Mozart wrote superbly in all genres, ranging from a magnificent but incomplete setting of the Requiem Mass to an enchanting piece for a mechanical clock.

Mozart's operas

It is as an opera composer that Mozart must first be considered, not only because he was passionately concerned with opera all his life, but also because his operatic achievement is the culmination of opera in the late eighteenth century—and the pinnacle of all operatic history.

Idomeneo

Mozart's first mature work for the stage was an opera seria, *Idomeneo*, written for Munich and first performed there in 1781. The libretto was written by a mediocre Salzburg poet, the Abbé Varesco, with considerable assistance from Mozart himself, who was an eager, if unwelcome collaborator. Although the resulting text conforms in general to the Metastasian pattern, the influence of reform ideas, and of Gluck in particular, is also evident: the chorus plays an important role, and there are independent instrumental movements. Even more important for Mozart, there are—in addition to the expected recitatives and arias—a duet, a trio, and a quartet. The latter two, especially, are not mere set pieces; they are significant dramatic ensembles in which the simultaneous and conflicting emotions of different characters are portrayed. Mozart here, even though his libretto gives him only the stock figures of opera seria, begins to show his genius for dramatic characterization. Each singer's music is expressive only of that character's emotion (except, of course, when all join together in some common conventional expression, such as the line "no one has ever suffered more" of the quartet, which is appropriate for all four characters). The unity necessary in ensembles containing such diverse sentiments is achieved largely by the symphonic treatment of the orchestra, and by the shaping force of tonality.

Although the ensembles may be the finest numbers in *Idomeneo*, the rest of the opera is almost equally fine. There are many pages of secco recitative, but the more important recitatives are accompanied by the orchestra, in brilliantly dramatic style. The arias range from the purely lyrical to the passionately intense. Da capo form, by now old fashioned, is suppressed in favor of a shape resembling a sonata form without development section. A first section contains two key areas, marked by different thematic materials and using different phrases of the text; in the second section, after a brief transition, the same sequence of ideas appears in the tonic throughout, often with a climactic, coda-like extension. On occasion, especially when the aria text consists of two contrasting stanzas, Mozart writes a two-part aria in which a slow opening section is followed by a thematically unrelated quick one.

Idomeneo is rarely staged today, presumably on the grounds that modern audiences can no longer accept the conventions of opera seria. But it is by no means a conventional work. Mozart had heard Gluck, and incorporated many of the reforms into his work—on a far higher musical level.

In 1782, at a time when there was considerable enthusiasm for native German opera, Mozart composed the singspiel *Die Entführung aus dem Serail* (The Abduction from the Seraglio). Like most Viennese singspiels, it includes many Italian traits, while preserving the characteristic features of German text and spoken dialogue. Thus while some of the arias—particularly those associated with characters of lower social standing—are German and folk-like in character, others, notably the celebrated "Marten aller Arten," are huge virtuoso pieces entirely in the Italian manner. Not all musicians find this mixture of styles wholly convincing: it was only at the end of his life that Mozart achieved a singspiel in which the national elements were not merely juxtaposed, but organically fused.

In 1786 Mozart found for the first time a librettist fully worthy of his talents: Lorenzo da Ponte. Da Ponte supplied Mozart with the librettos for *Le nozze di Figaro* (The Marriage of Figaro; 1786) and *Don Giovanni* (1787)—as well as one for *Così fan tutte* (roughly: Women Are Like That; 1790), a work differing from the other two only in its avoidance of serious matter. All three are Italian *opere buffe*, with sung recitative, but both *Figaro* and *Don Giovanni* contain scenes of the utmost seriousness, as well as conventional buffoonery.

Figaro is perhaps the most nearly perfect opera ever written. The libretto is closely adapted from an excellent play by the French dramatist Pierre Beaumarchais (1732-99). The play itself, which contains a good deal of social criticism, was condemned by the Viennese authorities as subversive, and spoken performances of it were forbidden. Mozart and da Ponte took some risk in making an opera of it, presumably hoping that the controversy surrounding the subject would attract audiences—a hope that proved largely vain. In any event, the book, even in da Ponte's somewhat toned-down version, is full of genuinely comic incidents involving a variety of real and believable people, and yet allows the characters to be taken seriously when this is appropriate. To this Mozart responds with music ranging from the near-tragic to the purely burlesque. In principle, Mozart accepted the Italian opera buffa tradition wholly—or at least he made no conscious attempt at "reform." But the result is quite different from the operas of his contemporaries. For one thing, the musical substance is far richer; this is evident particularly in the use of the orchestra, which is extensively employed in a more than accompanimental role. Even more important is Mozart's increased reliance on ensembles. Less than half of the separate numbers of the opera (excluding the recitatives) are solo arias. This emphasis allows Mozart free deployment of his greatest dramatic gift: the accurate musical realization of his characters. Even more than in *Idomeneo*, every note remains true to the character who sings it: through Mozart's mastery the listener comes to know Figaro, the Countess, and the others as real people—more real than most dramatic characters.

Mozart's lengthy finales are far more sophisticated than those of his predecessors: the development of symphonic forms and styles provided means whereby the numerous sections of a finale could be given at least the appearance of a unified and progressive whole. Thus in the finale of the second act of *Figaro*, the complexities of the plot

Die Entführung
aus dem Serail

Lorenzo da Ponte

Le Nozze di Figaro

require no less than 10 separate sections. These are grouped in 3 larger parts, with the tonal plan

$$E\flat \ B\flat \ B\flat \ / \ G \ C \ F \ B\flat \ / \ E\flat \ E\flat \ E\flat$$

Although the thematic recurrence typical of the symphony is necessarily absent for the most part (only sections 2 and 7 are thematically related), the sequence of keys looks very much like that of a sonata form. This, together with the fully symphonic style of the orchestral writing, welds the entire finale into an impressive unit.

Don Giovanni

In *Don Giovanni*, Mozart and da Ponte presented a new version of an old tale that had often been treated musically: that of the libertine who kills the aged father of a girl he has just seduced (or tried to seduce: the point is not made clear), and who is later dragged off to Hell by a stone statue of the murdered father. Da Ponte's libretto garnishes this tale with a number of incidents in the best comic manner, in order to make a full-length opera out of material that could in fact be treated much more briefly. Although the libretto is inferior to that of *Figaro*, it gives Mozart the opportunity—absent from the earlier work—of displaying the power of what might be called the daemonic side of his genius. In addition to the purely human emotions aroused by the violence of the action—in which the passion of *Idomeneo* returns, refined and enriched by a decade of experience—Mozart creates a unique style for the supernatural scenes. This appears only in the slow introduction to the overture (overtures were by now regularly single movements in sonata form), and in Act II: in a few brief pronouncements by the statue; and in the finale, during which Don Giovanni is dragged off to his punishment. (The finale actually quotes and amplifies material from the introduction to the overture.) In these places, Mozart reaches far beyond the normal confines of eighteenth-century style to find a literally terrifying musical representation of the nether world. Naive as the story may be, no spectator can help believing—at least as long as the music lasts—in the Don's supernatural destruction.

For the rest, *Don Giovanni* is a normal, if superb, example of the opera buffa type. The serious elements are balanced by lighthearted and comic scenes: even the Don's descent into the flames is immediately followed by a moralizing epilogue sung by the surviving characters in the most cheerful buffo style.

In *Don Giovanni*, as in *Figaro*, Mozart uses ensemble scenes extensively, with his usual gift for musical characterization. Donna Elvira, for example, a rather conventionally serious character, has fully embarked on a formal aria when Don Giovanni and his comic servant Leporello begin to interpolate their own ironic comments beneath her grandiose utterances, each character maintaining his or her individuality, intensified by the mutual interaction. Mozart's uncanny technical skill is also demonstrated in the finale of the first act, in part of which three small on-stage instrumental ensembles, each playing a different dance in a different meter, serve as background for the sung dialogue.

Don Giovanni has been called the greatest of all operas, and certainly nowhere else does Mozart show a wider range of emotions or a deeper dramatic insight. His next stage work (his last collaboration with da Ponte), was *Così fan tutte*, an elegant and artificial comedy, which Mozart clothed in music exquisitely appropriate—if sometimes not artificial enough.

In the next year (1791), Mozart was called on to write an opera seria for a court ceremony at Prague. The libretto was prescribed for him, *La clemenza di Tito* (The

Some of Mozart's finest works belong to a category not yet mentioned in this chapter: the concerto. There are concertos for relatively unusual instruments, such as the horn, the bassoon, and the clarinet (the last one of Mozart's greater works). There are also several for the violin, relatively early but impressive works. The finest and most numerous of the concertos, however, are those for the piano, most of them composed for concerts in Vienna in the 1780s, at which Mozart himself played the solo part, in an ultimately vain attempt to impress the Viennese public. (There is good reason to believe that the piano parts Mozart wrote are simpler than what he actually played—that he enriched the music by improvisation—but there is of course no way of recovering such additions, and most performers simply play what was written.)

Mozart's concertos

By Mozart's time, the concerto had developed forms that combined classical and Baroque elements. The traditional Baroque alternational of orchestral ritornellos with sections played by the soloist left no room for the essential sonata-form principle. A compromise resulted, in which the ritornello structure was integrated into an altered sonata movement. The first movement of a Mozart concerto begins with a lengthy orchestral section, still called the ritornello, and containing a considerable number of different themes but no important modulation: thus it is not an exposition, for it lacks the tonal contrast an exposition must contain. Only then does the soloist enter, ordinarily with the material used to begin the movement. There follows a regular sonata-form exposition, in which both soloist and orchestra participate. Some of the themes of this exposition may already have been heard in the opening ritornello, but some, at least, will be new. Often, but not necessarily, the end of the exposition will be identical to the end of the ritornello.

Formal characteristics of the Mozart concerto

The remainder of the movement consists of a development section of the usual sort, for both soloist and orchestra. (Since the ritornello-exposition section is never repeated, the dividing line between this part and the beginning of the development is often intentionally obscured.) The recapitulation, however, presents a problem: it must function simultaneously as a reprise of the ritornello and of the exposition, if redundancy is to be avoided. Thus, in the interest of brevity, some of the interior themes of both ritornello and exposition may fail to appear in the recapitulation, although naturally the principal materials—the main key-defining themes—are present. Towards the close of the recapitulation, the piano is given a formal cadence, and the orchestra continues alone, invariably building up to the antepenultimate chord of a typical final cadence. Then, however, the orchestra falls silent, and the soloist improvises, to the best of his ability, a "cadenza"—a sort of free fantasy on the materials of the movement, designed to show off the best of his technical powers. By convention, this always ends on a trill, which serves as signal for the conductor to reactivate the orchestra, and the movement concludes with the end of the original ritornello, or some variant of it. (Improvised cadenzas were normal in the eighteenth century, but even Mozart, perhaps distressed by the cadenzas of other players, wrote out cadenzas for many of his concertos later in life.)

The other two movements of a concerto (this form also lacks the minuet) generally employ forms similar to those of the symphony, enriched, of course, by the soloist-versus-orchestra contrast, which Mozart exploits in many ingenious ways. Notable in all of the concertos is the extreme care Mozart lavishes on the orchestration: the woodwinds are given particularly prominent treatment, and in general the scoring is richer in variety than that of the symphonies. This feature, added to the profusion of melodies abounding in the concertos, makes of them a repertoire especially enchanting even by Mozartean standards.

Mozart's church music

Although Mozart wrote a good deal of music for the church, notably during the period of his employment by Archbishop Colloredo, much of it is little more than occasional music: well made but not especially expressive. There are, however, a number of exceptions, among which the principal are the great Mass in C minor (K. 427; 1782-83) and the Requiem Mass (1791). Both are incomplete; the former for reasons unknown, the latter because Mozart did not live to finish it. The existing sections of the C minor Mass show that Mozart intended to write a cantata Mass, unlike Haydn's late symphonic Masses: the text is broken up into smaller sections, each composed as a single movement, for chorus, solo, solo quartet, or whatever. The style ranges from the purely operatic (as in the "Et incarnatus," a true concerto movement for soprano solo and solo winds), to a severe, nearly Baroque contrapuntal idiom. All the movements are of powerful expressivity, some of them containing unsurpassed inspirations (e.g., the "Benedictus" quartet). Even incomplete, the work must rank as one of the greater settings of the Mass.

Mozart's Requiem

The Requiem had a peculiar history. In July of 1791, a stranger visited Mozart and offered him a commission to write a Requiem Mass. Mozart accepted, and began at once, but had to interrupt his work to write *La Clemenza di Tito* and *Die Zauberflöte*. After the latter had had its first performance (30 September 1791), he tried to return to the Requiem, hampered by illness and depression. He became convinced that the Requiem was for his own death, and that the stranger who had commissioned it had been a supernatural messenger. After Mozart's death, his pupil Süssmayr finished the work, to some extent, perhaps, on the basis of ideas Mozart told him of but did not live to write down. In the end it turned out that the mysterious stranger was merely a steward to a nobleman who commissioned music that he then passed off as his own, and the Requiem was first performed in 1793 as a composition by Count Franz von Walsegg.

In any event, Mozart seems to have distilled all the pain—and much of the joy—of his life in this last work. Every movement is intensely individual, and the violent moods of the *Dies irae* text elicited unprecedented intensity from Mozart's music. It is hard now to imagine Mozart's ending his career otherwise.

APPENDIX: Chapter XI

THE CLASSICAL PERIOD

I. **Forms.**

   A. Sonata form.

      1. Development from Baroque binary dance form.

        a. Basic binary form:

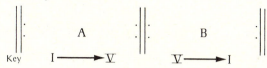

        b. Rounded binary form:

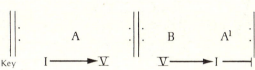

        c. Sonata form:

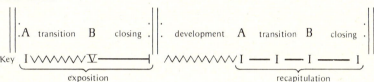

      2. Formal elements.

        a. Introduction (optional).

        b. Exposition.

           Opening theme group—tonic key

             Transition passage—modulates to key of

             second theme group.

           Second theme group—in contrasting key

           Closing passage—in contrasting key

        c. Development: unpredictable; generally deals with thematic material from exposition; normally modulates frequently.

        d. Recapitulation: repeats exposition in tonic key.

           Opening theme group—Transition—remains in tonic key

           Second theme group—now in tonic key

           Closing passage—in tonic key

        e. Coda (optional): ending for entire movement.

   B. Rondo form.

      1. Classical rondo form:

A	B	A	C	A	B	A
I	V	I	mod.	I	I	I

      2. Note the close similarity to sonata form. The principal difference is the first restatement of opening theme in tonic key

Sonata	expo.			dev't.	recap.		coda
Rondo	A	B	A	C	A	B	A
Key	I	V	I	mod.	I	I	I

355

C. Multi-movement pieces.

  1. All use the same sequence of movements and forms.

    a. Opening fast movement in sonata form.

    b. Slow movement; its form is not standardized: possible forms are ABA or some variant; theme and variations.

    c. Minuet and trio: two binary-form dances, of which the first is played first with repeats, and returns again, but without repeats, after the second.

    d. Concluding fast movement: rondo or sonata form.

  2. Compositions which use this sequence of movements (pieces preceded by an asterisk normally *omit* the minuet-and-trio movement):

    Symphony

    String quartet

    *Concerto (first movement is in altered sonata form)

    *Piano sonata (a good number do have minuets)

    *Violin (or 'cello, or flute, etc.) and piano sonata

    Miscellaneous chamber music

      String trio (violin, viola, 'cello)

      String quintet (adds one viola or one 'cello to string quartet)

      Piano (clarinet, etc.) quintet: adds one piano (clarinet, etc.) to string quartet

      Piano trio (violin, 'cello, piano)

II. **The principal works of Haydn and Mozart.**

A. The works of Joseph Haydn.

  1. Vocal works.

    13 operas

     5 marionette operas

     3 oratorios:

      Il ritorno di Tobia (1775)

      Die Schöpfung (The Creation; 1796–98)

      Die Jahreszeiten (The Seasons; 1801)

    14 Masses, including:

      Missa in tempore belli ("Paukenmesse"; 1796)

      Missa Sancti Bernardi von Offida ("Heiligmesse"; 1796)

      Missa in angustiis ("Nelsonmesse;" 1798)

      "Theresienmesse" (1799)

      "Schöpfungsmesse" (1801)

      "Harmoniemesse" (1802)

    Sacred choral works, including a *Stabat mater; Te Deum;* and two settings of the *Salve regina*

    48 songs with keyboard

    ca. 35 arrangements of Scottish and Welsh folksongs with keyboard accompaniment

    A few cantatas and concert arias with orchestra

    A few partsongs and canons

2. Instrumental works.
   104 symphonies, including:
       nos. 93–104, two sets of six "London" symphonies
       nos. 82–87, the six "Paris" symphonies
   16 overtures
   47 divertimenti
   Concertos:
       4 for keyboard
       4 for violin
       3 for 'cello
       3 for baryton
       5 for two solo *lyre organizzate*
       1 each for horn; two horns; trumpet; flute
   Marches and dances for orchestra
   Baryton music:
       126 trios
        24 duos
        11 divertimenti
   83 string quartets
   21 string trios (2 vlns. and 'cello)
    7 divertimenti with keyboard
   31 piano trios
   52 piano sonatas

B. The works of Wolfgang Amadeus Mozart.
   1. Vocal works.
      20 operas and singspiels:
          Apollo und Hyacinthus (1767)
          Bastien und Bastienne (1768)
          La finta semplice (1769)
          Mitridate, rè di Ponto (1770)
          Ascanio in Alba (1771)
          Il sogno di Scipione (1772)
          Lucio Silla (1772)
          La finta giardiniera (1775)
          Zaïde (1779)
          Il rè pastore (1775)
          Idomeneo (1781)
          Die Entführung aus dem Serail (1782)
          L'oca del Cairo (unfinished; 1783)
          Lo sposo deluso (unfinished; 1783)
          Der Schauspieldirektor (1786)
          Le nozze di Figaro (1786)
          Don Giovanni (1787)
          Così fan tutte (1790)
          Die Zauberflöte (1791)
          La clemenza di Tito (1791)
      18 Masses
      Requiem

Litanies, vespers, offertories, antiphons, etc., for church use
64 concert arias with orchestra
33 solo songs
Canons

2. Instrumental works.
41 symphonies
Divertimenti, cassations, and serenades for orchestra
Concertos:
  25 for piano
  4 for horn
  7 for violin
  2 for flute
  1 each for clarinet; flute and harp; bassoon.
6 string quintets
23 string quartets
2 piano quartets
7 piano trios
Other pieces for various chamber ensembles (clarinet quintet; horn quintet; 3 flute quartets; clarinet trio; quartet for piano and winds; etc.)
Many sonatas for violin and piano
17 piano sonatas; other pieces, including many sets of variations

III.   Brief notices of other composers of the classical period.
(N.B. From the late 18th century on, most important music is available in modern
edition—often several editions of the same work. In consequence, the bibliography of editions given in earlier chapters is herewith discontinued.)

Bach, Johann Christian (1735–82). Youngest son of J. S. Bach; a leader of operatic
and concert life in London. Composer of delicate, smoothly melodic music.

Bach, Karl (or Carl) Philipp Emanuel (1714–88). Son of J. S. Bach; harpsichordist
at the court of Frederick the Great of Prussia, prolific composer, especially for
keyboard. He emphasized expression, sensibility; composed operas, symphonies, chamber music, keyboard sonatas.

Bach, Wilhelm Friedemann (1710–84). Son of J. S. Bach; brilliant improviser, virtuoso organist. He held several positions, and spent many years unemployed
in Berlin; composed harpsichord and organ pieces; trio sonatas; symphonies
and keyboard concertos.

Boccherini, Luigi (1743–1805). Italian violoncellist and composer. Known for his
playing throughout Europe, he composed symphonies and much chamber music; his style is often likened to that of Haydn.

Cimarosa, Domenico (1749–1801). Italian composer of operas, the best-known
being *Il matrimonio segreto*. The acknowledged rival of Paisiello, he excelled
in comic operas in a simple, witty and natural style.

Dittersdorf, Karl Ditters von (1739–99). Austrian violinist and composer. He composed enormously popular operas and singspiels, including *Doktor und
Apotheker.*

Gluck, Christoph Willibald (1714–87). German composer of operas, also active at Paris. His attempts to reform opera by purifying it of extraneous action and musical virtuosity resulted in a simple and pure classical style.

Hiller, Johann Adam (1728–1804). Leipzig author and composer. He composed music for the earliest German singspiels.

Holzbauer, Ignaz (1711–83). Austrian composer, conductor of Mannheim opera. Considerable symphonic music; he is best known for his operas, especially *Günther von Schwarzburg*, an early attempt at a fully-fledged German opera.

Jommelli, Niccolò (1714–74). Italian opera composer, active in Stuttgart and Naples. His frequent rejection of conventional da capo form and his imaginative orchestration give his works greater expression than those of some of his contemporaries.

Paisiello, Giovanni (1740–1816). Italian composer of ca. 100 operas. Best known for his comic operas; his best asset is a direct and memorable melodic grace.

Pergolesi, Giovanni Battista (1710–36). A Neapolitan composer whose intermezzo *La Serva padrona* (1733) achieved enormous popularity and affected the subsequent history of opera.

Scarlatti, Domenico (1685–1757). Harpsichord virtuoso and composer, son of Alessandro Scarlatti. His brilliant keyboard sonatas (*essercizi*) are imaginative, virtuosic, idiomatic pieces of rococo elegance.

Stamitz, Johann (1717–57). Composer and conductor at the court of Mannheim, whose orchestra, under his direction, set new performance standards. His orchestral music is important both for its quality and for its influence on the development of classic symphonic forms.

XII

THE EARLY
NINETEENTH CENTURY

BEETHOVEN

THE BEGINNINGS OF ROMANTICISM

It was Mozart's Requiem, ascribed to its true composer, that was played in Haydn's honor just after the latter's death in 1809. This appropriate but apparently rather unimportant gesture marks the beginning of a radical alteration in the nature of musical repertoire. Up to this time, almost all music played was relatively new, by composers either living or only recently deceased. There were some exceptions: Palestrina was remembered and occasionally performed, and other sixteenth-century works were preserved in Germany and Italy, both as teaching pieces and as music for solemn church ceremonies; Lully's operas remained in the Paris opera repertoire for generations after his death; and, as has already been remarked, Handel continued to be performed in England. For the most part, however, music more than a generation old was either destroyed or stored away and forgotten.

Haydn and Mozart, however, had earned international reputations too powerful to be so easily forgotten. Even though later generations reduced Haydn to the genial "Papa Haydn," and Mozart (mostly) to a master of mere elegance, those generations went on playing at least some Haydn and rather more Mozart. This state of affairs—certainly very desirable for audiences, for which it vastly increased the available repertoire of first-rate music—created a new situation for composers. They could see the perfection their predecessors had achieved: a young composer's new symphony might share the program with Mozart's "Jupiter." They could not merely imitate the past, for no truly creative artist can *merely* imitate. Thus they were forced to become consciously original: stylistic self-consciousness, which had first flared up around 1600, entered a new phase.

Around 1800, that phase was just beginning, but even then it influenced—and even more was influenced by—the man whose music was an inspiration and an obstacle to the entire nineteenth century: Ludwig van Beethoven.

LUDWIG VAN BEETHOVEN

Beethoven's life

Beethoven's Character and Music.　Beethoven was born in Bonn and spent his youth there, receiving musical instruction from his father and from other local musicians, especially from C. G. Neefe, the court organist, who was apparently an excellent teacher. Beethoven paid one early visit to Vienna, where he met and impressed Mozart. In 1792 he moved there and began studying with Haydn. The younger man appears to have become impatient with Haydn's leisurely methods, however, and the lessons soon ceased. Beethoven continued his studies with men who, though less celebrated, seem to have given him the instruction he wanted.

Beethoven stayed in Vienna for the rest of his life, living on the proceeds of his music—concert receipts, publishers' fees, teaching fees—and on the patronage of aristocratic friends. He remained independent to the end, succeeding—barely—where Mozart had failed, and in so doing he established the pattern by which most later composers were to live.

His younger years were successful and relatively happy, despite his sensitive and suspicious temperament. He was much in demand as a pianist, and his compositions were highly regarded. In 1798, he experienced the first symptoms of a deafness that later became total—probably the worst affliction that a composer can be called upon to bear. His increasing isolation from society, and the anti-social elements of his character—both exacerbated by his deafness—made many of his later years painful. Beethoven, however, met his troubles not with resignation but with defiance. A proud

Fig. XII-1: Wax relief of Beethoven, between 1815 and 1818, attributed to Joseph Nikolaus Lang. (Courtesy of the Historisches Museum der Stadt Wien.)

man, dedicated to freedom, he delighted in treating the dukes and princes who helped to support him as if they were his equals, or indeed his inferiors. One cannot imagine his ever consenting to take his meals at table with his patron's personal servants, as both Haydn and Mozart perforce had done. It is to Beethoven more than to any other man that we owe the modern concept of the composer as a free artist, responsible only to his own conscience.

Although Beethoven was a prolific composer, his works are not as numerous as those of Haydn or Mozart. The latter wrote some 150 symphonies between them: Beethoven wrote nine. In large part, this reduction in productivity springs from the increased individuality of each work. His music, as it became more intensely personal, also became more demanding. Standard formulas, still normal even in the mature works of Haydn and Mozart, would no longer serve. Every note of a score had to be laboriously worked out, every problem solved individually, as if it were occurring for the first time—as in a sense it was. *Beethoven's approach to composition*

Furthermore, Beethoven wrote slowly and with difficulty, constantly revising and improving his original ideas. Often he writes in his notebook what seems a rather trivial theme (Ex. XII-1a): he has sensed that something important lies in it, but has not yet discovered what it is. A later version will realize more of the material's potential, and further revisions will finally bring it to the ultimate shape (Ex. XII-1b), which is so natural and so unforced that only the fortunate survival of the notebook sketches could convince one that the theme was not conceived in an instant.

Further proof of Beethoven's care in his approach to composition is his increased use of specific directions to the performer. The number of dynamic signs, marks of phrasing, and other indications is far greater than was normal in classical scores. Since each work is in fact so individual, the performer naturally needs more guidance in executing it properly (the more so as much of Beethoven is ferociously difficult technically: the player needs all the help he can get).

Scholars have generally agreed in dividing Beethoven's output into three periods. In the works of the first period, Beethoven is still to some extent a learner, and his *Style periods*

Ex. XII-1

music, while by no means lacking in personal character, is still strongly imprinted by the model of Haydn and, to a much lesser extent, of Mozart. In the second period, he reaches a triumphant and aggressive maturity, and produces music of enormous power and brilliance. In the third—corresponding to his late, isolated years—he turns inward, away from his audience. His late works are therefore less showy, more obscure, but also more profound. (Much the same sort of division can be applied to almost any composer's work, but the distinctions are particularly clear in Beethoven's case.)

Although Beethoven, like his predecessors, cultivated nearly all of the forms and media then in use, his works show a bias in favor of instrumental music. In fact, the core of the Beethoven repertoire—a core that permits a nearly complete understanding of Beethoven's style—is almost entirely instrumental: the 9 symphonies, 16 string quartets, and 32 sonatas for piano. In these works the essence of Beethoven's style is fully revealed, and without intending any disparagement of the numerous masterpieces that lie outside this list, the discussion here will deal primarily with these works.

Early Period. Beethoven's early style may be seen in the piano sonatas of Opus 2 (published in 1796; from Beethoven on, opus numbers—which indicate order of publication—are frequently, although by no means invariably, a guide to order of composition). The first, in F minor, opens with a concise and vigorous allegro movement that owes a good deal to Haydn—to whom the sonatas are dedicated. But there is already in the music a dynamism—one might almost say a violence—that is foreign to Haydn, and that lies at the heart of Beethoven's style.

Even in this early work, sonata form has been subtly used to produce overtly dramatic effects. The exposition is made to sound rushed by the avoidance of any cadence in the new key (A♭) until far later than was then normal. More concrete evidence of Beethoven's dramatic leanings may be found in the recapitulation of the initial theme. The left hand chords, most of which were on weak beats in the exposition (Ex. XII-2a), are now placed on the strong beats (Ex. XII-2b), so that the theme, originally light in weight, becomes immeasurably more forceful. There are, to be sure, precedents for such treatment in Haydn and Mozart, but one should not underestimate the portent suggested here: Beethoven, who had relatively little to do with actual drama on the stage, was nonetheless from the beginning a dramatic composer in a more general sense, and some of his successors eagerly took up the idea of a *specific* dramatic action expressed in music alone.

The same passage is symptomatic of another, related, change: Beethoven's music often speaks more specifically to the emotions than, say, Haydn's. The delight in pure music-making—in the fitting-together of notes to produce pleasure—yields in some works to the need for direct personal communication. Again, this is by no means entirely new, but it is another sign of a changing balance. That Beethoven himself was aware of this is shown by the inscriptions he placed on some of his works: the piano sonata Op. 13 is entitled "Pathétique," and a movement of one of the string quartets of Op. 18 is marked "adagio affettuoso ed appassionato" (slow, tenderly, and passionately).

In some works this subjectivism causes Beethoven to break away from conventional patterns. The piano sonata Op. 27, no. 2 (1801; the celebrated "Moonlight" sonata—a title *not* applied by Beethoven) lacks a conventional first movement: it consists of a slow movement, an allegretto somewhat in the manner of a minuet (a type

Ex. XII-2 (a)

Ex. XII-2 (b)

Beethoven often used in piano sonatas), and a rapid finale. And the slightly later sonata Op. 31, no. 2 (1801-02) begins with a quick alternation between a very slow tempo and a very rapid one, before the first principal theme is heard. The slow section returns in the middle of the movement, expanding into a wordless recitative, then into rapid arpeggios, after which the recapitulation begins—but only the second half of the exposition recurs.

This aspect of Beethoven's work should be observed, but not exaggerated. There are precedents for Beethoven's innovations, and for his emphasis on subjectivity: it is a quantitative rather than a qualitative change, for the most part. Indeed, the majority of Beethoven's early works are cheerful and unproblematic; they are original but not eccentrically so, and make deft use of familiar techniques. In these works Beethoven appears—and appeared to his contemporaries—as a worthy successor to Haydn, although as yet even Beethoven did not have the supreme command of the mature Haydn, let alone Mozart.

The "Eroica" Symphony

Middle Period.   The sonatas just mentioned (Op. 27, no. 2, and Op. 31, no. 2) might well be considered examples of Beethoven's second period, rather than his first; but in 1804, what is perhaps the archetypal work of the second period, the Third, or "Eroica," Symphony in E♭, appeared, a work of unprecedented force and vigor, and one in which the new characteristics can be seen with exceptional clarity. Its mere size is unprecedented: a first movement of 691 measures, of which more than half fall in the development and coda—the latter being, as often in Beethoven, a kind of second development. This is a departure both in size and proportion from classical precedent. The movement is about twice the normal classical length, and the center of gravity, as it were, has shifted away from the exposition of ideas to their manipulation—a process well begun in Haydn and Mozart, but here carried much farther. It is a measure of the change in proportion that Beethoven builds one of his most ferocious climaxes in the development section and follows this with the statement of a new and lyric theme in

Treatment of sonata form

the remote key of E minor: a new character has, as it were, been introduced into the drama. Thus the traditional shape of sonata form is subtly altered, and the change is allied with an increased permeation of the developmental process through all parts of the form. Even at the very beginning of this movement, Beethoven is not content merely to state a "tune:" the unexpected C♯ is already developmental. Still, Beethoven remains strictly faithful to the fundamental principle of sonata form—tonality. It is the relation between keys, a relation now spread over vast areas, that gives ultimate unity to this and indeed to all of Beethoven's works. However liberated the vocabulary, the underlying technique is securely classical. (The listener need not be concerned if he cannot follow Beethoven's intricate modulations accurately; not all professional musicians can do so. Beethoven, like his predecessors, makes perfectly clear what the hearer needs to know—that a new key has been reached, that the tonality is temporarily unstable, that the home tonic has finally been regained. Naturally it is interesting to see *how* all this is done, but it is not aesthetically necessary.)

If the first movement of this symphony seems to portray a kind of heroic self-confidence, representing the optimistic side of Beethoven's nature, the second, entitled "Marcia funebre" (funeral march), explores the dark regions of tragedy more explicitly than any earlier music. The overall form is conventional enough (roughly ABA'), but the material of the A section is of violent intensity, enhanced in its repetition by a severe fugal section. The final measures, in which the principal theme is literally shattered—broken into fragments separated by pauses—is again explicitly dramatic: the instruments attempt to speak, in the disjointed fashion of uncontrollable grief.

Scherzo

A minuet following such a conclusion would be unthinkable, but Beethoven had already often employed a new type of movement to replace the minuet, and he does so here. This is the "scherzo" (joke—although the humor is often grim). In essence, a scherzo is no more than the usual minuet-trio pairing, but at much greater speed and with a more violent or emphatic character. This sort of movement is ideally suited to Beethoven's purposes. The rapid tempo comes as a relief after a serious slow movement; the vehemence of the music prevents any sense of anticlimax; while the simple form and (usually) symmetrical phrasing provide a lightness that will not compete with the necessarily more complex finale. The scherzo of the Third Symphony illustrates not only Beethoven's vigor but also his tendency to expand whatever he touches. The movement is 441 measures long (not counting the internal repetitions). The orchestra is enlarged by the addition of a third horn to the by then standard two flutes, two oboes, two clarinets, two bassoons, two horns, two trumpets, tympani, and strings. The three horns, acting as a group, are prominently featured in the trio section.

For Beethoven, perhaps even more than for his predecessors, the finale of a symphony posed a problem: a movement was needed that was as serious and weighty as its predecessors, and yet did not compete with or in any way duplicate the effect of the first movement. In this symphony, Beethoven's solution is a free and complex set of variations. For Beethoven, especially in his middle and late years, the variation became a form capable of conveying the deepest musical thought. Beethoven's variation technique was basically that of his predecessors, but he gradually acquired the ability to extract from even a trivial theme a series of profound and personal statements. Since, then, the form itself is a serious one, Beethoven achieves the desired weight for his finale, while at the same time providing maximum formal variety. A special feature of this set of variations is that the apparent theme has more the character of a bass line than of a melody. Yet Beethoven proceeds to treat it as a true theme in the first two variations, saving what is obviously the "real," melodic form of the theme for variation 3. This in effect gives him two basic ideas on which to build further variations: the unison bass line, and the melodic form.

Beethoven's use of variation:"Eroica" finale

The "Eroica" is not merely a superb work of art: it is a landmark in the history of the symphony. What had begun as entertainment music in the 1730s had already grown capable of the most serious musical expression in Haydn and Mozart, while in the same process each work became more individual, more distinct from all other symphonies. Not only does the "Eroica" go much farther in the same direction: it changes the symphony's qualitative nature. The "Eroica" is explicitly concerned with self-expression—almost with confession. One need compare it only with its nearest neighbors—Beethoven's Second and Fourth symphonies—to understand the measure of the distance that separates the purely musical work from the work that also is an urgent personal communication. This is in no sense a matter of value—one may quite legitimately prefer the Fourth to the Third—it is the nature of the content of the work that has changed.

Beethoven's middle period was astonishingly fertile, especially considering his slow and painstaking approach to composition, and the intense individuality of each work. The dozens of major works produced during the years 1803-16 exhibit an enormous range of expressive types. There is the Fifth Symphony (1807-08), in which the bitter struggle of the first movement yields to the lyric interlude of the slow movement, then to the mysterious and ominous scherzo (in which a form of the main theme of the first movement appears), only to end in unambiguous triumph in the finale. There is also the "Appassionata" sonata (Op. 57; 1804-05), in which, despite the temporary serenity of the slow movement, savage despair persists until the end. In works such as these, Beethoven seems to be grappling with elemental problems. Yet in the same years there appeared the exquisite lyricism of the Fourth Piano Concerto, Op. 58 (1805-06), and the almost untroubled delicacy of the piano sonata Op. 78 (1809)—works fully as expressive, yet largely or wholly lacking the conflict found in the Third and Fifth symphonies. It would be naive to attempt any fundamental distinction between passionate and cheerful music, but it would be also short-sighted to ignore the difference between music that is explicitly problematic and that which is not.

Middle-period symphonies

The rich profusion of the music of these years includes most of the frequently performed works, several of which must be given individual mention. It is curious that the intense and vehement Third and Fifth symphonies are preceded by the relatively classical Second and Fourth. If this is a pattern, then the Sixth Symphony (1807-08) should also be a relatively lighter work—and so it is, but in an entirely different way. At the first performance of the work, known as the Pastoral Symphony, Beethoven had printed in the program "Recollections of Life in the Country," with the significant addition, "more expression of feeling than [tone-]painting." Moreover, each movement bears its own title: I. Cheerful Impressions on Arriving in the country; II. By the Brook; III. Peasants' merry-making; IV. Tempest and storm; V. The shepherds' hymn—Thanksgiving after the storm. Although there are a few classical precedents for this sort of thing (and many Baroque ones, unknown to Beethoven), this is in effect the first major classical work of "program music"—instrumental music in which the materials and structure are at least in part determined by a desire to depict extra-musical objects or events. The programmatic element is strongest in the coda of the second (slow) movement, in which the wind instruments imitate birdcalls, and in the fourth —the storm—which, standing outside the normal symphonic scheme altogether, owes its existence solely to the program. The storm movement is not separated from its neighbors, but is connected to them without pause—a procedure Beethoven often uses in other, non-programmatic works as well. Most of the Sixth Symphony is indeed "more expression of feeling than painting" and could be fully understood musically by one who had no idea what it was supposed to represent (although admittedly the peasants' merry-making, while formally a perfectly regular scherzo and trio, is so clearly rustic in sound that any listener would automatically associate it with the country).

Epoch-making as this approach to the symphony may now seem, and successful as the work was, Beethoven never repeated the experiment, although he came close to it in the piano sonata Op. 81a (1809-10), in which the three movements bear the very general titles: "The farewell," "Absence," and "Reunion;" and although he gave special titles to individual movements of other works. It may therefore be concluded that Beethoven, however specific his instrumental music often sounds, did not regularly conceive it—or wish his hearers to conceive it—as illustrative of extra-musical concepts or objects. In the overwhelming majority of cases, he preferred to let his music speak as music, without confining it by verbal specifications. It was left to later generations to enlarge upon the implications of the Pastoral Symphony.

The Seventh and Eighth symphonies form a pair like the Fifth and Fourth: the former is passionately rhythmical and intense, the latter lighter in tone but immensely sophisticated. Apart from the First, Beethoven's symphonies regularly alternate between the intense and passionate (3,5,7,9) and the lighter and more cheerful (2,4,6,8). In either type, it is hard to know what to admire most: the masterly expansion of the forms, without loss of clarity; the ingenuity by which relatively simple thematic materials are made profoundly expressive; the variety of developmental procedures; the enrichment of texture by the increased interest of subordinate parts; or the brilliant exploitation of the enlarged orchestra (trombones, long a part of the operatic orchestra, appear symphonically for the first time in Nos. 5 and 6; and the horns and trumpets are more and more treated as thematic instruments, rather than merely supportive ones).

Although Beethoven's harmonic vocabulary remained relatively conservative—he uses few chord-progressions that cannot be found in Haydn and Mozart—he gradually enlarged the tonal areas in which his music regularly moved, again with no loss of clarity. Thus in the C major piano sonata Op. 53 (1803-04), the second part of the exposition is not in the normal dominant G, but in the relatively remote key of E major (the connection is: E minor is closely related to C major, differing by only one sharp; major and minor keys on the same tonic are interchangeable; therefore E major is also related to C major). Although Beethoven never abandoned the dominant key as a basic tonal resource, his later works increasingly exploit relationships (such as this one) to keys a third rather than a fifth from the original tonic.

Beethoven's harmonic language

Another unusual tonal procedure appears frequently during the middle period. It had long been normal to juxtapose a phrase in the tonic with one in the supertonic (e.g., C major followed by D minor, as in the First Symphony, first movement, mm. 13-25), since the supertonic leads naturally to the dominant and hence ultimately back to the tonic. But the supertonic also exists in a more highly colored form, as a chord on the flatted second degree (e.g., D♭ in the key of C). This chord, known as the "Neapolitan," had also long been a commonplace, particularly at cadences. But Beethoven in certain works began to employ the flat supertonic not just as a chord but as a key area, in which context it is very remote indeed. Thus both the piano sonata Op. 57 and the string quartet Op. 59, no. 2, begin by repeating the opening theme directly in the flat supertonic. Indeed, the latter piece, while its first movement preserves outwardly orthodox tonal relations, is really "about" the conflict between E minor and F major, so baldly presented in the opening measures. The same two keys are again violently juxtaposed in the scherzo. The extraordinary finale, a rondo in E minor, is an ultimate echo of this conflict: its principal theme invariably begins in C major and remains there for some time before subsiding into the tonic; and its main subsidiary theme also sets its tonic (B minor) against its flat supertonic (C major).

Quartet Op. 59, no. 2

This same finale offers a good example of another aspect of Beethoven's mature style. The large scale of such movements demands a great accuracy of timing: it is necessary not only to arrive in a given key, for example, but to arrive there at precisely the moment demanded by the pace and scale of the whole movement. Beethoven often resorts to curiously "empty" passages to occupy the amount of time required. Thus in the movement under consideration, there are two passages of some length from which presentation of true themes is wholly absent: they consist merely of repetitions of a single rhythmic figure, (Ex. XII-3), in which, by gradually changing the pitches, a change of key is accomplished. By reducing his resources to a minimum—giving up themes, chords, and polyphony—Beethoven paradoxically succeeds in heightening the tension, while at the same moment calling attention to the importance of time as a musical factor.

Among the latest works of Beethoven's middle period, none is more characteristic than the string quartet in F minor Op. 95 (1810). The first movement is relatively short but ferociously concentrated. Here again the flat supertonic relationship is a primary feature, not only in the by now familiar repetition of the first theme a half-step higher, but also in the second part of the exposition, the main key of which is D♭ (another third relationship). Here two unison scales notated in A major and D major (properly B double flat and E double flat) interrupt the lyrical themes about them with violent reminders of the underlying key conflict. The development section is short, and stays surprisingly close to the main key of F minor. In the recapitulation, the chief point of interest is the manner in which the second group of themes is brought into the tonic major: Beethoven begins these themes in D♭, exactly as in the exposition; then, in an

Quartet Op. 95

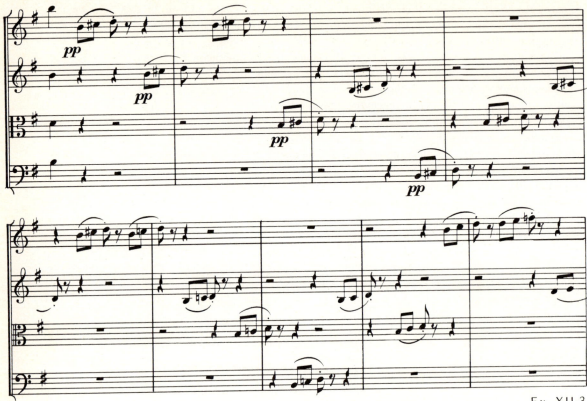

Ex. XII-3

abrupt shift of key simply settles in F major. The whole movement is so concentrated that transition—gradual motion from one tonal area to another—is almost wholly absent.

The slow movement that follows is set in the weirdly remote key of D major, and while this may have some connection with the scale in D of the first movement, it is probably better explained as an ultimate extension of the principle of identity of major and minor keys on the same tonic: D *minor* is related to F *major*, and if the modes of both are changed, D major must be related to F minor (this reasoning does not much lessen the shock of the opening measures of the slow movement, however). The overall form is not remarkable: ABB'A, with a brief reference to A between the two B's. The A section is basically a lyrical melody whose chief characteristic is its use of phrase extension—the internal lengthening of the phrase by avoidance of decisive cadences. Thus the first 8 measures form a unit that leads us to expect an 8-measure complement; the latter turns out in fact to be nearly three times as long.

The B sections are fugal, based on a chromatic subject, and written in a rich and complex counterpoint that owes almost nothing to Baroque technique. Beethoven here begins to go beyond Haydn and Mozart (he was to go even farther) both in the extent of his use of counterpoint and in the originality of his contrapuntal style. The second B section is an intensification of the first, the increase in intensity being achieved by more rapid figuration and more complex texture. The recurrence of the A section is also an intensification, again by means of the same device of phrase extension, now enormously amplified. This time the 8-measure fore-phrase is followed by a truly gigantic continuation—an unbroken line of no less than 80 measures, punctuated only by evasive and deceptive cadences that propel rather than restrain the line. It goes without saying that the lyric tension of this section is tremendous.

The remaining movements testify to Beethoven's efforts at achieving a perfect unity for the entire quartet. The scherzo, which follows the slow movement without pause, returns to the main key of F minor, and to the savage energy of the first movement. The trio, however, begins in the key of G♭—an unmistakable reference to the Neapolitan of the first movement—and makes extensive use of D (by equating G♭ with F♯), which was the key of the slow movement. As in certain earlier works, the scherzo form is extended by presenting the scherzo three times and the trio twice, in the pattern STSTS, with subtle variations in the repetitions.

The finale begins with a slow introduction—by now either of the outer fast movements may have such introductions—leading into an agitated and passionate allegretto. This is cast in sonata-rondo form, and runs its normal course until, after a moment of hesitation, the beginning of the coda is reached. The coda, however, turns out to be an extremely rapid, brilliant section in F major, which brings the work to an unexpectedly cheerful conclusion. Not all critics are convinced that this experiment is entirely successful. Without taking sides on the matter, one can certainly observe that Beethoven was intensely concerned with making the last movement a true "finale"—whether a summing up of problems, an affirmation of victory, or even a neutral evasion of the question. The variety of finale forms found in Beethoven's later works, and the absence of any true finale from several, testify to the depth of this concern.

The Late Works.   From Op. 101 (1816) on, Beethoven enters his third and last period. The works of these years are almost all difficult, not only for the performer, but also for the listener. In many cases, only repeated and attentive hearings will enable the student to understand what Beethoven is getting at, although there are of course passages and even entire works that are not so forbidding.

Beethoven's principal works of this period consist of five piano sonatas (Opp. 101, 106, 109, 110, 111; 1816-22), the Ninth Symphony (1817-23), the *Missa solemnis* (Solemn Mass; 1818-23), and the last string quartets (Opp. 127, 130, 131, 132, 135; 1824-26). In addition, there are numerous other compositions, including not only the monumental "Diabelli" variations for piano, in which Beethoven extracts a whole world of music from a trivial theme supplied by a publisher, but also a few short unconnected piano pieces, the *Bagatelles,* prophetic of a new type of piano work that later generations were to cultivate extensively.

Beethoven's late works and style characteristics

Certain characteristics are typical of Beethoven's late style: experimentation with novel effects of sound (this despite the composer's deafness, and indeed even partly because of it: he heard nothing from the outside world, and lived entirely in the sounds within his mind); contrast of different tempos within a single movement; extensive use of counterpoint; blurring of formal outlines (e.g., passing from exposition to development without formal articulation, or connecting successive movements by transitional passages); frequent reliance on variation, both as a form and as a technique; extensive use of the remotest areas of tonal space; fondness for feminine cadences (i.e., those in which the tonic chord falls on a weak rather than a strong beat); and, in general, a willingness to devise special new forms for individual movements, whether or not such forms had classical precedents.

Beethoven's late piano sonatas

The five piano sonatas strikingly illustrate Beethoven's experimentation with new sounds. In these works he delights in exploring the extreme ranges of the instrument (often using them simultaneously), and in creating other novel sonorities by means of trills and complex figurations. These sonatas also exhibit a wide range of overall forms:

Opus	Key				
101	A major	sonata	scherzo (canonic trio)	fragmentary slow movement	sonata
106	B♭ major	sonata	scherzo	slow movement (sonata)	introduction and fugue
109	E major	irregular slow-fast sonata	scherzo	slow variations	———
110	A♭ major	sonata	scherzo	slow movement (fragmentary) alternating with fugue	
111	C minor	introduction and sonata	———	slow variations	———

It should also be pointed out that Op. 106 is a work of enormous length and difficulty. The others, while very large by classical standards, are more modest.

The presence of fugues as finales in Opp. 106 and 110 is only one indication of the increased permeation of Beethoven's musical language by counterpoint: there are fugal developments as well, in the last movement of Op. 101 and the first of Op. 111; and innumerable contrapuntal passages throughout these works. That the two formal fugues are used as finales is also an indication of Beethoven's intense preoccupation with the problem of the last movement. Only Op. 101 has what might be called a conventional finale. Opp. 109 and 111 end with slow variations—a traditional fast concluding movement for either of these sonatas was evidently inconceivable to Beethoven.

As for the substance of these works, it is profound, difficult, and various. The tendency towards individualization of each work, to its formulation as the expression of some concrete but verbally inexpressible thought, is here—as in all late Beethoven—carried still farther.

Ninth Symphony

It is possible that Beethoven himself thought in some such terms, for in the Ninth Symphony (1817-23, overlapping the composition of some of the late piano sonatas), he undertook his most radical solution of the problem of the finale, and at the same time an acknowledgement of the "concreteness" of at least some of his musical thought: he introduced voices, and hence text, into the last movement. The first three movements of this symphony, while great in size and profound in content, are clearly based on classical models: a huge and tragic allegro in D minor; a demonic scherzo with bucolic trio; and a set of variations on two sublime themes. In the fourth movement, after a rapid introductory hubbub, the unaccompanied 'cellos and basses declaim a vigorous

THE EARLY NINETEENTH CENTURY 373

recitative. (This in itself is not new; recitative-like writing for instruments had many precedents.) Since there are as yet no words, only the general effect can be sensed: it is one of rejection. Thereafter, the themes of the first three movements are played in turn; a new recitative for 'cellos and basses follows the theme from each movement, again clearly rejecting what has just been played. Finally the beginning of a new theme appears, and this at last is greeted with enthusiasm by the lower strings, still in recitative. Then the new theme appears complete, followed by several variations.

By quoting themes of earlier movements, Beethoven has linked the finale in a specific way to what has preceded; this is not merely a matter of thematic relationship or allusion, but direct quotation. Moreover, by using the strings as if they were in fact saying something concrete, he has emphasized that each theme has—for him at least—some specific content. If this movement were to go on merely as an elaborate set of variations (like the finale of the "Eroica"), it would already be revolutionary. But there is more to come. After some development of the new theme, the introductory hubbub suddenly returns, followed this time by a *vocal* recitative; an invitation to sing the praises of joy. Now the new theme returns again, but this time sung, and the rest of the movement is a setting of Schiller's *Ode to Joy*. The purely instrumental beginning has thus become a prelude to a predominantly vocal main section scored for solo quartet, chorus, and orchestra, and cast in a unique form that combines variation technique, fugue, and other procedures. Evidently Beethoven felt impelled to make unequivocally plain what he regarded as the non-musical substance of at least this movement.

The Ninth Symphony is thus unprecedented, not only in its size and in its technical novelties, but also in its breaking of the barrier between vocal and instrumental music. In many ways, it is a work belonging more to the romanticism of the nineteenth century than to the past—except that Beethoven's supreme sense of musical form is always present and always felt.

In the last five string quartets, perhaps the greatest ever composed, Beethoven's late style appears in what is perhaps its purest form. There is no use of vocal elements here (perhaps because Beethoven had just completed a huge setting of the Mass). These works belong to the domain of "pure" or "abstract" music, as do the late sonatas: words are unnecessary and insufficient, except in the detailed directions to the performers. Like most works of Beethoven's last period, these quartets were not understood in their own time: most people felt that the composer had become more than a little mad, and perhaps on account of his deafness could not really mean what he wrote. Only gradually did later generations discover beauty and profundity in these difficult compositions.

Beethoven's late quartets

In these quartets, as in the late piano sonatas, we find Beethoven both accepting and altering the traditional four-movement pattern. The table on p. 374 shows the principal divisions.

In Opp. 127 and 135, the normal pattern is maintained without change, and in Op. 132 it is nearly so. Even so, the interpenetration of two tempos in a single movement appears several times: the slow introduction has become more than a mere gateway to the ensuing sonata form.

The extreme cases are Opp. 130 and 131—the first a basically cheerful, the second a deeply tragic work. In Op. 130 movements 2-4 are all related to the scherzo idea: the second directly, the third much less so (it is a semi-slow movement of playful character), and the fourth by its character as a rather naive-sounding country dance. In Op.

Opus	Key				
127	E♭ major	slow introduction and sonata (mixed)	slow variations	scherzo and trio	sonata (with long coda in new meter)
130	B♭ major	slow introduction and sonata (mixed)	short andante scherzo	rustic slow dance movement	sonata*
131	C♯ minor	slow fugue short allegro slow variations scherzo (most of these linked with transitional sections)			sonata
132	A minor	slow introduction and sonata (mixed)	scherzo	slow movement	short march and transition to rondo
135	F major	sonata	scherzo	slow movement	introduction and sonata (mixed)

*Beethoven had originally written an enormous fugue as finale for this quartet, but was persuaded to replace it with this long but infinitely less demanding movement. The fugue, called *Grosse Fuge* (Great Fugue), was published separately as Op. 133.

131, the main deviation occurs at the beginning, where the slow introduction has developed into a complete movement, and in so doing has caused the following allegro to shrink, both in length and weight: there has been a shift in the center of gravity. These two movements also represent the culmination of Beethoven's preoccupation with the contrast between the main key and its flat supertonic, for the fugue is in C♯ minor, and the succeeding allegro in D major. The remaining movements reconcile these two opponents: the variations are in A (dominant of D), the scherzo in E (dominant of A and relative major of C♯ minor), thus the C♯ minor finale is heard as tonally justified (a justification emphasized by an allusion to—not a quotation of—the fugue subject of the first movement).

No words can convey the peculiar qualities of Beethoven's style in these and other late works. Three quotations will have to suffice. The first consists of the opening measures of the third movement of Op. 130 (Ex. XII-4). Despite the grave beginning, the mood is light and cheerful. But note the complexity of the texture: the music is intensely, if informally, contrapuntal, and the cheerfulness is in no sense "easy."

The second is from the trio from the scherzo of Op. 135 (Ex. XII-5), in which a kind of demonic energy comes close to overwhelming the listener. The obsessive repetition of the pattern in the lower instruments must surely have been one of those moments that struck Beethoven's contemporaries as mad. Indeed even now it makes full sense only in the larger context of the whole movement.

The final example is part of one of Beethoven's most intimate utterances, from the slow movement of the string quartet Op. 132. This movement, headed by the composer "Holy Song of Thanksgiving, from One Who Has Been Healed, to the Godhead," is conventional enough in form: A B A B′ A″. It is the beginning of the last section that is quoted (Ex. XII-6).

Andante con moto, ma non troppo

poco scherzoso

Ex. XII-4

    Beethoven himself claimed to have invented a new style of counterpoint here, and his claim is just. Nothing could be more intensely polyphonic, nor more entirely unlike any traditional style of counterpoint. But the intensity is not merely of polyphony; it is of feeling as well: technique is swallowed up in the fervor of expression, and further analysis seems almost an impertinence.

Ex. XII-5

Ex. XII-6

Beethoven's Vocal Music.   So far this discussion has treated only Beethoven's instrumental music (except for the last movement of the Ninth Symphony): this is fair enough, for Beethoven wrote most of his best music in this area. He did write a considerable amount of vocal music as well, however, including two works that cannot be omitted from any survey of his work: his one opera (technically a singspiel), *Fidelio* (1805; and subsequent revisions), and the late *Missa solemnis* (completed in 1823).

Fidelio

Fidelio caused Beethoven endless problems. In the first place, he insisted on a libretto of high moral character. Much as he admired Mozart, he felt that too often Mozart had written sublime music to unworthy texts. Beethoven finally decided on a German translation of a French story, dealing with a heroic wife who saves her unjustly imprisoned husband from execution at the hands of a tyrant. The first part of the libretto is hardly more than a light and typical singspiel beginning, and Beethoven in dealing with these early scenes seems something like a giant trying to play with a baby's toy. His music is appropriate, but it is too fine, too musical, too impressive. The more serious scenes that follow Beethoven treats with supreme power and dramatic effect.

Still, despite the greatness of the work, and despite Beethoven's numerous revisions (more numerous than in any of his other works), Beethoven lacked the effortless stage sense of Mozart. *Fidelio* was not a great success in its time, nor has it ever become as normal a part of the opera repertoire as, say, *Don Giovanni*. In part, this is because it lacks the stage magic that attracts large audiences (necessary to make an opera financially viable); but part of the of the fault lies in the work itself: music and drama coexist, without always fusing into true unity.

Missa solemnis

The *Missa solemnis* is an entirely different kind of work. It was commissioned to be performed at the installation of the Archduke Rudolph as bishop of Olmütz in 1820; but Beethoven was carried away by the assignment, and the Mass was not finished until three years later. (It is in any case too long, too complex, and too personal to be used in the liturgy.) Formally, it descends directly from the symphonic Mass type of the mature Haydn, enormously magnified. It is a work that makes infinite demands on the performers—and on the hearers as well—but it stands with Bach's B minor Mass as one of the greatest settings of the text.

Beethoven's Influence.   In establishing himself as the first independent composer of international fame (Haydn achieved this also, but only late in life), Beethoven profoundly altered the position of the composer in society: he was no longer the employee or even servant of a court or church, but a free agent, responsible only to his own artistic conscience. The results of this change—and they were not all to the good, as will be seen—are still felt today. But even more important than this was the enormous musical influence Beethoven exerted on the nineteenth century. His style and his innovations opened doors leading to unexplored territories of all sorts, and if he himself remained firmly rooted in the classical tradition, his successors felt no such obligation of faithfulness.

Furthermore, his work presented posterity with a new and formidable obstacle. It was pointed out above that the continued performance of Haydn and Mozart after the composers' deaths tended towards the development of a new sort of style consciousness. But Beethoven's work was not only obviously "immortal;" it was also in some sense definitive. It seemed that Beethoven had said the last word in so many genres:

who could write a symphony after Beethoven's Ninth? A string quartet after his last five? Who would dare compete with this giant?

Thus nineteenth-century composers had to cope with two new problems: the preservation of masterpieces of earlier style in general, and the search for an escape from Beethoven's shadow in particular. Of course it was German composers who were first affected, but ultimately no musician in Europe could evade coming to grips with Beethoven's legacy.

THE BEGINNINGS OF MUSICAL ROMANTICISM

The preceding pages were devoted to the work of a single composer, as if the first decades of the nineteenth century were "The Age of Beethoven." In one sense, of course, they were, at least in retrospect; but many other composers were also active during these years, including some of great importance, and significant changes in musical style were taking place in which Beethoven had little or no share.

Indeed, the general intellectual climate changed profoundly in the early nineteenth century. The Age of Reason, which had confidently believed that the rational faculty could in the end solve all of man's problems, had once already been attacked by the *Sturm und Drang* forces of the 1770s. While rationalism—and with it classicism—had survived the attack, and perhaps even benefited from it, belief in the unqualified primacy of reason was moribund by the end of the century. A new force quickly gathered strength, a belief in the primary validity of man's subjective experience—of his own unique inner life. This new force—romanticism—was by no means anti-intellectual, but it did assert that the mere application of reason to external data was not enough. The personal experience of the individual should be the principal concern of thought, and especially of the arts.

The romantic movement

In literature, the romantic movement began about 1800 in Germany. It emphasized not only the subjective and emotional in general, but also certain more specific motives: Nature, unspoiled and uncontrolled by man; solitude, the state in which one's consciousness is at its height; the infinite and unattainable, exemplified by the "blue flower" of the romantic poet Novalis; night, when somehow the Infinite seems closest. More specific themes centered on a predilection for the exotic: the supernatural (ghosts, fairies, and the like); anything remote in time or place; and specifically the Middle Ages, greatly idealized by the romantics so as to include benevolent rulers, virtuous and happy peasants, knightly heroes, and so on. It should also be noted that many romantics were very fond of humor.

It is easy enough to see that almost all of these romantic themes are united by one common characteristic: their remoteness from the increasingly grim realities of Europe after the French revolution. Yet the romantic spirit was by no means purely escapist: it yearned for a perhaps unattainable but at least imaginable future in which man might be free to be truly himself.

When literary romanticism began in Germany, Haydn was still composing, and Beethoven was writing music still largely classical in spirit. Thus the change of style did not occur simultaneously in the two arts, nor need one have expected it to. Yet, as has been said above, musical classicism was always somewhat inclined towards subjectivism, and it is not surprising that romantic critics soon claimed Beethoven (and some of Mozart) for their own. If modern critics reject this view, considering Beethoven either as a classical composer or at most as a special post-classical but pre-romantic figure, it is because even his late works are deeply rooted in the classical past. The true musical romantics, even when they used classical forms and procedures, did so in a new way and in a new spirit. Romanticism and the post-romantic styles succeeding it in the later nineteenth century do not, perhaps, constitute a "period" in the history of music comparable to the Renaissance or the Baroque: their connection with and indebtedness to classical techniques is too great for that. Nevertheless, the nineteenth century is a clearly distinguishable era, with conscious aims and characteristics of its own.

The Place of Music in the Early Nineteenth Century.   Before discussing the formative stages of musical romanticism, it is necessary to consider briefly certain changes in the position occupied by music in nineteenth-century thought and life. Many nineteenth-century writers and philosophers assigned to music—especially instrumental music —an extremely exalted position. Schopenhauer, for example, regarded music as the truest representation of ultimate reality. There was in general much discussion concerning the nature of music and its proper aims (in contrast to the eighteenth-century emphasis on technical and didactic books about music). Many composers were prolific and expert writers on musical subjects—almost invariably from an aesthetic as well as a technical point of view.

At the same time the sociology of music underwent considerable change. By 1800, aristocratic and ecclesiastical patronage of music, although still powerful in some places, was rapidly waning. To the court entertainment had succeeded the public concert, open to anyone willing to pay the price of admission. Furthermore, the domestic practice of music was increasingly regarded as a normal and desirable pursuit by the middle classes.

These two tendencies led to two corresponding pressures on musical style. On the one hand, the public performer was successful to the extent that he was a brilliant executant, able to astonish audiences by his technical skill; this required music that not only *was* difficult, but that also *sounded* difficult. On the other hand, music to be played in the home had to be quite different: within the range of the amateur with a limited technique and a limited amount of time for practice. While both requirements could of course be met by music of high artistic quality, the two pressures created two corresponding temptations—to write for the virtuoso music full of musically empty technical display; and to write for the amateur music that was not only simple (in terms of technique), but also simple-minded.

This problem was not wholly new, but its intensity was. In the eighteenth century the gap between the professional and the amateur had not been so wide, and Mozart could write for his pupils music that he would not disdain playing himself. Now, however, much of Haydn and Mozart was too difficult for a mediocre amateur, and little of their work was brilliant enough to satisfy the true virtuoso. That the nineteenth century produced an abnormal amount of music that had ephemeral success but little value is not surprising—most of the music produced in any age is less than great. But the distinction became almost intentional. There were composers who hardly pretended to be taken seriously as composers—who were, rather, artisans: successful makers of products that happened to be in demand.

Some men successfully combined careers as virtuoso performers with distinguished accomplishments as composers. Among these was Muzio Clementi (1752-1832), an Italian who spent most of his life in England. Although some of Clementi's work is of minor importance, he contributed to the repertoire a number of fine piano sonatas which, in addition to their purely musical qualities, show great inventiveness in their treatment of the instrument. Beethoven was acquainted with Clementi's music, and may well have been influenced by it.

While there were other men comparable to Clementi, there were all too many composers of the artisan type. In consequence, the truly serious composer, especially if he was not a virtuoso, found himself in a difficult position. In the very instant of his liberation from the often relatively enlightened patronage of the church or the aristocracy, he was delivered into the hands of the lower standards of the middle class, to compete with far inferior but sometimes more attractive products. The isolation of the artist had begun: it seemed at times as if only he and perhaps a few friends could be the judges of a new work.

Early Nineteenth-Century Opera.   Opera, at least in its comic forms, had been a leader in the transition from Baroque to classical style in the middle of the eighteenth century. It did not play the same role in the change from classicism to romanticism. The loss of aristocratic patronage had strengthened the need for opera to be commercially viable, and, partly for this reason, opera remained at first relatively conservative. For reasons not entirely clear, Paris gradually became the European capital of opera, and the Parisian public the arbiter of operatic taste. For any opera composer, a success in Paris was necessary for success in general.

Gluck had had his greatest successes in Paris, and the Gluckian type of opera, composed by lesser but honorable composers, predominated for a time. Gradually, however, public interest changed, partly because of the growing romantic spirit, and even more because of the violent events of the French revolution. The tribulations of an Iphigenia or an Alcestis were nowhere near as exciting as the adventures that many men and women sitting in the theater had themselves actually experienced. Thus there arose the aptly named "rescue operas," on libretti rich in hair-raising pursuits and escapes—not a few of which were taken from the realities of recent history. In fact, Beethoven's *Fidelio* is an opera of just this type—the artistic, if not the popular culmination of the genre.

Opera in France

In France, one of the best of the rescue operas was *Les deux journeés* (1800), by the Gallicized Italian Luigi Cherubini (1760-1842), a composer for whom Beethoven had great respect. Technically it is an opéra comique, for it uses spoken dialogue and melodrama (spoken words with orchestral accompaniment); but it draws on the formal resources of the serious opera as well, and combines an exciting plot with well-made music.

About the time rescue operas were in vogue, the public ceremonies of the new French Republic (and later, the Empire) produced a demand for what might be called public music: works of massive sonority for outdoor use in large public places, yet in part simple enough for the populace to contribute at least the singing of refrains or the like. There was a natural tendency for the sonorous excitement of such music to find a place for itself in the narrative excitement of the rescue opera (without public participation, of course), and for these two ingredients to combine also with spectacular stage effects and virtuoso singing, creating an opera in which every element was intensified to the uttermost limit.

Grand opera: Gasparo Spontini

The result of this combination was "grand opera"—grand in both good and bad senses of the word. The first work of this type was *La vestale* (1807), by Gasparo Spontini, an Italian who spent a number of years in Paris, and later worked in Germany. Except for its setting—classical Rome—*La vestale* is in every other respect modern, combining a rescue-type plot with great scenic and musical opulence. Its success founded a tradition of grand opera that dominated the operatic scene in France—and strongly influenced developments in Italy—for much of the nineteenth century. Hardly any works of this type are now performed. They were written to satisfy the taste of their time, and taste has changed since then.

Giacomi Meyerbeer

The most successful composer of grand opera was Giacomo Meyerbeer (born Jakob Beer; 1791-1864), who, after a period of relative obscurity in Germany and one of considerable success in Italy, came to Paris to produce his most characteristic—and popular—operas. In them, real and original beauty is inextricably mixed with equally real vulgarity. His first work for the Parisian stage, *Robert le diable* (1831), mingles romantic subject matter, Italianate melody, dramatic recitative, brilliant orchestration, and scenic display in a fashion designed to please and to overwhelm the middle class audience for which it was written. In this and in later works, while the best passages are very fine indeed, one feels that Meyerbeer often adopts a style, not as a result of any inner necessity, but because popular success lay in that direction. If Meyerbeer failed as a serious composer, perhaps it was because he succeeded so well at the box office.

Characteristics of French opera

Structurally, the serious French opera of the early nineteenth century carried on, to some extent at least, the tradition of Gluck. Recitative was regularly accompanied by the orchestra, often in highly dramatic fashion; and the musical forms were generally flexible enough to accommodate themselves to the dramatic action. While the formal aria was by no means absent, the typical unit of organization was a larger section, in which recitative, arioso, instrumental sections, and choral passages might all occur, always, however, leading up to a formal musical number—either an aria or an ensemble, as the occasion might demand.

Paris also continued to cultivate the opéra comique—not necessarily a "comic" opera, but one that used spoken dialogue and required less elaborate resources. Ultimately the opéra comique split into two quite distinct sub-types: one was frankly humorous or parodistic; the other serious and sentimental (such works might bear the subtitle "lyric tragedy"). However serious the latter might be, however, they were "comique" in the technical sense of using spoken dialogue, and were never performed at the Opéra—the chief opera house of Paris, which admitted only works sung throughout.

Opera, of whatever type, soon came to dominate French musical life, and continued that domination until 1870 and beyond. While there were instrumental concerts as well, only one French composer of the early nineteenth century—Hector Berlioz (who is discussed in the next chapter)—contributed significantly to the instrumental repertoire, and he was not much esteemed by the French.

France therefore built up a solid musical culture centered around opera, and one that was influential in shaping operatic developments in other countries. But it was a culture tainted by commercialism, and produced little of lasting value.

That opera should have been the predominant musical genre in early nineteenth-century Italy is hardly surprising: it had been since the 1640s. In the late eighteenth and early nineteenth centuries operatic forms and styles underwent predictable changes. Opera seria in the conventional manner was in large measure extinct by 1800. Yet while the theoretical reforms of Gluck were not much imitated in Italy, some of the same objects had gradually been achieved in practice: rigid alternation of recitative and aria was replaced by more flexible dramatic forms that allowed for ensemble and choral participation. As in French opera, the basic dramatic unit was often an entire scene, rather than a single recitative-aria pairing. Still, attention was focused primarily on the virtuoso singer, and in general opera in Italy remained relatively conservative.

Italian opera

After the turn of the century, signs of romantic influence began to appear. At first this influence was evident only in the choice of subject matter, but later it appeared in certain musical elements, such as coloristic harmony and orchestration. The visual spectacle, so important in French grand opera, was not, however, so prominent in Italy. Opera was performed in all the major Italian cities, as well as many of the minor ones, and it was naturally impossible for every opera house to possess scenic resources comparable to the Opéra at Paris. The prudent composer therefore avoided calling for effects that would have severely limited the distribution of his work.

The most successful operatic figure of the early nineteenth century was Gioacchino Rossini (1792-1868), who, after a brilliant career in both serious and comic opera in Italy (his comic masterpiece, *The Barber of Seville* [1816], is still performed today), settled in Paris. There, after he had composed one grand opera in the French manner, *William Tell* (1829), he abandoned opera altogether. His works, however, exerted enormous influence all over Europe, for Rossini had all the gifts necessary for popular success: the ability to write catchy melodies that would stick in the memory of the audience; a sure orchestral hand; and an even surer sense of what was theatrically effective. Yet, although he courted and enjoyed popular success, he was no mere hack, and his music is always well made and often distinguished.

Gioacchino Rossini

One of Rossini's chief contemporaries was Gaetano Donizetti (1797-1848), a facile and popular composer whose music is primarily dominated by vocal melody. Donizetti's chief gift was an ability to invent tunes that aptly mirrored the emotional states of his characters, and at the same time, allowed for full display of the virtuosity of the singers. His most famous opera, *Lucia di Lammermoor* (1835), contains certain romantic elements as well. The libretto is adapted from Sir Walter Scott, and is consequently romantic in subject matter. While the musical style does not always succeed in expressing the romantic spirit, certain techniques—notably the dramatically motivated recurrence of the same materials in different parts of the opera—are decidedly progressive.

Gaetano Donizetti and Vincenzo Bellini

More important was Vincenzo Bellini (1801-35), a serious composer of discriminating musical taste. While Bellini too was primarily a melodist, capable of writing elegant and deeply expressive arias, he was also a master of powerful declamatory recitative. *Norma* (1831), his most famous work, is notable for its romantically exotic setting (Gaul in the time of the Druids); for its flexible dramatic forms, based on the large-scale scene, containing a mixture of recitative, aria, ensemble, and sometimes chorus; and for the truly romantic style of much of the music. Bellini's enlarged harmonic vocabulary and often highly colored orchestration are well suited to his romantic subject matter.

Like Rossini and Donizetti, Bellini often followed the old tradition of writing his operas with specific singers in mind, tailoring the parts to fit their special abilities (or even limitations). Since many of the singers involved were apparently of extraordinary ability, this has naturally created difficulties in modern performances of such works, since singers able to cope with the virtuoso parts are by no means easy to find. Nevertheless, some works by all three composers have remained in the repertoire, and others have been recently and successfully revived.

While Italian opera of the early nineteenth century did not represent the forefront of advanced musical thought, it did produce a repertoire of works that provided, especially in the relative freedom of their dramatic forms, a solid basis for the subsequent achievement of one of the greatest of all opera composers: Giuseppe Verdi. If it seems surprising that Italian opera derived so little from the achievement of Haydn and Mozart (to say nothing of Beethoven), this was not the result of indifference. Vocal melody was still the essence of opera in Italy, and symphonic styles and procedures were not yet necessary for dramatic purposes.

German-speaking Countries: Weber, Schubert, and Mendelssohn. Like Italy, Germany was politically divided in the early nineteenth century, with a further division between the Protestant north and the Roman Catholic south. The Austrian Empire, German-speaking in Austria itself, was as a whole an uneasy ethnic mixture, loosely held together by a weakening central authority in Vienna. While Italy achieved a more or less homogeneous musical style—in opera, which alone was important there—such homogeneity was less to be expected in the German-speaking areas. Cultural differences were greater, and the classical tradition weighed most heavily on German and Austrian composers, provoking diverse reactions. Moreover, no single genre predominated, as opera did in Italy. Hence German music (i.e., music of German-speaking composers) of the early nineteenth century became extremely diverse. The three major composers to be treated in the following pages—Carl Maria von Weber (1786-1826), Franz Schubert (1797-1828), and Felix Mendelssohn-Bartholdy (1809-47), all of whose careers overlapped that of Beethoven to some extent—differ from each other far more strikingly than do Donizetti, Rossini, and Bellini.

Carl Maria von Weber

Weber, the oldest of the three, naturally stood closest to the classical tradition. He passed his earlier years moving from one musical center to another, writing music of all sorts, vocal and instrumental, as occasion demanded. Much of it was frankly virtuoso music, either for himself (he was a pianist) or for other performers, and relatively little of it is played today.

Der Freischütz

It was, however, Weber's good fortune and good sense to hit upon an idea for a truly German and truly romantic opera (or singspiel, to be more precise), *Der Freischütz* (1821). The story is a tissue of romantic motives: good and evil magic, true love, a benevolent ruler, a happy peasantry, and a strong emphasis on Nature, in both its enchanting and horrifying aspects.

Although E. T. A. Hoffmann (1776-1822), a major romantic literary figure as well as a composer, had presented his *Undine*, an opera with an equally romantic libretto, only five years earlier, he had relatively little success. The music of *Undine* is well made, but not as romantic in style as the subject matter, nor of a sort likely to appeal to a wide audience. Weber's *Freischütz*, in contrast, became immediately and broadly popular. It satisfied the desire for an opera that was both thoroughly romantic and thoroughly

German (the latter in part a nationalistic reaction to the extensive importation of Italian opera in Germany and Austria). But the popularity of *Freischütz* was even more the consequence of Weber's musico-dramatic gift, which in this work came for the first time to complete fruition.

In its use of spoken dialogue, melodrama, and folk-like songs and choruses, *Freischütz* stands squarely in the singspiel tradition (although there are also elements from other operatic styles, particularly the French). Weber's particular contribution was his ability to write dramatically evocative music—music that is essentially romantic in spirit. The most celebrated example of this is the Wolf's Glen Scene (Act II, Scene 2). Here, in an eerie midnight landscape populated by unseen evil spirits, magic bullets are cast with the aid of diabolical spells. Weber combines evocative scoring and harmony, weird sounds from an unseen chorus, with deliberately harsh and discordant spoken dialogue. The recurrence in this (and other scenes) of material from the overture is another instance of the increasing interest in giving music an independent dramatic role in opera: recurrent themes can by themselves remind the spectators of what has gone before, and even foreshadow what is yet to come.[1]

Also notable in the score of *Freischütz* is the musical differentiation made among different social classes. Servants and peasants receive, for the most part, folk-like tunes (Ex. XII-7a), while the more important characters are given material deriving from the serious operatic-symphonic tradition (Ex. XII-7b).

A comparison of Weber's work with what Beethoven was doing at the same time is illuminating. Beethoven also was exploring recondite harmonic and instrumental effects—in the interests of profound, abstract musical structures. Weber's novelties were hardly more extreme, and certainly less profound, but they were turned outwards, as it were, to the audience—made palpable as brilliant musical colors. For in fact color, whether expressed in terms of orchestral sounds or of harmonic effect, stands—along with fine melodic invention—as a primary ingredient in the success of *Der Freischütz*.

Weber next set to work on a German opera that would be sung throughout: a true grand opera in the French and Italian form, but in the German spirit. The result was *Euryanthe* (1823), a romantic tale of medieval chivalry, spiced with heavy doses of the supernatural. Here Weber makes further use of recurrent musical means—themes, instrumental colors, and key areas—to identify characters or recurrent ideas of the plot. Although *Euryanthe* was not a public success, it is an important work, not only intrinsically, but in its attempt to give to opera at least the beginnings of an overall unity—an

Weber's later operas

Ex. XII-7 (a)

[1]In point of fact, the overture was probably written after the opera was completed: Weber used melodies from the opera as themes for the overture (a common practice in the nineteenth century). But to the spectator, who hears the overture first, it appears that scenes in the opera were prefigured by the overture.

Kommt ein schlanker Bursch ge-gan-gen,

Should a slender lad come along

(b)

blond von Lo-cken o-der braun,

süss   ent – zückt   ent - - ge - - - gen

blond or brown-haired.   Ex. XII-7(a)

ihm,   süss ___ ent – –zückt ent – ge – – gen ihm!

Cello

Sweetly enraptured by him.

Ex. XII-7(b)

attempt continued in Weber's last work, *Oberon* (1826). While *Der Freischütz* was the progenitor of a respectable but relatively minor school of German opera, the two later operas pointed the way towards the all-important work of Richard Wagner.

Franz Schubert   The second of these three German composers, Franz Schubert (1797-1828), was a Viennese, who passed his life, relatively unrenowned, in his native city, pouring out music with the precocity and the abundance of Mozart. Like Weber, he was still enough of a classicist to write in almost all genres, vocal and instrumental, sacred and secular. His most characteristic vehicle, however, was the song (Ger., *Lied*; pl., *Lieder*) with piano accompaniment. The German Lied had been extensively cultivated in the second half of the eighteenth century, but little music of importance had been produced. The traditional form was strophic: a simple folk-like melody, with simple accompaniment, repeated for each stanza of a poem. While Schubert was by no means the only composer of his time to raise this modest product to the level of a serious art form, he was by far the greatest, and his Lieder became the model for future song composers of the century.

Schubert's Lieder output—over 600 songs—is so various as to defy generalization. His choice of texts ranges from the poetry of Goethe to trivial rhymes of no literary importance. The range of forms is almost as great. Some songs are purely strophic; some are basically strophic, but incorporate alterations that render the music more suitable to the poetic content in later stanzas; some are cast in ABA form or in some similar pattern; and some again are through-composed, that is, they follow no set pattern, but develop freely according to musical and textual needs.

Schubert's Lieder

Schubert's treatment of the accompaniment is similarly various. More often than not, it is clearly subordinate to the vocal line, and consists mainly in the repetition of one or two rhythmic-harmonic figures. Yet Schubert's ingenuity in the invention of such figures was enormous: they range from simple chord-repetition to complex and expressive piano parts that pose a real challenge to the performer. Occasionally the piano takes the primary role, leaving the voice with little more than a declamatory line. There are even songs that are clearly operatic in concept, in which the piano represents an entire orchestra, and in which traditional recitative and aria types are present.

Fig. XII-2: Moritz von Schwind, "A Schubert evening." Schubert is shown at the piano. (Vienna, Wiener Schubertbund.)

What is common to all of the Lieder is the perfect matching of music and text, usually by means of exquisite and appropriate melody, but in some of the more dramatic songs, by other methods as well. The celebrated *Erlkönig* (Elf-king; 1815) is a setting of a ballad by Goethe, which tells of a father riding home through the night, his sick child in his arms. The child hears—but the father does not—the at first enticing, then menacing words of the Elf-king, who invites him to the pleasures of the afterlife. The

Who rides so late, through night and wind?   Ex. XII-8(a)

You lovely child, come with me; lovely games . . .

Ex. XII-8(b)

poem ends with the child's death. Schubert's setting creates a fundamental tension at once, in the constant throbbing of the accompaniment (Ex. XII-8a), which represents the horse's hoofbeats. Only when the Elf-king speaks does the music become truly lyrical, but in a sinister way; at the same time, the accompaniment changes to a seductive strumming (Ex. XII-8b). The sudden change to a major key paradoxically intensifies the chilling effect. The tragic conclusion is set to a couple of measures of recitative, a simple but overwhelming effect.

At the opposite pole stands *Wer ist Sylvia* ("Who is Sylvia?" translated from Shakespeare; 1826), in which almost all of the interest is centered in the lyrical voice part, with the piano contributing only the harmony, a little rhythmic figure, and an occasional echo of the melody (Ex. XII-9).

Ex. XII-9

Most of Schubert's songs are separate entities, but late in life he composed important cycles of songs—groups of up to twenty-four songs that were intended to be performed complete and in proper order. The songs in the cycles do not differ in technique from the separate songs, nor are the cycles unified by musical interconnections or quotations. In the last group (*Schwanengesang*; 1828), even the texts are unrelated (indeed there is considerable question whether Schubert considered this set a cycle or merely a collection of unrelated songs). But the cycle *Die Winterreise* (1827; poems by Wilhelm Müller), with its pictures of the winter journey of an unhappy lover, has an undeniable inner unity, despite the wide range of style, form, and key. Schubert here effortlessly evokes a whole world of unhappy passion, infinitely more intense than that provided by the poet; yet the means often remain extremely simple. The first song, "Gute Nacht," is basically strophic, with simple accompaniment. For the last strophe, Schubert moves from D minor to D major, a favorite device of his; here, as often, it has

Schubert's song cycles

the paradoxical effect of making the major sound even more forlorn than the minor. Almost all of the late songs are of great intensity of feeling, and many are no more than two pages long. Schubert's refined melodic and harmonic sense reached a peak of effectiveness in these works, which alone would have served to secure for him a place as one of the great composers.

Schubert was, however, much more than a writer of songs. Although already conscious of the overwhelming legacy of Haydn, Mozart, and especially Beethoven, he wrote symphonies, string quartets, piano sonatas, and other works, not competing with, but continuing in the classical tradition as he understood it. Of the symphonies, the last two are undisputed masterpieces, representing opposite extremes of Schubert's art.

Schubert's instrumental music: the last two symphonies

The Eighth, or "Unfinished," Symphony (1822) consists of only two movements: an Allegro in B minor and a slow movement in E major. This key sequence suggests that Schubert had not planned a two-movement work like Beethoven's piano sonata Opus 111 (introduction and allegro in C minor; slow variations in C major). Moreover, Schubert made a piano sketch of the beginning of a scherzo in B minor, but did not orchestrate it. Nothing is known of his plans, if any, for a finale. Whether Schubert regarded the two completed movements, despite their difference in key, as a "finished" symphony is something that will doubtless never be known; but audiences have always accepted it as such. It is essentially a tragic and romantic work, in which the lyrical world of the Lied is somehow reconciled with the dramatic world of the symphony.

The last symphony, in C major (1828; usually called the "great C major," and variously numbered 7, 9, and 10), is a spiritual descendant, not of Beethoven, but of Mozart's "Jupiter" symphony—proud and vigorous, filled with tension and climax, and yet untinged by autobiography. It is one of the last representatives of the world of pure music—music that exists for its own sake alone. Its overall structure is wholly classical in sequence and types of movements, and nearly so in key relationships. While it is thus a true—and fully worthy—successor to the classical symphonic tradition, it also contains clearly romantic elements. The first notes of the slow introduction, a simple melody scored for two horns in unison, unaccompanied, are already romantic in atmosphere; for the horn, by its association with the hunt and the outdoors in general, is the romantic instrument par excellence (Weber had made similar use of its evocative power). Later in the first movement, Schubert combines harmonic with sonorous means to create another magical effect: a theme played quietly at first by the trombones in the remote key of A♭ minor, that works its way to a climax for full orchestra in the orthodox dominant.

Classicism and romanticism in Schubert

For all its harmonic and sonorous richness, however, the C major symphony is basically a classically oriented work, just as the "Unfinished" is primarily a romantic one. The same fluctuating allegiance may be seen as one surveys Schubert's considerable output of chamber music. The "Trout" quintet, for piano, violin, viola, 'cello, and string bass (1819; so named because one of the movements is a set of variations on Schubert's song of that title), belongs to the tradition of "pure" music; while the "Death and the Maiden" string quartet (1826; so titled for the same reason) is fiercely personal and passionate.

Yet certain technical means remain relatively constant in Schubert's mature instrumental music, whatever their expressive purpose. His treatment of form seems on the surface to be thoroughly classical: one finds movements in sonata form; scherzos (or minuets) with trios; rondos; variations; and other traditional types. Closer examination, however, shows that, in the sonata-form movements at least, Schubert's methods are rather different from those of his predecessors. It is not, of course, surprising to find keys other than the dominant used for the second part of the exposition: this is common in Beethoven and not unknown even earlier. But Schubert often firmly establishes a new key (the mediant, for example), only to abandon it eventually in favor of the dominant. Such is the case in the C major symphony, where the first "new key" is E minor, which is maintained for some time before yielding to G major. Thus the exposition can be a three-key rather than a two-key section, with the implication that the recapitulation will contain two keys rather than one (ending, of course, in the tonic). While there is also precedent for this in late Beethoven, Schubert's usage is more extensive and more frequent.

There are also subtle changes in the nature of the development section. While it is often asserted that Schubert's developments suffer because his predominantly lyrical themes are unsuitable for development in the classical manner, this statement is refuted both by classical movements with lyrical themes (Mozart's G minor symphony, first movement), and by many of Schubert's own developments. Yet is is true that in some of his weaker movements, the developments are somewhat mechanical and repetitive. One has the feeling that Schubert has made his important points in the exposition, and that development is more of an obligation than a musical necessity.

This is a sign—although still only a faint and intermittent one—that classical form, and sonata form in particular, was on the way to being treated as a kind of abstract pattern, a rule that should normally be obeyed, rather than as simply the way in which a first movement was ordinarily written. Such a change of attitude was more or less inevitable once the concept of a repertoire of great music by classical composers had developed. One could not write a new symphony or sonata without remembering, at least, how the "masters" had written such works, and one would have to have good reason for rejecting their solutions. Schubert was fortunate in living as early as he did, for the process was just beginning. He could for the most part accept or modify inherited forms at his pleasure: the age of self-conscious confrontation with the classics (and especially with Beethoven) was yet to come.

If Schubert was essentially rather conservative with regard to form, the same cannot be said of his treatment of harmony (nor, of course, of melody, but his melody cannot be described—only experienced). Some of his harmonic devices have already been mentioned—the use of third-related keys, for example, and the frequent alternation between major and minor on the same tonic. But these are only fragments of Schubert's harmonic ability, which combined effortless modulation to the remotest keys with small-scale (often chromatic) effects involving only two or three chords. His ability to exploit the evocative, coloristic qualities of harmony created a warmth of harmonic feeling hitherto unknown. During precisely the same years, Beethoven also was expanding the harmonic domain, but with a different purpose: Beethoven explored the vast territory of harmony as a cartographer, intent on bending his discoveries to the service of form. Schubert was a traveler—a collector of exotic and exquisite harmonic specimens to be naturalized and used for expressive purposes.

Schubert's harmonic language

Certain other categories of Schubert's music remain to be mentioned. The first is opera, in which he was consistently unsuccessful, partly because hardly anyone could compete with the vogue of Rossini in Vienna, and partly because Schubert was not really at home in extended dramatic situations. He could compress a whole drama into

Other Schubert works

two pages of a song, but on the stage he was not comfortable. The second category is church music, especially the Masses, of which the best (those in E♭ and A♭) are worthy descendants of Haydn's late Masses.

The third is a rather miscellaneous repertoire of piano music (apart from the sonatas). Schubert wrote a number of dances, marches, variations, and the like for piano (often for piano duet), many of which are very fine, but of limited historical importance. More characteristic for the future are two small groups of independent piano pieces, six *Moments musicaux* (Musical Moments) and eleven *Impromptus*, all written in the last few years of his life. The neutral titles are suggestive: these are not monumental works in the sonata tradition, but spontaneous lyrical pieces—the first group short and episodic, the second longer and more complex. Quite apart from their intrinsic value they are, with Beethoven's late *Bagatelles*, among the earliest representatives of a new genre, in which the composer, not bound by any formal prescription, confides to the piano his intimate thoughts, in apparently casual (although in fact carefully wrought) manner. One might compare them with the entries in a skillful writer's diaries—records, seemingly spontaneous, of thoughts and impressions.

Schubert's work thus consists of two sorts of music—the intensely personal on the one hand, and the "purely musical" on the other. This is by no means new, of course: the same types may be found in Beethoven and even in Haydn and Mozart. But Schubert was the last great composer who could comfortably inhabit both worlds. After him the doors of unconscious classicism began to close.

This last statement may appear to be contradicted by the career of the last composer to be considered in this chapter, Felix Mendelssohn-Bartholdy (1809-47). But if many of Mendelssohn's works are as classical as any of Schubert's, the other world—that of the intensely subjective—was largely closed to him: there is nothing of his that can be compared to the "Unfinished" symphony or the "Death and the Maiden" quartet. Mendelssohn, the precocious son of a wealthy and cultured family, grew up with every educational advantage. He made his first public appearance as a pianist at the age of nine, and was an accomplished composer by his teens. Throughout the rest of his short life, he enjoyed public acclaim, and his wealth provided him with more material comforts than most composers have had.

His precocity at once suggests an analogy with Mozart, with whom his admirers compared him, and the analogy is not without some basis in fact. He wrote easily and well in all the current genres of composition except opera, thereby continuing the classical tradition of universality. He produced symphonies, concertos, chamber music, sonatas, oratorios, and other works as well, all of them assured in technique and style, and many of them very distinguished indeed. Even the lesser pieces are well made: it is merely that there is a certain blandness—a lack of urgency—in their musical substance.

Still, while the composer of such impressive pieces as the Octet for Strings (1826) and the Concerto for Violin in E minor (1844) need stand aside for nobody, it is Mendelssohn's more romantic vein that is important historically. This shows clearly in such pieces as the concert overtures, intended as preludes to spoken plays, or as isolated concert pieces (Beethoven had written overtures of this sort). In pieces such as the *Fingal's Cave* overture, and in the overture and incidental music to Shakespeare's *Midsummer Night's Dream*, Mendelssohn carries on from Beethoven's Sixth Symphony, emphasizing atmosphere rather than tone-painting, but with richer and more highly colored harmony and scoring. Especially brilliant is his treatment of the fairy

Felix Mendelssohn-Bartholdy

Romantic aspect of Mendelssohn's music

music in *Midsummer Night's Dream*, a style in which he excelled, and which also appears in some of his abstract music (e.g., the scherzo of the Octet).

The concert overtures are specifically designed to suggest extra-musical concepts; and some of Mendelssohn's symphonies bear programmatic titles—"Scotch," "Italian," "Reformation." While extra-musical content does not yet seriously influence the basis of Mendelssohn's manner of writing—it provides little more than a veneer of "local color"—the increasingly close association of music with verbal concepts and visual effects should be noted, for it is a tendency that later composers were to carry much farther.

Prophetic in a different way were Mendelssohn's *Songs without Words*. These are short pieces for piano solo, very much in the manner of a song: each presents a lyrical melody with appropriate accompaniment, for which the listener himself may imagine the proper sentiment (the lacking "words"). They are roughly analogous to Schubert's *Moments musicaux*, although Mendelssohn's pieces are even more song-like than Schubert's. Their importance lies not in their musical content, which is generally slight, but in their contrast to works involving the sonata principle. The latter type, even when relatively short or lyrical, is a complex architectural construction. Pieces like the *Songs without Words* are by contrast microcosms, in which all that is needed is melody and harmony: the form is simply that of the melody itself. The contrast between the two types of composition is basic for the nineteenth century. Mendelssohn and Schubert were perhaps the last composers for whom both modes of expression were equally natural.

Out of the rest of Mendelssohn's considerable output, mention should be made of his oratorios, especially admired by the English, for whom Mendelssohn became a model composer for most of the century. The oratorios are perhaps most notable for their exceptional choral writing, although they also contain scenes of considerable dramatic force. Mendelssohn also wrote a number of choral works for German choral societies, as well as other works, both vocal and instrumental, intended primarily for amateur musicians. By providing well-made music of various types for non-professionals, he helped to raise general musical standards.

Mendelssohn was important in two areas other than composition. He was one of the first truly professional conductors in the modern sense—not mere time-beaters, but interpreters of orchestral music. The famous Leipzig Gewandhaus concerts, under his direction, set new standards for the performance of both classical and new music. He was also one of the first "practical musicologists." Like his classical predecessors, he came to know and admire the music of J. S. Bach and, like them, absorbed some Bachian elements into his own style. But Mendelssohn went further: he prepared and conducted a public performance of Bach's St. Matthew Passion (1829), thus taking the first step in acquainting the general public with the forgotten glories of Baroque music.

This added a new element to the general tendency towards preservation of earlier music: the repertoire began to be expanded backwards in time, in a process that is only now being completed (and now being supplemented by an expansion in space so as to include music of other cultures). Henceforth the "growing past" was an increasing factor in the thought of almost all composers.

Summary. There is no single unifying thread that connects the wide variety of musical types considered in this chapter. Indeed, it is characteristic of the early nineteenth

Songs without words

Mendelssohn's oratorios

Other aspects of Mendelssohn's career

century that each composer reacted individually to the circumstances of his times. Certain recurrent problems can be observed—the virtuoso-amateur dualism; the potential conflict between self-fulfillment and public success; the weight of the Beethovenian legacy; and the degree to which a composer was willing to allow the novelties of Romantic subjectivism to influence normal classical procedures—but even these did not affect all composers (e.g., it is difficult to see any way in which Donizetti was a "problematic" composer).

Yet new attitudes were in the air, especially among the Germans, and one of the more important of these is also among the most elusive. It concerns a change in the relation between purely musical thinking as contrasted to conceptual thinking applied to music. While all composers think primarily "in music"—as Frenchmen think in French—so that their basic musical ideas are patterns of tones, they differ in the extent to which they subject these ideas to conscious conceptual patterns. In the sixteenth century, such a concept as parody is clearly put to deliberate intellectual use. Throughout the Baroque, from the theoretically generated recitative of the first operas to Bach's *Art of the Fugue*, conceptualization plays an important part. This of course is neither good nor bad, nor—more important—may one equate intellectually controlled music with expressive neutrality. Baroque composers frequently chose a highly intellectual device, the basso ostinato, for expressive climaxes.

For this writer, at least, the classical period appears as one in which purely musical thinking was paramount (especially, perhaps, in Mozart). The classical musical idea generated the entire work with a minimum of conceptual intervention. Already in late Beethoven there are signs of change: the quotation of earlier themes in the finale of the Ninth Symphony is clearly an intellectual idea, not a musical necessity. So also are the recurrent, character-related themes in Weber's operas, and, in a different way, so is the idea of form as an abstract pattern to be filled by new "content," as in some works of Schubert. Yet these instances are only a beginning. It is a paradox of romanticism that the search for more intensely personal means of expression regularly led to increased reliance on non-musical concept.

APPENDIX: Chapter XII

I. **The works of Ludwig van Beethoven.** (In this and following tables, pf. is the abbreviation for piano. Keys are indicated where useful: a capital letter indicates a major key, a lower case letter a minor key.)

A. Symphonic works.

Symphonies (9)
1. Op. 21, C
2. Op. 36, D
3. Op. 55, E♭ (Eroica)
4. Op. 60, B♭
5. Op. 67, c
6. Op. 68, F (Pastoral)
7. Op. 92, A
8. Op. 93, F
9. Op. 125, d

Concertos
5 piano concertos: Op. 15 (C); Op. 19 (B♭); Op. 37 (c); Op. 58 (G); Op. 73 (E♭; "Emperor")
Violin concerto in D, Op. 61
Triple concerto (vln., 'cello, pf.), C, Op. 56

Overtures
Leonore overtures nos. 1, 2, and 3
Overture to *Coriolanus*, Op. 62
"Birthday" overture, Op. 115
"Wellington's Victory," Op. 91

Incidental music
to *Egmont*, Op. 84
to *The Ruins of Athens*, Op. 113
to *King Stephen*, Op. 117

Ballet *The Creatures of Prometheus*, Op. 43

B. Solo piano music.
32 piano sonatas, spanning his whole career
21 sets of variations, including "Diabelli" variations, Op. 120
Collections of Bagatelles, Opp. 33, 119, 126
A number of individual pieces

C. Chamber music.

String quartets
Early: Op. 18, six quartets, F, G, D, c, A, B♭
Middle: Op. 59 (the "Rasoumovsky" quartets), F, e, C; Op. 74 (the "Harp" quartet), E♭; Op. 95, f
Late: Opp. 127 (E♭), 132 (a), 130 (B♭), 133 (B♭, "Grosse Fuge"), 131 (c♯), 135 (F)

String trios
  Op. 3
  Op. 9, three trios, G, D, c
Piano trios
  Op. 1, three trios, E♭, G, c
  Op. 11, clarinet (or vln.) trio
  Op. 70, two trios, D, E♭
  Op. 97 ("Archduke" trio), B♭
Piano and wind quintet, Op. 16
Septet, Op. 20
Solo sonatas
  Violin sonatas: 3 sonatas Op. 12 (D, A, E♭); Op. 23 (A); Op. 24 (F); 3 sonatas
    Op. 30 (A, c, G); Op. 47 (A, "Kreutzer"); Op. 96 (G)
  5 'cello sonatas: 2 sonatas Op. 5 (F, g); Op. 69 (A); 2 sonatas Op. 102 (C, D)
  Horn sonata, Op. 17

D. Vocal music.

Opera *Fidelio*, Op. 72
Oratorio *Christus am Ölberg*, Op. 85
Mass in C major, Op. 86
Missa solemnis in D, Op. 123
Cantatas *Die glorreiche Augenblick*, Op. 136, and *Meeresstille und glückliche Fahrt*, Op. 112
Many songs, including the cycle *An die ferne Geliebte*, Op. 98
Many arrangements of Irish, Scottish, etc., folk-songs

II.   Brief notices on some composers of the early 19th century.

Auber, Daniel-François-Esprit (1782–1871). French composer of opéra comique (*Le maçon*, 1825; *Le dieu et la bayardière*, 1830; *Le cheval de bronze*, 1857) and of the enormously popular grand opera *La muette de Portici* (also called *Masaniello*, 1828).

Bellini, Vincenzo (1801–35). Italian composer of 10 serious operas in aristocratic, lyrical style. *La sonnambula* (The Sleepwalker, 1831); *Norma* (1831); *I puritani e i cavalieri* (The Puritans and the Cavaliers, 1835).

Cherubini, Luigi (1760–1842). Italian-born composer whose work and influence were mostly in France, where he directed the Paris Conservatoire. He composed operas (*Médée*, 1797; *Les deux journées*, 1800) and much sacred music.

Clementi, Muzio (1752–1832). Italian pianist and composer who worked in London. Composer of sonatas, études (*Gradus ad Parnassum*), and virtuoso piano music; he also manufactured pianos.

Donizetti, Gaetano (1797–1848). Prolific Italian composer, principally of operas. *L'elisir d'amore* (The Elixir of Love, 1832); *Lucrezia Borgia* (1833); *Lucia di Lammermoor* (1835); *La fille du régiment* (The Daughter of the Regiment, 1840); *Linda de Chamounix* (1842); *Don Pasquale* (1843).

Field, John (1782–1837). Irish pianist and composer. Along with other piano music, his 18 nocturnes had considerable influence on Chopin and other 19th-century composers.

Halévy, Jacques Fromental (1799–1862). French composer of operas. Despite his haste, and his sometimes indiscriminate choice of libretto, his music is often remarkable. *La juive* (1835); *L'éclair* (1835); *La reine de Chypre* (1841).

Hummel, Johann Nepomuk (1778–1837). Hungarian pupil of Mozart; pianist and composer. He published an influential piano treatise, and composed much piano music, chamber music and several concertos and operas.

Mendelssohn, Felix. See appendix to Chapter XIII.

Meyerbeer, Giacomo (1791–1864). German-born composer of French opera; his popularity was enormous, and established the universal fame of French grand opera. *Robert le diable* (1831); *Les huguenots* (1836); *Le prophète* (1849); *L'Africaine* (1865, posth.)

Rossini, Gioacchino (1792–1868). Italian opera composer of enormous popularity and influence. *La scala di seta* (The Silken Ladder, 1812); *Tancredi* (1813); *L'italiana in Algeri* (The Italian Woman in Algiers, 1813); *Otello* (1816); *La cenerentola* (Cinderella, 1817); *Il barbiere di Siviglia* (The Barber of Seville, 1816); *La gazza ladra* (The Thieving Magpie, 1817); *La donna del lago* (The Lady of the Lake, 1819).

Schubert, Franz. See appendix to Chapter XIII.

Spohr, Ludwig (1784–1859). German violinist and composer. A conservative composer, his music sometimes suffers from a repetition of similar ideas. Opera *Jessonda*; orchestral works, including symphonies and violin concertos; chamber music.

Spontini, Gasparo (1774–1851). Italian composer of French operas. In his seriousness a successor to Gluck, he is Meyerbeer's antecedent because of his grand designs.

Weber, Carl Maria von (1786–1826). The best-known composer of German romantic opera: *Der Freischütz* (1821); *Euryanthe* (1823); *Oberon* (1826). Also symphonic music; overtures; piano music; songs.

XIII

THE
ROMANTIC
PERIOD

The first generation of composers committed to romanticism was a highly diversified group, as might be expected from the very nature of romantic principles. Of the six most important composers to be considered, three—Hector Berlioz, Franz Liszt, and Richard Wagner—came the closest to forming a "school:" they espoused many of the same aesthetic principles, furthered each other's work, and considered themselves to be the leading radicals of their day. Two others—Robert Schumann and Frédéric Chopin—were by no means so close to each other: they shared chiefly a certain skepticism about the work of the preceding three, and what might, with some stretching of the term, be called a relative conservatism. Verdi, the only Italian, stands alone.

Robert Schumann.   Of these romantics, Robert Schumann (1810–56) was the closest to the classic tradition (indeed most histories treat Schumann along with Mendelssohn). Destined by his family for the law, he turned passionately to music instead, first aiming for a career as a pianist. An injury to his hand having precluded this, he took up composition. Although he had had little professional instruction, he was bristling with new ideas, over which he acquired control with remarkable rapidity. His substantial output shows signs of a peculiarly nineteenth-century phenomenon: extreme specialization. First came a flood of works for piano solo (Opp. 1–23); then, in 1840 and the years immediately following, an even greater number of Lieder. Thereafter, Schumann's work became more diverse, but he still tended to concentrate on one genre at a time (e.g., all of his three string quartets were written in a few months in 1842).

Schumann's life and works

Schumann shared with most other romantic composers an interest in and talent for literature. In 1842, largely through his efforts, the first issue of the *Neue Zeitschrift für Musik* (New Musical Magazine) appeared, a periodical devoted to combatting prevalent mediocrities and encouraging the performance of serious music, whether of the past or, more especially, of the present. Schumann edited and contributed extensively to the *Neue Zeitschrift* for about ten years, and much of his criticism (however odd it may now seem in its romantic expression) is as valid today as it was when it was written.

Schumann's literary activities

Fig. XIII-1: "The Cross in the Mountains," by Casper David Freidrich (1774-1840). The Romantic motives of untamed Nature and the mysterious are admirably combined in this painting. (Dusseldorf, Kunstmuseum; photograph Landesbildstelle Rheinland.)

The appearance of the *Neue Zeitschrift* was symptomatic. The alienation between composer and audience, begun in Beethoven's time, was increasing. Even the word "new," which had been proudly printed on the title page of a book of sixteenth-century madrigals or of a Haydn symphony, was suspect to the conservative music-lover (the "Philistine," as Schumann called him): to him it meant formlessness, cacophony, lack of melody—all of the attributes that the conservative ascribes to what he does not understand. For the *Neue Zeitschrift*, on the contrary, "new" meant the vitality and excitement of music that represented the contemporary world. While the periodical wielded considerable influence, neither it nor any other force could succeed altogether, and the gap between composer and audience has grown ever deeper —leaving to the former only the cold consolation that generations yet unborn will understand his music (an idea first voiced by Beethoven about his late works).

Like Mendelssohn, Schumann was active in reviving interest in J. S. Bach: both were among the founders of the Bach-Gesellschaft, an organization that ultimately published all of Bach's works. But Schumann also had the good fortune, on a visit to Vienna (1839), to discover a number of unknown Schubert manuscripts, including that of the great C major Symphony—works that might well have otherwise been lost—and to give them the critical recognition that was their due.

Thus, even if he had never composed a note, Schumann would have been an important musical figure; but his compositions are far more important than his critical work. In his first period, as a writer of piano music exclusively (1830–38), he exhibited an extraordinary variety of forms, styles, and techniques. These range from the formally classical (although passionate and lyrical) G minor Sonata (Op. 22; 1838), to the celebrated *Carnaval* (Op. 9; 1834–35), a series of short character pieces, each bearing a fairly specific programmatic title. These latter include "Pierrot," "Harlequin," "Chiarina" (a reference to Clara Wieck, later Schumann's wife), "Chopin" (an imitation of that composer's style), "Florestan," "Eusebius" (Schumann's names for the fiery and dreamy sides of his own temperament), and others. Common to both the large and small works are the brilliance of the piano writing (first-class technique is required almost throughout); the adventurous, often quite dissonant harmony; and sudden contrasts in mood and tonality. A violent rhythmic energy is characteristic of the quick pieces, and an intimate lyricism of the slow ones.

Schumann's early piano works

One of the most important of Schumann's early works is the Fantasy in C (Op. 17; 1836). While there are classical prototypes for the fantasy as a quasi-improvisational piece, usually in only one movement, Schumann had more in mind than this: his thought was of a piece with the length and depth of a sonata, but free from the normal sonata conventions. The result still resembles the sonata plan—a fast first movement, a scherzo, and a slow movement (only the finale is lacking)—but the resemblance is superficial. The very opening (Ex. XIII-1), with its then shocking dissonances and passionate urgency of expression, sets the tone. Out of this Schumann intuitively evolves an ad hoc form that succeeds not because of any outward logic, but by the unanalyzable fitness of the procession of tonalities and themes. The second movement is less eccentric, but the last is less a formal movement than a reverie: it begins with simple arpeggios, out of which themes gradually arise and reach a climax, and into which they ultimately subside. One should not interpret the above as implying a total absence of recognizable form—all three movements have an overall ABA pattern—but rather as proof of Schumann's ability to create large-scale movements without reference to classical formal patterns.

Ex. XIII-1

Schumann's Lieder

    The great outpouring of Lieder that began in 1840 (the year of Schumann's marriage) represents a continuation both of the Schubertian Lied and of Schumann's short character piece—translated to the medium of piano and voice. Schumann's choice of poetry is generally distinguished, and his settings are always meticulously faithful to both the sentiments and rhythms of the poems. While the often quite complex piano parts sometimes take over much of the musical interest, the effect of the majority of the songs still depends primarily on warm vocal lyricism, supported by pungent harmonies and delicate figurations. Schumann wrote many single songs, but some of his best work may be found in the song cycles, notably *Dichterliebe* (Poet's Love; poems by Heinrich Heine) and *Frauenliebe und Leben* (Love and Life of Woman; Adalbert von Chamisso), both from 1840. In the latter cycle, a high degree of unity is obtained, in part from the text, which describes the various stages of a woman's love, from first sight through widowhood; and in part from the music: at the end of the last song, that of bereavement, the piano introduction to the first recurs—a simple but deeply moving effect.

    With his early piano works and his songs, Schumann had established himself as one of the major figures of the romantic movement. His later career was, however, somewhat problematic. His creative power, unlike that of most composers, seems on the whole to have weakened over the years (although the decrease has often been grossly overemphasized by critics). His mental health weakened also, and this decline led ultimately to insanity and death. Yet during these often painful years, Schumann was engaged in what now appears to have been an almost deliberate challenge: an attempt to make a major contribution to every type of composition that the classical masters had cultivated. In this venture Schumann seems to have been encouraged by his wife, herself a celebrated pianist, and by his own admiration for the classicizing Mendelssohn. But while Mendelssohn used the classical genres spontaneously and naturally, Schumann did so as it were from the outside, as a newcomer bent on a deliberate trial of strength. In the end, it may well have been this trial that destroyed his mind; but it was by no means wholly unsuccessful: in these later years Schumann composed symphonies, concertos, chamber music, oratorios, an opera, and various other works, many of which (even among those relatively little known) are among the finest of the period.

It is often remarked that Schumann's music for media other than piano solo or piano and voice is defective in its treatment of the instruments: that his musical thought was so deeply rooted in the piano that he scores even an orchestra in pianistic fashion. There is some truth in this. Many pages in his symphonies and quartets can be read off at the piano far more easily than scores of Beethoven or Mozart, and his symphonies, in particular, are not often especially interesting in terms of pure sound. But there are other pages—in the celebrated Piano Concerto (1841–45), in the opera *Genoveva* (1847–50), or in the passage from the A minor string quartet (Ex. XIII-2; Op. 41, no. 1)—that are as imaginative in their scoring as in their content. It would be better to say that while Schumann often preferred a thick and pianistic scoring, he was capable, when aroused, of treating any medium with great imagination.

In more general terms, Schumann's later works display an odd mixture of relative conservatism sprinkled with startling innovation. The style, on the whole, is less adventurous than that of the early works, in a perhaps conscious deference to classicism. In matters of form, the situation is more complex. From the beginning, Schumann had employed both free forms of his own devising and, less often, clearly clas-

Form in Schumann's late works: intellectual devices in romantic music

(continued on the following pages)   Ex. XIII-2

Ex. XIII-2

sical patterns. Both options remained available in the later works, but there are strong hints that Schumann's later formal thinking is more conscious and less intuitive. Thus the first movement of the Piano Concerto (1841) is clearly an ad hoc structure, owing virtually nothing to classical concerto form—for the good reason that it was at first intended to be complete in itself, a one-movement fantasy for piano and orchestra. It is basically monothematic, as almost all of the themes derive from the motive of the beginning. Four years later, Schumann added the remaining movements; and in the linking of the second with the third (achieved by quoting the principal theme of the *first* movement), one can see a kind of self-conscious rationalizing *about* music quite absent from the first movement.

There are plenty of other examples of such rationalizing in Schumann (and even more in other romantic composers). Thus the first movement of the A minor string quartet begins with a slow introduction, naturally in the tonic. But the Allegro following is in F major, and A minor does not return as a basic tonality until the scherzo and the finale. Of course Schumann knew that the Allegro "should have been" in A minor; but he chose to attempt an experiment instead. Less spectacular but equally indicative is the Fourth Symphony (revised in 1853; the original version, now hardly known, dates from 1841). This is a "cyclic" work, one in which all of the movements are connected by thematic relationships. Some are immediately obvious—like the recurrence of the principal theme of the first movement at the beginning of the last—while others are more subtle (the main theme of the scherzo is an inversion of the first theme of the opening slow introduction); but they have in common an intent—a conscious will to impose overall unity on the work.

It is paradoxical that the romantics, dedicated to intuition and subjectivity, needed so often to rely on intellectual devices (many more of which will be discussed below), while the classical composers did so only rarely. Although there is no full resolution of this paradox, the following observations are relevant: (1) For an intelligent musician, subjectivism brings with it an intellectual curiosity as to the nature and potential use of the subjective material: the mind, focusing on its own experience, can and must consider that experience as an objective fact. (2) The accomplishment of Beethoven literally drove later composers into devising originality—hence into thinking out intellectually new ways of achieving what classical composers had mostly done by musical intuition, not conscious verbal thought. (3) The increase in published musical criticism naturally led musicians into verbal speculation about their own music, and about the music of the past; and indeed the literary orientation of most romantics tended towards the same result. One can hardly imagine Beethoven writing a technical review of some new composition, whereas almost all the romantics did so.

By no means all of Schumann's later works are "planned" in an intellectual fashion. Some appear to be as intuitive as any classical work (the short pieces and the songs are almost invariably of this type). But for Schumann, there were potential dangers either way. An intellectually conceived experiment may work out well musically (as the Fourth Symphony does), or it may not. And in writing intuitive music on a large scale, Schumann, lacking something of the energy that propelled pieces such as the piano fantasy onward, fell back on classical models. His difficulty in writing really effective development sections—the heart of the sonata form—often created weaknesses. Just as in some works of Schubert, one finds developments in Schumann that consist mainly of repetitions of the same material in different keys—a device that may produce attractive moments, but lacks the propulsive tension necessary to an effective sonata movement. It is this that partially justifies the common criticism that Schumann is at his best in his short character pieces for piano and in his songs (and thus, inferentially, in his earlier works).

This judgment appears to be based primarily on the four symphonies, which are frequently performed, and which, despite their great overall value, all lie open to some criticism. Even among musicians, however, there are few who are acquainted with the later works involving voices, such as the opera *Genoveva* (1847–50), the *Requiem for Mignon* (1849), the incidental music to Byron's *Manfred* (1848–49), and the *Scenes from Goethe's Faust* (1844–53). In the first of these, Schumann achieves a flexibility of dramatic form that goes far to redeem an unusually poor libretto: the work is full of strong music, and does not deserve the complete neglect into which it has fallen. The other works cited are perhaps even more successful, and owe rather less to traditional antecedents. It would seem that Schumann was often at his best when his classical models were most subject to radical alteration. In any event, Schumann's last years were productive ones: what he had lost in spontaneous originality he made up (in the best works) in increased breadth and scope.

Chopin's life and works

Frédéric Chopin.   While even Schumann's more conservative works are indisputably romantic, Schumann remains the last composer (except for Brahms, to be discussed later) who could achieve versatility while still for the most part retaining some semblance of classical forms. The work of Frédéric (originally Frydryk) Chopin, Schumann's exact contemporary (1810–49), makes this especially clear. Chopin was born in Poland, the son of a French father and a Polish mother, but passed most of his adult life in Paris. His work is one of the primary examples of nineteenth-century specialization: almost all of his output (itself considerably smaller than that of Schumann) is for piano, and even of this the greater portion is cast in relatively small forms—short dances, such as waltzes and mazurkas (the mazurka was a Polish dance); études (studies); preludes; and nocturnes (an indeterminate title suggesting night time). Among the larger works, only a few—two piano concertos (1829 and 1830), three sonatas for piano (a youthful work plus two major sonatas of 1839 and 1844), and one for 'cello (1847)—are related to classical forms. The others are all single-movement pieces: scherzos (as independent movements), polonaises (another Polish dance, treated by Chopin in a heroic manner), and ballades—pieces, almost symphonic in style, whose progression of moods suggests an underlying story. Moreover, the majority of the larger works are clearly sectional, so that even these are more a mosaic of short sections, rather than an organically developing whole like a sonata movement.

Traits of Chopin's style

Certain characteristics remain constant for almost all of Chopin's work. First is Chopin's exploitation of the possibilities of pianistic sound—an achievement unmatched in the previous literature of the instrument. While Schumann considerably increased the expressive range of the piano, and other, earlier composers of the period, notably the Irishman John Field (1782–1837) had gone even further in their exploration of piano sound, Chopin outstripped all his predecessors in drawing from the instrument an immensely variegated spectrum of sonorities, ranging from the most delicate to the most heroic (his free use of the extremes of the piano's range and of its sustaining pedal were important factors in this achievement). Chopin's music is intimately and inextricably bound with its medium, to an extent only rarely seen. The strength of this tie may be demonstrated by the fact that all of the numerous attempts that have been made to orchestrate Chopin's piano music emasculate its substance.

As in the case of Domenico Scarlatti, Chopin's brilliant effects sometimes suggest greater technical demands than they actually require (one may compare Beethoven, whose piano writing is difficult even when it is *not* brilliant). Most of Chopin's music, however, demands a great deal from the pianist, who is richly rewarded by the dazzling effects created.

Chopin generally maintains a consistent figuration throughout a piece or a section of a piece. In some classes of his works, this consistency is natural: in the dance-type pieces, for example, and even more in the études, each of which is devoted to a specific technical problem (arpeggios, double thirds in one hand, etc.). But the same kind of consistency occurs in, for example, the preludes and the nocturnes, where there is no exterior necessity for it. A comparison between Bach's prelude in C from the first book of the *Well-Tempered Clavier* and Chopin's prelude in the same key (Ex. XIII-3a, b) is revealing. Each piece, having begun with a particular rhythmic-melodic figuration, continues the same pattern to the end. But Bach's prelude is essentially a study of a tonal progression: modulations to related keys and the ultimate return to the tonic are the essence of the piece. Chopin's prelude, much shorter, does not even modulate. It presents a single passionate melody, and, having done so, subsides into silence. Neither the consistency nor the passion is peculiar to Chopin, for the romantic character piece by its nature favored both. But Chopin's use of characteristically pianistic sonorities emphasizes both qualities.

Chopin's preference for shorter forms has already been mentioned, but this point deserves further examination. Unlike Schumann, whose short pieces are usually put together in groups that are intended to be played as a unit (e.g., *Carnaval*), Chopin quite regularly wrote a single waltz (or mazurka, or whatever) as a wholly separate entity; even when three or four of the same genre were published under a single opus number, the keys utilized rarely suggest successive performance.

There are certain exceptions. The two sets of études (Op. 10, 1829–32 and Op. 25, 1832–36) are often played as if each set were a sort of huge suite, and the sequence of

Ex. XIII-3(a)

Ex. XIII-3(b)

keys suggests that some grouping may have been intended. And the 24 preludes (1836–39), with their systematic progression of keys (C major, A minor, G major, E minor, D major, etc.) bear, and were intended to bear consecutive performance much better than Bach's *Well-Tempered Clavier* (C major, C minor, C♯ major, C♯ minor, and so on). No doubt Chopin, who knew and admired Bach's music, used the *Well-Tempered Clavier* as a kind of model. But Bach's preludes are in fact preparations for the fugues they precede, whereas Chopin's are preludes only to each other—or indeed to nothing at all, being merely the perfect expression of a "musical moment," to use Schubert's term. Thus, even in the preludes, there is no attempt at making an overall unity out of the set: each piece is a world in itself, having little or no contact with its neighbors.

Chopin's larger works

The larger pieces, of whatever sort, are, as has been mentioned, usually sectional—most often in some variant of the ABA pattern. Within each section (or in some cases sub-section) one finds the same consistency of figuration that dominates complete, shorter pieces. Thus, in the Polonaise in E♭ minor, a work of considerable length, the overall form is a literal ABA; but the "A" itself is a smaller aba, with the material of the small "a" differing from that of the small "b".

Needless to say, this method of construction is not suitable for sonatas and concertos. In works of these types, Chopin employs classical forms expertly and for the most part rather literally. As in certain works of Schubert and Schumann, the sonata-form movements lack something of the inner tension of their classical models. Chopin is fundamentally a lyrical composer. His melody, always expressive and graceful, is typically cast into the four-measure periods characteristic of song-like tunes (Ex. XIII–4; it is often suggested that Chopin owes more than a little to Bellini both in the contour and in the embellishment of his melody). While some movements of Mozart, and many more of Schubert and Schumann, demonstrate that lyrical melodies can be used as materials for sonata form, such melodies do have a tendency to form static

Ex. XIII-4

units that resist development. The melodies of Chopin, precisely because they are so perfect in their original form, do not encourage developmental procedures.

Chopin's treatment of harmony also affects the structure of his larger movements. While many of his works are prevailingly diatonic, others make extensive use of chromatically altered chords, rapid modulations, and lengthy passages of tonal instability. The end of the Prelude in E major, a piece only 12 measures long, shows the extent of this chromatic freedom. The tonic has just been reached, after a climactic modulation to Ab (really G#) major. In the measures shown (Ex. XIII-5), Chopin manages to confirm E as tonic, while introducing chords as remote as Bb major. In this case, it is the rising chromatic line of the top voice that controls the overall progression. Elsewhere, the harmonic logic, while always present, is less obvious: there are sudden modulations to keys a third distant (by means of a single tone common to both); irregular resolutions of seventh chords; exploitation of the Neapolitan relationship; and many other devices. The ingredients are not new, but Chopin's concentrated and original use of them makes his chromaticism both novel and important.

This chromaticism can easily be handled in smaller forms. When, however, it is applied to sonata or concerto movements, it ultimately weakens or even destroys the large-scale tonal tensions that lie at the heart of the form. The intensity of chromatic detail virtually prevents the listener from identifying structurally important modulations. In the Sonata in B minor, for example, only a listener with absolute pitch could be sure that the recapitulation is in fact in B minor—the preceding modulations have been so complex that the ordinary ear will accept any key as the tonic.

Nevertheless, Chopin's larger compositions, especially the sonatas, are major works. Their urgency of content sweeps away any question as to their form. If critical

Chopin's harmonic language

Ex. XIII-5

opinion on the whole gives an even higher place to the shorter pieces, this is perhaps because the latter so brilliantly illustrate the full range of Chopin's expression, from the heroic polonaises to the most intimate of the nocturnes, mazurkas, or preludes. Chopin was the foremost piano composer of the nineteenth century, and one of its most inventive musical minds.

General radical trends in romantic music

Hector Berlioz. Those composers who are regarded as representing the more radical side of musical romanticism have earned their reputations as radicals by their own literary pronouncements, often rather aggressively modernistic; by innovative features of their musical styles; and by their almost total rejection of "pure" or "abstract" music. Despite their profound differences, they shared one basic doctrine: that music could and indeed must represent something beyond mere tones, whether the representation was relatively explicit or narrative, as on the musico-dramatic stage; or implicit and evocative, as in instrumental music to which verbal programs were attached. (Naturally these categories should not be understood too rigidly: most works for the musical stage use music only intermittently for truly narrative purposes; and there are occasional narrative elements in instrumental music.) In their music, titles such as "Symphony in C major" disappear almost entirely in favor of "Symphonie fantastique" or "Faust Symphony"—or in other cases mere designations such as "Hamlet" or "Tasso." These titles should not be equated with the vaguely similar titles that Schumann, for example, gave to some of his piano works: the works now under consideration are for the most part of symphonic dimensions, not miniatures. Indeed, if the modernists shared another characteristic beyond their devotion to programmatic music, it was a predilection for bigness in all its manifestations.

Berlioz's life

The oldest of this group of composers was Hector Berlioz (1803–69), the only important French representative of musical romanticism. His life was a difficult one. His music was not successful in France: such triumphs as he enjoyed were mostly in Germany and in Russia. In consequence, he had to earn much of his living by writing musical criticism, at which he was as expert as Schumann. Despite his literary talent, he came to detest his critical work as a drain on his musical energies.

His most famous (though not his best) work is the *Symphonie fantastique* ("symphony of the fantasy," perhaps; 1830). The hybrid title implies some relation to the classical symphony and some sort of romantic extension of the symphonic principle: both implications are fulfilled. In its general structure, the work is clearly a symphony, the usual four movements being supplemented by a waltz, standing in second place, so that in effect the slow movement is surrounded by two scherzos (of very different types). The forms, moreover, except for that of the last movement, are normal enough as well. But a closer look—still on the purely musical level—discloses romantic traits. The large orchestra is treated with extraordinary imagination: Berlioz was the greatest orchestrator of his day, superbly skilled at inventing new and exotic sounds by means of unusual combinations or unusual uses of instruments (e.g., the haunting duet between English horn and oboe at the beginning or the chords for timpani at the end of the third movement). Even this early work is masterfully scored, and contains many passages in which orchestral color is more important than melody or harmony.

So great a dependence on sonority is not characteristic of the classical symphony, nor is the cyclical structure of the *Fantastique*. The principal theme of the first Allegro is quoted in the second, third, and fourth movements, and, wholly transformed in character, becomes an important part of the material of the last.

In this case, however, the quotations and transformation of the theme are not entirely musically motivated, but are manifestations of a detailed program that Berlioz provided for the work. This program presents scenes from the dream-world of an opium-drugged artist. Although Berlioz verbally characterized each movement at some length, it will suffice here to give their titles: 1. Reveries and passions: 2. A ball; 3. A scene in the country; 4. March to the scaffold; 5. Dream of a witches' sabbath. Beethoven's Sixth Symphony is clearly the ancestor here, but Beethoven's conception is romantically transformed.

The program justifies and reinforces the cyclical form, for the principal theme of the first movement (Ex. XIII-6a)—the *idée fixe*—represents the musician's beloved. The recurrence of this theme in the second and third movements, with which it has no organic connection, represents the sight or recollection of the beloved—at the ball, or in the country. The same is true in the fourth movement, except that here the *idée fixe* is truncated by an almost shocking orchestral picture of the guillotine in operation. In the last movement, the theme, transformed into something grotesque and vulgar (Ex. XIII-6b), suggests that the beloved has now joined the troop of evil spirits celebrating the witches' sabbath—a particularly forceful demonstration of the dramatic powers of thematic transformation.

The last movement—with its mysterious bells, its brilliant orchestral coloring, its ominous quotation of the plainsong *Dies irae* (day of wrath) from the Mass for the Dead—is without doubt the most imaginative of the symphony. It is a unique solution to the perennial "problem of the finale:" a kind of negative counterpart of the last movement of Beethoven's Ninth.

It is also the only movement that would appear arbitrary or unintelligible without the program: the only one in which knowledge of the extra-musical content of the

Symphonie fantastique: *cyclical form and thematic transformation*

Idée fixe

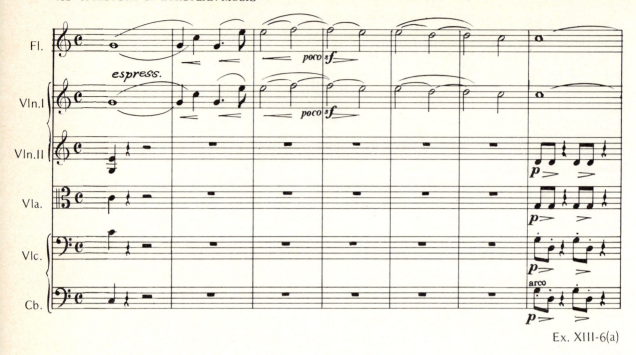

Ex. XIII-6(a)

Ex. XIII-6(b)

work is essential to musical understanding. This point deserves a certain emphasis, for it is too commonly thought that in program music of the nineteenth century, the program consistently controls and shapes the music. In point of fact, this is only occasionally true. Berlioz himself asserted that his music should make sense even to a listener ignorant of the program; and there are several instances of composers' adding programs to music that had been completed with no program in mind (or, conversely, of composers' deleting from works, prior to publication, programs that had at one time been intended). In general, romantic program music still conforms to purely musical principles (however original these may sometimes be), to which the program contributes a special focus, making specific what the music can only suggest.

Other works of
Berlioz

The *Symphonie fantastique* contains no sung text: only the program and the implied text of the *Dies irae* are verbal. Most of Berlioz's later works are vocal at least in part. There are operas, of which the grandiose *Les Troyens* (The Trojans; 1853-56) is the most important; enormous settings of the *Te Deum* (1849) and the Requiem Mass (1837), both impossible for liturgical use because of their length and the number of performers required. These continue, in their imposing dimensions, the tradition of French "public music" mentioned in the preceding chapter. The huge *Symphonie funèbre et triomphale* (1840) is an even clearer descendant of that tradition. By way of contrast, there is a surprisingly intimate and restrained oratorio, *L'enfance du Christ* (The Childhood of Christ; 1850-54), proving that Berlioz was not dependent on size for his success.

La damnation de
Faust

Especially interesting are two musical versions of major literary works, *Roméo et Juliette* (after Shakespeare; 1839), and *La damnation de Faust* (after Goethe; 1846). The former is aptly entitled "dramatic symphony," and the latter is a "concert opera." For both of them, Berlioz himself supplied the text (with some assistance in the case of *Faust*), as was his habit. His versions are not translations, but adaptations, sometimes quite free, of the originals. His Faust, to cite an extreme example, is transported to Hungary so that Berlioz can include his rousing *Rakoczy March* in the score. It is possible that Berlioz felt that Goethe and Shakespeare were too lofty to be set directly; or perhaps the adaptations were merely more amenable to musical treatment.

The dramatic
symphony: Roméo
et Juliette

Since *Roméo et Juliette* employs extensive vocal sections, it is necessarily further removed from the conventional symphonic tradition than the *Symphonie fantastique*. Although there are four purely instrumental sections, corresponding roughly to the four movements of the traditional symphony, the intervening movements with voices—especially the closing section, which is largely operatic in form—produce a symphonic-dramatic hybrid. Berlioz's treatment of Shakespeare's play is curious and original. While most of the primary events—the antagonism between Montagues and Capulets; the love of Romeo and Juliet, their separation, their death; and the reconciliation of the families—are represented in some form, only Friar Lawrence and Mercutio are actually impersonated by solo singers. The loneliness of Romeo and the ecstatic scene between the two lovers are entirely instrumental, as are their reunion and death. The two principal characters are thus evoked by the orchestra, without the aid of words. The chorus functions both as narrator, in a novel choral recitative near the beginning, and as the people, in Juliet's funeral procession and in the final scene. Berlioz's freedom of treatment is further evidenced by his expansion of Mercutio's delightful but peripheral speech about Queen Mab into two large sections: a vocal "scherzetto," and a full-size orchestral scherzo before the funeral procession.

All this makes for a strange and apparently arbitrary structure, yet it remains one of Berlioz's finest achievements. The orchestra is handled even more brilliantly than in the *Symphonie fantastique*, and some of the materials, most notably those of the love scene, are among the most beautiful in romantic music. The work is also more restrained than the *Symphonie fantastique*: Berlioz's taste has become more refined. There is no longer the rather dogmatic insistence on the *idée fixe*, as in the earlier work: themes recur from movement to movement, but only when the dramatic context demands their return.

Berlioz's niche in musical history is curiously uncertain. It is quite natural that nineteenth-century composers, so intent on projecting their personal feelings in their music, should provoke a variety of responses from modern listeners: there are people who love Schumann and dislike Chopin, or the reverse, others who cannot abide Wagner, and so on. The same is true for Berlioz, but with a certain difference. Some critics see him as the greatest of his generation; others as a gifted composer whose works are marred by technical flaws. Perhaps the truth is that—even for a romantic—Berlioz formed for himself an intensely individual style, one standing somewhat outside the mainstream of musical developments. Like some exotic food, the music of Berlioz is a delicacy for some people, and may be unattractive to others.

Liszt's life and works

Franz Liszt.   Franz Liszt (1811–86) is the second of the three radical romantics. Although born in Hungary, he belongs primarily to the German musical tradition. Liszt became known at an early age as an exceptional pianist, and went on to become one of the great instrumental virtuosi of the nineteenth century (among the others were Chopin and the violinist Niccolò Paganini). After extensive travelling on concert tours, he became attached to the court of Weimar in 1842, where he took up conducting and, increasingly, composing. Later in life he spent much of his time in Rome, and ultimately received minor orders in the Roman Catholic Church.

As might be expected, most of Liszt's early works are for the piano. Some are little more than concert display pieces: fantasies on popular operatic tunes, for example, or brilliant études, designed both to improve the technique of the performer and to dazzle the audience at a public concert. Even in these there is evidence of a powerful musical imagination; and there is more in the character pieces for piano without virtuoso elements. These latter are generally given quite specific programmatic titles—referring to places he had visited or literature he had read. (Liszt often set a poem to music as a song, and then later transcribed the song for piano solo, evidently regarding the transcription as the definitive version.) These character pieces show a masterly treatment of the piano, and, in addition, a striking freedom of harmony.

Liszt gave the title "sonata" to only one of his piano compositions, the Sonata in B minor (1852–53). A comparison of this piece, dedicated to Schumann, with the latter's Fantasy, dedicated to Liszt, gives the impression that the titles might well have been reversed. For while Schumann's work, though very free, has a superficial connection with the classical sonata idea—three separate movements, roughly analogous to the first three of a Beethoven sonata—Liszt's sonata is an entirely different type of piece. It is in a single movement that includes sections sharply contrasting in tempo, thematic material, and tonality. Liszt appears to have isolated the different kinds of ingredients found in a traditional sonata and mixed the results into one continuous movement—a movement moreover marked by large-scale recurrence of themes. These recurrences (sometimes involving thematic transformation) guarantee the overall unity of a piece that might otherwise have better been entitled "rhapsody" or "fantasy."

Liszt's symphonic poems

Liszt's procedures in this work are directly connected with his contemporary orchestral compositions. Feeling that Beethoven had said the last word in true symphonic form, Liszt devised a new type of orchestral composition, the "symphonic poem" or "tone poem," in which elements of the symphony, the character piece, and the concert overture are combined. The symphonic poem is not an absolute novelty: some of the concert overtures of Beethoven, Mendelssohn, and others might be given the title; and some of Liszt's tone poems were in fact written to serve as overtures. But there is still much that is new, particularly in regard to harmony and form.

Predictably, the symphonic poems all bear programmatic titles: *Hamlet, Orpheus, Prometheus,* to name three familiar subjects. Each is in a single movement, which, like the piano sonata described above, often combines sharply contrasting materials. The overall structures are various: some are fairly close to sonata form (although usually including the romantic type of thematic transformation), others are large ABA structures of varying degrees of complexity, and still others are ad hoc constructions falling into no regular category. Naturally, the form is to some extent influenced by the program, and even (to a lesser degree) by the narrative, if any, implicit in the program. But the tone poems are by no means stories told in music: Liszt is still largely faithful to Beethoven's motto in the Sixth Symphony—more expression of feeling than tone-painting.

Nonetheless, his musical language is thoroughly romantic. The style is vigorous and passionate (sometimes verging on the bombastic), or tenderly lyrical. The larger harmonic structure is often strongly chromatic, with sudden modulations to remote keys—often achieved merely by blazing forth an unexpected chord that the ear is forced to hear as a tonic. Since the smaller-level chord-to-chord progressions also are frequently chromatic, the overall force of tonality as a shaping agent in these works is somewhat weakened. The structure of the tone poems is achieved more by the recurrence of themes (often transformed radically in their expressive implications) than by the recurrence of the main tonality.

Larger than the tone poems, but basically similar to them in technique, are the two piano concertos (E♭ major, final version, 1856; A major, final version, 1861), the *Faust Symphony* (1854), and the *Dante Symphony* (1856). The concertos, like the B minor piano sonata, are "abstract" music, without programmatic titles or intentions. Their similarities to the tone poems further demonstrate that Liszt's music, whether programmatic or not, is based primarily on purely musical principles. Thematic transformation, a technique especially suitable for the conveyance of extra-musical content, is used prominently in the A major concerto (Ex. XIII–7a, b), as it was earlier in the piano sonata. It is thus apparent that this is above all a musical device, intended to achieve both unity and variety, whether or not a program is involved.

Faust Symphony and later works

Ex. XIII-7(a)

Marziale un poco meno allegro

Woodwind and brass parts omitted

Ex. XIII-7(b)

The *Faust Symphony* is one of Liszt's finest (and largest) works. It might be regarded as an interlocked set of three tone poems: the three movements are entitled
"Faust," "Gretchen," and "Mephistopheles;" and there are extensive thematic interrelations between them. The work also has affinities with the traditional symphony,
having a first movement in a sort of sonata form, then a slow movement, and a last
movement that serves as both scherzo and finale. Once again, there is no musical
story telling. Liszt contents himself with psychological portraits of his characters.
Liszt later added a choral section, using the final words of Goethe's play, to the end of
the *Faust Symphony*, but the work stands up perfectly well without it.

Liszt's later works include large sacred pieces—Masses and oratorios—as well as
a number of piano compositions. As he grew older, Liszt pushed his harmonic experimentation even further: from the free chromaticism he had long used, he proceeded
to experiments involving the whole-tone scale (e.g.,C, D, E, F♯, G♯, B♭, C; the scale has
no implied tonal center), and the use of violent dissonances that seem wholly to obscure the tonality at least for a time. Some of his more extreme passages sound more
like music written in the 1930s than "romantic" music; and indeed they are "post-

romantic," in the sense that the spontaneous lyricism of the romantics has given way to a more abstruse, intellectual style.

One other aspect of Liszt's style deserves mention. As he was Hungarian (although of course Hungary was then a part of the Austrian empire), he wrote a certain amount of music based on "Hungarian" themes—in fact mostly gypsy, rather than true Hungarian melodies. Although such pieces are neither the most numerous nor the best of his works, they are significant as a manifestation of musical nationalism (one may compare Chopin's use of Polish dance forms). Nationalism ultimately became an important factor in music of the later nineteenth century, and in the change of style that occurred before the First World War.

Of all the major romantics, Liszt is perhaps the least performed today. No doubt part of this neglect results from Liszt's occasional lapses into excessive rhetoric and sentimentality, and from his quite undeserved reputation as a mere composer of virtuoso piano works. But part also lies in the fact that his best works are difficult for the listener: they require close attention—and they amply reward it. Liszt was one of the most inventive musicians of the century, and a powerful influence on other musicians—especially on Wagner.

Richard Wagner.   Richard Wagner (1813–83) culminates and surpasses romanticism just as Beethoven did classicism. Although few would now give him a status equal to that of Bach, Mozart, or Beethoven, Wagner was beyond doubt the most important composer of his century, and one of the most controversial and influential figures of his or any age.

Wagner's early interests were divided between music and the theater, and he had relatively little formal training in either. Music finally gained the upper hand—in part owing to the impression made on him by hearing some of Beethoven's works—and he began his career as musical director at a provincial opera theater. Although his earliest works include some purely instrumental pieces (among them a *Faust* overture), he soon devoted himself to opera, and never thereafter turned away from the musical stage. His first three operas, written during the 1830s, are of relatively little importance: they show, successively, the influence of Weber, of Bellini, and of Meyerbeer, as if the young composer were trying on styles in order to find which one fit the best. Perhaps their most original feature is that in each case Wagner was his own librettist—a practice he adhered to throughout his life.

In the next decade, Wagner's musical personality began to assert itself with increasing force; and at the same time, certain dramatic themes that were to become crucial for his later work made their appearance. In both *Der fliegende Holländer* (The Flying Dutchman; 1841) and *Tannhaüser* (1845), the central dramatic motive is the redemption of the hero by a woman's love. In *Lohengrin* (1848), the legend of the Holy Grail forms part of the background, while the central tragedy is caused by the heroine's failure to surrender unquestioningly to love's command.

Musically, these three works represent the formative period of Wagner's mature style. One finds in them an increasing interpenetration of the traditional operatic types, to the point where many passages cannot be called either recitative or aria. This greater continuity is made possible by the greater use of the orchestra: it is the orchestra that supplies the continuum upon which the vocal utterances—which can be declamatory, fragmentary, or lyrical, as the occasion demands—are superposed. Finally, Wagner makes more—and more effective—use of recurrent musical motives

Wagner's early works

representing characters, situations, or ideas in the drama. These "Leitmotives" (leading motives) not only make for greater overall unity, but also enrich the dramatic potential: a motive played by the orchestra when a character is silent may allow the audience to discover his state of mind; or such a motive played when a character is singing about something else may give the audience information unknown to those on the stage. Naturally, thematic recurrence was not Wagner's idea: it was a commonplace among composers at this time and even earlier; but Wagner soon took the lead in applying the method.

In consequence of all these technical changes, *Lohengrin*, the most advanced of this group of works, is no longer an opera in the conventional sense, but—to use Wagner's phrase—a music drama. Each of its three acts is a near-continuous whole, freely mixing declamatory and lyrical singing, with only occasional recourse to "closed" musical numbers. The large orchestra, handled with extraordinary skill, compensates for the lack of formal arias by presenting a nearly constant flux of music in symphonic style, fortified by easily recognizable recurrent motives. The beginning of the second act is probably Wagner's finest achievement in this part of his career: a lengthy and impressive scene that owes nothing to normal operatic conventions, and follows faithfully every nuance of emotion suggested by the drama.

Lohengrin

Lohengrin represents an end as well as a beginning: although it was considered advanced—even radical—in its own day, its roots in the romantic past are now clear enough. And 1848 was a turning point in Wagner's life. After many tribulations and failures, Wagner had obtained in 1843 a good position at Dresden. But the political upheavals of 1848 found him on the losing side. Threatened with arrest, he left Dresden in 1849, settling in Switzerland. It was not until five years later that he completed a new music drama, and in the interval, he was occupied more with literary and philosophical writings than with music.

He had already begun at Dresden the writing of a drama freely based on Northern mythology and the *Nibelungenlied*. This work, entitled *Siegfrieds Tod* (The Death of Siegfried), was completed in 1850, and some few snatches of music for it may have been written at that time. He also wrote and published a number of essays, aimed at providing theoretical and philosophical justification for the type of art-work he had in mind for the future. The most comprehensive of these essays was *Oper und Drama*

Wagner's aesthetic writings: Oper und Drama

(Opera and Drama; 1852), written in Wagner's characteristically prolix and contentious literary style, but containing much important material. Wagner dismisses almost all contemporary opera as mere entertainment, debased and debasing. For him, all art must have serious moral as well as aesthetic validity. His own future work, he claims, will be addressed not to the "public"—the wealthy who go to the opera to be entertained—but "the people"—those who, whatever their social station, aspire to high ideals. Its center will be the drama, the most communal of the arts. The subject matter will be drawn from mythology, not that of ancient Greece, which is foreign to German ideals, but that of the Northern peoples. Mythology alone can provide dramatic substance capable of conveying eternal truths in symbolic but comprehensible form. To the drama music will of course be added, but as servant, not as mistress (here Wagner echos Monteverdi, of whom he knew nothing, and Gluck, whom he knew but misunderstood). Music is necessary because it alone can express the ineffable—can pass beyond the inadequacy of speech into the highest realms of the emotions. The union of drama and music will be further enriched by the other arts: acting, of course, but also the visual arts, in the designing and construction of the stage settings. Thus the work as a whole will be a *Gesamtkunstwerk* (literally, "all-the-arts-work), capable of overwhelming the spectator.

Since for Wagner, melody is the soul of music, his music drama will consist of "endless melody." By this, Wagner does not mean symmetrical tunes. The orchestra is, in practice, given developmental material. The vocal parts, however, are to be assigned a rhetorical speech-song, varying in lyrical content with the intensity of the emotion to be expressed. The qualification "endless" is merely another way of saying that there will be no formal divisions into recitative and aria sections. To strengthen the musico-dramatic relationship, the melody will incorporate "motives of reminiscence"—themes that, having been heard once fitted to a particular text, will when they recur remind the spectator of that text. (This is Wagner's theory of the Leitmotive at this time; in practice he often introduces a Leitmotive for the first time in the orchestra, in which case it is the general dramatic context at that moment, rather than any specific words, that will be suggested on later occurrences.)

"Endless melody"

Leitmotive

Wagner had already used most of these concepts, elaborated at length in *Oper und Drama*, in *Lohengrin* and even before. He now intended to go much further along the same lines. Finding that his play on the death of Siegfried required of the audience too much background information, he worked backwards from it, writing a total of three other dramas to introduce it. These were (in their proper order) *Das Rheingold* (The Gold of the Rhine), *Die Walküre* (The Valkyrie), and *Siegfried*, leading up to the final play, now retitled *Die Götterdämmerung* (The Twilight of the Gods). This gigantic tetralogy, which requires four evenings for performance, was given the general title of *Der Ring des Nibelungen* (The Ring of the Nibelung). Its principal dramatic themes are the Hero, who comes to supersede the gods; the curse of materialism; and the redemptive power of love. Through *Siegfried*, the text may also be read as a political allegory advocating socialism. (Other allegorical interpretations are also possible.) The poetic style is deliberately archaic; rhyme is avoided in favor of alliteration and assonance, devices borrowed from medieval German verse. While the result is certainly not great literature, the text of the tetralogy offers Wagner precisely the musical and scenic opportunities he needed to put his new theories into practice.

The Ring

Although he had written the texts in reverse order, Wagner composed the music in the proper sequence. *Rheingold* was finished in 1854, *Die Walküre* in 1856, and the first two acts of *Siegfried* in the following year. But the apparent impossibility of ever bringing such a gigantic work to performance finally discouraged Wagner, and he laid the project aside: the tetralogy was not completed until 1874.

The parts of the *Ring* completed in the 1850s represent the practical embodiment of the theories expounded in *Oper und Drama*—although not without some deviations, for Wagner's musical sense was always more powerful than his sometimes restrictive theories. While the musical style represents a continuation and intensification of the romanticism of *Lohengrin*, the *Ring* is no longer romantic music drama; for Wagner has imposed a strict realism on the imaginary world he has created. In the parts of the *Ring* composed in the 1850s, there is scarcely any choral or ensemble singing: even lovers are not allowed to sing simultaneously. Real people do not properly speak at once, and therefore the characters on the stage should not sing at once. Words are not repeated (except where they would be repeated in speech for emphasis), nor in general is any syllable of text given more than a single note. The vocal line is modeled on the rhetorical speech of an actor—more emotional than ordi-

Characteristics of the earlier portions of the Ring

nary speech, but less lyrical than ordinary song. For the most part, the singing is what might be called musical prose. It is only at points of intense dramatic emotion (and not always then) that Wagner permits his characters to sing in truly lyrical fashion, with symmetrical melodic phrases.[1] (Wagner's severity in this respect decreased as his work proceeded: *Die Walküre* contains more lyrical melody than *Das Rheingold*.)

This necessarily places the main burden of maintaining musical continuity on the orchestra (which Wagner enlarged enormously). It is the orchestra that gives emotional life to the vocal parts, and, by extensive use of Leitmotives, both reinforces the text and on occasion supplements it by adding further meanings not made explicit by the words. The first act of *Die Walküre* is concerned with the meeting of Siegmund and Sieglinde, and with their emotions, which quickly ripen into passionate love. The opening scene contains relatively little text, and the speeches, mostly quite neutral in tone, are often separated by long instrumental passages. These latter make perfectly clear the growing emotions of the characters—feelings of which they themselves are hardly yet aware. The orchestral material is woven out of Leitmotives, but almost all of them are new to the hearer: their evocative force lies primarily in the nature of the themes, rather than in connotations derived from previous occurrences. Later in the act, however, there is a particularly striking use of a motive that had been extensively used in *Das Rheingold*. Sieglinde is describing the visit of a mysterious stranger, and the orchestra, by playing the motive associated with Valhalla, the castle of the gods, identifies the visitor as Wotan, chief of the gods—but the characters on stage remain unaware of this.

Use of the orchestra

The orchestra thus functions in a manner analogous to the chorus in Greek drama, aiding in narration, explanation, and commentary on the stage action. Its texture is close to that of a continuous development section: Wagner's admiration for Beethoven, and particularly for Beethoven's developmental techniques, was boundless; and his Leitmotives, despite their great variety, are almost all so designed as to be suitable for development, and many for transformation as well. (The rare exceptions are the purely lyric vocal themes, like Siegmund's famous "Winterstürme" passage, which is almost un-Wagnerian in its aria-like effect.) Although Wagner never gave names to his motives, he made no objection when commentators did so, and there are numerous publications that print the several hundred motives of the *Ring* with suitable titles, as an aid—one might almost say a lexicon—for the heavily taxed memory of the spectator. A few typical themes (Ex. XIII–8) suggest the types of material Wagner used.

Harmony and form

An important feature of Wagner's developmental texture is its constant modulation and nearly constant avoidance of conclusive cadences. Both devices enhance the overall continuity: there are few large areas of clear tonal stability, and cadential dominant-tonic progressions are usually evaded by replacing the expected tonic with some other chord (except, of course, at the end of an act).

Such continuous flux could easily become amorphous and confusing. Naturally, the text helps greatly in keeping order; but since many lovers of music find Wagner satisfying even when they are ignorant of all but the main outline of the story, there must be other principles at work also. In fact, many analysts now agree that Wagner

---

[1] It is evident that Wagner's ideas closely resemble the Florentine dramatic aesthetic of the early 1600s. Wagner knew nothing of Peri and Caccini, and the resemblance is merely the inevitable result of the attempt to make music the "servant of the drama."

The curse   **The sword**

Treaty   **Siegfried**

Ex. XIII-8

organized his material into elusive but structurally potent musical units. Thus, on the smallest level, motives are presented in patterns like ABA or AAB. The phrases thus produced are then organized in larger but similar patterns, and these larger forms are grouped to produce entire acts—or indeed even larger units. In *Die Walküre*, the first part of Act II presents a series of events that have almost exact counterparts in the same order in the whole of Act I: the overall dramatic form of the two acts is therefore

Fig. XIII-2. V. J. Hoffmann, painting for the original stage setting for the first act of Wagner's Die Walküre. (Original in the Richard-Wagner-Gedenkstätte, Bayreuth.)

AA'B. In writing his libretti, Wagner frequently built such structures directly into the dramas, either on a large scale, as in the instance just cited, or on a smaller, local level—for example, by following two similarly constructed lines with one of contrasting structure. Such patterns naturally invited parallel musical treatment. Wagner's highly complex musical forms frequently pass unperceived by the listener, but they play an important role in articulating music that might otherwise be merely rhapsodic.

Already in the *Ring* music of the 1850s, Wagner's style is fully mature. His orchestral mastery is as great as that of Berlioz, although very different in kind. Wagner prefers warm, dense, and rich sonorities to the brilliant clarity of Berlioz. His harmony is often strongly chromatic (a trait that may owe something to the music of Liszt) and makes free use of dissonance (chords of the 9th, containing the three simultaneous dissonances of diminished fifth, seventh, and ninth, are common). As with other chromaticists, this harmonic richness is achieved at a price: basic tonal relations are less obvious when set in a sea of continuous modulation.

Tristan und Isolde

It is in Wagner's next work, *Tristan und Isolde* (1859), that his harmonic audacity reaches its peak. From the very first chords of the prelude, about which theorists have argued for over a century, the music is saturated with a dissonant chromaticism (Ex. XIII–9) that was unintelligible to most contemporaries—even to such an apparent radical as Berlioz. The harmonic style derives directly from the subject matter. Wagner freely works a medieval legend into an almost expressionistic love story, in which only the two principal characters have any significant role. There is little outward action, no opportunity for scenic display (so important in the *Ring*): the drama is an interior one, unfolding in the passions of the ill-fated lovers. Hence the chromaticism, for chromatic harmony had been the language of passion since the late sixteenth century. And hence too the even greater importance of the orchestra in *Tristan*: what the lovers feel is more important than what they say, and it is the orchestra that must communicate their feelings. *Tristan* has been called a symphonic drama, and it is quite natural that its climaxes—the love duet in Act II and the *Liebestod* (love-death) at the end—are often performed at concerts with instruments replacing the vocal lines.

The theories of *Oper und Drama* are no longer valid for *Tristan* and later works. Wagner wisely changed his theories to suit his musical purposes, and here there is simultaneous singing (in the love duet) and even choral writing. Leitmotives are still much in evidence, but since the dramatic subject is so restricted, they are not as sharply differentiated as they are in the *Ring*. Since most of them represent some aspect of love or longing, and since most are chromatic, they are heard as mere patches of color in the great flood coming from the orchestra, not as events of real dramatic importance.

Tristan is even less romantic than the *Ring*. While the old literary motives are still present—night, the Middle Ages, the yearning for the Infinite—Wagner's music is not romantically suggestive or evocative: it is literally overwhelming (the love music of the second act is an almost clinical portrayal of love-making). The spectator is engulfed by passion—is compelled to feel what Wagner wants him to feel. In literary criticism, the style subsequent to romanticism is often called "realism." It has already been noted that Wagner's *Ring* is "realistic" on certain levels. Nevertheless, "realism" is not generally accepted as a description of musical style, nor is any substitute term in common use. It is perhaps enough to ignore terminology and merely note the

Den ich ge—braut der mir ge-flos — sen

den Won — ne schlür—fend je ich ge — nos-sen

ver — flucht sei fürcht—ba-rer Trank

That which I brewed, which flowed, whose rapture I tasted as I drank—be accursed, frightful potion!

Ex. XIII-9

distinction: between genuine evocative romanticism (exemplified in Wagner's work by *Lohengrin*), and the post-romantic hyper-expressivity of *Tristan* and its descendants.

While the *Ring* is in one sense the essence of Wagner, *Tristan* is the more important work historically. Its harmonic style was a milestone: ultimately all composers had somehow to come to terms with it, for Wagner seemed to have squeezed every possible effect out of the tonal system—to some he seemed to have gone beyond it. The trials and accomplishments of composers of the post-*Tristan* period will be the principal subject of the next chapter; here only the epochal nature of the work itself need be noted.

Wagner had temporarily stopped work on the *Ring* out of fear it would never be performed, but *Tristan* hardly fared better. Even *Tannhaüser* was a failure in Paris in 1860 (despite a newly written ballet for the dance-loving French); and in 1861, after over fifty rehearsals, *Tristan* was abandoned by the Vienna Opera. Wagner's name was certainly well known, and his earlier works often played in Germany, but this brought him no money; and his mature music, with its immense demands on singers, players, and especially audiences, was greeted with hostility when even fragments of it were played. Unperturbed, still certain of his course, Wagner turned to comic opera, completing *Die Meistersinger von Nürnberg* in 1867. This stands at an opposite pole from *Tristan*: it is a historically accurate portrayal of the middle-class singers' guilds of late medieval Germany, with a mild love element and a good deal of real humor. Wagner had become interested in theories of the drama as an act of improvisation, and *Die Meistersinger* contains—in sharp contrast to the *Ring* and *Tristan*— scenes in which the action appears spontaneous, as if the characters were inventing the play on the spot. In consequence, Wagner also makes extensive use of a seemingly improvisatory type of counterpoint: originally independent themes are presented simultaneously, in accordance with the demands of the dramatic situation. (Counterpoint is also used parodistically, to portray musical pedantry.) The music also includes real arias, duets, ensembles, and choruses, all embedded, to be sure, in continuous music, but all more independent than had become normal for Wagner. The harmony, while complex, is largely diatonic. Nothing could be more surprising than such a work at such a time, but *Die Meistersinger* is as genuinely Wagnerian as the *Ring* itself.

In the midst of his work on *Die Meistersinger*, Wagner was the beneficiary of an almost unbelievable piece of good fortune. The young king Ludwig of Bavaria summoned the composer to Munich and offered him full financial and moral support for his work, extending eventually to a special theater at Bayreuth, built expressly for Wagner's works. (The theater, an unparalleled tribute to a living composer, is still the site of annual Wagner festivals.)

Thus, free of financial cares—either for his own luxurious tastes or the extravagant demands of his operas—Wagner turned back to the *Ring*, for which a suitable performance could now be envisaged. The cycle was finished in 1874; and while the last act of *Siegfried* and all of *Götterdämmerung* continue to employ the Leitmotives of the *Ring* music of the 50s, they clearly show results of the experience of *Tristan*. The orchestra is overwhelming, bursting with hundreds of Leitmotives, often combined in intricate counterpoint. And the style is in general more extreme, both in the ferocity of the evil characters and the exaltation of the good ones. Still, Wagner was

Die Meistersinger

The later parts of the Ring

careful not to go too far, and the cycle succeeds as a whole despite the stylistic differences of the later parts.

Wagner's last work was another surprise: the explicitly Christian *Parsifal*, a mystical treatment of the Grail theme. Although some critics find in it evidence of a decline in inventive power, it remains a profound, if demanding work. Wagner called it a "Festival Dedication Play"—as if the theater at Bayreuth were a cathedral—and directed that it never be performed except at Bayreuth. Naturally this prohibition was not kept after the composer's death.

Parsifal

Despite Wagner's lifelong emphasis on the importance of his drama, and on the moral and redemptive character of his work, it is primarily Wagner the musician who survives. This is no disparagement, for his musical accomplishment was enormous. His reform of operatic structure, although it did not ultimately work out quite as he had intended, was an exemplary achievement. While it can scarcely be said that he made music once again the servant of the drama—his music was too powerful for that—it remains true that the music is always dramatically relevant (indeed in *Tristan* one might say that music has *become* the drama). The outward signs of Wagnerian dramaturgy—the unbroken musical continuity and the use of Leitmotives—exerted enormous influence, but they are less important than Wagner's steadfast adherence to an aesthetic in which every note, whether played or sung, made some contribution to the dramatic action.

Wagner's achievement as an orchestrator has already been mentioned, as has his revolutionary harmonic style. Both of these accomplishments are especially important; for the first could be (and was) applied to any type of orchestral music, whether operatic or not; while the second was applicable to music for any medium. Thus, while his verbose philosophizing is now read only by specialists, and while even some aspects of his music and his drama no longer receive the uncritical praise his admirers once lavished on them, Wagner remains the colossus of the nineteenth century—the man who irreversibly changed the nature of the musical world of his time.

Giuseppe Verdi.   In retrospect, Wagner dominated the German operatic stage for over half a century, for his contemporaries, though numerous, prolific, and often very successful, rarely rose above the merely respectable (Schumann's *Genoveva* is an exception). The French opera had no Wagner of its own, and its composers were men of no great stature; only towards the end of the century did France begin to rise above mediocrity. In Italy, however, there arose a composer who was to eclipse his contemporaries as much as Wagner did in Germany—an exact contemporary and an almost exact opposite of Wagner, Giuseppe Verdi (1813–1901).

Few composers have had a longer career. Verdi's first opera appeared in 1839, his last in 1893. In this half-century of composing, there is one constant element: growth. Verdi began by unquestioningly accepting the Italian operatic conventions of his time: the formal division of each act into several large sections, each concluding with an aria, duet, or ensemble; the primacy of the virtuoso singer, and the concomitant subordination of the orchestra; and a musical style based on simple, memorable tunes, vigorous rhythms, and commonplace harmonies. This had been the method of Rossini and Donizetti—a style untouched by the work of Beethoven and little influenced even by Haydn and Mozart. Along with all this, Verdi also accepted—at the beginning—the libretti he was commissioned to set, and the reaction of the public as an

Verdi's career

almost infallible judgment on the value of the final product. The Verdi of 1839 was thus a wholly conventional musician, and if he had died young, he might not be remembered today.

Verdi's early works

Yet even Verdi's earliest work shows signs of remarkable dramatic vigor: there is nothing of the refinement of Bellini, but rather a forcefulness that was capable of making even conventional opera convincing. Verdi therefore became successful and, over the years, experienced; and success coupled with experience enabled him to write more freely, and to demand more of his performers, his librettists, and his public. All this led to profound changes in style, but they were gradual ones: Verdi was never a revolutionary or even a reformer. He aspired only to raise Italian opera, as he understood it, to the highest possible level; and he succeeded brilliantly.

His early operas are of relatively little interest today. The unrelenting succession of four-measure phrases, the conventional accompanimental figures, the commonplace harmonies no longer sound interesting. Yet there are scenes of real dramatic power—some of them especially appreciated in their day because of their oblique political implications. Verdi was an ardent patriot, and saw to it whenever possible that his audiences could read nationalist meanings into some of his stories, despite the efforts of Austrian or papal censors. His popularity was certainly not diminished by the curious fact that the letters of his name could be—and were—used as an acronym for Vittorio Emmanuele Re D'Italia (Victor Emmanuel, king of Italy). A shout of "Viva Verdi" could have more than one meaning. Nevertheless, any political implications in Verdi's work are incidental to his main purpose. Unlike Wagner, he deals in his operas with individual men and women, not types. Symbolism is foreign to his nature.

Operas of the middle period

It was in the 1850s, in three operas that still remain among his most popular, Rigoletto (1851), Il trovatore (The Troubadour; 1853), and La traviata (The Fallen Woman; 1853), that Verdi achieved full maturity of style. These are richer than their predecessors in all respects—melody, harmony, flexibility of dramatic forms, and orchestration. Verdi's increased mastery of the orchestra is especially important. While the "guitar-type" accompaniment is still common, there are passages of highly imaginative, evocative scoring in purely instrumental sections, and even the aria accompaniments are often more complex and interesting. Act III of Rigoletto is particularly noteworthy in this respect: the orchestral depiction of a storm, in which Verdi supplements the normal orchestra with an invisible wordless chorus to represent the wailing of the wind, is a masterly stroke.

But the new formal flexibility was in the end even more important. The still plentiful formal arias are usually cast in a traditional bipartite slow-fast form (cavatina and cabaletta are the names for the two sections), but they are now consistently real revelations of character rather than mere vocal display pieces. And, as often as not, Verdi tampers with the traditional structures in the interests of dramatic realism. Thus the beginning of the second act of Rigoletto is labeled "scene and aria" for the Duke, one of whose numerous beloveds has mysteriously disappeared. It begins conventionally enough with a recitative and arioso, followed by the Duke's cavatina. Then a chorus enters and holds forth for some time, conveying important information, so that when the expected cabaletta finally appears, much delayed, it is dramatically justified, for the new information has radically affected the Duke's feelings. Indeed the entire act consists of only three such "scenes," in which formal arias (or duets) take up less space than freely unfolding music occasioned directly by the dramatic action.

Verdi also makes increased and more sophisticated use of ensembles. In the inimitable quartet from Act III of *Rigoletto*, each character is given music that profoundly reveals his or her feelings, even when all are singing at once (Ex. XIII–10). Ensembles of this quality had not been written since the great finales of Mozart.

While still in his forties, Verdi had acquired an international reputation: both Paris and St. Petersburg had commissioned works from him, and his popularity in Italy was enormous. It is curious that although his growth as a composer clearly continued in the years that followed *La traviata*, not one of the operas preceding *Aïda* (1871) has achieved the consistent popularity of the three works of 1851–53, despite some considerable initial successes—and some failures. (*Simon Boccanegra*, for example, was a failure when first produced in 1857, although a much later revision in 1881 had considerable success.) It may be that Verdi was perhaps unconsciously working his way towards a new concept of opera as pure musical drama (though not in the Wagnerian sense: Verdi admired Wagner's work, but felt strongly that German methods were not suitable for Italian composers). However this may be, these works of the late 50s and the 60s are curiously uneven. They contain some of Verdi's most splendid pages, along with some decidedly lesser ones.

(continued on the following page)   Ex. XIII-10

Ex. XIII-10

Ah do not break, unhappy heart, heart betrayed. Do not break from anguish.
I am accustomed, good sir, to this sort of game. Ah, I laugh heartily.
Only you can heal my distress; ah, with a word only you can [heal].
Be assured. Be quiet and I shall see to the hastening of revenge.

Aïda was commissioned by the Egyptian government, to celebrate the opening of the Suez canal. Circumstances dictated that it be a "grand" opera, full of pomp and display, and set in the great days of ancient Egypt. The music partly reflects the nature of the commission, in its effective evocation of "local color" by means of vaguely Oriental-sounding melodies. But Aïda is no more an opera about Egypt than Hamlet is a play about Denmark. While the great crowd scenes are probably the most thrilling in all opera, the heart of Aïda lies—as always in Verdi—in the vivid emotional life of the principal characters. After twenty years of practical experience, Verdi carries freedom of form and intensity of expression far beyond what he had achieved in the 1850s. The big arias and ensembles are still there, but they are now hardly more than especially lyric moments in music that enjoys uninterrupted continuity for long stretches. The harmony (even when untouched by local color effects) is rich and often strongly chromatic, and both melody and orchestration are far more subtle and distinguished. Aïda is thoroughly worthy of the immense popularity it has always enjoyed.

After a magnificent setting of the Requiem Mass (1874)—operatic in form and style, but profoundly sincere—Verdi was inclined to rest on his laurels. But temptation appeared, in the possibility of a first-class libretto based on Shakespeare's Othello. (Many of Verdi's earlier libretti are based on important literary works, by Schiller, Hugo, Dumas *fils*, and Shakespeare himself; but the versions Verdi set are generally little better than the ordinary Italian libretto.) It happened that the composer Arrigo Boito (1842–1918) was also a man of considerable literary gifts. In an unusual gesture of generosity, he offered to prepare Othello for the Italian musical stage, and, some years later, Falstaff (based on The Merry Wives of Windsor, strengthened with elements from the Henry IV plays). These were by far the best

Aïda

Otello *and* Falstaff

Fig. XIII-3: A rehearsal of Verdi's Falstaff in 1893, with Verdi (extreme right) present.

libretti Verdi had ever had, and he could not turn them down. *Otello* was finished in 1887, and *Falstaff* in 1893, when Verdi was 80, but no trace of old age is apparent in the scores.

In these last two operas, each act is as continuous as an act of Wagner's. Yet Verdi arrived at continuity by his own means—the fragmentation and elision of old forms—rather than by Wagner's method of building out of motivic units. In both *Otello* and *Falstaff* the lyrical and declamatory elements flow smoothly into one another: even when traces of the traditional aria are present, each section is interlocked so carefully with its neighbors that no gaps are discernible. And Verdi's declamation is by now so intense as to transcend the concept of recitative: Otello's first entrance (in Act I) is certainly not an aria, yet it is as powerfully expressive as anything in the opera (Ex. XIII–11). The love duet at the end of the same act is wholly free of traditional forms—a rhapsodic outpouring of feeling, whose structure is perfect because it perfectly embodies the text.

glo-ria.   Do - po l'ar — — mi lo vin — se l'u — ra — ga — — no

Rejoice! The Moslem pride is buried in the sea. Ours is the glory from heaven. After the
battle, the hurricane conquered them.

Ex. XIII-11

Both late operas treat the orchestra with astonishing refinement, and allot to it a
larger share of the musical interest (*Falstaff*, in particular, demonstrates the fruit of
Verdi's admiration for Beethoven). But there are few recurrent themes and no true
Leitmotives at all: at the center is the human voice—the voice of the individual, and
not the anonymous mass of orchestral sound.

It is more than strange that two men, born in the same year, should have dominated the operatic stages of their countries for over half of the century. Comparisons
are inevitable—not qualitative ones, for the best of Wagner and of Verdi is literally   *Verdi and Wagner*
incomparable. It is, however, valid to contrast Wagner's symbolism, his constant developmental treatment of Leitmotives, his symphonic use of the orchestra, with
Verdi's purely human plots, his lyricism, and his emphasis on the human voice. Such
comparisons emphasize the nature of German and Italian musical thought of the time.

There is also one final contrast. Like Beethoven, Wagner was an immense force
acting on the musical world about him—a force that persisted well into the twentieth
century. Verdi was an isolated figure, with no important successors and no "school."
The history of music would scarcely have been different had he never lived, but it
would have been immeasurably poorer.

APPENDIX:

Chapter XIII

Comparative table of the compositions of major 19th-century composers

	Franz Schubert (1797–1828)	Robert Schumann (1810–56)	Felix Mendelssohn (1809–47)
Symphonic	8 symphonies; no trace has been found of a "Gastein" symphony of 1825. Incidental music to *Rosamunde* (1823)	4 symphonies: B♭ ("Spring"); C; E♭ ("Rhenish"); d Concertos: piano, a ; 'cello, a; violin, d	5 symphonies: c; *Lobgesang* for chorus & orch.; a ("Scottish"); A ("Italian"); D ("Reformation") 6 overtures 2 pf. concertos: g; d Vln. concerto: e Music for *A Midsummer Night's Dream*
Chamber music	2 string trios. 15 string quartets String quintet, C 2 pf. trios Piano quintet ("Trout") Octet for winds and strings Rondo; Fantasy; Sonata; and 3 sonatinas for vln. and pf.	3 quartets: a; F; A 3 pf. trios: d; F; g Pf. quartet; pf. quintet 2 vln. sonatas: a; d	2 'cello sonatas 6 quartets: E♭; A; D; e. E♭; f Octet, E♭ 2 pf. trios: d; c 3 pf. quartets: c; f; b Sextet (w. pf.), D
Piano music	22 sonatas (several unfinished) *Wanderer-Fantasie* 6 *moments musicaux* 8 impromptus Many dances Much music for piano duet	Mostly titled collections of pieces, including: *Carnaval* (20 pieces) *Papillons* (12) *Davidsbündlertänze* (18) *Kinderscenen* (13) *Jugendalbum* (40) *Waldscenen* (9) *Noveletten* (8) *Albumblätter* (20) 3 sonatas: f♯; g; f Variations	*Songs without words* (48) *Variations sérieuses* Other character pieces Capriccios, fantasias Organ works: 3 preludes & fugues, 6 sonatas
Songs	ca. 600 songs, written throughout his life, including the cycles *Die schöne Müllerin* (20 songs) and *Die Winterreise* (24)	ca. 250 songs, incl. cycles *Frauenliebe und leben*, *Dichterliebe*, *Liederkreise* opp. 24, 39 Duets, quartets, partsongs, some with pf. accomp.	ca. 75 songs 12 accomp. duets ca. 50 unaccompanied partsongs
Opera and choral music	*Alfonso und Estrella*, 1821–22 *Fierabras*, 1823 Six Masses; other choral music Vocal quartets with pf.	Opera *Genoveva* Choral wks. w. orch. incl. a Mass, a Requiem, *Paradies und die Peri*, *Requiem für Mignon*	Oratorios *Elijah*; *St. Paul* *Die erste Walpurgisnacht*, chorus & orch. Choral church music, both accompanied and unaccompanied

Frédéric Chopin (1810–49)	Franz Liszt (1811–86)	Hector Berlioz (1803–1869)	Johannes Brahms (1833–97)
2 pf. concertos: e; f Concert rondo; Polonaise Variations for pf. and orch.	*Faust Symphony* *Dante Symphony* 12 symphonic poems, incl. *Les Préludes, Mazeppa, Tasso* 2 pf. concertos: E♭; A *Totentanz,* pf. & orch	*Symphonie fantastique* *Lélio* (symph. w. narrator, chorus) *Harold in Italy* (w. viola solo) *Romeo and Juliet* (w. soloists, chorus) *Symphonie funèbre et triomphale* (for wind band) 6 overtures	4 symphonies: c; D; F; e Haydn variations 2 serenades 2 overtures Vln. concerto, D 2 pf. concertos: d, B♭ Double concerto (vln. & 'cello), a
Sonata; Polonaise for 'cello and pf. Pf. trio Variations, flute and pf.			3 quartets: c; a; B♭ 2 quintets: F; G 2 sextets: B♭; G 3 pf. trios: B; C; c 3 pf. quartets: g; A; c pf. quintet, f Horn trio Clarinet trio Clarinet quintet 3 vln. sonatas: G; A; d 2 'cello sonatas: e; F 2 clarinet sonatas: f; E♭
Polonaises (10) Ballades (4) Impromptus (3) Mazurkas (50) Nocturnes (19) Préludes (25) Rondos (3) Scherzi (4) Waltzes (14) Etudes (27) Berceuse; Barcarolle 2 sonatas: b♭; b	Transcendental études Hungarian rhapsodies (20) Sonata, b *Album d'un voyageur* (12 titled pieces) *Harmonies poétiques et réligieuses* (10 titled pieces) *Anneés de pélérinage* (26 travelogue pieces) Many other pieces, as well as many arrangements of his own and others' works		3 early sonatas: c; f♯; f Ballades (5) Rhapsodies (3) Capriccios (7) Intermezzi (8) Variations
17 Polish songs	ca. 75 songs	Songs for voice and orch. 28 solo songs	ca. 200 songs 25 duets Quartets with pf. (incl. *Liebeslieder* waltzes) Folk-song settings

	Oratorios *The Legend of St. Elizabeth; Christus*
	Masses; psalms; Requiem
	Choral church music
	Secular choral wks. w. pf. or orch. accomp.
		Operas:
		  Benvenuto Cellini
		  Les Troyens
		    I. *La prise de Troie*
		    II. *Les Troyens à Carthage*
		  Béatrice et Bénédict
		  La damnation de Faust (concert opera)
		
		Requiem
		Te Deum
		L'Enfance du Christ (oratorio)
			Requiem
			Schicksalslied
			Alto Rhapsody
			Unaccompanied choral works

Table 2. The operas of Verdi and Wagner

Giuseppe Verdi (1813–1901) (dates are first performance)	Richard Wagner (1813–1883) (date of composition)
Oberto, 1839	Die Hochzeit (unfinished), 1832
Un giorno di regno, 1840	Die Feen, 1833–34
Nabucco, 1842	Das Liebesverbot, 1835–36
I Lombardi, 1843	Rienzi, 1838–40
Ernani, 1844	Der fliegende Holländer, 1841
I due foscari, 1844	Tannhäuser, 1843–44
Giovanna d'Arco, 1845	Lohengrin, 1846–48
Alzira, 1845	Der Ring des Nibelungen
Attila, 1846	Das Rheingold, 1853–54
Macbeth, 1847	Die Walküre, 1854–56
I masnadieri, 1847	Siegfried, 1856–69
Il corsaro, 1848	Die Götterdämmerung, 1868–74
La battaglia di Legnano, 1849	Tristan und Isolde, 1857–59
Luisa Miller, 1849	Die Meistersinger von Nürnberg, 1862–67
Stiffelio, 1850	Parsifal, 1877–82
Rigoletto, 1851	
Il trovatore, 1853	
La traviata, 1853	
I vespri siciliani, 1856	
Simon Boccanegra, 1857	
Un ballo in maschera, 1859	
La forza del destino, 1862	
Don Carlos, 1867	
Aïda, 1871	
Otello, 1887	
Falstaff, 1893	

Bibliography.

Einstein, Alfred. *Music in the Romantic Era.* New York, 1947.
Complete editions of the works of all the composers listed here have been published; each composer has had several biographies written about him; it seems unnecessary to list them all, and unfair to cite only a few. Most are easily accessible.

XIV

THE LATE
NINETEENTH
CENTURY

Nationalism in music. The preceding chapter was concerned primarily with the work of German and Austrian composers, reflecting the preeminence in the nineteenth century of what may for the sake of brevity be called the German tradition. Of the exceptions, Liszt was largely Germanized, and Berlioz, Chopin, and Verdi all stand in one way or another outside what seems to have been the mainstream of musical development. They do so in fact precisely because they were *not* German, and because the "mainstream" was. Both the later Baroque and the classical periods had been international: Bach could transcribe Vivaldi, and borrow from the French style; and Mozart borrowed from everywhere. Such borrowings did not affect overall style in any significant way. There are Italians, Frenchmen, Spaniards, and Czechs among the classical composers, and it is rarely possible to deduce their nationality from their music.

In the nineteenth century, however, nationalism was one of the primary intellectual and emotional movements, not merely a political phenomenon, and its effects were also felt in the arts. Weber and Schumann used or imitated German folk tunes; and they, along with Wagner and others, were intensely concerned not only with music in general, but with German music in particular. So, also, Verdi felt it his duty to advise younger men to adhere to the Italian tradition, and to be wary of innovations from the North.

The nineteenth century also saw, if not the birth, at least the first important consequences of musical nationalism among peoples that had previously contributed relatively little to the central musical tradition. (Some of these have already been noted: Chopin's use of Polish dance-rhythms and melodic turns in his mazurkas and polonaises; "Hungarian" melodies in certain works of Liszt.) Such conscious attempts to utilize characteristic folk-idioms of the "peripheral" nations in art music are rather more striking than the folk-manner of, say, Weber, and the reason is both obvious and important. In the central nations—Italy, Germany, and France, in particular—folk- and art-music had long interacted, to the point where the more common folk tunes did not differ radically in style from simple art tunes (except in remote districts). Thus when Haydn bases a set of variations on what was apparently a French folk melody, the tune sounds neither French nor folk-like: it sounds like Haydn.

The same cannot be said for the nations of eastern Europe or for the Scandinavian countries. Their folk musics have styles differing widely from one another and from the prevailing styles of Western art music, and the introduction of such melodies, or of tunes composed in imitation of them, also introduces a new stylistic element into the work in which they appear. This is far from being a disadvantage: especially in the latter part of the nineteenth century, the problem of achieving something really original—in the face of the growing repertoire of accepted masterpieces—was increasingly difficult, and anything that could give music a new flavor was eagerly welcomed.

Nonetheless, nationalist music cannot be defined simply as music that contains or imitates folk melodies. (Here and in the following pages, the reference is to folk melodies as they were then understood by composers, not to scientifically exact reproductions of such tunes.)

Nationalist composers

Nationalist composers also attempted to evoke the historical and legendary past of their people, usually by employing or suggesting native literary materials. Even this, however, does not necessarily produce nationalist music. Verdi's *Aïda* glorifies the Egyptian past, and makes some attempt at suggesting the musical atmosphere of ancient Egypt: this does not make of Verdi an Egyptian nationalist. The truly nationalist composers offered their works to the public with the explicit intent that the music should be heard as a manifestation of national spirit, and the composers' countrymen, in their turn, agreed to receive such works in that spirit.

This compact between composer and public was an essential ingredient in the *creation* of national music, but of course the same music, performed outside the composer's own country, took on an exotic, not a national, flavor. The extent to which such music was successful in the Western world at large was, inevitably, a function of its composer's originality and talent. There are many works that have remained popular in their own countries without gaining more than token acceptance elsewhere.

Several nations produced nationalist music of great value and in considerable quantity. Bohemia (then still part of the Austrian empire, but with a culture of its own) can boast of Bedřich Smetana (1824–84) and Antonin Dvořák (1841–1904), Norway of Edvard Grieg (1843–1907); and there were others besides—all of whom combined elements from their native folk styles with methods derived from the primary European tradition. Some nationalists of a rather later period include Jean Sibelius (1865–1957) from Finland, Manuel de Falla (1876–1946) from Spain, Carl Nielsen (1865–1931) from Denmark, the Czech Leos Janáček (1854–1928), and the Hungarian Zoltán Kodály (1882–1967). In the work of these and other composers, national elements are combined with some features of twentieth-century style.

Music in Russia.   Without disparaging the contributions of other nations, it may safely be said that musical nationalism found its most typical and most important manifestation in Russia; and it is on Russian nationalism that this discussion will concentrate. For several centuries, art music imported from the West had coexisted with native Russian music, although the two had made little contact with each other. It was, of course, the aristocrats who preferred the sophisticated Western art, and the lesser folk who enjoyed and practiced the indigenous music. The success of Italian opera in Russia has already been mentioned, as has the personal success of Hector

Berlioz. But as early as the eighteenth century, Russian musicians (often serfs) were sent to the West to learn the techniques of European music, and European (mostly Italian) composers continued to be employed in Russia. The serfs, when they returned home, were of course "Russian composers," but their style hardly deviated from that of their Italian contemporaries. Even when Russian folk idioms were introduced into operas whose libretti depicted aspects of Russian life—as happens in works of both Russian and imported composers—the stylistic effect is apparently almost imperceptible (this music is as yet little known).

In any case, none of this music is of much artistic significance, and it was not until well into the nineteenth century that Russian music found composers capable of bearing comparison with the major composers of the West. The first of these was Mikhail Glinka (1804–57). After a period of travel and study in Europe, Glinka returned to Russia on fire with the idea of writing a truly Russian opera. The result was *A Life for the Tsar* (1836; also called *Ivan Susanin*), which—despite its fervently nationalistic subject matter—employs a rather conventional and Italianate musical style. The outstanding progressive feature of *A Life for the Tsar* is its extensive use of recurrent themes for dramatic purposes, well before Wagner's systematic development of the Leitmotive technique. Far more remarkable stylistically is Glinka's second opera, *Ruslan and Liudmila* (1842), which contains much music in Russian and vaguely "Oriental" idioms. Here Glinka also shows himself as an extraordinary innovator in matters of harmony and orchestration: the work is in several respects more advanced than anything in Western music at the time.

Mikhail Glinka

Another composer of the same period was Alexander Dargomizhsky (1813–69), author of a number of fine songs and several operas. Of these, the most important is *The Stone Guest*, a version of the Don Juan story. In this work Dargomizhsky restricts the vocal parts almost entirely to realistic (i.e., non-rhetorical) declamation, leaving the orchestra to provide most of the musical interest. While the result is by no means wholly successful, the work exercised considerable influence, particularly in the area of text-setting, on later Russian composers.

The next generation saw an intensification of Russian musical nationalism, made possible in part by the work of Glinka and Dargomizhsky. It is curious that most nineteenth-century Russian composers were in one sense or another amateurs: men without extended formal training in Western music, several of whom combined composition with a non-musical profession. This was, on the whole, an advantage. It was easier for such men to evolve an individual and striking Russian style precisely because they had not been carefully brought up on rules and practices based on Western music; while at the same time they could also turn to the international repertoire and select from it whatever techniques and devices they felt could be useful to them. In fact, nineteenth-century Russian music quite regularly embeds native elements into forms and contexts of Western provenance. Berlioz and Liszt were especially favored as models—and it is no accident that they were two of the more eccentric European composers, and that both had visited Russia.

One of the Russian "amateur" composers was Alexander Borodin (1833–87), whose professional studies and career were in the field of chemistry; and who, although he traveled extensively and knew much Western music, was never committed to Western style as a conservatory graduate would be. His life left him little time for composition, and his works are few but important. The largest is the opera *Prince Igor*. Unfinished at Borodin's death, it was completed by the younger composers Rim-

Alexander Borodin

sky-Korsakov and Glazounov, and first performed in 1891. (The Russian composers left many unfinished works, and even among those completed, there are a number of which the composer made several versions over a period of years: the lack of formal training may have resulted in a lack of confidence as well.) Borodin's style may also be seen in the fine Symphony in B minor (1876), some passages of which were originally intended for the opera. Even in this abstract and non-programmatic work, the Russian flavor is unmistakable from the very beginning. The basically monothematic first movement opens with a theme that is at once Russian and symphonic (Ex. XIV–1). The work is also remarkable for its unusual treatment of key-relations (the second movement is in F and the third in D♭: only the finale returns to B).

Ex. XIV-1

Modest Mussorgsky: Boris Godunov

An even greater composer was Modest Mussorgsky (1839–81), whose opera *Boris Godunov* (1874) is one of the major stage works of the nineteenth century. *Boris* is a remarkably original score, owing almost nothing to Western opera, and only a little (mainly in the area of declamation) to Mussorgsky's Russian predecessors. The plot is a gloomy tale out of Russian history, arranged as a series of juxtaposed static tableaux. (The shaping of an opera into a series of "pictures" with little internal dramatic action is a characteristically Russian device.) Although the music is saturated with Russianism, it makes little use of actual Russian folk melodies—the most famous being the one in the Prologue (a tune that Beethoven had used in his quartet, Op. 59, no. 2). The vocal writing in *Boris* is not lyrical in the conventional sense, being a more musical treatment of the song-speech of *The Stone Guest*. The rhetorical declamation of Wagner is conspicuously absent, as is any sort of aria in the Italian manner.

Yet it is vocal melody—a melody that derives more from speech than from conventional song—that lies at the heart of the work, effectively delineating the characters and carrying the movement of the drama. The orchestra is often treated quite elaborately—Mussorgsky was fond of brilliant, sonorous colors—but it is clearly subordinate, not central as in Wagner's operas. So also the harmony, often highly inventive—to the point of sounding "faulty" to Western contemporaries—is designed to heighten the impact of the melody. Mussorgsky was not interested in harmony for its own sake, and still less in academic correctness. In *Boris*, as in Mussorgsky's many fine songs, all musical means are placed at the service of the text.

The original versions of *Boris* and many other Russian works of the later part of the nineteenth century have only recently become known to the public, owing primarily to the editorial activities of Nicolai Rimsky-Korsakov (1844–1908), who extensively revised, edited, and in some cases completed works of his compatriots. Unfortunately, his zeal for stylistic propriety—in the Western, not the Russian sense—often outstripped his editorial discretion, and in attempting to "improve" his originals, he sometimes falsified the composer's intent. Mussorgsky's version of *Boris*, with all its "crudities," is now generally regarded as far finer than Rimsky-Korsakov's more sophisticated revision (to say nothing of later revisions by lesser men).

Nicolai Rimsky-Korsakov

As a composer, Rimsky-Korsakov was versatile and prolific, and somewhat more receptive to Western ideas than Mussorgsky. He achieved a profound mastery of orchestration, deriving ultimately from Berlioz rather than from Wagner (although there are Wagnerian pages as well), and his scores are particularly impressive as pure sound. While his numerous operas are seldom performed in the West, his *Scheherezade*, a symphonic suite, is well known. An extended tone poem in clear, bright colors, it makes a striking contrast with the gloom of Mussorgsky's *Boris*.

Not all Russian composers were nationalists: Peter Ilyitch Tchaikovsky (1840–93), the most famous of them all, was basically committed to Western musical methods. While Tchaikovsky often quotes Russian folk tunes in his music, his music remains fundamentally international in style. His most popular works, the later symphonies and the B♭ minor concerto for piano, are written in a passionately romantic, autobiographical style, and are more successful in their conveyance of violent emotion than in structure or refinement. His "overture-fantasy" *Romeo and Juliet* (final version 1880), more convincing in terms of structure, contains as well one of Tchaikovsky's most beautiful lyric melodies (Ex. XIV–2). But it is probably Tchaikovsky's ballet music (e.g., *Sleeping Beauty*, 1889; *Nutcracker*, 1892) that represents the composer at his best. In these works, Tchaikovsky has created a successful fusion of the symphony, the sequence of character pieces, and the old stylized dance suite. The attractive melodies and delicate scoring of these works are more convincing than the violent outbursts of the symphonies.

Peter Ilyitch Tchaikovsky

Tchaikovsky was also active as a composer of operas, some of which are again being performed in Western countries after many years of neglect. Compared to *Boris*, they are conventional, even a little old fashioned. But *Evgeni Onegin* (1879) and *The Queen of Spades* (1890), both with libretti after Pushkin, are thoroughly convincing works, stylistically closer to the ballets than to the symphonies.

A later Russian internationalist was Alexander Scriabin (1872–1915). He began by writing rather conventional piano music based on the style of Chopin. Gradually his style became more chromatic and more dissonant, to the point of losing almost all contact with a triadic or tonal basis: fundamental sonorities in his later works are frequently constructed of superimposed and chromatically altered fourths, with little or no tonal implication. These and other musical innovations were inextricably con-

Alexander Scriabin

Ex. XIV-2

nected with Scriabin's mystical philosophy. While he anticipated some of the methods used by composers of the twentieth century, Scriabin remained an isolated figure, with no successors and little historical influence.

Nationalism in Russian music

Indeed it may be said that only the nationalists were of real historical importance, not so much for the intrinsic value of their works—considerable though this is—but for their demonstration that Western (and more specifically German) methods and materials were not the sole possible vehicles for musical expression. Those Russian composers who assimilated and/or quoted native folk melodies in their music introduced, as it were, new words into the musical vocabulary: tunes using only a few different pitches, arranged so that similar melodic patterns fall in different rhythmic positions; underlying scales differing from the major and minor ones and often lacking the leading tone; hence, different types of chord progressions, made necessary when such melodies were harmonized; and, finally, different rhythms and meters (e.g., 5/4, which was extemely rare in Western music). When, in the late nineteenth century, Russian music became known in Europe, which was then hungry for stylistic novelties, such factors, translated into the language of other styles, took on considerable significance.

POST-ROMANTIC MUSIC IN GERMANY AND AUSTRIA

Bruckner and Brahms.   The search for such "new words" was still in the future for German and Austrian musicians of the second half of the century, although the problem of novelty was not. Composers had already felt the weight of Beethoven's legacy. To this was now added the problem of surpassing the innovations of the romantics and, increasingly, of coping with the stylistic self-consciousness induced by the growing knowledge of Bach, Handel, and sometimes even earlier composers. Finally, there was the challenge of Wagner. With the first performance of *Tristan* in 1865, the tonal system seemed to have been stretched to its limits. What more was there to write?

Still, the end was not yet at hand, even though it was not far off. There remained two possibilities: either somehow to reconcile the subjectivity of the romantics with the great structures of Beethoven; or, again somehow, to outdo Wagner on his own ground, or to apply Wagnerisms to areas Wagner had not cultivated. The choice of one of these alternatives was in a sense a pledge of allegiance—either to a conservative or to a Wagnerian school; but in fact the "schools" did not work out quite as might have been expected.

The apparently antipodal cases of Johannes Brahms (1833–97) and Anton Bruckner (1824–96) illustrate this clearly. Brahms, after a few youthful ventures in unrestrained romanticism, turned back for the most part to classical forms, and wrote structurally conservative quartets, symphonies, and the like. Bruckner, a passionate admirer of Wagner, never touched either the romantic character piece or the opera: he wrote primarily symphonies and some liturgical music. Both composers lived in Vienna and were aesthetic opponents, yet they were in a sense less opposed than they then imagined.

Brahms and Bruckner

An Austrian, Bruckner was intended for a career as a teacher. He turned gradually to music, was active as an organist from 1856, and as a teacher at the Vienna Conservatory from 1868. He was an ardent Roman Catholic, and most of his early music is sacred—Masses and smaller compositions for the church. Although he continued to write sacred music—his mature Masses and his *Te Deum* are fine works—it is as a composer of symphonies that he is chiefly remembered.

Bruckner's life and works

For a man attached so deeply to Wagner, the symphony would appear a curious choice of genre; yet Bruckner persisted in it, from the so-called Symphony No. 0 of 1863–64 to the incomplete Symphony No. 9, on which he was working at his death. Moreover, these are in some respects quite conventional symphonies: they are in the traditional four movements; they have no programmatic titles; and their forms, while ample, are basically classical. Indeed, on first examination, Bruckner's symphonies remind one more of Beethoven and Schubert than of Wagner. The Wagnerism is there, nevertheless. It lies in the richly modulatory, often strongly chromatic harmony; in the intensity of the expression; in the great size of the pieces (a Bruckner symphony averages about three or four times the length of one by Mozart). Bruckner's counterpoint and his use of thematic recurrence and transformation also derive from the Wagner-Liszt tradition. His counterpoint, except in the latest works, is more a matter of fitting together separate themes for a climactic combination than a continuing independence of different voices; and his transformation of an originally quiet or ominous theme into one of triumph (cf. the beginning and end of the Eighth Symphony) is clear evidence of his stylistic orientation. His use of the orchestra, while Wagnerian in the choice of instruments and sometimes in the manner of their employment, often appears to stem from his early work as an organist: it is as if stops were being added or taken off, something quite different from Wagner's subtly shifting colors. (Bruckner's orchestration, and indeed some other aspects of his music, have long been obscured by the first published versions of his scores. These first editions contain many changes—most, but not all, in matters of scoring—from Bruckner's original conceptions. Some of the changes were apparently accepted, perhaps reluctantly, by the composer; others are wholly unauthorized. The original versions, insofar as they can be determined, have only recently come into common use.)

Bruckner's style

Certain of Bruckner's mannerisms recur in several of the symphonies: mysterious beginnings, in which a theme arises out of string tremolos (a device obviously derived from the opening of Beethoven's Ninth Symphony); vigorous, peasant-like scherzo themes; climactic finales, often using lyrical chorale-like tunes as secondary themes; and favorite rhythms, such as ♫♩♫♩ and ♩♩♩♩ Still, each symphony has a personality of its own, and the familiar elements acquire a new and different life each time they appear.

Bruckner has been described as a naive composer, and his symphonies have been criticized as being too long and sometimes defective in structure. If Bruckner is naive, then so also are Mozart and Schubert. If his symphonies are long, it is generally for good reason. With a theme like that which begins the Seventh Symphony (Ex. XIV–3), one can and must expect a lengthy movement. It is true that not all of his movements are wholly convincing structurally; but the same may be said of many nineteenth-century composers. The tonal tensions that formed the essence of the classical symphony become less urgent and more difficult to hear when the individual phrase is saturated with chromatic harmony—a point noted earlier. Thus while the classicists had both tonality and thematic contrast at their disposal, Bruckner had to rely more heavily on themes. It would be surprising if he had invariably succeeded. In any event, although Bruckner is still played less frequently than many other composers of the century, he was one of the few major symphonists of his age.

Brahms's life and works

Brahms was a man of a much different sort. A North German who spent most of his adult life in Vienna, he was closely associated with Schumann in the latter's final years, and began composing in a violently romantic style. Despite Schumann's praises, however, Brahms soon became dissatisfied, and began a lifelong attempt to blend romantic fervor with severely classical structure. For this he earned from one critic (Alfred Einstein) the title of "posthumous musician"—which, despite its unfairness, contains some germ of truth.

(continued on following page)

(doublings omitted)

Ex. XIV-3

Brahms's output was considerable, and he contributed to most of the principal genres of composition—symphonies, concertos, string quartets and other chamber music, choral music, Lieder, and character pieces for piano. He also made a number of solo and choral arrangements of folksongs. There are, however, no dramatic works: Brahms preferred the internal drama provided by musical development to that supplied by extra-musical content. Most of his character pieces carry only such neutral designations as "intermezzo," "cappriccio," and the like.

Unlike many nineteenth-century composers, Brahms turned easily from one type of work to another; these are, for example, piano music, chamber works, and songs from all periods of his career. Exception must be made, however, for his large orchestral works. Brahms waited long before presenting his First Symphony (1876): the shadow of Beethoven lay heavily upon him. But by 1885 the remaining three symphonies, a (second) piano concerto, and a violin concerto were completed; his last orchestral piece, the double concerto for violin and 'cello, was finished two years later.

Brahms's symphonies

Brahms's concept of a symphony was quite different from that of Bruckner, even though both composers kept to the traditional four-movement pattern and relied on sonata form as their most important structure. The difference is basically a psychological one: for Bruckner, the symphony was primarily a mystic vision; for Brahms, it was first of all a solid piece of music. Bruckner's ancestry includes not only the lyricism of Schubert, but also some, at least, of the world of Wagner. Brahms, although he too received the inheritance of Schubert—and also that of Schumann—based his work on that of Beethoven far more directly than did Bruckner. In their solidity and tension, Brahms's symphonies closely resemble those of Beethoven, with the difference that Beethoven's violent and dramatic conflict (in the Third, Fifth, and Ninth Symphonies, for example) has mellowed in Brahms to a more instrospective, almost philosophical contemplation.

Three characteristics may clarify the distinction between Brahms and Bruckner. First, Brahms writes for what is essentially the classical orchestra—somewhat enlarged, to be sure—instead of Bruckner's Wagnerian ensemble, in which the brass section is often the dominating element. And Brahms is even less a colorist than Bruckner. His musical substance is almost as little dependent on the medium as the non-piano music of Schumann—as Brahms himself showed when he published his *Variations on a Theme of Haydn* in two versions, one for two pianos and the other for orchestra, both equally satisfactory.

Second, Brahms is consistently contrapuntal, in the sense that there are almost invariably present two or more simultaneous melodic strands, and even the hidden inner voices have their own integrity. This is a far different matter from the occasional climactic theme-combinations of Bruckner, who is only intermittently contrapuntal otherwise.

Third, and related to the preceding point, Brahms's musical materials, even when lyric, generally have a motivic basis—the first theme of the Fourth Symphony, for example, is built out of only two motives (Ex. XIV–4). This both encourages contrapuntal writing and provides material almost automatically suitable for development. It also provides means by which to avoid the excessive dependence on four-measure phrases that is so often a consequence of lyrical symphonic writing. The opening of the Fourth Symphony is a good example in this respect as well: its forephrase is four measures long, but what follows is greatly extended, with the result that a high degree of tension is achieved from the start.

(continued on following page)

Ex. XIV-4

Each of Brahms's symphonies has its own character. The First is a post-romantic counterpart to Beethoven's Fifth—a progress from despair to triumph; the Second is pastoral; the Third heroic; and the Fourth subdued and pessimistic. The Fourth also shows an important aspect of Brahms's musical thought—his concern with music of the past. His knowledge of musical history was greater than that of any other important composer of his time: he was familiar with the work of such long-forgotten masters as Heinrich Schütz, among many others, and was active as an editor and arranger of early music. For the finale of the Fourth Symphony he reached back into the Baroque for a formal scheme—that of the passacaglia. The movement is a chain of variations on one theme (Ex. XIV–5), ending with a free coda. This is more significant than it may first appear. While the tradition of imitative counterpoint had never died out, forms such as the passacaglia had, for all practical purposes. Brahms is thus borrowing not from the immediate past, but from a relatively remote period—the first sign of a historicism that was to grow even stronger in the next century.

Ex. XIV-5

All four symphonies share a basically diatonic harmony (with the result that the sonata movements are able to profit by tonal as well as thematic tensions); a certain severity of style, relieved on occasion by Viennese lyricism;[1] and a careful attention to detail. They are perhaps the only symphonies of the nineteenth century to recapture the structural urgency of Beethoven. This does not make them "better" or "more symphonic" than other nineteenth-century works, but it does make them different, and more strictly classical.

Brahms's "intimate" style

Although the symphonies and other large works fully deserve the high reputation they enjoy, an important part of the essence of Brahms lies elsewhere: Brahms in his heroic or public character is often less revealing than he is in his more intimate works. The difference in character does not depend entirely on the medium, for a work like the String Quartet in C minor, Op. 51, no. 1 (1873), is as grim and forbidding as the First Symphony. It is rather a difference in attitude, a kind of relaxation that Brahms achieves, perhaps when he is least preoccupied with the shadow of Beethoven. At such times, the lyricism of Brahms's music becomes more pronounced (although there is no relaxation of technical control). The mood ranges from nostalgic warmth to undisguised pessimism, the latter especially in some of the late works.

Naturally some of these more relaxed works are in the smaller romantic forms—songs and short pieces for piano—but the same quality also appears in pieces of classical structure. The Sonata in G for violin and piano, Op. 78 (1879), is an excellent example. It is a true sonata, well built and cogent, but its materials are largely lyrical (Ex. XIV–6). Its air of nostalgia is that of a composer looking back on the freer days of true romanticism, and wistfully reconstructing its spirit within the framework of classical discipline.

---

[1] In addition to continuing the lyric tradition of Schubert, Brahms also imitates from time to time the idiom of the Viennese waltz, immensely popular in the nineteenth century both as an actual dance and as a style. It is no accident that Brahms had great respect for Johann Strauss the younger, a composer of light operas that are saturated with waltz tunes.

Ex. XIV-6

Yet Brahms does not ignore romantic formal innovations. The last movement of this sonata contains two important reminiscences: the three repeated D's of the beginning of the piece, which serve also as beginning of this movement; and a transformation of the slow movement theme, which serves here as an episode. Thus the work is cyclic, but one senses that Brahms's reasons for making it so are musical rather than intellectual—that he is a classicist also in his way of thinking in tones, rather than in abstract extra-musical schemes. Indeed, while numerous works of Brahms contain thematic relations within and between movements, these are more often than not of a semi-concealed nature, often unnoticed by the casual listener (who hears, nevertheless, the inner unity of the piece). One may legitimately compare this discreet treatment with the styles of Liszt and Berlioz and their successors, where cyclical recurrence and transformation are regularly climactic effects that no listener could miss. The difference is not one of value, but of temperament: Brahms was no longer a romantic, as Bruckner (despite his debt to Wagner) was, but rather a neo-classicist.

Brahms wrote extensively for the piano, both as a solo instrument and as a participant in chamber music. His piano writing is more often solid than brilliant, deriving from Schumann, but thicker and more polyphonic; it shows few traces of the pianistic innovations of Chopin and Liszt, even in the brilliant and difficult pieces. Among his best pieces for solo piano are the late sets of character pieces—intermezzi, cappriccios, and rhapsodies. Most of these are simple in form (ABA being the commonest pattern) but rich and complex in content. Though clearly descended from the romantic character piece, they are even more abstract than Chopin's preludes: one could hardly imagine trying to read an extra-musical "program" into these austere but impressive works.

Brahms's piano works and chamber music

Brahms also produced much chamber music, including several pieces for piano and strings, and several involving the clarinet. One of the finest of his chamber works is the Quintet for clarinet and strings, Op. 115 (1891), in which Brahms's late, elegiac manner is effortlessly molded into classical forms of ample dimensions; while the passionate outbursts in the midst of the otherwise tranquil slow movement show that the romantic fire, while under strict formal control, was still alive in Brahms's old age.

Brahms's vocal music

Brahms was as productive in vocal music as he was in instrumental. He wrote a large number of songs, ranging from simple folk-song settings to complex art-songs. The latter continue the Lieder tradition of Schubert and Schumann, and while they offer no striking technical innovations, many of them rank among the finest songs of the century, and offer a wide variety of expressive types (e.g. the exquisitely lyrical "Die Mainacht," and the passionate "Von ewiger Liebe," both from 1868).

But Brahms had also another and rarer gift—that of writing for chorus with a skill as sure as that of Handel. In addition to numerous smaller works for chorus with or without accompaniment, he produced several major compositions for chorus with orchestra and solo voice (or voices). Chief among these are the *German Requiem* (1857–68), which is not a liturgical Requiem, but a setting in seven large movements of appropriate Biblical texts; and the *Alto Rhapsody* (1869), a setting of a text by Goethe. The latter is a particularly fine illustration of the severe and the lyrical Brahms juxtaposed: the first section pictures the plight of the lonely misanthrope, in appropriately harsh and uncompromising music; the second is a prayer for his deliverance, expressed in one of the loveliest of Brahms's melodies.

The German Requiem

The *German Requiem*, a much larger work, exhibits almost the whole range of Brahms's expressive palette, from the despairing to the exquisitely consolatory; or, in technical terms, from the purest lyricism to the strictest neo-Baroque counterpoint. While the *Requiem* is neither Brahms's last nor even his greatest composition, it forms an appropriate conclusion to a consideration of his work, for it demonstrates the range of his talent—as great indeed as that of any musician since Beethoven, and yet also limited, like that of all composers of the nineteenth century. His boundaries were imposed by the lateness of his time, and by his own commitment to conservatism: thus neither the innocence of real romanticism nor the genuinely heroic manner of Beethoven were available to him. Yet the middle ground he worked in was ample, and he exploited it superbly.

The post-Wagnerians.   It should by now be evident that the late nineteenth century was a period of special solutions to a general problem—that posed by the search for a fresh and vital style based (however tenuously) on tonality. Nationalism was one answer—one that took many forms; conservatism was another. Both honorably evaded the central problem, that of Wagner, who was for this period the same kind of stumbling block that Beethoven had been earlier. The 1860s saw the birth of the first important composers who were in a real sense followers of Wagner—who were able to assimilate what they wanted from his style, and then go on to formulate individual styles of their own. Of course, Wagner had had his imitators—lesser men who copied as well as they could, and quite naturally failed. And there was also a curious fad late in the century for the *Märchenoper* (fairy-tale opera), in which the whole panoply of Wagnerian dramaturgy was put in the service of some simple children's story. This produced only one work that has survived, the *Hansel and Gretel* (1893) of Engelbert Humperdinck (1854–1921), which somehow succeeds despite the disparity between means and end. But this late date merely confirms the fact that German Wagnerism produced nothing important until the last two decades of the century.

Of the three major composers of the Wagnerian school—Gustav Mahler (1860–1911), Richard Strauss (1864–1949), and Hugo Wolf (1860–1903)—the last named will be considered first. Wolf's short career (in Vienna) was almost totally lacking in public success. This failure, combined with his extreme sensitivity, doubtless contributed to the insanity that seized him in 1898, and to his early death. Like Chopin, Wolf was a specialist, for although he wrote a tone poem and an opera, and often dreamed of other large works, he is remembered almost solely for his Lieder.

Hugo Wolf

Wolf's songs are arranged, not in cycles, but in collections. It was his habit to seize upon the work of a single poet and set a large number of his lyrics in an astonishingly short time, and then to write nothing at all for a while. Then some new body of verse would rouse him from his depression, re-ignite his creative power, and the process would repeat itself. His choice of texts was discriminating. About half are German poems of high literary quality. The rest are German translations of Spanish and Italian poems, including some of Michelangelo's most serious sonnets. By no means all the songs are serious, however. Many of the Spanish and Italian poems, especially, are light in character, and permit Wolf to exhibit his exceptional gifts as a musical humorist. Wolf evolved a particular style for each set of songs: while his underlying musical personality is evident in all he wrote, each collection differs from all the others in detail, and forms a special unity of its own.

Wolf was a passionate admirer of Wagner, and publicly attacked Brahms as a pedant—in Vienna itself, where Brahms was all-powerful. Wolf's Wagnerism is evident in the irregular, asymmetrical phrasing of the melody, which often produces a kind of rhetorical declamation similar to that of Wagner; in the frequently chromatic and dissonant nature of the harmony; and in the importance of the accompaniment (always for piano), which often assumes a large part of the musical interest.

Wolf treats his texts with the utmost care, preserving and enhancing their natural rhythms, while faithfully reflecting every emotional and psychological implication of their meanings. In consequence, his forms are extremely varied: there are miniatures lasting a minute or so, held together by a recurrent figure in the piano; and there are large, serious songs five times as long. The latter generally contain some sort of sectional repetition (often varied), but such recurrence is always justified by the text. The music is indeed the servant—though a proud one—of the words.

Wolf's songs are always intensely expressive, but in an intimate, non-theatrical fashion. Their range is wide—from the coquetries of an Italian peasant girl to the profundities of Goethe. Although his entire output occupies no more than a few volumes, and although he was a composer without successors (if only because he had carried the Lied to a point that could not be surpassed without a radical change of style), Wolf made a priceless contribution to musical literature. He stands as the last heir of Schubert: although the effortless melody of the old days is gone, it is amply replaced by harmonic richness and psychological insight.

The pathetic career of Wolf finds its opposite in that of Richard Strauss. Born into a musical but conservative family, Strauss began by writing music of an almost academic sort. In the mid 80s, however, he was converted to the modernism of Liszt, Berlioz, and Wagner, and became, for a considerable period of time, the foremost German Wagnerian, simultaneously achieving celebrity as a conductor. His first important works are orchestral tone poems, which continue the tradition of Liszt, but

Richard Strauss's orchestral music

in a somewhat different manner. While Liszt treated the tone poem as a character study, with only occasional bits of musical pictorialism, Strauss leaned more to the pictorial and the narrative: representations of non-musical events (the attack on the windmill and the bleating of the sheep in *Don Quixote* [1897], for example) are more frequent than in Liszt.

Although one might expect that this tendency would demand that each work develop its own ad hoc form, Strauss often makes apt use of traditional formal schemes, treated very freely. Thus *Don Quixote* is a set of free variations, and *Till Eulenspiegel* a free rondo. For other works, Strauss does create a new structure, episodic in nature, with such thematic recurrences and transformations as the literary program may suggest.

The range of subject matter, and hence of expression, is very broad: from the *Symphonia domestica* (1904), describing a day in the life of Strauss's own family, to the heroic *Ein Heldenleben* (A Hero's Life; 1898; the hero is again Strauss), and not excluding the comic. The musical means are essentially Wagnerian, with less persistent chromaticism than *Tristan*, and a rather more venturesome treatment of dissonance. The latter may derive in part from Liszt's late experiments, but it owes more to Strauss's persistent use of highly contrapuntal textures, in which the moving voices are constantly colliding to form dissonant sonorities. In general, Strauss is an extremist, pushing every known means to what seems to be its utmost limit. There is a hectic intensity in his music, curiously relieved at times by sweetly lyrical melodies of an almost Italian cast.

Strauss was a superb orchestrator, blending the brillance of Berlioz with the richness and power of Wagner—while adding much of his own invention. He makes enormous demands on his players, but the opulent palette of sound that results is ample justification.

Strauss's operas   Some of Strauss's symphonic poems are best regarded as program symphonies in one movement; others (the more narrative ones) are more like operas without words. In 1895 and 1901 Strauss wrote real operas, but these may be considered as experiments: they are not highly regarded today. In 1905, however, he made a definitive turn to the musical stage, for which he thereafter wrote almost all of his important works. In his first two mature operas, *Salome* (1905) and *Elektra* (1909), he found a way of using Wagnerian methods without competing with Wagner: he chose subjects that are frankly revolting, rather than morally uplifting. *Salome*, based on Oscar Wilde's play, is a study in perversion: Salome's love for John the Baptist can be satisfied only by her kissing John's severed head. *Elektra* explores pathological vengeance, in a text (after Sophocles) by Hugo von Hofmannsthal, who remained Strauss's literary collaborator for the next twenty years.

Both operas are short and almost frenzied in their intensity. They are faithfully Wagnerian in their use of Leitmotives; in their declamatory vocal writing, often involving wide leaps and extreme range; and in their scrupulous fidelity to the text. But Wagner sounds almost tame by comparison. As always, Strauss was equal to his subject, and the two works are overpowering, if not unduly pleasant.

Strauss's next opera, *Der Rosenkavalier* (The Knight of the Rose; 1911) is quite different. The text, again by von Hofmannsthal, is a comedy of manners set in eighteenth-century Vienna; and the musical extremes of *Salome* and *Elektra* are replaced by a score that is still very complex, but much more pleasing. The more intense passages are often relieved by simple lyrical passages with diatonic harmony; and much of the music is based on popular Viennese waltz idioms. The ensemble scenes are especially impressive, showing a power of simultaneous character-delineation surpassed only by Mozart, Verdi, and Wagner (note especially the trio near the end of the opera, in which relatively simple musical means are employed to achieve a superb effect).

Der Rosenkavalier hints at, but does not make explicit, a basic change in Strauss's style: a turn away from the excesses of post-romanticism towards a classical—or rather neo-classical—style. Always an admirer, but to this point never an imitator, of Mozart, Strauss in his later works becomes more cool and more restrained. The vast Wagnerian orchestra is reduced, sometimes almost to chamber dimensions; sung lyrical melody begins to take precedence over declamation; and Wagnerian dramaturgy yields to some extent to a Mozartian formalism (there are true arias, some of which include superb virtuoso writing for the singers). It was along these lines that Strauss pursued the remainder of his long career, with only occasional reversions to his earlier style. His later works have not achieved popular success, although they have a number of admirers. Still, whatever their intrinsic interest, they are of little interest in the general history of style. One of the watchwords of the twentieth century was "neo-classicism"—but not Strauss's kind. After *Der Rosenkavalier*, Strauss withdrew increasingly into a world of his own.

The nineteenth century remains one of the great ages of music, and also one of the most problematic. It has left incomparable miniatures, but few of its larger works are beyond criticism of some sort. There are dull patches in Wagner, vulgarities in Verdi, academicisms in Brahms, chaotic passages in Bruckner, and so on.

Two types of adverse criticism are made: the frequent one that a composer has imperfectly realized a great conception; and the less common one that he has done perfectly something that, in the last analysis, was not worth doing that well. Obviously Strauss belongs among those whose execution was faultless: one can argue only with his purposes. With the last composer of the present group, the case is different, for Gustav Mahler had ideals as high and visions as broad as those of Beethoven: the only question concerns the extent to which he was able to realize them. Like Strauss, Mahler was celebrated as a conductor, with the important difference that Strauss conducted when he chose to, while Mahler was dependent on regular conducting for his living. Tied to a heavy schedule of rehearsals and performances, he was forced to limit his composition almost entirely to brief summer vacations. Although he was by no means the first composer thus encumbered, his career illustrates a trend that has continued and intensified to the present day—a trend towards the part-time composer, whose livelihood comes from performance or (more recently) teaching, and who must find time in the odd hours of his working day for composing, which will bring him little or nothing financially.

Partly for this reason, Mahler's works are rather few in number. But there is another reason as well: many of them are gigantic—in length, in the number of performers required, and in richness of detail—and pieces of such scope require much time and thought. Although some of Mahler's youthful works are large, most of his earliest published works are groups of Lieder, showing no sign of any inclination towards enormous size. The best of these are the *Lieder eines fahrenden Gesellen* (Songs of a Wayfarer; 1883), with orchestral rather than piano accompaniment: they are beautifully wrought, sensitive settings of folk-like texts. But, even though Mahler's conducting was primarily in the opera house, it was the symphony that drew

Gustav Mahler's life and works

him. Although he wrote several more songs in later years, most of his energy was poured into his symphonies—nine completed ones (1888–1909) and an incomplete tenth on which he was working at his death.

Mahler's conception of the symphony derived ultimately from Beethoven, by way of Wagner and Bruckner. (This is no justification for coupling the names of Mahler and Bruckner in the manner of "Bach and Handel:" their differences are greater than their similarities, and Bruckner was old enough to have been Mahler's father.) For Mahler, each symphony was to be "a world, with everything in it." Thus, while each has its own character, each also has a wide range of expression, so as to contain "everything."

Mahler's symphonies

The symphonies are about evenly divided between purely instrumental works (1, 5, 6, 7, 9, and 10), and those with voices (2, 3, 4, 8). The Eighth is the "symphony of a thousand," with eight soloists, double chorus, boys' choir, organ, and an enormous orchestra. One further large-scale work, *Das Lied von der Erde* (The Song of the Earth;

(continued on following page)

Gustav Mahler, *Das Lied von der Erde*. Copyright 1911, Universal Edition. Used by permission of the publisher. Theodore Presser Company, sole representative, United States, Canada, and Mexico.

Ex. XIV-7

1908), may be considered either as a song cycle for two soloists and large orchestra, or as another symphony, with extensive vocal passages. Whichever view one takes, it is perhaps Mahler's finest achievement (Ex. XIV-7).

Mahler's use of the orchestra

As a professional conductor, Mahler naturally had a profound knowledge of the capabilities of the orchestra, and his musical substance is inseparably linked to its medium. While less brilliant than that of Strauss, his orchestration is extraordinarily rich in felicitous sound colors, from the most delicate to the most grandiose. The attitude of the conductor is also evident from the numerous detailed instructions Mahler wrote into his scores: he knew exactly what he wanted, and took the greatest care that any performance would conform to his wishes.

Mahler seems to have thought of his instrumental music as essentially programmatic, even though the surviving versions of the symphonies are not given programs. Several movements of the early symphonies suggest aspects of Nature, in a kind of intensification of Beethoven's Sixth Symphony. From the Fifth through the Seventh, one's impression is that the music is concerned with spiritual struggle—by no means always ending in triumph. The last works seem increasingly resigned, sometimes restrained—"late" works by a composer who was still not fifty years old.

His style is not easy to describe or illustrate, if only because each symphony is "a world." Long lyrical melodies, complex and asymmetrical in shape, are mixed with violent motivic passages based on incisive rhythms. Pronounced folk-like elements are often found, and even intentional vulgarity of the German beer-garden variety makes an occasional appearance. All these elements are combined in large forms, some of which are clearly related to classical prototypes, while others are not. Themes often recur from one movement to another, although not systematically; and Mahler likes to quote his song melodies in his symphonies (thus presumably evoking their texts).

Mahler's harmony

Mahler's harmony is surprisingly diatonic for his time. Although there are frequent sudden changes of key, persistent, Tristanesque chromaticism is rare. Also absent is Strauss's deliberately shocking use of dissonance. From the Fifth Symphony on, Mahler's music becomes more contrapuntal, and its dissonance content increases; but the clashes are mostly heard as by-products of the part-writing, and are rarely exploited for their own sake.

Even so, the music is intensely expressive and subjective: one senses the moral convictions of the man in every measure. Thus it comes as no surprise that one symphony ends in a key different from that in which it began; that some have the traditional four movements, but others either more or fewer; that some are cyclically unified, others not; and so on. Each "world" has its own inner laws, which may or may not agree with normal symphonic conventions.

Most musicians would agree that Mahler's larger works are often defective, in the sense that he has not wholly or faultlessly conveyed the vast vision he has glimpsed. Nonetheless, Mahler's sincerity and force make him the leading German-speaking composer of his time. While Strauss seems to exhaust the possibilities of everything he touches, Mahler, even when he is not wholly successful, points the way to paths not yet explored.

FRANCE

Opera in Italy and France.   The end of the century in Italy produced little of lasting value. Opera still dominated the musical scene, and Wagnerian methods were cautiously imported and transformed to suit the lyric Italian temper. Two ephemeral trends appeared in the libretti: realism (*verismo*) and exoticism. The former is apparent in the popular *Cavalleria rusticana* (Rustic Chivalry; 1890) by Pietro Mascagni (1863–1945); the latter in several works of Giacomo Puccini (1858–1924); *Madame Butterfly* (1904; set in Japan); *The Girl of the Golden West* (1910; the first musical "Western"); and *Turandot* (1924; set in China). Puccini was less a Wagnerian than a Verdian, aiming to recapture the intense pathos of *Otello*. Although much of his work remains extremely popular, it never rises to the level of Verdi's better music. Puccini was nevertheless a sound musician and an adroit manipulator of dramatic effect.

In France, matters were rather different, and one may with justice speak of a renaissance of French music in the late nineteenth century. Although opera dominated the French musical scene until well after 1870, it was not the focus of new musical thought. Both the Opéra and the Opéra comique were basically conservative institutions, and the music composed for them was expected to be attractive to the general public. One prominent opera composer was Charles Gounod (1818–93), whose well-made and melodious works (including the popular *Faust* of 1859) have a good deal of charm, but fall short of true greatness. The only real masterpiece of French opera between Berlioz and Debussy is Georges Bizet's *Carmen* (1875), which remains as fresh today as it was at its first performance. But Bizet died young in 1875, and the normal, conservative French tradition was carried on: a successful composer was Jules Massenet (1842–1912), whose sensuous melodies lack the force of opera at its best.

The revival of French instrumental music.   Meanwhile, there were new, non-operatic stirrings. César Franck (1822–90), a Belgian who made his career as an organist in a Parisian church, wrote symphonic poems, a symphony, and chamber music, as well as much organ music and many sacred works. His music is by no means strikingly French in sound: the often strongly chromatic harmony is reminiscent of Liszt and Wagner, and his forms ultimately derive from the classical (i.e., Germanic) tradition, with frequent application of the cyclical principle. His best works—the violin sonata (1886), the symphony (1888), and the string quartet (1889) for example—are major contributions to the literature, despite Franck's lack of success with the French public. But even more important than his work was his role as one of the two principal founders of a new French tradition of serious instrumental music.

César Franck

The other was Camille Saint-Saëns (1835–1931), a versatile composer who wrote in all genres, including opera. An immensely talented musician, he was eclectic in style: his music, clearer and more elegant than Franck's, is less personal and less compelling. Therefore, even more than Franck, Saint-Saëns is important for historical rather than musical reasons—his enthusiastic promotion of French music, both old and new, and his dedication to high standards in instrumental as well as vocal music. His influence was a powerful and beneficent one.

Camille Saint-Saëns

It was in the 1870s, spurred by the revival of French patriotism that followed the disastrous Franco-Prussian war, that the new French music began to flourish. A national society of composers was formed, with a wide membership. New schools of music were founded. Even the public cooperated to some extent, so that orchestral and chamber concerts became far commoner than they had been. Of the many composers of this time, two must stand for all: Gabriel Fauré (1845–1924) and Vincent d'Indy (1851–1931).

Gabriel Fauré

Fauré, a pupil of Saint-Saëns, is known chiefly as a writer of songs, but he also produced important piano works and chamber music, as well as one major opera, incidental music for several plays, and a well-known Requiem (1887). Fauré's music is wholly French: clear, delicate, restrained, and "accurate" in the best sense, while still strongly expressive and even passionate. Its most striking feature is its harmony, which is strongly chromatic without being at all Wagnerian. Fauré succeeds in devising irregular and unexpected chromatic progressions that are nonetheless entirely convincing. His frequent use of "modal" flavoring (that is, of scales differing from both the major and the minor) is another contributing factor to the originality of the result.

In general, Fauré's songs (whether single ones or members of cycles) show an advance from the salon-like prettiness of the earliest works to an increasingly serious style wholly appropriate to the carefully chosen texts. The middle period cycle *La bonne chanson* (1891–92) is a fine example of his treatment of a major work by the important poet Paul Verlaine. The later songs are more austere, as Fauré gradually strips his style down to its essentials.

Much the same may be said of the instrumental music. A comparison of the two violin sonatas (1876 and 1917) is instructive. The first is certainly the more immediately attractive and tuneful. The second is by no means simpler in the obvious sense—indeed it is very complex—but it is more concentrated and more economical, without being any less expressive.

Fauré's other instrumental pieces, like the sonatas just mentioned, make use of forms clearly derived from classical prototypes, but individually treated. Indeed, Fauré was no more an innovator than Mozart: he merely took what was at hand and, over a long career, continued a long process of refinement. His music (apart from a few favorite songs) is not widely performed outside France, although the French place him among the great composers: perhaps its very Frenchness weakens its impact on those who are not partly French at least in spirit.

Vincent d'Indy

The second representative of this period in France is Vincent d'Indy, a pupil of Franck, and himself of major importance as a teacher. D'Indy was an ardent Wagnerian—Wagner's work had an enormous influence in France after about 1875—and was in general more German-oriented than Fauré. He was a musician of immense learning and formidable technique, a French counterpart of Brahms in this respect. He cultivated the principal genres of vocal and instrumental music, including opera. His operas are thoroughly Wagnerian in technique and yet wholly personal in style. The French opera public, at least, remained unchanged, however, for both these and other progressive operas of the time were public failures.

D'Indy's most celebrated work is the *Istar Variations* (1897). Since the legend that gives the work its title describes Istar as removing one garment after another, d'Indy reverses the usual procedure and presents a set of variations in which the most complex variation comes first, and the true theme last—an intellectual device that is nonetheless successful musically. Another aspect of his style may be seen in the *Symphony on a French Mountain Air* (1886; also *Symphonie Cévenole*). D'Indy took a scientific interest in the folk songs of his native Auvergne, and here (as in other works) uses one as a symphonic theme. The effect is predictably less striking than that of similar works by Russian nationalists, simply because French "airs" are less exotic than Russian songs.

D'Indy's mature style is so severe—chromatic, contrapuntal, intellectual—that at times his imaginative power seems crushed under the weight of technique. But there are many fine pages in his work, which certainly does not deserve the almost total neglect into which it has fallen.

Debussy and impressionism. The same period produced a number of other composers whose stature is hardly less than that of the two chosen for discussion here. But it also produced one of far greater importance—a man whose work was a true musical revolution, and whose influence is still potent today: Claude Debussy (1862–1918). Without Debussy the whole nineteenth-century French revival might have been regarded as a minor movement, suitable to Francophiles only.

Impressionism

Debussy's earliest works give scant warning of what was to follow. They are intense, sensuous music reminiscent of the fashionable operas of Massenet. But in that sensuous quality lies the root of all that Debussy was to accomplish—a rejection of the nature of music as it had been understood for several centuries.

Debussy's mature style is known as "impressionism," after the roughly analogous contemporary movement in French painting, in which literal representation of objects was avoided in favor of apparently casual brush-strokes that evoke the "impression" the object makes on the eye. These evocations (usually of outdoor scenes) are necessarily imprecise in detail, and often intentionally misty and blurred overall as well. The contemporary symbolist movement in French poetry supplies another analogue: the sense of words is subordinated to their sonority, and direct statement to oblique reference. As will be seen, "impressionism" seems a wholly suitable designation for Debussy's musical style also, but it should be observed that the composer himself disliked the term.

The aim of musical impressionism is to present the ear with sensations of tones—impressions—evocative of, but not specifically describing, a mood, feeling, or even object. Put in this way, it sounds innocent enough: did not Chopin and Schumann aim at the same goal? Yet there is a profound difference. The earlier composers continued to treat music as a process, whose logical elements included tonality, themes, development, counterpoint, and the rest. Debussy discarded precisely this idea of process, in favor of simple succession and juxtaposition of impressions—and with process went most of the elements of its "logic."

Consider first the matter of harmony. In tonal music, any chord implied motion to another chord of the same or a related key—it thus had a latent dynamism that propelled it forward. For Debussy, a chord is a "brush-stroke"—a sonority to be perceived as such, with scarcely any inclination to move in a particular direction. For this reason, the chord need no longer be a triad or seventh chord, but may be almost any set of simultaneous pitches (limited, of course, by Debussy's sense of what was musically possible), and may move to almost any other such sonority. In fact, Debussy's music contains many chords that are only loosely related to triads: F♯–B♭–C–E, or G–C–D–E, for example. This does not mean that his music is not tonal. The listener generally feels the presence of some tonal center at any given time, and is made aware of changes of tonal center as they occur; but such centers are not normally defined by the traditional hierarchy of triads (tonic, dominant, subdominant), but rather by devices like pedal points, prominent single tones, repeated figures suggesting a key, and the like.

Similar remarks apply to the concept of themes. While melody naturally arises whenever tones follow one another, impressionist melody is fragmentary, at most motivic, and almost never organized into the symmetrical patterns of earlier music.

Fig. XIV-1: Pierre-Auguste Renoir (1841-1919), "Young girl at the piano," an example of impressionist technique applied to a musical subject. (Cliché des Musées Nationaux.)

Moreover, while the melodic fragments may and do recur, either literally or—more often—in varied form, they are never systematically "developed" in the usual sense of the term. They appear and disappear at the composer's pleasure. This freedom naturally affects both rhythm and form. Earlier music is metrically defined by its thematic content, and by the rhythm of its chord changes. With both of these absent or irregular, the overall rhythm naturally becomes less clear, subsiding to a subdued, often irregular pulsation that almost always avoids the symmetrical periods of classic or romantic style. Similarly, clear formal schemes have no place in impressionism, not only because they negate the feeling of freely flowing sensations, but also because the technical features just listed make their building almost impossible. (Again, a reservation must be made. Overall schemes such as ABA' are quite common in Debussy: it is the forms based on systematic progression, such as fugue and sonata, that are absent.)

The above paragraphs constitute a sketch of musical impressionism. Its literary and artistic connections have already been mentioned. Its musical genesis is more complex. In part, it represents a conscious attempt on Debussy's part to create a musical analogue to contemporary painting and poetry. In this he was also influenced by the music of the Russian nationalists, whose irregular melodies and harmonies have already been discussed. He was also much impressed by the performances of a Javanese gamelan orchestra at a Paris fair in 1889, which suggested even more exotic types of material. And, of course, however radical he was, he drew upon the work of his own predecessors: he was at first attracted and then repelled by the work of Wagner; he certainly owes more than a little to some of the works of Liszt; and he was influenced also by much in the works of his French contemporaries.

Debussy's style

In any event, Debussy's music varies considerably in its adherence to impressionist technique. His first major impressionist work, the *Prélude à l'après-midi d'un faune* (1894), is still a compromise. Cast in an overall ABA' form, its first section is truly impressionistic, while the middle part is lyrical in a traditional, almost old-fashioned way. And in the much later *Préludes* for piano (Book I, 1910), the first is clearly, if unconventionally tonal, while the second, the celebrated "Voiles" (Veils), again in ABA form, is almost free of tonality in its outer sections, despite the persistent low B♭.

If one looks more closely at Debussy's music, several features that contribute to its novelty—to its impressionism—may be isolated. One feature has already been mentioned: the use of chords that are neither triads nor sevenths. Another is the use of triads in parallel motion, a device wholly foreign to classic and romantic music, since it implies the equality of triads, and hence inhibits tonal feeling (it also vaguely evokes the Middle Ages, in its suggestion of parallel organum). Still a third is the employment of scales other than major or minor. These range from modal scales to the pentatonic scale (one example of which is the piano black notes) and the whole-tone scale. These are listed in decreasing order of tonal implications. The modal scales may lack a leading tone or a major dominant triad, or both. The pentatonic ones used by Debussy generally lack both; and the whole-tone scale, with its equal steps (C–D–E–F♯–G♯–B♭–C), clearly implies no tonal center whatsoever. The passages in Example XIV–8, all from the piano *Préludes*, will give an idea of Debussy's treatment of these possibilities.

Above and beyond these new harmonic usages, however, there stands Debussy's use of pure sonority as a basic musical value. This was not wholly new, of course, but Debussy went far beyond any predecessors in this direction. His characteristically

Ex. XIV-8

misty (but occasionally brilliant) sounds are fundamental to his musical thought. Whatever the medium, Debussy creates a whole new complex of sonorities, any one of which may be a mere "impression," or a recurrent aural landmark that has real structural value. Such landmarks are especially valuable in a style that is otherwise so free—a style in which the listener or even the composer might otherwise lose himself.

Debussy's style having been discussed in detail, his works may be treated more briefly. His instrumental music is mostly programmatic, to the extent that each work bears a title, generally an evocation of some scene in nature: "Gardens in the Rain," "The Sunken Cathedral," *La mer* (The Sea; a large orchestral work with three titled movements). Important exceptions are the string quartet (1893) and the three late sonatas (1915–17), the sonatas being a reversion to a more abstract, classical style. For the most part, however, Debussy's music is clearly intended to illustrate extra-musical scenes; and, given the extreme freedom of impressionist style, it succeeds admirably in doing so, the "illustrations," of course, being like impressionist paintings, not photographs. (One may here legitimately compare the photographic realism of Strauss with Debussy's evocative style.) Certainly no music has succeeded more than Debussy's, in its own way, in evoking the world of nature. Yet it would be a mistake to regard his music as no more than illustration. A person ignorant of the title would certainly understand that he was listening to music of the highest order when "The Sunken Cathedral" was played. He might also sense that the music dealt with something ancient and solemn, and this realization might enhance his enjoyment. But on the whole Debussy is closer to Schumann and Liszt in his program music than he is to some of Strauss: the title adds to and clarifies the substance of the music, but is not really an essential element. (In the piano *Préludes* Debussy has the title printed at the end, not the beginning, of each piece, implying that the listener should be allowed to hear with an open mind before being told what the piece was "about.")

Debussy's vocal music includes a number of very fine songs, some large works for chorus and orchestra, and a single opera, *Pelléas et Mélisande* (1902), possibly his greatest work. In Maeterlinck's symbolist drama (for which Fauré, Jean Sibelius, and Arnold Schoenberg also wrote music), Debussy found the perfect—perhaps the only —vehicle for an impressionist opera: the play takes place in some ancient nowhere; its characters move in a reality qualitatively different from our own, thinking unguessable thoughts. Its affinity with Debussy's musical style was so close that the opera is almost a word-for-word setting of the play (a few of Maeterlinck's scenes are omitted).

Debussy's vocal music: Pelléas and Mélisande

Since *Pelléas* is a love story, and since Debussy was all too conscious of the shadow of Wagner's *Tristan* and *Parsifal*, the work gave him great difficulty. He accepted the essentials of Wagnerian dramaturgy—the Leitmotives, the continuous music, and the largely declamatory singing style. His task was to translate these into his own language, and he succeeded triumphantly in creating an original, indeed a unique, work. The key to his success lies in the extreme restraint he imposes on his music. His orchestra is as large as Wagner's, but it is almost never called upon to produce loud sounds. Most of the scoring is almost like chamber music: a few fragments of melody in the oboe, accompanied by whispering tremolos in the strings, perhaps; or a quiet chord played by muted horns. The Leitmotives, no more than landmarks, are so unobtrusive that many listeners miss them altogether. And the vocal writing is close to ordinary speech. Instead of the rhetorical declamation of Wagner, Debussy employs the natural cadences of ordinary French (here too he learned something from the Russians). One need only compare the love scene in *Pelléas* with that in *Tristan*: in the former, all is suggestion and evocation; in the latter, the listener is overwhelmed by passionate vehemence. Debussy achieves with a whisper what Wagner achieves with a shout, for there is a hard core of dramatic force despite the impressionist surface.

For all the perfection of individual works, it is primarily the style of his music that is historically important. At a time when any serious composer was forced to search intensively for some corner of the tonal system in which he could achieve something new, Debussy showed that the system itself could be in large part discarded, and its suppositions replaced by others. He had no important direct successors—simply because his own achievement was so personal that it could be carried no further—but no composer of the twentieth century could escape coming to terms with his technical innovations.

It has been mentioned that Debussy turned late in life to a more classical, abstract style. Maurice Ravel (1875–1937), whose name is often coupled with Debussy's, continued and emphasized this tendency. (A reaction in favor of some sort of "neo-classicism" was characteristic of the years after about 1910.) While Ravel wrote a certain amount of impressionistic music, he produced a good deal more that is not impressionistic. The two composers influenced each other mutually (much like Liszt and Wagner) for a time, but Ravel's temperament was closer to that of Fauré, with whom he studied, than to that of Debussy.

Maurice Ravel   Thus Ravel's music is cooler and more intellectual than Debussy's. Many of Ravel's works appear to be responses to specific technical challenges. This is obvious in the popular *Boléro* (1927), with its deliberate restriction of materials; and only slightly less so in the first movement of the *Rhapsodie espagnole* (1907), which is almost entirely dominated by a single descending four-note scale fragment. But to relegate Ravel to the role of a solver of musical puzzles is a gross injustice. His style is various—much more so than Debussy's—and his accomplishments equally so. In *Gaspard de la nuit* (1908), he turns impressionist techniques to macabre ends. In the partly impressionist ballet *Daphnis et Chloë* (1912), he provides a suitably erotic yet pastoral atmosphere for the ancient legend. In his settings of exotic folk material, especially the *Chansons madécasses* (Songs of Madagascar; 1925), he is able to convey with conviction an exotic world; while in abstract works like the Sonatina for piano (1905) and the string quartet (1903) he invests European music with a fully original new style.

Technically, Ravel's music is often as advanced as Debussy's, with free use of dissonant chord-formations, modal and pentatonic scales, and virtuoso writing for whatever medium is used. But Ravel is consistently more forthright: his melodies are not motivic wisps, but real melodic lines (although complex and sophisticated). His harmony, even when it departs radically from previous common practice, is more clearly tonal than that of Debussy. The tonally neutral whole-tone scale is rarely found in Ravel, and persistent chromaticism is also avoided. In short, his adventures are tempered by his classicizing outlook—and some of them appear that much the bolder for being presented without the softening Debussyan haze. Particularly in the years following the First World War, Ravel strove for a style of extreme concentration and severity in most of his works. As will be seen, this was in keeping with the stylistic attitudes of younger composers at that time. Yet Ravel, for all the intrinsic value of his works, and for all his influence on twentieth-century music, remained essentially attached to the nineteenth century. His study with Fauré is more than a mere historical accident: although Ravel's music is radically different from that of his teacher, it continues the same tradition.

The same cannot be said of Erik Satie (1865–1925), a composer whose work, much of it consisting of short piano pieces, is still a matter of some argument. Famous above all for the queer titles he gave to some of his music ("Three pieces in the shape of a pear," "Dried embryos," and the like), which are obviously parodies of the evocative titles of Debussy, Satie may be called an anti-impressionist—a down to earth composer, as it were. The apparent simplicity of much of his music, its modal diatonicism, its occasional deliberate employment of café-music style, and the frequent obsessive rhythmic repetitions all tend to support this view. The ballet *Parade* (1917) is expressly entitled "realistic." But Satie was more than anti-impressionist: he was also anti-romantic, anti-classical, anti-Baroque—a sometimes mocking, sometimes quite serious negator of three centuries of music. While other composers were deploying forces and techniques of great complexity in the interests of a revolution in musical style, Satie was quietly making his own revolution, often with no more than a few oddly related triads on the piano.

Erik Satie

SUMMARY

This chapter has been concerned with three types of late nineteenth-century music: nationalist, German (in its two sub-types of conservative and post-Wagnerian), and French (more specifically, impressionistic). On several occasions, a reversion to a deliberately "neo-classic" style has been noted—in most of Brahms, in much of Ravel, and in the late work of Strauss and Debussy, for example. This archaizing tendency, in whatever form it appeared, must be added to the three main types of music as one of the streams that were to flow into the new music of the twentieth century. But, since music is not water, but a living product of living musicians, the confluence of these streams was multiple, and the combination of any two or more of them in the mind of any composer produced an individual result. The sometimes bewildering variety of forms and styles exhibited by the new music of the first half of the twentieth century will be less confusing if the basic sources are kept clearly in mind.

Brief notices of some composers of the late 19th and early 20th centuries.

Bizet, Georges (1838–75). French composer. The son of musicians, he entered the Paris Conservatory at age 9. Some operas: *Les pêcheurs de perles* (1863); *La jolie fille de Perth* (1867); *Carmen* (1875); music for the play *L'Arlésienne* (1872).

Borodin, Alexander (1833–87). Russian composer, the illegitimate son of a Georgian nobleman. A distinguished chemist, he composed laboriously in his spare time. Opera *Prince Igor* (unfinished, completed by Rimsky-Korsakov and Glazounov); 2 symphonies, a 3rd unfinished. *In the Steppes of Central Asia* for orch. Chamber music includes 2 quartets.

Brahms, Johannes (1833–97). German composer. See text; for works, see appendix to Chapter XIII.

Bruckner, Anton (1824–96). Austrian organist and composer. Admirer of Wagner. Much early church music. Ten symphonies, numbered 0–9, the last unfinished. Masses, Requiem, Te Deum.

Debussy, Claude (1862–1918). French composer (see text). Opera *Pelléas et Mélisande* (1902). For orch.: *Prélude à l'après-midi d'un faune* (1894); *La mer* (1905); *Images* (1908). Ballets *Jeux* (1912); *Khamma* (1912). Chorus and orch.: *Le martyre de Saint Sébastien* (1911); *La damoiselle élue* (1887–88). Piano wks. include 2 bks. of Préludes; *Images* (2 bks.); *Estampes*; *Etudes* (2 bks.); *Children's Corner*. Sonatas for 'cello; for violin; for flute, viola, and harp. String quartet. Many songs.

Dvořák, Antonin (1841–1904). Bohemian composer, director of Prague Conservatory; traveled to England, U.S.A. Director, National Conservatory, New York, 1892–95. Opera *Russalka* (1901). Nine symphonies. Symphonic poems; overtures. Concerto for piano; for 'cello; for violin. Much chamber music.

Elgar, Edward (1857–1934). English organist, conductor, composer. Little formal training; wrote in traditional 19th-cent. idiom. *Froissart, Cockaigne* overtures. 2 symphonies. Violin, 'cello concertos. *Enigma Variations* (1899). Oratorio *The Dream of Gerontius* (1900). *Pomp and Circumstance* marches (1901–1930).

Falla, Manuel de (1876–1946). Spanish composer; studied in Paris; adopted a somewhat impressionistic style; Spanish flavor retained in his music. Opera *La Vida breve* (1913). Ballets *El amor brujo* (1915); *El sombrero de tres picos* (1919); *Nights in the Gardens of Spain* for piano and orch. (1916). Harpsichord concerto (1926).

Fauré, Gabriel (1845–1924). French composer, teacher, director of Paris Conservatory (1905–20). Incidental music for plays, incl. *Pelléas et Mélisande* (1898). *Pavane* for orch. (1897). *Ballade* and *Fantaisie* for piano and orch. (1881, 1919). *Romance* for violin and orch. (1882). Requiem (1887). Chamber music: 2 piano quintets, 2 piano quartets, 2 violin sonatas, 2 'cello sonatas, string quartet. Piano works. Songs, incl. cycle *La bonne chanson*.

Franck, César (1822–90). Belgian-born composer, organist of Ste-Clotilde, Paris. Teacher of d'Indy, Chausson, Duparc. Symphony (1889). Violin sonata (1886). Piano quintet (1879). Symph. poems *Le chasseur maudit*; *Psyché* (1883, 1888). String quartet (1889). Much organ music. Sacred vocal music.

Glinka, Mikhail (1804–57). Russian composer. Well-educated, friend of Pushkin. Composer of nationalist Russian operas. *A Life for the Tsar* (1836); *Ruslan and Liudmila* (1842).

Gounod, Charles (1818–93). French composer of sacred music and opera. Of his several operas, only *Faust* (1859) and *Roméo et Juliette* (1867) are still performed. Much sacred music, including *La Rédemption, Mors et Vita, St. Cecilia Mass.*

Grieg, Edvard (1843–1907). Norwegian composer; studied at Leipzig. Strong champion of Norwegian music. Performed his piano concerto at age 25. Incidental music to Ibsen's *Peer Gynt*, from which are drawn the two well-known suites. Ten sets of *Lyric Pieces* for piano. Many songs.

d'Indy, Vincent (1851–1931). French composer and teacher. With Alexandre Guilmant and Charles Bordes founder of music school called Schola Cantorum (1896). Published an important composition treatise. Operas include *Fervaal* (1897). Symphonic trilogy *Wallenstein*. Symphony on a French Mountain Air, for orch. and piano (1887). *Istar Variations* (1897). Chamber music. Piano music. Songs.

Janáček, Leoš (1854–1928). Czech composer; taught at Brno, conducted Czech Philharmonic. Strong interest in folk music. Operas include *Jenufa* (1904), *The Cunning Little Vixen* (1924), *From the House of the Dead* (1928). Choral works include *Slavonic Mass* (1927). Chamber music.

Kodály, Zoltán (1882–1967). Hungarian composer; collected folk songs with Bartók. *Psalmus Hungaricus* for tenor, chorus and orch. (1923). Opera *Háry János* (1926). *Merosszek Dances, Galanta Dances* for orch. Te Deum; Missa Brevis.

Mahler, Gustav (1860–1911). Austrian composer and conductor. Conducted Metropolitan Opera, N.Y. Philharmonic (1908–11). Nine symphonies. *Das Lied von der Erde*, for alto, tenor, and orch. Song cycles: *Lieder eines fahrenden Gesellen; Kindertotenlieder; Des Knaben Wunderhorn.*

Massenet, Jules (1842–1912). Influential composer of operas, whose works held the French stage through the turn of the century. His operas include *Manon* (1884), *Werther* (1892), *Thaïs* (1894), *Cendrillon* (1899), *Le jongleur de Notre Dame* (1902).

Mussorgsky, Modest (1839–81). Russian composer. Informal musical education led to a compelling originality seen by some as crudeness. Operas *Boris Godunov* (1874); *Khovanshtchina* (completed by Rimsky-Korsakov). *A Night on the Bald Mountain* for orch. Piano music, including *Pictures at an Exhibition* (later orchestrated by Ravel). Songs include the cycle *Songs and Dances of Death.*

Nielsen, Carl (1865–1931). Danish composer, violinist, conductor. Chromatic, descriptive music. Six symphonies. Operas *Saul and David; Maskarade*. Cantatas. Chamber music.

Puccini, Giacomo (1858–1924). Italian composer of operas, including *Manon Lescaut* (1893), *La bohème* (1896), *Tosca* (1900), *Madama Butterfly* (1904), *La Fanciulla del West* (1910), the three one-act operas *Il Tabarro, Suor Angelica* and *Gianni Schicchi* (1918), *Turandot* (unfinished).

Ravel, Maurice (1875–1937). French composer; brilliant orchestrator. One-act operas *L'Heure espagnole* (1911); *L'Enfant et les sortilèges* (1925). Ballets *Daphnis et Chloë* (1912); *Boléro* (1927). For orch: *Le tombeau de Couperin* (1917); *La valse* (1929). Two piano concertos (1931, for left hand alone; and 1932). Chamber works. Songs include *Trois poèmes de Mallarmé; Chansons madécasses*. Piano works include *Jeux* d'eau, Gaspard de la nuit, Valses nobles et sentimentales, Ma mère l'oye (for piano duet, later orchestrated).

Rimsky-Korsakov, Nicolai (1844–1908). Russian composer. Taught at St. Petersburg Conservatory. Famous treatise on orchestration. Finished (and arranged) works of Mussorgsky. Operas The Snow Maiden (1882); Sadko (1898); Le coq d'or (posth.) Orchestral works include Schéhérezade, Capriccio espagnole, Russian Easter Overture.

Saint-Saëns, Camille (1835–1921). French composer; brilliant pianist; organist of La Madeleine, Paris. Opera Samson et Dalila (1877). Carnival of the Animals for orch. (1886). Symphonic poem Danse macabre (1875). Three symphonies. Five piano concertos, three violin concertos, two 'cello concertos. Chamber music. Songs.

Satie, Erik (1865–1925). French composer. Eccentric and revolutionary; cabaret pianist. Enormously influential on 20th-century music in France and elsewhere. Socrate for 4 sopranos and orch. (1920). Piano suite Gymnopédies (orch. by Debussy). Ballets Parade (1917); Relâche (1924). Many piano pieces with remarkable titles: Descriptions automatiques; Crépuscule matinal; Trois morceaux en forme de poire, etc.

Scriabin, Alexander (1872–1915). Russian composer, pianist. Complex chromaticism; harmonic innovation. Poème de l'extase for orch. Prometheus (original score calls for a "color organ"). Piano works: 10 piano sonatas; 15 sets of preludes; études. No chamber music; no vocal music.

Sibelius, Jean (1865–1957). Finnish composer, the last of the romantic nationalists. Composing nothing after 1929, he was greatly venerated in his own lifetime. Many symphonic poems, including En Saga, Finlandia, The Swan of Tuonela. Seven symphonies; chamber music; music for violin and piano.

Smetana, Bedřich (1824–84). Bohemian composer, pianist (especially known for his playing of Chopin), conductor, directed Bohemian National Opera (1866–74). Operas include The Bartered Bride (1866), Dalibor (1868), The Kiss (1876), The Secret (1878). Set of six symphonic pieces with the collective title Ma Vlast (My Country). String quartet Aus meinem Leben.

Strauss, Richard (1864–1949). German composer, conductor. Brilliant orchestrator; especially well known for the literality of his descriptive music. Tone poems Don Juan; Tod und Verklärung; Macbeth; Till Eulenspiegels lustige Streiche; Also sprach Zarathustra; Don Quixote; Ein Heldenleben. Operas include Guntram (1894), Feuersnot (1901), Salome (1905), Elektra (1909), Der Rosenkavalier (1911), Ariadne auf Naxos (1912), Die Frau ohne Schatten, (1919), Arabella (1924).

Tchaikovsky, Peter Ilyitch (1840–93). Russian composer. Studied with Anton Rubinstein; taught at St. Petersburg Conservatory. Sentimental, melodic music. Not much inclined to nationalism. Operas Evgeni Onegin (1879); Queen of Spades (1890). Ballets Swan Lake (1876); Sleeping Beauty (1889); Nutcracker (1892). Six symphonies; two piano concertos; violin concerto. Orchestral works include Overture Romeo and Juliet, Marche Slave, 1812 Overture, Capriccio Italien, Francesca da Rimini. Variations on a Rococo Theme for 'cello and orchestra.

Wolf, Hugo (1860–1903). Austrian composer, known principally for his songs. His major collections are: 53 Mörike Lieder; 20 Eichendorff songs; 51 Goethe songs; Spanisches Liederbuch (44 songs); Alte Weisen (6 songs); Italienisches Liederbuch (pt. 1, 22 songs; pt. 2, 24 songs); Drei Gedichte von Michelangelo.

XV

THE
TWENTIETH
CENTURY

Temporal overlapping of musical styles is by now familiar to the reader, who has seen the *style galant* take hold while J. S. Bach was still committed to the ideals of the late Baroque, and has observed the appearance of romantic works such as Schubert's songs and Weber's *Der Freischütz* when Beethoven was working on his severest and most abstruse string quartets.

The first decades of the twentieth century saw the beginnings of several radical changes in musical style; yet many works composed during those decades have been shown to be essentially post-romantic in style, and not in any real sense revolutionary. If such men as Fauré or Strauss remained nineteenth-century musicians even into the 1920s and beyond, it was not because they were reactionaries, but simply because they were older men, whose goals had become fixed. Even Debussy and Ravel, the most advanced composers of their time (in certain ways, at least), remained attached to the nineteenth century in important respects: their innovations were for the most part radical *within* the context of a tradition they respected. Musical revolutions, in contrast, are generally made by young composers—men in search of a basically new vision.

RADICAL TRENDS: THE MAJOR DEVELOPMENTS

The pre-World War I years.   Several forms of musical revolution were already in the making in the early years of the twentieth century, revolutions corresponding to the various "confluences" mentioned at the end of the preceding chapter. The most spectacular of these resulted from a mixture of a form of Russian nationalism with impressionism. From 1909 on, a Russian ballet troupe led by the impresario Sergei Diaghilev had been an annual sensation in Paris. For his ballets, Diaghilev frequently commissioned music from outstanding composers of the day—Debussy and Ravel, for example. Surprisingly, he entrusted the music for some of his major productions to a young and scarcely known pupil of Rimsky-Korsakov, Igor Stravinsky (1882–1971). The first result of this collaboration was the ballet *Firebird* (1910), an original score,

Igor Stravinsky

but not a revolutionary one. The second was *Petrouchka* (1912), which aroused less sensation than it might have: in it, Stravinsky combined the bright clear colors of traditional Russian orchestration with the harmonic innovations of Debussy. The latter's strong dissonances were thus presented unveiled, often in pounding rhythmic ostinatos, with no impressionist haze to temper them. Parallel triads appear set against counterthemes in a different key, and in one celebrated passage, the same melody appears simultaneously in the unrelated keys of C and F♯.

Le sacre du printemps

It was not, however, until the next year that these explosive ingredients detonated publicly in Stravinsky's score for *Le sacre du printemps* (The Rite of Spring). In the full glare of Parisian publicity, Stravinsky and Diaghilev produced a ballet that *had* to be recognized as revolutionary. Its subject matter—"pictures of pagan Russia," culminating in human sacrifice—was shocking enough when seen on the stage, and the music more than amply matched the ferocity of the action. There was a riot at the first performance, and many musicians, even some progressive ones, were scandalized.

Yet *Le sacre* merely gives additional and violent emphasis to elements already present in *Petrouchka*: the high dissonance content and generally violent style are thrown into even greater prominence, however, by the savagery of the stage action. Most striking in *Le sacre* are the rhythms—which are, at least in the climactic dances, absolutely original (although they often preserve and intensify the ostinatos of *Petrouchka*). These climactic sections are not based on patterns of regularly recurrent beats and measures, but on short irregular groups consisting of multiples of a single short value (♩ or ♪). Perception of these groups is further complicated by irregularly placed accents, and by melodic fragments whose natural stresses do not coincide with anything. The beginning of the final section (Ex. XV-1a) and a passage from the "Dance of the Adolescents" (Ex. XV-1b) show two extreme—and celebrated—instances of this type of rhythm. In both cases, the ear has no way of predicting where the next stress will fall: the whole concept of a "measure" in the traditional sense becomes irrelevant. (It makes little difference whether the music is notated in regular or changing meters, as the example shows.)

As prominent as the rhythm is the consistently dissonant harmony. While this is tonal in the sense that the hearer is generally conscious of a tonal center, it makes almost no use of traditional tonal functions. Stravinsky later spoke of tonal "poles" and "polarity" in his music, so that one is justified in finding tonal centers in it. To observe that these are not traditionally treated requires no justification.

The striking dissonance of the harmony springs from several sources. One is the superposition of one triad (or seventh chord) on another. The harmony in Example XV–1b is a repeated chord consisting of an F♭ major triad with the E♭ major seventh chord above it. Another is the sounding of a foreign note in an otherwise normal triad (e.g., C–E–G with F♯ added), or the use of a triad with both major and minor third. Still another is the doubling of a melodic line at the seventh, instead of the traditional third or sixth. And finally, there is the already mentioned assertion of two keys simultaneously, most typically by having the melody in one key and the accompaniment in another.

Although melody seems less important in *Le sacre* than in Stravinsky's earlier ballets, appearing often to be overwhelmed by the rhythms and the harmony, it nevertheless plays a critical role. Most of the tunes are fragmentary, and all of them resemble folk song (the opening bassoon melody is a Lithuanian folk melody). Several

(continued on following page)

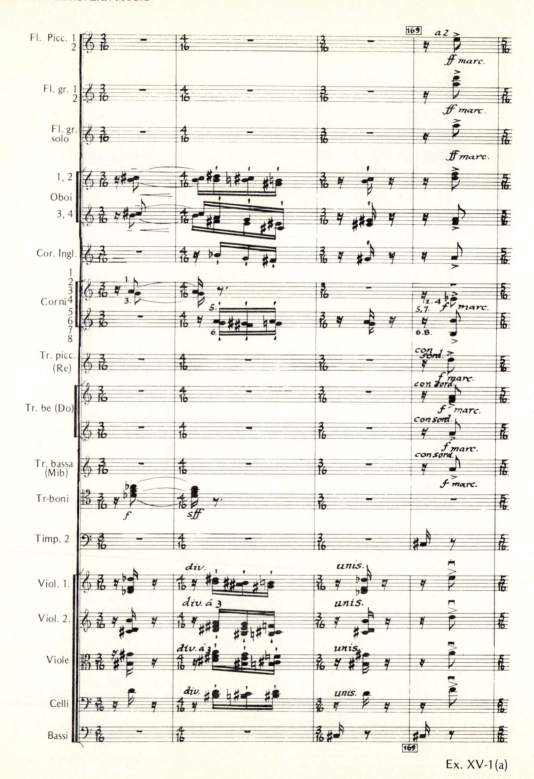

Ex. XV-1(a)

(continued on the following page)

Ex. XV-1(b)

are of the "Russian" type mentioned in the preceding chapter, with a limited range and a tendency for the same melodic patterns to recur in different rhythmic positions. Although the tunes are not formally related, they seem somehow akin to each other, and this apparent kinship, along with the pulsating rhythms, is a powerful unifying force in a score that discards conventional structural devices: recurrent themes or sections, development, and the like. The resultant structure is intuitive, not schematic, but fully compelling even apart from its dramatic content. Although Stravinsky generally made shorter versions of his ballet scores for concert use, he made no such changes in *Le sacre*, and the work survives transplantation into the concert hall without damage.

Much more could be written about *Le sacre*—especially about its brilliant and imaginative orchestration—but enough has been said to indicate its rank as one of the cornerstones of twentieth-century musical style, a position granted it by almost all musicians. It was also, for Stravinsky, the end of an era. While many lesser composers tried to imitate it, Stravinsky himself preferred to turn to different paths, to be considered later in this chapter. Meanwhile, he had become an international celebrity, and the example of *Le sacre* had opened up new possibilities for composers all over the world.

Arnold Schoenberg: the break with tonality

At about the same time, however, another equally explosive but quite different style had come into being, this one a direct descendant of the German chromatic style of Wagner and his followers. The Austrian Arnold Schoenberg (1874–1951) began his career in Vienna as a late hyper-romantic. His string sextet *Verklärte Nacht* (Transfigured Night; 1899) carries the chromaticism of *Tristan* to extreme limits. Schoenberg also had a strong sense of musical discipline (which he admired in Brahms), and was coming to believe that the musical language of the nineteenth century was nearly exhausted.

Slowly Schoenberg began to work his way towards new principles of composition. His already strongly chromatic style led him to question the necessity of a tonal center: if all twelve tones of the chromatic scale are to be used, why should any one of them be accorded a prominence denied to the others? Schoenberg found no satisfactory answer to this question, and concluded that all twelve tones should be treated equally—thereby discarding, of course, traditional tonality in almost all its aspects.

This resulted also in a different treatment of intervals. Consonances tend to define triads, and triads to define keys. Hence the dissonant intervals, instead of being the exception, became the rule, while consonances appeared less frequently. Although dissonances can also be used to define keys, their key-implications can easily be neutralized if their expected tonal resolutions are avoided. Thus Schoenberg relied heavily on seconds, sevenths, and tritones, building out of them complex chords carefully constructed to avoid the implication of any persistent tonal center.

The rejection of tonality resulted in further corollaries. Exact repetition of almost any succession of tones will tend to suggest a key; so also will symmetrical melody, especially if it is largely stepwise. Chordal music, however dissonant the chords, is more likely to evoke a tonality than is contrapuntal music of comparable dissonance content. In consequence, Schoenberg's new style would employ repetition only when varied; would use disjunct, asymmetrical melody; and would favor a strongly contrapuntal texture. These features, combined with the chromatic, non-tonal dissonance already described, and with extreme concentration and brevity, produced a music more radically new than anything else written in the early years of the twentieth century. (Schoenberg's principles have here been presented as a set of logical deductions, in order to expose their inner unity of purpose. In practice, Schoenberg arrived at his new style quite as much by musical as by logical means.)

The most celebrated work in the new manner is *Pierrot lunaire* (Moonstruck Pierrot; 1912), a cycle of twenty-one songs for vocal soloist and small chamber ensemble, on German versions of surrealist poems by Albert Giraud. This work exemplifies all the technical features already mentioned, and includes further innovations as well. Of the latter, the most striking is Schoenberg's treatment of the voice: the singer is to deliver the part neither in song nor in speech, but in *Sprechstimme* (speech-voice), a style intermediate between the two. The part is written in ordinary notation, but with small crosses added to the stems, and Schoenberg explains in the preface to the score that the singer is to follow the melodic contour exactly, but speaking rather than singing. The effect, however rendered (and it is doubtful that any performance can be really definitive in this respect), adds an especially eerie quality to music that, even today, is already very disquieting. The few notes marked "gesungen" (sung) have a special force of their own.

Formally, *Pierrot* is very complex. The poems all have refrains, but Schoenberg avoids literal recapitulations, while allowing varied returns of an ABA′ type. Schoenberg himself observed that, having decided to do without the unifying force of tonality, he found it difficult to write long pieces. In consequence, all of the songs in *Pierrot* are quite short, and many are held together by contrapuntal devices such as canon, or by elaborately worked out motivic consistency, as in the "passacaglia," a piece wholly permeated by the pitch-succession E-G-E♭.

Pierrot lunaire

Forms in Pierrot lunaire: *serial principle*

In this and other pieces of the time, a single set of pitches may be used to generate not only melodic motives, but also chords (by using the pitches simultaneously instead of successively). Music so constructed may be called "serial" (i.e., based on a series of pitches), and the serial principle was, as will be seen, the principal ingredient in Schoenberg's later style.

The content of Schoenberg's music about the time of *Pierrot* is intense and personal: a violent and at times anguished reaction to the events of the outer world (tempered, in the case of *Pierrot*, by a good deal of irony.) The term "expressionist" is often applied to music and other arts cultivated by certain German and Austrian artists in the early twentieth century. Both expressionism and *impressionism* deal with the artist's perception of what he sees and what happens to him, but in quite different ways. The expressionist is introspective, and his work is an intense autobiography of his emotional life. The impressionist looks outward—often towards the world of nature—and while his work is also personal, as all art of recent times has been, there remains in it an element of objectivity. One may legitimately contrast the expressionism of Schoenberg with Stravinsky's *Le sacre*, which presents a drama Stravinsky has imagined, but not directly participated in.

Thus while *Pierrot* is a landmark comparable to *Le sacre*, it is one of a very different kind. Moreover, Schoenberg did not benefit from the extensive publicity Stravinsky received. His name gradually became known to forward-looking musicians; but performances were few, and the musical public was (and still largely is) unaware of his music.

This was the more unfortunate because the new styles then coming into being posed problems even for the serious listener. The new forms, the new harmonic language, and above all the apparent rejection of the methods used by the established masters would, even under the best of circumstances, have required repeated hearings to win acceptance. And the circumstances were by no means the best. The catastrophe of the first world war not only claimed a dreadful toll of human lives; it also served as a primary cause of profound changes in the social order—almost all of them unfavorable to music in general and to new music in particular, however beneficial they may otherwise have been. Chief among these was the virtual cessation of private patronage, owing to the decline in number and influence of wealthy families. Since both aristocratic and ecclesiastical patronage were long since gone, this left composers dependent on their audiences at a time when audiences were least likely to be receptive to new ideas. Only shortly thereafter, the rise of radio, motion pictures, phonograph records, and, much later, television engendered two new difficulties: entertainment (usually including music) became readily available, thus reducing the need for "live" music; and the economic requirements of the entertainment market precluded the use of any "difficult" material. The split between composer and public necessarily deepened, and shows no sign of improvement at present. The profession of composer, far from offering a living to its practitioners, is now unlikely to yield any reward whatever. Patronage has become almost entirely institutional. A composer may receive one or two grants or commissions, but must depend on another profession (usually performance or teaching) for his livelihood. And, as the public has disregarded him, he often disregards the public when he writes, thus widening the rift even more.

Schoenberg suffered especially from these difficulties, and never achieved, even among musicians, the wide recognition he sought. In the years during and after the first world war, Schoenberg also had problems of a purely musical nature. He completed no major works during this period, as he was searching for some sort of order that would serve to replace tonality as a unifying force—some means that would permit the composition of large-scale works in a non-tonal style.

The Viennese school: Schoenberg, Berg, and Webern. Schoenberg's search was rewarded in the early 1920s, in the discovery of what he called a "method of composition with twelve tones which are related only to one another" (i.e., not to a tonic). This method had its origin in the intense motivic unity of many of Schoenberg's earlier works. It is simple in principle, although liable to considerable complication in actual practice. As the basis of each composition, a series of pitches is chosen. Now, however, the series must consist of all twelve tones of the chromatic scale, arranged in an order chosen by the composer. Such a series is called a tone-row, or simply a row. The row is in itself neither a theme nor a motive, although it can be used in either capacity. It is, rather, a generative element, out of which themes, motives, and chords may be derived.

The twelve-tone method

The basic rule of the row is simple: while any of its tones may appear in any register, from the highest to the lowest, with any duration and any degree of loudness, no tone of the row may recur until all the remaining tones have been sounded. Certain exceptions are allowed: directly repeated notes and trills are permitted, for they are no more than special forms of sustained tones. Also, when two statements of the row appear at once—as, for example, when the main melody and the accompanying voices both use the row—recurrences produced by their overlapping are permitted. Otherwise the rule is strict: once a C♯ (or D♭—spelling makes no difference in the absence of tonality) has been sounded, it may not reappear until the other eleven notes have been heard in their proper order.

Since the derivation of all musical materials from a single row might lead to excessive emphasis on unity, Schoenberg added a second principle, derived at least in part from traditional contrapuntal procedures: the row may appear not only in its original (O) (or prime [P]) form, but also melodically inverted (I), or backwards (retrograde: R), or both retrograde and inverted (RI). This yields a total of four row forms, which can be increased to forty-eight by permitting the row in any of its forms to begin on any of the twelve tones of the octave.

It is of course unlikely that all forty-eight forms of a row would be used in a single composition: one or two forms might suffice for a short piece, and even a longer one might use only four or five. But the freedom obtained by using different row forms is most important, for it provides a simple means of achieving variety while adhering to a single basic row. If one were to build the first section of a piece on the original row, the second on a transposed inversion, and the last again on the original, an ABA' form could easily be created, even without direct repetition of themes or motives.

The last movement of the Suite for Piano, Op. 23, is apparently Schoenberg's first piece to make consistent use of a twelve-tone row. The row is given complete in the opening melody (Ex. XV–2). The accompaniment in these measures is also based on the row: the first chord consists of tones 6 through 8 (note the difference in spelling), followed by the single notes 9 and 10. The chord in measure 2 is made up of 11, 12, and 1, followed by 2 (low A), and 3–5 in the next measure. Thereafter the double presentation of the row, in melody and accompaniment at once, is abandoned, and the notes are distributed between the two hands, continuing from the A♭ of measure 3. (Schoen-

Schoenberg's Suite for Piano, Op. 23

Ex. XV-2

berg allows himself a small liberty in measure 5, for the left-hand E—note 9 of the row—precedes the chord containing 6–8 in the right hand. Like all good composers, Schoenberg is always ready to sacrifice theory in favor of musical effect.)

The example is intentionally cut off in the middle of a phrase in order to show that the row is neither a theme nor a chord-succession, but rather a source of such materials, somewhat like a tonal scale. It differs from the latter principally in having no center, so that the ends of tone-rows need not, and probably will not, coincide with the ends of phrases (see especially measures 8–9 of Ex. XV-2). A row also differs from the kind of "series" Schoenberg had used in earlier works, in that it includes all twelve tones of the octave. Thus while all twelve-tone (or dodecaphonic) music is serial, the converse is not true.

While it is interesting and instructive to follow Schoenberg in his sometimes very complex manipulations of tone rows, it should be remembered that this is mere technique—as Schoenberg himself was careful to emphasize. One can write twelve-tone music that is cheerful or despairing, complex or simple, non-tonal or tonal, good or bad. The method may appear to be an intellectual one, and so it is. But so also were fourteenth-century isorhythm, sixteenth-century parody, and eighteenth-century fugue, to name only a few. Even tonality, however "natural" it may sound, is a highly sophisticated intellectual construction, with its hierarchically arranged chords, its modulations, its accommodation of non-chord tones into the texture, and so on. Tonal music seems natural to Western listeners because they have been brought up on it, whether in its popular or "serious" form. It does not sound at all natural to an African or Asiatic listener without previous exposure to Western music.

Thus the tone row in twelve-tone music may be inaudible, at least on the conscious level—like isorhythm, or indeed modulation. It functions as a constructive device, a means by which the composer can give order to his material. When order has been achieved, the details of the achievement are of interest only to the composer—and of course to the serious and advanced student of his music.

It is best, therefore, to turn away from Schoenberg's technique—enormously influential though it turned out to be—and consider his music. It is clear from the example above that the adoption of the twelve-tone system was essentially a codification of elements already latent in works such as *Pierrot lunaire*. All of the earlier characteristics are still present: high dissonance content; persistent chromaticism; wide-ranging, asymmetrical melody; tense counterpoint; avoidance of direct repetition; and extreme compression. Such elements naturally produce a strongly subjective emotional effect (as the same elements do when used by Mozart or Monteverdi). But the discipline inherent in twelve-tone technique makes a significant difference: free expression gives way to a stricter and more formal effect—not less expressive, but more controlled. This is, in fact, a kind of neo-classicism, and might well be so termed, had not the phrase already been preempted by the more obviously retrospective neo-classicism of other composers.

Once the system had been evolved, Schoenberg broke his long silence, and began once more to compose regularly, not only in small forms, but also—at last—in larger ones: he now had the organizing power he had so long wanted. Among the works written in the years immediately following his formulation of twelve-tone technique, the Variations for Orchestra (Op. 31; 1928) may well be the finest. Here Schoenberg builds a large symphonic structure, consisting of an introduction, a theme, nine variations, and a long finale, out of the various forms of a single row. The variations are of the late Beethovenian type: each has its own expressive character and its own relation to the theme. Especially noteworthy is Schoenberg's treatment of the large orchestra required for the piece. While there are occasional overpowering effects, much of the scoring is like chamber music in its delicacy. The instruments are used less often for doubling than in small and often unusual groups, with frequent employment of special effects (fluttertonguing for the wind instruments, harmonics for the double bass, bowing at the bridge for the strings, and so on).

In choosing variation form for this work, Schoenberg was following not only his own natural bent, for the principle of variation had long been an essential part of his stylistic equipment, but also a conscious impulse towards a rapprochement with classical forms. In his later chamber music—especially the third and fourth string quartets (1926 and 1936)—this rapprochement is even more evident. Here there appear structures clearly derived from classical models, now rethought and reworked in terms of the twelve-tone technique. Even the String Trio (1946), despite its anguished exploitation of unusual string effects and its generally hyper-emotional style, is more disciplined in its expression than the works of the pre-twelve-tone period.

Special mention must be made of Schoenberg's principal dramatic work, *Moses and Aaron*, on which he worked intensively in 1932 and again in 1950. The libretto, by Schoenberg himself, is theological: Moses can see God's purposes, but cannot communicate them to his people; Aaron can communicate, but is unable to understand. Schoenberg gives visual interest to this austere conflict by supplying some spectacular stage effects, most notably the orgy of the people before the altar of the Golden

Calf. The music, all based on forms of a single tone row, is immediately and profoundly expressive, offering ample proof of Schoenberg's mastery of technique for purely communicative ends. No spectator need worry about the use, or even the presence, of a tone row as he watches this powerful drama unfold.

It should also be observed that Schoenberg, while he used serial methods for most of his music, did not find it inappropriate to write some pieces not based on the system: there are even mature tonal pieces. These caused some embarassment to his more orthodox followers, but are clearly in accordance with Schoenberg's lifelong practice of creating musical values by whatever means seemed most appropriate.

Schoenberg's influence

Although Schoenberg's position as one of the principal figures of his time—many would say *the* principal figure—now seems unassailable, his career was not an easy one. In addition to suffering from a lack of public recognition and a paucity of performances of his music, he became, like most other progressive composers in German-speaking countries, an exile from the horrors of the Hitler regime. His wanderings ultimately brought him to the United States, where he became professor of music at the University of California at Los Angeles. In this post, he exerted considerable influence, and his teaching was a major factor in the education of many American composers. His two most celebrated pupils, however, were men of about his own age, with whom he had become associated early in his Vienna years.

Alban Berg

The first of these pupils, Alban Berg (1885–1935), emphasized in his music a kind of romantic expressivity—almost a nostalgia for the sounds of nineteenth-century music. Although he also made frequent use of classical (and Baroque) forms, these generally serve as frames for an intense emotional utterance, rather than acting, as in Schoenberg, as the means by which that utterance is expressed. Thus in the *Lyric Suite* for string quartet (1925–26), there are elements of the classical quartet—notably sonata form and scherzo style. There is also an overall schematic design: the movements are alternately fast and slow, with each fast movement faster and each slow movement slower than the preceding one. Yet the listener carries away with him not the formal symmetries, but the almost hysterical emotionalism of the music. The last movement is especially characteristic: wide, despairing melodic leaps give way eventually to a simple, monotonous figure that dies away in the viola; and in the midst of the movement, a quotation from Wagner's *Tristan* is embedded.

Berg's most famous work, the opera *Wozzeck* (1921), resulted from the composer's reaction to his own degrading military experience in the first world war, illuminated by a strangely prophetic play by Georg Büchner (1813–37). The play, which describes the crushing of the "little man"—the simple but sensitive soldier Wozzeck—by malignant forces he cannot understand or combat, is a precursor of literary expressionism. Berg, in creating a libretto from the play, followed his source closely, omitting a few scenes, but taking over most of the play verbatim. He imposes a formal structure on each short scene, but these structures are less important to the total effect than the expressive intensity of the music, which derives much more from Wagner than it does from any classical or Baroque models. In both *Wozzeck* and his later opera, *Lulu*, Berg maintains the essentials of Wagnerian dramaturgy, with Leitmotives, continuous music (despite the formal structures), and a predominant orchestra with overlaid, often declamatory vocal lines (*Sprechstimme* is used in some scenes). The forms in *Lulu* are larger, and the music is strictly composed in the twelve-tone system, but the two operas are basically similar in their effect.

Berg, following closely in Schoenberg's footsteps, had adopted the twelve-tone technique as soon as it became available. But the warmth of his expression often appeals strongly to audiences that find Schoenberg difficult. Berg's attachment to the past—the source of that warmth—may be seen with especial clarity in his last completed work, the Violin Concerto (1935). The basic series of this piece has strong and obvious triadic elements (Ex. XV–3). With such a row, tonal feeling can be introduced whenever it is desired, without sacrificing any of the unifying force of the serial system. In the last movement, Berg quotes a chorale melody, "Es ist genug"—surely an adequate testimony to his desire to preserve elements of the old within the context of the new.

Ex. XV-3

Schoenberg's other principal pupil, Anton Webern (1883–1945), took a much different path. If Berg chose to emphasize the potential warmth of Schoenberg's style, Webern seized instead upon its concentration. For all three composers, brevity had been a necessity prior to the formulation of the twelve-tone system. For Webern, it persisted in his twelve-tone works as well: there are no long pieces in his oeuvre, nor are there any that can be closely connected with classical models. Webern's music packs the maximum information in the minimum time—a time, moreover, in which silence plays almost as great a part as sound, further emphasizing extreme economy of means. Webern's harmony, also, is often pared down to a thin texture based wholly on minor seconds, major sevenths, and minor ninths; and his melody is dominated by the same intervals, adding yet another element of unification.

Anton Webern

Along with concentration, Webern's music emphasizes the intellectualism of Schoenberg's style. Like Berg, Webern adopted the twelve-tone system as soon as it was formulated. But Webern's choice and treatment of tone rows is stricter and more obviously ordered. His rows often are constructed on the basis of internal symmetries: one, for example, contains a single three-note series on three different pitches (Ex. XV–4). Naturally such a choice reinforces the tendency towards compression and economy, for relatively few melodic and harmonic progressions will ordinarily result from such a row.

Ex. XV-4

Partly in order to compensate for these self-imposed restrictions, but much more as an expression of his own compositional preferences, Webern made extensive use of a technique first used by Schoenberg, but most extensively employed in Webern's works, the so-called *Klangfarbenmelodie* (sound-color melody), in which the successive notes of a melodic line are assigned to different instruments—the first perhaps to the horn, the second to the clarinet, the next to a solo violin, and so on—instead of the more conventional practice of giving instruments complete phrases to play. By this means each tone is emphasized and isolated—made into a unique and notable event—again with the result of packing information more tightly into a minimum space.

Klangfarbenmelodie

Within this extremely terse style, Webern generally employs further unifying devices, especially canon and variation. Nevertheless, the use of such devices does not operate, as it does in Berg or even Schoenberg, as an evocation of or reference to earlier styles. Webern's music is too radical and individual for that: it absorbs and transforms whatever procedures it employs.

A portrait of Webern as merely an intellectual composer would, however, be incomplete. Much of Webern's music is vocal, and in this domain he shows not only a highly sensitive—if demanding—treatment of the voice, but also an extraordinary feeling for appropriate musical treatment of the texts he chose.

Still, given the presence of so many highly cerebral devices, and the absence of the emotional urgency of Berg, Webern's music poses a considerable challenge for the listener. Fortunately, its economy results in clarity as well as brevity, so that the problem is now by no means insoluble. Webern long remained enigmatic, however. While his techniques were generally understood by serious musicians, his "message"—the intent of his music—remained obscure to almost everyone until after 1950. At that time, the intensity of Schoenberg and Berg began to appear as a continuation of nineteenth-century aesthetics, despite the novelty of technique and style; and it was Webern alone who seemed genuinely prophetic. However correct this evaluation may have been, it was an extremely recent one. During the first half of the century, Schoenberg, Berg, and Webern—the Viennese school, as they are often called—were taken together as the chief representatives of the twelve-tone method of composition.

Neo-classicism: L'Histoire du soldat and Pulcinella

Stravinsky: neo-classicism and beyond.   Twelve-tone music stands as one of the stylistic poles of the period. The opposing pole, loosely termed neo-classicism, was considerably more diverse, if only because it claimed, for some decades, the allegiance of a far greater number of composers. Chief among them was Stravinsky, who, after *Le sacre*, undertook an astonishing change of style, leading him to a position almost entirely unconnected and indeed incompatible with the aesthetic of Schoenberg and his followers.

Stravinsky had perceived that *Le sacre* was an end rather than a beginning: that its audacities, however explosive, were still embedded in a declining style. Thus, while some characteristics of Stravinsky's earlier music—the Russian type melodies, the irregular pounding rhythms, the frequent use of ostinato, as well as certain harmonic usages—persist in later works, there is really only one piece, *Les noces* (The Wedding), that seems to descend from *Le sacre*. And even in *Les noces* (completed in 1923, but begun in 1914), there is a significant change: the large orchestra of the ballets is replaced by an ensemble of four pianos plus percussion instruments (the pianos also are treated percussively). Although the presence of chorus and soloists results in a considerable performing force, the tendency towards reduction and economy of means is still evident.

It is even more apparent in *L'histoire du soldat* (Story of the Soldier; 1918), scored for narrator and six contrasting instruments, again with percussion. Such a small group of instruments necessarily produces a transparent and "dry" sound, and the music has a cool and ironic cast (although the attentive listener may discover that Stravinsky is not quite as detached as he appears to be). Although the French text is derived from Russian folk sources, the music no longer sounds Russian: Stravinsky, by then resident in Paris, had found a style that was both personal and international—one in which the pungently dissonant harmony and irregular rhythms of *Le sacre* could coexist with elements derived from jazz.

In 1919, Diaghilev asked Stravinsky to arrange some "old" music for a new ballet. Stravinsky's choice fell upon pieces then believed to be by Pergolesi. Not surprisingly, Stravinsky went beyond mere arrangement: he rescored, reharmonized, and adapted his material. The result, the ballet *Pulcinella*, is a genuinely original piece, despite its eighteenth-century material.

L'Histoire du soldat and *Pulcinella*, taken together, may serve to define the principal elements of neo-classicism: economy of means; clarity of sound and form; avoidance of romantic sentiment in favor of (apparently) cool detachment; maintenance of some sort of tonal centers within a dissonant harmonic style; avoidance of excessive chromaticism; and finally—but not invariably—reference to or use of techniques or materials from the pre-nineteenth-century past. The term "neo-classicism" is thus misleading, for the "classicism" employed may be (and often is) earlier than the classical period; but despite this ambiguity, and in the face of objections by composers, "neo-classicism" remains the normal term for this stylistic orientation. One must be on guard, however, to distinguish twentieth-century neo-classicism from the superficially similar tendency in the later works of composers such as Strauss and Debussy. These latter were in essence drawing back from and tempering the extremes of their own styles. Stravinsky, on the other hand, and other composers of similar stamp, were aiming forward—towards a *new* style—and their intermittent use of older techniques was merely a means to that end.

The astonishing variety of works produced by Stravinsky in the years between 1919 and 1950 defies generalization. Each new piece appeared to be the definitive expression of a new and fundamental style, only to be followed by an equally distinguished work that appeared to point in a quite different direction. Seldom has a major composer exhibited such versatility.

From the early 1920s there is the *Symphonies for Wind Instruments* (1921; "symphonies" here has its ancient meaning of "soundings together"), a study in sonorities, and the Octet (1921), a strongly contrapuntal piece—also for winds—that makes considerable use of both classical and Baroque formal procedures. The two, despite their similar medium, are quite different, and yet both are equally typical of Stravinsky.

At this time, and for many years thereafter, Stravinsky, in his often polemical public pronouncements about his work, took the position that music was powerless to express anything except itself: it existed merely as music, with the ability to delight the ears and the mind, but without the power of suggesting specific states of mind or emotion. This rather extreme view—obviously a reaction against the subjectivism of German romantic and post-romantic thought—is partially supported by the coolness of Stravinsky's early neo-classical works, which stand closer to the "purely musical" works of Haydn and Mozart than to Beethoven or the nineteenth century. But even Haydn and Mozart wrote a good deal of music having quite specific expressive connotations—one need think only of the Mozart Requiem—and Stravinsky, whatever his theoretical position, was not long in doing the same.

His first large neo-classic work to embody more specific emotional expression was the opera-oratorio *Oedipus Rex* (produced in 1927). It clearly shows, however, Stravinsky's attempt to minimize the subjective element. The text, adapted from Sophocles by Jean Cocteau, was then translated into Latin—thereby deliberately pre-

Oedipus Rex *and*
Symphony of
Psalms

venting the audience from overreacting to the sense of the words. The actors are to wear masks, and the narrator is to appear in modern dress. All of these devices serve to keep the audience at a distance, as does Stravinsky's reversion to eighteenth-century dramaturgy, with closed-form arias and choruses. Nevertheless, the score is an intensely moving recreation of the ancient Greek tale. The concluding choral section, set over a typically Stravinskyan ostinato, may be cool technically, but only an insensitive hearer could miss its emotional force.

Even warmer in expression is the *Symphony of Psalms* (1930), a large-scale setting of psalms 39, 40, and 150, for chorus and orchestra (without violins or violas). Of its three movements, the first is tense, continuous, and climactic; the second is a double fugue, with an elegant neo-Baroque subject for the woodwinds; and the third is a movement of symphonic dimensions in which alternately quiet and tumultuous passages are followed and somehow reconciled by a serene hymn-like conclusion over (again) an instrumental ostinato. The *Symphony of Psalms* is generally ranked as one of Stravinsky's finest achievements, a work charged with a grandeur that only great composers can achieve.

Orpheus

This tendency towards lyricism and warmth of expression reaches a climax in *Orpheus* (1948), a ballet which, like most of Stravinsky's dance works, is also highly successful as a concert piece. *Orpheus* is constructed in a series of independent sections or movements, of which the last is an intensified variant of the first. The tone is for the most part warm and lyrical—more neo-romantic than neo-classic. The single shattering climax, occurring when the Bacchantes set upon the bereaved Orpheus, is inevitably reminiscent of *Le Sacre*; but even this violence is achieved with remarkable economy, and it is in any case the sole loud passage in the entire score.

In its time, *Orpheus* appeared to many musicians as the cornerstone of a flourishing musical style—one that would perpetuate the virtues of Baroque, classical, and romantic music, while still remaining genuinely contemporary. The Mass (1948), an austere work evoking the fourteenth and fifteenth centuries, seemed to expand still further the possibilities of revivifying old styles with new substance.

The Rake's Progress

Perhaps only Stravinsky knew better. In 1951 he completed his largest—and last—neo-classic work: *The Rake's Progress*, an opera on a libretto by W. H. Auden and Chester Kallman, freely based on a series of eighteenth-century engravings by Hogarth. Here the model is obviously the Mozart of *Figaro* and *Don Giovanni*. Mozartian dramaturgy is taken over intact: there are recitatives (accompanied by the harpsichord!), arias and ensembles in closed forms, and even a moralizing ensemble conclusion, directly modeled on the ending of *Don Giovanni*. The musical style is also neo-Mozartian, especially in the vocal melody. The harmony is generally diatonic and basically tonal, although liberally spiced with dissonance. Yet the whole is unmistakeably Stravinskyan, especially in the rhythm and the elegant orchestration.

The Rake's Progress is perhaps the most specifically neo-classical of all Stravinsky's works. The audience is invited to accept eighteenth-century dramatic values, and must be acquainted with classical models in order to understand Stravinsky's treatment of them. (It seems less important that the audience recognize the semi-concealed forms in Berg's operas.) No doubt it is one of the great stage works of the century, but it is unlikely to conquer the affection of a large public: it is music for the connoisseur.

The Rake's Progress also marks another important turning point in Stravinsky's career. In the early 1950s, he began, apparently for the first time, to take seriously the music of the Viennese school. Serial technique begins to appear in his work, at first hesitantly, then with increasing rigor. The influence of Webern becomes apparent. Nonetheless, the septuagenarian composer by no means abandons his musical personality: the old stylistic traits are disguised, not effaced, by the overlay of serialism. Of the last works, few are frequently performed, except perhaps for the brilliant, plotless ballet *Agon* (1957), and it is too early to judge their position within the Stravinsky canon. Nothing, however, can affect Stravinsky's own rank as one of the two or three greatest musical minds of his time.

Stravinsky's serial works

EUROPEAN MUSIC 1920–1950

In the years between the two wars, Stravinsky and Schoenberg were seen as representing opposite poles of musical style, a view that now seems oversimplified, if still basically sound. It would therefore be theoretically possible to classify other composers according to their proximity to one or the other of these two figures—a procedure that would disclose a large number of more or less neo-classical composers, and a much smaller group of twelve-tone adherents. Such a simplistic method would, however, fail in two particulars: it would leave no room for certain important men who owed little to either Schoenberg or Stravinsky; and it would ignore the point of view of the general public (and of many musicians), which regarded all "modern music" as a relatively undistinguishable and generally very unpleasant mass of sound.

This attitude is deftly summarized in a cartoon showing a composer bowing to acknowledge the (doubtless scattered) applause of a concert audience, while one lady turns to another, saying, "How nice! I thought they were all dead." She may be excused for thinking so. At that time, and indeed to a lesser extent in the present, teachers of music brought up their pupils on a diet of classical and romantic music (with perhaps a little Bach), and public concerts presented music of the same sort. Debussy and Ravel, together with the first three ballets of Stravinsky, were the most advanced music in the general repertoire. (There were, however, heroes also in those days— Serge Koussevitsky, for example, who conducted a good deal of new music whether his audience liked it or not.) The recording industry had begun to grow, but its repertoire was even more conservative than that of the concert stage. It is hardly surprising that audiences accustomed to Mozart, Beethoven, and Brahms found the new music incomprehensible, and rejected it out of hand.

In order to secure performances, composers banded together in societies, from the International Society for Contemporary Music down to ephemeral local groups. Such organizations were responsible for the first performances of many major works, but they rarely could follow up these premières with further hearings, and never succeeded in attracting a significant proportion of the "ordinary" concert audience. This naturally strengthened the tendency of composers to write for other composers, or for persons they knew to be sympathetic, rather than for the public: they could always hope for posthumous fame.

This background is essential to an understanding of the proliferation of musical styles in the years between 1920 and 1950. The innovations immediately preceding the first world war had shown that the old laws were not immutable. With audiences indifferent and hostile, the composer was left with almost total freedom to do whatever he wanted. As a result, individual styles were extremely diverse, and an orderly historical pattern for the period is by no means easy to discover—especially since value judgments on music so recent are often unreliable or even impossible. The following pages first treat two important composers only distantly related to either Schoenberg or Stravinsky, and then proceed to a nation-by-nation survey of men who achieved considerable reputations before 1950.

Béla Bartók

Individual styles: Bartók and Hindemith.   Béla Bartók (1881–1945) was a major figure, both as a composer and as a serious collector of folksong from his native Hungary, the Balkans, and Turkey. The many years he spent in the latter pursuit resulted in important critical editions of thousands of folk melodies. At the same time, his absorption in folk music inevitably helped to form his style as a composer, making of him in a sense a twentieth-century nationalist. His many published folk song settings, all distinguished by extreme skill in fitting original and appropriate harmonies to melodies that are by no means tonal in the Western sense, almost invariably (and quite naturally) have an eastern European flavor; and there are many folk-like turns of phrase in his free compositions. But Bartók is no more a Hungarian composer than Stravinsky is a Russian one. In his personal style, folk music is only one ingredient among many.

Bartók's works and style

Bartók's output was considerable, ranging from the *Mikrokosmos* (1926–37), a collection of piano studies in twentieth-century style, suitable for teaching purposes, to large-scale orchestral and dramatic works. Like most of the composers to be considered here, he wrote music that is chromatic and freely dissonant, yet basically tonal, in the sense that one perceives tonal centers at least at critical points. Some of the early works, in particular, employ ostinato, sharply dissonant percussive chords, and extremes of dynamics to produce an almost barbaric ferocity (one of his most popular early piano pieces is entitled "Allegro barbaro"). The later works incline often to a warmer, more lyrical style.

While Bartók often employs free variants of older forms (sonata, fugue, rondo), his principal means of achieving musical coherence are a tightly knit motivic web and, when necessary, forceful repetition of crucial pitches or harmonies. His motives, often strongly chromatic, generally create an intensely contrapuntal texture, sharply defined rhythmically in the fast movements, but sometimes impressionistically nonmetric in slow ones. While the insistence on interval patterns derived from motives may occasionally resemble serial technique, Bartók does not use tone rows, and maintains tonal relations as an important shaping force. Thus the beginning of the fifth string quartet is clearly in (or "on") B♭, and thereafter there is an equally clear motion away from B♭ and, at the end of the movement, a return to it. The second movement shows a less obvious but equally effective procedure: the forceful bass line slowly but securely establishes D as tonal center (Ex. XV–5). Here all twelve tones of the octave are used, but there is no question of their equality.

On a larger level, Bartók employs a wider variety of patterns. The Fifth Quartet is symmetrical. Of its five movements, the first and last are fast, the second and fourth are scherzos, with a slow movement at the center. The Sixth Quartet is, by contrast, a progressive form. The first three movements—allegro, march, and burletta (scherzo)—are each preceded by a slow introduction, based on essentially the same melody. This melody also begins the last movement (the only slow one), where it is allowed to expand as the principal material. The whole is a unique but fully satisfying construction.

The six string quartets, dating from 1908 to 1939, provide a good overall view of much of Bartók's stylistic development. Taken together, they are among the most im-

Béla Bartók, String Quartet No. 5. Copyright 1936 by Universal Edition; renewed
1963. Copyright and Renewal assigned to Boosey and Hawkes, Inc., for the
U.S.A. Reprinted by permission.

Ex. XV-5

portant achievements in the area of twentieth-century chamber music. Beethovenian
in their deep seriousness, their careful craftsmanship, and their exacting demands on
the players, they repay careful listening and study. Bartók's larger works include the
brooding, symbolic opera *Bluebeard's Castle*, three concertos for piano, a concerto
for violin and one for viola, as well as the popular Concerto for Orchestra (1944).
There are also important compositions for less orthodox media, such as the Sonata for
Two Pianos and Percussion (1938), and the Music for Strings, Percussion, and Celesta
(1937), of which the first, especially, reveals a joyous energy rarely found in music of
this period.

Even in this purely instrumental music, echos of folk melody and rhythm—sometimes very distinct ones—can be heard. The underlying scales are often neither major
nor minor; and such rhythms as 3+2+3, while they may owe something to Stravinsky's earlier work, are more directly derivable from east European dance
rhythms. Bartók's peculiar success was in internationalizing such idioms. While authentically nationalistic music—that of Mussorgsky, for example—seems always to

evoke the land of its origin, Bartók's work stands squarely in the main European tradition: its folk elements have been wholly assimilated into a larger style.

Unfortunately, Bartók's career was also unsuccessful. When he died, in poverty, his music was only slightly better known than that of Schoenberg. By a cruel caprice of fashion, Bartók's work began to be widely played in the years immediately following his death. By the 1950s, he had become, after Stravinsky, the most popular composer of his generation and his music performed valuable service in helping wider audiences to approach the complexities of twentieth-century style.

Paul Hindemith

Bartók had made no concessions to win a larger public, although the gap between composer and audience had naturally worried him, as it did most composers. One of the most active in attempting to bridge that gap was Paul Hindemith (1895–1963), a German whose early career produced radical and experimental works, many of which still sound fresh today. Gradually, he came to the conclusion that the apparently chaotic state of music in his time was an evil, to be combated whenever possible. His combat took three principal forms. First, he developed his own style of tonal neo-classicism, in which dissonant harmonies were embedded in forms and textures clearly derived from classical and Baroque models. His motivic counterpoint is often strongly reminiscent of Bach, and is often cast in formal fugues; his harmonies, often complex and dissonant in mid-phrase, usually depart from and end in triads.

Secondly, he took special pains to write music that would fulfill a real need, and hence be played. He composed sonatas for practically every instrument, giving even the double-bass player something for a recital. Similarly, he wrote pieces for children, and works in which the audience could take a part.

His third contribution was in the area of musical theory. His *Craft of Musical Composition* (German version, 1937–39; English translation, 1941) was an attempt to set forth an all-embracing theory of music that would both explain the music of the past, and regulate that of the present and future. Since Hindemith believed in an inherent human feeling for tonality, his theory was naturally not acceptable to twelve-tone composers; nor did it satisfy Stravinsky either. Indeed, few musicians would admit that Hindemith succeeded in his intention, although he himself was sincere enough to rewrite some of his earlier works so that they would conform to the precepts he had evolved.

His failure to bring order to what he regarded as musical chaos does not invalidate his musical works. While he wrote too much, perhaps, in his efforts to reunite composer and audience, his best work is first rate. His most celebrated compositions are the "symphony" *Mathis der Maler* (Mathis [Grünewald] the Painter; 1934), consisting of three instrumental movements adapted from his opera of the same title; and the song cycle *Das Marienleben* (The Life of Mary; 1923, revised in 1948). These show his predilection for chords and melodies built on superposed fourths (rather than thirds), his masterful counterpoint, and his relatively traditional formal schemes. In

Hindemith's music

some ways, Hindemith's position in the twentieth century resembles that of Brahms in the nineteenth. Both emphasized craftsmanship and restraint, while remaining capable of vigorous expression. Of course, Brahms's reputation is now secure, while that of Hindemith is still subject to considerable difference of opinion.

Music in the Soviet Union. "Dissonant but in some way tonal" describes much of the music between the two wars, except, of course, for that of the Viennese school and its adherents. In the following survey of the more important musical nations, it will become clear that the phrase applies to most composers; although its extreme generality naturally does not preclude the development of thoroughly personal styles.

In Russia, the fall of the Czarist autocracy and its replacement by the soon equally autocratic Communist regime introduced important political factors into the musical scene. After a brief flirtation with artistic freedom and egalitarianism (orchestras without conductors, for example) which produced some ephemeral "modernistic" music, the authorities concluded that the arts must serve the state and "the people." Many aspects of twentieth-century style—including serialism and the music of Stravinsky (who had emigrated)—were banned, and composers were instructed to cultivate "socialist realism." In musical practice, this meant retention of tonality and avoidance of any kind of extreme. Deviations from acceptable style were treated in the same way as political dissent, although not as harshly. The offender was required to make public confession of his errors, to promise amendment of his ways, and to keep his promise. Composers were thus in theory compelled to seek the approval of mass audiences, while in practice attempting to please their political leaders. Their efforts to do this, while still preserving some individuality, produced music that in general ranges from frankly post-romantic effusiveness to mildly dissonant tonal harmony, often with folk-like tunes. Nationalist—and specifically Soviet—subject matter was of course favored, but much abstract music was also composed.

Music after the Russian Revolution

Sergei Prokofiev (1891–1953) stands head and shoulders above his contemporaries in the Soviet Union, perhaps because he passed part of his career (1918–27) abroad, and was thus able to hear much music that was not performed in Russia. Nevertheless, his native talent would doubtless have obtained for him an outstanding position even without this advantage. While many of Prokofiev's works were officially condemned, he maintained a surprising independence even after his return to the Soviet Union at least until the general condemnation of "bourgeois formalism" in 1948, which castigated almost all the leading composers of the time.

Sergei Prokofiev

A musician, hearing Prokofiev's name, is apt to think at first of satire and wit, and there are indeed many passages and some whole works in which sardonic mockery—achieved by means of sprightly melodies supported by unexpected and often dissonant harmonies, presented in a brilliantly colored texture—is the chief effect. But this is only one species of Prokofiev's music, and not the most important. His major works, which include operas, ballets, symphonies, sonatas, and other types, are serious and distinguished. His music is based essentially on melody, lyrical or forceful as the occasion requires, and, in the fast movements, on a propulsive rhythmic energy that resembles that of early Stravinsky and of Bartók. His harmony is always basically tonal, but varies widely in dissonance content from work to work. On the whole, lyrical passages are more apt to be triadic (although of course without the regular functional progressions of the preceding centuries), while vigorous ones often employ sharp dissonances. The Fifth Symphony (1944) displays these qualities, and also demonstrates that Prokofiev was no mere follower of politically derived stylistic rules.

Prokofiev had more success than many in gaining and holding a considerable public, both in and outside the Soviet Union: his music has been and continues to be frequently played. While some of his popular reputation rests on deliberately "simple" works like *Peter and the Wolf* (1936), he was both a skillful and honorable composer, and the best of his music commands the respect of any serious musician.

Dmitri Shostako-
vich

Another Soviet composer is Dmitri Shostakovich (1906–   ), whose copious but uneven output appears to reflect a vacillation between a sincere desire to conform to the dictates of socialist realism and a compulsion to express his own musical personality. His vigorous tragic opera, *Lady Macbeth of Mtsensk* (1930–32), was at first a considerable success, but soon after incurred the disapproval of the government. Although this work and many others (e.g., the Fifth Symphony, 1937) contain many fine pages, and although Shostakovich obviously has given much thought and labor to the reconciliation of personal and official standards, his achievement does not measure up to that of Prokofiev. Much the same must be said for numerous other Russian composers of the period, talented though many of them certainly are.

Germany

Music in Western Europe.   The situation in the German-speaking nations was in some ways even worse. After the members of the Viennese school, Hindemith, and many others were well into their careers, the rise of Hitler put an end to almost all new or experimental music—simply because Hitler and his advisers did not understand, and therefore disliked, any sort of artistic innovation. In consequence, most progressive composers emigrated, many to the United States (much to the enrichment of American musical life); and Hitlerian Germany became nearly a musical vacuum. Of the major figures, only Webern stayed—unmolested, for the most part, because he was then so little known.

A much lesser man, Carl Orff (1895–   ) managed to remain for different reasons. He made extensive contributions to musical pedagogy: his system for introducing music to children is still in considerable use. As a composer, he sought to create a style that was at once simple enough for instant comprehension and yet free from romanticism. This involved the blending of vigorous irregular rhythms with simple diatonic tunes. His *Carmina Burana* (1937) has been much appreciated by audiences, but generally regarded with disdain by composers. His simplification of musical means may eventually appear to be either an ephemeral popularization of Stravinsky, or perhaps a real achievement in its own right.

Italy

In Italy, Mussolini's Fascism was also repressive of new developments. Although less violent than Nazism, Fascism lasted considerably longer. Still, two gifted composers, both basically neo-classical in orientation, pursued careers in Italy without undue interference: Alfredo Casella (1883–1947) and Gian Francesco Malipiero (1882–   ), the latter also the editor of the complete works of Monteverdi. Probably more important is Luigi Dallapiccola (1904–   ), who turned, more or less in solitude, to the twelve-tone technique in the late 1930s. The *Canti di prigionia* (Songs of Prison; 1938–41) combine modified serialism with highly original scoring for chorus and an unusual ensemble of percussion instruments, both pitched and non-pitched. His later works show strong traces of the influence of Webern, but without loss of individuality.

England

The beginning of the twentieth century found England shaking off at last the Mendelssohnian torpor of the preceding decades. Already Edward Elgar (1857–1934) had been a distinguished representative of the German post-romantic tradition, and

Frederick Delius (1862–1934) had produced his own version of impressionism. Gustav Holst (1874–1934) wrote music more specifically English in sound—in large part because of his interest in English folk song—and made some use of twentieth-century techniques. But it is Ralph Vaughan Williams (1871–1958) who typifies English music of the first half of the century. Vaughan Williams also took a deep interest in English folk music, although he does not quote it extensively in his compositions. His style is eclectic, and varies considerably from work to work: tonality in some form is always present, but the amount of dissonance ranges widely. The *Fantasia on a Theme of Thomas Tallis* (1909) is basically triadic, while the Fourth Symphony (1934) represents a much more aggressively "modern" manner.

After Vaughan Williams, the most celebrated English composer is Benjamin Britten (1913–   ). Like his predecessor, he gained international renown, especially with his opera *Peter Grimes* (1945). His music is written in yet another variant of the tonal but moderately dissonant idiom that dominated so much of the period. Other English composers could also be cited as evidence of a British musical renaissance in the twentieth century: for the purpose of this discussion, it is sufficient to note that such a movement occurred, and is still continuing.

In France, as has been seen, the renaissance had begun earlier: Debussy was certainly the most important precursor of twentieth-century style. He was followed, not by disciples, but by a reaction (already begun by Satie) in favor of clarity, coolness, and wit. In consequence, most French composers of the period between the wars were neo-classically inclined. Among them, the prolific Darius Milhaud (1892-1974) is well known for light, humorous, and satirical pieces in an almost self-consciously French manner. The greater part of his work, however (especially his dramatic music), is entirely serious and often deeply impressive. He is also celebrated for his frequent use of polytonality—a technique in which melodic lines, or even chord progressions, in different keys are sounded simultaneously. Milhaud himself warned against giving undue attention to this technique, and his music is based primarily on his ability to invent and manipulate appropriate melody, not on any specific harmonic system.

France: Milhaud, Honegger, and Poulenc

An exact contemporary of Milhaud, Arthur Honegger (1892–1955), tried deliberately to make the new music palatable to a large audience in his oratorio *King David* (1921), and its frequent performance indicates that he succeeded. Most of his music, however, is more complex, often austere—more German-sounding than French at times. His harmony is basically tonal but freely dissonant; his textures frequently chromatic and contrapuntal.

Francis Poulenc (1899–1963) is best known for his many fine songs and his late opera *Dialogue of the Carmelites* (1956), although he contributed to other genres as well. His music, like Milhaud's, strikes the listener as being intensely French, although his style is somewhat warmer and less obviously brilliant than Milhaud's.

Although the ultimate importance of these men—and indeed of any but a very few composers of this century—is still a matter for argument, their styles are clearly situable. Tonality is generally retained, although not by traditional means; triads are used, but so also are more dissonant chords; forms are either derived from classical or Baroque models, or are free but clearly recognizable structures invented for a specific work.

One French composer stands apart from his contemporaries: Olivier Messiaen (1908–   ), a strange and, for a long time, isolated figure. Messiaen, a devout Chris-

Olivier Messiaen

tian, wrote a great deal of organ music for the church. The pieces from the 30s, still often played, sound rather innocuous today, rather like post-impressionist fantasies, rich in organistic effects. Closer inspection, however, shows remarkable innovations. *La nativité du Seigneur* (The Birth of the Lord; 1936), for example, uses artificially constructed scales (e.g., one proceeding by alternating tones and semitones) and curious rhythms produced by adding "a half unit of [rhythmic] value"—a single sixteenth note in a passage of eighths, for example: ♪♪ ♫. These devices undermine both tonality and meter. In later works, Messiaen employs rhythms far more complex than the one just cited, and adds experimentation in other areas as well: one finds elements derived from Indian (and other non-Western) music, large numbers of unusual percussion instruments, bird songs, and sounds produced by electronic means. The vast symphony *Turangalîla* (1948) is typical of Messiaen's later style—a style that remains radical even at present, while retaining a certain slightly old-fashioned rhapsodic quality.

Edgar Varèse

If Messiaen arrived at a radical style gradually, Edgar Varèse (1885–1965), a Frenchman who passed much of his life in the United States, directly continued the experimental tendencies of the period around the first world war. Varèse was another isolated figure. Trained in both music and engineering, he brought to music a scientific attitude that became widespread among composers only after 1950. Titles like *Ionisation* (1931) and *Density 21.5* (1935), the first for massive percussion ensemble, the second for flute solo, suggest a frame of mind and a use of the medium quite different from that of any other composer of the time—when even Schoenberg, Stravinsky, and Webern were using labels like "symphony" and "variations." The music, which Varèse preferred to call "organized sound," is as startling. While there are certainly connections with *Le sacre*, the overall style is highly original. The mere writing of a large piece for percussion alone—hence without much dependence on pitch-succession as a primary factor—as early as 1931 shows a remarkable independence from conventional values. Varèse discards tonality entirely, and builds his structures out of sonorities and rhythms, combined with widely disjunct, asymmetrical melodies. Like Messiaen, Varèse remained a lonely experimenter, whose hour came only toward the end of his life.

THE UNITED STATES

Music before 1900

Early contributions. The history of music in the United States, naturally of special interest for American readers, belongs properly in this chapter, for only in the present century did the Americas begin to achieve musical equality with the major European nations. This is not to deny the value of various earlier American musicians, such as William Billings (1746–1800), Louis Gottschalk (1829–69), and many others. Nonetheless, Western art music acquired a secure foothold in the United States only gradually; even during the nineteenth century, when important new (European) music was beginning to be regularly performed here, the performers were generally Europeans.

At first, the German tradition predominated: the worthy if not great composer Edward MacDowell (1861–1908) received much of his training in Germany. While MacDowell occasionally used indigenous materials in his music, his style is essentially German. After the first world war, French influence became more important among composers, although the public repertoire remained (and still remains) largely German. Needless to say, the pressure of the European traditions was enormous, and most Americans felt it necessary to study composition in Europe, thus to some extent slowing the emergence of a distinctively American "school" of composition. An important turning-point was the immigration, mostly during the 30s, of many of the foremost European composers—Stravinsky, Schoenberg, Bartók, and Hindemith, among others. They greatly strengthened the United States as a musical nation, and by their presence as well as their teaching, helped it to take a place with the traditional leaders.

Meanwhile, the United States became internationally famous as a producer of music for a quite different reason: through the emergence and subsequent diffusion of jazz. While a study of jazz lies outside the scope of this book, some mention of it is essential, for its influence on composed music was (and to some extent still is) considerable. The origins of jazz are obscure: its practice is thought to have begun in New Orleans, before the first world war. Its technique was developed mainly by black musicians, who mingled elements of their own traditions with the triadic basis of Western music. A jazz performance is basically improvisatory, even when several players are involved. The basis for improvisation is, in theory, a known melody; in practice, it is more often a simple tonal succession of triads. The harmonic basis is thus Western, but the improvised parts are less so. They depart both rhythmically and melodically from traditional European norms: rhythmically in their constant syncopation and frequent use of rhythms employing values unnotatable in the conventional system; melodically in their employment of "blue" notes—tones deliberately out of tune with the normal scale. No notated version of a jazz performance can succeed in communicating the essence of the style.

Jazz

While jazz cannot be said to have created masterpieces comparable to the great works of European composers, it was nevertheless an extremely vital and persuasive style: its content was both immediate and significant. It quickly became the leading popular style in the United States, and was soon practiced extensively in Europe (by American performers) as well. It is to the honor of the Europeans (especially the French) that they recognized its freshness sooner than most American musicians did. Many "serious" composers were impressed to the point of introducing jazz elements into their works: the new style seemed a new source of strength, a new way of revivifying musical language.

The diffusion of jazz made America known as a music-producing nation throughout the Western world and, as a felicitous by-product, helped towards giving some status to black musicians. But there were other, not wholly favorable, consequences. While American composers after the first world war were, by and large, capable of equaling the work of comparable European musicians, they were rarely taken seriously in Europe: was not America the land of jazz? Before 1950, American composition was known to Europeans almost exclusively through the work of George Gershwin (1898–1937), a highly competent composer whose work, which combines jazz elements with late nineteenth-century style, is for the most part closer to popular or entertainment music than to the central art tradition. While his great success was well deserved, it tended to obscure the merits of an increasingly important school of American composers who deserved more international attention than they received.

In point of fact, an older American composer, Charles Ives (1874–1954), had already achieved a degree of distinction that should have placed him among the leaders of his time, but Ives's music remained unknown to almost everyone until the 1940s.

Charles Ives

Ives was another solitary figure, who combined a successful career in business with an obscure one as a composer. Although he had virtually no contact with European music after Debussy, one can find in his music anticipations of almost all the major technical innovations of the first half of the century: extreme dissonance, polytonality, highly complex rhythms, atonality, and even serial method. His most characteristic music is strongly national, often quoting melodies (especially hymn tunes) familiar to almost all Americans of his time—although the quotations are frequently embedded in a ferociously complex mass of dissonant and rhythmically unstable sound.

While Ives wrote pieces entitled "sonata" and "symphony," his works of these types owe almost nothing to convention—less than contemporary European works bearing the same titles. Thus his evocation of New England in the *Concord Sonata* (1909–15), for example, which might well have delighted a nation becoming conscious of its own importance, was too strange and too exotic to command public attention.

Ives's numerous songs show an astonishing range in every respect. Ives even labeled some of them as bad, and asked that they not be sung. The texts include popular or folk poems, serious art poetry, and a number of poems written by Ives or his wife. As to the music, it ranges from the direct and simple to the unperformable (or nearly so). The first song contains sixteen-note chords (or "tone clusters") for one hand at the piano, to be played by the forearm, or by a board. Others are notated in extraordinarily complex rhythms, with or without barlines. Still others are quite traditional.

Ives stopped composing in the early 20s and, during the remainder of his life, showed no interest in having his music performed, or in enhancing his reputation in any way. Although he slowly became recognized as an important figure, he remained aloof. This may partly account for his relative lack of influence on other American composers during his lifetime, but the very variety of his music was also responsible. A style so rich in innovations of so many different kinds does not serve easily as a model for imitation. Ives was an extraordinary pioneer, but one without direct successors.

Developments after World War I.   The real coming of age of the United States may be dated from the years after the first world war, when American music began to approach equality with that of any European nation. The Old World still played its part, to be sure. Many Americans were trained by the Frenchwoman Nadia Boulanger (1887–   ), whose talent as a teacher of composers attracted (and still attracts) musicians from all over the world to her studios in Paris and Fontainebleau. And, of course, there was no very solid "American tradition" on which young composers could build, so that they quite naturally modeled their own work on European prototypes. Shortly two quite different attitudes made their appearance: an American might more or less disregard his nationality, simply working out for himself the style that best suited his purposes; or he might attempt to produce specifically American music, using or alluding to American materials—folk songs, hymn tunes, jazz, spirituals, or whatever. While some composers consistently maintained one or the other of these positions, it would be a mistake to attempt a simplistic distinction between nationalist and internationalist composers. The danger of such a classification is made evident by the career of one of the most celebrated of the Americans, Aaron Copland (1900–   ). Some of his works are devoid of "Americanisms." The Piano Variations of 1930, for example, employ sharp dissonance and strict thematic economy to create a forceful piece that would be at home anywhere in the Western nations. His celebrated ballets, on the other hand, show a nationalist intent even in their titles—*Billy the Kid* (1938), *Rodeo* (1942), and *Appalachian Spring* (1944). These and other works make liberal use of folk-song idioms, and are written in a relatively simple style, intended to appeal to a wide audience. Yet this turn to nationalism is not a mere matter of chronology, for some of Copland's later works are again international, such as the Piano Quartet (1950), which employs a modified form of twelve-tone technique.

More consistently international in style are the works of Walter Piston (1894–   ), like Copland a fundamentally neo-classic composer. While his forms and techniques are clearly traceable to traditional models, his use of them is indisputably personal; and, although he generally avoids the use of quotations of any sort, recognizably American as well. (The occasional appearance of jazz rhythms in Piston and other composers can hardly be counted an Americanism, since European composers used such rhythms nearly as frequently.) Roger Sessions (1896–   ) absorbed rather more of the influence of Schoenberg and was generally hostile to the imitation of earlier styles, however disguised. His music is austere and difficult, and has been too little played, despite the composer's great reputation. It is important not only in its own right, but also as a bridge between the neo-classical and twelve-tone worlds. The somewhat younger Elliott Carter (1908–   ) developed relatively slowly, to become a leading figure in the 40s. One of the few composers with an early acquaintance with Ives, he has continued—in his own way—Ives's tradition of experimentation, notably in the area of rhythm: his "metric modulation" is an attempt to create a rhythmic analogue of a change of tonal center. His music is complex, difficult, and distinguished; and his continued search for new solutions to technical problems has maintained his position as an important innovator in the decades after 1950.

Among the more explicitly nationalistic composers may be mentioned Virgil Thomson (1896–   ), who, despite a long period of residence in Paris, remained musically rooted in the United States. He is best known for two operas written to texts of Gertrude Stein: *Four Saints in Three Acts* (1928) and *The Mother of Us All* (1947; the latter on the life of Susan B. Anthony). The apparent simplicity of the music only partly conceals an extreme sophistication. Thomson owes more than a little to Erik Satie, of whom he was in a certain sense a follower. Roy Harris (1898–   ) is chiefly famous for his Third Symphony (1939), a moving and indisputably American work.

Almost all these men were teachers as well as composers, with the result that younger musicians no longer needed to go abroad for their training (although many still spend time in Europe, if only for their own pleasure). This, coupled with the dissemination of recorded performances, has made of the United States a fully independent musical nation. The reader should, however, be wary of drawing chauvinist conclusions: much the same independence exists in such countries as Greece, Poland, Romania, and Japan—none of which had previously made consistently significant contributions to the Western tradition.

SUMMARY

On a superficial level, the first half of the twentieth century bears some resemblance to the first half of the seventeenth. In both cases, the first decade or two was a period of intense and radical experimentation, followed by a period of at least relative consolidation and stability. The analogy, however, is weak. By the 1640s, Italian composers were well embarked on the creation of a unified musical style, which was in time imitated by all the other principal nations except France. In the twentieth century, this was not the case. While it is too much to say that each composer created his own style, it is equally untrue to claim that anything resembling a stylistic common practice had emerged by 1950. It is perhaps more fruitful to argue that each decade had a certain quality—an ethos—of its own, however differently it might be expressed by different composers. Thus one finds the greatest concentration of satirical and humorous music in the 20s. The music of the 30s appears austere and sober by contrast, moving gradually towards the warmer lyricism of the 40s. And the middle of the century appears at the present to have been a turning point of a more decisive character—one whose consequences will be briefly considered below.

Brief notices of some composers of the 20th century.

Babbitt, Milton (b. 1916). American composer and teacher, the spiritual head of an American school of serialist composers. *Three Compositions* for piano (ca. 1957); *Composition for four instruments* (1949); *Ensembles for Synthesizer; All Set* (1957) for jazz ensemble; *Philomel* for voice and tape.

Barber, Samuel (b. 1910). American composer of lyric, basically tonal music. *Overture to The School for Scandal* (1933); *Adagio for Strings* (1938); opera *Vanessa* (1956); *Knoxville: Summer of 1915* for soprano and orchestra (1948).

Bartók, Béla (1881–1945). Hungarian composer; eminent collector of folk tunes. Terse, rhythmic, dissonant and sometimes percussive music. Opera *Bluebeard's Castle* (1911); ballet *The Miraculous Mandarin* (1919); *Music for Strings, Percussion, and Celesta* (1937); *Concerto for Orchestra* (1944); three piano concertos; violin concerto; viola concerto; six string quartets; sonata for two pianos and percussion; much piano music, incl. *Allegro barbaro,* and *Mikrokosmos* (six books of piano pieces of progressive difficulty).

Berg, Alban (1885–1935). Austrian composer, pupil of Schoenberg, though usually more lyrical and rarely so strictly twelve-tone as he. Piano sonata (1908); *Lyric Suite* for string quartet (1926); operas *Wozzeck* (composed 1914–21), *Lulu* (unfinished).

Berio, Luciano (b. 1925). Italian composer, known especially for the use of spoken language as a musical element. *Omaggio a Joyce* (1958). *Circles* (1960). *Passaggio* (1963).

Boulez, Pierre (b. 1925). French composer, student of Messiaen. Three piano sonatas. *Structures* for two pianos (bk. I, 1951–52; bk. II, 1967). *Le marteau sans maître* (1954), a cantata for contralto and instrumental ensemble. *Pli selon pli,* for voice and orchestra, on texts of Mallarmé.

Britten, Benjamin (b. 1913). English composer. Operas include *Peter Grimes* (1945); *The Rape of Lucretia* (1946); *Albert Herring* (1947); *The Little Sweep* (1949); *The Turn of the Screw* (1954). *War Requiem* for soloists, chorus, orchestra (1962); *A Young Person's Guide to the Orchestra* (1946). Many songs; much choral music.

Cage, John (b. 1912). American avant-garde composer, whose theories have been at least as influential in the other arts as in music. His attempts to create random music cause him regularly to be considered a charlatan. Compositions include *Four Minutes and Thirty-three Seconds* for piano; *Imaginary Landscape* for 12 radios; *Indeterminacy; Concerto for Prepared Piano and Chamber Orchestra.*

Carter, Elliott (b. 1908). American composer; polyphonic, chromatic, but not serial style. *Variations for Orchestra* (1955); Double concerto for piano, harpsichord, and two chamber orchestras (1961); Concerto for piano (1964–65); three string quartets.

Copland, Aaron (b. 1900). American composer. Among his popular works are the ballets *Appalachian Spring, Rodeo,* and *Billy the Kid.* More serious works, sometimes employing serial techniques, are the Piano Variations (1930); the Piano sonata (1939–41); the *Connotations for Orchestra* (1962).

Cowell, Henry (1897–1965). American composer; editor and biographer of Ives. A constant innovator, he is known for his "tone-clusters," produced by the hand, fist, forearm, etc., on the keyboard. Fourteen symphonies; chamber music; much piano music.

Dallapiccola, Luigi (b. 1904). Italian composer, mostly of vocal music in the Webern tradition. Operas *Volo di notte* (1940), *Il prigioniero* (1949). Cantata *Job* (1950). *Canti di liberazione* (1955).

Foss, Lukas (b. 1922). German-born composer, conductor, pianist; came to U.S.A. in 1937. Earlier works are in a modern tonal style: two piano concertos; cantata *The Prairie* (1944); string quartet. Later works generally have a significant element of improvisation: *Time Cycle* (1960); *Echoi* (1963).

Harris, Roy (b. 1898). American composer in a symphonic, neo-tonal style. Seven symphonies; other symphonic works; much chamber music, incl. three string quartets. Piano sonata. Choral works.

Henze, Hans Werner (b. 1926). German composer, best known for his dramatic works. An eclectic, popularly- and dramatically-oriented dodecaphonic style. Five symphonies. Operas include *Prinz von Homburg* (1960); *Elegie für junge Liebende* (1961); *Der junge Lord* (1965).

Hindemith, Paul (1895–1963). German composer, also an influential theorist and teacher. Lived in U.S.A. 1940–53. After ca. 1927, his music reflects his personal compositional system based on the degree of tension between chords. Works include the operas *Mathis der Maler* (1938), *Die Harmonie der Welt* (1957); a series of seven *Kammermusiken* (1922–28) for various combinations of instruments; the song cycle *Das Marienleben* (1923, revised 1948); *Ludus Tonalis* (1943) for keyboard—a sort of latter-day *Well-Tempered Clavier*; and a great number of keyboard, vocal, and chamber pieces designed as utilitarian music *(Gebrauchsmusik)*.

Honegger, Arthur (1892–1955). Swiss-born composer, one of the French group called "Les six." Works include oratorios *Le Roi David* (1921), *Jeanne d'Arc au bûcher* (1938); opera *Judith* (1926); Symphonic movements *Pacific 231* and *Pastorale d'été*; five symphonies; vocal and chamber music.

Ives, Charles (1874–1954). Innovative, individualist American composer, largely unknown in his lifetime. His many works include five symphonies; *The Unanswered Question* and *Three Places in New England* for orchestra; *Concord Sonata* for piano; 114 songs.

Jańaček, Leoš. See appendix to chapter XIV.

Kabalevsky, Dmitri (b. 1904). Soviet pianist and composer of direct, rhythmical, tonal works. Opera *The Family of Taras* (1947). Three symphonies; patriotic cantatas; much piano music. Music designed for young performers, incl. concertos for violin, 'cello, and piano.

Khatchaturian, Aram (b. 1903). Armenian-born Soviet composer. Ballet *Gayne* (1942); piano, violin concertos; three symphonies; several piano pieces.

Kirchner, Leon (b. 1919). American composer. Studied with Schoenberg; linear, chromatic style. Three string quartets (the third includes an electronic tape); piano sonata (1948); piano concerto (1952–53); toccata for strings, winds, and percussion (1956).

Krenek, Ernst (b. 1900). Austrian composer. His opera *Jonny spielt auf,* written when he was 26, scored a huge success. About 1933, he was perhaps the first composer, except for Schoenberg's pupils, to adopt the twelve-tone method, notably in his opera *Karl V.* Four piano concertos, two-piano concerto; eight string quartets; choral music.

Lutoslawski, Witold (b. 1913). Polish composer. A post-serial avant-garde style, dealing with shifting planes and blocks of sound; the senior member of a significant group of Polish composers. Concerto for orchestra (1954); *Funeral Music* (1958); *Jeux Vénétiens* for orchestra (1961).

Maderna, Bruno (b. 1920). Italian composer. Serialist at first, he worked in the Milan electronic studio in the 1950s. *Serenata* for 11 instruments (1946); *Musica per due dimensioni* (1952); opera *Hyperion* (1964).

Menotti, Gian Carlo (b. 1911). Italian-born composer; he has lived most of his life in the U.S.A. Composer of operas, in a tonal style, with immediate popular appeal. *The Old Maid and the Thief* (1939); *The Medium* (1946); *The Telephone* (1947); *The Consul* (1950); *Amahl and the Night Visitors* (1951).

Messiaen, Olivier (b. 1908). French composer and influential teacher; his principal sources of inspiration are religious mysticism, bird songs, and Oriental rhythms. Works include *Quatuor pour la fin du temps* (1941); *Vision de l'Amen* for two pianos; *Trois petites liturgies de la présence divine* (1945); *Turangalîla* for orchestra (1949); *Mode de valeurs et d'intensité* for piano (1949); *Oiseaux exotiques* (1956).

Milhaud, Darius (1892–1974). Exceptionally prolific French composer; one of the group known as "Les six." Often mentioned for his occasional use of jazz rhythms and of simultaneous tonalities. Enormous number of works, including *Les choéphores* (1919); *Le boeuf sur le toit* (1919); *La création du monde* (1923).

Nono, Luigi (b. 1924). Italian composer. At first identified with serial techniques; worked with electronic procedures; his music has strong social-political commitment. *Variazioni canoniche* (1950); *Canti* for 13 instruments (1955); opera *Intolleranza* (1960); *La fabbrica illuminata* (1964).

Penderecki, Krzysztof (b. 1933). Polish composer. His style seems directly concerned with the manipulation of the medium of sound itself. Works include a string quartet (1960); *Threnody for the Victims of Hiroshima* (1960); *Fluorescences* (1961); *Stabat Mater* (1962).

Piston, Walter (b. 1894). American composer and teacher. Relying on classical forms and a basically tonal harmonic structure, he produces instrumental music of great craftsmanship. Six symphonies; ballet *The Incredible Flutist* (1938); *Concerto for Orchestra* (1934); *Toccata* for orchestra (1948); viola concerto (1958); three string quartets; wind quintet.

Poulenc, Francis (1899–1963). French composer; one of the group known as "Les six." Composer of small, elegant pieces in the salon tradition. A notable composer of songs. Works include operas *Les mamelles de Tirésias* (1947); *Les dialogues des Carmélites* (1957); ballet *Les biches* (1924); concertos for harpsichord; for organ; for piano; for two pianos. Choral works. Songs include the cycles *Tel jour telle nuit* (1937); *Fiançailles pour rire* (1939).

Prokofiev, Sergei (1891–1953). Russian composer. His style is direct, melodic, with a constantly modulating tonality and strong rhythmic drive. Works include the operas *Love for Three Oranges* (1921); *The Flaming Angel* (1919); ballets *Le pas d'acier*

(1924); *L'enfant prodigue* (1928); *Romeo and Juliet* (1935–36); 7 symphonies; symphonic fairy-tale *Peter and the Wolf* (1936); film scores, including *Lieutenant Kije* (1933); *Alexander Nevsky* (1938); much piano music, including 5 concertos, 10 sonatas.

Schoenberg, Arnold (1874–1951). Viennese composer and teacher; professor at U.C.L.A., 1935–1951. His music progresses from post-Wagnerian chromaticism through free atonality to his method of twelve-tone composition. Early tonal works include *Verklärte Nacht* (1899) for string sextet; *Gurrelieder* (1900–1901, orchestrated 1910) for voices, chorus and very large orchestra; *Kammersinfonie* (1906). Atonal works include *Three Piano Pieces* (1909); *Five Orchestral Pieces* (1909); the song cycle *Pierrot Lunaire* (1912). Twelve-tone works include the *Serenade* (1923); *Piano Suite* (1921–23); *Variations for Orchestra* (1928); the unfinished opera *Moses und Aron*; String Trio (1946); *Phantasy* for violin and piano (1949).

Sessions, Roger (b. 1896). American composer. Numerous large-scale works in a complex, somewhat austere style. Operas *The Trial of Lucullus* (1947); *Montezuma* (1963). Four symphonies; concertos for piano, for violin; string quintet; two string quartets; two piano sonatas.

Shostakovitch, Dmitri (b. 1906). Soviet composer, principally of tonal, classically oriented symphonic works. Operas *The Nose* (1930); *Lady Macbeth of the Mtensk District* (1938); 13 symphonies; ballet *The Golden Age* (1930); concertos: 2 for piano, 2 for violin, 1 for 'cello; much film music; 10 string quartets.

Stockhausen, Karlheinz (b. 1928). Prominent German avant-garde composer; beginning as a post-Webernian serialist, he worked with electronic music, and beginning with his *Klavierstück XI*, produced music in which a significant role is assigned to decisions made during performance. Works include *Kontrapunkte* (1953); *Gesang der Jünglinge* (1955–56; electronic); *Zyklus* for percussion (1957); *Gruppen* for three orchestras (1958); *Kontakte* (1959) for tape (another version is for two pianos and percussion).

Stravinsky, Igor (1882–1971). Russian-French-American composer, one of the masters of the twentieth century. His variety of styles—"Russian," "neo-classical," "serial," etc.—make his music difficult to characterize. Among the features to be found throughout his career are formal clarity, the manipulation of blocks of sound often based on ostinatos, and a predilection for the theater. Works include the ballets *L'oiseau de feu* (1910), *Le rossignol* (1914), *Petrouchka* (1911), *Le sacre du printemps* (1913), *Renard* (1922), *Pulcinella* (1920), *Les noces* (1923), *Apollon musagète*, *Le baiser de la fée* (1928), *Perséphone* (1934), *Jeu de cartes* (1937), *Orpheus* (1948), *Agon* (1957), *The Flood* (1962). Vocal dramatic pieces include *Histoire du Soldat* (1918), *Oedipus Rex* (1927), *The Rake's Progress* (1951), *Symphony of Psalms* for chorus and orchestra (1930), *Mass* (1948); *Cantata* (1952); *Canticum sacrum* (1956); *Threni* (1958); *A Sermon, a Narrative and a Prayer* (1962). Symphonies in E♭; C; in Three Movements. Violin concerto; concerto for piano and winds; *Movements* for piano and orchestra. *Symphonies of wind instruments* (1920); Octet (1923); Septet (1954); Piano music; songs; choral pieces.

Thomson, Virgil (b. 1896). American composer and critic. Spent much time in Paris, where he was particularly associated with Gertrude Stein, the librettist of his operas *Four Saints in Three Acts* and *The Mother of Us All*. Critic for *New York Herald Tribune* 1940–1954. Other pieces in his witty, uncomplicated tonal style are several tone poems; two string quartets; four piano sonatas; two symphonies.

Varèse, Edgar (1885–1965). Paris-born composer who lived mostly in U.S.A. Composer of spatially conceived, textural music, making much use of unpitched sound in some compositions. *Octandre*, for winds and double bass (1924). *Ionisation*, for 21 percussion instruments and two sirens (1931). *Density 21.5*, for flute alone (1935). *Poème électronique* (1958), composed for Brussels World's Fair.

Vaughan Williams, Ralph (1872–1958). English composer; important collector of folk tunes. Nine symphonies. *Five Mystical Songs*, for baritone, chorus and orchestra; *Fantasia on a Theme of Thomas Tallis* for string orchestra. Cantatas include *Hodie*, *Five Tudor Portraits*. Film scores. Operas *Hugh the Drover; Sir John in Love*. Much choral music.

Xenakis, Yannis (b. 1922). Greek-born composer and architect. Student and colleague of Le Corbusier. His music employs statistical methods and probability theory in attempts to create new materials and forms. *Metastasis* for orchestra, (1955). *Pithoprakta* for strings (1957). *Achorripsis* for 21 instruments (1958). *Strategy* for two orchestras (1964).

EPILOGUE

The reliability of one's judgment of an artist's work is in part a function of the passage of a certain amount of time. If Western culture should survive the various dangers that threaten it, one may be tolerably sure that Michelangelo, Rembrandt, Dante, Shakespeare, Josquin, Bach, and Beethoven will continue to be revered—perhaps in different ways and for different reasons, but revered all the same. They are safely dead, and far enough off in time to be visible as standing head and shoulders above their contemporaries. As the time gap decreases, the possibilities of uncertainty increase. While hardly any normal musician denies the importance of Beethoven, there are quite a few who do not think highly of Mahler—who, after all, has been dead for over half a century. Narrow the gap still more, and the disagreement increases proportionally. While a majority of well-informed musicians would probably agree that the greatness of Stravinsky, Schoenberg, and perhaps a few others is an established fact, the position of many of the other composers mentioned in Chapter XV is by no means as secure. It may well be that they had something to say to their own time, but did not possess the power of speaking to later generations. Many years—and, one hopes, many performances—will be required before such questions are settled.

In writing of music since 1950, the mere notion of making historical evaluations becomes presumptuous: one may have opinions, but no more. (Naturally, practicing composers can and indeed must judge the works of their contemporaries, but they do so as composers, not historians—and even they are prisoners of their own time.) Thus this epilogue, even more than the preceding chapter, will attempt merely to relate what has been happening in music, without any pretense at separating the important from the ephemeral. The reader will make his own private judgments (and is free to suspect that the author has made his), but—once again—they will be opinions, and no more.

It should first be said that a number of composers—young ones as well as old—are continuing to write in styles not radically different from those prevalent in the period between the two world wars. Such styles must be reckoned as relatively conservative, compared to some of the methods now in practice. But the thoughtful critic

Leonard Meyer has suggested that the coexistence of such conservative styles with more radical music may well continue for a considerable period of time—that the continuing "evolution" of style hitherto characteristic of Western music may give way to a conservation of existing styles, such as has been the case in some Eastern cultures. This, of course, is no more than speculation; but it may serve to warn the reader that some apparently reactionary music might possibly turn out to be, in the long run, as important as more obviously "new" compositions.

This having been said, it is necessary to consider those things that were in fact new in the years after 1950. The point of departure for new compositional techniques was the posthumous celebrity of Webern, who soon acquired an influence exceeding that of Schoenberg himself. Stravinsky's turn to the twelve-tone system was like the breaking of a great dam. Younger composers turned increasingly to serialism and, attracted by Webern's pure and static sounds, as well as by his intellectualism, to a specifically Webernian serialism. His strictness was first emulated, then surpassed. Not only were pitches subjected to serial technique, but also rhythmic values, dynamics, and even such elements as the manner of attack of individual notes. There thus arose the totally organized piece, in which all possible elements were subject to serial treatment; and the act of composition centered primarily on choosing the series, not in the nearly mechanical application of them to the notes. Such music is characterized by complete avoidance of any feeling of tonality; by disjunct melody split up among different instruments; by irregular, non-pulsating rhythms, and exploitation of unusual sound effects; and by extreme difficulty of performance. This last is caused in part by ordinary technical difficulty, but in part also by the fact that nearly every single note must be executed in an exact and specific manner, different from that of the notes before and after it—the ultimate consequence of composers' increasingly specific directions to performers from the time of Mozart on.

Thus the role of the performer was at once made more difficult and reduced in importance. He was given little or no latitude to "interpret"—merely the job of conforming exactly to specifications. Hence it is not altogether surprising that a dramatically different attitude towards performance made its appearance. Some composers (often the same ones who also used total organization) produced music in which the performer was required to choose for himself, within certain limits, what he was to play. For example, a piece for piano solo might consist of a number of short sections, fully notated, whose order was to be determined by the pianist during the course of the performance. Or, in a work for orchestra, a player might find the instruction "play a rapid chromatic scale in the highest possible register" in a part otherwise fully notated. Finally, some chamber groups have extensively practiced simultaneous improvisation on the basis of given rules and perhaps a few given bits of musical materials. Naturally, each performance of a piece of this sort will, in varying degrees, be different from every other one; but oddly enough, such music often is similar in sound to totally serialized music. (This, of course, is the consequence of the types of rules imposed on the performers' improvisation.)

Another fertile area of exploration was found in the incorporation of "non-musical" sound—whether from the world of nature or the world of the machine—into music, or even in creating music entirely out of such sounds. This is perhaps not so much a discovery as a rediscovery, for primitive man had, probably from the first, made use of the sounds of sticks, bones, and the like, in the making of his music. In recent times, however, the range of available "non-musical" sonorities has become vastly greater, and the musical possibilities of their use has increased proportionately. While a number of experimental works involving non-musical "noise" had appeared as early as the 20s, sustained interest in this type of composition—sometimes referred to as *musique concrète* ("real" music)—is of recent origin.

There is of course good reason for this. A composition employing bird-songs, pneumatic drills, automobile horns, and bomb explosions could hardly be brought to the concert stage in its "real" form: some form of phonographic recording would be indispensable. Thus *musique concrète* began to flourish only after the invention of sophisticated recording techniques. But these electronic advances quickly led to even more advanced devices of far greater potential: machines capable of producing almost any kind of sound, musical or non-musical, at the will of the operator, or of altering in any desired way any sound fed into them. Music produced by such machines is referred to as electronic music. Here, too, there were prototypes—instruments operated on an electrical rather than a physical basis—quite early in the century. But only advanced technology has made systematic exploitation of this medium possible.

Fig. A-1: *An electronic music synthesizer, the "Synthi 100," capable of producing an enormous variety of sounds. (Photo by Stanley Goldberg, courtesy of Electronic Music Studios of Amherst, Inc., Amherst, Mass.)*

At the time these pages are being written, it is possible to acquire equipment capable of producing an almost incredible variety of sounds, for about the same price, and occupying about the same space, as a grand piano. Such equipment can of course be used to imitate traditional musical effects, but its principal value is not in duplicating, but rather enlarging the possibility of musically usable sonorities. The natural adjunct of electronic music-producers is the tape recorder, for sounds produced by the machine are imprinted directly on tape. Hence a notated score is rarely necessary, and often impossible. Hence also, no performers are required, and even the need for a concert-hall audience disappears: once the tape has been reproduced and made available for sale, it may be heard with greater convenience in the home than in the concert hall.

Electronic music is still, necessarily, in a relatively early stage. Many styles have been tried, most of them similar in a general way to the more advanced styles used in conventionally performed music. But the practice of composers suggests that the future of music does not lie entirely in the direction of the solitary listener playing tapes or records in the privacy of his living room. For one thing, a number of composers do not use electronic sound sources at all, even when they are easily available. Further, even composers of electronic music often choose to combine artifically produced sounds with those of human performers. While such pieces can, of course, be recorded and heard privately, they appear to acquire greater force in the presence of an audience—even when that audience is faced with the unusual spectacle of a single singer competing with a powerful accompaniment produced by invisible means. This at least suggests that the assembly of a considerable number of people in one place to hear music will continue to have at least some importance—that, especially in a society so menaced by individual isolation, an "audience" is not merely a certain number of people, but an interacting entity.

The same suggestion is borne out by recent experiments in music designed for stage performance, where the presence of an audience is taken for granted. Works have been composed in which all sorts of visual, kinetic, and audible effects are freely mingled. Such works may employ conventional performers, electronic sounds, conventional actors, still and animated projections, song and speech—in short, any ingredients the composer chooses. Recently a still further dimension has been added to this already potent mixture: the use of multiple channel stereophonic systems to create the illusion of moving sound sources, so that an audience may be given the impression of sounds advancing upon it, or receding from it, while the visual components may either confirm or deny that impression. All of this is still in an experimental stage, but it is already obvious that technology has given the composer potent new sources of expressive power.

Some of the techniques just described have been used by several of the composers mentioned in the preceding chapter. A few of those who have recently achieved prominence primarily by their use of "advanced" methods may be mentioned here. The selection has been made with a view to representing several different radical approaches, and is not intended as a judgment of value either on those composers mentioned, or on those, much more numerous, who are not.

The oldest, John Cage (1912–   ), is by no means the most conservative. Some of his works are clearly intended to startle the audience—to puncture the traditional solemnity of the formal concert. In the most extreme of these, *Four Minutes and Thirty-Three Seconds*, a pianist sits in front of his instrument for the time indicated in the title, but plays absolutely nothing. But others are serious attempts to demonstrate the doctrine that anything whatsoever may be perceived aesthetically and, more specifically, that anything in the world of sound is at least potentially musical. To this end,

Cage makes extensive use of indeterminacy: the performer may be given only a series of pitches, with an approximate graphic indication of duration and loudness; or he may have before him no specific pitches at all, but only a general instruction as to relative register. In *Imaginary Landscape*, the "instruments" are radios, and the score an indication of wavelengths and durations. Naturally the actual sounds produced will vary enormously according to the time and the place the work is performed.

At another extreme stands the music of Pierre Boulez (1925–   ), influenced by Messiaen as well as Webern. While Boulez also makes occasional use of indeterminacy, by permitting the performer some latitude in the order of sections to be played, his music is for the most part dominated by extremely strict intellectualism. All elements of the composition are subjected to serial ordering, and the manipulation of the series is effected by highly sophisticated mathematical operations. Nevertheless, in a work like *Le marteau sans maître* (1955), one senses a powerful musical imagination at work: the mathematical complexities of the work (which are largely inaudible anyway) are of less importance than the delicate sonorities they bring into being.

Karlheinz Stockhausen (1928–   ) uses methods rather similar to those of Boulez, but has also worked extensively with electronic music. In general, his choice of medium is less traditional than that of Boulez: there are pieces for percussion alone, as well as purely electronic pieces and works combining conventional instruments with electronic sounds. A notable feature of *Gesang der Jünglinge* (1956) is the combination of taped vocal sounds with artificially produced vowel and consonant sounds. Luciano Berio (1925–   ) has also experimented extensively with electronic modification of naturally produced vocal sounds (*Omaggio a Joyce*; 1958): "normal" singing and speech are subjected to various sorts of calculated distortion, producing eerie effects often suggestive of the operation of the subconscious mind.

Milton Babbitt (1916–   ), another distinguished representative of totally serialized and electronic music, is noted for the rigor of his theoretical method. By way of contrast, Iannis Xenakis (1922–   ), an architect as well as a composer, has never employed strictly serial procedures. He has instead evolved a probabilistic ("stochastic") method, in which the exact sound of a given performance is not foreseeable, although the structure and general outline are. Xenakis has made considerable use of computers as an aid to composition, as have other composers; and some attempts have been made to give the computer the primary role in musical composition.

All of the composers just mentioned (and many others) have also written extensively about music, both from an aesthetic and a theoretical point of view. Naturally there is a good deal of divergence among their views, but they seem generally agreed that "expression" (in its nineteenth- and twentieth-century sense of conveyance of personal emotion) is not a primary aim of their music, if indeed it is an aim at all. Music is an object to be contemplated, not a message to be communicated.

The reader who turns his mind back from these complexities to the first chapters of this book may quite properly be struck by the contrast between a simple antiphon sung from memory by a choir of monks and the enormously complex and expensive apparatus of a contemporary multi-media production. The contrast is certainly real enough, and yet human beings remain, for the most part, what they have been for several millenia. Music may be regarded as a means of communication—a language by which the composer initiates the listener into some part of his own experience—or as an organization of sounds intended only to give sonorous pleasure to the hearer: both positions are valid, depending on the style in question. But in both cases the ultimate criteria are the same. The music communicates, or it does not. It gives pleasure, or fails to do so. The honest composer of the present day, however vast his means and sophisticated his technique, is still the direct inheritor of the anonymous creators of Gregorian chant. His job is to take the raw materials of sound, and to arrange them in such a way that his listeners will be moved—or pleased, or edified, or perhaps even horrified. How he does this is of course a matter of the greatest importance as far as the history of music is concerned. But the history of music is the history of works of art—works that have, in their own way, succeeded. After the most searching analysis of the art work, the undecipherable residue remains—the very essence that makes it art and not mere technique. In the end, the means do not matter. Only the work itself, as it is, stands as testimony to the genius of its creator.

APPENDIX A

Notation of pitch; intervals. The pitch (highness or lowness) of a musical sound is indicated by the position of a "note" on a "staff." The note is an oval-shaped mark, either entirely black or void in the center. The staff consists of five parallel lines running horizontally. A note may be placed directly on one of the lines, or in one of the spaces between them. Counting the space above the highest line and below the lowest one, there are thus eleven positions available (Ex. A–1). When necessary, short additional lines, called ledger-lines, may be added above or below, providing additional positions (Ex. A–2).

Ex. A-1   Ex. A-2

The distance, or "interval," between two pitches may be readily computed by counting the number of positions, beginning with that occupied by the first note, continuing with all intervening positions, and including the position of the second note. Thus two adjacent notes are a "second" apart, two notes on adjacent lines (or spaces) a "third" apart, and a note on the lowest line is a "fifth" from a note on the middle line (Ex. A–3). The same nomenclature is used for other intervals, as the example shows, except: (1) notes of the same pitch are called "unisons" (not "firsts"); (2) the term "octave" is used in place of "eighth;" (3) beyond "tenth" the proper interval term is usually replaced by the name of the interval an octave smaller (e.g., sixth instead of thirteenth.

Ex. A-3

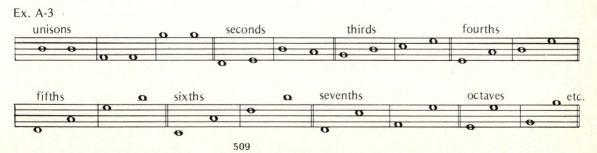

The last exception results partly from the nomenclature of the notes, and partly from physical fact. Notes are named by the first seven letters of the alphabet, A–G. The eighth note (octave) above an A is also called A, and picking out octaves on the piano or other instrument will demonstrate the extremely close relation between pitches an octave apart. An analogy with the days of the week has often been used: one Monday is not the same as the next Monday, but still duplicates it in a certain sense. If not pushed too far, the comparison may be useful.

The staff by itself gives no indication of the specific pitches indicated by the various line and space positions. This information is supplied by a "clef" (French: key), placed at the beginning of each staff. Of the several clefs once in use, the commonest now are the G and F clefs, represented by stylized (indeed unrecognizable) forms of those letters. The G clef (treble clef) fixes the note G on the next-to-bottom line of the staff; the F clef (bass clef) fixes F on the next-to-top line of the staff. These clefs also specify the octave of the two pitches involved: the G is a fifth above, the F a fifth below "middle C"—a pitch that in fact is roughly in the middle of the usable musical range, being approximately the middle note of the piano keyboard, and about the joining point between the normal ranges of male and female voices (Ex. A–4). A C clef is also often found. Unlike the G and F clefs, it may be placed on different lines of the staff, depending on the purpose intended: wherever it is placed, it fixes the position of middle C (Ex. A–5)

Ex. A-4

Ex. A-5

G middle C   F

middle C   middle C

middle C

Once the staff is supplied with a clef, the letter names of all the pitches may be determined by reference to the note indicated by the clef. There is, however, a further and most important complication. One might reasonably expect that the distance between any two adjacent pitches would be the same; or, in other words, that all seconds would be equal in size. Unfortunately, this is not the case. For both historical and acoustical reasons, the second exists in two sizes, called "major" (Latin: greater) and "minor" (Latin: smaller). The major second is also called a whole tone, or simply a tone, and the minor second a half tone or semitone. For all practical purposes, the major second may be considered to be twice the size of the minor second. The distance from B to C and that from E to F is a *minor* second; all other adjacent pitches are a major second apart. It is essential to memorize the two minor second (or semitone) pairs B–C and E–F if facility in reading music is to be achieved. Examination of a piano keyboard may be of help here. There is no black key between B and C, or between E and F; whereas all other adjacent white keys are separated by a black key. This correctly implies that G–A, for example, is a larger interval than E–F.

Since the second exists in two sizes, it follows that all other intervals may have two sizes as well. The third C–E, for example, is the sum of the major second C–D and the major second D–E: it is thus a "large," or major, third. The third D–F is the sum of the major second D–E and the *minor* second E–F: it is therefore a "small," or minor third. The reader should try to verify that the upward sixth D–B is major, and that the upward sixth E–C is minor.

The terms major and minor are used for seconds, thirds, sixths, sevenths, and for larger intervals formed by adding an octave to any of these. This is appropriate, since for each interval, the major and minor sizes sound clearly similar. A major seventh is not the same as a minor seventh, but neither one could be mistaken for any sort of sixth.

With fifths and fourths, however, the situation is different. If one plays or sings the fifth A–E, for example, the strong, open quality of the interval is evident. The fifth B–F, however, sounds entirely different: it is a more complex, almost harsh, sound. Experiment will show that in any octave, only one fifth has the latter quality—is, in other words, "abnormal." It can easily be shown that the normal fifth is made up of 3 1/2 tones (3 major seconds plus 1 minor second). This is called a *perfect* fifth. The abnormal fifth B–F is smaller: 2 major seconds plus 2 minor seconds. It is called *diminished*, to call attention to its lesser size and its special quality.

Fourths present an analogous picture. Most fourths consist of 2 1/2 tones (2 major seconds plus 1 minor second): these are called perfect fourths. The fourth F–B, is too large (3 major seconds): it is thus an "augmented" fourth. Augmented and diminished intervals are qualitatively different from their perfect forms: the terms major and minor would not be appropriate, for they would fail to express this difference. (The attentive reader will have noticed that the diminished fifth is the same size as the augmented fourth—three major seconds. Their nomenclature differs because the basic rule for naming intervals is invariable: the number of "steps" on the staff from one note to another determines the name of the interval, whatever its quality. From B up to F is five steps, hence a fifth; from F up to B is four steps, hence a fourth.)

If all the adjacent tones of an octave are played or sung in order, the result is called a "scale." Assuming the lowest tone of a scale to have special importance (to be, for example, the final tone of a melody), it is clear that the intervals between the starting tone and the other notes will differ according to the "final" chosen. A scale beginning on D will have a minor third as its third note, one on F a major third, and so on. Each of the seven notes of the octave will generate its own scale, different in at least some respects from all the others.

Every scale, however, will contain either the diminished fifth B–F or the augmented fourth F–B (and indeed both, if the scale is continued through two or more octaves). These intervals were long regarded as difficult to sing and as having unpleasant musical effect. From before the eleventh century, therefore, an expedient was adopted whereby these intervals could, at need, be made perfect: the B was replaced by a "B flat" (B♭)—a B lowered by a semitone. This in fact accomplishes the desired aim: the fifth B♭–F and the fourth F–B♭ are now perfect (Ex. A–6). Inevitably, the E–B♭ intervals are no longer perfect. The balance of intervals is a delicate one, and changing one relation is bound to alter others. But the B♭ is often useful. (As will be seen, both the flat and its opposite, the sharp, came to be used freely on any note.)

Ex. A–6

Notation of rhythm; meter. In the twelfth and thirteenth centuries, various methods were developed of indicating the duration of a note, as well as its pitch. These are discussed, where necessary, in the text (Chapter III). Here only the modern system of durational signs will be considered.

In principle, this system is very simple: the mark indicating pitch on the staff is supplied with auxiliary graphic features showing duration, in such a way that any note-length differs from any other by a multiple of two. Thus the theoretical unit of value is the "whole note" o (larger values are not now used). The additional of an upward or downward "stem" (♩, ♩) results in the half note, occupying, as its name implies, one-half the value of a whole note. A further reduction, producing a quarter note, is made by blackening the entire note head, while retaining the stem (♩, ♩). Still further reductions are made by (1) adding one or more "flags" to the stem of the quarter note (♪, ♪, ♪), producing eighth and sixteenth notes, and so on; or (2) joining two or more notes by single or multiple "beams" (♫, ♬). The two methods produce identical results, and the choice of the one to be used in any given situation is based on various graphical considerations.

Durational notation came into being simultaneously with what is now called "meter." If rhythm is defined as the durational or temporal aspect of tones, meter may be likened to a temporal grid or graph paper, with which the actual rhythm may have varying relations. The commonest modern unit of meter is the quarter note. (In modern practice neither the quarter note nor any value has *absolute* temporal value: in any performance, the absolute value of the basic unit is determined either by the musical intuition of the performers, or, in more recent music, by specific instruction of the composer.) Imagine first an unarticulated succession of quarter notes, each lasting, say, one-half second. These correspond to the vertical lines of graph paper. But most music is like metrical poetry: the series of time units is divided into groups, each beginning with a stress. Thus, in one of the commonest meters, the quarter notes fall into groups of four, the beginning of each group being marked by a (sometimes imperceptible) stress: ♩ ♩ ♩ ♩ | ♩ ♩ ♩ ♩ | etc. Each group is followed by a vertical "bar line," and is called a "measure" or "bar." The commonest meters are shown in the table below. Their designations, shown at the left, are not really fractions. The upper figure shows the number of units in a measure; the lower, the note-value chosen as a unit. Thus 4/2 indicates a measure of four units, the unit being the half note, and 3/8 a measure of three units, the unit being the eighth note.

Meter, however, is still merely a grid. It resembles the sort of graph paper in which every tenth line is darker than the rest, creating a regular grouping but nothing more. In actual music, a measure may be occupied by a variety of durational values, provided only that their sum be equal to the proper sum of values in the meter chosen. Thus in 4/4, ♩ ♩ ♫ | ♬ ♫ ♬ ♫ | o | are all possible *rhythms* within a single meter. There is a nearly inexhaustible flexibility in creating varied rhythmic patterns within a given meter: the grid serves simply as a frame of reference for a potentially complex variety of rhythms.

The durational system so far described has, however, certain limitations. It cannot adequately express ternary (as opposed to binary) values, and it cannot express values exceeding a measure in length. The first of these deficiencies is met by the use of the dot: a dot following a note increases its normal value by one half. Thus ♩. = ♩ + ♪ or ♪. ♪ + ♪ In ternary meters (3/4, 6/8, etc.), the dotted note is the normal means of expressing the measure-length or half-measure-length value 6/8 ♩. ♫♪ | ♩.; 3/4 ♩ ♩ ♩ | ♩. . In binary rhythms, a dotted note followed by a single note of the next smaller value is often found: ♩. ♪ or ♪. ♪ , equal to ♩ and ♩ .

Values exceeding a measure in length are expressed by means of a curved line called a "tie." Thus, in 3/4 ♩. | ♩ ♩ ♩ | , the tie indicates that the value of the second note is to be added to that of the first, to form a single unbroken duration equal to four quarter notes. The tie may also be used within a measure, sometimes in combination with the dot, to express a variety of lengths: 6/8 ♩. ♩ ♪| ♩.; 4/4 ♩ ♫♫ | .

Certain special rhythmic effects include syncopation, in which a longer note is displaced from its normal place in the measure: 6/8 ♩ ♪♫♫♪ ♩ ♩|♩. | ; and the replacement of two notes by three occupying the same time: 2/4 ♩ ♩ | ♫♫♩ | or the reverse: 6/8 ♫♫♩₂ | ♩. |. The manner of writing shown is the normal one, but the reader may wish to verify that the second example could also have been written: ♫♫ ♩♩ ♩. |♩. |.

In later music, the principle of the dot has been extended to include double-dotting: ♩.. ♪ = ♩ + ♩ + ♪ ♪ ; and replacement of a normal group by an abnormal one: 3/4 ♩ ♩ |♫♫♫♫♩ ♩ |. Some styles have employed simultaneous use of different meters in different parts, and rapid changes from one meter to another.

Harmonic intervals; the triad; tonality. Two pitches sounded simultaneously form what is called a "harmonic" interval. Such a sonority may strike the ear in one of two basic ways: as a "consonance," a stable sound, more or less fully at rest; or as a "dissonance," an unstable sound requiring movement to a consonance to resolve the instability. While acoustical law has often been invoked to support the classification of intervals into these categories, it has been the nature of musical style that has ultimately determined the category of harmonic intervals.

The classifications of intervals in early polyphony are discussed in the text (Chapter III). By the end of the fourteenth century, a classification had been developed that was to remain standard until the twentieth century. This is a three- rather than a two-fold categorization: perfect consonances (intervals of absolute stability); imperfect consonances (intervals of relative stability); and dissonances (intervals requiring motion to a consonance):

Perfect consonances	Imperfect consonances	Dissonances
unison	third	second
octave	sixth	seventh
fifth		all diminished
		and augmented
		intervals

The fourth presents a peculiar case: it is a dissonance when its lower note is the lowest sounding pitch, but otherwise a consonance. There seems to be no explanation for this anomaly.

Given such a scheme, it was naturally desirable that all fourths and fifths be perfect, except when a dissonance was specifically desired. The use of B♭ could often, but not always, achieve this. If, for example, a cantus firmus (which could not be altered) contained a normal B, and a perfect fifth above it was wanted, the normal F had to be *raised* a semitone, made into an F sharp (F♯). Moreover, from the fourteenth century and even before, it was increasingly felt that the best final cadence of a melody was made by preceding the final by a note a semitone below. If, then, the final note was to be A, the note preceding should not be G, a whole tone distant, but G♯, a semitone below (Ex. A–7).

Ex. A-7

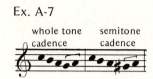

There thus came into regular use the signs ♭ and ♯, applied to any desired tone of the scale. In all cases, the flat lowers and the sharp raises the note affected by a semitone. The letter name of the note is not changed, even though its pitch is: the sharp and flat are in a way like adjectives modifying a noun. Reference to a piano keyboard will show that sharps and flats generally require the use of the black keys. The keyboard will also suggest that, for example, G♯ is "the same pitch" as A♭, since the same black key serves for both. Such pairs of notes are called enharmonic equivalents, but they are the same pitch only on keyboard instruments, to avoid an excessive number of keys. On other instruments, G♯ is played very slightly higher ("sharper," as a musician would say) than A♭.

In practice, sharps and flats are used in two different ways. A sharp or flat may be placed immediately before the note to be altered: this "accidental" then affects that note and any further recurrence of that note in the same measure. When, however, it is anticipated that a given note or notes will be sharped or flatted frequently throughout a composition, the appropriate sign or signs will appear at the beginning of each staff, directly after the clef. This then affects all notes of the same letter name, regardless of the range in which they lie, throughout the piece (Ex. A–8).

Ex. A-8

In either case, it will often be necessary to cancel the effect of a sharp or flat. This is done by use of the "natural" sign ♮, which, placed before a note, simply annuls either a flat or a sharp, whether an accidental or at the beginning of the staff. The natural is normally valid only during the measure in which it occurs (Ex. A–9). The double sharp 𝄪 and double flat ♭♭, raising or lowering the pitch of a note by two half tones, are also found.

In the fifteenth and sixteenth centuries, music came increasingly to be based on a sonority of a particular type: the triad. As its name implies, a triad consists of three tones in a specific relationship to each other. A triad may be thought of as (1) a fifth with a third "filling in;" or (2) two superposed thirds above a given tone (Ex. A–10). In

Ex. A-9   Ex. A-10

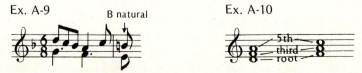

either case, the three tones of the triad are called, as shown, the root, the third, and the fifth. (The fifth may be omitted from a triad: the ear will supply it from imagination.)

In most cases, the interval from root to fifth is a perfect fifth. Such triads are called major if the third immediately above the root is major, and minor if that third is minor. When, as sometimes happens, the fifth is diminished, the triad is also called diminished. Much more rarely, one finds triads consisting of two superposed major thirds. These are called augmented triads, since their fifth is augmented.

When the root of the triad is the lowest sounding tone, the triad is in "root position." A triad in root position gives much the same effect regardless of the number and disposition of the upper voices (Ex A–11). If the third of the triad is the lowest note, the triad is in "first inversion" (this is often called a "sixth-chord"). Placing the fifth lowest produces the second inversion ("six-four chord"), an unstable sonority primarily used at cadences (Ex. A–12).

Ex. A-11

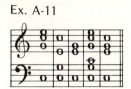

Ex. A-12

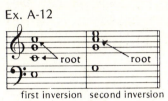

first inversion   second inversion

The essence of triadic music is the motion from a triad on one root to one on another. The effect of course varies depending on the interval between the two roots. Especially important is the progression of a major triad to a major or minor triad whose root is a perfect fifth lower (Ex. A–13). This, the "authentic cadence," was a standard concluding formula for many centuries, and was extensively used elsewhere as well. The reverse—root movement up a fifth, the "plagal cadence"—is also common, but less decisive in its effect. Many other triad progressions are possible and musically useful: it is not, however, necessary to attempt to catalogue them.

Ex. A-13

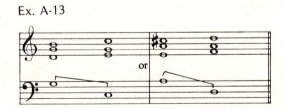

While some music consists of nothing but pure triads and their inversions, far more is triadically based, but includes many notes having an ornamental or embellishing function—notes that are not usually members of the triad prevalent at a given moment. These "non-harmonic" tones, as they are called, do not obscure the triadic basis of the harmony, but give it variety and animation (Ex. A–14). In the example, all non-harmonic tones are marked by an asterisk. Musical theory has classified non-harmonic tones into a variety of types. For the present purpose, it is sufficient to note that most such tones fall in rhythmically weak positions. (The suspension, discussed in Chapter V of the text, is the principal exception.)

Ex. A-14

The basic principles of tonality are discussed in the text (Chapter IX). For convenience, these principles are again presented here, in slightly different form.

1. In tonal music, one major or minor triad—the tonic—serves as the tonal center of a piece or a movement. Its primacy is assured by some form of the triad-succession in which the subdominant (root a perfect fifth below the tonic) is followed by the dominant (root a perfect fifth above the tonic) and then by the tonic (Ex. A–15). (The dominant must always be a major triad, even if the tonic is minor.) When this chord progression is used, it unequivocally defines a scale, and the scale thus defined is peculiar to the tonic of the chord progression. The major scale (i.e., the scale defined by a major tonic) is invariable for any given tonic. In the minor scale, the sixth and seventh notes may be raised or lowered for melodic purposes (Ex. A–16).

Ex. A-15

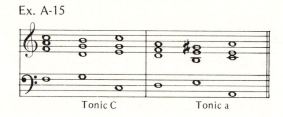

Tonic C   Tonic a

Ex. A-16

The triad acting as tonic of a piece gives the name of the "key" of that piece. If a D major triad is the tonal center, the piece is said to be in the key of D major. With appropriate use of sharps or flats, music may be written in any key (Ex. A–17). As the example shows, such sharps or flats are generally placed at the beginning of each staff, and the particular sharps or flats required for a given key are called the "key-signature" for that key. (When there is only one sharp, it is on the note F; each succeeding sharp is on a note a perfect fifth higher. The first flat is on B; each succeeding flat is on a note a fifth lower. The sharp or natural required to make the dominant triad major in a minor key is never placed in the signature, but is entered as an accidental whenever required [Ex. A–18]).

Ex. A-17(a)   (b)

Ex. A-18

g minor

2. The theory of music refers to the triads of a key by Roman numerals indicating the relation of their roots to the tonic. The tonic triad is called "I," that on the second degree of the scale "ii," and so on. (By convention, capitals are used for major triads, lower case for minor. Thus the progression subdominant-dominant-tonic may be written IV–V–I in a major key, iv–V–i in a minor key.)

3. While the tonic, dominant, and subdominant are the "primary" triads of a key, the other triads are freely used as well for variety—most often in sequence. Non-harmonic tones are also freely used in tonal music. The non-harmonic tone passing from the root of one triad to the third of another ultimately acquired the status of a chord tone (Ex. A–19). As may be seen, such a tone lies a seventh above the root of the first triad, and may be thought of as another third piled on to the superposed thirds of the triad. When such a sonority is used independently (i.e., where the seventh is not obviously non-harmonic), it is called a "seventh chord." While the dominant seventh (V⁷) is by far the commonest, any seventh chord may be used either in root position or in any of its three possible inversions.

Ex. A-19

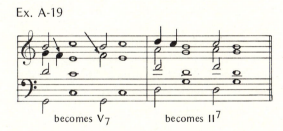

becomes V₇   becomes II⁷

The "figured bass" of the seventeenth and eighteenth centuries is for the most part merely a means of indicating by suitable numbers the triad or seventh chord (or inversion thereof) to be played above the written bass note. Figures are often used also to call for sonorities including non-harmonic tones, so that the number of figure-combinations used is considerably greater than would be required to indicate triads, seventh chords, and their inversions.

4. The chief structural resource of tonal music is modulation: the temporary suppression of the tonic triad in favor of a different triad as temporary tonic, followed by a return to the original tonic. The reader need not expect to identify specific modulations consciously, but will invariably be aware somehow when the original tonic has been left, and when it is restored.

Modulations may be roughly classified into (1) those moving to closely related keys—keys whose scales share most of the notes of the original scale; and (2) those moving to more remote keys. In the first case, the modulation is generally effected by use of a triad common to both keys, and is a gentle, almost imperceptible process (Ex.

A–20). Remote modulations are usually more sudden and more obvious: their effect is often more coloristic or dramatic than structural. Until the nineteenth century, they are less common than modulations to closely related keys. The commonest of all modulations are those from a major tonic to its dominant, and from a minor tonic to its "relative major" (i.e., the major key having the same number of sharps or flats).

Ex. A-20

C major I   V   I·V VI   V   I
          G major II

Modulation occurs in all tonal music: the motion away from and back to the original tonic is one of the most powerful devices ever discovered for achieving both unity and variety. Music containing modulations must necessarily contain both tonally stable areas (areas in which a key is established or confirmed) and tonally unstable areas (areas in which a modulation is or appears to be taking place). The contrasts between such areas are an important feature of tonal styles.

5. Tones foreign to the prevailing key—"chromatic" tones—are freely used in tonal music even where no modulation has taken place. Many are non-harmonic tones, "altered" from the normal scale tone for expressive purposes (Ex. A–21). Others result from the momentary borrowing of a scale tone from the minor scale in a piece predominantly in major (Ex. A–22). Still others are produced by an extension of the basic V–I relation, so that any major or minor triad of a key may be preceded by its own dominant (Ex. A–23); this is an analogue of modulation on a microscopic scale.) Finally, some chords may include chromatically altered tones to intensify the harmonic color (Ex. A–24). Properly handled, chromaticism of any kind need not weaken, and may indeed strengthen, the basic tonal feeling.

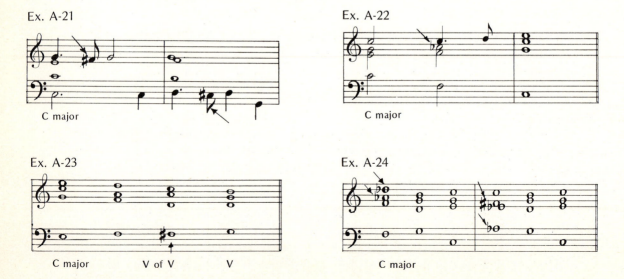

Ex. A-21

C major

Ex. A-22

C major

Ex. A-23

C major   V of V   V

Ex. A-24

C major

Musical instruments. The principal musical instruments in common use today are keyboard instruments, stringed instruments, woodwind instruments, brass instruments, and percussion instruments. The commonest keyboard instrument is the piano (short for pianoforte—Italian for "soft-loud"), an instrument capable of a vast variety of effects. The volume of sound produced varies with the force with which the keys are struck. The organ, a much older instrument, possesses a wider variety of tone colors, since any organ has a large number of "stops"—sets of pipes of a particular tone quality—and the stops may be combined in any desired way. Since most organs have two or more keyboards, plus a pedal keyboard, the simultaneous use of two or more tone colors is normal, but continuous changes of color or volume are not idiomatic to the organ. The recently revived harpsichord and clavichord have less volume than the piano or organ (the clavichord very much less). The harpsichord resembles the organ in often having two keyboards, and hence the possibility of simultaneous contrasting tones; and resembles it also in its inability to produce continuing changes of volume. The clavichord is capable of subtle dynamic changes, but its small sound restricts its use to solo playing in a small room.

The remaining categories comprise the standard orchestral instruments. The strings are a closely related family. There are four types: violin, viola, violoncello ('cello), and double bass. They share a basic shape, a basic method of tone production (the hairs of a "bow" are drawn against the string to cause vibration), and a basic technique of playing (the right hand operates the bow, while the left, by pressing the string against the "fingerboard," alters the sounding length of the string and hence its pitch). The difference between the four instruments is simply one of size: the violin, being the smallest, produces the highest pitch; the double bass is the largest and lowest. Among them, the strings can produce any musically useful pitch, with extensive overlapping through most of the range (e.g., middle C is possible on any stringed instrument, as a very high tone for the double bass, and a rather low one for the violin). While each instrument has its own special quality, the group as a whole is remarkably homogeneous. This helps to account for the central position of the string section in much orchestral music, and for the importance of the string quartet as a chamber medium.

The woodwinds do not form such a homogeneous group. There are four basic types: flute, oboe, clarinet, and bassoon. All of them share a basic playing technique: air is blown into a tube, whose sounding length (and hence pitch) is altered by opening and closing holes placed in its sides. (The recorder shows the basic process most clearly: orchestral woodwinds have far more complex mechanical systems.) The tone-quality of any woodwind instrument is determined in part by the shape of the tube (whether cylindrical or conical), and in even greater part by the means by which the air in the tube is made to vibrate. In the flute, the breath is directed past the edge of a hole in the side of the tube; in the oboe and bassoon, the air is blown past a "double reed"—a thin folded piece of cane whose ends are free to vibrate; in the clarinet a single reed is used. The resultant differences in sound are readily perceived by the ear, but do not lend themselves to verbal description.

Of the four basic woodwinds, only the bassoon can play in the low register; the other three have ranges lying entirely or mostly in the octaves above middle C. In order to gain more variety in range, and also to produce subtle differences of tone color, each type exists in two or more different sizes, producing correspondingly different ranges. Thus the bass clarinet is a large clarinet, sounding about an octave below the normal size. The contrabassoon, similarly, sounds an octave below the normal bassoon. The piccolo (short for "flauto piccolo"—Italian: little flute) is a small flute sounding an octave above the ordinary flute. Also common is the misnamed English horn, a large oboe sounding a fifth below the regular oboe. There are several other less frequently encountered woodwinds as well. For historical reasons, and also for the practical purpose of allowing a player to change from one instrument to another of the same family without changing technique and fingering, the parts for many woodwinds are notated as "transposing" parts. Notes for the piccolo, for example, are written an octave lower than they are to sound. A flutist need only lay down his flute and take up his piccolo: if he fingers the notes on the latter as they are written, they will automatically sound in the higher octave as they were intended to. Other transpositions are regularly found. Even the normal clarinet is usually a clarinet "in B♭" or "in A." A written C *sounds* B♭ in the first case, and A in the second. Reading scores that contain several transposing parts can be quite difficult. For the present purpose, it is sufficient to warn the reader that such parts are found in most scores. The apparent presence of a clarinet playing in the wrong key in a classical symphony is not an early instance of polytonality, but merely the consequence of a transposing part.

The brass family includes the trumpet, horn (French horn), trombone, and (since the nineteenth century), tuba. Like the woodwinds, they vary considerably in quality of tone, owing to differences in the shape of the tubing and of the mouthpiece. In all brass instruments, the vibrating medium consists of the player's lips. As the lips are tightened, higher tones are produced, according to the "harmonic series." (Ex. A-25). This series is obviously not a complete scale, and some of its notes are out of tune.

Ex. A-25

fundamental

To enable the brasses to play any desired pitch, all except the trombone are equipped with "valves." The valves activate an ingenious mechanism that acts to increase the sounding length of the tube, thus lowering all the notes in the series given above. By using the valves, the player can produce any pitch in the instrument's range. (Valves came into common use only after about 1850. Before that, while horns and trumpets could be adjusted to play in any key, the key could not be changed easily in the course of a piece. The player was thus restricted to the harmonic series of one key. Composers could either write parts in the extreme high range of the instrument, where the notes of the series lie close enough together to be used melodically—the method used in Baroque music; or could use the brass chiefly for harmonic support, taking advantage of the fact that the lower notes of the series are the tonic and dominant of the key of the instrument—the method used in classical music).

The trombone has always had its own method of adjusting pitch: the familiar "slide." As the slide is pushed out, the tube length is obviously increased, and the pitch is lowered; pulling the slide in reverses this. The trombone part is written as it is to sound. The other brass instruments are almost always written as transposing instruments.

The harp stands outside the basic categories of orchestral instruments. Its forty-seven strings are tuned to a major scale of nearly seven octaves. The strings are plucked by the player's hands, producing a sound only remotely similar to that of the harpsichord or piano. Seven pedals permit the harp to play in different keys. Depressing one pedal will raise all the A's of the harp by a semitone; depressing it still further will raise all the A's a whole tone; and the other pedals act similarly ony all the B's, C's, and so on. Thus the harp, like the other orchestral instruments, can play any note in its range.

Many percussion instruments may be used in an orchestra. The timpani (kettle-drums) are perhaps the most important, and certainly the oldest percussion members of the orchestra. They are drums that emit a definite (very low) pitch when struck (modern timpanists are able to tune their drums to different pitches rapidly during the performance of a single piece). Other types of drums may also be used, as well as dozens of different instruments or objects—cymbals, castanets, wood blocks, and so on—that give characteristic sounds when struck or otherwise sounded. These special sounds are generally used in a sparing fashion, to provide special effects of momentary color. In some relatively recent works, however, they have been promoted to a more central role, and some works require as many as five or six percussion players, each one responsible for several different instruments. Since most percussion instruments (apart from the timpani) produce sounds of indefinite pitch, their increased use is generally found in relatively radical styles, in which pitch is less important than other factors.

Performance indications. Besides symbols of pitch and duration, written music from the eighteenth century and later contains words and signs regulating the manner of performing the notes. A curved line resembling a tie, and placed over a group of notes, indicates that those notes are to be closely connected as a single phrase. A dot placed over (not after) a note indicates that it is to be played shorter than its written value, and hence detached from the note following. There are various signs that call for the accentuation of a note. The symbol ⟨crescendo⟩ indicates a gradual increase in volume, and ⟨diminuendo⟩ signifies a gradual decrease.

Even more numerous than these signs are words—mostly in Italian—that serve to govern various aspects of performance. Some of the most important of these are:

1. Words that indicate the tempo (speed) of the music. These are regularly found at the beginning of a piece or movement, but may occur within if the tempo changes. The commonest tempo-words, from fastest to slowest, are: presto, allegro, allegretto, andante, largo, lento, and adagio. They may be modified by "molto" (much) or less often "poco" (a little). "Molto adagio" would indicate an extremely slow tempo. Since the time of Beethoven, most composers have supplemented these designations by metronome markings, which give the number of beats per minute, and are hence more exact.

2. Words (and abbreviations) that prescribe the volume of sound desired. These are usually given as abbreviations of Italian words, the two basic ones being f (forte, loud), and p (piano, soft). Ff stands for fortissimo, very loud; and pp for pianissimo, very soft. Sometimes three or even more f's or p's may be found, obviously calling for dynamic extremes. In mf and mp, the m stands for "mezzo" (half), and calls for a moderately loud or moderately soft sound.

3. Words that suggest the type of expression desired. Almost any word or words may be used for this purpose. Most composers have used Italian, but German, French, and other languages have been used also. Even a selective listing would be impractical in a book such as this. Some directions are obvious in meaning: "con forza" correctly suggests "forcefully." Others, like the common "dolce" (sweetly) are not immediately clear to someone who does not know Italian. While any musician is familiar with quite a number of "expressive words" of this type, some are so rare that they must be looked up in a dictionary.

Indeed the above listing of musical terms includes only a few of the commonest words and signs. A "Dictionary of Musical Terms"—of which several have been made—is a book-length work in itself. The reader who wishes to enlarge his musical vocabulary in this direction should consult such a work, bearing in mind, however, that most performance directions are at best relative, and that many words have suffered significant change of meaning over the years.

APPENDIX B

Anyone interested in music will need to make at least occasional use of printed editions of musical works (scores), books about music or musicians, and recordings (disks or tapes). The quality of any of these may be excellent, or it may be poor; and while there is no certain way of distinguishing the good from the bad—except in extreme cases—there are some criteria that may help the uninitiated to make reasonably informed choices.

Scores are perhaps the easiest to evaluate. In principle, the score that most accurately reproduces the composer's intention is the best. Thus any good edition should clearly indicate the editorial procedure that has been used. A volume of piano music should, for example, distinguish by typographical means those dynamic signs, pedalings, and fingerings that originated with the composer, from those added by the editor. In music for strings, similarly, editorial bowings should be readily distinguishable from original ones. Such editorial additions are not at all an evil—they are often of much help to the performer and even the listener—but their observance is of course optional, in contrast to the normally obligatory indications supplied by the composer himself. When there are several editions of the same work or works, it is often enlightening to compare them (at a library or music store): the method and intent of the several editors will usually become quite clear.

Ideally, the editor should also make clear the *source* of his musical text: the composer's own autograph manuscript; the first edition, known to have been approved by the composer; or whatever. In most of the works of the standard repertoire—Mozart, Beethoven, and the like—this is not necessary, since the text is generally known and agreed upon (although there are some surprises even in Mozart). But for almost all earlier music, including that of J. S. Bach, the information is important, and its absence from an edition should be considered a serious defect. Often a work is known to us from several copies, differing in detail, and all made by persons other than the composer. It is the editor's job to collate the versions, decide which is best, and inform the reader of his decision and the reasons for it. In many cases, variant readings should also be included, as footnotes or in an appendix: it may not be clear which is the "best" reading, and the user should be given the opportunity to decide for himself.

As a very general rule, with many exceptions, miscellaneous collections are apt to be inferior to editions of a complete, specific repertoire. A volume devoted to the complete piano works of Mozart is likely to be a better edition than a volume containing piano pieces by Mozart, Beethoven, Chopin, and others—simply because the former is addressed primarily to serious musicians, the latter to amateurs unlikely to insist on scrupulous editions. Recently, however, a number of excellent anthologies have appeared on the market, often drawing their content from a wide variety of good published editions. These latter generally contain music for several different performing media, while the collections designed for amateurs are almost always exclusively for piano, or for violin, or for voice or whatever.

In music prior to the eighteenth century, fidelity to the composer's intention is frequently not enough: the user must also know something about the conventions of the style, since the composer has left nothing but a pattern of notes, with no indication that these notes are to be performed in certain specific ways—often not suggested by the notation. Thus a volume of seventeenth-century German organ music should give the user some idea of what type of organ was in use at the time, or refer him to an accessible source of such information. Without this, the inexperienced organist would be unable to select the appropriate sounds from the wide resources of a modern organ. In still earlier music, the meaning of the notation then used may still be in doubt, and the editor must explain how he has interpreted it, and for what reasons. In these, as in all the preceding cases, the basic rule is the same: the editor must make his own role clear, and failure to do so should be regarded as a serious fault. This principle is far more important than attractive appearance, recent date, or even convenience of use. While a good deal has been written about the differing needs of "scholarly" as opposed to "performing" editions, the criteria for the two are not really so different. The real difference lies primarily in the manner in which the edition is sold. A choir wishing to perform a Josquin Mass obviously cannot afford to buy thirty copies of a large and expensive volume containing ten such Masses: it needs, rather, an inexpensive, unbound edition of the Mass to be performed. But the musical text of the latter should be governed by the same principles that produced the former.

Books about music are almost incredibly various, ranging from "biographies" of composers that turn out to be romantic novels loosely based on a few incidents in the composer's life, to minute technical studies in which the footnotes take up more space than the main text. It is usually easy enough to recognize a seriously intended book. It will give due credit to others who have worked on the subject, will give objective evidence to support its conclusions, and will avoid sweeping generalizations, personal diatribe, or obviously personal and peculiar positions. But not all such books are good, and, on the other hand, much valuable material may be found in informal volumes that do not look at all scholarly. In cases of doubt, it is best to consult a reliable recent dictionary or encyclopedia of music: the article on the subject at hand will generally warn against or ignore worthless publications, and call attention to unlikely but useful material. And, of course, the reader will make up his own mind also, evaluating a book by the same standards he applies to any factual or interpretative writing.

Recordings present problems that are sometimes insoluble. While records and tapes regularly list the performers, as well as the work(s) performed, they rarely go further. The edition of the music used in the performance is not often given; and, for early music, the specific instruments employed are only occasionally listed. (Phrases like "performed on authentic instruments" should be regarded with caution, if not skepticism.) The purchaser of a record is in a particularly awkward position: unlike the buyer of a book or score, he is not generally allowed to examine the product—that is, listen to at least part of the record—before parting with his money; nor can he recover the price if he does not find the record satisfactory.

For standard repertoire music of the eighteenth and nineteenth centuries, the ability and reputation of individual performers is as good a guide as any. In most cases, the musical text has been firmly established, and performances differ only in the style and taste of the performers. Even here, however, some caution is in order. A conductor who has produced fine recordings of, for example, Brahms may turn out insufferable Mozart. Where possible, it is desirable to hear a recording at a public library (the copy will probably be badly scratched, but the style will still be perceptible) before purchasing it. And there are, even in the standard repertoire, some works whose musical text has *not* been fixed—the symphonies of Bruckner being perhaps the most striking example. If the record does not unequivocally state that the original form was used, one may assume that an altered edition is being performed.

With music prior to about 1750, the situation is more difficult. Famous virtuosi have often recorded "old" music, using defective editions, and treating even these with a great deal of freedom, and little knowledge of the proper style. This is certainly their right, and the results are sometimes extremely attractive. It could be wished, however, that such products be clearly identified for what they are: personal modernizations of music that, in its own time, sounded very different.

On the other hand, there are all too many musicologically oriented recordings that remain faithful to the letter of earlier styles, while failing almost completely to capture their spirit—or even, at times, any spirit of musicality whatsoever. While such attempts may occasionally be helpful in conveying the overall sonorous feeling of the music performed, they are on the whole a disservice to the art, in that they unintentionally but firmly convey the impression that all music prior to J. S. Bach is not only old, but dead. Out of the many recordings of Renaissance vocal music, for example, it is hard to think of more than a half dozen that transmit the vitality and exuberance of the music.

This being the case, the listener must proceed by experiment. If he finds that a certain performer, or group of performers, has issued a particularly lively recording of Italian lute music or madrigals, he can perhaps hope that a new issue of sixteenth-century French music by the same person or persons will be as successful. There is some hope that it will be—more, certainly, than that an organist who has issued one disastrously unmusical record will miraculously acquire sensitivity in his next. For here the criteria that identify a good edition are useless. The record jacket may meticulously list every relevant piece of information about the music, its sources and editions, even about the performers and their training and experience; but if the performance itself is lifeless and unmusical, the recording is worse than useless.

Fortunately it is not necessary to end on a note of pessimism. A great deal of music—far more than most people imagine—is well within the range of amateur performance. Almost anyone can learn to sing well enough to participate in informal chamber singing groups; and, with a little patience, almost anyone can learn to play some of the simpler instruments (notably the recorder and its relatives). Half a dozen people so equipped can spend years playing and singing, without coming near to exhausting the available repertoire. While performances such as these are unlikely to satisfy professional standards of accuracy, they have the enormous advantage of actively involving the participant in the music being played. One can hear a recording in the morning, and forget it entirely by afternoon; but once one has actually helped to play or sing music, the memory will endure for years, and the understanding gained will last even longer.

GLOSSARY

(Note: This glossary contains for the most part technical terms that occur in two or more chapters of the text, often with somewhat different meanings, as well as a few semi-technical terms, like "score," that are not elsewhere defined. For terms restricted to a single period or style, such as "parody," or "isorhythm," the reader should refer to the index. For terms relating to the rudiments of music—names of intervals, of note values, and the like—and for names of musical instruments, Appendix A should be consulted.)

Absolute (abstract) music. Music not intended to depict or refer to extra-musical ideas, feelings, or objects.

Accidental. A sharp, flat, or natural not appearing in the *key signature, and valid only in the *measure in which it occurs.

Acoustics. The science that examines the nature and activity of sound, whether musical or non-musical.

Aesthetics. The branch of philosophy devoted to analysis of the "beautiful" in the arts and elsewhere. "Aesthetic" (as a noun) is often used to refer to the artistic aims of an artist or school of artists.

Alteration. A change in *pitch caused by preceding a note with a sharp, flat, or natural (less often, a double sharp or double flat). The letter name of the note remains unchanged.

Appoggiatura. A note dissonant to the prevailing sonority, falling in an accented rhythmic position. It differs from the *suspension in that the appoggiatura is not prepared.

Aria. A formal composition for solo voice with accompaniment in an opera, oratorio, or cantata, etc. Arias for more than one singer are called *duets, *trios, etc.

Arpeggio. The sounding of the notes of a *chord in (usually rapid) succession, rather than simultaneously.

Atonality. Absence of any perceptible tonal center.

Augmentation. The presentation of previously heard musical material in time values systematically larger than those of the original statement. In music since 1600, augmentation is generally literal, producing values twice, three times, or four times the length of the original. In earlier music, the rules of the notational system sometimes produce an apparently irregular increase when triple meter is involved.

Authentic. (1) A *mode whose range lies largely in the octave above the *final. The first, third, fifth, and seventh modes are authentic. (2) A cadence made by preceding the *tonic by the *dominant *triad.

Ballet. Formal (as opposed to social) dancing, generally to music especially composed for the purpose. A ballet may be either an independent work or a part of a larger composition (usually an opera).

*The asterisk indicates that there is a separate entry in this Glossary under the word asterisked, or under a form of it (e.g., a reference from "polyphonic" is to "polyphony.")

527

Bar. (1) The form AAB. (2) A *measure of music (bar is not used in that sense in this book). (3) a bar line—the vertical line that separates one measure from the next.

Basso continuo (also figured bass, thoroughbass). A system of musical shorthand. An accompanist, playing either a lute or keyboard instrument, is supplied with a *part giving only the bass notes, to which numbers and other symbols have been added. The bass notes are played as written, and chords above them are supplied by *improvisation according to the directions contained in the numbers.

Binary. (1) A form consisting of two sections. More specifically, the form used for dance and other pieces in the late seventeenth and early eighteenth centuries. (2) A meter, such as 4/4, in which all values are related to the others by multiples of two.

Cadence. A musical point of articulation, indicating the end of a *phrase, section, or of an entire composition. The term is used both for the articulation itself ("there is a cadence in measure 34") and for the means of achieving the articulation ("an *authentic cadence").

Canon. The duplication, over an extended period of time, of musical material first presented in one *voice in one or even more following voices. The term is also used to denote a composition in which this device is the most prominent technique.

Cantus firmus. A melody, usually preexistent, that functions as the basis of, or as an important element in, a *polyphonic composition.

Chord. Properly, a sonority consisting of at least three different pitches sounded simultaneously. In practice, the term is often applied to some two-note sonorities as well, and it is not necessary that the simultaneity be absolute (e.g., a chord may be given in the form of an *arpeggio).

Chordal. A style in which two or more *voices have the same rhythms, with the result that the music is perceived as a succession of chords.

Chromatic. A tone or tones foreign to the basic *scale of a composition. The chromatic scale consists of all twelve tones of the octave sounded in order.

Coda. A concluding section of a *movement. Usually applied to music since about 1650, although concluding sections functioning in the manner of a coda can be found in many earlier styles.

Color. The particular sonorous quality of a sound or combination of sounds, whether in itself, or in relation to adjacent sounds.

Compound. (1) Compound meter combines binary and ternary elements, as in 6/8, consisting of two groups of three eighth-notes. (2) Compound intervals are those consisting of a basic interval enlarged by one or more octaves (e.g., the twelfth is a compound interval, consisting of a fifth plus an octave).

Concerto. (1) From about the end of the seventeenth century, a composition for one or more featured solo instruments with orchestral accompaniment. (2) At the beginning of the seventeenth century, a composition in the then modern style, usually involving both voices and instruments.

Conjunct. Of melodic motion, proceeding by step (tone or semitone).

Consonance. In any given style, an interval giving an impression of stability and repose.

*The asterisk indicates that there is a separate entry in this Glossary under the word asterisked, or under a form of it (e.g., a reference from "polyphonic" is to "polyphony.")

Contrary motion. In *polyphony, two voices moving in opposite directions.

Counterpoint. The combination of two or more melodic lines simultaneously; or, more generally, a *texture in which two or more *voices have independent melodic interest.

Cross-relation. The presence of a note in both its *altered and normal forms in two different voices, either at the same time or in rapid succession.

Development. The treatment of musical materials in such a way as to exploit their latent possibilities. Materials may be developed by changing the original harmonies or the original *key, by breaking larger units up into smaller ones, or in general by retaining some features of the original material while changing others. Development generally conveys an impression of temporary instability.

Diatonic. Pertaining to the basic (usually seven-note) *scale of a composition.

Diminution. The presentation of previously heard material in time values systematically smaller than those of the original statement; the opposite of *augmentation.

Disjunct. Of melodic motion, proceding by intervals larger than a whole tone.

Dissonance. In any given style, an interval giving an impression of instability, requiring *resolution to a *consonance.

Dodecaphonic. *Twelve-tone.

Dominant. In tonal music, the tone a perfect fifth above the *tonic, and the major triad with that tone as root.

Duet. (1) An *aria for two singers. (2) A composition for two singers or players, with or without accompaniment.

Enharmonic. Having, in equal *temperament, the same pitch, but different notation. G♯ and A♭ are "enharmonic equivalents."

Ensemble. (1) A formal composition for several singers in a dramatic work. (2) All of the players and/or singers required by a given work. (3) The mutual adjustments of performers necessary to produce a good performance ("the members of the quartet exhibited an extraordinary ensemble").

Episode. In general, a section contrasting in some way with the principal material of a composition. Specifically, those sections of a *fugue in which the complete *subject is not present, and the sections of a rondo that alternate with recurrences with the main section.

Equal temperament. *Temperament.

Figuration. A generic term for musical patterns (*scales, *arpeggios, or more complex schemes usually combining these) that are repeated, using different pitches, to create continuity. Figuration may serve as the primary element (as in some Baroque music), or as a means of organizing the accompaniment (as in much classical music), or it may be absent altogether.

Figured bass. *Basso continuo.

Final. The concluding tone, especially of a melody. The final generally has an important role in the hierarchy of tones out of which a melody is constructed.

*The asterisk indicates that there is a separate entry in this Glossary under the word asterisked, or under a form of it (e.g., a reference from "polyphonic" is to "polyphony.")

Finale. (1) The last movement of an instrumental work. (2) A special technique used for the end of an act of an opera, characterized by rapid developments in the plot, increase in the number of characters on stage, and relatively short, thematically unrelated sections of music.

Form. The structure of a piece of music, or the arrangement of its constituent parts in some perceptible order. While some elements of form may be verbally or schematically represented (e.g., "ABA;" "exposition, development, recapitulation"), the essential inner unity of a work of art can be perceived only intuitively, and does not lend itself to description.

Fugato. A section of a piece in a style resembling that of a *fugue.

Fugue. A tonal composition in *imitative texture, usually based on a single *theme or "subject." There are fugues for as few as two *voices and for as many as six or even more. Most fugues alternate presentations of the subject with *episodes.

Ground bass. *Ostinato.

Harmonic. (1) Pertaining to *harmony. (2) A tone produced on a musical instrument by causing the sounding length to vibrate in parts (1/2, 1/3, etc.) rather than in its full length.

Harmonic rhythm. The temporal effect produced by changes from one *chord to another. Harmonic rhythm is usually different from and slower than the rhythms of the melody (or melodies).

Harmonic series. The tones produced by the fractional vibration of a sounding body. Almost all musical sounds consist of a "fundamental" (the sounding body vibrating at its full length), combined with vibrations of 1/2, 1/3, 1/4, etc., of the total length. The special quality or *color of a single sound depends largely on the strength of these "harmonics," or "partials," relative to the fundamental. (The ear does not hear the partials as separate tones, but merely as enrichments of the fundamental.) For the use of the harmonic series in the playing of brass instruments, see Appendix A.

Harmony. The "vertical" aspect of *polyphonic music, i.e., the way in which *chords are treated in a musical style. Often opposed to *counterpoint—the "horizontal" or linear aspect. In reality, all polyphonic music contains both harmonic and contrapuntal elements, interacting in various complex ways. For a discussion of tonal harmony, see Appendix A.

Homophony. A style of *polyphonic music in which each voice moves in the same rhythm, producing a succession of *chords.

Imitation. The presentation in one or more following voices of material already heard in a preceding voice. The term is generally restricted to cases in which the material imitated is relatively brief. Consistent imitation over a long period is called *canon.

Improvisation. The performance of some or all of the elements of music without either written music, memorization, or specific prior determination. A wholly improvised piece is one made up by the performer entirely, as appropriate musical ideas "come into his head." More commonly, some or most of the elements of a piece are fixed by *notation, leaving the performer free to improvise other elements, such as *ornamentation.

---

*The asterisk indicates that there is a separate entry in this Glossary under the word asterisked, or under a form of it (e.g., a reference from "polyphonic" is to "polyphony.")

Inversion. (1) Of an interval: the transfer of one of the notes up or down one or more octaves, so that, e.g., the third C–E becomes the sixth E–C. (2) Of a melody: the replacement of all ascending intervals of the original melody by equivalent descending intervals, and the reverse. (3) Of counterpoint: the placing of what was originally the top voice in the bottom, and the bottom voice in the top (double counterpoint); or, in more than two voices, the possibility of placing any voice in the top, middle, or bottom position (triple, quadruple counterpoint). (4) Of a *chord: sounding a chord with some tone other than the root in the bass.

Key. In *tonal music, the major or minor *triad serving as tonal center for a composition or *movement. Keys are referred to by the letter name of the triad *root, plus the qualification *major or *minor (e.g., a quartet in D minor, a symphony in E♭ major).

Key signature. The sharps or flats needed to produce the proper *scale of a *key, and placed at the beginning of each staff, directly after the clef.

Line. Short for "melodic line"—the aspect of melody concerned primarily with the relation between successive pitches. ("A jagged, disjunct bass line;" "a smooth, often chromatic line for the oboe.")

Major. Literally, larger. (1) Of intervals, the larger type of second, third, sixth, seventh, and their *compounds. (2) Of triads, the type having a perfect fifth and a major third above the root. (3) Of keys, one having a major triad as *tonic.

Mass. Musically, a setting of the ordinary (unchanging) parts of the Mass liturgy.

Measure. The music contained between one *bar line and the next. When, as is usually the case in music employing *meter, the meter remains unchanged, the measure is a temporal unit of music.

Melisma. A melodic passage of a considerable number of notes set to a single syllable of text.

Melody. A succession of tones having an inner unity and hence heard as a whole. A melody may be either a complete composition in itself, or may be a constituent element in a larger work. Melody is often loosely used in the sense of "tune."

Meter. A regular pattern of strong and weak rhythmic pulses. See Appendix A.

Minor. Literally, smaller. (1) Of intervals, the smaller type of second, third, sixth, seventh, and their *compounds. (2) Of triads, the type having a perfect fifth and a minor third above the root. (3) Of keys, one having a minor triad as *tonic.

Mode. (1) Generally, the specific nature of the scale underlying a composition. For the eight modes of Gregorian chant, see the end of Chapter I. *Tonal music has only two modes, *major and *minor, depending on the quality of the *tonic *triad. (2) One of a set of rhythmic patterns used in twelfth- and thirteenth-century *polyphony. See Chapter III.

Modulation. In tonal music, a temporary change of tonal center from the original *tonic to another *key.

Monody. A type of speech-like declamatory singing developed for dramatic and other purposes early in the seventeenth century. Sometimes loosely used as equivalent to *monophony.

*The asterisk indicates that there is a separate entry in this Glossary under the word asterisked, or under a form of it (e.g., a reference from "polyphonic" is to "polyphony.")

Monophony. Music in which only one pitch is sounding at any given moment. Cf. *polyphony.

Motet. (1) In the thirteenth and fourteenth centuries, a *polyphonic composition over (usually) a liturgical *cantus firmus. (2) In the fifteenth century and after, a sacred vocal polyphonic composition.

Motive. In general, the smallest meaningful unit of musical material in a given style. Thus a *theme or *melody may be made up of several motives, or of varied forms of a single motive.

Movement. A complete, self-contained composition that serves as a part of a larger work consisting of two or more such units. Occasionally, for special purposes, a movement may be fragmentary or incomplete.

Non-harmonic tone. A tone foreign to, and usually dissonant with, the *chord prevalent at any moment.

Notation. Any system for representing elements of music in graphic form. For the system of notation used at the present, see Appendix A.

Note. Properly, a graphic sign indicating a musical sound, or *tone. The word is regularly if somewhat loosely used to refer to the sound itself.

Oblique motion. Two voices moving in such a way that one remains stationary while the other ascends or descends; or in such a way that both move in the same direction, but by different intervals. (The latter is also called similar motion).

Ornament. A tone or group of tones serving a decorative rather than a structural function in a *melody. Also, a graphic abbreviation representing such a decoration.

Ornamentation. The process of adding *ornaments, whether written or *improvised, to a composition.

Ostinato. A repeated melody, usually in the bass (basso ostinato), above which other voices sound constantly varying material. Ostinato is an important means of producing unity, especially in Baroque music.

Parallel motion. Two voices moving in the same direction by the same interval.

Part. (1) A section or, especially in sixteenth-century music, a *movement of a larger work. (2) A continuing melodic line or *voice of a *polyphonic composition. (3) The written or printed music for one or more performers ("the second violin part;" "the bassoon part").

Phrase. A meaningful unit of music, roughly analogous to a phrase (clause, sentence) of speech. Those who write about music differ in terminology as regards larger (e.g., "period") or smaller (e.g., "antecedent, consequent") units.

Pitch. The location of a musical tone with respect to highness or lowness. *Absolute* pitch is measured by the number (frequency) of vibrations per second (the A above middle C is commonly given as 440 v.p.s.). Scientific determination of pitch dates only from the nineteenth century. Earlier, absolute pitch was determined conventionally by instruments of fixed pitch (e.g., the organ), and varied considerably at different times and places. *Relative* pitch is merely the distance between a given tone and an arbitrarily chosen tone of reference.

*The asterisk indicates that there is a separate entry in this Glossary under the word asterisked, or under a form of it (e.g., a reference from "polyphonic" is to "polyphony.")

Plagal. (1) A *mode whose range is such that the *final lies in about the middle. The second, fourth, sixth, and eighth modes are plagal. (2) A *cadence made by preceding the *tonic by the *subdominant triad.

Polyphony. Music in which different pitches are sounded simultaneously. Sometimes loosely used for *counterpoint. More exact are the pairs monophony/polyphony and homophony/counterpoint.

Program music. Music that suggests or portrays extra-musical ideas, feelings, or objects. Program music may range from the mere depiction of a verbally defined mood to an attempt at actual narrative.

Quartet. (1) An *aria for four singers. (2) A composition for four singers or players, with or without accompaniment, especially a piece scored for two violins, viola, and 'cello (string quartet).

Range. The interval between the highest and the lowest *pitch performable by a given instrument or voice. Also, the interval between the highest and lowest pitches actually used in a composition.

Recitative. Speech-like declamatory singing employed for the dialogue and narrative portions of dramatic music. See also *monody.

Requiem. The *Mass for the Dead. Musically, a setting of the Requiem Mass.

Resolution. Motion from an unstable sonority to a stable one. Specifically, motion from a *dissonance to a *consonance.

Retrograde. The presentation of a series of pitches in reverse order, beginning with the last, and ending with the first. Unlike melodic *inversion, retrograde presentation does not generally produce a result that is heard as similar in some way to the original.

Rhythm. Anything that pertains to the temporal aspect of music. "Rhythmic," however, is often loosely used to refer to rapid and prominent rhythms ("a rousing and highly rhythmic finale").

Ritornello. A recurrent section of music whose appearances are separated by contrasting material.

Root. The fundamental tone of a *chord, more specifically of a *triad or *seventh chord.

Root position. A disposition of the tones of a *triad or *seventh chord in which the *root is the lowest sounding tone. See also *inversion.

Scale. Theoretically, the arrangement of the *pitches used in a composition in order, beginning with the lowest and ending with the highest. In most *polyphony and some *monophony, *pitches occur that are clearly foreign to what is perceived as the basic scale of the composition. These are considered *chromatic tones, not part of the basic scale.

Score. The writing or printing of music so that *notes intended to sound simultaneously are vertically aligned. More generally, a graphic representation of the roles of all the performers needed for the execution of a composition, as contrasted with *parts.

---

*The asterisk indicates that there is a separate entry in this Glossary under the word asterisked, or under a form of it (e.g., a reference from "polyphonic" is to "polyphony.")

Serial. Based on a series, originally of pitches (early twentieth century). Later the pitch-series was invariably an arrangement of all twelve tones of the octave (*twelve-tone music), and later still, other musical elements (dynamics, rhythm) were subjected to serial treatment.

Seventh chord. A dissonant sonority formed by adding a third above the upper note of a *triad. See Appendix A.

Signature. *Key signature.

Sonata. Literally, something played, as opposed to a composition involving voices. For sonata form, see Chapter XI.

Stop. A set of organ pipes of the same sound quality, one for each *pitch of the organ keyboard (certain stops require two or more pipes for each pitch). Most harpsichords also have two or more stops—in this case sets of strings, not pipes—but they are less different, and far less numerous, than the stops of the organ.

Stretto. (1) The presentation of two or more entries of the *subject of a *fugue in such a way that the second entry begins before the first has ended. (2) An increase in tension, achieved by an increase in *tempo and *volume, in an opera.

Subdominant. In tonal music, the tone a perfect fifth below the tonic, and the *triad with that tone as *root. Unlike the *dominant, the subdominant may be replaced by related triads and seventh chords that serve the same function while differing in harmonic *color.

Subject. The principal musical material of a *fugue.

Suspension. A type of *non-harmonic tone: the tone to be suspended appears first as part of a *triad, is then sustained while the triad is changed, thus becoming dissonant, and is then resolved conjunctly. See Chapter V.

Syncopation. A rhythmic effect produced by the placement of a long or stressed tone where a short or light one is expected.

Temperament. Any system for tuning all of the *pitches of the *chromatic scale to produce musically usable results. Temperament is necessary because the use of acoustically perfect intervals is impractical, especially with keyboard instruments, for which it would require an excessive number of keys. Since about 1700, "equal temperament" has supplanted earlier tunings. In equal temperament, the octave is divided into twelve equal semitones, with the result that no interval is perfect (except the octave), but all are at least tolerable.

Tempo. The speed or pace of a piece of music. For designations of tempo, see Appendix A.

Tenor. (1) A male voice having a high range. (2) In much *polyphony through the sixteenth century, the *voice having the *cantus firmus, or in general the fundamental material.

Ternary. (1) A form having three sections, e.g., ABA. (2) A *meter such as 3/4, in which the primary subdivision is into groups of three beats.

Texture. The vertical, or simultaneous, elements of music, apart from *harmony. Textures may be classified according to the extent to which they are *contrapuntal or

---

*The asterisk indicates that there is a separate entry in this Glossary under the word asterisked, or under a form of it (e.g., a reference from "polyphonic" is to "polyphony.")

*homophonic; according to the extent to which tones are packed close to each other (dense texture) or widely spread (thin texture); and, more subjectively, according to the *color of the total sound ("a very rich texture").

Theme. A piece of musical material, often but by no means always melodic in nature, that serves as an important element in a composition. In normal usage, theme suggests a larger entity than *motive, and in practice, a theme is often made up of several motives.

Thoroughbass. *Basso continuo.

Timbre. The specific quality or *color of the sounds made by a particular instrument (or, less often, voice).

Tonal. Usually, pertaining to *tonality.

Tonality. In the broadest sense, any means by which a composition uses one *tone or *chord as a center, and assigns different functions to other tones or chords. Usually employed to refer to the triadic tonality in use from the seventeenth through nineteenth centuries, for which see Appendix A.

Tone. (1) A musical sound, indicated graphically by a *note. (2) More loosely, the quality or *color of a sound ("the nasal tone of the oboe").

Tonic. The *triad that serves as tonal center of a piece employing triadic *tonality (see Appendix A), or, more generally, the *tone or sonority having this function.

Transition. A passage that effects some kind of significant change. Most commonly used of passages that effect a change of *key.

Triad. A three-note sonority consisting of a basic tone or *root, a tone a third above the root, and a tone a fifth above the root. For the different types of triads and their *inversions, see Appendix A.

Trio. (1) An *aria for three singers. (2) A piece scored for three voices or instruments, with or without accompaniment.

Tritone. An interval equal to the sum of three whole tones. The tritone may be either an augmented fourth or a diminished fifth, depending on the *pitches involved.

Twelve-tone. Pertaining to that type of *serial music in which the basic series is always a "row" consisting of all of the tones of the *chromatic scale. See Chapter XV.

Variation. In general, the presentation of previously heard material with some elements changed and some retained, so that the new presentation is heard as related to the original. As a musical form, variation normally consists of a short section called the "theme," followed by anywhere from three to thirty or more further sections, each of which retains some elements of the theme, while changing others.

Virtuoso. A performer having extraordinary technical skill. Applied adjectivally to music in which the display of such skill is an important element.

Voice. (1) The human voice, as opposed to "artificial" musical instruments. (2) A contunuing melody or line through a *polyphonic composition or section (used in this sense normally when there are two or more such lines, and a contrapuntal *texture).

Volume. The degree of loudness of sound at any given moment. For methods of indicating volume, see Appendix A.

---

*The asterisk indicates that there is a separate entry in this Glossary under the word asterisked, or under a form of it (e.g., a reference from "polyphonic" is to "polyphony.")

INDEX

This index is primarily one of proper names, of musical forms and techniques, and of other essential concepts. Individual works are not indexed by title, but can be readily found by looking up the composer's name (if the section devoted to a composer is larger than two or three pages, subentries will help find the work wanted). The abbreviation "(ex.)" following a page number indicates that a musical example of that composer's work will be found at the page indicated. The chapter appendices are indexed only for composer's names, and, in the earlier chapters, for principal musical forms. Page references to chapter appendices are given in italics. The Appendices and Glossary are not indexed.

Double-chorus writing, *see* Polychoral music
Double concerto, 444
Double fugue, 299–300, 484
Dowland, John (1563–1626), *176*, 193 (ex.)
Doxology, 9, 10, *28*, *29*, 36
Drama, liturgical, *see* Liturgical drama
Drama, Renaissance, music in, 214
Duetting, 132, 136, 137, 140
Dufay, Guillaume (1400–77), 109–18, 121, 134, 140, 167, 170
    hymns, 115 (ex.)
    Masses, 112–15 (ex.)
    motets, 112, 116–17
    secular music, 109–12 (ex.)
    table of works, *126–27*
Dunstable, John (d. 1453), 107–11 (ex.), 170
    table of works, *126–27*
Duplum, 54, 56–57, 60
Dvořák, Antonin (1841–1904), 436, *466*

Echiquier, 99
Eleanor of Aquitaine, 70
Electronic music, 506–507
Elgar, Edward (1857–1934), *466*, 490
Empfindsamer Stil, 327
Encina, Juan del (1468–1529), 164–65 (ex.)
"English manner" (*contenance angloise*), 110–11
English music
    features of in 13th–14th c., 66
    15th-c., 106–109
        influence on Continental style, 107–109, 112
    16th-c., 170–74
    17th-c. 264–68
Ensemble music, 184, 185, 188, 190, 231, *235*
Ensembles in opera, 330, 344–47, 424, 427, 429, 453, 484
Episode
    in fugue, 275, 283, 298–99
    in rondo, 327
Epistle, 5, 6, *25*
    farsed, 38

Equality of voices in polyphony, 111, 114, 118, 120–21, 131, 134, 139
Estampie, 99–100, *103–104*
Eton Choirbook, 170
Etude, 406, 407, 414
Exit aria, 315
Exoticism, 347, 379, 383, 457
Exposition, 324, 326, *355*
Expressionism, 476, 480
    and impressionism, 476
Eye music, 161

Faenza Codex, 100, *104*
Falla, Manuel de (1876–1946), 436, *466*
Familiar style, 132, 137, 140
    see also Chordal style
Fancy, *see* Fantasia
Fantasia, 188–91, 193, *207*, *208*, 264, 266–67, 272, 273, *277*, 303
    for later works see Fantasy
Fantasy, 327, 351–52, 401, 405, 414
Fauré, Gabriel (1845–1924), 458, 459, 463, 465, *466*, 469
Fauvel, Roman de, 80–83, *101*
Fauxbourdon, 115, 117, 120, 150
Festa, Costanzo (d. 1545), 158, *175*, *176*
Field, John (1782–1837), *396*, 406
Figured bass, *see* Basso continuo
Final, 8, 12, 18
Finale (instrumental), 338–39, 367, 369, 371, 373, 411
Finale (operatic), 320, 345–46
Florence, role in early Baroque, 196, 214–18
Folksong, 435–36, 438, 440, 444, 450, 458, 472, 486, 487, 491, 494
Formes fixes, 70, 87, 120, 137
Foss, Lukas (b. 1922), *498*
Four-voice writing, beginnings of, 121
Francesco da Milano (1497–1543), 189 (ex.), *207*
Franck, César (1822–90), 457, *466*
Franco of Cologne (13th c.), 62–63, *75–76*, 80, 90
French music
    Baroque, 255–64, *277*
        influence in Germany, 276
        Italian influence on, 293